P9-DNU-741

Emily Post's
ETIQUETTE

Published by Funk & Wagnalls
for the EMILY POST INSTITUTE, INC.

Etiquette: The Blue Book of Social Usage
Etiquette for Young People
Etiquette in Society, in Business, in
Politics and at Home (Replica Edition)
Children Are People
The Emily Post Cook Book

Emily Post's
ETIQUETTE

TWELFTH REVISED EDITION BY

Elizabeth L. Post

FUNK & WAGNALLS · NEW YORK

Emily Post's Etiquette

TWELFTH REVISED EDITION

4-73

Library of Congress Catalog Card Number: 68-55996

Composed, printed, and bound in the United States of America
ISBN 0-308-10037-9 (Plain)
0-308-10038-7 (Thumb indexed)

PREFACE

to the Twelfth Edition

When my husband and I became engaged, one of the first things he wanted to do was to take me to Edgartown, Massachusetts, and introduce me to his grandmother, Emily Post. In spite of his reassurances, and obvious devotion to her, I had all the natural reservations about meeting the famous First Lady of Etiquette, and I was a very nervous young lady when we arrived at her lovely island home that day in June, 1944. And I remained nervous for at least five minutes! In that space of time, I found that the supposedly unapproachable authority on all our manners and behavior was the sweetest, most natural, warmhearted, unaffected person I had ever met. From that day on, we were as close as two people separated by a span of some years can be, and I was never once made uncomfortable or self-conscious in her presence. That, to me, is the proof of the value of etiquette. To practice perfect manners without appearing to be "stiff" and at the same time to let those about you feel that *they* are equally well-mannered is a goal that can be achieved only by making consideration and unselfishness an integral part of your behavior.

My husband and I, and our children, spent a great deal of time with "Grandmama," as we always called her, and the children loved her as much as we did. Even they felt the gracious atmosphere that radiated from her and were almost invariably at their best in her presence, not because they had to be, but because they wanted to be.

We often discussed etiquette in those years, both the subject itself and the book she wrote about it. Emily Post was thoroughly aware of the changing pattern of modern living and made a point of keeping in constant touch with the changes, both through her correspondence with readers and through the activities of the members of her own family. Furthermore, she fully realized that the time would come when etiquette would necessarily be affected by these changes. She herself eliminated and changed parts of her original work in frequent revisions over the years, and she foresaw that one day still other parts would no longer be applicable. And, conversely, she recognized that new aspects of modern life, nonexistent then and therefore unmentioned in earlier editions, would need to be considered.

As a result, Emily Post founded—in 1946—the Emily Post Institute. The purpose of the Institute was, and is, to perpetuate the traditions of gracious living by making available the most recent information on etiquette today. The staff of the Institute worked closely with Mrs. Post herself, and she actively supervised all phases of the work until her recent death. She insisted from the beginning that I take an active part, and it is for this reason that I have undertaken this revision of *Etiquette*.

All of us connected with this project have constantly kept in mind the need to maintain the high standards set by Emily Post, although in the less formal life that most of us lead today, some of the rules may seem more stringent than ever. If we have succeeded in making this revision of her book a useful, readable, and practical guide on all questions of etiquette for young and old alike, then we will know that we have carried on the work started by Emily Post as she would have wished.

ELIZABETH L. POST

CONTENTS

Part ONE

THE ART OF CONVERSATION

Part TWO

CORRESPONDENCE

Part THREE

AS OTHERS SEE YOU

Part FOUR

ADVICE FOR TRAVELERS

Part FIVE

FORMAL ENTERTAINING

Part SIX

INFORMAL ENTERTAINING

Part SEVEN

SPECIAL OCCASIONS

Part EIGHT

WEDDINGS

Part NINE

ON THE SUBJECT OF INVITATIONS

Part TEN

CARDS AND CALLS

Part ELEVEN

PROTOCOL IN OFFICIAL CIRCLES

Part TWELVE

GOOD MANNERS FOR EVERY DAY

Part THIRTEEN

ON HOW TO DRESS

Part FOURTEEN

THE WELL-APPOINTED HOUSE

Part FIFTEEN

FAMILY LIFE

Emily Post's
ETIQUETTE

Part ONE

THE ART OF CONVERSATION

1

Introductions, greetings, and farewells

The words we say when we meet someone, whether or not we ever expect to see him again, can create an impression with far-reaching consequences. This also applies to our manner of leaving a new acquaintance. As a result, the forms used on such occasions are more important than their brevity and simplicity suggest. An automatic and easy familiarity with them leaves us free to turn our minds to the more complicated arts of conversation and listening.

THE UNBREAKABLE RULES OF INTRODUCTION

Although rules for introductions have become much less rigid in recent years, and there is considerable variation in the phrases used, certain forms must be followed.

First, a younger person is presented *to* an older person. Second, a gentlemen is always presented *to* a lady, even though she is no older than eighteen. Third, no woman is ever presented to a man, unless he is: the President of the United States; the recognized head of another country; a member of a royal family; a cardinal or other church dignitary.

THE USUAL FORMS OF INTRODUCTION

The simplest form of introduction, suitable for all but the most formal occasions, is the mere pronouncing of the two names: "Mrs. Woodman, Mrs. Norman."

A man and a woman may be introduced in the same way: "Mrs. Woodman, Mr. Schley." A mother introducing a man to her grown daughter would say, "Mr. Schley, I'd like to introduce you to my daughter, Mary." If Mary is married, her last name may be added: "My daughter, Mary Smartlington."

The same form may be used when introducing a stepparent and an acquaintance. In order to avoid confusion you say, "Mrs. Brown, my stepfather, Mr. Jones." This is really much more pleasant and affectionate than saying, "Mrs. Brown, my mother's husband."

Although the name of a stranger or of the older or more prominent person is properly said first, this is not really too important—except that a woman's name must be said before a man's unless the preposition "to" is used before the lady's name. For instance, if you find yourself saying Mr. Norman's name first, it is quite simple to correct this slip by saying, "Mr. Norman, may I introduce you to Mrs. Maddox?" Or, with greater friendliness, "Mr. Norman, I'd like to introduce you to Mrs. Maddox."

Formally, a man introduces another man to his wife: "Mr. Brown, may I introduce you to my wife?" If this seems awkward to you or seems to imply that you are asking Mr. Brown's permission to present him to your wife, you can say, "Mr. Brown, I'd like to introduce you to my wife."

To a friend a husband would say, "Jim, I want you to meet my wife" (never "the wife"!). Then he adds, "Mary, Jim Buyer." If they are all the same age, he probably just says, "Mary, this is Bob Ace," indicating that he expects his friend to call his wife "Mary."

A lady introduces her husband to friends as "John" and to acquaintances as "my husband." You may always use the forms "my husband" and "my wife," because they are proper no matter to whom you are talking. "Mr. Jones" or "Mrs. Jones" are only used when introducing an employee to one's husband or wife.

When said with an enthusiastic inflection, an introduction prefaced by "This is" can express a warmth and charm that other introductions lack. This feeling was once illustrated in *Punch* by a drawing of a small boy leading an abashed small girl by the hand to his mother and radiantly exclaiming, "Mummy! THIS IS HER!" In the same way, a youngster might introduce a favorite teacher enthusiastically, "Mother, *this* is Miss Brown," or "Miss Brown, *this* is my mother!"

INTRODUCING RELATIVES-IN-LAW

A woman formally introduces her son's wife to acquaintances as "My daughter-in-law," but to friends she simply says "Mary, Dick's wife." The more formal "my daughter-in-law" depends for its warmth on the tone of voice in which it is spoken. And this is, of course, an extremely important point in all introductions: by tone, the same words can convey every shade of feeling, from cool indifference to adoration.

The introduction of a parent-in-law as simply "Father" or "Mother" is well meant, but can be confusing. It is better to say, "This is my mother-in-law" or, if you prefer, "This is Bill's mother." When introducing other relatives-in-law, say, "My brother John's wife," or "John's wife." These identifications are clearer than "My sister-in-law."

INTRODUCING STEPPARENTS

When a child has always lived with his stepparents and has been given their name, he almost invariably calls them "Mother" and "Father" (or derivatives of those names) and introduces them in that way. When he has come to live with one stepparent, or two, later in life, the situation is different, because he may well retain his own name. Since this can be extremely confusing when introductions are necessary, the relationship should be made clear at once. There is nothing objectionable or derogatory in the terms "stepmother" or "stepfather," and the simplest form of introduction, said in the warmest tone to indicate an affectionate relationship, is, "Mrs. Jones, I'd like you to meet my stepfather, Mr. Casey," or "Mr. Fulbright, may I introduce you to my stepmother?" In the latter case it is not necessary, although perfectly proper, to say her name, as it would be the same as a son's or unmarried daughter's.

The same rule holds true when the parents are the introducers. A man would correctly introduce his wife's son by a former marriage, "Jack, I'd like you to meet my stepson, Jimmy Winters."

TEEN-AGERS AND YOUNG ADULTS

Informality is the rule among young adults and teen-agers. Muriel Manners, for example, taking a friend to the country club, greets a group of friends with "Hello, everybody. This is Sally Stranger." Everyone says "Hi" or "Hello, Sally," and further introductions are made individually by those she has just met: "Sally Stranger, Lucy and Bob Gilding." Or "Lucy, this is Sally Stranger," and then to Sally, "This is Bob Gilding, and this is Tom Brown."

OTHER PERMISSIBLE FORMS

Many other forms of introduction could be called conversational introductions. For example: "Mrs. Parker, do you know Mrs. Norman?" or "Mrs. Robinson, have you met Mrs. Parker?"

A few words of explanation will make the introduction of a stranger pleasantly smooth: "Mrs. Worldly—Miss Jenkins. She writes as Grace Gotham," or "Mr. Neighbor, I'd like you to meet Mr. Tennis. He just won the tournament at Forest Hills." Such well-meant explanations can be overdone, however, for you may create the effect of trying to impress one acquaintance with another's importance.

FORMS TO AVOID

Never say, "Mr. Jones, shake hands with Mr. Smith," or "Mrs. Jones, I want to make you acquainted with Mrs. Smith." And in introducing one person to another, don't call one of them "my friend." You may say "my aunt" or "my sister" or "my cousin," but to pick out one person as "my friend" implies that the other person is not.

An agreeable form of introduction is "Mrs. Smith, I want (or, I'd like) you to meet Mrs. Jones." But never say, "Mrs. Smith, meet Mrs. Jones." This last phrase is neither friendly nor courteous.

Do not repeat "Mrs. Jones—Mrs. Smith. Mrs. Smith—Mrs. Jones." To say each name once is enough, except when one is foreign or difficult to pronounce, in which case repeating the name a second time, and slowly, is helpful.

Some people dislike being asked their names, and "What is your name?" is abrupt and unflattering. If giving your own name doesn't elicit the information, you can almost always find a third person later and ask, "Who was the attractive woman with the gray hat?" The next time you see her, you will be able to say, "How do you do, Mrs. Green?"

FORMAL AND CEREMONIAL FORMS OF INTRODUCTION

The most ceremonious introduction possible is: "Mrs. Cartwright, may I present Mr. Traveler?" *Present* is somewhat more formal than *introduce*, but "may I introduce" is equally proper.

TO THE PRESIDENT OF THE UNITED STATES

The correct introduction of a man or a woman is: "Mr. President, I have the honor to present Mrs. (or Mr.) Williams," or "Mrs. Williams of Chicago," if further identification is really necessary.

Both men and women respond in the same way. That is, Mrs. Williams (as well as Mr. Williams) bows. If the President offers his hand, Mrs. Williams gives him hers. She does not offer hers if he fails to make this gesture of courtesy—as is most unlikely.

TO A REIGNING SOVEREIGN

Because the formality of having one's name put on a presentation list has been gone through beforehand, the "accepted" name is repeated at the actual presentation from one functionary to another, and nothing is said to the king or queen except "Mrs. (or Mr.) Williams."

Mrs. Williams curtsies, and if the king offers to shake hands, she curtsies again as she gives him her hand. If she has any objection to curtsying, she should not ask to be presented to the sovereign. Mr. Williams follows the same procedure, bowing instead of curtsying.

On less formal occasions a woman is presented to a member of a reigning family: "Your Royal Highness (or whatever the title), may I present Mrs. Williams?"

TO CHURCH DIGNITARIES

To a cardinal one says, "Your Eminence (or in England, Your Grace), may I present Mrs. Williams?"

A non-Catholic behaves exactly as he would to a king, but a Roman Catholic drops on the right knee, places the right hand, palm down, under the cardinal's extended hand, and kisses his ring.

A woman is always presented to church dignitaries. Mrs. Williams would reply to these introductions by saying to an archbishop, "How do you do, Your Excellency?" or to a monsignor, "How do you do, Monsignor Ryan?" She would speak to a priest as "Father Kelly" or simply "Father."

TO OTHER DISTINGUISHED PERSONS

With the exception of heads of state and church dignitaries, the following persons are all presented *to* women by their proper titles. A foreign ambassador is presented, "Your Excellency, may I present you to Mrs. Williams?" A senator is introduced, "Mrs. Williams, may I present Senator Davis?" A senator is always "Senator Davis," even when he is no longer in office. But the President of the United States, once out of office, becomes "Mister."

Former governors or ambassadors are both properly "The Honorable." On ceremonial occasions you would present "The Honorable John Jones, former Governor of the State of Blank." Among friends, of course, "The Honorable John Jones" may be introduced simply as "Mr. Jones."

Doctors and judges are always introduced and addressed by their titles. Protestant clergymen are "Mister" unless they hold the title of doctor, dean, or canon, in which case the surname is added to the proper title. But a Catholic priest is "Father," whatever his other titles may be.

If you are introduced to a prominent person and the one making the introduction has not spoken clearly or has not used a title (as he should have), the safest thing for you to say is "How do you do?" If the conversation continues and the person's title is still not mentioned, you may address any gentleman as "Sir." In fact, to avoid repetition of long titles like "Your Royal Highness" or "Mr. President," it is preferable to say "Ma'am" or "Sir" occasionally.

For a chart of titles to be used in addressing and introducing important persons, see Chapter Seven.

WHEN TO INTRODUCE

Introductions are always required at the presentation of other guests to a guest of honor. If you arrive after the receiving line has dispersed, you must present yourself, because it is the height of rudeness to go to an entertainment given in honor of someone and fail to greet him.

RECEIVING LINES

If the party is a very big one for a stranger, the hostess receives, standing with the special guest. As each guest approaches, the hostess say, "Mrs. Famous, this is my neighbor Mrs. Johnson"; "Mr. Prominent, our headmaster, Mr. Riley"; or, simply, "Mrs. Notable, Mrs. Stokes." If the guest of honor offers his or her hand, the other guest says "How do you do?" or "I'm so glad to meet you," and moves on. At a smaller, friendlier party given for someone known to most of the people present, the guest of honor does not receive with the hostess, but sits or stands in a convenient place so that everyone can go up and talk to him or her.

Even at large balls and receptions the receiving line should be limited to four whenever possible. One thinks of a receiving line as being composed entirely of women, yet there are many occasions when men also are included, and men sometimes receive alone.

WHEN A GUEST IS UNKNOWN TO HOSTESS

When you are taking a houseguest with you to a party who is not known to your friends, remember to introduce him or her to everyone you meet. This does not mean that you should make a grand tour of the room—but it is unfair to your hostess to expect her to look after *your* guest and to have a stranger's name at the tip of her tongue in order to introduce him to her other guests.

FORMAL DINNERS

At a formal dinner the host should try to see that every gentleman either knows or is introduced to the lady he is to take in to dinner, but this is not always practical at a very large dinner. The man who does not know Mrs. James Jones, whose name is in his "dinner envelope," should try to find out who she is and ask to be introduced to her. If even this is difficult, it is entirely correct for him to go up to her and say, "Mrs. Jones? I'm Henry Smith, and I believe that I'm to have the pleasure of taking you in to dinner."

Strangers sitting next to each other at the table should introduce themselves. A gentleman says, "I'm Arthur Robinson," and an older lady replies, "I'm Mrs. Hunter Jones." A younger woman says, "I'm Mary

Brown," and perhaps adds, "Bob Brown's wife." Your neighbor's place card is a handy reminder if you do not quite catch, or do not remember. the name he or she gives you.

When a woman finds herself next to an unknown man at a dinner party, she may or may not start talking to him without telling him her name. But if he introduces himself to her, she immediately says, "I'm Mary Smith."

Whether they exchange names or not, all people who find themselves seated together at any table must accept the obligation of talking. To sit side by side without speaking is a great discourtesy to your hostess, let alone the person next to whom you are sitting.

ONE PERSON TO A GROUP

On formal occasions when a great many people are present, an arrival is not introduced to every person there. He should be introduced to one or two people, or he may talk with those nearby without exchanging names.

Let us suppose you are the hostess at a small luncheon. Your position is not necessarily by the door, but it is near it. Mrs. King and Mrs. Lawrence are sitting quite close to you. Miss Robinson and Miss Brown are farther away. Mrs. Jones enters. You go and shake hands with her, then stand aside to see if she goes to speak to anyone. If she apparently knows no one, you say, "Mrs. King, Mrs. Jones." If Mrs. King is younger she rises, shakes hands with Mrs. Jones, and then sits down. If Mrs. King is about the same age as Mrs. Jones, or older, she merely extends her hand and does not rise. Having said "Mrs. Jones" once, you do not repeat it immediately, but turning to the other lady sitting nearby, you say, "And this is Mrs. Lawrence." You can also look across the room and continue, "Miss Robinson, Miss Brown, Mrs. Jones." The two nod but do not rise. When the group is made up of young people, first names may be used instead of "Miss" and "Mrs."—"Ann Brown, Mary Jones."

It is much more practical to name those already present before naming the new arrival. Mrs. Jones is paying attention, of course, but one who is chatting may need to hear her own name before she hears the name of the new arrival.

The well-meant practice of leading a guest on a tour around the room to make sure that he—or more especially she—is introduced to everyone is usually a failure. The poor stranger is hopelessly confused by too many names, and the hostess is often interrupted by the arrival of other guests.

The best procedure is to seat a stranger with a nearby group, introducing her to them. Even if the hostess does not complete these introductions the stranger will not be marooned, because in a friend's house people *always* talk with those seated near them. The good hostess, however, will make every effort to see that all her guests are introduced during the course of any party of moderate size.

INTRODUCING ONESELF

At all informal gatherings the home of a friend serves in itself as an introduction. But at a very large party (a dance or a wedding reception, for example) it is not necessary to speak with those whom you do not know, unless you and another guest find yourselves apart from the others. In such a case, you simply make casual conversation, and if the other seems happy to talk, you should introduce yourself with an identifying remark: "I'm Sally's cousin," or "I live next door to Bill."

There are many occasions when you have a good reason for knowing someone, and then it is quite proper to introduce yourself. For instance, you would say, "Mrs. Worldly, aren't you a friend of my mother's? I'm Jane, Mrs. John Smith's daughter." Mrs. Worldly says, "Yes, I am. How nice to see you."

When a strange man says, "Aren't you Sally Patterson?" Sally says "Yes, I am" and waits for an explanation. He tells her his name and where he thinks they met—at a college prom or a friend's house, perhaps. If Sally remembers the occasion she acknowledges it by saying, "Oh, yes. How nice to see you again," and the introduction is complete. But if Sally never went to the college he mentions, or never heard of his friend, she must say so at once. She need not cut him dead, but she should not continue the conversation under false pretenses.

WHEN INCORRECTLY INTRODUCED

We have all, at one time or another, been incorrectly introduced. One's title may be wrongly given, the name can be confused or mispronounced, or the identification may be erroneous. It is only sensible and kind that the person being introduced correct the error immediately. If, for example, a hostess introduces him to a group as "a surgeon who has just moved to Greenwich" when he is really a general practitioner, he should explain this to the new acquaintances—and the hostess, if she remains there—at once. He should also make a correction should she refer to him as "Mister" instead of "Doctor," or call him "Dr. Donald" instead of "Dr. McDonald."

When someone is introducing a stranger to a number of people and consistently says the name wrong, the person being introduced should correct the host as soon as he realizes it is not just a slip of the tongue. He should do so not with annoyance but, if possible, making light of it.

WHEN NOT TO INTRODUCE

At a small social gathering it is quite all right for the hostess to introduce as many people as she can, but at a large party or wedding reception repeating never-to-be-remembered names is a mistake—unless there is some good reason for doing so. For instance, a friend might be chagrined if he were not introduced to a celebrity or a person in whom he had a special interest.

An arriving visitor is never introduced to someone who is taking leave. Nor is an animated conversation between two persons interrupted to introduce a third.

CONVERSATION WITHOUT INTRODUCTION

Sometimes it happens that in talking to one person, you want to include another in your conversation without making an introduction. Suppose you are talking in your yard to a gardener, and a friend joins you. You greet her and then casually include her by saying, "Mr. Smith is suggesting that I dig up these daisies and put in delphiniums." Whether or not your friend comments about the change in color of your flower bed, she has been made part of your conversation.

There are other occasions when a halfway introduction seems most appropriate. Suppose, for example, you wish to make a maid's name known to a guest. "Olga, would you please take Mrs. Jones's bag to her room?" Or you might say to your guest, "Mary, this is Hilda, who will be glad to take your bag for you."

Even in formal households, loved and respected servants, especially those who have been with a family for many years, are often introduced to close friends. A young man might say to his fiancée, "Mary, this is Lizzy Smith, who brought me up," and to Lizzy, "Lizzy, I know you'll be as crazy about Mary as I am."

In many homes one person is employed who helps in so many ways that she becomes more than a "housekeeper" and is often known as a "mother's helper." These wonderful people frequently are almost members of the family and rightfully expect to be treated as such. They are always introduced to guests, especially to houseguests. The hostess might say, "Mary, this is Sally Jones, whom we couldn't manage without. Sally, this is my friend Mrs. Charles." If Sally is on hand to take wraps from dinner guests, she is introduced in the same way. An older woman, especially one whose employers are a young couple, may be called and introduced as "Mrs. Jones."

WHAT TO DO WHEN INTRODUCED

WHAT TO SAY

"How do you do?" followed by the name of the person you have just met is a traditional and acceptable response to a formal introduction. However, if you think about it, the phrase "How do you do?" has little meaning. Therefore, except on very formal occasions when tradition is important and desirable, I prefer the less formal responses: "Hello," or "I'm very glad to meet you." In the case of an older or prominent person, the addition of the name adds a note of respect, and repeating the name is a great help, too, in committing it to memory.

If you have not heard the new name clearly, you may ask to have it repeated, but it is perfectly correct to say simply, "How do you do?" It may be said gladly or casually, and it may be varied in emphasis, depending on the degree of warmth you wish to convey. In any event, when Mrs. Worldly has been introduced to Mr. Struthers and replies, "How do you do, Mr. Struthers?" he nods and need not say anything more, or he may say, "I'm very glad to meet you."

When you meet someone whom you have heard a great deal about and have wanted to meet, you may of course say, "Oh, I am so *glad* to meet you," and then go on to say, "John Brown speaks of you all the time," or whatever may be the reason for your special interest.

WHEN TO SHAKE HANDS

Men usually shake hands when they are introduced to each other, even if they have to cross a room to do so. Ladies may do as they wish. Boys and girls both follow the example of their fathers and shake hands when introduced to adults.

When a man is introduced to a woman, she generally smiles, nods, and says, "How do you do?" Strictly speaking, it is her place to offer her hand or not, as she chooses; but if he should extend his hand, she must give him hers. Nothing could be ruder than to ignore any spontaneous friendliness. Technically, it is the place of a man to whom another is being introduced to offer his hand first, but the gesture is usually simultaneous.

There is no fixed rule about shaking hands on parting. Nearly all rules of etiquette are elastic, but there is a wide distance between rudeness and reserve. You can simultaneously be courteously polite and reserved with someone who does not appeal to you, or you can be welcoming and friendly to another whom you like on sight.

THE PERSONALITY OF A HANDSHAKE

A handshake can create a feeling of friendliness or of irritation between two strangers. No one likes a "boneless" hand extended as though it were a spray of seaweed or a boiled fish, and what woman does not wince at the viselike grasp that cuts her rings into her flesh and temporarily paralyzes every finger?

The proper handshake is brief, but there should be strength and warmth in the clasp, and one should at the same time look at the person whose hand he takes. In giving her hand to a foreigner, a woman should relax her arm and fingers, for it is customary in many countries for him to lift her hand to his lips. A hand should have life even though it is passive—a relaxed hand does not mean a wet rag.

WHEN TO RISE

On formal occasions the hostess always stands at the door with the host nearby, and both shake hands with every arrival. On informal occasions, they both stand up and go to greet each guest. Children should rise for every grown person who enters the room (or to be introduced to another child) and stand until the older person is seated. Members of the family other than the host and hostess rise to greet guests, but do not necessarily shake hands.

A woman does not stand when being introduced to someone at a distance, nor when shaking hands with anyone, unless that person is much older.

A man always rises when a woman comes into a room, and remains standing until she is seated or leaves his vicinity. In public places, men do not jump up for every strange woman who happens to approach, but if any woman stops to talk to him, he stands as he answers her.

When a woman goes to a man's office on business, he should stand up to receive her, offer her a chair, and should not sit down until after she is seated. When she rises to leave, he gets up instantly, stands for as long as she remains and then goes with her as far as the door, which he holds open for her.

In a restaurant when a woman greets a man in passing, he merely makes the gesture of rising slightly from his chair and nodding.

For additional details, see Chapter Twelve, "In Restaurants."

THE YOUNG GREET THE OLD

It is very rude for young people not to go and shake hands with an older person whom they meet away from home, especially someone to whose house they have often gone. It is not, however, necessary for either young women or young men to linger and enter into a long conversation, unless the older person detains them, which he should not do beyond a minute or two.

NAME "BLACKOUTS"

When you are talking with someone whose name you are struggling to remember and a friend joins you and looks inquiringly from you to the nameless person you are obviously helpless to do anything other than introduce your friend to the stranger by saying to the latter, "Oh, don't you know Mrs. Neighbor?"

The stranger should be tactful and understanding enough to announce his own name. If he says nothing, however, and Mrs. Neighbor makes matters worse by saying, "You didn't tell me your friend's name," the situation reaches the height of embarrassment. The only solution then is to be completely frank, admit you do not remember the name, and ask them to complete the introduction themselves.

When meeting someone who may have forgotten you, never say, "You don't remember me, do you?" and then stop. Unless the person you speak to greets you by name, you should say at once, "I'm Mrs. Brown" or "Mary Brown." And if this does not bring a glimmer of recognition, "We met at the Robertses'."

INFORMAL GREETINGS

"Hello" is the universal form of greeting in America, and it is acceptable in any situation except after a formal introduction. Even comparative strangers say "Hello" in passing, and it is the friendly response to a first-name introduction. "Sally, I'd like you to meet Joan," and Sally says, "Hello, Joan, I'm glad to meet you."

Even more informal is the widely used "Hi." A friendly greeting for people who already know each other, it should never be said in answer to an introduction.

In the business world "Good morning" is the usual greeting before the lunch hour; after lunch, "Good afternoon" is proper. But because these sound somewhat stilted, they have largely been replaced by "Hello" and a smile.

"Good afternoon" is used, however, as a phrase of dismissal, indicating that an interview is ended, a class is over, etc. Among friends or business acquaintances who know each other personally, "Good-bye" or "Good night" is said on parting.

GREETINGS IN PUBLIC

A tipping or slight raising of the hat on the man's part and a nod and smile on the woman's is all that is necessary when casual acquaintances meet by accident. In theaters, restaurants, shops, or almost any public place, people speak to acquaintances as long as the greeting does not create a situation that may disturb others around them, as it would in the middle of a movie. If they are too far apart to speak without shouting, they simply smile and wave.

It is always safer to nod to someone whose face is familiar than to run the risk of ignoring an acquaintance. It is often difficult to recognize people whom one has met when they are wearing a different type of clothing—sports clothes rather than evening dress, for instance.

But the habit that causes most unintended rudeness is absentmindedness. Absorbed in their own thoughts, people do not hear the voice or see the motions made by someone trying to speak to them. They may walk right by a friend unaware of his proximity. Although it is annoying to be passed by an "unseeing" acquaintance, one should be careful not to confuse absentmindedness with intentional slight.

Except at a wedding, people greet each other in church with a nod and a smile. At weddings people do speak softly to friends sitting near them, but it would be shocking to enter a church and hear an undignified and unceremonious babel of voices. If you go to a church other than your own and a stranger offers you a seat in his pew, you should, of course, quietly say "Thank you." But you do not greet anyone aloud until you are out in the vestibule or on the church steps, when you naturally speak to your friends as you meet.

THE ANSWER TO "HOW ARE YOU?"

Tact produces good manners. To a chronic invalid or someone in great sorrow or anxiety, a gay "Hello, Mrs. Jones! How *are* you? You look fine!" is really tactless, however well intended, since a truthful answer would make the situation emotional. In such a case Mrs. Jones can only reply, "All right, thank you." She may be feeling that everything is all wrong, but to let go and tell the truth would open the floodgates disastrously.

"Fine, thank you" or "Very well, thank you" is normally the correct and conventional answer to "How are you?" unless there is reason to believe that the person asking *really* wants to know the state of one's health.

THE INTENTIONAL "CUT"

For one person to look directly at another and not acknowledge his greeting is a deliberate breach of civility. The "cut" is quite different from the slight caused by poor vision or absentmindedness. A direct stare of blank denial is not only insulting to its victim but embarrassing to every witness.

TAKING LEAVE

When a visitor is ready to leave, he or she stands up at a pause in the conversation. To those with whom he has been talking, he says, "Good-bye. I hope I'll see you again soon," or simply, "I'm glad to have met you." The others answer that they were delighted to meet him too. Or a woman replies to another who hopes to see her again, "I hope so, too," or merely, "Thank you."

In taking leave of a group of strangers—whether you have been introduced or not—you nod and smile a good-bye to those who happen to be looking at you, but you do not attempt to attract the attention of others who are unaware that you are leaving.

If you must leave a large party early, you find your hostess and say good-bye without calling more attention than necessary to your going. It might suggest leaving to others and so lead to the premature breaking up of the party.

2

Names and titles

A century ago it was not unusual for a wife to refer to her husband as "Mr. Jones" and to call him "Mr. Jones" when she was speaking to him, even in private. The use of first names was restricted to children, brothers and sisters, close cousins, a very few lifelong friends (of the same sex, of course), and perhaps a girl and her fiancé. Ridiculous as these customs now sound, the pendulum sometimes seems to have swung a bit too far in the other direction. First names, titles of respect, and descriptive phrases for members of the family have become a hodgepodge of informality and confusion.

THE USE OF FIRST NAMES

First names are so widely accepted today that even strangers who have just been introduced immediately start to call each other "Jack" and "Hugh." Certainly if two people find each other attractive and discover common interests, it is perfectly correct for one to say to the other, "Please call me Barbara." Furthermore, at an informal party in the home of friends it is customary to use first names after having responded to the introductions. If you don't, you will surely be thought stiff and unfriendly.

The times when first names may not be used *except by specific request* are:

To a superior in one's business, unless it is obviously the office custom.

To a person of higher rank (a diplomat, for example).

To an older person.

We all know people of middle age and older who seem to think that being called "Sally" or "Jack" by Doris Debutante and Bobby Freshman will take them back to the same age level. "Sally" or "Jack" may suggest a camaraderie that "Mrs. Collins" or "Mr. Sears" does not. But one wonders how Mrs. Collins would feel if she could hear those same youngsters calling her "Old Sal" behind her back.

When an older person calls a younger person by his first name, the younger is not to take it as an invitation to respond with a first name. But if Mrs. Collins and Mr. Sears prefer to be "Sally" and "Jack," no one else has a right to object.

PARENTS

Parents should insist on respect in the manner in which they permit their children to address them. *It is a flagrant violation of good manners for children to call their natural parents by their first names.*

STEPPARENTS

The question of what children should call their stepparents is difficult because the circumstances are so variable, and the answer must depend on what seems best in each case.

The most important thing is that a child should *never* be FORCED to call a stepparent "Mother" or "Father" or any nickname having that meaning, especially if his own parent is living. If the child *chooses* to do so, it is a compliment to the stepparent and should be encouraged.

If a child does not, and probably will not, know his own parent, then he would consider a stepparent who has brought him up as his own and say "Mother" or "Father." This is especially true if he has stepbrothers or stepsisters whom he hears using those names. But if the child is older when one parent remarries, the situation is quite different. If he has known the stepparent for some time, he may call him (or her) by a nickname or first name. Actually, a nickname seems to be the best solution, if one can be found that is appropriate and not a derivative of "Mother" or "Father."

NAMES FOR PARENTS-IN-LAW

The question of what a bride is to call her parents-in-law has no definite answer either, and the choice of names is purely personal. In unusually formal families, one hears "Mr." and "Mrs.," which to most of us sounds very cold. "Mr. and Mrs. B." seems warmer and more intimate than "Mr. and Mrs. Brown." More often, parents-in-law are called by names that mean mother and father, but are not the names that the bride uses for her own parents. Or perhaps they are called "Mr." and "Mrs." until a grandchild's nicknames—"Mimi" and "Poppy," for example—gradually become theirs. When a son or daughter has a special nickname for a parent, the new husband or wife usually uses that same name. And this is one case, especially if the parents are young, when a younger person may call the older by a first name.

The ban against "Mother" and "Father" results from consideration for one's own parents. Very few mothers or fathers would be happy to hear their own special names used for someone else.

The less intimate relationships of aunts, uncles, and even grandparents never come into question, because with the exception of his parents, the bride calls all her husband's relatives exactly what he does, and he in turn does the same.

OTHER ADULTS

Some adults dislike being called "Aunt," "Uncle," or "Cousin" when no such relationship exists. In other cases, really intimate friends are devoted to the children and feel that "Mr. (or "Mrs.) Surname" does not express the affectionate relationship. These friends or relatives may suggest nicknames for themselves or even specifically request that the youngsters call them by their first names. Otherwise, a child addresses all friends of his parents as "Mr. (or "Mrs.) Surname."

REFERRING TO HER HUSBAND OR HIS WIFE

Usually—and correctly—a lady says "my husband" when speaking of him to an acquaintance. But to a friend or to the friend of a friend, she speaks of him as "John." This usage does not, however, give anyone else the privilege of calling him "John" unless asked to do so.

In the same way, Mr. Worldly speaks of "Edith" to intimate friends and to every woman whom they both know socially, whether they themselves call her "Edith" or "Mrs. Worldly." But to a man who is not an intimate friend or to a woman who is a stranger, he speaks of her as "my wife." Thus, when the Duke of Edinburgh, accompanying Queen Elizabeth II, was hailed by a former shipmate in the British Navy, he correctly introduced him to "my wife."

NAME OF SAFETY

The so-called "name of safety"—properly used by every man, woman, or child when speaking to a stranger about any member of the family—is "my wife," "my husband," "my daughter," "my mother," or as necessary, "my sister, Alice," "my son, George." These forms are correct for every occasion; whereas, should Mrs. Jansen, whom you have met socially, speak of her husband as "Mr. Jansen," she would be very rude.

WHEN NOT TO REFER BY FIRST NAME

In speaking about other people, "Mr.," "Mrs.," or "Miss" is used if the person with whom you are talking does not know the one to whom you refer. You should not speak of absent friends by their first names unless you have referred to them often enough so that the person to whom you are talking realizes who they are. For example, to a close friend to whom you had often spoken of your college roommate you might say, "We are so delighted—Jane Stuart is coming East to visit us next month." But in speaking of someone you have mentioned only once or twice, a word of identification is necessary. "Yesterday I ran into that nice Mrs. Brown who was on the cruise with us last year."

ANNOUNCING ONESELF

ARRIVING AT THE DOOR

When an adult member of the family comes to the door in answer to your ring, you never call yourself "Mr." or "Mrs." or "Miss." If he does not know you, identify yourself by a sentence or two: "I'm John Grant, a friend of Jim's at the office. Is he home?" or "Susan and I met at the Barry's cocktail party. I told her I'd drop by."

If a child answers the door, you say, "I'm Mr. Grant" or "Mrs. Smythe" and "Would you please call your mother for me, if she is at home?"

If the door is answered by a maid who does not know you and if you are not expected, you say, "Mr. John Grant. Is Mrs. Jones in?" If you are expected, you merely say, "Mr. Grant," and you may add, "Mrs. Jones is expecting me." A woman uses "Mrs. Grant" in either case.

THE BUSINESSMAN ANNOUNCES HIMSELF

When you enter an unfamiliar office, say to the receptionist, "Good morning. My name is Roger Sailscurve. I have a ten-o'clock appointment with Mr. Byre." At this point, offer your business card. It helps the receptionist give your name correctly to the secretary of the person you with to see. And some firms keep the card as a record of each visitor.

If you do not have a specific appointment, it is helpful to give a little information about your business. "Good afternoon, I'm Roger Sailscurve of the Schmid Corporation. I'd like to see Mr. Byre about our line of lubricants."

ON THE TELEPHONE

Introducing oneself on the telephone is described in Chapter Sixty-two.

USE OF "DOCTOR"

When the title "Doctor" indicates a degree required for the practice of a profession, as in medicine, dentistry, or veterinary medicine, it is used instead of "Mister" at all times.

An earned title indicating that a man or woman has received a doctorate in divinity, philosophy, literature, etc. is always used professionally. In private life he may, if he prefers, continue to call himself "Mister." But in any situation where other people are introduced as "Mr.," "Mrs.," or "Miss" rather than by first names, it is a mark of recognition and respect to use the title "Doctor." The distinction, then, is in the social setting rather than in the type of degree.

He generally uses "Mister" or no title at all on social visiting cards or in social directories, and the initials of his degree do not follow his name.

THE USE OF JR., 2ND AND 3RD

A man with the same name as his father uses Jr. after his name as long as his father is alive. He may drop the Jr. after his father's death, or if he prefers, he may retain it in order not to be confused with his late father. This also helps to differentiate between his wife and his mother if the latter is still living and does not wish to be known as Mrs. Jones, Sr.

When a man is named after his father who is a "Jr.," he is called 3rd. A man named after his grandfather, uncle or cousin is called 2nd.

The following diagram may help to clarify these relationships

John Silas Acres

John Silas Acres, Jr.   Robert Smith Acres

John Silas Acres, 3rd   John Silas Acres, 2nd

The wife of each of these men uses the same suffix after her name as her husband does, i.e., Mrs. John Silas Acres, 3rd.

NAMES LEGALLY CHANGED

Whatever the reason for changing the name by which one has been known, social and business associates should be notified of the change if embarrassing situations are to be avoided. The quickest and simplest way of telling them is to send out formal announcements:

Mr. and Mrs. John Original-Name
Announce that by Permission of the Court
They and Their Children
Have Taken the Family Name of
Miller

SPECIAL USAGE OF WOMEN'S NAMES

A DIVORCEE'S NAME

Until recently, unless a divorcée took back her maiden name and used the title "Miss," her only possible form of address was her maiden name combined with her ex-husband's last name. Mary Jones who married John Smith, after divorcing him became Mrs. Jones Smith. This is still absolutely correct, but for those who find this unacceptable or confusing there is now an acceptable alternative.

Years ago divorce was uncommon, and when it occurred the divorcée, who was apt to remain in the same town or city where she was well known, seldom remarried. Therefore, her maiden name was known to all of the people around her, and its use identified her and also declared her divorced state. But today many divorcées move; they look for a new life in a community where their maiden names mean nothing and are a source of considerable confusion to people they meet. They are naturally introduced as Mary Smith, and new acquaintances have no way of making a connection with someone they hear of as Mrs. Jones Smith. By using the formerly unacceptable title "Mrs. Mary Smith" she established both her identity and her divorced status.

A divorcée may also prefer to use her given name as opposed to her maiden name when the combination of the two last names is ludicrous or unmanageable. Mrs. Mary Lipwitz is certainly easier for both Mary and her friends than Mrs. Hobenzollen Lipwitz. Mrs. White Black could not fail to cause considerable amusement, if not confusion.

It is quite true that the title "Mrs." should technically be used only in conjunction with one's husband's name, but in the interest of simplifying an awkward custom, an allowance may be made for those who prefer this form of address.

A MARRIED WOMAN'S LEGAL NAME

A woman's legal name consists of her given name, her maiden name, and her husband's name. Except in a few instances—for example, on income tax forms—the middle name is shortened to an initial. The title "Mrs." is never used with the legal signature since it should be used only with a woman's husband's first name. The only possible exception is in the case of a professional woman who wishes it to be known that she is married, but does not wish her husband's name to appear. In that case she may put "Mrs." in parentheses before her signature.

She uses her legal name as her signature on all business correspondence, on bank accounts, and all legal documents. On correspondence, to denote her marital status, she may write Mrs. Henry Smith below Barbara H. Smith.

PROFESSIONAL WOMEN IN SOCIAL SITUATIONS

A woman who has a degree in medicine, dentistry, etc., is always called "Doctor" professionally. She also may be introduced and referred to as "Doctor" socially. However, social correspondence to her and her husband is addressed "Mr. and Mrs. John Woods." In this instance she forgoes her professional title in the interest of convenience and social convention.

3

Words and how we use them

Nothing reveals our background, training, self-discipline, and education as quickly as the words we choose and how we pronounce them. Well-educated people, for example, invariably use certain expressions and appear to avoid others instinctively.

To speak English properly is not difficult. The dictionary is meticulous in its definitions, and rules of grammar determine each word's use. These matters can be learned by anyone who cares enough to try. Furthermore, the dictionary labels words as preferred, archaic, colloquial, popular, slang, or vulgar. The shades of meaning, however, may vary from one place to another, and there are, of course, local or regional dialects and accents. Usually, to speak as the educated people in one's hometown speak is sufficient for all social and domestic purposes. Be sure, though, not to confuse the educated or cultivated with the caricature—the "lady" with the comic-strip "society" manner who says "pahdon me" and "charmed" and talks of the elegant affairs she attends.

Of course, there are certain exceptional people with very little education who overcome all handicaps. They may say "He don't want to" and "I done it," proving their lack of grammatical training, but at the same time they are respected by everyone who knows them, because they are what they seem and pretend to be nothing more. This is far better than the extreme of pretentiousness. A genuine, sincere man or woman can go anywhere and be welcomed by everyone, provided that he is a person of some natural ability, wit, or charm.

PRONUNCIATION

Traits of speech typical of certain sections of the country or accents acquired from foreign-born parents are not to be confused with crude pronunciations whose origins are illiteracy or carelessness.

REGIONAL AND FOREIGN ACCENTS

An Irishman may have a brogue as rich as Irish stew, while another person may speak in soft Southern drawl, a flat New England tone, or a rolling Western style. The very crisp Boston accent is considered by some the best English spoken in America. In the South, there is a softness, with "I" turned to "Ah" and a tendency toward a drawl. People from Chicago say "Chicawgo," eat "chawklut," and drink "waaatuh." Philadelphia's "haow" and "caow" for "how" and "cow" are as typical as the twang of the Midwest. All these variations merely indicate the part of the country we are from. "Bot" and "thot" may sound ugly to those who pronounce "bought" and "thought" with lips shaped like an "O," but it is very possible that "bought" and "thought" sound equally ugly to the others. Yet regional variations are in no way unacceptable. Some people may think the speech of others sounds too flat, too soft, too harsh, too clipped, or too drawling, but it does not sound uncultivated. Only to those involved in making public speeches to the entire nation—perhaps as a candidate for federal office—could a markedly local accent be a handicap, because it might suggest to the listeners a mind limited to that particular locality and uninformed about the broader issues.

As a general rule, therefore, when you look up the pronunciation of a word in your dictionary, you need not be concerned because you may say the "ou" as in "out" or the "a" as in "add" in a way quite unlike that of a Bostonian or a San Franciscan. As long as the sound you produce is natural to you and consistent with your general speech pattern and your region's, you are quite correct—for *you*.

CARELESS AND IGNORANT PRONUNCIATIONS

Anyone can pronounce common English words properly with the help of a good dictionary and the willingness to use it. Too many errors are the result of nothing more or less than laziness. Differences such as those between "wash" and "wawsh" or "cahn't" and "can't" are unimportant, but an educated person doesn't commit errors such as "cherce" for "choice" and "the ay' ter" for "theater."

THE USE AND MEANING OF WORDS

REGIONAL EXPRESSIONS

The meanings of words as well as their pronunciations vary from one section of the United States to another. In one town the local grocer will put your purchases in a "bag," while in another, he provides a "sack." An expression common in Dallas might as well be Greek when the Texan uses it in Vermont. No one can be expected to know each and every one of these regional words and phrases. But we ought to be aware that such differences exist, especially when we find ourselves in another part of the country or talking with a visitor from another city. To use obscure colloquialisms with no concern for the listener's understanding —and hence his feelings—is hardly polite. If you are the listener, don't hesitate to ask the meaning of a word or phrase you do not understand. Otherwise, the conversation may slip into misunderstanding and confusion for no good reason.

SLANG

The *Standard College Dictionary* defines "slang" as follows: "Language, words, or phrases of a vigorous, colorful, facetious, or taboo nature, invented for specific occasions or uses, or derived from the unconventional use of the standard vocabulary." A slang expression, although usually short-lived, may achieve wide use, and in the evolution of language, many words originally slang have been adopted by good writers and speakers and have ultimately taken their place as accepted English.

The fact that slang is apt and forceful makes its use irresistible. Naturally, coarse or profane words are unacceptable, but so many entertaining or descriptive expressions are in common use that their exclusion from everyday conversation would be absurd.

To be an asset to your conversation, slang must be fresh and applicable or it is as unappetizing as cold gravy. Moreover, using slang is like underscoring written words; to be effective, it must be sparingly done. It is all too easy to fall into the habit of using too much or of depending on it to express ideas that it cannot adequately convey.

FOREIGN WORDS

Sprinkling foreign words indiscriminately through your speech is not a sign of great education—in fact it sounds pretentious—but an occasional word, used in its proper sense, adds color and interest to English speech and writing. There are many foreign words that have become an accepted part of our language, and we should be familiar with their meaning and pronunciation.

We cross paths so often with the many foreigners living in the United States that it is easy to increase one's knowledge of their languages. We have Italian grocers, German bakers, French and Spanish waiters—to name only a few—all of whom are delighted if you show an interest in their language, how it sounds, and what it means.

COMMON FRENCH WORDS

Among modern languages, French is the one from which we have borrowed the greatest number of words, and some, like "amateur," "fiancé," and "hors d'oeuvres," are used so frequently that it is essential to know how to pronounce them correctly.

The French and other foreign terms used on restaurant menus are too numerous to learn all at once. Many good cookbooks contain glossaries of these terms and provide an excellent source of reference. In any case, the waiter or headwaiter is always available to explain the dish to you if there is no translation, and you may make a note of the words for future use.

WORDS AND PHRASES TO AVOID

No one "arises," or "retires," or "resides" in a "residence." One gets up, takes a bath, goes to bed, and lives in a house. In other words, everything that is simple and direct is better form than the cumbersome and pretentious.

Other expressions are provincial; and if you want your speech to be pure, avoid them unless they are indigenous to you. They include such terms as:

reckon, guess, calculate, *or* figure, *meaning* think
visiting with, *meaning* talking with

WORDS CONFUSED AND MISUSED

Lady and gentleman. These meaningful words have become so discredited by misuse that those to whom they most accurately apply rarely use them. Instead they have substituted for them the less precise words man and woman.

However, an understanding of the true meaning of "lady" and "gentleman" is helpful to an understanding of the true meaning of good manners. To say that no man cheats at cards or strikes a woman in the face or to say that no woman tries to attract the attention of strange men would be false. Each of these statements is true of a gentleman and a lady but not necessarily of a man or a woman.

In practice, these words, though necessary in a book such as this, are very rarely used in ordinary conversation.

Home versus house. In its true meaning "home" conveys the spirit, the personality, and the hospitality of your house. "Home" is not a synonym for "house." A house is a solid structure built of wood or brick or stone. You can love your home, be at home, do whatever you please at home, and you can eat home cooking. But if you are sensitive to nuances, you never put a piece of furniture in "the home" unless you mean a charitable institution. You would say, "Our home was an old Georgian house," but not "We had a Georgian home."

Formal and informal. "Formal" is a synonym for "ceremonial." A formal party is conducted according to rules of established forms of ceremony.

In some houses—Mrs. Worldly's, for instance—formality is inevitable no matter how informal the invitation may be.

On the other hand, the Kindharts can invite a hundred guests and achieve a party that is strictly informal. Ordinary pleasant social intercourse between friends and neighbors could never be characterized as formal.

While the word "formal" used to mean the extreme degree of correctness, it is currently used to mean somewhat less.

An elderly gentleman and his grandson were sitting together at a beach club, when young George called out to a passing friend, "Hey, Jim, are we going formal tonight?"

Jim answered, "I think so."

Grandfather looked at George's shorts, bare feet, and T-shirt. "Tell me," he said, "what do you mean by 'going formal'?"

The boy shrugged and replied, "I don't know, exactly. I guess it means we've got to put on ties."

Gracious. Although the word "gracious" is one of the most beautiful in our language, it does imply an unavoidable flavor of condescension. It is therefore best applied to an elderly person who is bending down, as it were, from an earlier period of time rather than from an assumed position of superiority. Obviously, it is not suitably said of a young person who would prefer to be called friendly, responsive, or good-looking.

Party. In general speech "party" is correctly used to describe a social gathering, but never to refer to a person. "Do come and bring your guests or friends," never "you and your party." The word probably crept in as a synonym for "person" because of legal usage.

CULTIVATING AGREEABLE SPEECH

INCREASING VOCABULARY

Irritating speech is like a badly tuned car engine—each knock and thump disconcerts the listener. He hears the "er-er-and-er," shares the frantic search for a word or the effort with which each word is pronounced, and never hears the thoughts the speaker is trying so desperately to convey.

One of the best ways to cultivate taste in words is by reading good books. It must be remembered that there can be a vast difference between excellence and popularity and that many books on the best-seller lists have no literary merit.

Although we have many fine American authors, the works of two English writers, Rebecca West and Winston Churchill, are outstanding as sources of flawless English. And it is true that Winston Churchill's war memoirs have a value of "matter" as well as "manner" of writing English that sets a high standard. Rebecca West's writing is invaluable to those who are interested in finding an example of English at its *best.*

The best way to cultivate both vocabulary and a perfect pronunciation, apart from associating with cultivated people, is to get a small pronouncing dictionary and read it word by word, marking and studying any that you have used and mispronounced or those you wish to learn. Or choose a book and read it aloud to yourself, looking up words you come across that are not familiar to you and learning the meaning as well as the correct pronunciation.

There are excellent books available containing vocabulary-building instructions, with exercises to help you increase your knowledge of words and test your achievement. The consciousness of these exercises may initially make you sound a bit stilted, but by using your new vocabulary constantly, you will soon overcome this tendency.

A postscript of encouragement is that plain speech is much more pleasing and friend-making than the self-conscious use of a broad vocabulary that is not really natural to the speaker.

THE CHARMING SPEAKER

The often-heard but not-too-polite expression "You know she is a lady as soon as she opens her mouth" is not an exaggeration. A pleasing voice is the first requirement for charm of speech. A low voice—low in pitch, not in range—is always more pleasing than one forced up against the ceiling and apparently let out through a steam vent in the roof. On the other hand, a voice uttered with so little strength that it threatens to be extinguished is even more trying. Socially and in a business office, it is annoying to have to ask a "mumbler" to repeat what he has said. Making yourself heard is chiefly a matter of enunciation; if you breathe properly and pronounce distinctly, a low voice carries well and delights the listener's ear.

Screaming is not only ear-splitting but is also extremely bad form, since it attracts the attention of everyone within shouting radius. As a nation we do not talk too fast so much as too loudly. Tens of thousands twang and slur and shout and burr; many of us drawl and many others race tongues and breath at full speed, but the speed of our speech does not matter so much. It is pitch that is important, along with pronunciation and enunciation, both of which are essential to the listener's comfort.

Another outstanding attribute of charming speech is brevity. Speech that bores, exhausts, and exasperates is chatter that goes on and on and on with complete disregard of the increasing lethargy of its listeners.

See also Chapter Four, "Public Speaking."

4

Public speaking

Many excellent books have been published on the subject of parliamentary procedure, and in most high schools students are required to take courses in the subject and in public speaking as well. This chapter is intended not for experienced speakers or for those who have to run formal meetings frequently, but for the thousands of private citizens who may be called upon to speak at a club meeting, a P.T.A. meeting, or a testimonial dinner. To the novice, public speaking can be a terrifying experience, but there are many simple rules that can be a great help in making the occasion a success.

INTRODUCING A SPEAKER

Men are called upon more often than women to serve as masters of ceremonies or chairmen at dinners, and are expected to introduce the speakers. When the appointed time comes, if he is on a stage or platform, the chairman rises, steps forward, and taps firmly on the speaker's podium or table to attract attention. If he is at a dinner table, he simply rises, and the people near him immediately stop talking, which should be enough to bring quiet to the rest of the hall.

An introductory speech should be extremely brief in order not to divert time or attention from the main speaker. A few sentences to identify him are all that is necessary. If he is very well known, you might open your introduction by saying, "Our speaker tonight is Mr. Jim Jones. I know that it is not necessary for me to tell you about him as we have all read of his exploits in Africa. We are most fortunate in having persuaded him to fit this evening with us into his busy schedule, and it gives me great pleasure to introduce—Mr. Jones."

If the speaker is less famous, a few more remarks might be added to explain his background and the reason for his speaking to your organization. But avoid overdoing it, and confine your talk to two or three minutes at the most.

Having made the introduction, sit down quietly until the speech is over. Then you should rise, shake hands, and thank the speaker for his time, his effort, and his excellent speech. *See also Chapter Sixteen, "Conducting Meetings."*

PREPARING YOUR SPEECH

The greatest asset to a successful speech is having it well prepared and rehearsed in advance. It may be long or short, serious or humorous, but the confidence gained from the knowledge that your material is good and your presentation smooth is worth hours of preparation and practice. This does not mean that your speech should be rattled off like a memory exercise, and it should certainly never sound as if it were being read.

After you have written the speech, notes should be made (if it is long enough to warrant them) in large clear print on index cards or a small pad. These notes should be only an outline of the speech—a reminder in case you lose the train of thought. The speech should be rehearsed several times, first in front of a mirror and then, if possible, before family members or friends so that you will feel less strange when you stand before a larger audience. It is a good idea to try to express a thought in several different ways while you practice, for this tends to make your speech sound less "rehearsed" and more as if you were thinking about what you are saying.

OPENING WORDS

There is a set formula for opening a speech that is helpful to an inexperienced speaker because he hears the sound of his voice for a second or two while repeating exact phrases that he has committed to memory. He must turn to the chairman first and, calling him by name, thank him for his introduction; he greets any distinguished persons present and then the audience: "Mr. Chairman, Senator Brown, and fellow members of Delta Psi, good evening," or "Mr. President, Distinguished Guests, Ladies and Gentlemen."

Some speakers begin by giving the audience a suggestion of the points to be covered in the speech, others with an amusing story or a pertinent quotation to introduce the subject. It is wise not to make too important a point in the opening paragraphs because the audience may take a few minutes to settle down to listen. Also, most speakers "warm" to their subject and will make their salient points more forcefully after they have overcome any initial nervousness.

USE HUMOR AND PROPS

Everyone enjoys listening to a speaker who tells an amusing story well, but it must have some connection with his subject. There is nothing worse than a poor attempt at humor which fails either in the choice of the story itself or in its presentation. This distracts the audience and leaves them searching for the point rather than listening to the speaker. Jokes, anecdotes, and quotations are all useful means of giving a talk variety and interest. But remember that the audience wants to hear what *you* have to say, not just a collection of other people's thoughts and actions.

If your subject permits the use of illustrations or slides, by all means take advantage of this. Not only does it make your preparation easier (although you still must rehearse, using the slides and perfecting the timing and mechanical details), but the attention of an audience is held more firmly when it is seeing as well as hearing.

THE IMPORTANCE OF YOUR VOICE

Closely rivaling in importance your material and preparation is the quality of your voice. A low-pitched voice is vastly more attractive than a high one, but it must be loud enough so that the audience need not strain to hear. Speak slowly rather than fast (between ninety and one hundred and thirty words, or half a double-spaced typed page a minute), but vary the tempo or you will sound monotonous. A certain amount of variation in pitch is desirable, especially in telling a joke or story, and some words should be stressed for emphasis. All this is a matter of practice, and you should think of these points, as well as the content of your speech, while rehearsing.

If you are to use a microphone, try to arrive early enough to test it with your own voice. If this is not possible, make certain that someone has proved it to be working properly and try to watch the chairman while he is introducing you to see how close he stands, how loudly he speaks, and how he adjusts the height. Most people have a tendency to speak much too loudly into a microphone and to hold onto the stand, causing interference. If you have advance notice that a microphone is to be used, try to practice with one beforehand.

THE DANGER OF RAMBLING

The inexperienced speaker's most serious fault is a tendency to talk too long. Almost invariably, at meetings where a number of people are allotted five or ten minutes to speak, the speakers must be cut off long before they have made their points. When you have been told, or have decided for yourself, the length of the speech, you must plan your remarks to fit that time limit and stick to your plan. Notes will help you stay with the subject, but the extemporaneous speaker is in real danger of rambling too long on each thought as it occurs to him.

The most successful speakers say what they have to say, concisely, simply, and without pretentious language or repetition. When your point is made, go on to the next one—it is not necessary to explain the preceeding one in other ways. Your listeners will go away thinking you a wonderful speaker if you end your speech before they become restless and while they are still hoping that you have more to say.

IN CLOSING

When your time is up or you have said all that you have to say, a brief summary prepares the audience for the ending. Sometimes an entertaining story in conclusion will leave them with a pleasant memory, and some speakers like to close by thanking the audience for their attention. However you choose to end your talk, do not let yourself fade away. Memorize your closing remarks carefully so that you will make them firmly, and without apology.

WHEN CALLED ON UNEXPECTEDLY

If you happen to be called on unexpectedly to "say a few words," it is in very poor taste to contradict, out of embarrassment, the speech of the chairman who has graciously introduced you. To say "I'm afraid the chairman has greatly exaggerated my abilities" is an impulse of modesty, but besides being discourteous to the chairman, it all too seldom rings true.

If your knees begin to shake and you feel incapable of uttering a sensible word, you must acknowledge the chairman's introduction at least briefly by some such words as "I'm sorry, I'm not a speaker but I do wish to thank you all for attending (supporting our cause)," and sit down. But if you are able to speak, you should smile and think (whether or not you actually say it) "How nice of you to say that," and make at least a few remarks. Try to think of what you are saying rather than of the impression you are making. Remember, the speech that charms is the one that ends to its listeners' regret.

THE PROBLEM OF YOUR HANDS

One of the greatest problems for a public speaker is what to do with his hands. At a podium you may grasp the side edges with your hands and keep them there, moving them only to turn the pages of your notes or to make an occasional gesture. At a dinner table you may press your hands against the table, but only if it is high enough so that you need not bend over. Avoid the temptation to pick up a piece of silver or to finger your napkin or glass. And wherever you are speaking, if you are a man, be sure that you do not have loose change or keys in your pockets. It is a perfectly natural gesture for a man to put his hand in his pocket, but if it results in rattling or jingling, it is most distracting to the audience.

If you are using slides, be sure that a pointer is available. Not only is it practical for indicating details in the pictures, but it also serves as a prop for you to grasp during the rest of your speech.

If there is no support of any kind available, you must do your best to keep your hands reasonably still, clasping them before you or behind your back or simply letting them hang at your sides. Gestures are important to add emphasis to your speech, but avoid repeating the same movement again and again. Do not throw your arms about or move around so much that your listeners' attention is diverted from what you are saying.

DRESSING FOR SPEAKING ENGAGEMENTS

The keynote of a woman's costume for speaking in public is simplicity. If the occasion is an afternoon meeting, wear a neat suit or a simple wool dress in winter; choose a short-sleeved or sleeveless cotton or silk dress in summer. Jewelry in the daytime should be confined to simple earrings, a pin, a necklace, and a bracelet, which must not jangle. A small hat or a veil should be chosen, although younger women often prefer not to wear hats. At an evening meeting, a slightly more elaborate dress or a cocktail suit is appropriate.

For a dinner speaking engagement, the woman speaker should find out what the other women will wear and dress accordingly. The variety of costume might range from a very plain cocktail dress to a short dinner dress or a long evening dress, depending on the formality of the occasion. In all cases, however, the dress should not have a very low neckline and should not be ruffled or elaborate in design. A veil or small hat may be worn with a cocktail dress or suit. Jewelry for evening naturally may be more elaborate than that worn in the daytime, but it should not be so brilliant or worn in such quantity as to attract attention or criticism.

Shoes should go with the rest of your costume, but be sure that they are very comfortable, especially if the speech is to be long.

A man speaking in the daytime wears a business suit with a conservative tie. In the evening he may wear anything from a business suit to white tie and tails. For a dinner engagement, he must find out what the other men at the speaker's table will wear and dress in the same way. If he is speaking from a stage or if he knows for certain that his audience will be informally dressed, he should wear a tuxedo. If the men in the audience are to wear tuxedos, he may do the same or, if he wishes, wear white tie and tails. But he must always be dressed as formally as, or more formally than, his audience.

TOASTS

Men are frequently called on to make a toast, an often perplexing experience for those who are not accustomed to it. Unless one knows he will be called on and can plan in advance, his mind is apt to go completely blank.

The best solution is simply to say exactly what you feel. Toasts never need be long, and if you do panic when called on unexpectedly, you can get away with something as brief as "To Joe, God bless him," or "To Jack—a wonderful friend and a great boss."

But if you wish to appear more poised and more eloquent, you must add a few remarks—a reminiscence, praise, or a relevant story or joke. The toast should, however, always be in keeping with the occasion. A touch of humor is rarely out of place, but toasts at a wedding should be on the sentimental side, those in honor of a retiring employee nostalgic, and so on.

The following toasts are intended only to give you some ideas for various occasions. They must be changed to fit the particular circumstances, of course, and a word or two of your own feelings will always add a personal touch.

A FATHER'S TOAST AT HIS DAUGHTER'S ENGAGEMENT PARTY

1. Now you know that the reason for this party is to announce Mary's engagement to John. I would like to propose a toast to them both, wishing them many years of happiness in their life together.

2. Mary's mother and I have always looked forward to meeting the man Mary would choose to marry. We knew she'd pick a winner, but we never dared hope he'd be as fine a person as John. We want you all to know how pleased we are to announce their engagement tonight. Please join me in wishing them a long and happy marriage.

A BEST MAN'S TOAST AT THE REHEARSAL DINNER

1. For some time I have been worried about Mary and John's apparent incompatibility, but looking at them tonight I see how wrong I have been. So, please join me in a toast to John's income and Mary's patibility.

2. John and I have been friends for a long time now and I have always known what a lucky guy he is. Tonight all of you can see what I mean when you look at Mary and realize she is to become his bride tomorrow. Please join me in a toast to Mary and John. May this kind of luck continue throughout their lives together.

A BEST MAN'S TOAST TO THE BRIDAL COUPLE AT THE WEDDING RECEPTION

1. To Mary and John—a beautiful girl, a wonderful man—and the happiest couple I ever hope to see!

2. To Mary and John—may they always be as happy as they look today.

A BRIDEGROOM'S TOAST TO HIS BRIDE AT THE WEDDING RECEPTION

1. I'd like you all to join me in a toast to the girl who's just made me the happiest man in the world.

2. All my life I've wondered what the girl I'd marry would be like. In my wildest dreams I never imagined she would be as wonderful as Mary, so please join me in drinking this first toast to my bride.

A BRIDEGROOM'S FATHER'S TOAST AT THE REHEARSAL DINNER

1. I would like to ask you to join me in drinking a toast to two wonderful people without whom this wedding could never have been possible: Mary's mother and father, Mr. and Mrs. Brown.

2. I don't need to tell you what a wonderful girl Mary is, but I do want to tell you how happy John's mother and I are to welcome her as our new daughter-in-law. To Mary and John.

TOAST TO A RETIRING EMPLOYEE OR A MEMBER OF THE FIRM

1. It is often said that nobody is indispensable, and that may sometimes be true, but for all of us there will never be anyone who can replace Joe. Although we will miss him greatly, we know how much he is looking forward to his retirement and we wish him all the happiness he so richly deserves in the years to come.

2. I know that everyone of us here tonight thinks of Bob (Mr. Smith) not as an employee (employer) but as a friend. When he leaves, we will suffer a very real loss both in our organization and in our hearts. At the same time we rejoice that he will now be able to enjoy the things he wants to do, so let us rise and drink a toast to one of the finest friends we have known.

ANNIVERSARY TOAST

1. Many of us who are here tonight can well remember that day twenty-five years ago when we drank a toast to the future happiness of Mary and Bob. It is more than obvious that our good wishes at that time have served them well, and therefore I would like to ask that all of you—

old friends and new—rise and drink with me to another twenty-five years of the same love and happiness that Mary and Bob have already shared together.

2. John, I'd like to propose a toast to you on your fiftieth birthday. It has been a wonderful party tonight and all of us wish you health, wealth, and the years to enjoy them.

TOAST TO A GUEST OF HONOR AT A TESTIMONIAL DINNER

1. We are gathered here tonight to honor a man who has given unselfishly of his time and effort to make this campaign so successful. Without the enthusiasm and leadership that Bob Jones has shown all through these past months, we could never have reached our goal. Please join me in drinking a toast to the man who more than anyone else is responsible for making it possible to see our dream of a new hospital wing finally come true.

2. Ladies and gentlemen, you have already heard of the magnificent work our guest of honor has accomplished during his past two years in Washington. Right now we would like to tell him that no matter how proud we are of his success in his chosen career, we are even more pleased to have him home with us again. It's great to have you back, Jim!

5

The good conversationalist

Ideal conversation is an exchange of thought and not an eloquent exhibition of wit or oratory. Fortunately for most of us, it is not necessary to have a special gift of cleverness to be a person with whom others are delighted to talk. An ability to express our thoughts and feelings clearly and simply is sufficient for ordinary conversation among friends.

Conversation should be a matter of equal give and take, but unhappily it is too frequently all "take." The voluble talker or chatterer plunges ahead without giving anyone else a chance to do other than wait for the turn that never comes. Only once in a while does one meet a brilliant person whose continuous talk is a delight.

As a rule the man who has been led to believe that he is a brilliant talker has also been led to make himself a pest. He is the authority on all subjects. No conversation is possible among others who find themselves near him. There is a simple rule by which one who is voluble can at least refrain from being a pest or a bore. Stop and think.

BE CALM! THERE IS NOTHING TO FEAR

If you dread meeting strangers because you are afraid you won't be able to think of anything to say, you might do well to remember that most conversational errors are committed not by those who talk too little but by those who talk too much. A bore is almost always one whose voice is never still, and a tactless person invariably rushes in with what ought never to be said.

Many people for some reason are terrified of silence, and they generally have great difficulty in carrying on a conversation. This terror is very like the terror of sinking felt by those who are learning to swim. It is not just the first stroke that overwhelms them, but the thought of all the strokes that must follow. Finding the endless effort of thinking of further remarks dismaying, the frightened talker doesn't hear a word that is said to him because he is trying so desperately to think of what to say next. So the practical rule for continuing a conversation is the same as that for swimming: Don't panic. Just take it calmly.

The old sign at the railroad crossings—*stop, look, listen*—is excellent advice in many circumstances other than when waiting to cross the tracks. In conversation *stop* means not to rush recklessly forward; *look* means to pay attention to the expression of the person with whom you are talking; and *listen*—meaning exactly that—is the best advice possible,.because the person most people love to sit next to is a sympathetic listener. Remember, though, that a sympathetic listener really listens. To hold a fixed expression of sympathy and let your mind wander won't do at all.

THINK BEFORE YOU SPEAK

Nearly all the faults or mistakes in conversation are caused by not thinking, that is, by lacking consideration. One of the primary rules for behavior in company applies particularly to conversation: Try to do and say only that which will be agreeable to others. Many people who really should know better and who are perfectly capable of intelligent understanding let their brains remain asleep—they are too lazy to be considerate. They go night after night to dinner parties, day after day to other social gatherings, and absentmindedly chatter away without ever taking the trouble to think about what they are saying and to whom they are saying it!

Would a young mother describe her baby's cunning tricks to a bachelor who has been helplessly sitting next to her at dinner if she *thought?* A more considerate woman would understand that only the closest friend would care for more than an *hors d'oeuvre* of the subject. The older mother is even worse, unless something makes her realize that she not only bores her hearers but prejudices everyone against her children by her unrestrained praise. That great love seldom has perfect wisdom is one of the real tragedies in the drama of life. In the case of the doting wife or mother, someone should love *her* enough to make her realize that her lavish praise is not merely boring her friends but unfairly handicapping those whose image she most wants to enhance.

The rest of us are just as unlikely to have anyone to instruct or remind us about thoughtless and inconsiderate talk. Only by careful listening to our own words and strict attention to the reactions of our listeners can we discover our personal infelicities. The burden of thinking before speaking is our own.

PLEASANT TALK

HUMOR: THE RAREST OF GIFTS

If you know anyone who is bright and amusing, you will, if you are wise, do everything you can to make him prefer your house and your table to any other, for he can "make" your party. His subject is unimportant; it is the twist he gives to it, the intonation, the personality he puts into his observation that delights his hearers. To him the ordinary rules do not apply.

There are those who could tell a group of people that it had rained today and would probably rain tomorrow and make everyone burst into laughter—or tears, if they chose. But the forced wit is a bore, and the rest of us, if we wish to be thought attractive or agreeable, are safer if we rely on sincerity, clarity, and an intelligent choice of subject.

FISHING FOR TOPICS

In talking to a person you have just met and about whom you are in complete ignorance, there is really nothing to do but try one topic after another just as a fisherman searches for the right fly. You "try for nibbles" by asking a few questions: "Are you fond of the theater?" If the answer is "Yes, very," you can talk theater. When the subject runs down, you try another. Or perhaps you take your turn and talk of something you have been doing or thinking about—planting a garden, planning a trip, contemplating a vacation. Don't snatch at a period of silence. Let it go for a little while. Conversation is not a race that must be continued at breakneck pace.

MY NAME IS BETSY JAMES

Introducing oneself is sometimes the most practical way to begin a conversation with a stranger seated next to you at a party. "I'm Betsy James. That's my husband sitting opposite you." The stranger will reply, "I'm Bob Ashley. I'm very glad to meet you." This formality over, you can start your "fishing."

"I understand you're the man who went out on the Roberts' boat last summer. You must have had a wonderful time."

If you know nothing about him: "Do you live in Homeville, or are you just visiting?" From his answer, hopefully, you can carry on a conversation. He will probably ask where you live, and what your husband does. It's really quite simple, but be sure to give him the opportunity to talk.

Another helpful gambit is to ask advice. "We are planning to drive through the South. Do you know any particularly good places to stop on the way?" or "I'm thinking of buying a television set. Which make do you think is best?" In fact, it is safe to ask his opinion on almost anything: politics, sports, the stock market, the current fad—anything. Or if you are a man talking to a woman, ask her what she thinks about life, love, work, amusement—almost any question about the values people hold or aspire to. If she is an older woman, she will probably talk to *you!*

FORBIDDEN GROUND

AVOIDING SORE SUBJECTS

Even though you are very sure of your ground, certain subjects should be shunned: for example, criticism of a religious creed or disagreement with another's political conviction. And since few people can parry an opponent's thrusts with good temper as well as skill, be careful not to let amiable discussion turn into argument. The tactful person keeps his prejudices to himself, and even when involved in a discussion, he says, "It seems to me" thus and so. One should never say, "That's not so!" which is tantamount to calling the other a liar. If he finds another's opinion unreasonable, he tries to find a more pleasant subject as soon as possible.

If you care too intensely about a subject, it is dangerous to allow yourself to say anything. That is, if you can only lecture about your fixed point of view, then you should never mention the subject except as a platform speaker. But if, on the other hand, you are able to listen with an open mind, you may safely speak on any topic.

Mrs. Oldname and Mrs. Kindhart, really the most devoted of neighbors, are so violently opposed to each other on a certain political question that their neighbors have made a rule to which both have amiably agreed: the first person who mentions the forbidden topic must pay a fine.

After all, conversation between two people is very easy. You find a mutually interesting topic, although it may lead to one about which you don't agree. Then take care! Much better to withdraw unless you can argue without bitterness or bigotry. Argument between cool-headed, skillful opponents may be a delightful, amusing game, but it can be very, very dangerous for those who become hot-headed and ill-tempered.

THE TACTLESS BLUNDER

Inner or sacred thoughts and feelings are ruthlessly laid bare by such remarks as "Bobby's complexion has gotten so much worse since he went away to school!" "I suppose you feel lonely since the death of your daughter?" "Are you really going to be divorced?" These examples may sound unbelievable, yet each of these remarks was made by a person who should have known better and who had not a semblance of excuse for cruelty.

Commonplace examples of tactlessness include such remarks as "Twenty years ago you were the prettiest girl in Philadelphia." Or in the pleasantest tone of voice to a woman whose only son has just married, "Why is it, do you suppose, that young wives always dislike their mothers-in-law?"

If you want to be sought after, you must not talk about the unattractiveness of old age to the elderly, about the joys of dancing and skating to the lame, or about the advantages of ancestry to the self-made. It is needlessly unkind to ridicule or criticize others, especially for what they can't help. A young girl who admired her own witticisms said to a casual acquaintance, "How *can* you go about with that squint-eyed girl!" "Because," answered the young man whom she had hoped to impress, "she is my sister."

PERSONAL REMARKS

Although personal remarks can be in bad form, it is proper to say and always pleasant to hear an appreciative comment about something one has done. "Your speech was splendid!" "You gave us such a delicious dinner." "What a lovely dress!" But never, never ask about expense or other money matters. "What a beautiful lamp! How much did it cost?" is the height of rudeness. When one wishes to avoid answering such an impertinent question, the simplest thing to say is, "I really don't remember."

UNPLEASANT TYPES

THE BORE

It has been said of the bore that he is "one who talks about himself when you want to talk about yourself." This is superficially true, but a bore might more accurately be described as one who insists on telling you at length something that you don't want to hear about at all. He insists that you hear him out to the bitter end in spite of your obvious boredom.

There are certain delightful people who refuse to be bored. Their attitude is that no subject need ever be utterly uninteresting, so long as it is discussed for the first time. Repetition is deadly dull and there is no reason why you should be bored when you can be interested. When you find yourself sitting in a field with nothing but weeds, don't shut your eyes and see nothing; find what beauty you can in the weeds. Cynically, life is too short to waste in drawing blanks; therefore, it is up to you to find as many picture as possible to put on your blank pages.

THE WAILER

One of the fundamental and common-sense rules of all conversation is that one must talk about things that will be interesting and agreeable to the listener. It seems unbelievable, therefore, that so many people use as the staples of their conversation misfortunes, sickness, and other unpleasantness. Don't dwell on your own problems. Your audience has them, too, and won't be entertained by yours. Only your nearest and dearest care how many times you have been in the operating room.

THE CUTTING WIT

The man or woman of brilliant wit is in great danger of making enemies. Sharp wit tends to produce a feeling of mistrust even while it stimulates. Furthermore, the applause that follows every witty sally becomes in time the breath of life, and perfectly well-intentioned people who mean to say nothing unkind often "see a point" and are unable to resist underscoring it with a cutting remark.

The mimic is a joy to his present company, but eccentric mannerisms are much easier to imitate than charm, and the subjects of the habitual mimic are all too likely to become enemies.

THE SENTENCE-FINISHER

Some people are quicker to find a word or phrase than others. They have an irresistible urge to supply that word or to finish a sentence for one who is slow in finding the exact expression he wants. If you are inclined to do this, use all your strength to resist the urge. It makes the other speaker feel inadequate, you may change his meaning by supplying a word he did not intend to use, and finally, you put yourself in the position of appearing to try to steal the limelight from him.

"I'D SAY IT TO HER FACE"

A good resolve to make and keep, if you would like to keep your friends, is never to speak of anyone without, in imagination, having him or her overhear what you say. One often hears the exclamation "I would say it to her face!" Be very sure that this is not just a meaningless phrase, and then—nine times out of ten—think better of it and refrain. Preaching is all very well in a textbook, schoolroom, or pulpit, but it has no place in society. Society is supposed to be a pleasant place; telling people disagreeable things to their faces or talking behind their backs is not a pleasant occupation.

FOR THOSE WHO TALK TOO MUCH

The faults of commission are far more serious than those of omission; there are seldom regrets for what you left unsaid. "Better to keep your mouth closed and be thought a fool than open it and remove all doubt."

Don't pretend to know more than you do. To say that you have read a book and then make it evident that you have understood nothing of what you have read proves you a halfwit. No person of real intelligence hesitates to say, "I don't know."

The most important rule, above all, is: Stop and *think* about what you are saying. If you stop, you can't chatter or flounder ceaselessly; and if you *think*, you will find a topic and a manner of presenting it that will stimulate rather than bore your neighbor.

FUNDAMENTALS TO REMEMBER

People who talk too easily are likely to talk too much and at times imprudently. And those who have vivid imaginations are often unreliable in their statements. On the other hand, the "man of silence," who never speaks except when he has something worthwhile to say, tends to wear well among his intimates, but he is not likely to add much to the gaiety of a party. In conversation, as in most things, the "middle road" is best. Be neither too silent nor too glib. Know when to listen to others, but know also when it is your turn to carry the conversation.

Try not to repeat yourself, either by telling the same story again and again or by going back over details of your narrative that seemed to interest or amuse your hearer. Many things are interesting when told briefly and for the first time; few bear repeating.

Remember that the sympathetic listener is the delight of delights. The person who is eager for your news or enthralled with your conversation, who gives you spontaneous and undivided attention, is the one to whom you would rather talk than any other.

Part TWO

CORRESPONDENCE

6

The appearance and style of your letters

The letter you write, whether you realize it or not, is a mirror that reflects your appearance, taste, and character. A sloppy letter—the writing running up and down, badly worded, badly spelled, paper and envelope unmatched, smeared—proclaims the sort of person who probably has uncombed hair, run-down heels, or a run in her stockings. Conversely, a neat, precise, evenly written note portrays a person who has those happy characteristics. Therefore, while it cannot be said that a person's future can be read in his handwriting, his character may well be revealed. Furthermore, a messy letter is discourteous, clearly implying a lack of interest and care on the part of the writer.

The businessman picks his secretary not only because her neat and efficient letters are a credit to him every time he signs one, but because they indicate that she herself is well-organized and tidy.

Excellent secretaries have an advantage over most of us in that they have had training in the preparation of business correspondence. And, of course, the mechanical nature of the typewriter itself simplifies such matters as the evenness of margins and the regular spacing of lines and words. Writing letters by hand is more difficult, but it is possible to make graceful letters, to space words evenly, and to put them on a page so that their appearance is pleasing. No matter how badly formed each individual letter may be, the page as a whole will look fairly neat if the writing is consistent and the lines level. Avoid such exaggerated styles of writing as dotting "i" with a circle, for no amount of attention to other matters can compensate for such childish habits.

You can make yourself write neatly and legibly. You can—with the help of a dictionary if need be—spell correctly. You can be sure that you understand the meaning of every word you use. If it is difficult for you to write in a straight line, use the lined guide that comes with some stationery, or make one yourself. If you find it impossible to keep an even margin, draw a light perpendicular line at the left of the page so that you can start each new line of writing on it. A guide line one inch from the right edge of your paper to tell you where to stop will also help. Far better to use these guides than to send envelopes and pages of writing that slide uphill and down in uncontrolled disorder, so that the recipient must all but stand on his head to read them.

These calligraphic complications may be avoided by using a typewriter. All business letters—from home as well as office—should be typed if you have access to a machine, and letters to friends certainly may be if you wish. However, some forms of correspondence must always be written by hand, and the following rules are unbreakable except for physically handicapped people who otherwise could not write at all.

Never type an invitation, an acceptance, or a regret.

Never type letters of congratulations or thanks.

Never type letters or notes of condolence.

STATIONERY

Suitability should be considered in choosing your stationery, just as it is in choosing your wardrobe. For a handwriting that is habitually large, pick a paper of a larger size than you would choose for writing that is small. The shape of paper should also depend somewhat upon the writer's usual spacing of the lines and on whether a wide or narrow margin is used. Low, spread-out writing looks better on a square sheet of paper; tall, pointed writing looks better on paper that is high and narrow.

Whether the paper is rough or smooth is entirely a matter of personal choice—but its quality should be good and its shape and color conservative. Paper should never be ruled or highly scented or oddly shaped, nor should it have elaborate or striking ornamentation.

When the paper is thin, envelopes with colored linings should be used so that the writing cannot be read through the envelope, or you may fold a blank sheet outside the pages. The monogram or address may be stamped on the paper in a color to match the lining. Young girls may use gay envelope linings and paper, and the device on the paper may correspond, but it must not be so large or loud as to be ostentatious. Oblong envelopes are excellent for business, but those more nearly square are smartest for personal use.

Linings for Christmas-card envelopes may be as bright as the ornaments that decorate a Christmas tree. This is the time one may go overboard. But unrestrained masses of red and gold, swirls of purple and green, or other striking colors are in poor taste at any other time.

PAPER FOR A MAN

A man's writing paper should always be conservative. White or cream, gray- or granite-colored paper, medium size or larger, is the best choice. The color of the engraving (or printing) should be black, gray, or dark blue. Writing ink should be black or blue-black.

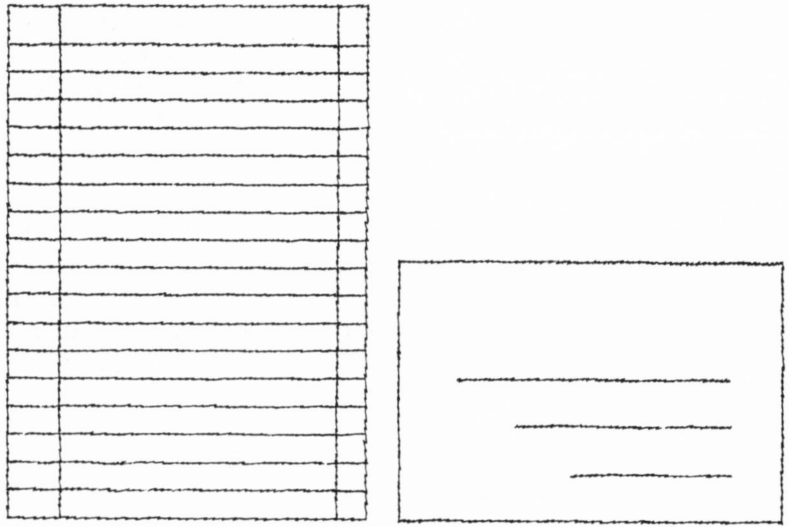

A very practical man's paper is a single sheet seven or seven and one-fourth inches by ten or ten and one-half inches marked in plain block letters in dark blue at the top. His name (without title), his address including zip code, and his telephone number all appear. This paper can be used for typewriting or handwriting and for all types of correspondence. It is folded in threes to fit into a seven-and-one-fourth- or seven-and-one-half-by-four-inch envelope. For purely social correspondence, he may use paper of the same color and size, with initials in block letters or a crest if he has one. A man who has occasion to write short notes frequently may also have single sheets in a slightly smaller size, so that the message will not look as lost as it would on the larger paper.

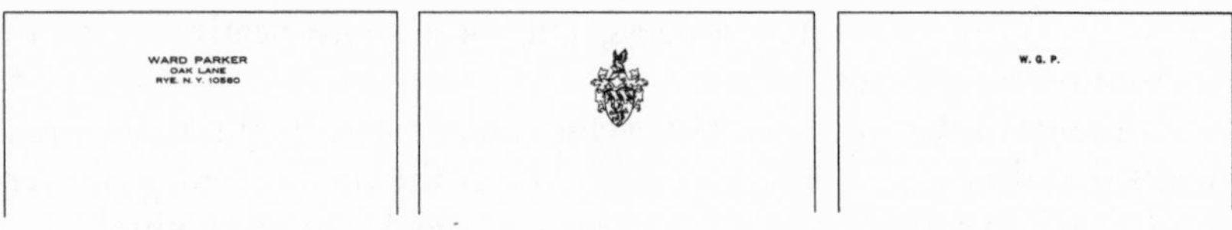

PAPER FOR A WOMAN

White, cream, light blues, grays, and light greens are in best taste. Paper should be of small or medium size, single or double sheets, plain or with colored border, stamped with a monogram, initials, or name and address in color to match the border. Writing ink should be black or blue, and green may be used if that is the color of the paper.

A married woman's paper is engraved "Mrs. William Frost," not "Mrs. Mary Frost" or "Mary Frost." An unmarried woman uses "Miss" only in the return address on the envelope. A professional woman may use her professional name without title—"Jane Author" rather than "Mrs. Robert Author"—on paper used for business correspondence.

PAPER FOR EVERYONE IN THE FAMILY

Paper suitable for use by all the members of a family has the address engraved or printed in plain letters at the top of the first page. Frequently the telephone number is put in small letters under the address or in the upper-left-hand corner with the address in the center. This paper is especially practical if you have a country or vacation home, as it can also be used by your guests.

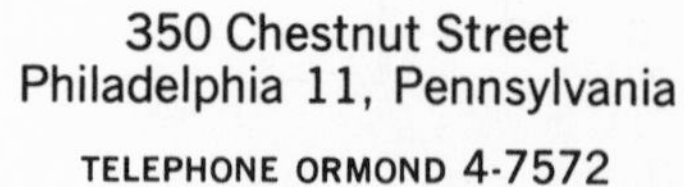

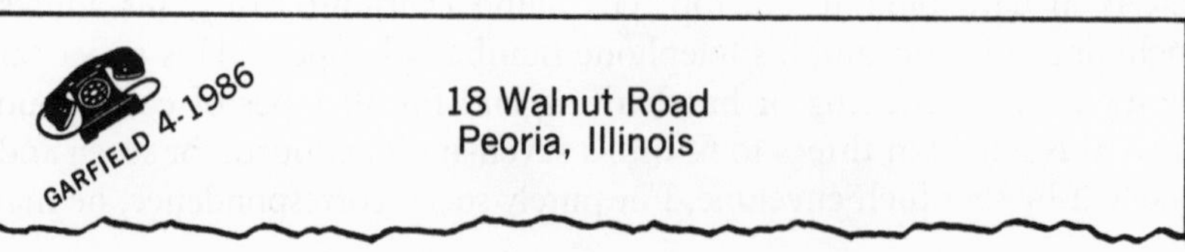

FOR THE YOUNG CORRESPONDENT

A girl's first name—either Elizabeth in full or Betty—is popular for all of a young girl's personal correspondence, but it should not be used by an older woman. If her first name is not distinctive, the young girl may wish to use her surname also. Available for very young ladies are attractive papers with designs in the upper-left-hand corners or along the left or top borders, usually flowers, birds, or perhaps a kitten or puppy. A name or monogram is not used, and the style of the picture varies with the age of the girl. The paper illustrated below would be suitable for a young teen-ager.

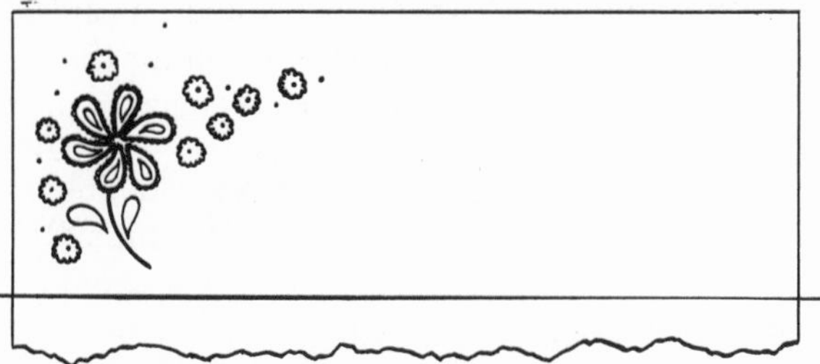

Many stationers also sell paper for very young girls or boys. It is ruled, usually has an illustration of animals, toys, or something from a familiar story or nursery rhyme, and may come in a variety of shapes. It is designed to amuse the young child and make him consider letter writing a pleasure rather than a chore.

NOTEPAPER

For short notes, for acceptances or regrets, and for invitations, a supply of fold-over notepaper, half the size of a single sheet of lady's writing paper, is invaluable. It may be of any color properly used for letter paper and engraved or printed with initials or with the owner's name and address, and possibly telephone number. If not marked with initials or a name, it is useful for every female member of the family.

OFFICIAL WRITING PAPER

An ambassador or minister has his country's coat of arms—usually in gold—stamped at the top of writing paper and on cards of invitation for official or formal use. For his personal use and for the use of all who live at the embassy or the legation, notepaper is engraved merely

AMERICAN EMBASSY
LONDON

A governor's letter paper is stamped

EXECUTIVE MANSION
COLUMBUS
OHIO

and is usually surmounted by the state coat of arms. EXECUTIVE OFFICE is also correct as the heading for official letters. Paper engraved with EXECUTIVE MANSION, but without the coat of arms, may be used by the Governor's family if the address is also that of their home. Otherwise their paper is engraved with their personal address.

A senator's wife has no right to use stationery headed THE SENATE, nor may the wife of a representative write on paper engraved HOUSE OF REPRESENTATIVES.

MOURNING PAPER

Few people use mourning paper at all, and plain white paper has almost replaced that with a black border. A one-fourth-inch border is considered deepest mourning; borders of three-sixteenths, one-sixteenth, or one-thirty-second of an inch are also appropriate.

PRINTING AS WELL AS ENGRAVING

Years ago the paper used by a lady was either engraved (die-stamped) or left plain. Today paper upon which one's full name and address are printed has become indispensable to everyone who must write many letters. Therefore, a small supply of engraved paper at unavoidably higher cost is used only for formal correspondence and is augmented by a larger supply of printed paper for informal social correspondence and for business letters.

CRESTS

Because heraldry, with its medieval origins, is not an institution in America, the use of a coat of arms is as much a foreign custom as the speaking of an alien tongue. But when an old family has used its family arms continuously since the days when they brought the device—and their right to it as certified by the colleges of heraldry—from Europe, its use is proper, if somewhat conspicuous.

It must be remembered, however, that the crest is the exclusive property of male members of a family, although it may be used jointly by husband and wife on some occasions. Its appearance on the paper of a widow or a spinster is as absurd as it would be to put "Esquire" at the end of her name. Surprisingly few Americans, however, seem to be aware of this heraldic rule. A widow has no right to use her husband's crest on her letter paper. She may properly use the device on the shield of his coat of arms, transferred to a diamond-shaped device called a lozenge. She may also, if she chooses, divide the lozenge perpendicularly into two parts and crowd the device from her husband's shield into the left half and the device from her father's shield into the right half. A spinster uses her paternal arms on a lozenge without crest or motto.

THE MECHANICS OF THE LETTER ITSELF

SEQUENCE OF PAGES

Folded stationery may cause problems about the proper order in which to use the pages. If a letter is longer than one page but shorter than three, it is customary to use the first and third pages, as this leaves the fourth page blank and prevents the writing from showing through the envelope. For longer letters, one may write first, second, third, fourth, in regular order; or first and fourth, then, opening the sheet and turning it sideways, write across the two inside pages as one. The sequence is not important, and there is no fixed rule.

One may write on both sides of single sheet stationery, but not if it is airmail weight, as that shows through and makes the letter difficult to read.

On fold-over or informal notepaper, when the address is at the top and there is nothing in the center, the letter or note begins on the first page and follows into the center pages. The paper is opened flat and written on vertically as if it were a single page. If there is an initial or name in the center of the front page, the note begins at the top of the opened center pages if it is long enough to cover more than half, and on the lower half if it is to be only a few words.

YOUR HOME ADDRESS AND THE DATE

If your stationery is not marked with your address, it is only courteous to provide it for your correspondent's convenience in replying. The upper-right-hand corner of the first page of your letter is the usual place for an address, but sometimes, especially on a short note, it may be included in the lower left-hand part of the page, just below the level of your signature. In either case the date goes below the address.

Sincerely,
Mary Swenson
(Mrs. John Swenson)

45 Barton Street
Racine, Wisconsin
May 5, 1968

When your address is already engraved or printed on the stationery, the date is placed in the same place—in the upper right-hand corner of the first page of a letter or at the end and to the far left of the signature of a note. May 9, 1968, is preferable to 5–9–68.

At the end of a note "Thursday" is sufficient unless the note is an invitation for more than a week ahead, in which case you write, as in a letter, "January 9." The year is not essential, for it can hardly be expected that a year will be required for a letter's delivery.

RECIPIENT'S ADDRESS

The correct form for business letters demands that the receiver's address be put at the left, below the level of the date and two lines above the salutation, exactly as it appears on the envelope.

June 7, 1968

Mr. James Johnson
Smith, Johnson & Co.
20 Broadway
New York, New York 10027

Dear Mr. Johnson:

June 7, 1968

Smith, Johnson & Co.
20 Broadway
New York, New York 10027

Dear Sirs:

Personal letters and notes, however, never have the address of the receiver anywhere except on the envelope itself.

THE SALUTATION

For business letters, the salutation may be "Dear Sir," "Dear Sirs," or "Gentlemen." When writing to a firm or organization composed of women, the salutation is "Dear Madams." You never use "Mesdames," any more than you would "Messieurs" instead of "Sirs."

An impersonal business letter to a woman begins:

Mrs. Richard Worldly
4892 Third Avenue
New York, New York 10017

Dear Madam:

A personal business letter, meaning a letter from a business or professional man to a customer or client he knows personally, begins:

Mrs. Richard Worldly
4892 Third Avenue
New York, New York 10017

My dear Mrs. Wordly: (or, if they are friends, "Dear Anne,")

The most formal beginning of a social letter is "My dear Mrs. Smith." Increasingly intimate are "Dear Mrs. Smith," "Dear Sally," and "Dearest Sally." In this area, your own feeling must be your guide, although it is perhaps better to err on the side of formality when you are not absolutely certain of your recipient's feeling.

Except in the most intimate correspondence, a man is always addressed "Dear Bob," when something less formal than "Dear Mr. Smith" is suitable.

Forms used in addressing distinguished persons or those in special categories are discussed elsewhere. *See Chapter Seven.*

THE CLOSING

It is too bad that, for personal letters and notes, the English language does not permit the charming closing of letters in the French manner, those little flowers of compliment that leave such a pleasant glow. But ever since the eighteenth century, English-speaking people have been busy pruning away all ornament of expression; even the last remaining graces—"kindest regards," "with kindest remembrances"—are fast disappearing, leaving us little but an abrupt "Sincerely yours."

The best ending to a formal social note is "Sincerely," "Sincerely yours," "Very sincerely," or "Very sincerely yours."

"I have the honor to remain . . ." is used only in correspondence to certain very prominent people in the government, diplomatic corps, or church.

The close of a business letter should be "Yours truly" or "Very truly yours." "Sincerely" is also correct. "Respectfully" is used only by a tradesman to a customer or by an employee to an employer. No lady should ever sign a letter "Respectfully," except as part of the long, formal "I have the honor to remain" close of a letter to the President of the United States or to a bishop or a mother superior.

"Faithfully" or "Faithfully yours" are appropriate for a man when he is writing to a woman or for any formal social correspondence, such as a letter to the President of the United States, a member of the Cabinet, an ambassador, a clergyman, etc.

"As always" is useful to someone with whom you may not be on intimate terms, especially when you have not seen the person for some time.

"Sincerely" in formal notes and "Affectionately" or "Love" in friendly notes are the most frequently used closings at present. Between the first and last two there is a blank; in English we have no adequate expression to fit sentiment more friendly than the first and less intimate than the others. "Cordially" was brought into use no doubt to fill this need, but it sounds a bit condescending.

"Yours in haste" and "Hastily yours," while not bad form, are rather carelessly rude unless for some reason your communication indicates real and necessary haste.

"Gratefully" is used only when a benefit has been received, as to a lawyer who has skillfully handled a case or to a friend who has gone to unusual trouble to do you a favor.

In an ordinary letter of thanks, the signature is "Sincerely," "Affectionately," "Devotedly"—whatever your usual close may be.

Forms used in letters to distinguished persons or those in special categories are discussed elsewhere. *See Chapter Seven.*

THE SIGNATURE

John Hunter Titherington Smith, finding his name too much of a penful for letters and documents, may choose J.H.T. Smith instead, or perhaps at the end of personal letters, John H.T. Smith. Of course, if he is writing a business associate with whom he is on terms of close personal acquaintance, he signs simply "John" or "Jack" over the typed "J.H.T. Smith." Mail is addressed to him in the typed form (or the printed form, if the letterhead carries his full name).

A married woman always signs a letter to a stranger, a bank, a business firm, etc., with her legal name. If her stationery is marked with her full married name and address, her signature—Mary Jones Mathews or Mary J. Mathews—needs no further explanation. But if it is not, she should give her married name (to which the reply will be sent) in one of several ways. When she writes by hand, she adds her married name beneath her signature, or to the left of it, in parentheses, thus:

Very truly yours,
Mary Jones Mathews
(Mrs. John Mathews)

When the letter is typed, her married name is typed beneath the space left for her signature, where it need not be enclosed in parentheses.

Very truly yours,
Mary Jones Mathews
Mrs. John Mathews

The only times when a woman actually uses "Mrs." in her signature are in a hotel register, on a business telegram, on a charge account, or in a letter ordering a purchase from a store. And then it must be "Mrs. John Smith." To a servant who works for her, it is "Mrs. Smith."

An unmarried woman uses much the same form in a typed letter:

Sincerely,
Mary Mathews
Miss Mary Mathews

When she writes by hand, she may use this style:

Sincerely,
(Miss) Mary Mathews

And a final warning about the signature: Avoid a flourishing, unrecognizable one. While the reader may be able to decipher a word in a sentence because of its context, he cannot possibly make sense of an illegible signature if he does not already know who wrote the letter.

A PROFESSIONAL WOMAN'S SIGNATURE

When an unmarried woman starts her career using her maiden name, she naturally continues to do so throughout her professional life. She uses "Miss" in combination with that name even after she marries.

Many women start their careers after their marriage and wish to have it known that they are married. Professionally called Mary T. Forsyth or Helen Horton Hughes, they should use business stationery with their names printed that way. This can be most confusing to a correspondent. In order to make it clear what title he should use in addressing a reply, Mary or Helen may precede her typewritten signature with (Mrs.). This should *never* be done except on business correspondence—in all other cases their husbands' names are used below the handwritten signature when it is necessary.

FOLDING A LETTER

One need not worry about which edge of a letter is inserted first into the envelope, but for those who wish to be strictly proper—insert the open, or unfolded edge, first. It is sufficient that the paper be folded neatly—once, of course, for the envelope that is as deep as half the length of the paper, and twice for the envelope that is a third as deep.

The paper that must be folded into thirds is used only as personal stationery for men or for business purposes. Women's personal letter paper should fold only once and fit into its envelope. Notepaper is the same size as the envelope and goes into it flat with only the original fold.

THE OUTSIDE ADDRESSES

Write the name and address on the envelope as precisely and as legibly as you can. If your writing is poor, print.

When you are writing to someone who lives in an American city with a zip code, write it on the envelope, as it is an essential part of the address. Zone numbers are used in many foreign cities, and are an integral part of the address.

The address may be written with each line indented a few spaces:

Mr. Harvey S. Simpson
  4 Hillside Lane
    Clinton
      Ohio 20567

or with a straight margin on the left:

Mr. Harvey S. Simpson
4 Hillside Lane
Clinton, Ohio 20567

Either form is correct.

CORRECT USE OF "ESQUIRE"

The use of "Esquire" has virtually gone out of general use in the United States—except among the conservative members of the older generation and among lawyers and justices of the peace. Its correct use, furthermore, is confusing. For example, engraved invitations are always addressed to Mr. Stanley Smith on both invitation and envelope. Handwritten invitations, as well as all other personal letters, may be addressed to Stanley Smith, Esq.

A WIDOW AND HER HUSBAND'S NAME

No note or social letter should ever be addressed to a married woman—even if she is a widow—as Mrs. Mary Town. Correctly and properly a widow keeps her husband's name, always. If her son's wife should have the same name, she becomes Mrs. James Town, Senior, or simply Mrs. Town, if there is no other in her community with the same name.

ADDRESSING DIVORCEES. *See Chapter Two*

YOUNG PEOPLE

Young ladies are addressed as "Miss" from the very day they are born. Both the first and last names are used on envelopes—the only time a girl is addressed as "Miss Taylor" is on the inner envelope of a wedding invitation.

Boys may be addressed as "Master" until they are six or seven. After that they are addressed without title until they graduate from high school at approximately eighteen. At that time they take the adult title of "Mister."

"Messrs." may not be used to address a father and son. It is correct only in writing to unmarried brothers.

"PERSONAL" AND "PLEASE FORWARD"

Because in writing to someone at his home address you properly assume that no one else will open the letter, it is rude to write "Personal" on it. But if you are writing a social note to a friend's business address, it is entirely correct. "Please Forward" is correct if you know only a former address but not the current one.

RETURN ADDRESS

It has always been customary to place a return address in the upper left-hand corner on the face of a business envelope. When it was necessary to use one on a personal letter, it was put on the flap. Whatever the real reason for making this distinction, it did separate the two types of letters in our mail.

Today (in response to requests made by the United States Post Office) it is preferable to put any return address on the face of the envelope. If handwritten, it should be very small. Remember that zip codes are a part of the return address.

UNSEALED LETTERS

Properly, any letter given to a person (other than a commercial messenger) for delivery by hand is unsealed. Customarily, the person who will carry it seals it immediately in the presence of the writer, but this is not obligatory.

Exceptions may be made, of course, should there be a heavy or particularly valuable enclosure that might slip out after the time of writing. In this case, it is polite to explain why the envelope has been sealed.

7

Addressing important persons

At one time or another nearly every one of us either meets or has to write a letter to someone important, a senator or a judge, perhaps, a clergyman or a professor, and we certainly do not want to be thought ignorant because we address him or her improperly. Neither can we remember all the proper forms of address for all the personages we might ever need to speak to or write to. The chart in this chapter has been prepared to cover as many as possible of the situations likely to occur in the ordinary course of events—and some not so ordinary.

The chapter is devoted to official and formal occasions, for naturally a governor's friends continue to call him by his first name at purely friendly functions, and their wives continue to address their dinner and luncheon invitations to the governor's wife. In fact, no matter how important the personage or what your degree of acquaintance with him, his wife receives the invitations just as she did before her husband entered public life. Only when wedding or other formal invitations are sent to both husband and wife is it necessary to use the special forms included below in the "Social Correspondence" column.

"THE HONORABLE"

"The Honorable" is an expression that causes considerable confusion. Federal custom in the United States bestows the title "Honorable," first officially and then by courtesy for life, on the President and Vice-President, United States Senators and Congressmen, Cabinet members, all federal judges, ministers plenipotentiary, ambassadors, and governors of all states. The title is not used by the person himself on his visiting card or letterhead or in his signature. The people of the state address their state senators as "The Honorable Lawrence Hamilton, State Senator," as a courtesy title only.

Best usage dictates that "The Honorable" (spelled out in full) appear on a separate line, as shown in the chart, and that when his wife is included, she have a line to herself below his name and slightly indented.

WITH OTHER NATIONS

We refer to our country briefly and casually as "America," but when we address anyone elsewhere in the Western Hemisphere, good manners should remind us that we have no monopoly on the name. Thus, although it is customary in both Europe and Asia to speak of or write to the American Embassy or the American Legation, it should not be done in Latin America or Canada. The address on a letter to one of our government representatives there always specifies "the United States of America."

Representatives of other countries who are living in the United States present no particular problems, since the ways of addressing them are firmly fixed by governmental protocol. But whether their wives are addressed as Mrs., Madame, Señora, or some other title depends upon the usage of their particular nations. In many instances the wife uses whatever she would in her own country (that is, the wife of the Mexican Ambassador is Señora Ortega), but sometimes, especially when hers is a difficult or little-known language, she uses Mrs. or Madame.

In this age of international travel we may well find ourselves in need of information about the important personages of countries other than our own. Customs vary, of course, and no general rules can be made for the more than one hundred nations in the world. However, should you find yourself about to leave for Ghana or Japan or Finland, there are many sources of help. Try the consulate nearest you or the embassy in Washington or the mission to the United Nations in New York. Information officers from all over the world are ready to help you and eager to facilitate your communication with their homelands.

Personage	ENVELOPE ADDRESS	SOCIAL CORRESPONDENCE	INFORMAL BEGINNING OF LETTER
THE PRESIDENT	The President The White House Washington, D.C.	The President and Mrs. Washington The White House Washington, D.C.	My dear Mr. President:
THE VICE-PRESIDENT	The Vice-President United States Senate Washington, D.C.	The Vice-President and Mrs. Hope Home address	My dear Mr. Vice-President:
CHIEF JUSTICE, SUPREME COURT	The Chief Justice The Supreme Court Washington, D.C.	The Chief Justice and Mrs. Page Home address	My dear Mr. Chief Justice:
ASSOCIATE JUSTICE, SUPREME COURT	Mr. Justice Katsaros The Supreme Court Washington, D.C.	Mr. Justice Katsaros and Mrs. Katsaros Home address	My dear Mr. Justice Katsaros:
CABINET MEMBERS	The Honorable Gary George Gussin The Secretary of the Treasury *or* The Attorney General *or* The Postmaster General Washington, D.C.	The Honorable The Secretary of the Treasury and Mrs. Gussin Home address *or* (*for a woman cabinet member*) Mr. and Mrs. Henry Leo Woods	My dear Mr. Secretary: *or* My dear Mr. Attorney General: *or* My dear Mr. Postmaster General: *or* Madam Secretary:
FORMER PRESIDENT	The Honorable Alfred Edward Work Office address	The Honorable Alfred Edward Work and Mrs. Work Home address	My dear Mr. Work:
UNITED STATES SENATOR	The Honorable John Wandzilak United States Senate Washington, D.C.	The Honorable John Wandzilak and Mrs. Wandzilak Home address *or* (*for a woman senator*) Mr. and Mrs. John Row Doe	My dear Senator Wandzilak:
THE SPEAKER OF THE HOUSE OF REPRESENTATIVES	The Honorable Walter James Grevesmuhl The Speaker of the House of Representatives Washington, D.C.	The Speaker and Mrs. Grevesmuhl Home address	My dear Mr. Speaker:
MEMBER OF THE UNITED STATES HOUSE OF REPRESENTATIVES	The Honorable Henry Cobb Wellcome United States House of Representatives Washington, D.C.	The Honorable Henry Cobb Wellcome and Mrs. Wellcome Home address *or* (*for a woman member*) Mr. and Mrs. John Knox Jones	My dear Mr. Wellcome:
AMBASSADOR OF THE UNITED STATES	The Honorable John Wilson Smith The Ambassador of the United States American Embassy London, England	The Honorable John Wilson Smith and Mrs. Smith Home address *or* (*for a woman ambassador*) Mr. and Mrs. Leeds Walker Home address	My dear Mr. Ambassador: *or* My dear Madam Ambassador:

ORMAL EGINNING F LETTERS	INFORMAL CLOSE OF LETTERS	FORMAL CLOSE OF LETTERS	IN CONVERSATION	TITLE OF INTRODUCTION	PLACE CARDS FOR FORMAL OCCASIONS
r:	Very respectfully yours,	I have the honor to remain, Most respectfully yours,	Mr. President *or* Sir	*Only the name of the person being introduced is spoken*	The President (Mrs. Washington)
r:	Sincerely yours, *or* Faithfully yours,	Very truly yours,	Mr. Vice-President *or* Sir	The Vice-President	The Vice President (Mrs. Hope)
r:	*Same as above*	*Same as above*	Mr. Chief Justice *or* Sir	The Chief Justice	The Chief Justice
r:	Sincerely yours,	*Same as above*	Mr. Justice *or* Mr. Justice Katsaros *or* Sir	Mr. Justice Katsaros	Mr. Justice Katsaros
r: *or* ear Sir: *or* ladam:	*Same as above*	*Same as above*	Mr. Secretary *or* Mr. Attorney General *or* Mr. Postmaster General *or* Sir *or* Madam Secretary	The Secretary of the Treasury *or* The Attorney General *or* The Postmaster General	The Secretary of The Treasury *or* The Attorney General *or* The Postmaster General
r:	*Same as above*	*Same as above*	Mr. Work *or* Sir	The Honorable Alfred Edward Work	Mr. Work
r: *or* ladam:	*Same as above*	*Same as above*	Senator *or* Senator Wandzilak *or* Sir *or* Madam	Senator Wandzilak of Alaska	Senator Wandzilak
r:	*Same as above*	*Same as above*	Mr. Speaker *or* Sir	The Speaker of the House of Representatives	The Speaker
r: *or* ladam:	*Same as above*	*Same as above*	Mr. Wellcome *or* Mrs. Jones *or* Sir *or* Madam	Representative Wellcome of Nebraska	Mr. Wellcome
r: *or* ladam:	*Same as above*	*Same as above*	Mr. Ambassador *or* Madam Ambassador *or* Sir *or* Madam	The American Ambassador *or* (*if necessary*) Our Ambassador to England	The Ambassador of The United States *or* (*if more than one present*) to (*name of country*)

Personage	ENVELOPE ADDRESS	SOCIAL CORRESPONDENCE	INFORMAL BEGINNING OF LETTERS
MINISTER PLENIPOTENTIARY OF THE UNITED STATES	The Honorable James Lee Row The Minister of the United States American Legation Oslo, Norway	The Honorable James Lee Row and Mrs. Row Home address *or* (*for a woman minister*) Mr. and Mrs. Arthur Johnson Home address	My dear Mr. Minister: *or* My dear Madam Minister:
CONSUL OF THE UNITED STATES	Mr. John Smith American Consul Rue de Quelque Chose Paris, France	Mr. and Mrs. John Smith Home address	Dear Mr. Smith:
AMBASSADOR OF A FOREIGN COUNTRY	His Excellency Juan Luis Ortega The Ambassador of Mexico Washington, D.C.	His Excellency The Ambassador of Mexico and Señora Ortega Home address	My dear Mr. Ambassador:
MINISTER OF A FOREIGN COUNTRY	The Honorable Carluh Matti The Minister of Kezeah Washington, D.C.	The Honorable Carluh Matti and Mrs. Matti Home address	My dear Mr. Minister:
GOVERNOR OF A STATE	The Honorable Joseph L. Marvin Governor of Idaho Boise, Idaho	The Honorable Joseph L. Marvin and Mrs. Marvin Home address	Dear Governor Marvin:

State Senators and Representatives are addressed like United States Senators and Representatives, with appropriate addresses

Personage	ENVELOPE ADDRESS	SOCIAL CORRESPONDENCE	INFORMAL BEGINNING OF LETTERS
MAYOR	His [or Her] Honor the Mayor City Hall Easton, Maryland	His Honor the Mayor and Mrs. Lake Home address *or* (*for a woman mayor*) Mr. and Mrs. L. T. Wayne Home address	Dear Mayor Lake:
JUDGE	The Honorable Carson Little Justice, Appellate Division Supreme Court of the State of New York Albany, New York	The Honorable Carson Little and Mrs. Little Home address	Dear Judge Little:
BISHOP, PROTESTANT	The Right Reverend John S. Bowman Bishop of Rhode Island Providence, Rhode Island	The Right Reverend John S. Bowman and Mrs. Bowman Home address	My dear Bishop Bowman:
CLERGYMAN, PROTESTANT	The Reverend David Dekker Address of his church *or* (*if he holds the degree*) The Reverend David Dekker, D.D. Address of his church	The Reverend David Dekker and Mrs. Dekker Home address	Dear Mr. [*or* Dr.] Dekker:
RABBI	Rabbi Paul Aaron Fine Address of his synagogue *or* (*if he holds the degree*) Paul Aaron Fine, D.D. Address of his synagogue	Rabbi [*or* Dr.] and Mrs. Paul Aaron Fine Home address	Dear Rabbi [*or* Dr.] Fine

FORMAL BEGINNING OF LETTER	INFORMAL CLOSE OF LETTER	FORMAL CLOSE OF LETTER	IN CONVERSATION	TITLE OF INTRODUCTION	PLACE CARDS FOR FORMAL OCCASIONS
Sir: *or* Madam:	*Same as above*	*Same as above*	Mr. Row *or* Mrs. Johnson	Mr. Row, the American Minister *or* (*if necessary*) Mrs. Johnson, the American Minister to Denmark	The Minister of The United States to (name of country)
Sir: *or* My dear Sir:	*Same as above*	Sincerely yours,	Mr. Smith	Mr. Smith	Mr. Smith
Excellency:	Sincerely yours, *or* Faithfully yours,	Very truly yours,	Mr. Ambassador *or* Excellency *or* Sir	The Ambassador of Mexico	The Ambassador of (name of country)
Sir:	Sincerely yours,	*Same as above*	Mr. Minister *or* Sir	The Minister of Kezeah	The Minister of (name of country)
Sir:	*Same as above*	*Same as above*	Governor Marvin *or* Sir	The Governor *or* (*if necessary*) The Governor of Idaho	The Governor of (name of state)
Sir: *or* Madam:	Sincerely yours,	Very truly yours,	Mr. Mayor *or* Madam Mayor	Mayor Lake	The Mayor of (name of city)
Sir:	*Same as above*	*Same as above*	Mr. Justice	The Honorable Carson Little, Judge of the Appellate Division of the Supreme Court	The Honorable Carson Little
Right Reverend Sir:	Faithfully yours, *or* Sincerely yours,	Respectfully yours,	Bishop Bowman	Bishop Bowman	Bishop Bowman
Sir: *or* My dear Sir:	Sincerely yours,	Sincerely yours, *or* Faithfully yours,	Mr. [*or* Dr.] Dekker	Mr. [*or* Dr.] Dekker	Mr. Dekker, *or*, (*if he holds a degree*), Doctor Dekker
Dear Sir:	*Same as above*	Sincerely yours,	Rabbi [*or* Dr.] Fine	Rabbi [*or* Dr.] Fine	Rabbi Fine, *or*, (*if he holds a degree*), Doctor Fine

Personage	ENVELOPE ADDRESS	SOCIAL CORRESPONDENCE	INFORMAL BEGINNING OF LETTER
THE POPE	His Holiness Pope Paul VI *or* His Holiness the Pope Vatican City		
CARDINAL	His Eminence Alberto Cardinal Vezzetti Archbishop of Baltimore Baltimore, Maryland		
ARCHBISHOP, ROMAN CATHOLIC	The Most Reverend Preston Lowen Archbishop of San Francisco San Francisco, California		Most Reverend and dear Sir:
BISHOP, ROMAN CATHOLIC	The Most Reverend Matthew S. Borden Address of his church		My dear Bishop Borden:
MONSIGNOR	The Right Reverend Monsignor Ryan Address of his church		Reverend and dear Monsignor Ryan:
PRIEST	The Reverend John Matthews [*and the initials of his order*] Address of his church		Dear Father Matthews:
MEMBER OF RELIGIOUS ORDER	Sister Angelica [*and initials of order*] *or* Brother James [*and initials*] Address		Dear Sister Angelica: *or* Dear Brother James:
UNIVERSITY PROFESSOR	Professor Robert Knowles Office address *or* (*if he holds the degree*) Dr. Robert Knowles *or* Mr. Robert Knowles	Professor [*or* Dr. *or* Mr.] and Mrs. Robert Knowles Home address	Dear Professor [*or* Dr. *or* Mr.] Knowles:
PHYSICIAN	William L. Barnes, M.D. Office address	Dr. and Mrs. William L. Barnes Home address	Dear Dr. Barnes:

FORMAL BEGINNING OF LETTER	INFORMAL CLOSE OF LETTER	FORMAL CLOSE OF LETTER	IN CONVERSATION	TITLE OF INTRODUCTION	PLACE CARDS FOR FORMAL OCCASIONS
Your Holiness:		Your Holiness' most humble servant,	*See Chapter Twenty-one*	*See Chapter Twenty-one*	His Holiness, The Pope
Your Eminence:		I have the honor to remain, Your Eminence's humble servant,	Your Eminence	*One is presented to* His Eminence, Cardinal Vezzetti	His Eminence, Cardinal Vazetti
Your Excellency: *or* Most Reverend Sir:	*Same as formal close*	I have the honor to remain, Your Excellency's humble servant,	Your Excellency	*One is presented to* The Most Reverend, The Archbishop of San Francisco	The Archbishop of San Francisco
Most Reverend Sir:	Faithfully yours,	I have the honor to remain, Your obedient servant,	Your Excellency	Bishop Borden	Bishop Bordon
Right Reverend and dear Monsignor Ryan:	Respectfully yours,	Respectfully yours,	Monsignor Ryan	Monsignor Ryan	The Right Reverend Monsignor Ryan
Reverend Father:	Faithfully yours,	I remain, Reverend Father, Yours faithfully,	Father *or* Father Matthews *or* Your Reverence	The Reverend Father Matthews	Reverend Father Matthews *or* Father Matthews
My dear Sister: *or* My dear Brother:	Faithfully yours,	Respectfully yours,	Sister Angelica *or* Brother James	Sister Angelica, [*or* Brother James,] may I present Mrs. Jones	Sister Angelica *or* Brother James
Dear Sir:	Sincerely yours,	Very truly yours,	Professor [or Dr.] Knowles (*within the college*) Mr. Knowles (*elsewhere*)	Professor [*or* Dr.] Knowles	Doctor Knowles *or* Professor Knowles
Dear Sir:	*Same as above*	*Same as above*	Dr. Barnes	Dr. Barnes	Doctor Barnes

8

The contents of business letters

Business letters written from offices depend so thoroughly on the nature of the concern that little can be said beyond an injunction to be clear, concise, and to the point. A rambling effusion never does the job of a well-organized and brief communication. If you know exactly what you want to say and give considerable thought to the initial statement of your most important point, you cannot go far astray. And by all means, when you have said what you intended to say, stop. A meandering last paragraph influences no one in your favor.

Business letters written by a customer or client differ very little from those sent out from a business house. They, too, should always be as brief and explicit as possible. For example:

May 17, 1968

H.J. Paint & Co.
22 Branch St.
New York, N. Y.

Dear Sir:

Your estimate of $300.00 for painting my dining room, living room, and hall is satisfactory, and you may proceed with the work as soon as possible.

Very truly yours,
Ida Town
(Mrs. James Town)

TO A STORE

An order letter to a store should contain precisely this information:

1. name or description of article
2. quantity, size, color
3. price
4. how paid for (C.O.D., check enclosed, or charge account)
5. how to be sent, when necessary
6. address and date

May 3, 1968

Brown, Green, and Company
Evanston, Illinois

Dear Sirs:

Please forward by Railway Express C.O.D. to
Mrs. J. B. Greatlake
20 Lakeshore Drive
Chicago, Illinois 20304
1 chair (No. 4433 in your catalogue), price $59.50
1 quilt (No. 1746 in rose color), price $22.00

Yours truly,
Alan K. Greatlake

TO A HOTEL OR A RESORT

LETTERHEAD
WITH ADDRESS

April 2, 1968

Manager
Loon Lake Lodge
Shiretown, Maine 12267

Dear Sir:

Would you be kind enough to send me your information folder and your schedule of rates for Loon Lake Lodge? Your hotel was recommended to me by Mrs. Arthur Simpson.

Would you also let me know what accommodations you have open for the month of August? We would require two double rooms with baths for my two daughters, my husband, and myself.

If the accommodations and your rates are satisfactory, I shall let you know our decision immediately.

Very truly yours,
Mary Newhouse
(Mrs. John Newhouse)

LETTERS OF INTRODUCTION

The letter that will introduce one business acquaintance to another or to a personal friend is considered elsewhere because of the many different possibilities, ranging from the extremely formal to the very casual. *See Chapter Nine.*

THE LETTER OF RECOMMENDATION

A letter of recommendation for membership in a club is addressed to the secretary and should follow this general form:

To the Secretary of the Town Club.

My dear Mrs. Brown,

Mrs. Walter Smith, whose name is posted for membership, is a very old friend of mine.

She is a charming and intelligent person. She has had a great deal of experience with fund raising, and her knowledge should be of great value to our activities. I feel that she will be a tremendous addition to the club, and when you meet her, I am sure that you will agree.

Very sincerely,
Ina Jackson

For other letters pertaining to clubs, see Chapter Sixty-five.

LETTERS OF RESIGNATION

A letter of resignation should be concise, but always polite. It should touch briefly on the reason for the resignation, but whatever that may be, it should never in any way give any indication of rancor or ill-feeling on the part of either the firm or the individual. Since resignations are almost always discussed in person and rarely come as a surprise, there is no need to do more than write a letter that will serve as a permanent record.

Mr. Henry Farthing
Associated Household Wares
14 Kent Place
Cincinnati, Ohio

Dear Mr. Farthing,

I regret that I must resign from the firm. My health has been very poor in recent weeks and my doctor has told me that I must retire from business if I wish to recover completely.

Our long association has been a very happy one for me, and I leave you all with sincere gratitude and best wishes for the continued success of the firm.

Sincerely,
Foster Hayes

In the case of an unpleasant parting, the letter should not reveal any signs of vituperation and should attempt to alleviate bitterness.

Dear Mr. Farthing,

I regret that I feel I must resign from the firm. An opportunity has been offered me by another company which will allow me more time with my family, and I feel that I should accept it.

I am sure a younger man will be better able to fill my position with your company. However, I leave Associated with the highest regard for you and the other members of the firm.

Sincerely,
Robert Pugh

For letters of resignation from a club, see Chapter Sixty-five.

REFERENCE FOR EMPLOYEES

The written recommendation that is given to an employee carries very little weight compared to the slip used by some employment agencies on which either "yes" or "no" has to be answered to a list of specific and important questions. Nevertheless, one is put in a trying position when reporting on an unsatisfactory servant.

Either a poor reference must be given—possibly preventing the employee from earning his or her living—or one writes what is not true. Consequently it is best to list truthfully any good qualifications and to omit the qualifications that are lacking except when the employee was disrespectful, neglectful, or dishonest.

This evasion helps solve the poor recommendation problem, but as a result the good servant suffers unless one is very careful. In writing for a satisfactory employee, therefore, it is most important to put in every good point that you can think of, remembering that omission implies a failing in those characteristics not mentioned. All good references should include honesty, sobriety, capability, and a reason, other than unsatisfactoriness, for the employee's departure. Special attention should be given to the recommendation for a baby's nurse, which cannot be too conscientiously written.

It is not necessary to begin a recommendation with "To whom it may concern" or "This is to certify." The form can be very simple. For example:

TWO HUNDRED MAPLE SQUARE

Selma Johnson has been in my employ as cook for two and a half years.

I have found her honest, sober, industrious, neat in her person as well as her work, of excellent disposition, and a very good cook.

She is leaving—to my great regret—because I am moving away.

I shall be very glad to answer personally any inquiries about her.

Josephine Smith
(Mrs. Walter Smith)

February 17, 1965

AN ENGRAVED CARD OF THANKS

An engraved card of thanks is proper only when sent by a public official to acknowledge the overwhelming number of congratulatory messages inevitably received from strangers when he has won an election or been otherwise honored by his state or country. Thus it falls into the category of business communications rather than personal letters.

Executive Mansion is the established name of the house in which a governor lives; but if he prefers, all official letters may be sent from the Executive Office. For example:

EXECUTIVE MANSION

My dear (*name inserted by hand*):

I warmly appreciate your kind message of congratulation, which has given me a great deal of pleasure, and sincerely wish that it were possible for me to acknowledge it in a less formal manner.

Faithfully,
(*Signed by hand*)

9

Personal letters

The practice of general letter writing is diminishing to such an extent today that the letter threatens to become a telegram, a telephone message, or just a postcard. Since daily events are communicated by newspapers, radio, and television with far greater accuracy and dispatch than they could have been by the efforts of a Voltaire himself, the circulation of general news—which formed the chief reason for letters in the stagecoach and sailing-vessel days—has no part in the hurried correspondence of the twentieth century. Still, people *do* write letters, and there are some who possess a gift for a fresh turn of phrase with which to charm the reader. It may be, too, that in the other days the average writing was no better than the average of today, for naturally, the letters of the unusually gifted are the ones that have been preserved for us over the years.

THE LETTER EVERYONE LOVES TO RECEIVE

The letter we all love to receive is the one that carries so much of the writer's personality that he or she seems to be sitting beside us and talking as if we were together, instead of by proxy in ink-made characters on paper. To achieve this happy feeling of *talking* through a letter, one must employ certain devices in order to detract from the stilted quality of the written word. Here are a few specific suggestions that may help to make your letters reflect your personality.

It is quite correct to type a personal letter, but only if the writer is a proficient enough typist so that the number of errors does not distract the reader.

Punctuation can add interest and variety to your letters, much as the change in tone of a speaker's voice adds zest and color to his story. Underlining a word or using an exclamation point after a phrase or sentence gives emphasis where you want it. A dash is effective instead of a longer, possibly more grammatical phrase. "We went to a dance last night—what a party!" is more colorful than "We went to a dance last night and it was a great party."

In a personal letter phrases typical of your speech should be used and not artificially replaced by more formal language. A young person who commonly uses the expression "a real doll" would sound most unnatural and self-conscious if she wrote "she is a lovely girl."

Occasionally inserting the name of the person to whom you are writing gives your letter an added touch of familiarity and affection. "And, Helen, guess what we are going to do this summer!" makes Helen feel as though it will be of special interest to *her*.

The use of contractions is another means of making your writing natural. Since you would probably never say "I do not know" for "I don't know" or "I am so glad" for "I'm so glad," why write it that way?

And, finally, don't stop too long to think of *how* to say it. Decide what you want to say, and then write it as quickly as possible; that way, it will seem as if you are truly talking to your friend.

LETTERS THAT SHOULDN'T BE WRITTEN

LETTERS OF GLOOMY APPREHENSION

No useful purpose is ever served by writing needlessly of misfortune or unhappiness—even to members of one's family. Our distress at hearing about illness or unhappiness among those we love is intensified by the number of miles that separate us from them.

The chronic calamity writers seem to wait until the skies are darkest and then, rushing to their desks, luxuriate in pouring out all their troubles to their friends.

"My little Betty ("my little" seems so much more pathetic than merely "Betty") has been feeling miserable for several days. I'm worried to death about her, for there are so many cases of mononucleosis around.

The doctor says the symptoms are not alarming, but doctors see so much of illness that they don't seem to appreciate what anxiety means to a mother," etc., etc.

Another writes: "The times seem to be getting worse and worse. I always said we would have to go through a long night before any chance of daylight. You can mark my words, the night is hardly more than begun."

THE DANGEROUS LETTER

Every day the mails carry letters whose fallout would be spectacular if they fell into the wrong hands. Letters that should never have been written are continually introduced as evidence in courtrooms, and many of them cannot, in any way, be excused. Silly girls and foolish women often write things that sound to a jury, for example, quite different from what was innocently intended.

Remember this above all: Never write a letter to *anyone* that would embarrass you were you to see it in a newspaper above your signature. Not that this means *you,* but thousands upon thousands of people, inspired by every known emotion, have poured words on paper, and few of the many made public have had charm or beauty.

However, if you are a young person—or even not-so-young—and are determined to write a letter to someone of the opposite sex that contains any possibility of emotion, then at least put it away overnight in order to reread it and make sure that you have said nothing that may sound different from what you intended to say.

The point to remember is that written words have permanency, and thoughts carelessly put on paper can exist for hundreds of years.

A FEW MORE WARNINGS

The light jesting tone that saves a quip from offense cannot be expressed in writing, and spoken remarks that would amuse can become sharp and insulting when written. Moreover, words that should be of a passing moment are made to stand forever.

Anger in a letter carries with it the effect of solidified fury. Bitter spoken words fade away once the cause is forgiven; written words are fixed on the page forever. Admonitions from parents to their children may very properly be put on paper—they are meant to endure and be remembered—but momentary annoyance should never be more than briefly expressed. A parent who gets into the habit of writing in an irritable or faultfinding tone to his children soon finds that his letters are seldom read.

One point cannot be overstressed: Letters written under strong emotion should be held for twenty-four hours and reread before being sent—or probably torn into small pieces and not sent at all.

THE DIFFICULTY IN BEGINNING

Most people who wonder how they will ever fill a blank sheet of paper find that the difficult part of a letter is the beginning. The instruction of a professor of English—"Begin at the beginning of what you have to say, go on until you have finished, and then stop"—is just about as much help as was the instruction of the celebrated artist who proclaimed, "You simply take a little of the right color of paint and put it on the right spot." Perhaps the following suggestions will be more helpful.

Even someone who loves the very sight of your handwriting could hardly be expected to enjoy a letter beginning "I know I ought to have written sooner, but I haven't had anything to write about." Or one saying "I suppose you think I've been very neglectful, but you know how I hate to write letters." Yet such sentences are written time and again by people who are utterly unaware that they are really expressing an unfriendly thought.

Suppose you merely change the wording of the above sentences, so that instead of slamming the door in your friend's face, you hold it open. "Do you think I have forgotten you entirely? You don't know, Ann, how many letters I planned to write you." Or "Time and time again I've wanted to write you but each moment that I saved for myself was always interrupted by—*something.*"

It is unfortunate when the answer to a letter has been so long delayed that it must begin with an apology—at best an unhappy beginning. The examples above, however, show that even an opening apology may be attractive rather than repellent. After all, if you take the trouble to write a letter, you have remembered someone in a friendly way; otherwise you would not be writing at all.

It is easy enough to begin a letter in answer to one that has just been received. You have fresh news to comment on, and the impulse to reply needs no prodding. Nothing can be simpler than to say, "We were all so pleased to hear from you this morning," or "Your letter was the most welcome thing the postman has brought for ages." Then you take up the various subjects in Ann's letter, which should certainly launch you upon topics of your own.

Remember to answer all of her specific questions. It is not only unflattering to be given the impression that you read them hurriedly, but often very upsetting if long-awaited information is not forthcoming.

ON ENDING A LETTER

Just as the beginning of a letter should give the reader an impression of greeting, so should its ending express friendly or affectionate leave-taking. Nothing can be worse than to flounder for an idea that will effect your escape. "Well, I guess you've read enough of this," and "You're probably bored by now so I'd better close" are obvious phrases of desperation.

When you leave a good friend's house, you don't have to invent a special sentence in order to say good-bye. Leave-taking in a letter is the same. In personal letters to friends or family, it is not necessary to use the standard forms of closing.

Will write again in a day or two.

Martin

Lunch was announced half a page ago! So good-bye for now.

Nancy

Counting the hours 'til next weekend!

Betsy

THE NOTE OF APOLOGY

The note of apology should offer a valid excuse for breaking an engagement. Although you may have telephoned or sent a telegram, a written explanation should follow.

BROADLAWNS

Dear Mrs. Town,

I do apologize for having to send you the telegram about Monday night.

When I accepted your invitation, I stupidly forgot entirely that Monday was a holiday and that my own guests, naturally, were not leaving until Tuesday morning; Arthur and I could not very well go out by ourselves and leave them!

We were disappointed and hope that you know how sorry we were not to be with you.

Very sincerely,
Ethel Norman

Tuesday morning

Occasionally, an unfortunate incident occurs, which, although it may have been entirely beyond our control, requires that we send another type of note of apology.

Dear Mrs. Johnson,

My little boy has just told me that our dog got into your flower beds and did a great deal of damage.

The fence around his pen is being built higher at this moment, and he will not be able to escape again. I shall send you some plants to replace those that were ruined, although I know that new ones cannot compensate for those you have lost. I can only ask you to accept my apologies.

Sincerely yours,
Katherine Pennybacker

THANK-YOU LETTERS

The most important qualification of a thank-you letter is that it sound sincere. Therefore, you use the expressions most natural to you, and write as enthusiastically as though you were talking. Even the letters of older people, although they are more restrained than those of youth, avoid anything suggesting smugness or affectation.

LETTERS OF THANKS FOR WEDDING PRESENTS

Insofar as possible, thank-you notes for wedding presents should be written as soon as the gift is received. This is not always possible, but if they are not sent before the wedding, they must be written as soon as the bride returns from her honeymoon. Even for a very large wedding, when the gifts are innumerable, all thank-you notes should be mailed within two months.

The notes sent before the wedding are properly written on plain white note paper, or paper engraved with the bride's maiden initials. Those mailed after the marriage may be written on paper marked with her married initials.

All wedding presents are sent to the bride, and she writes all the thank-you notes. But she generally words her letters to include the bridegroom, especially if the gifts have been sent by friends of his. Some girls prefer to sign the notes with both their names. This is not incorrect, but the first way is considered more proper. She might write something like this:

Saturday

Dear Mrs. Beck,

To think of your sending us all those wonderful glasses! They are perfect, and Jim and I want to thank you a thousand times!

The presents will be shown on the day of the wedding, but do come over this Tuesday morning for a cup of coffee and an earlier view.

Thanking you again, and with love from us both,

Joan

More formally, the bride-to-be might write:

Dear Mrs. King,

It was more than thoughtful of you and Mr. King to send us such a lovely clock. I have never been noted for my punctuality, and your gift will surely help me to improve. Thank you very, very much.

Looking forward to seeing you on the tenth,

Very sincerely,
Joan McCord

The salutation is addressed to Mrs. King only, but sometimes, as in the examples above, thanks to the husband is definitely expressed in writing to the wife. Usually, however, "you" is understood to mean "you both."

For a present received after the wedding, the bride might write:

Dear Mrs. Chatterton,

The mirror you sent us is going over our living-room mantel just as soon as we can hang it up! It is exactly what we most needed, and we both thank you ever so much.

Please come in soon to see how beautiful it looks in the room.

Affectionately,
Mary Smartlington

THANKS FOR CHRISTMAS AND OTHER PRESENTS

Thank-you notes for Christmas—and all other—presents should be written within two or three days of the time the gift is received. In the case of Christmas gifts, they should be sent before New Year's day, and certainly before young people return to school.

Dearest Aunt Lucy,

We just love our armchair! Jack says I'll never get a chance to sit in it if he gets there first. We both thank you so much, and are looking forward to seeing you at Easter.

With much love,
Sally

Dear Kate,

I am fascinated with my jewel box—it is so unusual. You are really clever at finding what no one else can, and what everyone wants. I don't know how you do it!

Again, thanks so much.

With love,
Edie

THANKS FOR A BABY PRESENT

Dear Mrs. Foster,

No one else in the world can knit like you! The sweater you made for the baby is perfectly adorable on her. Thank you, so much, from both of us.

Affectionately,
Robin

Dear Mrs. Cooper,

Thank you ever so much for the blanket you sent the baby. It is by far the prettiest one he has, and so soft and warm that I am really envious of him.

Do come in and see him, won't you? We love visitors, any day between 4 and 5:30.

Affectionately,
Helen

BREAD-AND-BUTTER LETTERS

When you have stayed overnight, or longer, at someone's house, it is absolutely necessary that you write a letter of thanks to your hostess within a few days after the visit.

Why bread-and-butter letters, as they are called, are so difficult for nearly everyone is hard to say unless it is because they are often written to those with whom you are on formal terms, and you want your letter to be informal in tone. Possibly you have been visiting a friend and must write to her mother, whom you scarcely know, or perhaps you are a bride and have been on a first visit to relatives or old friends of your husband who were strangers to you until now.

In the first case, when you have been visiting a girl friend and must write a letter to her mother, you write "Dear Mrs. Town" at the top of a page, and nothing in the memory of Mrs. Town encourages you to go further. It would be easy enough to write to Pauline, your friend. Very well, write to Pauline then—on a different piece of paper, about what a good time you had, how nice it was to be with her. Then copy the note you composed to Pauline on the page beginning "Dear Mrs. Town." You have only to add "Love to Pauline, and thank you again for asking me," end it "Very sincerely," or better, "Affectionately"—and there you are!

Don't be afraid that your note is too informal; older people are always pleased with friendly and spontaneous expressions from the young. Never think, because you cannot write a letter easily, that it is better not to write at all. The most awkward note imaginable is better than none—for to write none is the height of rudeness, whereas the awkward note at least fulfills the duty.

AFTER A HOUSE-PARTY WEEKEND

Dear Franny,

You and Jim are such wonderful hosts! Once again I can only tell you that there is no other house to which I go with so much pleasure, and leave with so much regret.

Your party over this last weekend was the best yet, and thank you very, very much for having included me.

With much love to you all,
Betty

Dear Mrs. Farthingham,

Last weekend was the high spot of the summer. Everything you planned was wonderful, but the best of all was the trip to the country fair on Sunday.

I truly enjoyed every minute with your family, and thank you more than I can say for including me.

Very sincerely,
Elliot Sandstrom

AFTER VISITING A CLOSE FRIEND

Dear Ellen,

It was hideously stuffy in town this morning after the coolness of Strandholm, and a back alleyway is not an alluring outlook after the beauty of your place.

It was so good being with you and I enjoyed every moment. Call me just as soon as you get back to town and we'll have lunch.

With love,
Caroline

Dearest Bett,

We both had a wonderful time! Bob's sunburn has turned to a beautiful tan, and the rest did him a world of good.

You were good to ask us so soon again, and we thank you very, very much. Call us as soon as you get home.

Yours,
Mary

TO A STRANGER WHO HAS ENTERTAINED YOU

When someone has shown you special hospitality in a city where you are a stranger:

Dear Mrs. Duluth,

It was so good of you to give my husband and me so much of your time. We enjoyed and appreciated all your kindness to us more than we can say.

We hope that you and Mr. Duluth may be coming East before long and that we may have the pleasure of seeing you then at Cottswold.

In the meanwhile, thank you for your generous hospitality, and my husband joins me in sending kindest regards to you both.

Very sincerely yours,
Katherine Starkweather

FROM A BRIDE TO HER NEW RELATIVES-IN-LAW

The following letter, written by a bride after paying a first visit to her husband's aunt and uncle, won her at a stroke the love of the whole family:

Dear Aunt Anne,

Now that we are home again I have a confession to make! Do you know that when Dick drove me up to your front door and I saw you and Uncle Bob standing on the top step—I was simply paralyzed with fright!

"Suppose they don't like me," was all that I could think. Of course, I know you love Dick, but that only made it worse. How awful, if you

didn't like—me! The reason I stumbled coming up the steps was that my knees were actually knocking together! And then you were both so perfectly adorable to me and made me feel as though I had always been your niece—and not just the wife of your nephew.

I loved every minute of our being with you, just as much as Dick did, and we hope you are going to let us come again soon.

With best love from us both,

Your affectionate niece,
Nancy

LETTERS OF CONGRATULATION

ON AN ENGAGEMENT

Dear Stella,

While we are not altogether surprised, we are both delighted to hear the good news of your engagement. Ted's family and ours are very close, as you know, and we have always been especially devoted to him. He is one of the finest—and now luckiest—of young men, and we send you both every good wish for all possible happiness.

Affectionately,
Nancy Jackson

Dear Ted,

Just a line to tell you how glad we all are to hear of your wonderful news. Stella is lovely, and, of course, from our point of view, we don't think she's exactly unfortunate either! This brings our very best wishes to you from

Arthur and Nancy Jackson

LETTER FROM A MOTHER TO A SON'S FIANCÉE

When it is impossible for a mother to go to meet her son's new fiancée, a letter should be written to her. The general outline is:

Dear Mary,

John has just told us of his great happiness, which, of course, makes us very happy, too. Our one distress is that we are so far away (or whatever else) *that we cannot immediately meet you in person.*

We do, however, send you our love and hope that we shall see you very soon.

Sincerely and affectionately,
Martha Jones

ON THE BIRTH OF A BABY

Dear Sue,

We were so delighted to hear the news of Jonathan Junior's birth. Congratulations to all three of you!

May I come to see you and the baby the first time that I'm in town? I'll call and let you know when that will be.

Much love,
Helen

OTHER LETTERS OF CONGRATULATION

Dear Mrs. Steele,

We are so glad to hear the good news of David's success; it was a very splendid accomplishment, and we are all so proud of him and happy for you. When you see him or write to him, please give him our love and congratulations.

Sincerely,
Mildred Bowen

Dear Michael,

We were all so happy to hear of the confirmation of your appointment. The state needs men like you—if we had more of your sort, the ordinary citizen would have less to worry about. Our warmest congratulations!

Jim

LETTERS OF INTRODUCTION

A business letter of introduction is somewhat different from a social one, although it carries the same implicit approval of the subject. It also implies the writer's request that the receiver pay due attention to the one being introduced. Since these letters are often written to important men with little time to spare, it is imperative that they not be written casually nor for people who do not truly merit the introduction.

A business letter of this type does not necessarily oblige the receiver to entertain the subject socially. If he wishes to, he certainly may, but generally his attention to the bearer's business is sufficient.

The social introduction is, in a way, more of a responsibility, because the writer must decide on the compatibility of the people he is introducing. Therefore, there is one firm rule:

Never *ask* for such letters of introduction, and be very sparing in your offers to write them.

Few people realize that a letter of social introduction carries an immediate obligation. The form might as well be "The bearer of this note has the right to demand your interest, your time, your hospitality—liberally and at once, no matter what you think of him." Therefore, it is far better to refuse to write a note of introduction in the beginning than to commit the greater error of inconveniencing a friend or acquaintance.

When you know someone who is going to a city where you have other friends and when you believe that it will be a mutual pleasure for them to meet, a letter of introduction is proper and very easy to write. But sent to a casual acquaintance—no matter how attractive or distinguished the person to be introduced—it is a gross presumption.

THE MORE FORMAL NOTE OF INTRODUCTION

Dear Mrs. Miller:

Julian Gibbs is going to Buffalo on January tenth to deliver a lecture on his Polar expedition, and I am giving him this note of introduction to you. He is a very great friend of ours, and I think that perhaps you and Mr. Miller will enjoy meeting him as much as I know he would enjoy knowing you.

With kindest regards, in which Arthur joins,

Very sincerely,
Ethel Norman

If Mr. Norman were introducing one man to another, he would give his card to the visitor, inscribed as follows:

> *Introducing Julian Gibbs*
>
> **Mr. Arthur Lees Norman**

Mr. Norman would also send a private letter by mail, telling his friend that Mr. Gibbs is coming.

Dear Jack,

I am giving Julian Gibbs a card of introduction to you when he goes to Buffalo on the tenth to lecture. He is delightfully entertaining and a great friend of ours. I feel sure that Betty would enjoy meeting him. If you can conveniently ask him to your house, I know he would appreciate it; if not, perhaps you could put him up for a day or two at a club or arrange for a reservation in a good hotel.

Faithfully,
Arthur Norman

INFORMAL LETTER OF INTRODUCTION

My dear Ruth,

I am giving this letter to George Perrin, a good friend of ours, who is going to be in Chicago the week of January seventh.

I want very much to have him meet you and hope that this will find you in town.

Affectionately,
Louise Hill

At the same time a second and private letter of information is written and sent by mail.

Dear Ruth,

I have sent you a letter introducing George Perrin. He is young, about thirty-five or so, very good company, and an altogether likable person.

He is very interested in modern art, and knowing that you count a number of artists among your friends, we thought you might be able to arrange some introductions for him.

I know it would be a pleasure for everyone concerned, and hope you will be able to get together.

Affectionately,
Louise

PROCEDURE ON ARRIVAL

A letter of introduction is always handed to you unsealed. It is correct for you to seal it at once in the presence of its author.

If you are a man and your introduction is to a lady, you go to her house soon after you arrive, introduce yourself, and give her your letter of introduction. She should, if it's possible, immediately invite you to cocktails, lunch, or dinner. If you feel presumptuous in going directly to her home, you may telephone and explain who you are and by whom you are introduced. She should, and undoubtedly will, set a time for you to meet, and when you arrive, you give her your letter of introduction.

A letter to a man is mailed to his house, unless the letter is a business one. In the latter case, if there has not been time to mail the introduction ahead, you go to his office and send in your business card and the letter. You wait in the reception room until he has read the letter and calls you into his office. If at all possible, it is much better to write or call him first, letting him know your business and when you will arrive. This will insure his having time to see you, as well as preparing him to discuss whatever your business may be.

A woman mails her letter of introduction and does nothing further until she receives an acknowledgment. But the obligation of a written introduction is so strong that only illness or absence can excuse the recipient from asking you to her house—either formally or informally.

When a man receives a letter introducing another man, he calls the person introduced on the telephone and asks how he may be of service. If he does not invite the newcomer to his house, he may arrange a hotel reservation or ask him to lunch or dinner at a restaurant, as the circumstances seem to warrant. But it is absolutely necessary that he show the stranger what courtesy he can.

THE INDIRECT LETTER OF INTRODUCTION

When the Franklins move to Strangetown, an indirect letter of introduction is better than a direct one. An indirect letter is one written by Mrs. O'Connor to a friend of hers in Strangetown. As already explained, a letter of introduction *presented* by Mrs. Franklin puts its recipient in a position where she must do something for the Franklins, no matter how inconvenient or distasteful it may be.

If, on the other hand, Mrs. O'Connor merely writes to Mrs. Hartwell, "My friends, the Franklins, are going to live in your neighborhood," the latter is free to make advances only insofar as she feels inclined.

Mrs. Franklin, knowing nothing about this letter and expecting nothing in the way of hospitality, is far more likely to be pleased when Mrs. Hartwell calls on her than when she is invited to Mrs. Hartwell's house because the invitation is obligatory. A letter of introduction, as you can see, is usually an inconvenience and on occasions a very real burden.

THE LETTER OF CONDOLENCE

The two most important things about letters of condolence are that they be written immediately after one hears of the death, and that they be sincere.

Intimate letters of condolence are like love letters in that they are too personal to follow a set form. One rule, and one only, should guide you in writing such letters. Say what you truly feel. Say that and nothing else. Sit down at your desk; let your thoughts be with the person you are writing to.

Don't dwell on the details of illness or the manner of death; don't quote endlessly from the poets and Scripture. Remember that a person with an aching heart will not wish to wade through interminable sorrowful thoughts. The more nearly a note can express a thought of sympathy, and a genuine love or appreciation for the one who has gone, the greater comfort it brings.

Write as simply as possible and let your heart speak truly but briefly. Forget, if you can, that you are using written words. Think merely how you feel—then put your feelings on paper.

Suppose it is the death of a man who has left a place in the whole community that will be difficult, if not impossible, to fill. You remember all he stood for that was fine and helpful to others and how much he will be missed. All you can think of is "Steve—what a wonderful man he was! I don't think anything will ever be the same again without him." Say just that! Ask if there is anything you can do at any time to be of service. There is nothing more to be said. A line into which you have put a little of the genuine feeling that you had for Steve is worth pages of eloquence. A letter of condolence may be abrupt, badly constructed, ungrammatical—never mind. Grace of expression counts for nothing; sincerity alone is of value.

An occasional letter from one who has suffered an undeniably equal loss, who in sincerity writes words of encouragement and assurance that in time the pain will grow less instead of greater, is of genuine help. But such a letter must never be written by anyone whose own suffering has not been equally devastating.

The few examples below are intended merely as suggested guides for those at a loss to construct a short but appropriate message.

My dear Mrs. Sutphen,

We are so very shocked to hear of the sorrow that has come to you. If there is anything that either my husband or I can do, I earnestly hope that you will call upon us.

Alice Blake

My dear Mrs. Conrad,

I know how little words written on a page can possibly mean to you at such a time. But I must at least tell you that you are in our thoughts and in our hearts, and if there is anything that we can do for you, please send us a message—whatever it may be.

With deepest sympathy,
Mary Newling

LETTER WHERE DEATH WAS A RELEASE

The letter to one whose loss is for the best is difficult in that you want to express sympathy but cannot feel sad that one who has suffered so long has found release. The expression of sympathy in this case should not be for the present death, but for the illness or whatever it was that befell long ago. The grief for a paralyzed mother is for the stroke that cut her down many years before, and your sympathy, though you may not have realized it, is for that. You might write: "Your sorrow during all these years—and now—is in my heart; and all my thoughts and sympathy are with you."

TO WHOM ARE LETTERS OF CONDOLENCE WRITTEN?

Letters of condolence may be addressed in various ways. If you knew the deceased well but do not know his or her family, the note is addressed to the closest relative—usually the widow, the widower, or the oldest child. Some like to add "and family" on the envelope, and this is permissible when you feel that you are sending your sympathy to all rather than to one special person.

When you did not know the person who died but do know one of his relatives, you write to that person rather than to someone who might have been closer to him. In writing to a married person who has lost a parent, you may write to the one whose parent it was, or if the other partner was close to his or her in-law, the letter may be addressed to both.

Letters to children who have lost a parent may be addressed to Miss Lucy Field (the daughter), with Mr. John Field (the son) underneath. The salutation would read, "Dear Lucy and John."

10

Greeting cards

Birthday and anniversary cards and all other messages of friendship are charming evidences of good wishes from family and friends. The wide variety of cards now available makes the choosing and sending of them a pleasure rather than a chore.

But a word of warning is in order. The very fact that they are attractive and easy to use may on occasion lead to their abuse. Elderly Aunt Margaret will enjoy her birthday card only if you take the trouble to add a little note in your own handwriting expressing something of your own feelings about the day or giving her a bit of family news. A printed message, however delightful, cannot always make up for lack of personal attention, and she may feel that troubling to write only your name indicates neglect or laziness on your part. Last names are used in signing cards only when the recipient might not recognize the first name or might confuse it with another. When a wife signs for herself and her husband, she generally signs her own name last. *See also Chapter Forty-two, on the proper (and improper) use of "Thank you for your sympathy" cards.*

CHRISTMAS CARDS

There is virtually no limit to the list of those to whom one may send Christmas cards, beginning with dearest friends and ending with mere acquaintances. However, the custom that has arisen in many communities of sending a card to everyone with whom you have a nodding acquaintance is ridiculous and contrary to the spirit of Christmas. In many areas it has become a contest to see who can receive the most cards—each person who sent a card the previous year must be sent one, plus all the new acquaintances made during the intervening months. The tradespeople in most towns now send cards to their customers. This practice, unless there is a personal relationship involved, can be for no other reason than to bolster business. Surely the idea of a heartfelt greeting and sincere wish for a happy holiday cannot go with each and every one of these messages!

Christmas cards should be sent to those whom you really wish to greet but who are not quite close enough to you to exchange gifts, to good friends whom you may not have seen for some time, and most of all to those who do not live near you and with whom your Christmas card may be your only communication. In this last case, a picture of your children or a new house is always appreciated. It need not be elaborate—a snapshot pasted on red paper, with "Merry Christmas" in green ink, is sufficient, although film stores and stationers do make these cards up to order in attractive folders, with or without a printed message.

CARDS TO BUSINESS ACQUAINTANCES

When it is company policy to send a Christmas card to a client, it is preferable to send it, addressed to the man at his business address, in the name of the company—"The Hollister Hardware Company wishes you a Merry Christmas and a Happy New Year"—rather than sending a card to his home in the name of the president or other officer. But if the client is known to the executive socially as well as through business, it may be addressed to husband and wife, even though he may not know her personally. It should be signed, however, by the executive alone, not by him and his wife. This also applies to people working with you, or for you, in your own company.

ENGRAVED CARDS

Very few people send engraved cards today unless they are prominent in public life or hold an official position. These cards are very simple—they may contain the message and no more, or they may have a little decoration, perhaps a straight gold border or a simple design of holly leaves around the edge. The title is included in the signature and the message usually reads, "Mr. and Mrs. Christopher Holly send you their best wishes for a Merry Christmas and a Happy New Year" or, "Governor and Mrs. Herbert Black wish you a Merry Christmas and a Joyous New Year."

It is important that the engraving of names on Christmas cards (as opposed to printing) follows the rules for the engraving of names on visiting cards. A woman's name should never be engraved without the title of "Mrs." or "Miss," and a man's card includes "Mr." or "Doctor" ("Dr.").

IS HUSBAND'S OR WIFE'S NAME WRITTEN FIRST?

When cards are sent by husband and wife, the one who writes the names courteously writes his or her own name last. To close friends, the last name need not be written; to others, it should be included. When cards are printed, there is no rule about whether the husband's or the wife's name should be first, but the last name is always used. Mary and John Godfrey may seem more polite to Mary, but John and Mary Godfrey does, of course, follow the conventional Mr. and Mrs. form. When children's names are included, the father's name comes first—always. For example: John and Mary and John Jr. Sometimes, by the way, a baby's arrival at any time during the year is announced by adding his name on the Christmas cards—John and Mary and their new son Timothy. Cards sent to intimate friends, by a family having several children, might be from The John Smiths—All Five; or from The Smiths—John, Mary, Johnny, Marie, and Tim. There is, of course, no rule about anything as informal as this.

On any other than engraved cards, a title—Mr., Mrs., etc.—is never used.

When cards are sent by a widow and her grown son together, or a widower and his grown daughter, the name of the parent goes on one line and that of the son or daughter on the line below. Or if written by hand, the parent's name would come first: Henry Brown and Mary, or to those who call the parent by the first name, Henry and Mary, each signing his or her name.

Engaged couples may send cards together to their intimate friends, with their first names either written by hand or printed to match the rest of the printing on an informal card.

ENVELOPES FOR CHRISTMAS CARDS

Although red and orange ink are not in the best taste for social correspondence, there is no objection to using colored ink to match the printing on a Christmas card. Also Christmas envelope linings can be as vividly colorful as you please. It is correct to paste return address stickers or write your address on envelopes. This not only complies with the Post Office's request but is a help to those receiving the cards in keeping their lists in order. The Christmas seals sold to help support various worthy causes look gay on the back of the envelope. They should be applied to the tip of the flap or to the center of a square flap.

A CARD FOR THE WHOLE FAMILY

When you intend a card for the whole family but dislike the ambiguousness of Mr. and Mrs. Brightmeadow and Family, address the envelope to Mr. and Mrs. Brightmeadow, and then on the card itself write in ink "Love to the children, too" below the printed message. If the message reads "A Merry Christmas and a Happy New Year" or "Holiday Greetings," you may simply add "to all of you" or "to all the Friendlys" below.

A CHRISTMAS CARD TO SOMEONE IN MOURNING

A card to someone who is in mourning will be gratefully received if in some way it illustrates the promise of peace or a comforting religious thought, or if its message is one of love or friendship. But please do not send a gay or humorous card shouting "Merry Christmas and Happy New Year" to one who probably feels that he will never laugh or be happy again. Whether or not those who are themselves in mourning send cards depends entirely upon their own feelings. Naturally they would not send cards to mere acquaintances, but certainly there is no impropriety in wishing their friends happiness, if they can forget their own unhappiness enough to do so. On the other hand, no one could possibly want them to do anything that could add to their difficulties or emotional burdens.

DISPLAYING CARDS

Christmas cards are joyfully displayed in any way the imagination can devise. They are hung from stair rails, mantels, in special containers, and even on streamers from the ceiling! They add greatly to the other decorations and express the warmth and love of the season.

After the holidays, they may be given to hospitals or other organizations who find many uses for them, or they may be kept to decorate your Christmas packages the following year. The pages with messages and names are, of course, removed before using the cards again for decorating packages. It is not necessary to remove names from those given to hospitals, however, unless there is also a personal message on the page.

Part THREE

AS OTHERS SEE YOU

11

The general rules

The cardinal principle of etiquette is thoughtfulness. This implies a concern with the effect of your actions on those around you, and attracting attention to yourself, because it is objectionable to others, is contrary to that basic principle.

"DO NOT ATTRACT ATTENTION TO YOURSELF IN PUBLIC"

Many of the specific suggestions that appear in this and the following chapters are simply applications of this all-important rule. Just by keeping this one injunction in mind, you can save yourself and others embarrassment in many situations.

Begin by avoiding conspicuous manners and conspicuous clothes. Don't stare at people or bump into them or point at them. Whether on the street or in a building, don't talk loudly. Nothing is in poorer taste than the noisy broadcasting of your achievement. One should avoid making personal remarks that may either attract attention or divulge another's identity. Never expose your private affairs, feelings, or innermost thoughts in public. You are knocking down the walls of your house when you do.

A young couple behaving in too devoted a manner is always conspicuous. Physical contact, other than a man's taking a woman's hand or arm to help her or keep her from falling, should be avoided.

WALKING ON THE STREET

Years ago it was necessary for a man walking with a lady to stay between her and the street to protect her from runaway or obstreperous horses. The most dangerous thing he might protect her from today would be the splash of a passing automobile going through a mud puddle. But while the old rule is no longer a necessity, most women feel more feminine and "cared for" when their escorts follow the established pattern. A man need not hop back and forth each time they cross the street, but when they are continuing in the same relative position for some time, he will appear more gentlemanly if he walks on the outside. Otherwise, if he prefers to ignore the curbside rule entirely, he should always walk on the lady's left.

A man should not sandwich himself between two ladies when walking or sitting with them. From one side he can look in the direction of both while talking with either one; whereas when he is between them, he must turn away from one when he talks to the other. In addition, if the women happen to be intimate friends, they may have a tendency to talk "across" him, forcing him to turn back and forth as if he were at a tennis match.

There is, however, an exception to this rule. When a bachelor is walking with two single girls, it might cause considerable consternation if he chose to walk beside one, leaving the other on the far side. Therefore, in this situation, in spite of the disadvantages it would be better if he walked between the girls.

THE PROBLEM OF PACKAGES

In Victorian days it was considered necessary for a man to carry anything and everything for the lady he was with, no matter how feminine in appearance or how light in weight the bundle happened to be. Today, however, the guide is practicality. A lady should certainly carry such feminine articles as her handbag, umbrella, and hatbox, and she should also carry any lightweight packages. A gentleman must carry the heavy items—suitcases, golf bags, or boxes of groceries—and he should ask if he can assist her when she has a lot of small packages. Obviously a woman should not ask a man to carry a heavy or awkward load for any distance. If she knows she will be in a situation where there are no porters available, she must plan to send luggage by other means or to restrict her pieces to manageable proportions.

THE PROFERRED ARM

A gentleman offers his arm to old ladies, to invalids, or to any lady on an occasion when he thinks she may need his support. In the daytime, she takes it or not, as she wishes. At night when going down steps or a slope, she is wise to accept his offer, not only because it is a courtesy, but because evening or high-heeled shoes can be difficult to manage when it is too dark for a woman to see clearly where she is walking.

A gentleman also offers his arm to a woman when he takes her in at a formal dinner or when he is an usher at a wedding. Otherwise, at parties couples walk side by side rather than hand on arm.

Etiquette does not permit a gentleman to grab a lady by the arm or the elbow and shove her along. It is only when he is helping her into a car, a taxi, or a bus that he should put his hand under her elbow.

GENTLEMEN BEFORE LADIES

In all ordinary circumstances, indoors or out, the lady precedes the gentleman. Over dangerous footing, he goes first and offers his hand, which the woman takes to steady herself. He steps ahead of her to open a car door for her when she enters it, and he gets out first and holds the door for her when they arrive, unless this necessitates his climbing over her in order to get out on the safe side. He also precedes her down a very steep or slippery stairway. Although the idea of protecting her should she slip is quite out of key with the capable women of today, etiquette requires that he make the gesture of stepping into a boat first, for example, to be ready to help her. Moreover, remember that charm in a woman still requires feminine grace rather than masculine capability and in no way denies the fact that a young woman's helplessness is a thing of the past.

ON GOING THROUGH DOORS

A gentleman always stands aside and allows a woman to pass through an open door ahead of him. When approaching a closed, heavy door, however, it is far more practical and simpler if he pushes the door open, goes through and holds the door while she follows. If the door opens toward them, he pulls it open and allows her to go through first.

A woman steps into a revolving door ahead of a man if it is already moving, or if there is a partition in such a position that he can push it to start the door turning. Otherwise he steps in first and gets the door moving slowly so that she may step into the section behind him.

A LADY NOT ON THE LEFT

In former days there was a rule of great importance: a lady was never seated on a gentleman's left, because according to the etiquette of the day a lady "on the left" was *not* a "lady." But today in America all that remains of this rule is that, when equally practical, it is always more polite that a gentleman seat a lady on his right. (The few surviving rules about placing a lady on the gentleman's right include the seating of a guest of honor on the right of the host or hostess or chairman, the rule that the bride walk up the aisle on her father's right and that she be seated on the bridegroom's right at all wedding festivities, and the military rule that the senior officer walk as well as sit on his junior's right.)

SEATING IN A TAXI

Ordinarily there is no problem—the woman enters the taxi first and her escort follows her. If, however, she is dressed in billowing evening clothes or a tight skirt so that it is awkward for her to slide across the seat, the man may get in first and let her follow. This is less impractical than having her seat herself first in the near corner so that he must climb over her to reach the far side. In either case, he must reach back across her to close the door. This is, at best, inconvenient, and should only be done when the lady's costume makes it almost impossible for her to edge her way to the far seat.

SMOKING IN PUBLIC

If for no reason other than a purely esthetic one, it is hard to imagine a true lady walking on a city street either chewing gum or smoking a cigarette. It simply does not look dignified or attractive. Nor does a gentleman smoke when he's walking with a lady in the city. In the country the rules are more relaxed, so that men and women alike smoke more or less whenever they please.

A new, unfortunate, and dangerous habit is smoking on the dance floor. This is inexcusable. Not only does it look unattractive, but there is a very real danger of burning your partner or his or her clothes.

In general, men and women in stores, at sports events, or in restaurants smoke as much as they wish, provided that it is legally permitted. *See also Chapter Sixty-four, "For Those Who Smoke."*

THE QUESTION OF PAYING

It is much less customary than it used to be for a man to offer to pay a woman's way, especially if they happen to meet by chance. For example, if a woman and a man find themselves taking the same train and she stops at the newsstand to buy magazines, the man may start to pay for them. If she knows him very well and the total is small, she perhaps lets him. But if he is someone she knows slightly or if she has bought several of the higher-priced ones, she says, "Don't bother; I have it!" and puts the money on the counter. It would be awkward for him to protest and bad taste to press the point. In this case, too, she buys her ticket and tips the porter for carrying her bag. On the other hand, if she has gone *on his invitation* to spend the day in the country, or to lunch, or to dinner, or to a theater, he of course pays for everything.

A group of people going on an excursion or dining together in a restaurant should agree beforehand on the handling of the finances. Going "Dutch" (each couple's or individual's paying his own way) is more often done than not. To avoid the confusion of dividing and then paying the bill, it is far better for one man (or woman, but only when it is a women's group) to pay the entire bill and the others to pay him their shares later. Another method is for each to contribute a sum in advance, based on the probable cost, from which fund he may pay and then return in equal amounts any money left over.

LIFE IN CROWDED CITIES

Considering others is essential for dwellers in city apartments so closely packed that every sound made by one family can be heard by several others. In fact, sound seems sometimes to be intensified by the walls between. In the same room with the children, their play does not seem overloud, nor does the radio or television set when we are engrossed in the program. But to the family living on the floor below, the patter of little feet sounds like a stableful of Percherons. The toys they drop seem to be made of iron! The disk jockey crashes through each separate convolution of a tired neighbor's brain. As for a musician's practicing—what manager of an apartment house has not been at his wits' end to solve this cause of complaint?

There are certain annoyances to others that can't be helped: babies must sometimes cry, children scream, dogs bark, or someone get a hacking cough. The best that considerate people can do is to try to soften such sounds as much as possible by shutting a window temporarily and by trying to train both children and dogs.

In nearly all apartment buildings there are always those who seem to have no feelings for others because their own sensitivity is, as it were, on another wavelength. It is very hard to keep in mind that there can be sounds that greatly annoy some of us—the unceasing sound of a television set, for example, or a record player—but that do not disturb others at all, whereas some of the things which we don't mind can quite possibly be unbearable to our neighbors. In today's congested cities, behavior that was once strictly private can all too easily become public.

PUBLIC CLEANLINESS

This subject is not pleasant; some aspects of it are almost too unpleasant to write about. But no one can be unaware of the increasing messiness (at times actual filthiness) of the lounges and powder and dressing rooms of hotels, theaters, and movie houses. Even the lounges of clubs are not kept in as perfect order as they ought to be. As for such places as waiting rooms in railroad terminals, rest rooms in overcrowded department stores, or sports stadiums, the problem is becoming overwhelming!

Food-container- and newspaper-discarders have always been conspicuous offenders, and the gum-scatterers have ranked with the wall-defacers in doing permanent damage. But in former years their destructiveness was held in check by employees whose present scarcity makes the orderliness of these places the responsibility of the public—in other words, each one of us.

In writing this, there are, of course, certain persons to whom I want to make a special appeal. At one extreme there are those who are really untidy. We all know people who throw ashes no matter where, set wet tumblers down on no matter what, drop wet raincoats on the nearest upholstered chair, and burn table edges with forgotten cigarettes. The women of this group wipe indelible lipstick on napkins and towels. They shake face powder on whatever is near them and leave hairs in the sink when they fix their makeups or arrange their hair-dos. Their behavior suggests that in their own homes they would not object if their beds were never made! In other words, those who live in disorder can hardly be keenly aware of the disorder they make others endure.

In the second group are those who are careless because they take it for granted that someone will come along after them with dustpan and brush. These people, if made to realize there is no one other than themselves to tidy up, would ordinarily be careful to leave no disorder.

If only all of us who care about our surroundings would become sufficiently conscious of our obligation to act as deputy wardens, the situation would be improved. In short, instead of courteously refraining from showing criticism of others, no matter what they do, it is sometimes our obligation not only to become conscious of our own behavior, but to do what we have been trained not to do—frankly to correct others. For example, when a women tosses a used paper towel at a receptacle and leaves it lying on the floor when it misses its mark, try to suggest that she make more effort by picking it up yourself, saying, "Did you notice that you missed the basket?"

In the powder rooms of many restaurants and clubs there are signs that say something like "Please leave this rest room as you found it." But they seem to do little good. Having an attendant on duty seems to be the greatest help—people apparently take a little more care if they feel they are being watched. This is a sad commentary, but in the case of rest rooms—true!

Most familiar and most troublesome to all who have the care of public places is the discarding of chewing gum. I was told by a railroad official that the chewing gum ground into the marble floor of a crowded terminal meant hours of scraping that cost the building maintenance department a small fortune.

Flagrant examples of sheer thoughtlessness are found in the washrooms in airports, department stores, and other public places. The greatest offenders are people who carelessly throw all manner of trash into toilets. In washrooms that have no attendants conditions are sometimes so bad that there is no answer other than a locked door. The owner of a department store was forced to hang a large sign on the door of the customers' rest room that read: "This washroom can remain open for your convenience only for so long as you cooperate in helping to keep it in order."

Every city has the same problem in keeping its streets clean. All the campaigns, the special "Keep Our City Clean" weeks, the signs, the trashcans on corners, and the fines imposed for littering fail to solve the problem completely. As in the public washroom, it is the duty of each and every one of us to take pride in keeping our cities and towns places of cleanliness and beauty and to impress others with the importance of the problem.

CONSIDERATION FOR THOSE WHO SERVE YOU

It is always an evidence of poor manners as well as inexcusable selfishness to show lack of consideration for those who serve us in restaurants, hotels, stores, or any public place. Only those who are insecure show neither courtesy nor consideration except to those whom they think it would be to their advantage to please.

12

In restaurants

Dining out is a necessity for a traveler or a man expected to conduct business at lunch or dinner, but it is also a pleasant form of relaxation for the family and a popular way of entertaining friends. Whether they are eating in a restaurant for social reasons or of necessity, there should be no appreciable difference in the conduct of the diners, and the rules and suggestions that follow are applicable in either situation.

ON ARRIVING

CHECKING HATS AND COATS

On entering a restaurant, a man leaves his hat and coat in the checkroom near the entrance. A woman may check her coat too, although some checkrooms are so small that the attendants will not accept women's coats. Generally she wears it until she is seated, then throws the shoulders back over her chair, with her escort's help if necessary.

In the daytime she may wear a hat or not, as she prefers. Despite today's trend toward hatlessness, a hat is always correct with a street dress. At night she wears a hat with daytime clothes, an evening hat or small veil with a cocktail or dinner dress, and no hat, ever, with a formal evening dress.

BEING SEATED

After the coats have been checked the couple or the group wait at the entrance to the dining room until the headwaiter or hostess comes forward to ask about the number in the group and about possible preference as to the location of the table. If there is no host (or hostess) one member of the group should assume the responsibility for a host's duties. If many people are involved, an informal kind of decision may be made beforehand: "John, why don't you handle things this noon?" This avoids the confusion that can arise when several people are addressing the waiter at once, leaving him in doubt about whom to listen to first and what to do next—a state that never improves the service or adds to the enjoyment of the meal. The person playing the host's role is only a spokesman, however, and is not expected to shoulder financial or other burdens that are not properly his.

When your group reaches the table the waiter pulls out the choice seat first (meaning the seat that he considers choice because it faces the room or the view or is out of the stream of traffic). If you are a woman with a man you naturally take it, unless for some reason you prefer another. In this case, you stand beside the other chair saying, "I'd rather sit here." A woman who has another lady as her guest offers her the best seat, but when the hostess is a much older person, the young guest would naturally refuse, saying, "Oh no, Mrs. Friendly, won't you sit on the banquette?"

If you do not like the table that has been offered to you you may always say, "We would prefer a table with a banquette if there is one free," or "Could we sit a little farther from the door, please?" Any good headwaiter will try to accommodate you, but if he says, "I'm sorry, all the other tables are reserved," don't argue. Just say, "All right, then, this will be fine," and if you really feel that you have been shabbily treated, don't return to that particular restaurant.

When there is no waiter at hand to seat people, the man seats his women guests. If he is with two women he helps first one and then at least makes the gesture of helping the second. He should always help a guest before his wife, who by that time should have seated herself.

The women walk behind the headwaiter and the men follow them. But if a man is giving a dinner for six or more, the women must wait at the table until told by their host where to sit. In this case it causes less confusion if he goes in ahead of his guests. When a husband and wife are hosts, the wife seats the guests, usually going first with the most important lady, and the host follows last.

If they are only four and none is married, the ladies seat themselves facing each other. When one married couple takes another to dinner, the host and his wife sit opposite each other exactly as they do at home. If, however, neither couple is giving the party, they may sit in any fashion they prefer. At a table of eight or other multiples of four the most important man sits opposite the host with the hostess on his left.

If there is dancing, and there is a lady guest of honor, the host invites her for the first dance; then he dances with the other ladies and finally with his wife. The other men should invite the women on either side of them to dance before asking others from seats farther away. A woman should never be left alone at a table.

In a restaurant that has continuous sofa-seats or banquettes along its walls, the seating is necessarily somewhat different. Two people dining together are seated side by side against the wall, and the table, which is two places wide, is pushed in front of them. If there are four, the women are seated on the banquette and the men face them across the table.

If the restaurant is very crowded, two diners who might otherwise be given wall seats are seated opposite each other at a narrower table. The lady would be seated on the banquette with the gentleman facing her.

In a restaurant with booths, the women go in first and sit against the far wall, facing each other across the table. The men then sit next to them on the outside. If a woman and two men are lunching or dining, the woman takes her place first against the wall. If one of the men is related to her, he sits across from her, and the one not related sits beside her. If this grouping is reversed, the two ladies sit next to the wall, and the man who is the husband of one sits beside the other.

MEETING PEOPLE AT A RESTAURANT

When a group of women arrive separately to have lunch at a restaurant, the first arrival should wait for the second rather than go in and sit by herself. When two have arrived, unless they are early, they should ask to be seated, explaining to the headwaiter that others are joining them and asking him to see they are promptly directed to the table. This avoids overcrowding the entry and sometimes is the only way of holding a reservation.

When a girl is meeting a man at a restaurant and arrives first, she may do one of several things. If she knows he has made a reservation she may say to the headwaiter, "I believe Mr. Rodgers made a reservation for us. Please show me to the table and tell him I'm here when he arrives." If no reservation has been made, however, it is better for her to wait in the entry for him rather than assume the responsibility of choosing the table. Finally, if it is a nice day, she may prefer to walk down the street, window shopping for a few moments, and return after she is sure he has arrived. This, however, is really a question of tactics rather than of etiquette.

A man, on the other hand, will always wait for a lady in the entry after first making sure that she has not already arrived.

COCKTAILS AND WINE

When the group is seated, the waiter may ask if anyone would like a cocktail. The host asks the others what, if anything, they would like and gives the order to the waiter, or if there is no host, each diner may give his own order.

No one should be urged to drink cocktails once he has refused, but neither should any guest feel uncomfortable because he would like one. If there are some who say "no" to liquor, the host should ask if they would like to have a soft drink or tomato juice while the others are having cocktails. It is most impolite to order more than one or two cocktails when others are left with nothing in front of them and only the hope of a meal to sustain them.

Wine should be ordered after the choices for the meal have been made, from the wine steward if there is one, or from the waiter, if there is not. The host, or whichever man may be best qualified, should choose a wine that goes well with the greatest number of choices of food. For instance, if more people have ordered chicken or fish, choose a white wine; but if more are having a steak dinner, pick a red. There are also many people who prefer a vin rosé, or pink wine, and it is often a happy compromise, as it goes well with almost any menu.

If you have a definite preference for red or white wine, it is not incorrect to order either with any food. The choices stated above are simply those which usually result in the most pleasing combination of flavors.

You may choose expensive imported wines if you wish, but there are many excellent domestic wines at a fraction of the cost. Some of the imported wines at lower prices are delicious, too, and one should not feel it necessary to spend a great deal to enjoy a good wine with dinner. If you do not recognize the names on the wine list, by all means ask your headwaiter's advice, giving him an idea of the type you prefer, and whether domestic or imported.

ORDERING THE MEAL

WHO GIVES THE ORDER?

For many years the rule was that the woman told the man what she would like and he gave the order—she never so much as spoke to the waiter herself. Presumably, the man was supposed to be the protector of his "shrinking violet," and in addition, no woman ever spoke to any strange man. Today this is obviously ridiculous. When one couple is dining in a restaurant it is correct and practical to follow the old rule, but when there are more than two people and the waiter asks each one for his choice, there is every reason that the ladies should give him their orders directly. It is certainly less confusing, and there will be fewer mistakes made, especially if the group is large. When the waiter looks straight at a woman and asks, "What kind of dressing would you like on your salad?" it would be almost insulting if she turned away and relayed her message through her escort. Many waiters ask the woman for her order first in an effort to be polite, and there is no reason why she should not answer him directly.

When the man knows the restaurant and its specialties well, and sometimes when foreign food is served with which the woman is not acquainted, he should suggest some choices to her. If they are both unfamiliar with the type of food served, he should ask the waiter to recommend one of the specialties of the restaurant.

Unless a woman knows that her host is very well off, she should show some consideration for his pocketbook and avoid ordering the most expensive items on the menu. She may ask for a *table d'hôte* dinner if one is offered, or choose only a soup or appetizer, a main course, and a dessert. The man may always add more, with her permission, but she should give him the opportunity of economizing.

THE DIFFERENCE BETWEEN *table d'hôte* AND *à la carte*

Table d'hôte means a set price for a complete meal, irrespective of how many courses are ordered. "Club" breakfasts and lunches, "blue plate" dinners, or any meals at fixed prices are *table d'hôte.*

À la carte means that you order from a list of dishes and you pay for each dish ordered, often including the bread and butter.

Usually it is very easy to know which is which, because the price follows each item on an *à la carte* menu, whereas no prices are listed on a *table d'hôte* bill of fare except at the top where the price for the complete dinner is printed. Very often a separate card or a box inset on the *à la carte* menu reads, "Special dinner $3.00," or whatever the price may be, and informs you that you can order whatever you choose on this special list for three dollars, but that any item taken from the regular bill of fare will be charged for as an extra.

A very popular type of menu is one that has a price following each entrée. This price includes the choice of an *hors d'oeuvre* or a soup, a salad, and a dessert, and choice of coffee, tea, or milk. If any other items on the menu are followed by a price, there is an additional charge for them.

RESTAURANT TABLE MANNERS

Although table manners are much the same whether you are eating at home or in a restaurant, there are a few special problems that do arise when dining out.

THE APPETIZER KNIFE

Restaurants offering appetizers requiring the use of a knife often fail to supply an extra one for this purpose. Use the knife that has been provided originally, leave it on your appetizer plate, and ask for a fresh one when the waiter brings the main course. Do not try to clean your first knife and then lay it on the table between courses.

INDIVIDUAL SIDE DISHES

Many restaurants serve vegetables and potatoes in small individual side dishes which the waiter places strategically around your dinner plate. You may eat these vegetables directly from the small dishes, or you may put them on your dinner plate by using a serving spoon or sliding them directly out of the small dish. If you then ask the waiter to remove the empty dishes, this avoids overcrowding the table.

CUTTING BREAD AND POURING COFFEE

When an uncut loaf of bread is placed on the table, the host slices or breaks off two or three individual portions and offers them with the rest of the loaf in the bread basket or on the plate to the ladies next to him. This is then passed around the table, and each man should cut or break off a portion for himself and the lady next to him.

If coffee or tea is placed on the table without first having been poured by the waiter, the person nearest the pot should offer to pour, filling his own cup last.

ICED-TEA AND ICED-COFFEE SPOONS

If iced tea or coffee has been served in a glass with a saucer under it, the spoon used to stir the drink is placed in this saucer. Often there is no saucer and the problem arises as to what to do with the spoon. If paper napkins are available, put one on the table next to your glass and then put the spoon on the napkin. If no paper napkins are available the spoon should be placed with the bowl upside down on the edge of your butter plate, or dinner plate if necessary. A used piece of silver should not be put on the table, especially when there is a tablecloth.

SUGAR AND STRAW WRAPPERS

These wrappers should be neatly tucked under the edge of your dinner or butter plate. They should not be crumpled and placed in an ashtray, where there is a danger of their catching fire.

SPECIAL TYPES OF MEALS

The smorgasbord is a delightful importation from Sweden. Actually it is simply a buffet, but a buffet of such variety and interest that it has become extremely popular in the United States.

When a man invites a woman to dine in this fashion, he may go to the buffet alone and fill a plate for her, but this eliminates much of the fun of dining in such a restaurant. Aside from the fact that they would be left sitting alone at the table, few women would want to miss the opportunity of seeing the delectable displays of food and choosing a little of everything that appeals to them.

At this type of meal, the individual tables are set as usual. The smorgasbord, which literally translated means "sandwich table," has one or more stacks of small plates to be served with reasonable amounts of food. Since you are expected to make as many trips as you wish from your seat to the smorgasbord and back, you should never overload your plate, and if you choose foods which do not go well together, you should use a clean plate for each trip. Leave your used plate and silver at the table for the waiter to remove while you are helping yourself to your next selection. You are intended to take your time. Start with fish, which should whet your appetite, then cold cuts, followed if you wish by cheeses and a bit of fresh fruit or jello. You then choose your hot food, and end with dessert if your appetite is still there. Plenty of coffee is served throughout the meal.

Japanese and Chinese restaurants offer interesting variations in service and food. Some of the Japanese have sections where the guests may remove their shoes, if they choose to, and sit on cushions on the floor at low tables, Japanese style. Naturally, if you are taking older or crippled people to such a restaurant, you would not sit in that section, but at the regular tables, which are always available for those who prefer them. Chinese restaurants have regular seating arrangements, but in many of them you may eat with chopsticks if you wish. Some suggest that the people at the table order different dishes, which are placed in the center of the table so that the diners may serve themselves from any or all of them. This is a delightful way to experiment with various dishes—and one that may be helpful in ordering the next time you go to a similar restaurant.

SUMMONING A WAITER

There is no hard or fixed rule for the best way to summon a waiter. In fact, ways which are considered proper in some countries are downright insulting in others. For example a waiter who is hissed, whistled, or clapped at in the United States would probably run in the other direction, and yet those gestures are perfectly correct in certain other countries. The usual way here is to catch his eye and then raise your hand, finger pointing up, as if to say "attention" or "listen." If he refuses to look in your direction, you may call "Waiter" or "Waitress" quietly or, if he is too far away to hear you, ask any other waiter nearby, "Please call our waiter." Writing this paragraph reminds me of one of my favorite stories—that of the waiter whose tombstone was marked, "God finally caught his eye."

PAYING THE CHECK

When everyone has finished his meal, the host catches the eye of the waiter or headwaiter and says, "The check, please." The check is brought face down on a small plate and presented to the man who ordered the dinner. He looks at it, checks it quickly for mistakes, and returns it to the plate with the necessary money. If he has found an error, he beckons the waiter and points it out quietly; the waiter makes the adjustment, either himself or with the help of the headwaiter or cashier. In no circumstances should a "scene" be made. If the management is unpleasant about making a correction, simply pay the check, leave as quickly as possible, and do not return to that restaurant.

Many restaurants ask their customers to pay a cashier on the way out. This practice is especially common in large city restaurants and in those which are used mostly at the lunch hour. It is a great time-saver, as very often a waiter, when he has finished serving a table, gives his attention to other customers, and those waiting for their checks find it difficult to attract his attention. When you read at the bottom of your check "Please pay cashier," put the tip on the table, collect your belongings, and leave, with the host following the group, who wait in the entry while he pays the bill. If he needs change in order to have the right amount for a tip, he pays the check and quickly returns to the table so that the waiter knows he has not been forgotten.

When a group is small the men wait for the ladies to precede them on leaving the restaurant. With more than six or eight people, however, this becomes unwieldy and each couple goes out together.

CREDIT CARDS

A popular and practical method of paying for restaurant dinners, entertainments, and even such necessities as gasoline and travel accommodations is to use a credit card. Numerous companies issue credit cards, which are a great convenience for those who dine out or entertain frequently but do not wish to carry large amounts of cash. The card is used as identification at any restaurant or establishment that is a member of the credit organization. All the customer has to do at the time is give the check and his card to the waiter for processing, after which he will be asked to sign a special voucher when his card is returned to him. The restaurant sends the voucher in to the credit-card company, which in turn bills the customer at the end of the month. The customer adds the tip to the voucher himself, after making sure that the bill is correct.

TIPPING

It is difficult to give definite rules for tipping, because it depends upon where you go and the service that is given you. That is, if you patronize luxurious restaurants or if you have special requirements or are difficult to please, greater "compensation" is expected than if you choose simpler restaurants and have less exacting demands.

WAITER AND HEADWAITER

Fifteen percent is standard in any restaurant, or possibly 20 if you have been very demanding or the service has been unusually good. Ten percent is too little almost anywhere, except perhaps at a lunch counter, and never less than ten cents should be left there.

Patrons who make a practice of tipping waitresses less than waiters are being unfair, because the service rendered is the same.

If you are having a party of ten, twelve, or more, 15 percent would be quite adequate divided among the waiters who serve you and five dollars would be enough for the headwaiter if he has taken pains to give you extra service. On the other hand, if he has done nothing beyond seating you and handing you a menu, you give him nothing.

WINE STEWARD AND BARTENDER

If a wine steward has served you, he should receive 12 to 15 percent of the wine bill. The bartender receives 10 or 15 percent if you have drinks at the bar.

CHECKROOM AND DRESSING ROOM

The fee to the checkroom attendant who takes care of a man's hat and coat in most restaurants is twenty-five cents—fifty cents in very expensive ones.

The maid in a ladies' room never receives less than twenty-five cents in any restaurant or hotel and sometimes fifty in an expensive one. There is almost always a small plate with a few coins on it in a conspicuous place. If the attendant hands you a towel or performs some other service for you, you are expected to leave a coin of the same denomination as those on the plate—usually a quarter—but if she does nothing but sit and look at you, you need not leave a tip.

A HOST'S RESPONSIBILITIES

The first thing a host must consider is the choice of restaurant. Do his guests like exotic food or good plain cooking? If they are from out of town, do they have the proper clothes with them for an elaborate restaurant? Do they wish to see a place with a worldwide reputation? If a man is taking a woman to dinner, would she like a small, intimate spot, or would she prefer to dance to a good orchestra?

Having reached a decision, the host must make every effort to see that the restaurant chosen meets the expectations of his guests. If he has picked a well-known restaurant he must reserve a table ahead of time; and should his party be on a weekend evening it is always safer to make a reservation in advance.

If he has ordered the dinner ahead of time, he must try to observe the dishes as they are served to make sure that everything is as he requested. If there are any omissions, he quietly calls them to the attention of the waiter and makes sure that the missing items are supplied.

If dinner has not been ordered beforehand, it is the host's duty to take his guests' orders and give them to the waiter or, if the party is large, to make sure that the waiter gets the order correctly from each person. Again, if there are mistakes, he must tactfully and politely see that they are corrected, without embarrassing his guests.

When he pays the check, the host does not display the total but puts the money (or the signed check if he pays by credit card) quietly on the plate and nods to the waiter that he may remove it. If he does not have the exact amount, including the tip, the waiter will bring his change, but if the sum includes both bill and tip, the host thanks the waiter and indicates that he is ready to leave by rising or by making some such remark as "Well, let's move along or we'll never make the first act."

If the headwaiter has been especially helpful, the host unobtrusively slips a tip (from two to five dollars, depending on the size of the group) into his hand and thanks him as he is leaving the restaurant.

WOMEN DINING OUT

WHEN A WOMAN INVITES A MAN

When a woman invites a man to dine with her for personal rather than business reasons and it is understood that she is paying the bill, there may be some embarrassment at the time the check is presented. The best solution is for the woman to have a credit card, or possibly a charge account at the restaurant. The act of signing a slip of paper does not somehow seem so objectionable as having the woman check over the bill and count out the money while the man sits helplessly by. In fact, this situation is so awkward that many women without charge privileges prefer to give their guest a sum of cash large enough to cover the bill before they enter the restaurant, thus relieving the man of any embarrassment before the waiter. Incidentally, this solution also serves for the husband who has left his wallet behind or has insufficient money with him. Rather than have him embarrassed in front of the waiters or his guests, his wife may pass him the necessary sum without calling attention to his situation.

When a woman entertains a customer for her company, she signs the check as her firm's representative. If they have not made arrangements for her to sign the check, she pays cash, and if her guest protests and tries to pay himself, she explains that he is her company's guest and that the amount of this check is going on her expense account. Or again, if she has a credit card, she may use it and present the bill to her employer.

WHEN A WOMAN INVITES A MARRIED COUPLE

A woman may invite a married couple to have dinner with her, but when she does she should make it clear that it's her party. She does this by saying when she invites them, "I'd like to *take* you to dinner." If the man offers to pay, as he probably will, she should be firm, saying, "No, this was *my* invitation and I really want it to be *my* party." She should follow the same procedures described above for the mechanics of paying the bill.

WHEN WOMEN DINE TOGETHER

When several woman are dining out together the problem of the check can cause concern to and confusion among the waiters, the nearby diners, and the women themselves. Women so seldom are able to separate a check into several parts with grace and speed that the cartoon of feminine heads clustered about the waiter's tab, captioned "Now let's see, Ethel, you had the Tomato Surprise," is familiar to all of us. One way to avoid such a scene is to get separate checks. Or one woman may pay the entire check, and the settling up can be done later. If each one's debt must be figured at the table, make sure at least that the best computer in the group gets the chore so that it is done as quietly and simply as possible.

WOMEN APPLYING COSMETICS AT TABLE

A thoughtful woman always avoids extensive making-up in public. At the end of a meal she may quickly powder her nose and put on a little lipstick, but to look in a little mirror and daub at the face for any length of time is in bad taste.

The one never-to-be-broken rule is: Never use a comb on the street or in any public place. Never even slightly rearrange or put your hands to your hair in any place where food is served. These rules apply to both men and women.

RESTAURANT COURTESY

When a group enters a restaurant and sees people whom some know and others do not, they continue directly to their table, nodding "hello" as they pass. A public restaurant is scarcely the place for mass introductions.

On the other hand, there are occasions when one or two introductions are suitable. All men at the table rise when a woman is being introduced, as they do whenever a woman stops to talk. But when a woman stopping at a table is introduced to other women seated there, the latter never rise—even though they be young and the visitor quite old.

All the men at the table do not rise when another man stops on his way by. When someone comes across the room to speak to one of the diners, that man only should stand to shake hands. The visitor should then ask him please to be seated while he finishes what he has come to say. If he intends to say more than a few words of greeting, he might ask a waiter for a chair or as quickly as possible arrange to meet later.

We all must have occasionally seen a thoughtless woman who, seeing her friend Mrs. Evans dining in a restaurant with Mr. Evans, cannot resist stopping for a greeting that lengthens into a chatty dialogue. She overlooks the fact that during her stay the polite husband is obliged to stand and watch the food on his plate grow colder and colder.

True, the visitor does from time to time earnestly urge, "Oh, *do* sit down! Oh, *please* don't stand!" Mr. Evans may quite properly do so, but undoubtedly he would feel most conspicuous if he were seated while the woman remained standing at the table.

One husband solved this problem quite effectively. Gustav Gourmet, just about to eat a perfect soufflé in a noted restaurant, was forced to stand for a friend of his wife who stopped at their table. "Oh, *please* sit down! You mustn't let your soufflé fall!" said she. Reluctant to sit down, he solved the problem by lifting the plate and eating—standing.

Let us hope that long-talking standees will take this anecdote to heart and pass the tables of their friends without pausing for too long a time.

LUNCH COUNTERS AND CAFETERIAS

When a couple goes to a lunch counter that is so crowded that there are not two seats together, it is permissible to ask a person sitting between two empty stools if he would mind moving down one place. Conversely, a person in this position should offer to move before he is asked. At a crowded cafeteria tables are meant to be shared, but it is only friendly and courteous to ask "Is this seat saved?" or "May I sit here?" before grabbing an empty chair at a table that is already occupied.

13

The opera, the theater, and other indoor entertainments

The basic principles of conduct are exactly the same in the formality of an opera house or in the free and easy atmosphere of a circus tent: Do not draw attention to yourself by noisy or conspicuous behavior. Do remember that others in the audience (as well as the performers) are entitled to your consideration.

THE OPERA

SEATING IN A BOX AT THE OPERA

Great dignity is required in a box at the opera. If people have dined together beforehand they all arrive at the same time. The gentlemen help the ladies to take off their coats, and one of them draws back the curtain dividing the anteroom from the box. The ladies enter, followed by the gentlemen, the last of whom closes the curtain again. If there are two ladies besides the hostess, the latter places her more distinguished or older guest in the corner of the front row nearest the stage. The seat farthest from the stage in the front row is always her own. The older guest takes her seat first, then the hostess takes her place, whereupon the third lady goes forward in the center to the front of the box and stands until one of the men places a chair for her between the other two. If there are eight, one of the ladies sits in the second row with two of the gentlemen beside her. The other two men sit in the back row.

One of the duties of the men is to see that the curtains at the back of the box remain tightly closed, so that the light from the anteroom does not shine into the faces of others in the audience across the house.

Three or four couples often subscribe to a box at the opera together, sharing the cost and enjoying each other's company during the season. So that each member of the group may enjoy the better seats and no two men be always relegated to the back row (especially if it is an off-center box that does not offer a full view of the stage from all of its seats), these friends may agree to switch their seating arrangements around, even though it violates the old rule of "no gentlemen in the front row."

BETWEEN THE ACTS

Both women and men may visit friends in other boxes between the acts, but the women should always have escorts. They may go out to enjoy the refreshments that some opera houses provide or simply to enjoy seeing the interesting people who are invariably at the opera. No lady should ever be left alone in the box, however, and no gentleman may stay in a box other than his own after the lowering of the lights. In fact, everyone should return as soon as the signal is given for the raising of the curtain, for it is very annoying to have people coming in after the performance has resumed, not only to the audience but to the performers as well.

It should not be necessary to point out that there must be no conversation during the overture or the performance. An enthusiastic audience may applaud at the end of an aria and, of course, after each curtain, but not for the entrances or exits of a performer.

DRESSING FOR MONDAY NIGHT

In New York and some other large cities, there has been a return to very formal dress for Monday night at the opera. In the boxes, many of the men wear white tie and tails, and their companions wear long evening dresses and brilliant jewelry. This formality is not required, however. Dinner jackets for men and evening, dinner, or cocktail dresses for ladies are acceptable.

In the orchestra, either a dinner jacket or a business suit is correct, and you will feel comfortable in whichever you choose. A lady may wear a long or short dinner dress or, if her escort is in a business suit, a silk dress or a cocktail suit.

In the balconies, daytime clothes are worn by both men and women.

DRESSING FOR OTHER EVENINGS

On evenings other than Monday, clothing is very much the same as that worn to the theater, but one may occasionally see tuxedos and dinner dresses. One rarely sees tails on other than an opening night, but for men who have the opportunity to change from business clothes, a dinner jacket is sometimes worn, especially by those in the boxes.

THE THEATER

DINNER AND A PLAY

In any audience there are almost certain to be married couples who are enjoying an evening away from home, serious devotees or students of the drama, and theater parties of various sizes. One of the more delightful ways of entertaining people is to ask them to have dinner and go to a play.

When an unattached man invites friends to go to the theater, he usually takes them to dinner in a restaurant; but if a host and hostess have a house or apartment in the city, they are likely to have dinner at home. Among young people this form of entertainment usually involves dining out, and the evening is Dutch treat. If one member of the group wishes to, he (or she) may ask the others to meet at his home for cocktails, but the cost of dinner and the tickets is divided among the group.

It is absolutely essential that a host arrange for theater tickets well in advance, and naturally he must get good ones. In New York, for instance, if you buy your tickets at the box office, you must plan weeks ahead in order to get the seats that you wish for the most popular plays. If you plan your party on the spur of the moment, at best you will have to settle for a less popular play or one that has been running for some time, or else you must buy the tickets from a ticket agency, which charges more than the box-office price.

ARRIVING AT THE THEATER

On arriving at the theater, the host (or hostess) holds the tickets in his hand so that the ticket-taker may see them, but he allows his guests to pass in ahead of him. If the usher is at the head of the aisle, the host gives her the stubs and steps back, and the women precede him down the aisle. If, however, the usher is already part way down the aisle, the host may lead the way until he reaches her. If the party is large, the hostess should tell her guests in what order they are going to sit, so that they may arrive at their row in more or less that order, avoiding a great deal of shuffling about and confusion in the aisle.

The only fixed rule about seating in the theater is that a man should sit on the aisle. When there are two couples, a woman should not go into the row first because it leaves her at the end of the line in a more difficult position for joining the conversation before the play starts and between the acts. Therefore, one man should go in first, followed by the two women, and finally the other man. Each woman generally sits next to the man who is not her husband.

When the party is larger, a woman does lead the way into the row, and the others alternate, men and women, leaving the host, or one of the men if there is no host, on the aisle.

In the case of a man and a woman alone, she, of course, goes in first, and he follows, sitting on or nearest to the aisle.

WHEN THE PLAY IS OVER

The first man to leave the row naturally stands in the aisle for a moment so that the lady who follows can walk with him or, if the crowd makes two abreast impossible, precede him. In nearly all situations, a lady goes first. Only when the crowd is really dense does a man go first to make a wedge for her. In a theater party of six or more, the first man should let the woman who sat next to him go ahead of him, but he does not wait to follow the others.

DRESSING FOR THE THEATER

It is perfectly correct for both men and women to wear daytime clothes to the theater. During the week, the audience is likely to be made up of a large proportion of couples from the suburbs, and the man who has been at his office all day and has had no opportunity to change his clothes would hardly wish to see his wife arrive to meet him for dinner dressed in an elaborate cocktail or dinner dress. So if Mrs. Franklin has decided to combine her trip to the theater with an afternoon's shopping, she need feel no embarrassment at appearing at the theater in a wool dress, or even a suit, although it should not be a sports suit. Many women carry an extra piece or two of jewelry in their purses with which to dress up their "basic" black dresses for the evening.

On the rare occasion when a hostess plans a large theater party, perhaps to celebrate an anniversary, she may wish to make the evening more gala by requesting that the men wear "black tie." The only other time that more formal dress is required is the opening night of an evening performance, when one attends by special invitation. Then the women wear cocktail or dinner dresses and the gentlemen wear tuxedos.

COURTESY AT THE THEATER

You must not be late! It is terribly unfair to others in your party to make them miss the beginning of a performance because of your tardiness. Other theatergoers, too, dislike being climbed over after the performance has started. If your taxi breaks down or a flat tire causes a truly unavoidable delay, it is far more considerate to wait at the back of the theater until the first scene is over; then the usher can show you to your seat. If the first act is not divided into scenes and there is no pause in the action, you should slip into your seat as quickly and noiselessly as possible.

Hats off! Even if a woman believes her hat too small to obstruct anyone's view she should be agreeable about removing it if asked to do so. Thoughtful women whose hats are likely to interfere with the view of those behind them take them off without having to be asked.

"Excuse me, please" is the natural thing to say when having to disturb anyone in order to get to or leave your seat in a theater, and if someone is obliged to get up to let you pass, you add "Thank you," or "I'm sorry." Should you by any chance have to pass someone a second time, you say "I'm sorry to disturb you again," and "Thank you" as they let you go by.

In passing strangers, men as well as women face the stage and press closely to the backs of the seats they are facing, remembering, however, not to drag anything across the heads of those sitting in the row in front of them. Some women are very careless about their handbags, which, if swinging from a strap handle, bump into people beside or below them.

When you are seated you must give others enough room to pass. If the seats are far enough apart so that you can do this by merely turning your knees sideways, so much the better, especially if the play has started. But if there is so little space that the passers-by have to step over your knees, you must stand and sit down again—quickly! Remember that during every second you stand, you are cutting off the view of all who are seated behind you.

There are certain ill-mannered men and women who practically refuse to allow anyone to pass once they are seated. It is quite true that having to gather up hat, program, and bag, and stand while each person on a long aisle leaves and comes back between each act can be far from pleasurable. But if you haven't sufficient self-control to be amiable about these annoyances you should forego the discomforts of the theater and take your entertainment in front of your television set at home. If, for example, you do not wish to leave your seat between acts, why not try to get seats away from an aisle instead of on it?

Quiet, please! Most theater audiences are made up of mature people genuinely interested in the performance, but even they may irritate their neighbors through sheer thoughtlessness. Especially annoying are those who cannot seem to settle down when the curtain first goes up, who must finish that one important story or find a misplaced glove that could perfectly well wait until the intermission. Not much better are those who feel they must explain all the jokes to their companions; rarely is anyone enlightened, and all too often those nearby miss the next punch line. If you want to discuss the plot or the performance, wait until the act is over.

SMOKING BETWEEN THE ACTS

A woman usually goes out to the lobby with her escort if he wishes to smoke between the acts. But if a man is with a woman who does not smoke and prefers to remain seated, he may leave her briefly during one intermission or, if she has no objections, during both. Of course, it depends somewhat upon whom he is with. He might possibly leave his wife or mother more often than a guest—but it really depends on the lady's reaction.

THE MOVIES

An evening at the movies is a good deal less formal than one at a play, but other considerations are not too different. Unless you are attending a premier or an elaborate benefit performance of some kind, when you would dress as you would for the opening night of a play, casual clothes are proper. "Casual," however, must be determined by the location of the theater and the other activities of the evening. For example, slacks might be quite proper in the country, but they would be quite out of place in the city, especially if you were going to a restaurant first or a night club later.

FINDING SEATS AT THE MOVIES

The order in which a couple goes down the aisle in a movie theater is unimportant. When there are no ushers, a man and woman go down the aisle together. Either one might say, "There are two—shall we take those?" The other agrees or suggests two somewhere else.

If you come in after the movie has started, wait at the rear until your eyes have become adjusted to the darkness. By doing this you may avoid stumbling into the center of a row only to find that there are not the necessary vacant seats, having to back out, and tripping over unsympathetic spectators.

AUDIENCE PESTS

Talking, coughing, jingling bangles—not to speak of rattling cellophane when opening candy boxes—are annoying and disturbing to everyone in the audience. Very young people who go to the movies in droves often ruin the evening for others who happen to sit near them. If Julie and Johnny and Susy and Tommy want to talk and giggle, they should arrange chairs in rows in a game room, turn on the radio or television, and sit there and chatter.

If those behind you insist on talking, it will do you no good to turn around and glare. If you are young, they pay no attention; and if you are older, you may discover that most young people think an angry older person the funniest sight on earth. The small boy throws a snowball at an elderly gentleman for no other reason! The only thing you can do is to say amiably, "I'm sorry, but I can't hear anything while you talk." If they persist, you can ask an usher to call the manager.

The romantically inclined should realize that every word said above a whisper is easily heard by those sitting directly in front of them, and those who discuss family or other private affairs might also do well to remember this.

But comparatively few people are anything but well-behaved. Most people take their seats as quietly and quickly as they possibly can and are quite as interested, and therefore as attentive and quiet, as you are, or they would not have come.

CIRCUSES, ICE SHOWS, AND RODEOS

As long as members of the audience obey the basic principles of consideration for others, behavior at such events as circuses, rodeos, or ice shows is unrestricted by rules. Clothing depends entirely on the weather. At a summertime circus held in a hot tent, women wear the coolest sleeveless dresses imaginable, and the young wear shorts. At a winter ice show, spectators would appear foolish if they did not wear warm boots and heavy coats into a cold arena. There is, however, one rule about clothing that should be followed: unless a woman is very young, she should not wear shorts to summer performances of this nature, nor slacks in the winter.

At any show where it is not necessary to hear the performers, the audience may talk as much as they please. In fact, at such competitive events as rodeos part of the fun is cheering your favorite on.

But in spite of all this informality, there are a few things to avoid. As at the theater, don't be late. Even here it disturbs others who have arrived on time. Don't blow your cigarette smoke into your neighbor's face, and don't let your enthusiasm get so out of hand that your voice may burst his eardrums.

14

Outdoor events

Football, baseball, soccer, ice hockey, and basketball are integral parts of American life. Few parents of young boys have not had to wait their turn for the sports page of the Sunday newspaper. Beginning in the earliest grades, children learn teamwork and loyalty through participating in team sports. It is natural, therefore, that Americans grow up with an avid interest in one or many sports, an interest that sometimes becomes almost fanatical. In fact, most professional games are so well attended that if you wish to get choice seats you must have season tickets or at least order them well in advance.

AT A PROFESSIONAL MATCH

At a sports event you need follow few rules other than those of ordinary courtesy. Arrive on time so that you do not disturb others in reaching your seat. You are expected to cheer for your team or your favorite player, but don't shout insults at the opposing team, as you may very well find yourself in a fight with your neighbor, and you will gain little by being escorted to the nearest exit by an usher or a policeman. Try to refrain from jumping up in moments of crisis; the people behind you are interested in seeing too, and you will be deluged with shouts of

"Down in front!" Since smoke going directly into someone's face can be most irritating, hold your cigarette or cigar in such a way that it does not offend. If possible leave very young children at home. They lose interest very quickly at a long game, and the spectators around you will not appreciate repeated requests for candy, ice cream, sodas, or trips to the bathroom. And last but not least, don't shove! If you have an appointment following the game, slip out quietly a minute or two before the end. If you leave when the game is over, walk slowly *with* the crowd, not *through* it, to the exit.

Clothing is as variable as the weather. At football or soccer games warmth is the first consideration. Above all, don't forget boots—a concrete floor is one of the coldest footrests known to man. At indoor arenas, people in the boxes generally dress more formally than those in the balconies, where any costume seems to be acceptable. For the better seats at evening games, suits or wool dresses for women and sports jackets with ties or business suits for men are usually worn. Baseball, although it is our National Sport, is perhaps the least formal of all, and even in the boxes (unless you are the guest of an official) open sports shirts for men, flat-heeled shoes for women—in short, the most comfortable clothes possible—are the rule.

To sum up, if you do not act or dress in a conspicuous manner, and if you observe the basic rules of consideration for others, you will be able to get the most enjoyment out of any sporting event, as well as add to the pleasure of neighboring spectators.

AT COLLEGE AND SCHOOL MATCHES

The rules of behavior are the same at any school or college match as they are at professional sports events. There are, however, a few suggestions for girls that may add to their enjoyment and to that of their escorts. In choosing your clothes remember to consider where your date may be taking you after the game. If there will be a cocktail party or a tea dance before you'll have a chance to change, carry a handbag that will hold a pair of suitable shoes to replace your boots, and wear a scarf or hat that will preserve your hairdo for the evening.

If you are unfamiliar with the sport you are going to see, try to get some information about it in advance. The girl who spends the afternoon asking stupid questions ("Why do they do that? What's the score? Which team is ahead?") is not likely to find herself invited to the next game. Even more important, don't show your boredom or ignorance by talking "girl talk" with your escort's roommate's date!

Whether you feel any enthusiasm for your date's team or not, let him think you do. Disinterest or lack of loyalty to his school is as bad as or worse than lack of knowledge of the sport.

AT A PUBLIC BEACH

At a public beach the first rule is to avoid crowding—at least as much as you possibly can. Those who have children should choose places as near as possible to the spot where the youngsters are going to wade in and out of the water and dig canals and build sand castles. Not only is it dangerous to have little children paddling in the water far away, but it is natural for a child to fill his pail and run back and forth from his family to the water, kicking sand and spilling water over those who may be sitting in his path. Even though the children may be enchanting, their charm is not apparent to a sleeping sunbather on whom they have just splashed icy water!

It is also important not to let a child thrust his attentions upon strangers. While spontaneous friendliness is one of the most appealing traits that a child can have—and most people are inclined to like children—remember that there are those who do not. Therefore, before letting Johnny make himself one of a group of strangers sitting nearby, be sure to notice whether the strangers are showing particular interest in Johnny or whether Johnny alone is showing interest in them! If the latter seems to be the case, call him back immediately.

Dogs are forbidden on most crowded beaches, but on more remote ones they are usually allowed and can give a lot of pleasure if they are properly controlled. In an area where there are other people, a dog must be kept on his leash so as not to alarm small children or adults who are distrustful of animals. If your dog is to be free to run and swim, you must find a deserted part of the beach, being sure to leash him again if a stranger approaches.

Children and dog owners are not the only offenders on the beach. Throwing a ball over, around, and between the sunbathers can be very annoying. An obvious display of affection is out of place, too. Couples who give languid back rubs, lie with heads resting on stomachs, or throw their arms across each other's shoulders, to say nothing of kissing and caressing, show their ignorance of good taste and make their neighbors thoroughly uncomfortable.

Although brief bathing suits, including bikinis, and trunks are now accepted wherever there is sun, it is not necessary to throw modesty to the winds and appear among people of all ages and backgrounds in a costume that barely conforms to the legal requirements of decency.

Bikinis can look superb on a young girl with a beautiful figure. On an older woman, however, or one who even tends toward overweight, they are a disaster. Far from adding to her charms by a display of seminudity, they draw attention to and exaggerate the imperfections in her figure.

PARKS AND PLAYGROUNDS

Behavior at a public park is virtually the same as at the beach. Again, don't crowd others if you can help it. Don't spread your picnic baskets and personal belongings over two or three tables when your share is one. Although picnic-table manners are less exacting than those at a set table at home, they do not grant to the children the privilege of eating like little savages and offending the sensibilities of neighbors who cannot help seeing them.

Public parks and picnic grounds are excellent training schools in that they teach a child to take his turn and be satisfied with his own share of time with the slides, swings, seesaws, and any other play equipment offered to all children.

Most important of all, always leave public grounds as clean or cleaner than you find them. Papers, cans, trash, and broken bottles, so frequently strewn over picnic grounds and beaches, completely destroy the beauty of the loveliest landscape.

15

Appearing on television and radio

Except for the special requirements of makeup and clothes for a television appearance, the rules are the same for a radio broadcast as for television. Since a radio program is always witnessed by members of the station's staff and sometimes by a studio audience as well, you should dress tastefully and appropriately; but because you are not appearing before a camera, the style of your dress, your makeup, and your jewelry is entirely up to you.

DRESSING FOR TELEVISION

You can always get help in choosing the clothing for your television appearance by calling and asking the advice of the producer. A more satisfactory way is to watch the program two or three times and decide which costumes you think are the most suitable or would be most becoming to you. Pastel or even dark colors televise better than white or black—men's shirts as well as women's dresses. Choose clothes that are "slimming," because the television camera tends to make everyone look fatter than he or she is. Almost all networks have makeup artists on hand for their regular performers, and they occasionally see that a guest is properly made up before appearing. Be sure, however, that they know what your role on the program is to be.

You may wear jewelry if it is necessary to your costume, but remember that brilliant stones will be sprayed with wax to dull the glitter, and the wax may be difficult to remove. Otherwise, choose clothing that is most flattering to your face and figure and appropriate to the time of day and the type of program. A sports suit would seem out of place on an evening variety show, as would a low-necked cocktail dress on a morning "quiz" program.

YOUR VOICE AND MANNER

The most important thing to remember when you are appearing on either radio or television is that you are really a guest in the home of the listener or viewer. Your manners, therefore, should be the same as if you were in their houses in person. You speak in a well-modulated voice, just as if you were in the same room with your audience. Remember, too, that a pocketful of jingling coins and a rattle of notes will sound far louder through the microphone than they would across a room, and check before the program begins to make certain you have eliminated all distracting and unnecessary noisemakers.

Once on the air, act naturally and try not to show off. If other people on the program become noisy or the discussion becomes heated, don't compete. By waiting until the moderator calms them down or changes the subject you retain your dignity.

If you are appearing on behalf of a charitable cause or on an intellectual program, be sure that the interviewer knows exactly what your subject is. Otherwise you may have difficulty in bringing out the points you wish to stress. If you are a participant in a discussion group or on a panel show, listen to the views of the other members and don't concentrate on pushing only your own opinions.

Don't talk down to or patronize your audience. You are a guest in the homes of people from every walk of life, and you cannot possibly know more than each and every one of them. In other words, don't *under*estimate the intelligence of your listeners. On the other hand, simply because they have chosen to listen to you, don't *over*estimate their knowledge of your subject.

16

Conducting meetings

Meetings may consist of three or four mothers who want to work out suitable arrangements for transporting their children to school, or they may involve hundreds of stockholders of the country's largest corporation. Almost all of us attend several kinds of meetings each year, and many of us find ourselves from time to time in the position of having to take charge. Situations vary, of course, but some rather generalized suggestions may be useful.

MEETINGS OF LARGE ORGANIZATIONS

The president or chairman of any large organization must run its meetings in strict accordance with the rules of parliamentary procedure. The standard reference book on the subject is *Robert's Rules of Order*, which is available in any library or bookstore. In addition to learning these rules and following them scrupulously, the person in charge must control the meeting politely but firmly, so that it does not get out of hand through unnecessary arguments or unpleasant wrangling, and he should prevent discussion from wandering from the business of the day.

Furthermore, he must be neatly dressed in the proper clothes for the time of day and the type of meeting. *See Chapter Four, "Public Speaking."*

BOARD MEETINGS

If you are elected chairman of the board of any organization, you will be called upon to hold meetings, probably once a month and possibly oftener. If the organization is of considerable size or importance (a hospital or a community-fund drive, for example), the meeting must be run with some degree of formality.

Before the members arrive, it is up to you and the secretary to see that the room is in readiness. The meeting should, if possible, be held in a room furnished for the purpose, with one large table, or several smaller ones, and adequate seating for all. There should be a clean pad and sharp pencil at each place, as well as copies of the minutes of the last meeting and the agenda for that day. If such a room is not available, then pad, pencil, and other materials should be placed on the seat of each chair that will be used.

When the board members have arrived (and you should not wait more than ten minutes for latecomers), you say, "Will the meeting please come to order?" If you wish, you may add a word of welcome. If your organization requires it, the secretary calls the roll at this point. You then ask him or her to read the minutes of the last meeting. When they have been read, you ask, "Are there any additions or corrections?" If not, you say, "The minutes stand approved as read." If there are corrections, the secretary makes them, and you say, "The minutes stand approved as corrected." When the minutes have been distributed to each board member in advance, you may wish to dispense with the reading, but you must ask for a motion and a second from the the floor to that effect. Next you call for the treasurer's report and then the reports of the committee chairmen. Even though you know that some chairmen may have no report, you ask each of them in turn, and he or she may simply say, "I have no report to make this month." If there are no questions about the reports, you bring up the business to be discussed, following your prepared agenda.

It is your duty as chairman to recognize those who indicate by raising their hands that they wish to speak and to prevent anyone's speaking for too long. If arguments develop you must avert their getting so heated or involved that the meeting ends in chaos. If possible wait for a break in the speech, but if the speaker is too excited to pause, rap your table or stand and break in, saying, "Mr. Smith, will you please confine yourself to the subject?" or, "Mrs. Harris, you have spoken for more than your allotted time, and I shall have to ask you to sit down," or even, "Mr. Robertson, it is not necessary to go into personalities, and if you insist on doing so, I must ask you to sit down immediately." By directing the discussion firmly along appropriate lines, limiting speeches, and staying in charge, a good chairman can hasten immeasurably the successful conclusion of a business meeting. Generally, if there is a guest speaker, the business is finished as quickly as possible, and the guest's speech concludes the program, with only a brief word of thanks from the chairman before the adjournment.

MEETINGS HELD IN THE HOME

When a group is formed for some special reason—to raise funds for a charity, back a political candidate, or put on a play—meetings are held in a home, not necessarily that of the leader or chairman, but that of any member of the group who volunteers. Coffee is usually served before or after a morning meeting, and tea or coffee in the afternoon. The member at whose house the meeting is held may provide the refreshments, or various others may volunteer to bring them. Or each member of the group may contribute a small sum, which the host or hostess uses to buy and prepare the food.

No matter how informal these gatherings are in some ways, certain formalities must be observed if the group is to be successful. First, a chairman should be appointed or elected, because without one person to plan and direct a meeting it is impossible to coordinate discussions and come to decisions. Second, there must be a secretary to take notes or minutes; a record of each meeting is necessary in order to be able to refer back to earlier ones—to resolve any arguments, to avoid repetition, and also to aid any other group that might continue the work in the future. And last, if there are funds involved in any way, there must be a treasurer to handle them and to keep an exact account of receipts and expenditures.

Beyond the formality of appointing these officers, the group need not follow any particular rules. The meetings may be run semiformally with minutes being read and the roll being called, or as social meetings with open discussion over a cup of coffee and a piece of cake. The chairman must still direct the discussion into the proper channels, however, or no business will be accomplished at all. It is all too easy for friends who become involved in a discussion of business, children, neighborhood politics, and other subjects close to their hearts to forget entirely the purpose of the meeting. It is the chairman's responsibility to get each member to make suggestions or express his or her views about the current topic. At the same time, each individual who has agreed to participate in the activity should have given it some thought and be willing to discuss and act on suggestions so that the chairman does not carry the full load.

Because these groups are made up of good friends, there are no rules about clothing other than the ordinary standards of neatness and cleanliness. Don't come straight from the garden with mud on your shoes. Ladies should certainly *never* have curlers in their hair! However, if a woman is dressed in a skirt and sweater, she need not change to more formal clothes. In fact, if she lives in the country where slacks are accepted as everyday wear, there is no need to change into a dress. And if the group is made up of young mothers, the children are usually brought along to play together in a safe yard or in a playpen if they are babies.

Part FOUR

ADVICE FOR TRAVELERS

17

Planning your trip

There are some people who find it so pleasant to make plans for a trip that they truly consider the preliminaries "half the fun." But to the joys of poring over maps and collecting suggestions from your friends must be added certain practical preparations without which travel can be a nightmare instead of an exciting adventure. Dream of castles in Spain if you will, but don't forget that you may well be footsore and weary by the time you have actually toured your first one. A good dinner and a decent bed may make all the difference in your enthusiasm for the next day's expedition.

RESERVATIONS

ADVANTAGES OF A TRAVEL BUREAU

The easiest way to plan your trip is to go to a travel bureau. If there isn't one in your own town, write to one that has been recommended to you by a friend. Tell the bureau just where you want to go and when and how—in fact, give all the details you can, and let them work out the best possible plan for you. This is their business, and they can do it better and more economically than you can. There is no extra cost to you, as they get their commission from the transportation company, the resort, or the hotel.

There is one important point that should be explained to the inexperienced traveler: A competent travel bureau can arrange the most elaborate accommodations—from the best rooms in deluxe hotels to automobiles with chauffeurs. With equal interest, the same travel bureau will provide the same quality service for those traveling on a limited budget.

MAKING YOUR OWN RESERVATIONS

If you do not use a travel agency, start well in advance to make your reservations. If you are refused at the first hotels or resorts you write to, you may have to wait days or even weeks before you have word from your alternate choice. It is not unreasonable to make the arrangements for an extensive trip to a popular area six months or more ahead of time. In this case the reservations must be reconfirmed a week or two before your departure. It is also essential to request a receipt or acknowledgment (and don't forget to carry it with you) to be shown on your arrival. It is all too easy for a careless innkeeper or hotel manager to fill up the rooms with earlier arrivals and tell you cheerfully when you arrive, hot and exhausted, "But, we have no record of your letter!"

Your travel reservations should be made at the same time as those for hotel rooms, and don't neglect your home-bound ticket. Many people have found themselves in Europe at the end of the tourist season with days of waiting for a plane seat still ahead of them. With a little forethought you can plan your return date as definitely as that of your departure, and thus prevent a last-minute case of jitters and impatience that could ruin your whole trip.

A tip to parents: When your son or daughter sets off for a summer of traveling, possibly with a knapsack on his back and no planned stopping places other than a list of youth hostels (inexpensive lodgings for bicyclists and motorcyclists found in every European country), be sure that he or she has a return reservation, either with him or held at the airline or steamship office for him. It is all too easy for a youngster to cable home, "Unable to get space until September 15"—three weeks longer than you had expected to finance him!

USING A GUIDEBOOK

If you are young enough so that you don't care where you spend the night—at an inn or in a field—or if you are fortunate enough to be able to travel during the "off" season when most of the tourists are at home, you may not need reservations. Nothing is more delightful than being able to drive at random, following whatever highway or byway catches your fancy and stopping for the night wherever you happen to be. And what a joy to have plans so flexible that you can leave a town that has little to offer the day after you arrive, or stay for ten in a city that has all the charm you have dreamed of!

To travel in this way is ideal, but there is one requirement—a good guidebook. By using its listings of available lodgings and eating places, you may avoid, first, hours of searching for a respectable hotel, and second, the danger of falling upon dirty accommodations or dishonest proprietors. Since the staffs of all good guidebooks regularly visit the places they recommend, their information is as accurate and current as can be found.

See also Chapters Eighteen and Nineteen for additional suggestions about hotels and transportation.

LEAVING YOUR HOME IN ORDER

WHEN THE CHILDREN STAY AT HOME

If you wish to enjoy your trip to the full with a minimum of worries, there are several precautions that you must take to insure the safety and well being of the people and things you have left behind.

The first and most obvious responsibility is that of parents who must leave children at home. If you already have a reliable housekeeper who is capable of taking charge while you are away, there is no problem. She simply takes over the house with a few extra instructions and possibly extra pay if her duties will be substantially increased during your absence. Otherwise, if you do not have relatives who can come and stay at your house or invite your children to stay at theirs, it is absolutely essential to find a trustworthy person to care for them. Occasionally a couple, or a man if the children are boys, can be found, but generally the position of sitter or temporary mother is filled by a woman. She should be recommended either by a friend whose judgment is sound or by a reputable agency. If you do not know her personally, she should arrive two or three days in advance so that the children may get to know her while you are there to help them over any rough spots, and so that she may become acquainted with your house and routine.

There should be definite rules laid down—especially if the children are teen-agers—about what hours they are to keep, what they are allowed or forbidden to do, and with whom they may go out. Otherwise the sitter has no way of knowing what your basic standards are, and the young people will soon find out that they can have many more liberties than they are ordinarily allowed.

Your household should have a complete list of addresses at which you may be reached and also a list of those people, relatives or friends, who may be counted on to help in an emergency. The sitter should also have a list of the stores you ordinarily deal with and the names of dentists and doctors, as well as any appointments that must be kept.

If you take care of these matters conscientiously before you leave, you will have little reason to be concerned about your family while you are gone.

WHEN NO ONE IS LEFT IN THE HOME

When you are leaving an empty house or apartment, there is a different set of precautions to consider. A house whose owners are obviously away is an open invitation to a burglar. Therefore, in order to make it appear occupied, the following suggestions should be followed. Don't forget to:

Cancel milk delivery.

Cancel newspaper delivery.

Request that the post office either hold or forward your mail. Nothing could better advertise your absence than mail and newspapers piling up at your door.

Have all laundry and cleaning delivered before you leave so that it is not left hanging outside for days or weeks.

Leave a light or two burning, or install an automatic light that goes on at dusk.

Check all locks on windows and doors, and be sure that you take a key with you! Not a few people have been horrified to find on arriving home in the middle of the night that they had so thoroughly closed up their house with the key inside that they must either break a window to get in or spend the remainder of the night in a motel.

Leave a spare key with a friendly neighbor and ask him to check the house occasionally.

Put potted plants outside or make arrangements to have them watered by a friend. A neighbor's child is often happy to take over this chore for, possibly, fifty cents a week.

Take pets to the veterinarian's or wherever they are to be left.

Notify the police of your absence, and ask them to keep watch over your house. Also, if you have a cleaning woman or anyone coming into the house legitimately, give the officer her name so that she will not be accused of unlawful entry.

Never give your travel plans or dates to your local newspaper in advance. There are people who watch the papers every day in order to take advantage of just such information.

There is no way that you can make your home one-hundred percent burglar-proof, but the above suggestions will help to discourage any but the most professional thief. If you travel frequently and wish to go away feeling confident that all will be in order on your return, make a list of the above suggestions that apply to your home and check it off carefully before every trip.

TRAVEL DOCUMENTS

Several weeks before your departure, you should apply for your passport, visas if they are required, and health certificates. If you already have them, make sure that they are still valid and in good order. These matters have to be attended to in person, although after you have filled out the forms and paid the fee at the passport office, your passport will be sent to you by mail. Your doctor will tell you where to get official health forms if he does not have them. You must go in person to the consulate of the country from which you wish to get a visitor's permit or visa. Everything else can be done for you; and if you are obliged to go on a suddenly planned trip, a great deal of valuable time can be saved by having an experienced agent make your reservations and deliver your tickets to you.

It is advisable to get some foreign money in small bills and change to have in your hand when you land. There are restrictions as to the amount you are permitted to take in or out of some countries, and these should be checked before you leave. It is also very important to take the bulk of your money in traveler's checks, which can be replaced if lost and are accepted everywhere as readily as cash. Even though you have a letter of credit—a good idea if you want to have something to depend on for extra and unexpected expenses—there are many occasions when it is inconvenient or even impossible to go to a bank. *See also Chapter Twenty, "Currency and Language."*

18

Motels and hotels

All over America, and recently in foreign countries as well, motels have sprung up like mushrooms. They are becoming more and more luxurious as the competition increases, with some of them actually taking the place of resort hotels. The larger ones and those belonging to national chains are equipped with every facility for the traveler's comfort and pleasure, including swimming pools, shuffleboard courts, sunbathing areas, television sets (apparently a must in every motel), and individual coffee-makers in each room. I know of one motel where there is a drive-in movie directly behind so that you may sit comfortably in bed and see a movie before going to sleep, with the sound piped into each unit through a private speaker!

Motels can claim many advantages over hotels for the automobile traveler. Because the majority are on the outskirts of towns or between cities, you need not drive into heavy urban traffic to reach them. There is no parking problem, as your car is left directly in front of your room or unit. You may unload only what you need for the night—the rest can be locked up in the car. Especially important to a woman is the fact that, unless she is traveling alone, she need not be seen at all on arrival. Therefore she may travel in shorts, slacks, or whatever costume is most comfortable for driving. Her husband simply goes to the office of the motel, registers, receives the key, and drives to the room allotted to them. There Mrs. Tired Traveler in her rumpled dress may slip in with scarcely a chance of being seen by anyone at all. Since one pays for the night on arrival, one leaves the next morning with no need to go to the office again, and as there has been no service, neither is there anyone to tip.

There are, of course, certain disadvantages to motels. There is rarely (except in the most luxurious resort type, which hopes to attract people to stay longer than overnight) room service. One unloads the luggage alone, gets ice for oneself from an ice machine (always found near each unit), and provides one's own refreshments. Often soft drinks are available in vending machines, and cigarettes, magazines, newspapers, etc. are sold in the offices of many motels. Restaurants are generally found on the premises of motels connected with a chain, but if you are staying at a smaller motel you may have to go some distance to find a good eating place. Also, if you are looking for entertainment—dancing, movies, and so on—you may find that you would be better off in a hotel in the heart of the city.

Because of the immense popularity of motels as stopping places, it is wise, especially for a woman alone, to make reservations in advance. If you choose to stay in a chain motel, the manager will be delighted to call ahead to the member motel in or nearest your next destination to reserve a room for the following night. Since you usually pay for this reservation at the time it is made and receive a written receipt, you need not fear that your room will not be held for you, no matter how late your arrival. The larger chains will also help you plan your trip, providing road maps and lists of restaurants, entertainments, and points of interest, as well as the location of their own or associated motels.

HOTELS

Because of their central locations in most cities and the services that they offer, hotels will never be completely replaced by motels. The business traveler arriving by plane or train naturally chooses a hotel in the center of town, near the offices of the companies he must visit. Tourists, other than those driving their own cars, usually wish to be in a central location where they can easily find transportation to museums, monuments, parks, historical sites, and other points of interest. Finally, many people, and certainly those making their homes in such accommodations, will never forsake the convenience and excellence of the services offered in first-class hotels.

TO ASSURE ACCOMMODATIONS IN HOTELS

You should write or telegraph in advance for accommodations in a hotel. A typical telegram reads:

PLEASE RESERVE DOUBLE ROOM WITH BATH AFTERNOON DECEMBER THIRD TO FIFTH. REQUEST CONFIRMATION.
JOAN HAWKINS

A letter is a little more explicit:

Manager of the Lake Hotel
Chicago, Illinois

Dear Sir:

Please reserve two single rooms with baths or with a bath between for my daughter and me from December sixth through December twelfth. We will be arriving in the late afternoon, so please hold the accommodations.

Very truly yours,
Mrs. George K. Smith

Kindly confirm reservation to
Brightmeadows, Ill.

(Note that this is one of the few occasions when "Mrs." belongs with a woman's signature.)

Both letter and telegram should state clearly the hour of your arrival, the number of persons, the accommodations you wish, and the approximate length of your stay.

THE ARRIVAL AT A HOTEL

When you arrive at a first-class hotel, a doorman opens the door of your car or taxi and deposits your luggage on the sidewalk. If the hotel is crowded, he will ask, "Have you a reservation?" If you say "Yes" all is well; but if you say "No" the reply may be "Very sorry, but there is not one room left." So you should not only wire or write, but ask for a confirmation. Usually a day or two is sufficient notice, but at the time of a convention, an exposition, or an important sporting event, you may have to write months in advance to assure your accommodations.

If your room reservation is in order, a bellboy comes out, takes your bags, carries them into the lobby, and deposits them not far from the desk. In a typical hotel there is a counter with one or two men behind it. In city hotels there are divisions of desks labeled "Rooms," "Cashier," "Information," etc.

In any case you go to the desk, or to the division marked "Room Clerk," and say, "I am Mrs. George K. Smith. I telegraphed you Tuesday and received your confirmation on Thursday." The clerk presents you with a form to fill in and sign. The length of your stay at the hotel should also be clearly established at this time.

A man registers as "John Smith, New York." He does not use "Mr." if he is alone, but with his wife he adds the title to their joint names: "Mr. and Mrs. John Smith, New York."

He fills in the blanks on the registration form, which will include one for his house address. If he is accompanied by his entire family, "John Smith and Family" is acceptable. Nurses, employees, or those with a different name should be listed separately so that they may receive mail or messages.

If for any reason children are registered individually, "Miss" precedes the names of all little girls. Boys are registered with no title—just "John" or "Henry" or whoever—until they are eighteen or over.

One exceptional occasion when a lady signs her name "Miss" or "Mrs." is in a hotel register. "Miss Jean McLean" is correct, or "Mrs. George K. Smith"—never "Sarah Smith."

If Mrs. Smith arrives first, she fills in the blank for both herself and her husband. When Mr. Smith arrives, he says to the room clerk, "Mrs. Smith has already arrived and registered. What is the number of our room, please?"

As soon as you have registered, the clerk hands the key not to you but to the bellboy, who gathers up your bags and starts in the direction of the elevators. You follow. In your room, the bellboy puts down your bags, turns on the lights, and opens the window or tests the air-conditioning unit. He receives a tip, usually twenty-five cents for each large bag, more if there are other packages, and an extra twenty-five cents for opening up the room.

SERVICE IN A GOOD HOTEL

Any service that you require is requested by telephone. You tell the operator if you wish to be called at a certain time or ask for the desk if you want to inquire about mail or give the name of a visitor you are expecting. You call the porter's desk if you have any inquiries about luggage or trains or reservations. You call room service when you want food or drinks sent up to you, and valet or maid service if you need a dress or suit cleaned or pressed.

If you want breakfast in your room you call room service and order it—this may be done the evening before or you can call when you awaken. Many hotels have breakfast menus in each room, and you may choose from them. Presently the waiter brings in a tray with your order. In a first-class hotel, he rolls in a long, narrow table that fits between twin beds or stands beside a single one. It is completely set: damask cloth, china, glass, silverware, thermos pitchers, and possibly chafing dishes to keep the food hot.

It is entirely proper when only dressed in a bathrobe to open the door for the waiter. He is used to carrying breakfast trays into the presence of all varieties of pajamas and negligees, and it is not necessary for even the most old-fashioned lady to be completely dressed to receive him.

After the waiter has arranged the breakfast and removed the covers from the dishes, you should sign the check and give it to him with a tip amounting to approximately 15 percent of the total. Most hotels will include an additional amount as a room service charge, but this does not take the place of the normal tip to the waiter. You may wheel the serving table outside your door when you have finished in order to give yourself more space in a small room and to avoid being disturbed when the waiter returns for it.

You telephone maid service to have your clothes washed unless, as is often the case, there is a bag or receptacle marked for laundry in the bathroom. Pressing is done by the regular valet or maid, but in a small hotel, a woman's dress as well as a man's suit may be sent out to a cleaner. It is against the rules in some hotels to use your own iron; therefore, if there is no regular valet service, you ask a chambermaid tactfully, "Where can I have my dress (or suit) pressed?" She answers, "I will do it for you," or tells you who will.

PILFERAGE

An inexplicable urge seems to come over many otherwise decent, honest citizens when they are guests in a hotel. This is the urge to pilfer —to help themselves to articles that can be hidden away in luggage—exactly as if such things were put out as gifts to the guests from the management! Bath towels with the hotel's name on them, ash trays, writing paper, soap, dining-room silver, and even bed linen disappear in such quantities as to be a major expense in every large hotel. These pilferers, when accused of stealing, say, "Not at all—the management expects these things to disappear!" How any normal law-abiding person can thus excuse what is technically petty theft, I cannot understand. All I can suggest is that the next time you, or anyone traveling with you, is tempted to take home such a souvenir, say to yourself or to them, "That ash tray is hotel property; if I take it home with me, it will have to be replaced, and I am no better than a common thief."

HOTEL MANNERS

A woman who entertains a man in her hotel bedroom leaves herself open to criticism. But if you have a private sitting room, you can invite anyone you please to take a meal there, or simply visit, as long as you break none of the ordinary conventions of behavior. Noisy parties, men visitors at unconventionally late hours, or anything that suggests questionable behavior is not permitted in any first-class hotel.

The woman staying alone in a hotel and having no private sitting room should receive any men visitors in one of the public rooms that all hotels provide. She is also free to ask anyone she wants to the bar or dining room. There is not the slightest reason why a woman—even though she be very young and very pretty—may not stay in a hotel by herself and have men come to see her and be invited by her to lunch or dinner. It is not so much a question of suitable age as of suitable behavior.

A hotel guest—whether a woman or a man—going down to the dining room alone usually takes a book or newspaper, because nothing is duller than to sit eating bread and butter and looking at the tablecloth, which is scarcely diverting, or staring at other people, which is impolite, while waiting for one's order.

When visiting people who are staying at a hotel, you can ask the desk clerk to telephone them in their rooms or you can call them yourself on the house telephone. If they are receiving you upstairs, they tell you the number of the room, and you go up to join them there. If there is an elevator operator, you can ask the way to Room 616, but the room numbers are usually clearly indicated by arrows or signs.

If the friends you are visiting answer that they are coming down, you wait for them in the lobby or the lounge, in view of the elevators.

WHEN YOU LEAVE THE HOTEL

When a guest is ready to leave, he goes to the cashier—or telephones from his room—to request that his bill be prepared. When he has finished packing, he telephones for a bellboy to carry down his luggage. Having tipped the boy, he goes to the desk marked "Cashier," pays his bill, leaves his key, gives a forwarding address if he wishes any mail sent after him, and departs.

TIPS

The following schedule of tips applies to transient visitors staying in the hotel (or the motel with services) for not more than a week. Perma nent or long-term residents tip on a monthly or even twice-yearly basis rather than having to produce a perpetual stream of small change for every service. The amount, of course, would vary according to the quantity and quality of the service. Hotel residents must arrive at their own conclusions, possibly with the help of other permanent guests and even the hotel management.

The usual tip for a dining-room waiter in a first-class restaurant is between 15 and 20 percent of the bill, but never less than twenty-five cents in a restaurant with tablecloth on table. If you are staying in an American-plan hotel, at the end of each week the waiter receives about

10 percent of the week's board per person, but less if the family is large. When going to the dining room for the first time, you give from two to five dollars to the headwaiter if you would like a table in a particular location. When you leave you tip him in proportion to the service rendered. You give him one or two dollars a week if he has done little, and five dollars a week if you are a family to whom he has been especially attentive. For a one-night stay you need not tip him at all.

The room waiter receives 15 percent of the bill for each meal. This is in addition to a set sum charged by the hotel for each meal taken to a room.

The chambermaid in a first-class hotel is given about two dollars a week a room, or one dollar a week in a small inexpensive hotel. If you stay one night only, fifty cents for each person in a room in a large hotel, or twenty-five cents in a small one, is given her if she can be found. If not, leave it on the bureau in an envelope marked "chambermaid."

Other tips:

Nothing to the doorman for putting a bag on the sidewalk, but twenty-five cents if he helps take the luggage into the hotel or on other occasions if he calls a taxi.

Twenty-five cents for each large bag the bellboy carries to the room.

Twenty-five cents for paging.

Fifty cents to a porter for bringing a trunk to the room, or fifty cents or a dollar if there is much baggage.

Twenty-five cents for delivery of ice, drink set-ups, newspapers, packages, telegrams, etc.

Twenty-five cents for checking a man's coat and hat.

Twenty-five cents to the attendant in the women's dressing room or twenty-five cents for the coat rack at the entrance to the dining room.

The valet receives a tip only if he brings a large amount of clothing back to your room when you are there. His charge for cleaning or pressing is included in the hotel bill.

Barbers, manicurists, and beauty-parlor specialists are tipped on the basis of 15 percent of the bill, but not less than twenty-five cents.

Bootblacks are tipped twenty-five cents.

One piece of advice: While you need not tip lavishly you will not get good service unless you tip generously.

Tipping is undoubtedly an undesirable and undignified system, but since it happens to be in force, travelers who like the way made smooth and comfortable have to pay their share of it.

EUROPEAN HOTELS

Large, first-class hotels in Europe—those most frequented by tourists—are essentially the same as our best hotels in the United States. Before venturing into less well-traveled areas, however, be prepared for certain differences in facilities and service.

In European hotels all services other than your actual accommodations and meals are provided by the concierge. He corresponds to our porter, but has a much wider range of responsibility and is as important as the hotel management. He presents a separate bill, or his bill appears as a separate item on the hotel bill. He and his staff handle luggage and mail, make reservations, rent cars, shop for you, deliver packages, arrange tours, and are altogether indispensable.

Many foreign hotels do not have a telephone in each room. Instead they have a push-button device with charming little pictures of waiters, maids, or valets beside each button to indicate which one you must push. This system certainly overcomes the language barrier—at least until the maid arrives!

Many small hotels do not have bathrooms with every room. Many rooms do have wash basins, although in very small towns there may just be a pitcher of water and a bowl. In these hotels you use the public bathrooms on each floor, which are usually marked "W.C."—a universally known abbreviation for "water closet." There may be two, marked for men or women in the language of the country, or there may be just one to be used by all guests. You must reserve a time for your bath with the maid on the floor. She will run the bath and give you the key and a towel. In many places an extra charge for each bath will be added to your bill.

Although the hotels in small towns may not be luxurious, the desire to please and the friendliness of the help more than make up for the lack of comfort. The chef who proudly invites you to see his spotless kitchen, the chambermaid who smilingly brings you a cup of coffee when she awakens you in the morning, and the concierge who takes great pains to insure that you miss nothing in this, the most beautiful town in Europe, all leave you feeling that it is the spirit of the place and not the physical comforts that enchant so many Americans who travel abroad.

19

On plane, train, or ship

Airplane travel is so much a part of our life and times that it is hardly necessary to point out its advantages. The speed of getting to one's destination by jet, the frequency of flights, the number of airlines and airports, and the safety of flying all combine to make the airplane the choice of almost all who travel. In this day of rising costs, air travel is one of the few areas where prices have actually gone down.

Of course, there are still many people who prefer to go by train, which is sometimes the only convenient way of reaching one's destination. Others prefer the relaxing days on shipboard to the long flight to Rome or Athens or Beirut. On a cruise your ship is your floating hotel as well as your means of transportation.

AIRPLANE TRAVEL

ACCOMMODATIONS

There are now two main classes of air travel—first class and economy. Many small airlines that fly twin-engine equipment or four-motor propeller planes do not offer any choice of accommodations; all seats are the same price and all passengers receive the same services. On the large, scheduled airplanes, however, you can choose between the two classes. The economy-class seats occupy three quarters or more of the space toward the rear of the plane and are divided from first class by a movable partition, the door of which is kept closed except at take-off and landing. These seats are more closely spaced with often three on each side of the aisle. Meals and snacks are included in the fare, but if you wish alcoholic drinks (cocktails are served before meals on overseas flights and on some domestic flights) you must pay for them. Service is somewhat slower than in the first-class section, as two or three stewardesses or stewards must take care of one hundred or more people on a full plane. On long flights many airlines show movies in both economy and first class. Because the difference in cost between economy and first class on an overseas flight is quite astronomical, a vast majority of people, even the well-to-do, put up with the discomfort of more crowded conditions on a flight that rarely lasts more than a few hours on a fast modern jet.

For older people who may have difficulty in getting in and out of crowded seats or cannot stand long in line for washroom facilities, for disabled persons, or simply for those who prefer, and can afford, a bit of luxury when they travel, the first-class section has far more appeal. The seats are roomy—two on each side of the aisle, widely spaced so that one may tip far back and stretch one's legs. Tables may be put between them so that passengers may play cards or comfortably spread out their business papers. Cocktails are free, meals are more elaborate, and champagne is sometimes served if you wish it. The steward or stewardess often has only ten or fifteen passengers to attend, and therefore every request is taken care of at once.

LUGGAGE

Airplane luggage should be light. There are strict weight limitations, varying according to class and whether the flight is domestic or overseas. In general, overseas economy-class passengers are allowed approximately forty-four pounds, and first class, sixty-six. You may carry more, but you pay for the excess at a specified rate per pound. At this writing, there is no weight limit on domestic flights if you carry no more than two pieces of luggage.

The ideal luggage is made of a lightweight metal, such as aluminum, or a composition. The soft bags made of synthetic materials or strong weaves are most attractive, but can be damaged or pierced if handled roughly.

On overseas flights the airlines weigh almost every piece of baggage, even those you carry with you onto the plane. The only exceptions are handbags, briefcases (except large, square, or bulging ones), knitting bags, or other lightweight articles obviously for use during the flight—baby's diapers, a book or two, embroidery, etc.

You may not carry any bag or package onto the plane unless it can be stowed under your seat. No one is allowed to put hard or heavy articles on the shelf above the seats.

At the airport or terminal your luggage is taken on a cart by a porter, and either put in line to be weighed when your turn comes to check in or taken directly to the plane. In this event you will receive your claim check directly from the porter. If it is overweight, you pay the extra charge at this time. The porter is tipped a minimum of twenty-five cents for each bag (not for small hand pieces) and goes off to help the next arrival. When your ticket is validated, the bags are tagged and the stubs given to you at the same time. You do not see the luggage again until it is brought into the "baggage claim" section at your destination. You should make it clear to well-meaning friends who come to see you off that they should not bring presents. They will only be added to your weight allowance, or if you have been checked in, you may not be allowed to take them onto the plane.

ARRIVING AT THE AIRPORT

For overseas flights you are requested to arrive at the airport one hour ahead of departure time, as opposed to the half hour required for domestic flights. This provides the extra time involved in checking travel documents other than tickets.

Until recently a chart of the plane was always hung in plain view at the counter of the airline so that you could choose your seat from those not marked as taken. Now, however, many airlines are giving up this practice and simply assigning the seats as the passengers arrive. You are given a boarding pass with the seat number on it, to be shown at the departure gate and again to the stewardess when you board the plane. Some airlines have now dispensed with any check-in except at the actual departure gate.

WHILE IN THE AIR

The seats are clearly numbered, but the stewardesses who greet you with a friendly smile when you board will direct you to your chair and assist you with coats and bundles. Coats are hung on a rack in the rear on some planes or folded and laid on the overhead shelf on others. During the trip the stewardesses, when not serving meals or drinks, will do their best to assist you in any way they can. You signal them with a light that you find above your head. They will bring magazines, hand out newspapers, bring food or extra pillows or blankets, and even help care for babies by heating bottles, etc. The steward or stewardess is never tipped, nor is any other member of the crew.

Be sure that you wear loose, comfortable clothing that is as wrinkleproof as possible. Men are entirely free to remove their jackets, loosen or remove their ties. Both men and women should carry a loose sweater if they can, as the temperature in an air-conditioned plane can be quite low.

When the sign flashes "Fasten Seat Belts," do so promptly. The stewardess has to check on each passenger. Also be prompt in obeying the "No Smoking" signal. When smoking is permitted, only cigarettes are allowed.

No animals are allowed in an airplane cabin except a Seeing Eye dog. If you take your pet he must be in a carrier. His weight is counted as part of the amount of luggage you are permitted. He rides in the luggage compartment if it is pressurized, or in a special compartment if it is not.

The same rules apply in using the washrooms or lavatories on a airplane as on any public transportation. The only difference is that an airline is one of the few places where men and women use the same facilities. You must wait patiently for your turn, and when it comes try to take as short a time as possible. You should leave the washstand and the dressing table in perfect order. When you have finished washing, wipe out the basin thoroughly with your used towel, and throw it into the receptacle marked for it. Before combing your hair, lay a fresh towel over the wash basin or counter. Leave it there until you have finished your hairdo and put on your makeup. Then gather up that towel and throw it into the receptacle. Complete neatness is a first essential of good manners. Never leave any unpleasant trace of untidiness *anywhere!*

A general spirit of friendliness among the passengers is so characteristic of air travel that it has, actually, brought about new rules of traveling etiquette. The on-the-ground custom of paying no attention to fellow travelers is not observed in the air. Those who are willing to talk—and in a plane nearly everyone is—are entirely free to do so. On the other hand, one who wishes to be left alone can avoid conversation with the explanation, "I'd rather not talk; I'm very tired," which should never be resented.

TRAIN TRAVEL

LUGGAGE

The official rate for a porter who takes luggage from the entrance of a railroad station to a train is twenty-five cents for each piece, and an additional tip is optional but expected. Since there are no porters at all in many small cities or towns, restrict your baggage to pieces that can be carried by hand when your destination is unknown. You can send larger bags and trunks ahead by railway express.

If you are spending the night in a single upper or lower berth, you must carry a small overnight case with you, as the remainder of your luggage will be stowed at the end of the car. Even in a compartment or drawing room space is limited, and if you can avoid having to open large, bulky suitcases you will be much more comfortable.

IN THE DINING CAR

On a day-long journey, there is no need to speak to your companions at the table, beyond a possible "May I have the salt, please?" although there is no objection to a casual conversation. On a longer journey, if you happen to sit next to or near the same person for a number of meals, it is extremely unfriendly to sit in wooden silence.

IN THE PULLMAN

During the day in a Pullman section, the seat that faces forward traditionally belongs to the occupant of the lower berth; the occupant of the upper berth rides backward. When you have the right to the seat facing forward, it is courteous to ask the person in the other seat whether he or she minds riding backward—and if he does, to make a place at your side. The window seat naturally belongs to you, unless you prefer the other.

In a bedroom, compartment, or drawing room, all of which have doors that can be closed, there is no reason not to have a friend or two in for a chat. But since the partitions between rooms are thin, voices must be kept low, and the porter should be called to make up the bed by ten or ten-thirty at the latest. If you wish to have another drink or continue your talk, you may go to the club or bar car. When your berth is in the open section of the car, divided only by curtains from the other passengers, you must cease all conversation as soon as neighbors are in bed. If you do not feel like sleeping, resort to a good book in the privacy of your berth. Occupants of a section, even though they are strangers, must consult each other as to what time they would like their berths made up for the night.

GOING TO BED IN A PULLMAN

Whatever your accommodation, you ring for the porter to make up your berth when you are ready to go to bed. If you have a roomette, drawing room, compartment, or bedroom, you simply shut your door when he is finished, and go to bed. In every variety of room, all bathroom facilities are included so that you do not go to the public dressing room at all. If, however, you are in an upper or lower berth, you wash and prepare for the night in the dressing room while the porter makes up your bed. This is especially necessary if you have an upper berth, so that when you have gone up the stepladder you will not have to come down again. You may remove your clothes in the dressing room and return to your berth, dressed for the night and in a bathrobe. But rather than keep others waiting, most people return to their berths after washing, close the curtains, and go through the gymnastics of undressing in an impossibly small space! In the morning when you want to get down, you ring the bell inside your berth and ask for the stepladder. Again, you dress as best you can in your cramped quarters to avoid monopolizing the dressing room.

IF YOU MUST TAKE THE CHILDREN

If you can possibly avoid it, do not travel on a train with very small children. If it is necessary, try to maintain their regular schedule of meals, naps, and bedtime. Those who are sufficiently well-to-do usually take a drawing room or compartment and keep the children in it. Those who travel in coaches should take special pains to plan diversions for the children ahead of time; it is unreasonable to expect little children to sit quietly for hours on end and just "be good." Whatever you do, don't let them race up and down the aisles.

TIPS

Dining-car waiters are tipped exactly as waiters are in any restaurant. They are given 15 percent of the bill, and never less than a quarter.

Waiters or stewards in the bar car or club car are tipped 15 percent of the bill, as well as a quarter if they bring "set-ups" (ice, glasses, water, and soda) to you in the Pullman car.

The Pullman porter receives fifty cents to one dollar for each person on an overnight trip—more if he has given additional service other than making up the berths.

TRAVEL ON A SHIP

LUGGAGE

On a ship where you will occupy the same cabin the entire time, particularly if you are to have it alone or with your husband or wife, the amount of luggage you take does not matter. On the other hand, if you are sharing a cabin with strangers, you must limit your luggage to one or two small bags. In other words, you have no right to expect your cabinmate to live in a baggage room. Luggage not needed en route is, of course, checked.

On your arrival at a pier, there is a porter to put your luggage on the escalator or elevator to the upper level, for which the tip is twenty-five cents or more a bag. Some steamship lines provide porter service and prominently post signs forbidding tipping. You take the elevator or walk up the stairs to the receiving end of the escalator. There the luggage is put on trucks for delivery to the point from which it goes on board the ship. On most piers a different crew takes over upstairs, and tips are also given to these porters. You then show your passport and ticket at the proper desk and board the ship.

Be sure to arrive at the ship in plenty of time to be certain that your luggage is on board. Any trunks sent to the pier by express or delivered by other means will be covered by numbered checks, the stubs of which will have been given to you. These stubs should be turned in to the baggage master, or to whoever is in charge of his desk on the pier. The luggage will be stored in the hold or sent to your stateroom, as requested.

RESERVING DINING-ROOM TABLE AND DECK CHAIR

Immediately after being shown to your cabin, you should go to the dining room and reserve a table at the sitting you wish—early or late, the times will be posted in the dining room. Next, go to the main deck and see the head deck steward about a steamer chair. If you have a preference about the location, this is your chance to get it.

SOCIAL LIFE ON BOARD

You may very well have friends coming to the ship to wish you "Bon Voyage!" It's a fine excuse for a party, and a happy beginning to your trip. There are two ways of giving such a party. If you have a large, comfortable stateroom, your steward will bring soda and soft drinks, hors d'oeuvres, ice, and glasses to your cabin. Often one of the guests will bring a bottle of liquor or champagne as a going-away present. If you are in a small room, possibly shared with strangers, you may have your party in one of the bars or lounges. In either case, you board the vessel as early as possible and make the arrangements with your cabin steward or with the headwaiter in whichever public room you choose.

During the rest of the trip you may entertain your new shipboard acquaintances in the same way. You should tip the stewards who serve such a party 15 percent of the bill at the time rather than adding it to your regular tip at the end of the trip.

If you are traveling first class on a luxury liner you will find that some people dress in evening clothes—tuxedos for the men and dinner dresses for the women—every night except the first on board. This is not necessary, however, except on the night of the Captain's party (usually the next to the last night out), and cocktail dresses and business suits are acceptable on other evenings.

Unless your own group is very large or you request a table to yourselves, you may be seated with other people in the dining room. No formal introductions are necessary on board—you introduce yourself to your neighbors, and with luck you quickly find congenial people with whom you will become fast friends for the length of the voyage. In deck chairs, around the swimming pool, in the lounges, or in the game rooms this holds true. You may open a conversation with anyone who appears to be congenial; but if a person does not respond with some enthusiasm, do not force yourself on him; he may honestly wish to be left alone. A

short transatlantic crossing may lead to very little friendliness, but a cruise always has a sociable atmosphere, like the holiday spirit of a large house party where the guests speak to each other as a matter of course.

On every cruise ship there is a "cruise director" who acts as host or hostess and tries to see that the passengers have a pleasant time. Anyone on board who is without friends is expected to go to the director and ask to be introduced to congenial people. If the passenger plays deck games or bridge or likes to dance, the director arranges for games and introduces partners. On the smaller ships, the purser, or possibly the chief steward, assumes the role of director.

By the time you arrive at your first port, you probably will have made a number of friends. If you especially like someone who was introduced to you or someone who sits next to you on deck or at table, you can go ashore with her or him. If this is not the case, then you may always go along with the general group.

Nothing is more mysterious than the way a group of people develops as in a photograph. At first you see a crowd of faces and none of them stands out. Little by little they take on identity, and more often than not, some inconspicuous person whom at first you hardly noticed is the one who becomes your most delightful friend.

On any ship the Captain usually entertains at cocktails—once for first-class and once for tourist-class passengers. He may also give smaller parties for prominent persons, personal friends, or those sitting at his table. These invitations should always be accepted if possible, and a written refusal sent if you cannot attend.

The Captain is always spoken to as "Captain Sawyer" and the other officers are called "Mister."

People seated at the Captain's table or at the tables of the other senior officers must treat them as they would a host in a private home. These passengers should arrive at the same time as the officer. If he is delayed, wait for him before starting unless he sends word to go on without him. At other tables it is not necessary to arrive all together, as long as each person or group sits down well within the limits of that sitting.

TIPS

There are definite minimum amounts that a passenger is expected to give. If you are traveling first class, your cabin steward should receive ten dollars. The dining-room steward receives ten dollars and the headwaiter five. One or two dollars to the bus boy, if there is one, would make him very happy. Lounge and bar stewards are tipped 15 percent at the time they render their services. The chief deck steward receives five dollars, and his assistant, if he has one, three dollars.

Fifteen percent of the amount of the wine bill is given to the dining-table wine steward.

To the bath steward you give a dollar.

All these suggestions for tipping are per person on a transatlantic trip.

Tips in the cabin and tourist classes are lower, in proportion to the difference in the passage fare. A good general rule for shipboard travelers is to allow approximately 10 percent of their fare for tips. Divide about half of this allowance between the cabin and dining-room stewards, and distribute the rest to others who have served you. Obviously, passengers occupying suites are expected to tip more generously than those in modest accommodations. To thank someone who has taken extra pains to please you, give a more generous tip to show him that you appreciate his efforts.

It should be unnecessary to add that you must on no account attempt to tip a ship's officer! Thank the purser as you would any other acquaintance for courtesy. If you consult the doctor on board, he will probably send you a bill for his services. If he does not and you have had a real illness, when you leave the ship it is proper to send him the amount that probably would have been charged by your own doctor. If you are ill enough to be hospitalized an extra charge will be added to your fare.

20

Currency and language

The two greatest problems for travelers abroad are language and currency. Lack of understanding of another country's currency can result in painful situations—you may grossly undertip someone who has done you a real service, or you may overpay highly, appearing to be either ostentatious or stupid. But worse than this is the ill feeling and misunderstanding that can result from being unable to communicate with someone who knows no more of your language than you do of his.

MONEY MATTERS

The rates of exchanging dollars for each country's currency vary from time to time, but revised and inexpensive wallet-sized guides may be bought at stationery stores or gift shops and are distributed by many travel bureaus, ticket agencies, etc. You can also buy adjustable ones that can be changed to give the current exchange. In any case, they are a great help to the tourist who (like myself) has great difficulty in equating seventy-five cents with several hundred (or thousand) lire, francs, pesos, or whatever the local currency may be. Whether you carry a computer or not, it is wise to memorize the corresponding sum for such standard amounts as a quarter, a dollar, and five dollars. If you know the amount equal to one dollar, it is not difficult to arrive at that corresponding to ten dollars, or one hundred dollars. How much more intelligent one looks in the market place if he says quickly, "Oh, no—that's too much!" than if he has to pull out a card, find the price and its equivalent sum in dollars, and then start to bargain!

A word about bargaining—in large city stores all over the world the prices are just as firm as they are at Macy's in New York City. Items are often marked or tagged exactly as they are in the United States, and frequently there are signs saying *Prix fixe* or "Fixed price."

In small towns or rural market places, however, especially in Latin countries, bargaining is part of the fun of making a sale. Not only is the tourist considered an idiot if he pays the "asking price," but he has ruined the day for the vendor, in spite of the exorbitant amount paid. In some countries like Mexico, which are overrun by tourists, you may at first be told that the price is fixed, but with persistence and a little firmness (an indication that you are about to walk away and forget the whole thing is usually effective) it is sure to be lowered.

In most restaurants in Europe there is a charge on the bill for service. When this is a substantial amount you need not tip an additional 15 percent, but you should leave something. The waiter will often bring your change in denominations that make it correct to leave only the coins on the plate, an accepted practice in most countries. If there is no service charge, or a very small one, you should tip the usual 15 percent.

THE LANGUAGE BARRIER

For years Americans have been criticized for their ignorance of the idioms of countries in which they not only travel, but sometimes live. Not even our diplomats have been required to learn to speak the lanluages of the countries to which they are accredited. The criticism is justified.

Although people will tell you time and again that it is not necessary to speak a foreign language because "everyone in Europe speaks English," it simply is not so. Outside the cities and areas frequented by tourists, there are literally millions of foreigners who neither speak nor understand one word of English. One cannot stress enough the importance, first, of knowing a few words of the idiom of whatever countries you are planning to visit, and second, of carrying a small pocket dictionary or phrase book with you. It is not necessary, of course, to take a course or buy a self-teaching system, but these few often-used words and phrases (the grammar need not be perfect—your inflection can indicate a statement, question, exclamation, etc.) will smooth your path in any strange land:

"Yes" and "No."

"Please" and "Thank you." (Most important of all!)

"Hello." "Good-bye." "Good morning." "Good evening." "Good night."

"How much?" "How much does it cost?"

"The check (or bill) please."

"Please speak slowly."

"I don't speak (whatever the language may be)."

"I don't understand."

"Where is . . . ?" and "How do you get to . . . ?"

"Ladies' room" and "Men's room."

"More, please" and "No more, thank you."

"Beautiful," "Wonderful," "Nice," "Kind," etc. These single words, said admiringly and sincerely about the place or people you are visiting, will warm the heart of the most skeptical native.

All phrase books will give more explicit sentences and questions on many subjects, but the above words should be learned by heart, so that they can be used quickly and easily without having to refer to a book.

For some reason we all have a natural reluctance to use foreign words if we do not really know the language. This results in a tendency to mumble or else to shout as if your listener were deaf. Obviously, neither of these mannerisms helps him to understand you. The best way to make yourself understood is to say a word or phrase slowly and distinctly. Look at the other person and use gestures if they are meaningful. Waving your arms about may mean nothing, but making a writing motion can certainly help the waiter to understand that you are asking for the check.

Nothing pleases a native of any country, including our own, more than the realization that a visitor has taken the time and made the effort to learn a little of the country's language. If we could all remember this we would be far more eager to enter into conversation with foreigners. A great stride would be made toward furthering friendship among all peoples, and we would derive much greater pleasure from our travels.

Anyone who has walked through a little alley in a tiny town on a Greek island and seen the beaming smiles and eager response of the old ladies who sit there in the sun and hear "*Calimera*" instead of "Hello" or "Good morning" will know that this is true.

21

An audience with the Pope

Any American tourist visiting Rome can be granted an audience with the Pope, for although there are often hundreds of people in a day who wish an audience, no one is denied. Obviously only relatively few can be granted one of the three types of audience that are considered to be personal; group or collective audiences are arranged for the great majority.

Requests by Americans for these group audiences as well as for the personal ones should be cleared by the North American College and then sent to the Office of the Master of the Chamber known as *Ufficio del Maestro di Camera di Sua Santita,* which is in the Vatican. They should be presented in person, or sent on arrival in Rome, to the Monsignor in charge, whose name, and the address, can be obtained from the concierge of your hotel. Each applicant must fill out a form requesting the kind of audience desired and show his credentials, which for a Roman Catholic may be simply a letter of introduction from his parish priest or a prominent layman. The length of his stay in Rome and his address and telephone number are also included on the form so that he can be notified of the day and hour of the audience. Non-Catholics as well as

Catholics are granted audiences, and their requests must be arranged through prominent Catholic laymen or members of the Catholic clergy.

The reply, and the invitation if the answer is favorable, will be sent to you within a few days. You may receive a general admission ticket, meaning no reserved seat, or if you are considered sufficiently important, a reserved seat in a special section.

THE GENERAL AUDIENCE

Although general audiences are usually held at noon, people without reserved seats should arrive very early if they want a location with a good view. Choice places are often filled as early as ten in the morning.

At noon the audience rises as the Pope appears, seated on a portable throne called the *Sedia Gestatoria,* carried by eight Swiss Guards. At the end of the aisle he leaves the portable throne for a fixed one, and when he sits down the audience may be seated also. He delivers a short address, and then the audience kneels as he gives his benediction to all those present, as well as to all the articles they have brought to be blessed. The group rises, and if the Pope has time, he greets each person in the special area. The audience is over when he mounts his portable throne and is carried out.

For general audiences it is only required that everybody be dressed in a sober and suitable manner. Women must have their hair covered, must wear black or dark dresses with necklines that are not too low and skirts that are not too short. They may not have bare arms or legs.

OTHER AUDIENCES

The "private" audience is reserved for cardinals, heads of state, ambassadors, or others in important positions. The second type, the "special," is granted only to people of high rank or to those who have an important subject to present to the Pope. The third type is the only special audience to which laymen are invited. At the "baciomano," each visitor comes into the personal presence of the Pope, kisses his ring, and exchanges a few words with him, addressing him as "Your Holiness."

In the third type of audience visitors stand in a single file around the room until the Pope enters. They then kneel and do not stand again until he leaves the audience chamber or makes a sign for them to rise. He passes from one visitor to another, extending his hand so that all may kiss his ring. He also may ask a question and exchange a few words with each. As in the general audience, visitors customarily take with them one or more rosaries or other small religious objects, which are also considered to have been blessed when the visitor has received the Papal blessing.

The rules of dress for visitors to the Pope are not so strict as they once were. But even now for a private or special audience, men traditionally wear evening dress with tails or sack coat, and women long-sleeved black dresses and veils over their hair. No one may wear any but the most functional jewelry.

NON-CATHOLICS

At a general audience every person present must kneel, rise, and sit at the prescribed time. Non-Catholics, if they do not ordinarily do so, need not make the sign of the cross.

In private audiences the people on their arrival will be told the proper manner of kneeling and kissing the Pope's ring. If they object to these requirements on the grounds of their own religion, there may be some slight modification. But since the procedures are strictly followed, these people would be wiser to forego the private audience rather than make an issue.

22

Representing America abroad

As a result of jet travel, people at the farthest reaches of the earth have become our neighbors. Every traveler will increase his enjoyment of his trip if he attempts to make friends and exchange ideas with the foreigners he meets. We should try to acquire an understanding of the customs of the countries we visit, and never presume that our own behavior is the only pattern to be followed.

The principal rule of conduct, abroad as well as at home, is to do nothing that either annoys or offends the sensibilities of others. Thus, it is necessary for us to consider the point of view of all those with whom we come in contact when traveling. We must learn something of the customs that determine the foreigner's attitude if we want to be accepted with warmth and understanding. The best way to learn about the customs of other lands is to read all the books you can find about the people and places you intend to visit.

OUR ATTITUDE

We don't love all the foreigners who come to our shores. We do love those individuals who are appreciative of our country and courteous to us. Plainly then, corresponding manners are expected of us in the countries where we are foreigners.

At first thought it would seem that there could be no difficulties between us and those whose language is the same as ours—especially the Canadians, Australians, and New Zealanders, who are said to be so similar to ourselves. But since frictions develop even when there is no language problem, thoughtful observance of other people's reactions to the things we do and say would be helpful. It is said of our soldiers stationed overseas, for example, not only that they have more money than those of other nations, but that they are careless—and ostentatious—in their manner of spending it. This naturally angers those who are less well off, or are more frugal by nature.

To our credit it can be said that we are straightforward; we honor our obligations; we keep our word. But sometimes we make overoptimistic promises, and tact is not one of our virtues. Sensitive perception of the feelings of others is something that few of us possess instinctively. It is necessary, therefore, that we try to remember that it is always the stranger who must adapt himself, just as the visitor does to the ways of the house in which he is a guest.

Our travel attitude serves a dual purpose; it determines, of course, the impression we make on those who meet us, but it also determines the amount of enjoyment we get from our trip. Who enjoys his travels more: the man who goes with an open mind, eager to see the best in each country and forget the inconveniences, or the man who finds it too hot in Spain, broods all day because he had no hot water for shaving, or can't find a hamburger stand to buy his favorite lunch? This may sound ridiculous, but I have lived abroad, and many a time I shuddered and tried to pretend that I was anything but American when I heard the boorish complaints of my compatriots repeated endlessly in a penetrating voice. The complainer was certainly not enjoying his trip, nor was he impressing his neighbors with the charm of Americans.

ENTHUSIASM

You will make yourself thoroughly popular in every part of the world if you show appreciation and enthusiasm for the customs and sights of the country you are in. Of course, there will be annoyances—service in many places is less efficient than that to which you are accustomed; neither the food nor the climate may appeal to you, but it is not necessary to voice your disappointments in public. You need not be falsely ecstatic, but you may be politely noncommittal and attempt to find and dwell on the parts of your stay that you *do* enjoy.

NO COMPARISON

Don't compare everything you see with the United States. We may have taller buildings, bigger automobiles, newer supermarkets, and less poverty, but because no one wishes to "suffer by comparison," this is the surest way of alienating your foreign acquaintances. Every country in the world has something to offer that we do not. Therefore, remember that not everyone necessarily envies us our material wealth—he may prefer his simpler, less complicated existence.

ADAPTABILITY

Life and culture in northern Europe are more similar to ours than those in Latin countries. In Germany, the Scandinavian countries, and the British Isles we have fewer problems understanding the people, whose way of life differs less from ours. Without exception Latins live in warmer parts of the world. The combination of temperament and the necessity of adapting themselves to hot weather has resulted in a relaxed, unhurried attitude in all things, and *mañana* is the order of the day. This is one of the most difficult adjustments for Americans to make. We are by nature hustlers, and to arrive in a country where no one cares about time, where people arrive for appointments hours late or forget to keep them at all, and where meals are served hours later than we are used to is quite a shock. Some Americans simply cannot get used to it, and they leave as soon as they can. Others, who are more adaptable, find that the Latin countries have something to offer that is unique. They find it as difficult to return to a clock-watching society as it was to leave it behind in the first place.

MERCENARY AMERICANS

American tourists generally have more cash than people of other countries. To learn to spend it graciously is essential. The fact is that some of us still don't understand that the payment we should make is something more than dollars—that is, if we are going to be given more than just what dollars can buy! Dollars, pounds, francs, pesos, lire—yes—all these buy material things, but they don't buy a single gesture of welcome, admiration, or sympathy.

A little thought, a little preparation, and a great wish to learn and understand are the attributes which will reap the reward—the foreigner's friendship.

OUR CONDUCT

When we are traveling abroad our conduct as much as our attitude determines whether the impression we leave is favorable or unfavorable. If our smile is friendly, our manners impeccable, and our actions above reproach, the foreigner cannot help but be left with a good impression of America and its people.

APPEARANCE

The first thing that the native of another country notices is our appearance. Neatness and modesty are the two most important features. Your clothing may be the least expensive you can find, and you may be traveling with only two or three outfits. But if you unpack your clothes when you arrive and keep them clean (always carry a good spot remover and soap powder) and pressed (use valet service or your own little traveling iron), you will appear well dressed. Clothing should, of course, be appropriate. You should always carry dark clothes for large cities. Women should include a "dressy" suit or dress for dining out, and both men and women should take the proper clothes for any sports they intend to participate in. And clothing should be modest. In resorts, on the Riviera or Majorca, for example, you may wear the same things you would wear at any American resort—even more daring if you wish—but foreign men and women do not wear shorts or slacks except at resorts, in the privacy of their own yards, or for golf, tennis, boating, etc. Tourists only proclaim their ignorance and lack of respect for convention if they appear on the street in such attire. In fact, apart from cities in tropical climates, clothing is more formal than that in our cities. Men are rarely seen in anything but business suits, and well-dressed women wear dark suits or dresses. This is not so in the tropics, however, where the women often wear sleeveless cottons. The men in many hot countries do not wear shirts and ties, but a loose cotton or linen shirt-jacket, worn outside the trousers and sometimes beautifully pleated or embroidered. Women should always have with them a head-covering, if only a scarf, for some churches ask that heads be covered, and it is only courteous to comply with their requirements.

No matter how you are traveling or for how long, your luggage should be neat and compact. There is no excuse for bags that look as if they'd been with you on a ten-year safari, since durable and lightweight luggage is available at moderate cost. Nothing looks worse or makes a traveler so uncomfortable as broken-down bags and numerous bundles.

GENERAL CONDUCT

The next thing people abroad will notice is your general behavior. Don't attract attention to yourself by talking in a loud voice. Americans have a reputation for being "loud," and it is true that foreigners, Latins especially, are brought up to admire a well-modulated voice. You will be far more attractive to people abroad if your voice carries only to those with whom you are talking. Your actions should be as inconspicuous as your voice. There is no need to gesture wildly because you are trying to speak a strange language—your movements should be natural but dignified. When you see a friend from home across the square or in a crowded restaurant, it is not necessary to shout and wave violently to attract his attention. Approach him quietly and greet him as you would ordinarily do at home.

Don't push ahead of others in lines or crowds. Most Europeans are more polite about waiting their turns than we are, and nothing could be ruder than shoving ahead of someone who is too polite to object.

Above all, don't stare! Of course you are interested when you see a Greek gentleman pull out his "worry beads" and toy with them, or when a peasant family approaches with mother burdened down with a heavy load while father rides the donkey. But don't stand rooted with your mouth open, obvious surprise or criticism written all over your face. Their customs are natural to them—it is not your place to judge them—and when you are in their country accept whatever you see as normal, storing it away in your memory as an interesting facet of life abroad.

Probably the best piece of advice was suggested to me by a young lady who had just returned from a most successful trip to Europe. She said, "Don't try to be different from what you are at home, but be the same as nicely as possible."

FOOD AND DRINK

Drinking and eating habits are different abroad, but if your table manners are good you will not be criticized because they are typically American. By this I mean that you will not be considered ill-mannered if you switch your fork from your left hand to your right hand after cutting your meat, but everyone in the room will know that you are from the United States.

Cocktails are not a part of life abroad as they are in our country. Because everyone suspects, thanks to the movies, that Americans drink whiskey and cocktails from morning to night, they are frequently offered to us in private homes, and they are served in bars in all big cities. But beware! They may not taste like any cocktail you have ever had before, and they will more than likely be served lukewarm, possibly with a peanut-sized piece of ice. They may soon cure you of any desire to continue your normal "cocktail habit." It is far better to follow the customs of most foreign countries and take, instead, the delicious local wine or beer served with your meals. There are drinks, alcoholic and nonalcoholic, in each country which are interesting to try at least once. Wines in France, aperitifs in Italy, beer in Germany, and retsina wine in Greece are examples. While you may not enjoy all (or any) of them, they are a part of the culture and economy of the country and should be sampled by all tourist visitors.

TAKING PICTURES

If you wish to include a citizen of the country in your pictures, have the decency to ask his permission. Although an impoverished farmer may appear unusual or picturesque to you, he may be ashamed of the very costume that to you seems "typical," and the last thing he wishes is to have his poverty recorded and distributed to strangers from another land.

In countries where the natives still wear a national costume (which are rare in Europe except on holidays, but common in Africa and the Middle and Far East), the people are accustomed to being photographed by tourists, but it is still polite to ask their permission unless you are just taking a picture of a large crowd.

Children may be frightened of you or the camera, but their fears can usually be overcome by a smile and perhaps some token—a coin, candy, or gum. In areas where there are many tourists, children will often crowd around you, offering their services as models.

If you happen to see a tourist couple, one of whom is taking a picture of the other, offer to snap the picture for them, so that they both may be in it. This is always greatly appreciated, and we should remember to be thoughtful to fellow-travelers as well as to the residents of the country in which we find ourselves.

CHAPERONS

Until very recently in Latin countries, no girl or young woman ever went out alone with a man unless he was her husband. Because more and more of them are now being sent away to schools and colleges in more liberal societies, standards are slowly changing, and the chaperon is becoming a thing of the past. In remote areas and in small towns the daughter's social life is still quite restricted, but in most parts of the world she may go out with a group of friends without an older chaperon. Brothers are considered excellent guardians, and a man wishing to go out with a girl may often arrange a "double date" through her brother.

Both men and women visitors to Latin countries should remember these customs. A man must not expect to meet a well-brought-up girl one night and take her out the next. He must be presented to her family, gain their approval, and then arrange, at least on the first few dates, to include mutual friends.

In many countries women do not go out alone after dark. A woman on the street by herself at night is an open invitation to improper advances by any Latin man. In fact, he would consider himself at fault if he did not attempt to approach her. Young girls should stay in groups of three or four, and older women must be accompanied by at least one friend.

EUROPEAN AND SOUTH AMERICAN MANNERS

The manners of Europeans and South Americans are more elegant than those of Americans. The men bow more deeply, the women always shake hands when introduced, and hand-kissing is still practiced. If you are a woman and you see that a handsome gentleman is about to lean over and kiss your hand, don't giggle or pull away. Accept the gesture for what it is—a compliment to your femininity—and act as natural as you can. European gentlemen not only tip their hats to ladies; they remove them and bow with a flourish. And ladies are always seated on the gentleman's right, except in a theater, when this would place her on the aisle.

FLOWERS AND PRESENTS

Europeans, and especially Latins, dearly love to give presents, not only at Christmas or at someone's birthday, but unendingly. Such gifts are usually foods baked in their own ovens or flowers grown in their gardens. Or they may be any trifling or more expensive things.

In accepting these, if we cannot speak the language, we bow and smile to show our pleasure in accepting the gift. As soon as possible thereafter we reciprocate with a simple present to prove our courteous intentions when fluency of speech is lacking. Flowers are always sent or taken to the hostess when you are invited to dinner. When you deliver them in person, remove the wrappings before you hand them to the hostess. They are also sent as a "thank you" and to greet visitors. In fact, almost any occasion can be called an excuse to send a bouquet.

If it so happens that you cannot speak a word of Spanish or Portuguese, or it may be French or Italian or Dutch, remember that a smile and a genuine handshake will be received with a cordial welcome. Such gifts are the most heartwarming of all.

Most Europeans shake hands all around when arriving at and leaving a place, or even when they meet each other on the street. Traveling Americans who adopt this custom will show their awareness and acceptance of local manners.

Part FIVE

FORMAL ENTERTAINING

23

Formal dinners

Although the truly formal dinner at home is almost a thing of the past, its every feature is a definite part of the complete pattern from which even the simplest dinner-giving is derived. Today the formal dinner is more commonly held at official residences, hotels, or clubs than in private houses. The requisites for a perfect formal dinner, whether for two hundred people or for eight, are as follows:

Guests who are congenial (by far the most important requirement)

Servants who are competent and suited to your needs

A *lovely table setting*—furnishings in perfect condition and suitable: immaculate linen, brilliantly polished silver, shining glassware

Food that is perfectly prepared, and a well-chosen menu

A *cordial and hospitable host*

A *charming hostess*—a requirement that includes tact, sympathy, poise, and perfect manners

Although these requisites are much the same for all dinners, the necessity for perfection increases in proportion to the formality and the importance of the occasion. Many a perfect or near-perfect dinner has been given that cannot be classed as a *formal dinner.* By definition, it is not possible give a formal dinner without the help of servants. No matter how elaborate the meal, if the guests have to help themselves from a buffet, or if the hostess has to rise to clear the table, the dinner immediately becomes informal. *For dinner-giving in a less formal style, see Chapter Twenty-eight.*

THE IMPORTANCE OF DINNER INVITATIONS

Invitations to formal dinners may be engraved or written by hand, or they may take the form of a card of general invitation. They may even be telephoned. *See Chapter Fifty-two.*

Invitations must be answered immediately—engraved or written ones, by return mail, or those which were telephoned, by telephone and at once! Also, nothing but a serious illness or an unavoidable accident can excuse the breaking of a dinner engagement. To accept a dinner at Mrs. Nobody's and then break the obligation upon being invited to dine with the Importants is inexcusable. But having declined the Nobody invitation in the first place, you are then free to accept Mrs. Important's or to stay at home. The rule is: Don't accept an invitation if you don't care about it.

If, for some unavoidable reason, a guest who has accepted a dinner invitation is forced to drop out at the last moment, the hostess must try to fill in by inviting an intimate friend. She always does this herself, by telephone. The one who receives such an invitation is virtually bound by the rules of good manners to accept if possible.

SELECTING YOUR GUESTS

The proper selection of guests is the first essential in all entertaining. Some people have a sense for it—others haven't. The first are the great hosts and hostesses; the others, unless they exert considerable effort, are mediocre.

Usually it is a mistake to invite too many great talkers to the same gathering. Brilliant men and women who love to talk want listeners, not rivals. If it seems advisable or necessary to invite two brilliant people, most hostesses think they should be put together. Possibly they should, but with discretion. If both are voluble or nervous or "temperamental," you may create a situation comparable to putting two opera stars in the same part and expecting them to sing together.

Very silent people should be sandwiched between good conversationalists or at least voluble talkers. Silly people should never be put anywhere near learned ones, nor the dull near the clever, unless the dull one is a young and pretty woman with a talent for listening and the clever one is a man with an admiration for beauty and a love of talking.

When seating her guests, a hostess must try to put together those who are likely to be interesting to each other. Professor Bugge might bore *you* to tears, but Mrs. Entomoid would probably adore him, just as Mr. Stocksan Bonds and Mrs. Rich would probably have interests in common. Making a dinner list is a little like making a Christmas list. You put down what *they* will like (you hope), not what you like. People placed between congenial neighbors remember your dinner as delightful, but those seated next to their pet aversions will need wild horses to drag them your way again.

While a friendly difference of opinion or even a mild argument is often stimulating, a bitter controversy is embarrassing and destructive to good conversation. It is thus safer to avoid inviting people who are deeply involved in, or rabidly opinionated about, opposite sides of a controversial issue.

The host who holds an official position may have more to say in the choosing of guests than the man in private life, whose wife generally decides on the guest list. He may, if he is in the diplomatic corps, for instance, be ordered by his government to entertain important visitors, and he may even be told in what way and to what extent he is to do so. He relays this information to his wife, who takes care of details of food, service, etc. as usual, but who follows his suggestions as to the date, what officials must be invited, and other matters important to the specific occasion. When the official list is complete, his wife will, as at any dinner, choose as the other guests those who will be most congenial to the ones who must be invited.

ANNOUNCING GUESTS

Guests are not always announced at formal dinners. But at large official functions it is often necessary, as even the hostess may not know some of those she has invited. A gentleman follows his wife to the drawing room. If the butler knows the guests, he merely announces the wife's name first and the husband's. If he does not know them by sight, he asks whichever is nearest to him, "What name, please?" He or she answers, "Mr. and Mrs. Lake."

The butler then precedes the guests a few steps into the room where the hostess is stationed and, standing aside, says in a low but distinct voice, "Mrs. Lake," and then after a pause, "Mr. Lake." Married people are usually announced separately, but occasionally people have their guests announced "Mr. and Mrs. Gray."

PERSONS OF RANK

Since formal dinners often include guests of rank, one should know the proper forms of announcement. All men of high executive rank are announced before their wives. The President of the United States is announced simply "The President." His title needs no qualifying appendage, since he, and he solely, is *the* President. He enters first and alone. Then "Mrs. Washington," after being announced, follows. The governor of a state is in courtesy announced as "His Excellency, The Governor of (name of state)," and then "Mrs. Goodland." He enters the room first and Mrs. Goodland follows. "His Honor the Mayor and Mrs. Lake" observe the same etiquette, or in a city other than his own he would be announced "The Mayor of Chicago and Mrs. Lake."

Other announcements are "The Honorable Chief Justice and Mrs. Law," "The Secretary of State and Mrs. Eminent," "Senator and Mrs. Jefferson." The senator, however, allows his wife to enter the room first, because his office is not executive. An ambassador must be announced "His Excellency the British Ambassador," and then "Lady Howard"; he enters the room first. But a first secretary and his wife are announced without other title than their own—"Count and Countess European" or "Mr. and Mrs. American."

"Excellency," though strictly a title belonging to none but an ambassador, is always granted by courtesy to a minister plenipotentiary. It may also be used for a chargé d'affaires, although this courtesy is temporary and ceases upon the return of his chief.

The President, the Vice-President, the governor of a state, the mayor of a city, the ambassador of a foreign country—in other words, all executives—take precedence over their wives and enter a room first. But senators, representatives, secretaries of legations, and all other officials who are not executives allow their wives to precede them, just as they would if they were private individuals.

SPECIAL SITUATIONS

On some occasions a question may arise about how to announce a foreigner of rank, whether his title is hereditary or political. There is only one general rule, always applicable in the United States: Whatever the title, it is invariably translated into English. Thus, *M. le Comte* becomes Count, *Marquise* becomes Marchioness, *Duc*, Duke, and so forth. (This, incidentally, eases the difficulty of pronouncing words from a language with which one is not familiar.)

When there is any doubt about the official title or its proper translation, check with the information officer at the embassy or consulate of the country from which the person comes. In almost every case, however, this information would necessarily have been obtained earlier when the invitation was properly addressed, and so would be available to whoever is announcing at the official function. *See also Chapter Seven, "Addressing Important Persons," and Chapters Fifty-eight, Fifty-nine, and Sixty-one on protocol.*

SEATING YOUR GUESTS

WHO IS THE GUEST OF HONOR?

The guest of honor is the oldest lady present, or someone whom you wish for some reason to honor. A bride at her first dinner in your house after her return from her honeymoon may be given, if you choose, precedence over older people. The woman guest of honor is *always* taken in to dinner by the host and placed on his right. A male guest of honor is seated on the hostess's right. The lady of next greatest importance sits on the host's left and is taken in to dinner by the gentleman on whose right she sits. The hostess is always the last to go into the dining room at a formal dinner unless the President of the United States or the governor (but only in his own state) is present. In these exceptional cases the hostess would go in to dinner with the guest of honor, who leads the way, and the wife of the President or governor would follow immediately with the host. Unless envelopes have been given to the men (see, "Envelopes for the gentlemen," page 170) the other guests walk in with whomever they are conversing.

One point to remember in making up your guest list is this rigid and unbreakable order of seating. If you are not careful, you may find your guest of honor placed next to a most unsuitable table companion.

In Washington, even though the dinner be given for a guest of medium rank, those present of highest rank have the honor places on either side of the host or hostess. The person for whom the dinner is actually given is merely "among those present," unless those of higher rank agree to waive precedence. When Mrs. Frances Perkins was Secretary of Labor, she waived her rank and said always to seat her wherever was most convenient.

THE ORDER OF TABLE PRECEDENCE

The lady of highest rank is on the host's right. The lady of next highest rank is on his left. The third lady sits on the right of the man of highest rank who is on the hostess's right. The fourth lady is on the left of the man of second rank who is on the hostess's left, and so on (see diagram). The lowest in rank is nearest the center. If the dinner is not official and there is no particular distinction in rank or age, the hostess may seat her guests in whatever order she thinks will achieve the most congenial and pleasant conversation. The lady she places on her husband's right is automatically the guest of honor. The "lady of honor" or of first rank must be "taken in" by the host and seated at his right. The hostess goes in to dinner with the man of the second highest rank, because she will be on his right and therefore will be seated by him. But if the man of honor is of such importance that she must go in with him as well as place him at her right, it is necessary to send the lady who sits on the right of the gentleman of honor and the gentleman who sits on the hostess's left in to dinner together and then to separate them. He sees her to her place, and discovering that his card is not next to hers, goes around the table until he finds his own. The diagram (with arrow lines indicating ladies and gentlemen who go in together) makes this seemingly complicated situation clear:

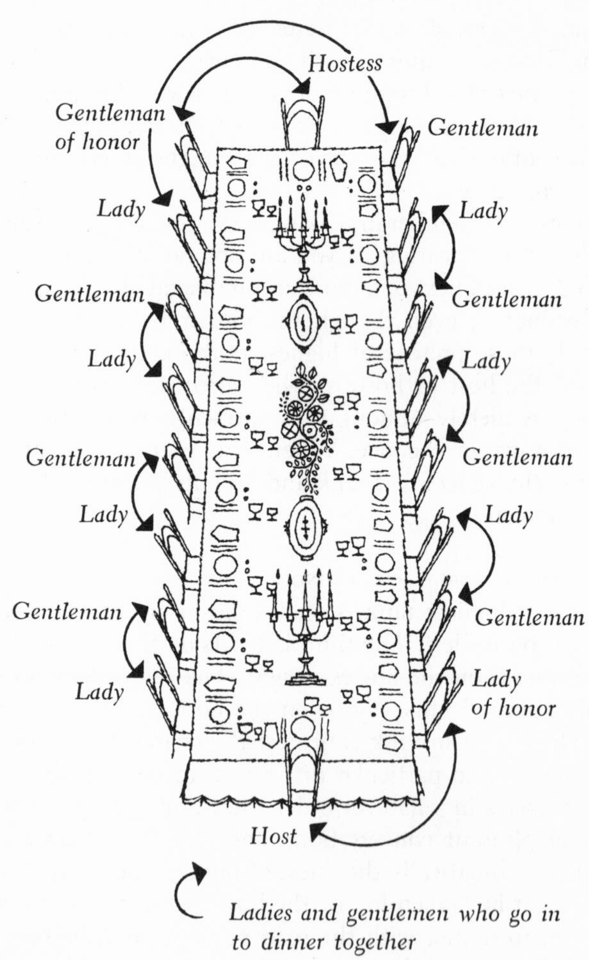

Ladies and gentlemen who go in to dinner together

SEATING A PARTY OF EIGHT, TWELVE, OR SIXTEEN

At dinners of eight, twelve, sixteen, twenty, and twenty-four, where either two ladies or two men must sit at head and foot of the table, the hostess usually relinquishes her place and the host keeps his. At a dinner of twelve, it is important that she take the place at her left instead of at her right, because otherwise she, instead of the lady at the right of the gentleman of honor, will be served first. The following diagram gives an example of this, with the lines showing service:

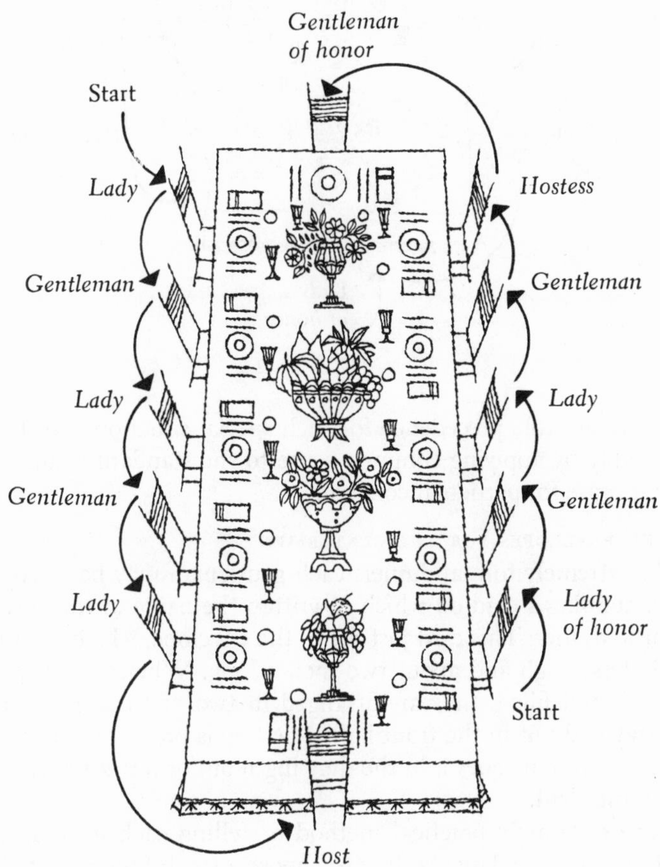

Occasionally other variations on the usual scheme are necessary for a specific reason. This diagram shows, for example, the correct seating arrangement for a group that has a hostess but no host:

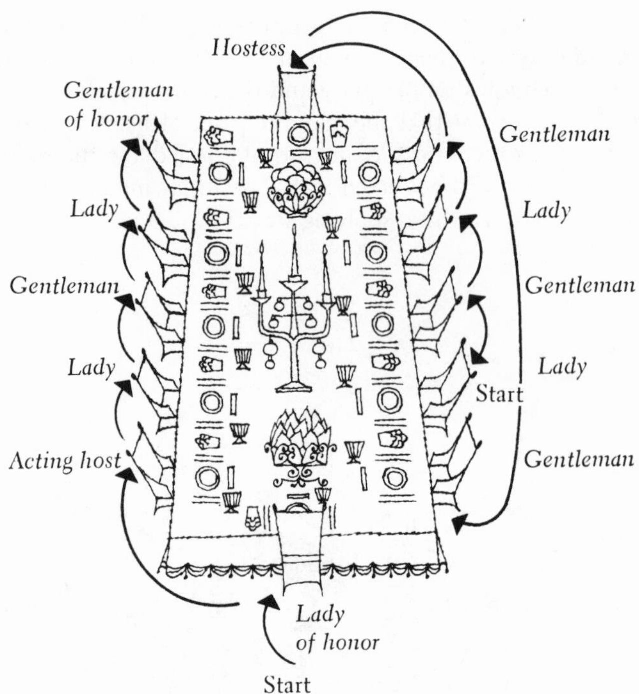

The order of table precedence for such special situations can be worked out suitably by applying common sense to the standard forms and need not be a cause for particular concern.

THE ENVELOPES FOR THE GENTLEMEN

At extremely formal dinners each gentleman may be given an envelope containing a card on which is written the name of the lady he is to take in to dinner. This card just fits in the envelope, which is an inch (or slightly less) high and about two inches long. When the envelopes are addressed and filled, they are arranged in two or three neat rows on a silver tray and put in the front hall. The tray is presented to each gentleman just before he goes into the drawing room or just after his arrival in the entrance hall.

An exceedingly practical method of telling each gentleman where he is to sit at a very large table is to choose a small fold-over card instead of the usual single one. His name is on its front fold and his partner's name inside, and below her name in the lower half of the fold is a small engraved diagram showing the table, the location of the door, and their seats.

If it is so big a dinner that there are many separate tables, the tables are numbered with standing placards (as at a public dinner) and the

table number written on each lady's name card. (Do not call it an "escort card.")

THE PLACE CARDS

Place cards are always used at formal dinners to indicate to each diner where he is to sit. Place cards are usually plain or marked with a simple monogram, about an inch and half high by two inches long, sometimes slightly larger. Fancy cards, while suitable on such special occasions as Christmas or a birthday, are out of place on a formal table. The courtesy title and surname—"Dr. Gooding," "Mr. Ashley"—are used except when there is more than one guest with the same surname, in which case "Mr. Russell Albright" and "Mr. Lee Albright," for example, should be used to make the distinction. *See also Chapter Fifty-eight, if your dinner involves government officials.*

EXPERT SERVICE WITH PERMANENT OR TEMPORARY HELP

The fact that few households except such official establishments as embassies have staffs that include butlers, footmen, or kitchen maids need not keep you from entertaining formally at home. The hostess who wishes her dinner to be formal can hire temporary help. All cities and many smaller communities have catering services that provide not only servants but excellent meals, either prepared by a cook sent to your home or partially cooked in their kitchens and finished in yours.

If the servants are efficient and well trained, a small (that is, for no more than twelve) formal dinner may be beautifully handled by a cook, a butler, and a footman. The footman may be replaced by a maid, but at a truly formal dinner, men should serve the meal. When the host does not have a chauffeur, a man should be hired to assist the ladies from the cars or taxis, to direct and help with parking, and to bring the cars to the door when the party is over. In the country his job is that of a chauffeur—in the city he acts as a doorman. If there is a permanent cook in the house, she prepares the meal, and only the butler and footman are hired for the evening. They serve and also assist the cook with the cleaning up.

When these temporary servants are used, the hostess naturally must do most of the advance preparation. She sets the table, arranges flowers, and does all else that will relieve her help of any responsibilities other than the preparation and serving of the meal.

The cook arrives early in the day so that after the hostess has given explicit directions as to the food and explained the whereabouts and workings of all the utensils and appliances to be used, there will be plenty of time for the careful preparation of the meal.

The butler and footman come a little later, but early enough to discuss all details of service with the hostess and to take care of any last-minute polishing or arranging that may be necessary. If cocktails are to be served, the butler mixes them in advance and has them ready to serve as each guest arrives, so that dinner will not be delayed. A few minutes before the hour of the guests' arrival the butler and footman put on their uniforms, which must be impeccable. The footman takes his place in the hall to direct the guests or help with their wraps. The butler stands near the hostess to announce the guests, or if they are not be announced, he passes cocktails or simply waits to assist her in any way he can. It is the responsibility of the temporary butler, as it would be if he were permanently employed, to see that all runs smoothly. The hostess should be able to devote her attention to her guests.

The butler, footman, and waitress (if one has been hired) may not leave until the guests have been ushered out, the last glass washed, and the last ash tray emptied. The cook, however, may leave as soon as the cooking utensils and dinner service have been washed and the kitchen made immaculate.

The method of paying temporary help varies in different localities and also depends on the policy of the agency through which they are hired. Some caterers send a bill for their services and prefer that you do not add a tip. Others send a bill but indicate that you may add a tip. If the help has been hired from an employment agency, or by you personally, you simply pay them before they leave at the rate you have agreed upon. In any case, it is most important to establish the method and amount of payment at the time the servants are hired to avoid embarrassment or unpleasantness that may ruin an otherwise perfect evening.

If your table—or tables—seat more than twelve and you wish to entertain a larger group, you will find it desirable and even necessary to hire more than one footman and possibly an assistant to work in the kitchen as well. Otherwise, the considerable delay in serving and removing courses will mean that the last guests will be served a cold dinner.

Temporary help of this sort is the only solution for almost all housewives today. But whether temporary or permanent, they have the same duties, which are thoroughly discussed in this chapter.

SETTING YOUR TABLE

The one unbreakable rule for a formal table is that everything must be geometrically spaced: the centerpiece in the actual center, the places at equal distances, and all utensils balanced. Beyond this one rule you may vary your arrangement and decorations as you choose.

If the tablecloth is of white damask, which for a formal dinner is always best, a pad must be put under it. (If you do not have a felt pad cut to the dimensions of your table, a folded white blanket serves very well.) To say that the cloth must be smooth and white—in other words, perfectly laundered—is, I hope, unnecessary. Damask is the most conservative tablecloth, especially suitable in dining rooms furnished in English or French style, or with formal "contemporary" furnishings. Lace tablecloths are better suited to an Italian room—especially if the table is a refectory style. Embroidered or lace-inserted tablecloths are suited to all quaint, low-ceilinged, old-fashioned rooms. Either lace or linen goes over the table without felt or other padding.

Whenever a damask or linen cloth is used, the middle crease must be put on so that it is an absolutely straight and unwavering line down the exact center from head to foot of the table. If it is an embroidered cloth, be sure the embroidery is "right side up."

First, arrange the centerpiece, which must never be so high that the guests cannot see over it. It can be composed of an almost unlimited variety of things: flowers or fruit in any arrangement that taste and ingenuity can devise; an ornament in silver that needs no flowers, such as a covered bowl; an ornament of glass or china; or perhaps an arrangement of distinctive conversation-piece objects that blend with the rest of the table setting.

THE INDIVIDUAL PLACES

Next comes the setting of the places. The distance between places at the table must never be so short that guests have no elbow room and the servants cannot pass the dishes properly. When the dining-room chairs have very high backs and are placed so close as to be almost touching, it is difficult for even the most skillful server not to spill something on someone. On the other hand, people placed a yard or more apart will find a shouted conversation equally trying. About two feet from plate center to plate center is ideal. If the chairs have narrow and low backs, people can sit much closer together. This is especially true of a small, round table, the curve of which leaves a spreading wedge of space between the chairs at the back even if the seats touch at the front corners. But on the long, straight sides of a rectangular table in a very large dining room there should be a foot of space between the chairs.

The service plates, with the pattern properly positioned, are first put around the table at equal distances—spaced with a string if the person setting the table does not have an accurate eye. The silver is placed in the order of its use, with the implements to be used first farthest from the plate. The salad fork is placed next to the left of the plate, then the meat fork, and finally the fish fork, which will be used first. Just to the right of the plate is the salad knife, next is the meat knife, and on the outside is the fish knife, the cutting edge of each toward the plate. Outside the knives go the soup spoon and then the oyster fork or grapefruit spoon.

No more than three forks (not counting the oyster fork) and three knives belong on the table when it is set. Therefore, if there is an additional course (rarely seen these days, but coming between the fish and the main dish when it appears), the fork for this course is placed between the fish fork and that for the meat, and the salad fork is left out to be brought in later. The salad knife is also omitted, as it is in any case when the salad does not require one.

In short, the silver is arranged so that one uses the utensils farthest from the plate first, taking the next in order for each succeeding course.

Butter knives and plates are never used on a formal dinner table.

The wineglasses chosen depend of course upon the menu, but their table-setting arrangement will have to be according to size, in that little ones should not be hidden behind the large ones. Therefore, the goblet for water is placed directly above the knives at the right of the plate; next to it, at a slight distance to the right, the champagne glass; in front and between these two, the claret or red-wine glass, or the white-wine glass; then, either in front of this or somewhat to the right again, the sherry glass. If there is to be a glass for burgundy, it should be back between the goblet and the glass for champagne. Or instead of grouping the glasses on the table, some prefer to have them placed in a straight row slanting downward from the goblet at upper left to the glass for sherry at lower right.

Such an array as this is scarcely ever seen except at a public dinner, which is more properly classified as a banquet. At the private dinner two or three glasses in addition to the goblet are usual—one for sherry, one for a claret or possibly a burgundy, and one for a light white wine.

A dinner napkin folded square and flat is laid on each place plate. Very fancy foldings are not in good taste, but if the napkins are very large, the sides are folded in so as to make a flattened roll a third the width of its height. If they have a corner monogram, they also may be folded diagonally in half and the two long ends folded under.

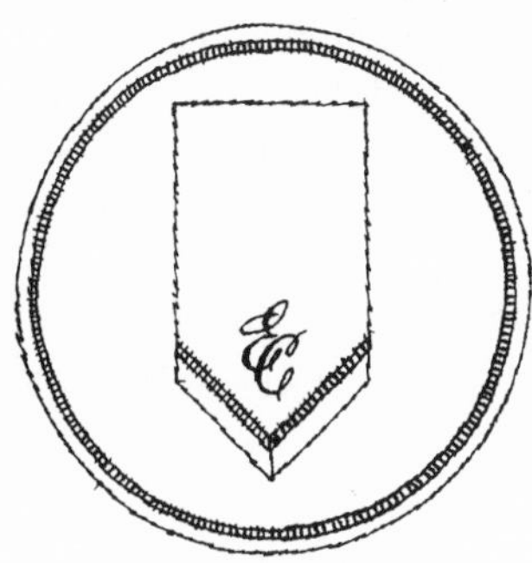

Napkins are put at the side only when it is necessary to put food on the table before seating the guests. To put the napkin at the side of the empty plate in order to display the plate is very much like wearing a ring over a glove—as well as being incorrect for formal table setting. The old custom of wrapping a roll in the napkin was most impractical. When the diner flicked open the napkin, he generally also flicked the roll right onto the floor.

Place cards are put on top of and in the center of the napkin, or if unsteady there, they may be placed on the tablecloth above the service plate at the exact center of the place setting.

FINISHING THE TABLE

When the places have been set, a pair of candlesticks are placed at each end, about halfway between the center and the edge of the table, or candelabra at either end halfway between the places of the host and hostess and the centerpiece. The number of candles depends upon whether the dining room is otherwise lighted or not. If the candles alone light the table, there should be a candle a person. You will need two or four candelabra, depending on the length of the table and the number of guests. But if the candles are merely ornaments, four candles will be adequate for a table of eight. Candlesticks or candelabra must be high and the candles as long as the proportion can stand, so that the light does not shine into the eyes of those at the table.

Dishes or compotes filled with candy, fruit, fancy cakes, or other edible trimmings are put at the corners, between the candlesticks or candelabra and the centerpiece, or wherever there are equally spaced vacancies on the table. They are left there through the entire meal and are sometimes passed around after dessert is finished. Nuts may be put on the dinner table either in two big silver dishes or in small individual ones at each of the places, but they are removed with the salt and pepper shakers after the salad course. The colloquial description of eating "from soup to nuts" could never apply to a formal dinner. After-dessert "nuts and raisins" belong only on the family dinner table—especially at Thanksgiving and Christmas.

Flowers are also often put in two or four smaller vases, in addition to a larger and dominating one in the center.

Pepper pots and saltcellars should be put at every other place. For a dinner of twelve there should be six (and never less than four) saltcellars and pepper pots.

Olives and celery are passed during the soup course and placed on the edge of the plate under the soup plate. When fish or meat or salad has its own accompanying condiment, sauce, or relish, it is also passed. Pickles have no place on the correct dinner-party menu, because they are served as an accompaniment or garnishing for cold meats, which belong to lunch, supper, buffets, and picnics.

CIGARETTES AND ASH TRAYS

Whether or not the hostess and her husband smoke, she sees that her guests are supplied with ash trays and cigarettes. A small ash tray is put at each place, and cigarettes are found on the table, either in a small holder in front of each diner or in larger holders spaced evenly about the table. Smokers should follow the usual rules of good smoking manners more strictly at the table than at any other time.

There are some hostesses even today who prefer that their guests do not smoke until coffee is served, and no ash trays or cigarettes are placed on the table. Others have them passed at the end of the salad course.

FOOD AND DRINK

COCKTAILS

If cocktails are served, they are prepared in the pantry or kitchen and passed (on a tray) to each guest as he arrives. Two or three varieties should be offered, with the butler indicating what they are: "Would you care for an old-fashioned or a martini?" There must also be glasses of tomato juice or some other nonalcoholic beverage on the tray for those who prefer something other than liquor. Unless dinner is delayed because of waiting for late arrivals, only one cocktail need be served. There will be wine with the meal, and formal dinners should start as nearly as possible at the hour stated on the invitation.

THE MENU

The menu, no matter how formal, does not consist of more than six courses:

1. soup *or* fresh fruit cup *or* melon *or* shellfish (clams, oysters, or shrimp)
2. fish course (*or* on rare occasions, a dish such as sweetbreads instead of fish)
3. the entree, or main course (usually roast meat or fowl)
4. salad
5. dessert
6. coffee

One should always try to choose a well-balanced menu; an especially rich dish is balanced by a simple one. Fish timbale with a thick creamed sauce might perhaps be followed by spring lamb, roast squab, or a filet mignon; broiled fish by an elaborate meat dish.

You may love highly flavored Spanish or Indian dishes, but they are not appropriate for a formal dinner. Consider the appearance of the food you serve. Avoid a dinner of white sauces from beginning to end: cream soup, creamed sweetbreads, followed by breast of chicken and mashed potatoes. Combine flavors intelligently. Don't serve all "sweet" dishes: beet soup, duck basted with currant jelly, a fruit salad, and a sugary dessert. In these examples, each dish is good in itself but unappetizing in the monotony of its combination.

In addition, although a dinner should not be heavy, neither should it consist of mere samples of the foods. The following menu might seem at first glance a good dinner, but it is one from which the average man would go home and forage ravenously in the refrigerator: clear soup; escargots (snails); broiled squab, potato croquette, and string beans; green salad; and sherbet.

If there had been a thick cream soup, or a fish with more substance —such as salmon, or a baked thick fish of which he could have had a generous helping—this would have been more adequate. But too many women order trimmings rather than food.

MENU CARDS

Menu cards are most often seen at official dinners or banquets, but they are sometimes used at a formal dinner at home. Usually there is only one, which is placed in front of the host, but sometimes there is one between every two guests.

Menus on fashionable tables never include obvious accessories such as celery, olives, rolls, jelly, chocolates, or fruit any more than they would include salt and pepper or iced water.

WINES

Wines have an important place on the menu of a perfect dinner. Let us consider some of them in detail.

Sherry is the first wine offered at dinner, and then usually only with a soup which contains sherry in the preparation. In other words, it should not be offered with cream of chicken soup or vichysoisse, but it would be an appropriate accompaniment to black bean or green turtle soup. Sherry should be put into a decanter at room temperature and poured into small V-shaped glasses. It can stand being decanted almost indefinitely without spoiling. Sherry, which is also served at lunch or supper, or as a hospitable refreshment at any time, is often included as an alternate choice with cocktails.

A dry white wine is served with fish or with an entree, and is often the only wine at a woman's lunch or at the family dinner table. White wine may be kept in the refrigerator for at least several hours or even days before being used, since it should always be well chilled before being served. The quickest and most efficient way to chill a bottle of uncooled white wine is to place it in a bucket or cooler filled with a mixture of ice and cold water. The actual melting of the ice in the water will cool the wine faster than if it is immersed in cracked ice alone. Drawing the cork and turning the bottle from time to time will hasten the cooling. Unlike red wines, a white wine is good to the last drop, and the bottle may be upended when pouring the final glass.

Red wine is normally served with red meats, duck, and game, but at less formal dinners it may be drunk from the beginning of the meal to its close. This would more likely be true with a claret, a light red wine, than with a burgundy, which is much heavier. All red wines should be served at room temperature, and the burgundy may be a degree or two warmer if the vintage is very good. It may be brought to this temperature by being left in a warm spot—never by warming over a burner or flame. The procedure for serving a fine vintage is somewhat complicated but should be followed carefully if its excellence is to be appreciated. A day or two before it is to be used the wine should be removed from the wine cellar or closet. This is done by transferring the bottle into a straw basket as gently as possible, maintaining the bottle in a semihorizontal position. Actually, in the basket it should be tilted 15 or 20 degrees more toward the vertical than it was in the bin, and it is left in this position for a day at least to permit any disturbed sediment to settle. If you do not have a wine cellar, purchase the wine several days before your dinner and follow the same procedure. The bottle should be opened an hour or so before serving. At this time, the foil is neatly cut away to prevent the wine from coming in contact with it while being poured. For the same reason, a damp cloth is used to wipe the mouth of the bottle, removing any accumulated dirt and grime. The cork is then carefully pulled and placed beside the neck of the bottle in its basket in order that the host or any interested guest may note that it is undamaged. During this hour the bottle is open, the wine is given an opportunity to "breathe" and rid itself of any musty or other unpleasant odor it might have absorbed in the cellar.

It should be served in the basket, with the label showing to permit each guest to note what he is being offered. Caution must be taken when pouring the wine to avoid any "backlash" or bubbling that can result if it is handled carelessly. This would agitate the sediment, which should now be resting in the bottom of the bottle. Finally, it is obvious that the last inch or so should not be poured from the bottle since this will be murky with sediment.

When a bottle of red wine is so heavy with sediment that the procedure given above will not result in a palatable drink, it may be decanted. Another less legitimate reason for decanting is to prevent a guest whose palate does not tell him otherwise from discovering that he is not being served a particularly high quality wine.

Champagne is, above all other beverages, that of the formal dinner party. When other wines are included, it is served with the meat course, but when it is the only wine, it is served as soon as the first course has begun. Its proper temperature depends upon its quality.

Champagne that is not of especially fine vintage is put in the refrigerator for a day and then chilled further by putting it into a cooler with a little salt as well as ice. Occasionally, holding the bottle by the neck, turn it back and forth a few times. In doing this take care not to leave the bottle in the salt and ice too long, or the champagne may become sherbet! Also, when opening, be sure to wrap the bottle in a towel or napkin as a protection in case it explodes.

An excellent vintage champagne, on the other hand, is packed in ice without salt, which chills it just a little less. Generally, champagne is served in a wide-brimmed glass such as the one shown on the left. Although this is correct, the type of glass shown on the right is preferred by many connoisseurs. This shape of glass tends to prolong the life of the

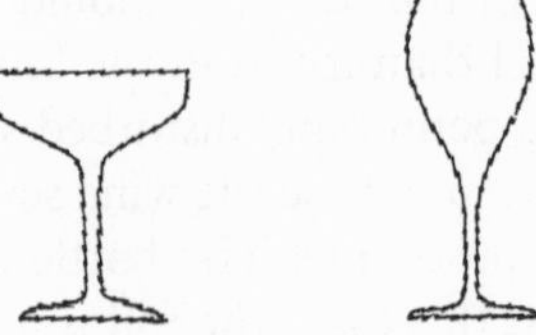

effervescent bubbles which contribute so much to the enjoyment of this particular wine. The old idea of stirring champagne to remove these bubbles has nothing to recommend it. If you dislike effervescence, a good white wine would be a much more preferable drink.

Champagne glasses ought to be as thin as soap bubbles. Thick glasses will raise the temperature at which a really good champagne should be served and spoil its perfection. If they must be used, the epicurean thing to do is to chill them in the refrigerator and put them on the table at the moment the champagne is served.

Other types of wine glasses:

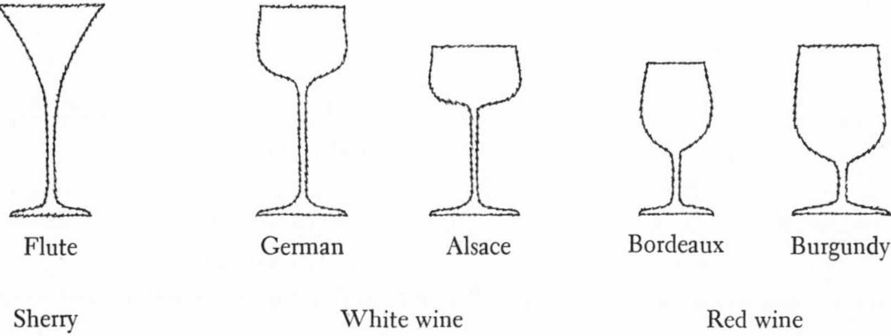

Wine glasses should be picked up by the stem rather than the bowl. In the case of white wine and champagne this helps to keep the wine cool, and in the case of all wines, including red ones, it enables you to appreciate the color.

THE CHARMING HOSTESS

GUESTS ARRIVE

On all formal occasions the hostess stands near the door of her living room. As guests enter or are announced, she greets them with a smile and a handshake and says something pleasant to each. What she says need not be important; her expression and manner can convey a far more gracious welcome than the most elaborate phrases, which, in fact, should be studiously avoided. She may simply say, "I am very glad to see you," or "I am so glad you could come!" No matter what she says, she takes your hand with a firm pressure and her smile is really a *smile* of welcome, not a mechanical exercise of the facial muscles. She gives you her complete attention, even if only for the moment. And you go into her drawing room with the feeling that you are under the roof of a friend and not of a mere acquaintance.

Some hostesses love to embellish their introductions: "Mrs. Jones, I want you to meet Mrs. Smith. Mrs. Smith is the author of *Dragged from the Depths*, all about psychic insight!" Or to a good-looking woman, "I am putting you next to Count Zilbo—I want him to carry back a flattering impression of American women!" But well-mannered people do not exploit their guests with embarrassing praises or make personal remarks. Both are in very poor taste. Don't take this to mean that helpful explanations can't be made; it is only that they must not be overdone. Mrs. Lovejoy might tell a lady just before going in to dinner, "Mr. Traveler, who is sitting next to you at the table, has just come back from Europe." This is not to exploit her guest but to give his neighbor a starting point for conversation at dinner.

Although personal remarks are never good form, it is permissible for one lady to casually remark on how attractive another lady looks.

THE RESPONSIBILITIES OF A HOSTESS

First of all, a hostess must show each of her guests equal and impartial attention. Also, although engrossed in the person she is talking to, she must be able to notice anything amiss elsewhere. The more competent her servants, the less she need be aware of details herself, but the hostess giving a formal dinner with inexperienced help must be constantly alert to the possibility of difficulties. No matter what happens—if all the china in the pantry falls with a crash, she must not appear to have heard it. Whatever goes wrong, she must cover it as best she can and at the same time hide the fact that she is covering it. To give hectic directions merely accentuates the awkwardness. If a dish appears that is unpresentable, she as quietly as possible orders the next one to be brought in. If a guest knocks over a glass and breaks it, her only concern must seemingly be that her guest has been made uncomfortable. She says, "I am sorry! It doesn't matter at all!" And she has a fresh glass brought (even though it doesn't match) and dismisses all thought of the matter.

Both the host and hostess must keep the conversation going if it lags, but this is less important at a large dinner. At a small dinner the skillful hostess has need of what Thackeray calls the "showman" quality. She brings each guest forward in turn to the center of the stage.

THE DUTIES OF THE HOST

Mr. Lovejoy, who stands near his wife as the guests arrive, grasps your hand and adds his own greeting to his wife's gracious welcome. Either you join a friend standing nearby, or he introduces you, if you are a man, to a lady; if you are a lady he presents a man to you.

At formal dinners introductions are individually made. People do not as a rule speak to strangers, except those next to them at table or in the drawing room after dinner. The host must therefore make introductions when necessary.

Since before dinner the hostess is standing, no gentleman may sit down. The ladies also usually stand until dinner is announced, as it is awkward to sit and talk with someone who is standing.

A hostess who is either a widow or unmarried asks the man she knows best—a relative if there is one present—to act as host. He gives his arm to the guest of honor and leads the way to the dining table, where he sits opposite the hostess. After dinner if the men do not remain at the table for their coffee, he leads them to the smoking room and later to the living room to "join the ladies."

WHEN DINNER IS ANNOUNCED

It is the duty of the butler to "count heads" so that he may know when all the guests have arrived. As soon as he has announced the last person, he notifies the cook. When the cook is ready, the butler, having glanced into the dining room to see that curtains have been drawn and the candles lighted, enters the drawing room, approaches the hostess, bows, and says quietly, "Dinner is served." Or if she happens to be looking at him, he merely bows. If cocktails have been served, he may wait a few moments to allow the guests time to finish their drinks.

SEATING YOUR GUESTS

The host offers his right arm to the lady of honor and leads the way to the dining room. If "envelopes" have been distributed, all the other gentlemen offer their arms to the ladies appointed to them and follow the host, two and two; the only order of precedence is that the host and his partner lead, while the hostess and her partner come last. If by chance a gentleman does not know the lady whose name is on the card in his envelope, he must find out who she is and be presented to her before he takes her in to dinner. At a very large dinner, if there is no table diagram in the hall, or if the table number is not marked on the "name card," the butler usually stands just within the dining-room door with one and, asking each gentleman's name, tells him "right" or "left." He has plenty of time to reach the chair of the hostess before her, as she always enters the dining room last.

At a dinner of less than ten, or if the men have not been given "envelopes," the ladies are not escorted in to dinner. They may walk in with whomever they please.

The guests look for their place cards, assisted by the hostess, who may carry her seating plan with her if she feels that she cannot remember where each guest is to sit. The gentlemen help the ladies on their right into their seats, with the exception of the male guest of honor, who seats the hostess, leaving the man on her left to walk around and seat the lady on the right of the guest of honor.

THE LATE GUESTS

Fifteen minutes is the established length of time that a hostess may wait for a late guest. To wait more than twenty minutes, at the outside, would be showing lack of consideration to many for the sake of one. When the late guest finally enters the dining room, it is he who must go up to the hostess and apologize for being late. The hostess remains seated, and if the guest is a lady, she merely shakes hands quickly so that all the men at table need not rise. The hostess must never take the guest to task, but should say something polite and conciliatory such as, "I was sure you wouldn't want us to wait dinner." In the past the latecomer was always served dinner from the beginning unless he was considerate enough to direct a nearby servant, "Let me begin with this course." But today etiquette is more practical, and it is not considered necessary to bring back any dish after it has left the dining room.

CORRECT SERVICE

At a formal dinner served by a large staff, the butler always stands behind the hostess's chair, except when giving one of the men under him a direction or when pouring wine. He is not supposed to leave the dining room himself or ever to handle a dish. At a smaller dinner when he has no assistant, he naturally does everything himself; when he has a second man or a waitress, he passes the principal dishes and the assistant follows with the accompanying dishes or vegetables.

In any case, whether there are two at table or two hundred, plates are changed and courses presented in precisely the same manner. No serving dishes are ever put on the table except the ornamental dishes of fruit and sweetmeats. The meat is carved in the kitchen or pantry; vegetables, bread, and condiments are passed and returned to the side table.

From the time the table is set until it is cleared for dessert, a plate should remain at every place. The plate on which oysters or clams are served is put on top of the place plate, and so is a plate holding fruit or cold seafood in a stemmed glass. At the end of the course, the used plate is removed, leaving the place plate. The soup plate is also put on top of this same plate. But when the soup plate is removed, the underneath plate is removed with it, and the plate for the next course immediately exchanged for the two taken away.

If the first course is passed instead of being served on individual plates, it should be eaten on the place plate. An exchange plate is then necessary before the soup can be served. That is, a clean plate is exchanged for the used one, and the soup plate then put on top of that.

Although all dishes are presented at the left of the person being served, it is better that plates be removed from the right. If more convenient, however, it is permissible to remove them from the left. Glasses are filled and additional knives placed at the right, but forks are put on as needed at the left.

The only plates that may be brought into the dining room one in each hand are for soup and dessert. The soup plates are put down on the place plates, which have not been removed, and the dessert plates need merely be put down on the tablecloth. But the plates of every other course have to be exchanged, and therefore each individual service requires two hands. Soup plates two at a time, however, can be dangerous, as it is while putting down one plate and balancing the other that the mishap of "soup poured down someone's back" occurs! If only one plate of soup is brought in at a time, this accident should not happen. Also, the spoon and fork on the dessert plate can easily fall off unless it is held level. Two plates at a time are therefore not a question of etiquette, but one of the servant's skill.

At one time good service required the removal of each plate the instant the fork was laid down on it, so that by the time the last eater was finished, the entire table was set with clean plates and was ready for the service of the next course. But the protests of the slow eaters were loud and clear, and the hostess who a few years ago prided herself on having no used plate left at any place more than a few moments now does not have the plates removed until the slowest eaters have finished.

At every well-ordered dinner there should be a separate service for each six persons; that is, no hot dish should be presented to more than six, or seven at most. At a dinner of eighteen, for instance, three dishes, each holding six portions, are garnished exactly alike and presented simultaneously: to the lady of honor, to the lady sitting six seats to her right, to the lady six seats on around the end of the table. Study the diagrams on the preceding pages, which explain seating precedence and partner arrangement.

The butler and his assistants pass the dishes to the right, or alternately right and left so that the same gentleman is not always offered the last piece on a dish.

Whenever the dinner is large enough to require two services it is not advisable to reverse the direction of service. Because the footmen can become confused by serving first to the right and then to the left, there is considerable risk they they will bump into each other.

THE HOSTESS IS NEVER SERVED FIRST

The hostess who has herself served first when there is another woman at the table forgets the first principle of good manners. Consideration is the basis of all courteous behavior, and the hostess who helps herself to the fresh and untouched dish and lets the others take what she leaves is either unthinking or rude.

FILLING GLASSES

As soon as the guests are seated and the first course is put in front of them, the butler goes from guest to guest, on the right-hand side of each, and fills the water goblet. He then serves the wine, asking each guest,

"Sherry, Sir?" (or "Madam?") All wines are poured at the right of each person and without lifting the glass from the table.

The proper way to serve champagne is from its own bottle with a napkin wrapped around it. The reason for this is to catch all drops—either of wine or of condensed moisture—that might fall, as well as to protect its proper chill from the warmth of hands.

SERVING BREAD

As soon as soup is served, dinner rolls are passed in a flat dish or a basket. An old-fashioned silver cake basket makes a perfect modern bread basket. The most popular type, perhaps, is a shallow wicker basket with a fringed napkin laid in it. Several sorts of breads are always displayed—finger rolls, crescent rolls, melba toast, and rye or whole wheat crackers are typical. A guest helps himself with his fingers and lays the roll or bread on the tablecloth. No bread plates are ever on a table where there is no butter, and no butter is ever served at a formal dinner. Whenever a guest has no bread left at his place, more should be passed to him.

PRESENTING DISHES

Dishes are held flat on the palm of the servant's left hand; every hot one must have a napkin placed as a pad under it. An especially heavy meat platter can be steadied if necessary by holding the edge of the platter with the right hand, the fingers protected from being burned by a second folded napkin.

Each dish is supplied with whatever silver is needed for serving it. A serving spoon, somewhat larger than an ordinary tablespoon, and a fork of large size are put on most dishes. Sometimes the spoon alone is used if the dish is not hard to help oneself to. String beans, braised celery, spinach *en branche,* etc. need both fork and spoon. Asparagus has various special lifters and tongs, but most people use the ordinary spoon and fork. With the spoon underneath, the fork prongs turned down hold the stalks on the spoon. Corn on the cob is taken with the fingers, but this dish, delectable though it be, is *never* served at a *formal* dinner party. For this occasion corn should be cut off, buttered, seasoned, and served in a vegetable dish. An aspic or mousse should have both fork and spoon, but peas, mashed potatoes, rice, etc. may be offered with a spoon only.

THE SERVING TABLE

The serving table is usually an ordinary table placed in the corner of the dining room nearest the door to the pantry or kitchen and behind a screen, so that it cannot be seen by the guests at table. In a small dining room where space is limited, a set of shelves like a single bookcase can be used.

The serving table is a halfway station between the dinner table and the pantry. It holds stacks of plates, extra forks and knives, finger bowls, and dessert plates. If the serving table is small or too crowded, the latter are sometimes put out on the sideboard.

At informal dinners all dishes of food after being passed are left on the serving table on a warming tray in case they are needed for a second helping. At formal dinners dishes are never passed twice and are therefore taken directly to the pantry after being passed.

CLEARING TABLE FOR DESSERT

At all dinners the salad plates or the plates used for the entree are removed before dessert is served. The saltcellars, pepper shakers, unused flat silver and nut dishes are taken off on a serving tray, and the crumbs are brushed off each place with a tightly folded napkin onto a tray held under the table edge.

DESSERT SERVICE

There are two methods of serving dessert. One is to put the fork and spoon on a china plate with or without a glass plate for ice cream on top of it. After the dessert the finger bowl is brought in on a plate by itself. In the other, more common, service the finger bowl, as well as the fork and spoon, are brought in on the dessert plate. The diner puts the finger bowl above his plate, and the fork and spoon each to its proper side.

When fruit is to be served, it is passed immediately after the dessert or ice cream; and decorative sweets are passed last.

FINGER BOWLS

Before leaving the subject of dessert, one should add that the finger bowl is less than half-filled with cold water; and at dinner parties a few violets, sweet peas, or rose petals may be floated in it.

This reminds me of a delightful story that one of my daughter's friends told about herself. She was invited for the first time to a dinner at her boy friend's home. She was somewhat nervous about it because she knew that his family lived on a grander scale than her own. Naturally, she wished to make a good impression and decided to watch carefully and simply copy other guests if she had any problems. Everything went beautifully through the entree: she chose the right silver, broke her bread before buttering it, and served herself impeccably. Then came the dessert—she thought! A pretty bowl of clear liquid with bits of pink icing or pastry floating in it. Flushed with her success until then, she forgot to look around her, picked up her spoon, and proceeded to eat the rose petals that were floating in the finger bowl!

Fortunately, her sense of humor and that of her boy friend's family carried her through, and the couple are soon to be married!

A slice of lemon is never used in an after-dessert finger bowl. After broiled lobster at an informal or family dinner, lemon in *hot* water is excellent.

Coffee is seldom served at a formal dinner table, but is served elsewhere later.

AFTER THE MEAL

LEAVING THE TABLE

At the end of the dinner, when the last dish of sweets has been passed and the hostess sees that no one is eating any longer, she catches the eye of one of the ladies and slowly stands up. Anyone who happens to be observing also stands up, and in a moment everyone is standing. The gentlemen offer their arms to their dinner partners and conduct them back to wherever they are to sit during the rest of the evening.

Each gentleman then leaves his partner and with the other men follows the host to the room where after-dinner coffee, liqueurs, and cigars and cigarettes are being passed. It is perfectly correct for a gentleman to talk to any other who happens to be sitting near him, whether he knows him or not. At the end of twenty minutes or so, the host must take the opportunity of the first lull in the conversation to suggest that they "join the ladies" in the living room.

In a house where there is not an extra room to smoke in, the gentlemen do not take the ladies to the living room, but stay where they are and have their coffee, cigars, liqueurs, and conversation sitting around the table.

The ladies leave the table and have coffee, cigarettes, and liqueurs passed to them in the living room.

AFTER-DINNER COFFEE

Coffee is served in one of three ways:

1. The footman proffers a tray of cups, saucers, and sugar; the butler follows with the coffee pot and pours into the cup held in the guest's hand.

2. A tray with filled cups is proffered by the butler to the guests, who help themselves.

3. The tray of cups and sugar is held on the servant's left hand. The guest puts sugar into one of the cups and the servant pours coffee with the right hand.

Liqueurs are offered exactly as coffee in the second or third manner. The guests pour their own, or they say "Cognac" or "Mint, please," and their choice is poured for them.

Cigarettes are arranged on a tray with matches or a lighter.

At a dinner for ten or twelve, the five or six ladies most often sit in one group, or possibly two sit by themselves, and three or four together;

but at a very large party they inevitably fall into groups of four or five or so. In any case, the hostess must see that no one is left to sit alone. If one of her guests is a stranger to the others, the hostess draws a chair near one of the groups and, offering it to her single guest, sits beside her. After a while, when the stranger has at least joined the outskirts of the conversation of the group, the hostess leaves her and joins another group. Even when there is no one who needs any especial attention, the hostess nevertheless sits for a time with each of the different groups in order to spend at least a part of the evening with all of her guests.

THE GENTLEMEN RETURN

When the gentlemen return to the living room, they naturally go directly to whichever group or person they are most interested in talking to.

Gentlemen should not, of course, continue to talk together after returning to the drawing room, as it is impolite to the ladies, who would be necessarily left without partners.

TAKING LEAVE

It was once so fixed a rule that the guest of honor must be the first to take leave, that everyone used to sit on and on, no matter how late, waiting for him or her to go. More often than not, the guest of honor was an absentminded old lady who was vaguely saying to herself, "Oh, my! are these people *never* going home?" until it dawned upon her that the obligation was her own!

Today, although it is still the obligation of the guest who sat on the host's right to make the move to leave, it is not considered ill-mannered for another lady to rise first if the hour is growing late.

She goes to her hostess and says, "Good night. Thank you so much." The hostess answers, "I am so glad you could come!"

In the dressing room the maid may be waiting to help the ladies with their wraps, or their husbands may help them put them on in the hall. When Mr. and Mrs. Sewell are ready to leave, the butler goes to the door and asks that Mr. Sewell's car be brought up by his chauffeur, if he has one, or by the man who has been hired to act as chauffeur-doorman. In the city, this same man would be responsible for getting taxis for the guests.

SOME ADVICE FOR GUESTS

STARTING A COMPLICATED DISH

When a dinner has been prepared by a chef who prides himself on being a decorative artist, the guest of honor and whoever else may be the first to be served may have quite a problem in knowing what parts of an intricate structure are to be eaten and what parts are scenic effect.

The main portion is generally clear enough; the uncertainty lies elsewhere. Are the flowers edible vegetables, and are the fancy puffs potatoes or trimming? If there is one for each guest, the chances are that they are edible; rings around food are nearly always to be eaten; platforms under food seldom are. Anything that looks like pastry is to be eaten; and anything divided into separate units should be taken on your plate complete. You should not try to cut a section from anything that has already been divided into portions in the kitchen.

REFUSING WINE OR FOOD

If you do not wish wine, it is best—because least conspicuous—to allow a little to be poured into your glass. Unless your host happens to be looking at your glass when the wine is poured, he will not know later on that your almost empty glass was never filled. On the other hand, if he does happen to notice he cannot feel that much wine is wasted. In any case, to turn your wineglass upside down is a needlessly rude way to say "No."

Not so many years ago, when diet fads had not yet come into fashion and the scientific study of balanced rations, vitamins, allergies, and so on was unknown outside the laboratories, it was considered very discourteous to refuse whatever one's host or hostess offered. A well-behaved guest took at least a little of everything passed and ate or drank that little. Today, the increasing use of the word "allergic" has been helpful in developing the acceptance of the phrase "No, thank you." After all, if a guest knows that lobster gives him hives, he would be stupid to eat it even though it *has* just been flown in from Maine.

GLOVES AND NAPKINS

Ladies always wear gloves to formal dinners and take them off at the table—entirely off. It is hideous to leave them on the arm with the hand part turned back. If the lady's bag is too small to hold the gloves, both gloves and bag are laid across the lap, with the napkin, folded once, placed across the lap on top of the gloves and bag. All three are supposed to stay in place on a slippery satin skirt.

It is all very well for etiquette to say "They stay there," but every woman knows they don't! If you obey etiquette and lay the napkin on top of the bag and gloves loosely across your satin-covered knees, it will only be a matter of time until the avalanche starts right, left, or forward onto the floor. There is just *one* way to keep these articles from falling: cover the gloves and bag with the napkin put cornerwise across your knees, and tuck the two side corners under you like a lap robe, with the gloves and bag tied in place, as it were. You either do that or have the gentleman next to you groping under the table at the end of the meal, hardly a fitting concluding ceremony at dinner.

CIGARETTES AT TABLE

At a truly formal dinner cigarettes are passed at the end of the salad course, even in conservative households. But there are numberless women who light their own cigarettes the moment they are seated at the table—and when young Mrs. Nicotinic lights her cigarette before laying her napkin across her knees and greets the man on her right from behind a veil of smoke, everyone else at the table, including the man next to her, feels free to follow her example. To stop this practice a hostess has no choice except to avoid putting ash trays on the table—a clear indication that she would prefer that her guests wait until the cigarettes are passed. Since no guest can know his hostess's wishes until the table is in sight, he should always put out his cigarette before going into the dining room.

TALKING TO DINNER PARTNERS

The "turning of the table" is an outmoded custom designed to make people divide their conversation time more or less evenly between their two dinner companions. The hostess, after the first two courses (or at any time she chose), would turn from the man on her right to the one on her left, and each woman at the table was supposed to notice this and switch at the same time. This was a rather forced means of achieving a change that should happen naturally at a convenient break in the conversation rather than at a signal. It is true that without a signal, if two diners are engrossed in their conversation, the diners on either side may be momentarily left with no one to talk to. A considerate woman will quickly notice this and find a way to end her conversation so that she may talk to her other neighbor. The first man is then free to turn to the lady on his other side.

One unbreakable rule of etiquette is that you must talk to both your neighbors at a dinner table. You must; that is all there is to it!

Even if you are placed next to someone with whom you have had a bitter quarrel, consideration for your hostess and the other guests dictates that you give no outward sign of your dislike and that you make a pretense, at least for a little while, of talking together.

24

Luncheons

The formal luncheon, although less formidable than the formal dinner, differs from it only in details. Therefore, this chapter will be confined to the variations. *For the handling of all other matters, you must read Chapter Twenty-three.*

The most significant difference is that luncheons are generally given by and for women. However, an equal number of men may be included on a Saturday, Sunday, or holiday, and their presence or absence affects certain considerations such as the heartiness of the menu.

THE INVITATIONS

The word "lunch" is used much more often than "luncheon." "Luncheon" is rarely spoken, but it is written in books like this one and sometimes in third-person invitations.

Although invitations may be telephoned, occasionally an engraved card is used for an elaborate luncheon, especially for one given in honor of a noted person. If written, a formal invitation to lunch is nearly always in the form of a personal note, which is rarely mailed more than a week in advance. For instance:

Dear Mrs. Swift (*or Martha*):

Will you come to lunch on Monday the tenth at half past one? I hope so much that you will be able to join us.

Sincerely (*or Affectionately*),
Jane (*Toplofty*)

If Mrs. Toplofty's luncheon were given in honor of somebody, the phrase "to meet Mrs. Lawrence" would be added immediately after the hour. If it is a very large luncheon for which the engraved card is used, "To meet Mrs. Lawrence" is written across the top. *See also Chapter Fifty-two.*

ARRIVAL OF THE GUESTS

The hostess receives in the living room in some place that has an unobstructed approach from the door. After removing her coat, each guest is preceded by the butler or the maid to within a short distance of the hostess, where he (or she) announces the new arrival's name and then stands aside. Or the guests may greet the hostess unannounced. The hostess takes a step forward, shakes hands, and says, "I'm glad to see you," or "I'm so glad you could come." She waits for a second or two to see whether the guest who has just come in speaks to anyone; if not, she makes the necessary introductions.

When all the guests have arrived and have had time to enjoy a cocktail if it is offered, the butler or maid notifies the kitchen, goes back to the living room, and approaches the hostess and bows slightly. If it is necessary to attract the hostess's attention, he or she says quietly, "Luncheon is served."

If there is a guest of honor, the hostess leads the way to the dining room, walking beside her. Otherwise, the guests go in in any way they wish, except that the very young make way for their elders. Gentlemen stroll in with the people they happen to be talking to. If alone, they bring up the rear. Gentlemen never offer their arms to ladies in going in to lunch—unless there should be an elderly guest of honor, who might be taken in by the host, as at a dinner. Even then the others follow informally.

COCKTAILS

Cocktails may or may not be served before lunch. If they are, they differ a little from those offered before dinner. Although a martini can be offered, sherry, Dubonnet, "Bloody Marys," or daiquiris are more usual. As always, there must be tomato juice or plain fruit juice available for those who wish it.

THE TABLE

Candles are not needed on a lunch table, but are sometimes used as ornaments. They should never be lit in the daytime. The plain white tablecloth that is correct for dinner is not used for luncheon, although colored damask is acceptable. Traditionally the lunch table is set with place mats made in any variety of linen, needlework, or lace. A runner, matching the mats but two or three times as long, may be used in the center of the table.

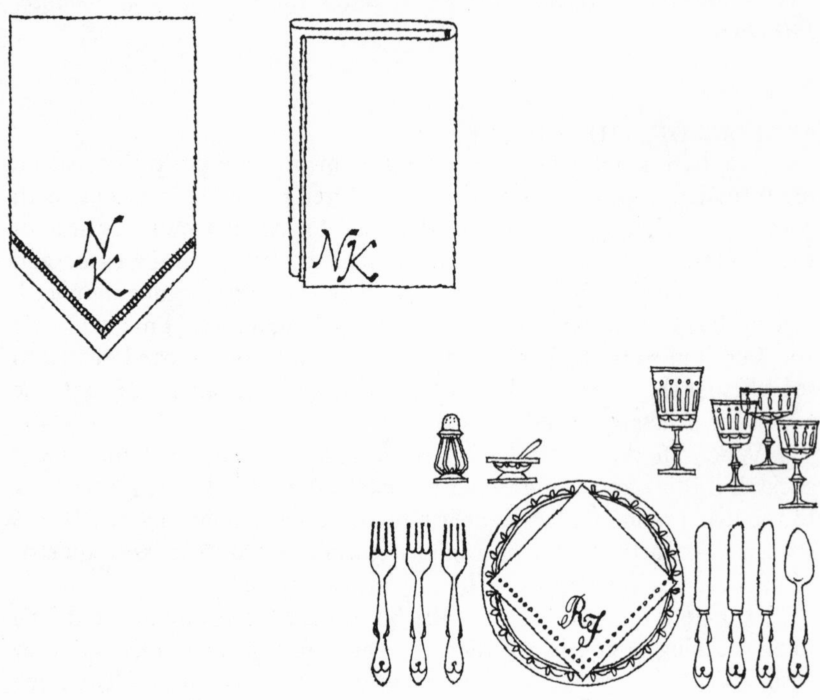

The decorations are practically the same as for dinner: flowers or an ornament in the center, and two or four dishes of fruit or candy where they look best. If the table is very large and rather too bare without candles, four small vases with flowers matching those in the centerpiece —or any other glass or silver ornaments—may be added.

The places are set as for dinner, with a place plate, a fork, a knife, or a spoon for each course. The lunch napkin, which should match the table linen, is much smaller than the dinner napkin and is not folded in the same manner. Generally it is folded like a handkerchief, in a square of four thicknesses. The square is laid on the plate diagonally, with the monogrammed (or embroidered) corner pointing down toward the near

edge of the table. The upper corner is then turned sharply under in a flat crease for about a quarter of its diagonal length; then the two sides are rolled loosely under, with a straight top edge and a pointed lower edge and the monogram displayed in the center. Or it can be folded in any simple way one prefers.

If it is a large luncheon, place cards are used just as they are at dinner.

THE BREAD-AND-BUTTER PLATE

The bread-and-butter plate is always part of the luncheon service. It is put at the left side of each place just above the forks. The butter knife is placed on the plate diagonally from the upper left to lower right, with the knife edge toward the table edge.

Hot breads are an important feature of every lunch—hot crescents, baking-powder biscuits, bread biscuits, dinner rolls, or corn bread. They are passed as often as necessary. Butter is usually put on the plate beforehand, and it is passed again, whenever necessary, until the table is cleared for dessert. Preferably it should be served as butterballs, or curls, rather than in squares.

Bread-and-butter plates are always removed immediately before dessert, with the saltcellars and pepper pots.

GLASSES

A goblet for water is at each place, and a wineglass if wine is to be served. If the hostess chooses to serve iced tea or a similar beverage in the summer, a highball glass on a coaster replaces the wineglass.

THE SERVICE

If the luncheon is to be formal, the hostess must have help, whether her own servants or temporary ones. Lunch, as opposed to dinner, may be served by one or two waitresses instead of by men alone.

The formal service is identical with that of dinner. Carving is done in the kitchen and, except for the ornamental dishes of fruit, candy, and nuts, no food is set on the table. The plate service is also the same as at dinner. The places are never left without plates, except after the salad course when the table is cleared and crumbed for dessert. The dessert plates and finger bowls are arranged as for dinner.

THE MENU

Five courses at most (not counting the ornamental sweets or coffee as a course) and more usually four are sufficient for the longest and the most elaborate luncheon possible. They include:

1. fruit, or soup in cups
2. eggs or shellfish
3. fowl or meat (not a roast)
4. salad
5. dessert

The menu for lunch eaten in a private house never consists of more than four courses. Any one of the courses just given may be omitted except for the fowl or meat.

Melon, grapefruit, or fruit cup, with or without a liqueur poured over it, is a popular first course. It may be served in special bowl-shaped glasses that fit into long-stemmed and much larger ones with a space for crushed ice between, or it can just as well be served in champagne glasses, after being kept as cold as possible in the refrigerator.

Soup at a luncheon is never served in soup plates, but in two-handled cups. It is eaten with a teaspoon or a bouillon spoon, or after it has cooled sufficiently the cup may be picked up and lifted to the mouth with both hands. It is almost always a clear soup: in the winter a bouillon, turtle soup, or consommé, and in the summer a chilled soup like jellied consommé, madrilene, or vichyssoise.

There are innumerable lunch-party egg and fish dishes. A second course that is substantial and rich, such as eggs Benedict or crab meat *au gratin,* should be balanced by a simple meat, such as broiled chicken served with a salad, combining meat and salad courses in one. On the other hand, if you serve eggs in aspic, or small portions of filet of sole *meunière*, you could have meat and vegetables, as well as salad and dessert. If you serve both fruit and soup, omit eggs, especially if there is to be an aspic with salad.

BEVERAGES

In the winter a wine is usually served with lunch. Sherry may also be served with soup, or a liqueur after dessert, but one wine is sufficient, and it should be a light wine such as a dry Rhine wine or a claret.

A chilled white wine may also be served in the summer, but iced tea or iced coffee are the usual choices. Iced tea at lunch is prepared with lemon and sugar and sometimes with cut-up fresh fruit or a little squeezed fruit juice. It is poured into the glasses and decorated with sprigs of fresh mint. Coffee should be passed around in a pitcher on a tray that also holds a bowl of granulated sugar and a pitcher of cream. The guests pour their own coffee into tall glasses that are half full of ice and accompanied by long-handled spoons.

After lunch the men, rather than having coffee in the library or at the table, accompany the ladies and have coffee with them in the living room.

25

Formal afternoon entertaining

Afternoon parties range from the very dignified reception, through the more or less formal tea dance, to a tea.

RECEPTIONS

The reception today is primarily a state affair, a public or semipublic gathering in honor of a prominent person or an important event. Receptions most frequently take place on the diplomatic or civic levels and are handled, like official dinners, by a household staff or a caterer.

The major difference between a reception at which tea is served and a "tea party" is one of atmosphere. A reception takes itself seriously. A tea, no matter how formal it pretends to be, should be friendly and inviting.

Receptions are rarely given for women only, and therefore the liquid refreshments served are generally different from those served at a tea. The food may be quite similar—sandwiches, cakes, etc.—but when men are present, coffee or punch or cold drinks, including cocktails and highballs, are served.

TEA DANCES

An afternoon tea dance occasionally takes the place of a debutante ball. It may also be given to honor a birthday or anniversary, or to celebrate a holiday.

Invitations are usually written on the hostess's visiting card or on the inside of a fold-over card or informal. They may also be telephoned.

Since houses with rooms large enough for dancing are comparatively few, a tea dance is usually given at a club or in a small ballroom of a hotel. Remember that it is a mistake to choose too large a room, for too much space for too few people gives an effect of emptiness that throws a pall on the party. Also remember that an undecorated public room needs more people than a room in a private house to make it look filled. Although a crush may be unpleasant, it does give the effect of success. Nothing is more dismal than a half-empty room with scattered guests.

The arrangements for a tea with dancing are much the same as for an evening dance. A screen of greens behind the musicians and flowers on the tables form the typical decorations.

Whether in a hotel, club, or private house, the curtains are drawn and the lights lighted as though for a dance in the evening.

Tea, coffee, tea sandwiches, and cakes are served. In addition there is usually a table nearby with pitchers or bowls of fruit juice or punch, and a bar for those who wish stronger drinks.

Guests go to the table and are served coffee or tea. They help themselves to the sandwiches or cakes, which they eat standing at the table or nearby while chatting with friends.

FORMAL TEAS

Afternoon teas are given in honor of visiting celebrities, new neighbors, to "warm" a new house, for a houseguest or, as is often the case, for no reason other than that the hostess wants to entertain her friends.

INVITATIONS

The invitation is a visiting card of the hostess with "Jan. 10, Tea at 4 o'clock" in the lower corner, opposite the address. Or it may also be telephoned. If you have no visiting cards a fold-over or informal card will do just as well.

THE TEA TABLE

At a gathering of this sort, the tea and the coffee (or hot chocolate) are sometimes passed on trays, but more often the hostess prefers to have them poured at a table. Many choose their dining-room table as the simplest and most comfortable place from which to serve. However, the tea table may be set up in any room that has adequate space and easy access and exit. The guests should be able to circulate freely without becoming trapped in a corner after they have been served.

Except on a glass-topped table a cloth must always be used. It may barely cover the table, or it may hang half a yard over the edges. A tea cloth may be colored, but the conventional one is of white linen, with needlework, lace, or appliquéd designs.

A large tray is set at either end of the table, one for the tea, and one for the coffee.

One tray is used to bring in all the equipment necessary for the proper serving of tea: a kettle with boiling water—with a flame under it—an empty teapot, a caddy of tea or tea bags, cream pitcher, sugar bowl, and thin slices of lemon on a dish.

The coffee tray is simpler. The coffee is in a large urn or pot—with a flame under it. A pitcher of cream and a bowl of sugar complete the tray. If chocolate is served instead of coffee, there is nothing needed other than the pot of steaming chocolate.

If the trays are carried by a maid, the flames under the pots are not lighted before the trays are set down in order to avoid setting her uniform on fire.

The cups and saucers are placed within easy reach of the ladies who are pouring, usually at the left of the tray, because they are held in the left hand while the tea (or coffee) is poured with the right. On either side of the table are stacks of little tea plates, with small napkins matching the tea cloth folded on each one. Arranged behind these, or in any way that is pretty and uncluttered, are the plates of food and whatever silver is necessary. Forks should be on the table if cake with soft icing is served. If the table is not large enough to hold all the plates, some may be placed on a sideboard or a small table in a convenient location.

SERVANTS NOT NECESSARY

Because nothing needs to be passed to the guests, it is perfectly possible for a hostess to give a formal tea without the help of servants. If she has no maid she sets out the tray with everything except the boiling water before her guests arrive, leaving the kettle on the stove in the kitchen. She greets the guests at the door, telling them where to leave their coats, and when she is ready for tea, she fills the tea-tray kettle from the kitchen kettle and carries it in to the tea table.

MAKING GOOD TEA

The most important part of the tea service is boiling water and plenty of it.

To make good tea, first, half fill the pot with boiling water, let it stand a moment or two to heat the teapot, and then pour it out. Put in a rounded teaspoonful of tea leaves or one tea bag for each person. Half this amount may be used if the tea is of superb quality. Then pour on enough *actually boiling* water to cover the tea leaves about half an inch. It should steep at least five minutes (or for those who like it very strong, ten) before additional boiling water is poured on. Now pour half tea, half boiling water for those who like it "weak." Increase the amount of tea for those who like it strong. The cup of *good* tea should be too strong without the addition of a little lively boiling water, which gives it freshness.

When tea has to stand a long time for many guests, the ideal way is to make a strong infusion in a big kettle on the kitchen stove. Let the tea actually boil three to four minutes on the range; then pour it through a sieve or filter into your hot teapot. The tea will not become bitter, and it does no matter if it gets quite cold. The boiling water poured over no more than the tablespoonful of such tea will make the drink hot enough.

DRINKS SERVED AT TEA

At a tea to which men have been invited, the hostess (or maid) often asks a guest who has refused a cup of tea if he or she would like anything else, a whiskey and soda, or a cocktail. If there is a maid she will serve the drink after it has been made in the pantry. If the hostess has no help, she may ask the guest to mix his own drink from a bar that has been set up in an inconspicuous place in a room separate from the tea table.

THE LADIES WHO POUR

The pouring is usually done by intimate friends of the hostess. These ladies are invited beforehand and are chosen because they can be counted on for their good manners and friendliness to everyone in all circumstances. Sometimes after an hour, the first two are relieved by two other friends of the hostess.

It does not matter that a guest going into the dining room does not know the deputy hostesses who are pouring. It is perfectly correct for a stranger to say, "May I have a cup of tea?"

The one pouring should smile and answer, "Certainly! How do you like it? Strong or weak? Would you like cream or lemon?"

If the visitor says, "Weak," *boiling* water is added and, according to the guest's wishes, sugar, cream, or lemon. (Good tea calls for milk, though it always seems to be called cream!) If the guest prefers coffee, she asks for it at the other end of the table. If the hostess is unoccupied and her momentary guest is alone, she makes a few pleasant remarks; but if there are a number of people around the table, she need only smile as she hands each guest her cup.

26

Balls and dances

There are two fundamental differences between balls and dances. First, while guests at a dance are of approximately one age, those at a ball are personal friends of the hostess, of any age. Second, since fewer people are asked to a dance, the decorations and refreshments may be simpler.

Although great private balls have become almost unheard of in recent years, this book would be incomplete if a description of them was omitted. Besides, the charity and debutante balls which have replaced private ones all over the country are similar to them in terms of customs, rules, and procedures. *For more details on debutante assemblies, see Chapter Forty.*

HOW AND WHERE TO START

The hostess who gives a private ball must, of course, assume the final responsibility for every aspect of the evening, but fortunately she may enlist the aid of many and various people. The club or hotel where it is to be held will provide the servants, the food, and the drinks; or if the ball is held at home, a caterer will provide the same services. A florist will see to the decorations, and there are social secretaries available who can help her with the lists and invitations. But no matter how much help she is able to amass, the hostess giving a private ball must make the final decisions on all the details that are so important to the success of the party.

A public ball is run by a committee, whose chairman is in some ways comparable to the hostess, but without the full burden of responsibility. Special duties are allotted to each member of the committee: one takes charge of invitations, one of decorations; others are appointed to be responsible for the orchestra, the food, the ticket money, etc. In the following paragraphs, wherever the word "hostess" is used, you may substitute "committee member" if the ball is other than a private one.

The first thing the hostess must do is to make an appointment to see the manager of the hotel, club, or any other suitable assembly room and find out which evenings are free. It is important to select an evening not already taken by another hostess or organization in order not to conflict on lists or, in a small town, on the services of caterers, florists, etc.

She then telephones and engages the best orchestra she can for the chosen evening. If it can possibly be arranged, there should be two orchestras so that the moment one finishes playing, the other begins. You cannot give a ball or a dance that is anything but dull if you have poor music.

Having hired the bands and engaged the ballroom and rooms where guests can talk and relax, the hostess next makes out her list and orders the invitations. They are sent out three to four weeks prior to the ball. Invitations to balls, private or public, are always formal. There are, however, many variations in good taste. *For these forms, and also for less formal invitations appropriate to the smaller dance, see Chapter Fifty-two.*

ASKING FOR AN INVITATION

You may always ask a hostess if you may bring a man who is a stranger to her; extra men are always in demand—the more the better. But it is rather difficult to ask for an invitation for an extra girl, no matter how pretty she is, unless the person asking for the invitation is willing to look after her. In that case, the hostess should be delighted to invite her. Invitations are never asked for persons whom the hostess already knows. This is a definitely established rule of etiquette, because if she knows them, she will send them invitations if she cares to. It is not at all out of the way, however, for an intimate friend to remind her of someone who may have been omitted by mistake.

The one who has arranged for the invitation for the stranger should accompany him to the ball and introduce him to his hostess. "Mrs. Norman, I would like you to meet John Franklin, my roommate," and John should promptly thank her for extending him an invitation.

A BALL IN A PRIVATE HOUSE

When a ball is held at home, there is always an awning and a red carpet down the front steps or walk of the house. A chauffeur at the curb opens the car doors, and there are men hired to park the cars. To protect the hostess and her guests from crashers you are expected to hand in your invitation—or admission card, if you have been sent one—to whoever is receiving them at the door.

All the necessities such as awning, red carpet, coat racks, and ballroom chairs, as well as crockery, glass, napkins, food, and the waiters can be supplied by hotels or caterers.

The room selected to serve as a ballroom should be emptied of furniture. Informal groupings of chairs in a hall or in the library is a far better arrangement than the stiff row or the wallflower exhibit suggested by the alignment of straight chairs around the dance floor. The floor itself, it goes without saying, must be smooth and waxed.

DECORATIONS

Decorations for a ball or dance may be as simple or elaborate as the pocketbook and the taste of the hostess or committee allow. When the ball is held during a holiday season—Christmas, for example—the decorations generally are in keeping with that time of the year. Christmas ornaments, a beautifully decorated tree in one corner, red, gold, or green ribbons, and so one would provide the central theme of a "Mistletoe Ball." Or the hostess might choose a type of decoration that goes particularly well in her house, perhaps Japanese lanterns and oriental flower arrangements. In any case, whether at home or in a public ballroom, some greens behind the orchestra, some flowers on the tables and wherever else they are most effective are all that are necessary for even the most elaborate ball.

THE GUESTS ARRIVE

The hostess must be ready to receive on the stroke of the hour specified in her invitations. If the ballroom opens on a hall or reception room at the head of a stairway, she usually receives there. Otherwise she receives in the ballroom near the entrance.

Guests are announced at private balls as they arrive, and after shaking hands with the hostess, they pass into the ballroom. (This formality is not usually observed at the public ball.)

THE PERFECT HOST AND HOSTESS

The duty of seeing that guests are looked after, that strangers are presented to partners, that shy girls are not left at the wallflower outposts, and that the older and honored guests are taken in to supper falls to the perfect host. But the hostess must also try to see that the guests are enjoying themselves.

THE PERFECT GUEST

Guests have responsibilities too. Once they have accepted an invitation, they must try to be pleasant and act as if they are having a good time, no matter how dull the party may be.

DUTY DANCES

Every young man must dance at least once with the hostess, the girl or girls the dance is given for, the hostess of the dinner he went to before the dance, and both girls he sat beside at dinner. At a dance to which he has brought a girl, he must of course dance the first dance with her. He must also watch during the evening to be sure that she is not stuck too long with any one partner, and he must take her home after the dance.

THE HELPFUL USHERS

The hostess who wants to insure the success of her dance chooses a number of young men who are tactful and self-possessed to act as ushers. They are identified by white or other distinguishing boutonnieres as deputy hosts. They must see that the wallflowers remain chair-bound as little as possible, and they must also try to relieve any young man who has been "stuck" for any length of time.

An usher has the right to introduce any man to any girl without knowing either one of them personally and without asking permission. He may also ask a girl (if he has a moment to himself) to dance with him, whether he has ever met her or not. He should also release every stag he calls upon by substituting another, and the second by a third, and so on. In order to make a ball "go," the ushers must sometimes spend the entire evening in relief work.

If they fulfill all their obligations, they have little chance to spend time with the girls of their choice, so the appointment—which cannot be refused—is a doubtful pleasure.

At a ball where there are ushers, a girl standing or sitting alone should at once be rescued by one of them, and a rotation of partners presented to her. If she is a hopeless dancer even the ushers are helpless! Even a lovely girl who is a stranger can spend a miserable evening when none of her friends happens to be present and when there are no ushers. Ushers can indeed be useful, and their greatest advantage is that their presence gives courage to many a young man because, knowing he will be rescued, he is willing to dance with a girl he would otherwise avoid.

DANCE PROGRAMS

The program or dance card had some undeniable advantages. A girl could give as many dances as she chose to whomever she chose, and a man could be sure of having as many uninterrupted dances as he wished with the one he most wanted to be with. But the dance card is unheard of today, probably because the young people do not care to be scheduled. They like to dance when the impulse moves them; they also like to be able to stay or to leave as they please. There may be two or three dances given on the same evening, and they like to drift from one to the other just as they like to drift from one partner to another—or not dance at all if they do not want to.

THE MANNERS OF THE GUESTS

ASKING FOR A DANCE

When a man is introduced to a girl, he says, "Would you like to dance?" She replies, "Certainly," or "Yes, I'd like to very much." At the end of the dance, whether it has lasted one minute or twenty, the man thanks the girl, and she may return the compliment if she wishes.

REFUSING TO DANCE

If a girl is sitting in another room or on the stairs with one man, a second man should not interrupt or ask her to dance. But if she is sitting in a group he can go up and ask, "Would you like to dance?" She either smiles and says, "Yes," or "Not just now." If she likes him, she may add to her refusal, "Come and sit with us!"

To refuse to dance with one man and then immediately dance with another is an insult to the first one—excusable only if he was intoxicated or otherwise offensive. In ordinary circumstances, if a girl is dancing she must dance with everyone who asks her; if she is not dancing, she must not make exceptions.

A girl who is dancing may not refuse to change partners when another cuts in. This is the worst phase of the cutting-in custom; those who particularly want to dance together are often unable to take a dozen steps before being interrupted. Possibly the current custom of dancing only with one's date the entire evening is a reaction against the old idea that to be popular, a girl must be constantly cut in on.

CUTTING IN

When one of the stags sees a girl with whom he wants to dance, he steps forward and taps the shoulder of her partner, who relinquishes his place in favor of the newcomer. The couple then dances until a third man cuts in.

When cutting in, the following rules must be observed:

1. The partner who was first dancing with a girl must not cut back on the man who took her from him. He can cut in on a third man if he wants to.

2. A man must not continue to cut in on the same man when the latter dances with other partners.

SUPPER IS SERVED

A sit-down supper may be served by the caterer at a very elaborate ball, but a buffet supper that begins at one o'clock and continues for an hour or more is pleasanter and easier to manage. People may serve themselves whenever they feel like it, and small tables are set up so that the guests may sit down to eat. They may sit where they please, with either a group making up a table or a man and his partner taking any two vacant chairs. A girl is always taken in to supper by the young man who is her escort. If there is an unescorted girl at the party, the ushers (or the host, if there are no ushers) should see that one of the stags takes her to supper or that she is included in a group.

Suppers are no longer as elaborate as they used to be. Although hot dishes are still served at some balls, many times the supper consists of a variety of sandwiches, platters of cold meats, and accompanying dishes. There may be hot drinks such as coffee, chocolate, or bouillon, or bowls of iced fruit punch. And if it is in accordance with the customs of your community and your own taste, and if the guests are of legal drinking age, nothing is more festive than serving champagne at a ball.

Part SIX

INFORMAL ENTERTAINING

27

Cocktail parties

In many parts of the country cocktail parties have become the most common form of entertaining, and they can be the answer to a busy housewife's prayer. Along with open houses, barbecues, and picnics they provide a relatively simple answer to the rule that all invitations must be repaid. Their advantages over a dinner party are many in a society in which relatively few households have servants, and in which the cost of hiring temporary help or a caterer is beyond the reach of many. Cocktail parties require little preparation, they are less expensive than a dinner party, they are limited as to time, and you can entertain many more people at once in a small house. On the other hand, no one invited to a cocktail party feels as honored as if he had been invited to dinner, and at a large party the host and hostess cannot spend as much time with any one guest as they would if they were seated at a dinner table. Cocktail parties do provide an excellent opportunity for entertaining new acquaintances, particularly if you also wish to include the people at whose house you met your new friends. (This, however, is in no way required at either cocktail parties or other forms of entertainment.)

"PAY-BACK" PARTIES

One of the least attractive customs that has arisen in recent years is that of giving large "pay-back" cocktail parties. A hostess who has been invited to many parties herself and thinks she has not the time or the energy to give a number of small parties creates one large horror by inviting everyone to whom she is indebted at once. The guests are not chosen for compatibility, there are not enough places to sit down, the crowd is likely to be such that no one can move freely from group to group (or table, or bar), and the noise level reaches such a pitch that it becomes intolerable. If you are a popular guest and incur social obligations with any frequency, make the effort to give small parties from time to time and avoid the necessity of a yearly "pay-back."

COCKTAILS BEFORE A DANCE

A pleasant form of entertaining is to have a group of friends for cocktails before a dinner dance or any other function that they would enjoy attending. Invitations are sent out on visiting cards, notepaper, or any printed cocktail-party invitation card, but they must state "Cocktails before the dance at the Happy Course Golf Club, 6:00 to 8:00," as well as the place and date. It is also necessary to add "R.S.V.P.," because the hostess usually makes the reservations for those of her guests who wish to go on to the other event.

A practical method is to extend the invitations by telephone, since the hostess knows immediately how many will be joining her at the club or dance and can make the reservations sooner. An invitation to this type of party should not be accepted if you do not intend to go on to the later party, unless a hostess specifically says, "Please join us first even though you can't come to the club afterwards." It is not up to you to make this suggestion, however, because if her group is small, your dropping out early in the evening could well spoil her plans.

When you are the guest, you must pay the cost of admission, dinner, drinks, and anything else at the later party unless your hostess specifically says or writes that she expects you *as her guest*. If you are not a member of the club involved, you must find out in advance whether you may sign as a member of another club or pay in cash. If neither is permitted, then you must ask your host if you may sign his name and add your initials to enable you to pay him your share when he receives his bill.

COCKTAIL BUFFETS

A cross between a cocktail party and a buffet dinner party, the cocktail buffet is the choice of many hostesses for entertaining all except the smallest and most informal groups. Because there is usually enough food presented so that the guests need not have dinner afterward and therefore are expected to linger longer, the invitation frequently states only the hour of arrival. In many sections of the country this is likely to be a little later than a simple cocktail party, often at six thirty or seven. It should be made very clear that the gathering is a "cocktail buffet" so that the guests realize that they will be served some substantial food and need not make other plans for dinner.

The menu may vary from simple to very elaborate, but even the simplest must provide more than just hors d'oeuvres. The least that one can expect is a platter of cold meat, ham, chicken, or roast beef, slices of buttered breads, accompanying dishes such as sliced carrots, celery, olives, raw cauliflower, and possibly some sandwiches. This minimum type of buffet may be eaten standing near the table without a plate. The meat can be placed on a slice of bread and eaten like a sandwich, and the raw vegetables picked up and dipped in a sauce if one is served. Often a smoked ham or turkey is placed whole on the table, and when the platters of meat are running low, the host, or any of the guests, may carve additional slices as they are required.

The table should be covered with a tablecloth, and napkins must be available. If there is room, a centerpiece of flowers or fruit is attractive, but it is better to leave it off and use a decorated cake (or even one of the main dishes) in the center rather than crowd the table.

For a more elaborate buffet you will probably include one or more hot dishes, generally casseroles that can be kept warm on an electric hot plate or served in a chafing dish over a flame. In this case, of course, there must be stacks of plates and rows of forks. If the main table becomes too crowded, the hot dishes and plates may be put on the sideboard or on a side table.

If you do not wish to go into the added complication of plates and silver, you may choose a hot dish such as bite-sized meat balls or frankfurters, tiny hot potatoes dipped in salt, and hot bread or rolls with a cheese fondue, all of which may be speared with a toothpick.

JUST COCKTAILS

Many cocktail parties, of course, involve neither a buffet nor a dance afterward. They may be as large or small, as simple or elaborate as you wish.

The ways of inviting people to such a party are as varied as the parties themselves. If the number of guests is small, the invitation is almost always by telephone. For a larger party they may be written on your own informal, on notepaper, or on a visiting card. (*See Chapter Fifty-three for the correct forms.*) Or you may buy attractively printed cards.

When there is to be no buffet, the time is usually stated "Cocktails

from 5:00 to 7:00" rather than "Cocktails *at* 5:00." While "R.S.V.P." is often omitted, thoughtful guests let the hostess know whether they are planning to attend the party. If there is an R.S.V.P., the telephone number is usually written beside it, as this type of invitation may always be answered by telephone.

At a cocktail party, you may serve literally every sort of hors d'ouevre or appetizer that you think tastes good and looks tempting—as long as it can be eaten with the fingers. Olives (either chilled or wrapped in bacon and broiled) or very thin broiled sausages; thin bread rolled around cheese or bacon, skewered and toasted; crackers spread with sandwich paste; crabmeat or lobster in small pieces, or shrimps on wooden picks with which to dip them in colorful sauces—are all favorites. Don't forget a pile of cocktail napkins—cloth or paper—on the tray. Most hors d'oeuvres are a little greasy, and also, since plates are not used, the napkin may be used to hold an appetizer which is, for the moment, too hot to eat.

WHAT DRINKS TO SERVE?

The most important thing about "what to serve"—whatever you decide on—is to have enough. As a general rule a host should count on each guest having two to three drinks.

In the winter, martinis, whiskey "on the rocks," and whiskey in a tall glass with water or soda are the most popular drinks. In warm weather cocktails mixed with fruit juice and gin or rum or tall drinks made from these same ingredients are more often served. But there is an infinite number of other drinks that are offered in different localities, and the host may choose according to his own taste or that of his guests.

Unless you know for certain that your guests all drink alcoholic beverages you must have nonalcoholic drinks available. Tomato or other fruit juices, colas, and ginger ale are all popular substitutes. To avoid remarks that may be annoying, a "nondrinker" may choose ginger ale, which looks exactly like a whiskey and soda.

Never urge a guest to have a drink—or *another* drink—if he has once refused. If as a guest you are pressed further, simply say firmly, "No—really, I can't," or "No thanks—honestly."

BARTENDERS AND WAITERS

If you are planning a cocktail party for more than eighteen or twenty people, and if you have no maid in your home, it is wise to consider hiring a bartender for the evening. If it is a really large party, the services of a waiter or waitress as well will make the evening much pleasanter for the hostess. She may prepare the hors d'oeuvres herself in advance, even days ahead if she has a freezer, or she may hire a waitress or caterer who will both prepare and serve the food.

The bartender attends to the drinks in any one of various ways, or he may combine several means of serving. He generally stands behind a large table loaded with ice, bottles of each kind of liquor and soft drink to be served, and every sort of cocktail glass. The guests go to the bar themselves and request the kind of drink they wish. A man usually asks the woman with him what she would like, and she waits at a little distance from the bar while he gives the order to the bartender and brings her the drink. If a group of women are talking together, it is perfectly correct for one of them who wishes another drink to go and ask the bartender to mix it for her, rather than to interrupt a conversation that her husband or escort might be having.

Another method of serving is for the bartender to pass a tray of drinks, already mixed, to each guest as he arrives. He may continue to do this, but it involves using an enormous number of glasses, because a fresh one must be passed each time. Therefore, after the first serving it is more practical for him to watch carefully for empty glasses and, when he sees one, approach the guest and say, "May I bring you another drink?" The guest replies, "Thank you, I'm drinking bourbon and soda," and hands him the glass to be refilled.

If your party is large enough to warrant having two men to serve drinks, one acts as a waiter. He may ask each new arrival for his order, go to the bar where the second man (as bartender) mixes the drink, and return with it to the guest. This method is too slow for one man alone, however, especially when a large group of people arrive at the same time.

One important note to remember: Be sure that you instruct the bartender in advance exactly how you like your drinks mixed, and insist that he use a measure. If you let him measure "by eye," you may find that your liquor supply is about to run out long before you had planned. Or you may have some unexpectedly boisterous guests on your hands!

WIDOWS, DIVORCÉES, AND BACHELOR GIRLS

When a woman who lives alone gives a cocktail party, she should, if she possibly can, hire a man to bartend for her. If the party is too small or too informal to warrant that expense, she may ask one of her male guests to take over the duty. If she has invited a single man as her "date," he would be the logical choice; if all the guests are married couples, she should ask a relative or one of her closest friends.

HINTS FOR HOSTS AND GUESTS

At a small party the hostess may present a newcomer to all the guests, but at a large one she leaves a stranger on his own after introducing him to two or three people. Her roof serves as an introduction, and unless he appears to be completely lost she may assume that he will talk to whomever he wishes, either asking the people he has already met to introduce him to someone else or introducing himself.

There is no need to shake hands. A girl has trouble enough managing handbag, hors d'oeuvres, cigarette, and cocktail—and hands that have been holding a drink are cold and clammy in any case.

Women remove their gloves so that they will not become grease-stained from the hors d'oeuvres or wet from the moisture that condenses on the glass.

SELF-HELP

When there is no extra help for the evening, the host is the bartender and the hostess is the waitress. She passes the trays of hors d'oeuvres once or twice, often with a close friend helping her. The food is then left in a conspicuous spot (on a hot plate or in a chafing dish if the hors d'oeuvres are hot), and the guests help themselves. She must watch carefully and remove trays or dishes even before they are empty. There is nothing more unappetizing than one remaining cold, limp shrimp, or a mayonnaise-smeared platter.

The host-bartender asks each guest as he arrives what he would like to drink. If the choice is limited, he may say, "Will you have a martini or bourbon?" rather than "What would you like?" This saves them both from the embarrassment of having the guest request a drink that is not to be had. Also, he may ask the men to refill their own glasses, as well as those of any women who wish another drink. He will have much more time to mix with the group and perform his other duties as host if he does not have to spend the entire evening at the bar.

If there are only a few guests, the host may hang their coats in a hall closet. If there are more wraps than a closet can conveniently hold, the men and women are asked to put them in separate bedrooms (or in the same bedroom if the house or apartment is small) neatly on the beds. This scheme is far better than having them piled on chairs or banisters in the entry, and furthermore the ladies have an opportunity to comb their hair and freshen up before they appear in the living room.

Either the host or the hostess should stay within sight of the door to greet arriving guests, but they should try to avoid both being out of the room where the party is held at the same time.

OVERSTAYING YOUR WELCOME

Cocktail parties rarely begin—or end—at the hours stated on the invitation. Although the hosts must be ready on time, the guests may—and do—arrive as much as an hour after the start of the party. However, a late arrival should not mean a late departure. Every experienced hostess knows that she must expect some of her guests to linger a half hour or so beyond the indicated time, but that is as much as she should be expected to endure. She may even take steps to hurry the last survivors out. The best way to get guests to leave is simply to remove the liquor and close the bar. Once the guests finish the drinks in their hands and find no more being served, the party will soon be over.

28

Informal dining

The degree of informality of a party depends entirely on the circumstances and taste of the host or hostess. The hostess who belongs to the great majority of women who entertain with no help at all, or with only a maid hired for the evening, should nevertheless consult the chapter on formal dinners. Many of the suggestions made there will be useful as she plans and prepares for a less formal occasion. For example, the consideration given to her guest list can be no less careful than that given by the hostess whose help includes a butler and two footmen. The rules for the informal dinner are derived from the rules for the formal dinner, and a knowledge of both will facilitate every step of the proceedings.

SIT-DOWN OR BUFFET?

Having decided to give a dinner party and knowing that it will not be a formal one, you have an immediate decision to make: Will it be a sit-down dinner or a buffet?

The first consideration is the size of your party. Eight is the maximum number that can be served comfortably at a sit-down dinner without help. Should it be possible to seat more than eight at your table, or if you plan to set up several small tables, you might choose a semibuffet, with the guests serving themselves from a sideboard but sitting down together at the table or tables. Otherwise, you must move on to the next chapter and plan a buffet dinner. In this chapter it is assumed that your guest list, your table, and your preference make it possible for you to give a sit-down dinner.

PREPARATION AND PLANNING

The careful planning and preparation of the meal are essential to the success of your dinner. If you wish to enjoy the company of your guests, you must choose dishes that can be prepared in advance and served with a minimum of last-minute fuss. You need not worry about fancy hors d'oeuvres—salted nuts or "niblets" available in packages are preferable to elaborate spreads if you don't wish to ruin your guests' appetites for dinner.

Because the normal routine of housework must continue along with the added work of preparing for your party, try to spread it out over several days. Cigarette boxes may be filled, flowers arranged (being sure to choose those that will last several days), silver polished, and even your table set in advance. Of course, your husband must agree to eat in the kitchen, and the children must be asked to play in other parts of the house, but any chores that can be attended to ahead make the day of the party much more enjoyable. If you have a freezer, by all means prepare in advance whatever dishes can be frozen.

THE INVITATIONS

Invitations may be written on visiting cards or notepaper, but they are usually telephoned. They are extended between ten days and two weeks ahead of time, and the person invited must answer promptly either by mail or by telephone. *See also Chapter Fifty-three, "Informal Invitations," for other details.*

SEATING YOUR GUESTS

Seating arrangements at an informal dinner follow much the same pattern as at a formal one, but they are more flexible. In spite of this flexibility, the seating of the guests should be considered when the list is drawn up, for the congeniality of dinner partners can make or break a party. In a group of six or ten the host sits at one end of the table opposite the hostess, who generally chooses the location nearest the kitchen for greater convenience if she must go back and forth herself. If there are eight or twelve at the table, she must move one seat to the left, putting the male guest of honor on her right opposite her husband. The lady who is guest of honor of course sits on the host's right. When there may be no particular guest of honor among a group of friends dining together, the hostess might choose the oldest lady present or one who has not visited her house for some time. Otherwise, she may seat her guests according to whatever arrangement she thinks they will enjoy the most, alternating the men and women and separating husbands and wives. If there is an uneven number of men and women, she must space them as evenly as possible. She may keep her place at the end of the table unless doing so puts too many women in a row. She still seats the honored guests at her and her husband's right.

SOME MENU SUGGESTIONS

Menus for an informal dinner are not limited by rules or conventions, but there are certain practical aspects to consider. Try to avoid dishes that require many extra condiments or sauces. Because you probably wish to eliminate extra plates or silver if you are to clean up alone, restrict your courses to two or three. If you decide on only two, a main course and a dessert, you may serve more substantial hors d'oeuvres beforehand. To make the serving of dinner less complicated some hostesses serve soup or a fish course, such as cold salmon or shrimp, in the living room. If this is done, the host may help his wife by removing the empty plates and ash trays quickly while she is seating the guests in the dining room. Or else the hostess must excuse herself while the guests are finishing their dessert in order to have the living room neat when they return there for coffee. If there is a maid, she should do this tidying up while the guests are eating their main course.

A roast is always delicious, and there is something mouth-watering about watching the meat being carved. If you follow a recipe that calls for it to "repose" (to be removed from the oven after a shorter cooking time than usual and to continue cooking from its own heat), even the gravy may be made before the guests arrive and kept hot in a double boiler. Creamed or curried chicken within a ring of noodles or rice is pretty and saves table space by eliminating an extra dish. Almost any meat-and-vegetable casserole, such as *coq-au-vin* or beef in red wine, is ideal. Or you may invite your guests for a special dinner—lobsters flown from Maine, or shrimp cooked in beer and shelled and eaten in the fingers. With these delectable and filling dishes, you need only serve a salad, rolls, and dessert.

In recent years an increasing number of men have become interested in cooking, especially in cooking meat on a grill or spit. A marvelous sight and a fine conversation piece is a golden, aromatic roast of beef turning over glowing coals in the fireplace when the guests arrive.

It is an excellent idea to keep a notebook in your kitchen in which you record the names of guests at your dinner parties and the menus you have given them. This avoids the possibility of serving someone the same dish twice, and it also provides a place to keep a list of those foods to which some of your friends may have a particular dislike or be allergic.

The imagination of the hostess (or host) is really the only limitation on an informal menu. But a word of caution—don't experiment with a new dish at a party. Try it out at least once on the family so that it will be perfect when you offer it to your guests. And remember, the appearance of a dish is almost as important as its flavor. Choose a menu that has variation in color and texture—never serve a white sauce on chicken with rice and cauliflower. Chops should be arranged in a pretty design rather than piled in a heap, just as asparagus neatly laid in the same direction has infinitely more appeal than a helter-skelter pile of broken stems.

CHOOSING AND SERVING WINE

Tradition has always decreed that one particular wine goes with one particular food, but unless the meal is strictly formal, there is no reason why the host may not choose any wine he thinks his guests would prefer. Many fine wines now come from American vineyards, and their lower prices have made wine available to almost every family. The most important consideration in choosing a wine is that it complements the food with which it is served. *For details about the traditional choices of wine, see Chapter Twenty-four, "Formal Dinners."*

The simplest way to offer wine at an informal dinner is to place the opened bottle on the table in front of the host, preferably on a coaster to prevent any drops from spotting the tablecloth. If there are enough guests to require more than one bottle, a second one is placed at the other end of the table and the host asks a man at that end to assist him in pouring. When the first course is served, the host, and his helper when necessary, informally fill the glasses of the guests at each end of the table. If a maid is present, she may pour the wine after she has served the first course. To do this, she removes the bottle from the table, serves the lady who is guest of honor, and continues around the table counterclockwise. She serves the host last, and replaces the bottle in front of him. Anybody who does not wish wine merely says, "No, thank you," but does not cover his glass with his hand nor turn it upside-down. Incidentally, when drinking white wine finish the glass completely, but with red wine it is better to leave a sip in the bottom to avoid swallowing any possible sediment. Those pouring the wine offer to refill a guest's glass whenever it is empty or almost empty.

SETTING YOUR TABLE

The table may be set as for a formal dinner, with a damask or lace cloth, or it may be set with individual place mats as for a luncheon. Gay, colorful cloths add much to a table set on a terrace or in an informal room. You can buy special tablecloths or doilies appropriate to the season; holly-decorated ones for Christmas, or those with designs of autumn leaves or turkeys in the fall. Fruit or a combination of dried plants and flowers can be an attractive variation on the more common floral centerpiece.

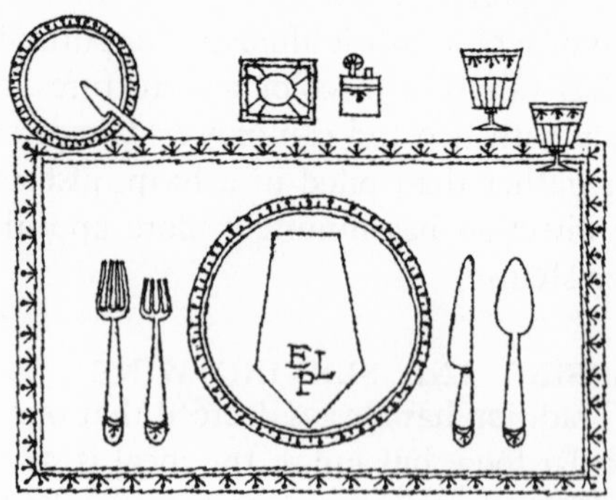

If a tablecloth is used, you need not set out butter plates, but with place mats they are necessary to avoid soiling the polished surface with the buttered or crumbly rolls.

All flat silver necessary for the meal is put at each place. As always, the silver to be used last is put nearest the plate, the ones to be used first on the outside. The service plate, which is an inseparable item of formal service, is put on the informal table only when it is to be used. Otherwise each place at the table is left plateless.

Whether or not you serve wine or beer (or milk if there are children present) is entirely up to you, but a glass of iced water should be at every place.

The butter should already be on the butter plates, the water glasses filled, and the wine in a cooler beside the host or in a decanter on the table. Salad is often served with the main course instead of as a separate one, and rather than putting a crisp cool salad on a hot plate or one swimming in gravy, a salad plate or a bowl may be set at the left of each place.

Cigarettes, ash trays, and condiments must all be in place, conveniently spaced around the table.

If the host is carving a roast, or serving the meat and vegetables, the stack of warm plates may be in front of him along with the foods to be served and the necessary implements. If there is a course already on the table, however, the hostess or maid must bring the entree in from the kitchen after the plates have been removed.

A course to be served before the entree may be on the table when the guests come in to dinner. Long-stemmed glass bowls containing fish or shrimp should have service plates under them. Both are removed to make way for the hot plates of the main course. If your first course is soup, the most practical soup dishes are little pots with lids, which will keep the contents hot while the guests are seating themselves.

In some houses the salad-dressing ingredients are arranged in a set of bowls and bottles that, with the salad bowl, are put in front of the hostess, who mixes the dressing herself. A few drops of this or shakes of that, according to the taste of the hostess, lend an excitement to a dressing which can never be duplicated in a store-bought bottle.

The same idea exactly has made certain internationally known restaurants famous—the head waiter, or the proprietor himself, cooks and mixes something before your eyes. The ducks of the Tour d'Argent, the noodles of Alfredo's in Rome, or Japanese sukiyaki seem to acquire a special flavor by the visible preparation. In short, preparing a dish at the table (which many hostesses think of as a handicap) may easily become a special feature of your hospitality.

GREETING THE GUESTS

The host and hostess stay near the door if possible, or if the living room is out of sight of the door, they go together to greet their guests when the doorbell rings. If the host is serving cocktails, he brings them what they wish; and the hostess introduces them to the people they do not know.

If cocktails are served, dinner should be planned for forty-five minutes to an hour later than the time on the invitation; twenty minutes later if drinks are not served, to allow late arrivals a moment of relaxation. During this period the hostess may slip out to the kitchen to attend to last-minute details. She should make her absence as brief as possible so that the guests will not feel that she is overburdened.

INFORMAL SERVICE

WITH ONE MAID

One maid cannot possibly do all the preparing and serving of a dinner party in an elaborate way, but she certainly may do a great deal toward making the dinner go smoothly and allowing the hostess more time to be with her guests. Before dinner, if she and the hostess have planned well and prepared in advance, she may be on hand to take coats from the guests and serve hors d'oeuvres if cocktails are offered. She should attend to all the last-minute details so that the hostess need not leave her guests. When all is ready she announces dinner, or signals the hostess, who tells the guests that dinner is ready.

If a first course is served it should be on the table when the guests sit down. The maid removes the plates when everyone is finished and either replaces each one with a hot plate or places a stack of hot plates in

front of the host, depending on how the main course is to be served. If all the food is ready in the kitchen, she passes it to each guest, the meat first and then the vegetables. If the host is carving and serving at his place, she takes each plate as he fills it and places it in front of a guest.

When the maid serves the food directly from the kitchen, she starts on the host's right with the lady who is guest of honor and continues around the table counterclockwise, serving the host last. Some hostesses insist that they be skipped and the maid return to serve them next to last, but this is awkward and delays the rapid serving that is so important in keeping food hot. The order is exactly the same when the maid passes plates that have been filled by the host.

All dishes are served from the left and, if convenient, removed from the right. Condiments, breads, and sauces are usually passed around the table by the guests themselves, but if the group is not large, the maid may pass one or more of them when she has finished with the main dishes. Dishes that hold two or three varieties of condiments and divided vegetable dishes can greatly facilitate serving. There is no reason why a competent maid may not pass two vegetable dishes at the same time, holding one in each hand.

When everyone is served the maid may remove the serving dishes to keep them warm in the kitchen; or if the dishes have covers or are of pottery or other heat-retaining material, they may be left in the dining room. When the host or hostess wishes to offer the guests another portion, the one nearest the bell rings for the maid and says, "Mary, would you please bring me Mrs. Harris' plate," or "Mary, would you please pass the meat and rice again?" If Mary is experienced, she will bring in the serving dishes without being asked.

While the guests are eating, the waitress neatens up the living room and prepares the dessert and the coffee tray. When the hostess sees that all her guests have finished, she rings and the maid clears the table. Everything is removed except the glasses and the silver for dessert. She then crumbs the table, using a clean folded napkin to sweep the crumbs onto a small plate held just below the edge of the table.

Dessert may be brought in from the kitchen already on the plates and placed before the guests in the same order as was the main course. Or the plates may be set before the guests and the dessert passed to each one in turn.

WITHOUT HELP

The ideal solution when one is giving a dinner party with no help is to have the guests serve themselves from a side table or buffet and then seat themselves at the dining-room table. This completely avoids the necessity of passing dishes around the table and makes dining easier and more pleasant for everyone.

However, some hostesses do not have the facilities to do this, or prefer that the food be served at the table after the guests are seated.

For this type of meal, start with the main course and provide the equivalent of a first course by serving plenty of substantial canapés with your cocktails or before you enter the dining room.

You receive your guests and stay with them until they have all arrived and until the "cocktail hour," if you serve cocktails, is over. Then you leave them with your husband, bring the meat from the kitchen, set the vegetable dishes beside it, and then invite everyone to "Come in to dinner."

When the food is served at one table, your husband carves the roast or serves the casserole. Preferably he also serves the vegetables, but the vegetable dishes may be handed around.

In either case, when the first plate is filled, the host hands it to the lady on his right. This first time, he says, "This is for you," since the guest of honor should be served first. The next plate is passed down the table on his right and is placed in front of his wife, or of whoever is seated at the opposite end. The rest of the guests on his right are served in order working back toward the guest of honor, and the process is then repeated on his left. He serves himself last. Since this procedure can consume considerable time and the food will surely be getting cold, it is important that the host or hostess ask the guests to start after three or four people have been served. If the host and hostess forget to do so, one of the guests is perfectly correct in beginning to eat.

When the salad is mixed, it is best that the guests pass the bowl, each one in turn holding it for the person on his right. Dessert may be put on each plate in advance, or you may serve it at the table as your husband did the roast.

In most cases, when the guests see you start to rise to clear the table, they will stand up, saying, "May I help you?" You *must* refuse, telling them, "No, really, it is easier to do it myself," or "Thank you, but we'll just get in each other's way." The only exception to this occurs when you have a daughter, sister, or very close friend at the table and have asked her in advance if she would mind helping.

In any case, alone or with help, you remove the dishes two at a time, not stacking them, and either put them on a side table or take them to the kitchen. Bread-and-butter plates, salt and pepper containers, and condiment dishes must be taken off also, but you need not crumb the table. Each time that you take something out to the kitchen, you may bring back dessert plates, salad and salad plates, or whatever is needed for the next course. If you wish, you may put a dessert plate at each place you have cleared as you return to take the next plate. Or as soon as you have removed your husband's plate, you may put a stack of dessert plates and the dessert in front of him and he may serve it while you are finishing the table-clearing. In other words, any system that speeds and smooths the changing of courses is acceptable, so that your guests do not feel that you are going to too much trouble.

There is no need to clear the dessert dishes unless your dining table is at one end of your living room. In that case you cannot subject your guests to the unappetizing sight of dirty dishes for the rest of the evening.

At this point, one of your guests is likely to say, "Let's just wash the dishes quickly. It won't take a minute and we don't mind at all." Even if they are close friends or relatives, do your best to dissuade them, or at least limit their efforts to getting a first load of dishes into the dishwasher. If they are only acquaintances, you must flatly refuse. After all, you have invited them to your home hoping to make a pleasant break in their routine, and allowing them to do the same unpleasant chores they must do every day at home is hardly the way to make their evening the most enjoyable possible. At the same time the considerate guest will not insist too stubbornly, because the embarrassment it may cause the hostess far outweighs the help that is given.

THE SINGLE WOMAN ENTERTAINS

When a single woman invites guests to a dinner party, she may well need to appoint one of her men guests to help her with the mechanics of mixing drinks and serving dinner. He should not be expected to act as a host insofar as greeting or entertaining the guests, but the hostess may ask him to carve meat, serve wine, and otherwise assist her in making the dinner run smoothly.

Unless the man is a relative or close friend, however, this can be an imposition. If there is a maid, she should take care of all the preparation and serving.

SERVING COFFEE OR TEA WITH THE MEAL

When the coffee or tea is to be served with the meal, the simplest method is to have the cups on the table when the guests sit down. After the meal is served, the hostess takes the coffee- or teapot and goes around the table filling the cups, starting with the woman on her husband's right. She fills her own cup last. It is not incorrect if she prefers to fill the cups while seated at her place—the guests passing them down the table from hand to hand. But this is inconvenient for the diners, and there is a strong possibility that an accident will occur.

AFTER-DINNER COFFEE

When the guests are seated in the living room, take the cream out of the refrigerator and pour the coffee into the pot you plan to serve it from—preferably one that has a flame under it to keep the coffee hot. It may be made and served in an electric coffeemaker, which can be plugged in again in the living room. Arrange the coffee and cream on a big tray, which is already set with sugar, spoons, cups, and saucers. Since it is a nice gesture to offer either a large cup or a demitasse, many hostesses put some of each size on the tray. When it is all ready, you or your husband carry it in and set it on a coffee table or on any table that has a chair nearby. You serve the coffee, asking each guest, "How many lumps of sugar?" and "Cream?" Either you or your husband may pass the cups around, or the guests may step up so you can hand it to them directly.

Just as every successful hostess has nonalcoholic drinks available for those who do not drink cocktails, she should be prepared to offer caffeine-free coffee as an alternate to regular after-dinner coffee. Or if she herself prefers caffeine-free coffee, she should offer her guests regular coffee as well.

HINTS FOR GUESTS

While most of the obligations lie with the hostess at a party, there are many things that you as a guest can do to make the evening a success.

When you know a party is being given especially for you, it is a thoughtful gesture to send flowers ahead of time. It is not necessary for other guests to do this, but a few flowers sent afterwards as a thank-you are always appreciated.

Do not arrive early! You should arrive within fifteen minutes of the time for which you were invited. More delay than that indicates that you have not made much effort, and it may ruin the hostess's carefully planned meal. This rule does have exceptions. In large cities especially, it is often expected that guests do not arrive until at least a half hour later than the stated hour.

When dinner is announced, don't ignore the invitation, sitting back and sipping slowly at your full cocktail glass. On the other hand, don't jump up and fly out as if you have been kept waiting to the point of starvation. Watch your hostess, and if she seems to be edging toward the door, take one more sip and rise. She may say, "Dinner is ready, but don't hurry. It will stay hot for a few minutes." Unless she says, "Please bring your drink with you," don't. She may be serving wine or a meal that she does not feel is complemented by a cocktail.

Wait until the hostess is ready to seat herself before you sit down, unless she says, "Please sit down. I have to bring in another dish." As at any meal, men should help the women on their right to be seated.

If there is a cold first course already on the table, you must wait for the hostess to pick up her fork or spoon before you start.

When your hostess rises to clear the table, don't jump up to help unless she has asked you to beforehand. You'll probably only get in her way. However, it can only be a help if you wish to offer to pass the cups around when she serves coffee after dinner.

And most important—remember to talk to the guests on either side of you or to enter with enthusiasm into a general conversation if the table is small.

If games are suggested after dinner, no matter how you feel about them, try to look as though you think it's a fine idea and help your hostess to organize the group. Very often, especially if the guests do not have a great deal in common, entertainment that a hostess would ordinarily avoid can be the means of pulling a party together and making a delightful evening out of what started out as a very dull one.

In some communities guests make it a custom to telephone their hostess the following day and to tell her how much they enjoyed her party. This is a very friendly gesture, but it is not obligatory since your verbal thanks when you leave are sufficient.

FAMILY MEALS

If the family has a maid, the meals are served exactly as they would be if guests were present. She may serve from the kitchen, or if the family is large she may pass the plates as the man of the house fills them.

In most households where Mother is cook and waitress, she fills the plates and brings them to the table two at a time, giving her husband the first one. She may, and should, enlist the aid of any one of the children who is old enough to help her. If the family is small she may remove the dishes herself, but if there are a number of children, those old enough should take their own plates to the kitchen. They should wait until everyone has finished eating.

If the meal is served by the father at the table, the dishes are passed from person to person. The first one filled is sent down the table on the host's right and stops at the mother's place. The others are served in order working back up the table, first on the right side, then on the left. Aside from the fact that the first plate is not given to the person on the father's right, the order is the same as that described for an informal dinner party.

At large family meals the vegetable dishes, instead of being at the father's place, may be further down the table. When this is done the person nearest the dish, as soon as he receives his own plate, helps himself and passes the vegetable in the direction of those who already have their meat.

When a person seated at one end of the table asks for something that is near the other end, the person nearest the food requested picks it up and passes it on. If he wishes some himself he may help himself before passing it to avoid his neighbor's having to send it back again.

29

Buffet dinners

There are three great advantages to a buffet dinner that appeal to all of us. First, you can accommodate many more guests than your dining-room table will seat. It is important, however, to restrict the number so that there will be places for everyone to sit down, and also so that there will be room for the guests to move about freely when serving themselves and returning to the living room.

Second, lack of service is no handicap. Because a buffet is truly a "do-it-yourself" party, even the hostess without a maid may spend almost the entire evening with her guests.

And third, it has the informality that most of us so much enjoy. There is something about sitting in one place before dinner, going into the dining room and foraging for yourself, then coming back to the same place or finding a new place, that makes buffet parties so popular. Either women or men not sitting beside someone they find particularly congenial are free to move elsewhere. If you have never given a buffet lunch or dinner, you can't begin too soon to discover the charm and ease of this delightful form of entertaining.

WITH OR WITHOUT HELP

The duties of a hostess serving a buffet dinner alone are far lighter than those at a sit-down dinner, providing that she has planned carefully and prepared the food well in advance. Just before she announces dinner, she must, of course, attend to such details as lighting candles, putting out iced water, and arranging the platters, casseroles, or serving dishes on the table. But the food can be all ready in double boilers or chafing dishes or, if it is to be served cold, in the refrigerator. Thus, a hostess's last-minute chores will take her away from her guests only briefly. After eating, the guests take their empty plates back to the dining room themselves, putting them on a side table—not on the buffet—and serve their own dessert. The host and hostess may remove the dessert plates, or the guests may assist. If the dining room has a door, it can be closed, or a screen can be pulled across the entrance once all the plates have been taken out. If, however, the dining area opens onto or is a part of the living room, the hostess should remove the soiled plates to the kitchen while the guests are drinking their coffee.

If she has a live-in maid or has hired a waitress for the evening, the hostess has very little to do at all. If cocktails are served she must watch to see that her guests are ready, and then advise the waitress when to put the food on the buffet table. The maid, in turn, signals to her when all is prepared in the dining room. The waitress should remove cocktail glasses and clean the ash trays while the guests are serving themselves, and she should take out empty plates as they set them down. She may or may not, as the hostess wishes, pass the dishes around for second helpings. Because every one will not finish simultaneously, the maid should have adequate time to remove the food from the buffet table and replace it with dessert plates and dessert, or salad and cheese, or whatever is to finish the meal.

After the maid has removed the last of the plates, she brings the coffee tray into the living room and the hostess pours. From then on the host takes over the serving of liqueurs and after-dinner drinks, and the maid is free to clean up the kitchen and dining room.

THE INVITATIONS

The invitation may be written on an informal, on your notepaper, across the top of the face of your "Mr. and Mrs." visiting cards, or on the attractive invitation cards available at every stationer's. *See Chapter Fifty-three, "Informal Invitations," for additional details.*

The invitation must be answered promptly or the hostess will have no idea how many to provide for. If the hostess's number appears on the card, the answer may be telephoned. Otherwise you may write a note or send your reply on a visiting card, merely saying "Sat. Oct. 2 with pleasure." *See also Chapter Fifty-five, "Acceptances and Regrets."*

SEATING ARRANGEMENTS

There are two ways of seating guests at a buffet dinner. First, they may simply take their plates into the living room (where there are enough chairs for everyone), hold their plates on their laps, and set their glasses on the nearest table. Your guests will be much more comfortable and there will be much less chance of an accident if you set a small table (the folding kind that fit in a rack are ideal and easy to store) by each chair, or at least by each chair not within easy reach of a coffee or side table.

Second, your guests may be seated at small tables—sturdy card tables, perhaps—in your living room, dining room, or library. This arrangement is, of course, dependent on your having large enough rooms so that the tables will not be in the way before dinner or while the guests are serving themselves. If you do have the space, most men and many women prefer to be seated in this way. The tables are covered with cloths of almost any color and style. The places are set exactly as for an informal dinner, and since the guests need not carry silver, napkins, or glasses with them, a great deal of space is saved on the buffet table. The guests serve themselves as at any other buffet, going for second helpings and removing their empty plates unless there is a maid to do it. If the living room is used, the hostess must take the tables out after the meal to make room for conversational groups or whatever activity she may have planned. For a bridge party, of course, she simply clears the tables and removes the cloth, leaving the tables ready to be used.

SEMIBUFFET

A pleasant way of serving a small group of friends or a family party is to arrange the food on the sideboard or a side table and set the dining-room table as for a sit-down dinner. Two variations are possible. First, the guests are seated, and the host serves each plate, asking the guests, "Do you like your meat rare or well done?" or "Do you take cranberry sauce and stuffing?" The hostess passes the plate and serves herself next to last. The host helps himself last. She should say as she hands the plates around, "Pleast start, so that your dinner won't get cold." Second, the guests may serve themselves as at a regular buffet and carry their plates to the table while the hostess watches to see whether she may help or if they have missed any of the sauces or side dishes. Again the hostess serves herself after the guests, and the host is last.

THE INVALUABLE ELECTRIC HOT PLATE

Whichever type of buffet you are serving, the most valuable piece of equipment you can have is one that keeps things hot. I recommend an electric hot plate or tray, because they can be used to heat your plates and keep your meal warm for an almost indefinite period of time. As long as your finished dish is covered so that it will not dry out, it may be placed on a hot plate an hour or more before dinner and be as delectable when it is served as it was the moment it was taken from the stove. The only exception, of course, is a soufflé, which must be served at once. For this reason soufflés are not recommended for any large serve-yourself party. Furthermore, with an electric appliance on the buffet table, there is no need to take the dishes to the kitchen to be kept warm for second helpings. And finally, it is unnecessary to watch and replace fuel for flame-heated chafing dishes.

SETTING THE TABLE

The difference in the principle of buffet and ordinary table setting is that necessary and useful objects are of first importance. Unless there is ample space, omit articles that are solely ornamental. Flowers in the center of the table are lovely, of course, but if it is a question of choosing between decorative flowers and edible fruit, a centerpiece of the fruit to be served for dessert is preferable.

In the same way, if the table is crowded and candles are not needed to see by, they are better left off. If candles are needed, candelabra are better than candlesticks because first, they give better light, and second, they are less likely to be knocked over by a guest reaching for a plate of food.

If the party is large, it is better to leave the table in the center of the room so that two lines of guests may serve themselves at once. Then the most important dish is divided into two parts, and one platter or casserole placed at each end of the table. The plates are in two stacks beside them, and the napkins and silver neatly arranged next to the plates. Dishes of vegetables, salads, bread and butter, and sauces and condiments are on each side of the table so that the guests need to pass down only one side—greatly speeding the service and keeping them from turning back and bumping into each other.

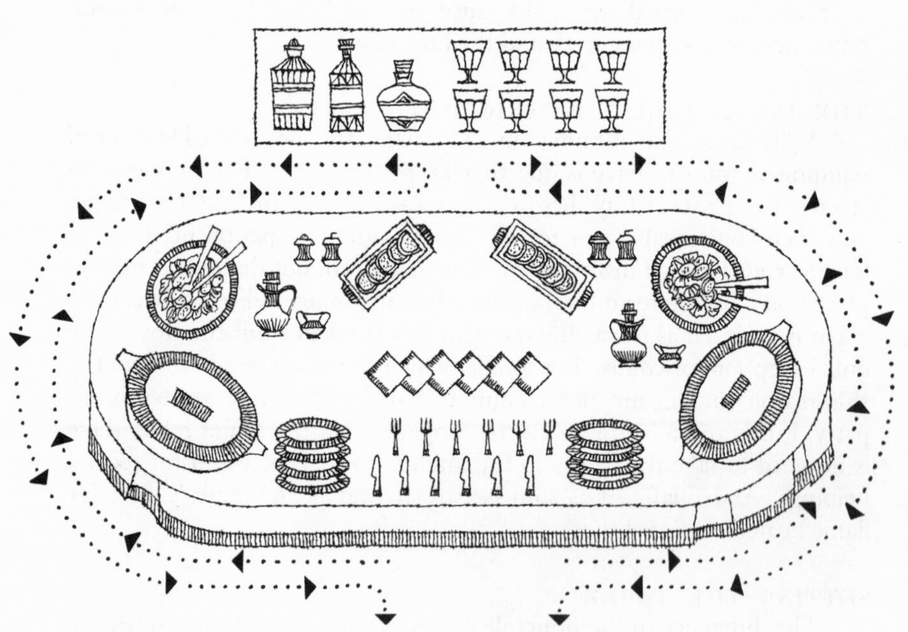

If the table is set against the wall, place your plates and main dish at the end that makes for the best flow of traffic. This is usually the one nearest the entrance so that the guests, after serving themselves, do not have to double back against the people coming in.

The table may be set as formally or informally as you wish. If you use a white damask cloth, silver candelabra, and an elaborate centerpiece, your buffet will appear quite formal. But you may go to the other extreme and use pottery dishes with nothing but a hot-plate pad under them and a bowl of fruit in the center of the table. What makes your table attractive is not the elegance of the utensils and decorations you use, but the combination of dishes, linen, and silver, and the way in which they are arranged.

Color plays an enormous part in the beauty of a buffet table. If you have copper bowls or a kettle to use as a centerpiece, red and yellow fruit—peaches, apples, grapes, bananas—or a combination of fall vegetables—squash, tomatoes, pumpkins—are most effective. Keep the autumn tints in mind: use green, red, russet, and yellow pottery on a bare table. Or if you prefer, a red or green or yellow tablecloth is warm and inviting. A coarse white damask cloth and napkins dyed a strong color make an ideal informal covering for a table.

Red or white wine, a punch or other cold drinks, iced water, or beer left in its cans or bottles, together with glasses, are on the sideboard. A large urn of coffee should also be available during the meal as well as afterwards.

Because the coffee is already on the sideboard, the guests may serve themselves. The hostess, if she wishes, may take an additional tray, set with cups, a coffee pot, cream, and sugar into the living room to serve people who may not have noticed it or wanted it with their dinner.

When there are no individual stands or tables, and guests must put their glasses beside them on the floor, it is wise to use iced-tea glasses or highball glasses because they are steadier than goblets. If the beverage is served with ice in the glass, it should not be put down on a table unless coasters are provided.

THE MENU

It does not matter what foods you happen to choose so long as they are well prepared and easy to eat with fork alone (although this is not important if your guests will be sitting at tables). Otherwise, merely use a reasonable amount of common sense in selecting dishes that will be satisfying to the people invited. Don't feed hungry men bouillon, daubs of hors d'oeuvres, samples of fruit salad, and meringues. Food may be lighter for women alone, but for men with good appetites, three or four substantial dishes should be provided, at least one of them hot.

Substantial dishes would include most meats, fish in a sauce such as Newburg, potatoes, and the heavier desserts. Nearly everything made in a baking dish or casserole is ideal for a buffet meal, not only because it is hearty, but because it is easily kept hot.

There are countless delicious menus to be tried; the only limit is your imagination. If you wish to be very elaborate, or if you have a great many guests, you may wish to serve two main dishes, possibly a lobster Newburg at one end of the table and beef stroganoff at the other. But choose two dishes that will be complemented by the same vegetables and condiments, or you will have more preparation than you can easily handle and not enough space on your table for all the dishes.

Here are some menu suggestions, ranging from an elaborate buffet to a very simple family-type menu. You may, of course, use any combination that appeals to you, omitting or adding to each menu as you wish.

Veal Scallopini   Roast Turkey
Mashed Potatoes
String Beans with Mushrooms
Cranberry Sauce, Stuffing, Gravy
Buttered Rolls
Fresh Fruit Compote
Cookies
Coffee

Italian Spaghetti and Meatballs or Lasagne
Mixed Green Salad
Choice of Roquefort, French, Italian Dressing
French or Italian Bread, Butter
Lemon Ice
Coffee

Hungarian Goulash or Beef and Kidney Pie
Noodles
Glazed Carrots
Green Salad with Mandarin Oranges
Buttered Rolls
Coffee

Curried Lamb or Chicken
Rice Ring
Chutney, Raisins, Ground Nuts
French Bread, Butter
Raw Spinach Salad
Ice Cream and Cake or Cookies
Coffee

For a summer evening:

Three or four varieties of cold sliced meats such as
Ham, Turkey, Roast Beef, Lamb, or Cold Cuts
Scalloped Potatoes
Vegetable Salad
Buttered Rolls
Vanilla Ice Cream with Green Mint Sauce
Cookies
Coffee

A good suggestion for a Friday evening, when some of your guests may not wish to eat meat:

Lobster or Shrimp Newburg or Beef Stroganoff
Rice
Green Peas and Onions
Croissants
Caesar Salad
Cheese and Crackers
Fresh Fruit (Apples, Pears, Seedless Grapes)
Coffee

THE PARTY ITSELF

The table is set with all the cold foods, the dining-room lights are lighted, and the hot foods are ready to be brought in from the kitchen—or are already on the electric hot plate or in their chafing dishes. Let's go with the host and hostess into the living room and wait for the guests to arrive.

As people enter the room, the host and hostess go forward to greet them and perhaps introduce any who may for the moment find themselves alone. It must always be remembered that the roof of a friend's house serves as an introduction, and one talks with anyone nearby, whether he knows him or not.

When the guests have arrived and the cocktails, if served, are finished, the door into the dining room is opened, and people in more or less of a queue file around the dining table. The guests go first, urged along by the hostess, if necessary, but whether it is a seated dinner or a buffet, the hostess should *never* serve herself first. The women as well as the men help themselves—it is fun to see what there is to eat and to take just what one wants. Sometimes, however, and quite correctly, a man may ask a woman what she would like, fill a plate, and take it to her.

A man seeing a woman sitting without a plate or with an empty one asks her (whether he knows her or not), "Can't I get you something to eat?" or "Would you like more of anything?" If she says, "Yes, please," he brings her whatever it is she would like. But most likely she says, "Thank you, but I'm going into the dining room in a moment."

If people continue to sit and wait to be served, the hostess has to prod them a little, saying, "Please go into the dining room and help yourselves to dinner." If they remain standing, carrying on a long conversation and blockading the table, she should suggest they take their plates into the other room.

Important item: Have plenty of ash trays. For a large buffet supper recently, a wise hostess I know went to a ten-cent store and bought two dozen ash trays. She put them on several steps of her staircase, on the mantle, on every table, on the piano, on the window sills, and in every space that could possibly serve as a cigarette-parking place.

The only serving detail of importance in a buffet meal is the clearing-away of used dishes and the unceasing emptying of ash trays. In a house with servants, every plate is removed as soon as it is put down and filled ash trays are constantly replaced. Also, if there are servants, they refill the glasses of seated guests from time to time, and the main dishes may be passed for second helpings. The servantless hostess can ask one or two members of her family—or her most intimate friends—to help her take the used dishes to a convenient table or sideboard, from which she can stack them and take them to the kitchen as easily and unobtrusively as possible.

30

Informal luncheons

Just as the informal dinner is a less elaborate version of the formal dinner, so the informal luncheon resembles the more formal one. Because of the hour the guests are usually all women, although on weekends or special occasions mixed groups are not uncommon. If men are included in the guest list, the meal is likely to have a stronger resemblance to the informal dinner, for the menu must be fairly substantial or half the guests will go away hungry.

Again, the type of luncheon you give depends upon the size of your dining room, the number that can be seated at your table, and the help that you will have with the serving. If you have extra rooms or a large enough living room, you may set up one or more card tables to increase the number of guests you can accommodate. In this case you seat an intimate friend or member of your own family as hostess at the card table and you sit at the head of the dining-room table. If you are one of those who have a very small dining room, or perhaps no dining room at all, but have a living room or a patio large enough to permit two or three small tables to be set up ahead of time, a luncheon for eight or twelve people, perhaps followed by bridge, is one of the nicest parties imaginable.

Each card table should be set with a white or colored cloth—the best covering for lunch as well as dinner on small tables. The tablecloths may be of any style, but they should, if possible, be exactly alike. It is better to have simple, matched ones than assorted, elaborate ones. A small flower arrangement makes the prettiest centerpiece. The tables are set as for an informal dinner (*Chapter Twenty-eight*) except that candles are never used in the daytime.

SERVING THE LUNCHEON

THE HOSTESS ALONE

If you are serving without the help of a maid, you will be wise to make your party a buffet luncheon. The food is set out as for a buffet dinner, on the dining-room table or on any table with sufficient space. For a ladies' luncheon the fare is much simpler than for a dinner. Among a group of eight or twelve women, there are almost always some who are watching their calories, so a delicious but light meal is far more appreciated than one dressed with rich sauces and ending with gooey sweets.

As soon as you announce that luncheon is served, your guests file past the table and serve themselves, taking their plates to the card tables and seating themselves wherever they wish. If you are having a course before the entree, it should already be on the tables when your guests arrive, and they sit down and finish it before going to the buffet table for the main course. If there is no maid to help, the guests should take their empty plates and leave them on a side table as they go to get their next course. While they are helping themselves, you may remove the soiled dishes to the kitchen.

The same procedure is followed when the guests are ready for the salad or dessert. When they have finished you ask them to go to another room, or at least to leave the tables and sit on more comfortable chairs to have their coffee. This gives you a chance to clear away the glasses, silver, and cloths from the table, and if bridge is to follow, set out the cards. There should always be two decks of *clean* cards and at least two score pads and two pencils on each table. *For further details about card parties, see Chapter Thirty-five, "Other Informal Gatherings," and Chapter Sixty-eight, "In Games and Sports."*

WITH THE HELP OF A MAID

When a maid is there to help you, she can serve eight or twelve guests quite easily if the first course is already on the table. She may clear the plates by standing at the table corner, taking away one plate in each hand. The main course should be limited to a single dish and salad, or it will take a rather long time to serve, as the maid must pass the food in the usual way, from each person's left. The salad may be all ready in small bowls or plates, which are brought in two at a time and placed on the guests' left. If there is no first course, the salad may already be on the table. Rolls, butter, and iced water and any other beverage should also be put on the table beforehand.

When dessert is finished, the waitress carries the coffee tray to another room and, if it is a bridge party, readies the tables while the hostess pours the coffee.

ON FOOD AND DRINK

If you wish to serve cocktails before lunch, you may, but the time should be limited, especially if everyone is looking forward to playing cards. And the drinks should be of a milder type than those served before dinner. Sherry, Dubonnet, and vermouth, either "on the rocks" or in a wineglass, are ideal luncheon cocktails, but you may, if you know your friends prefer them, serve drinks such as martinis, daiquiris, or Bloody Marys.

Two or three courses are sufficient at any informal luncheon. If you serve many more than that and then move to the bridge table, you will find some of your players falling asleep over their hands!

While cold food is both appropriate and delicious, no meal—except on the hottest of hot summer days—should ever be chosen without at least one course of hot food. Some people dislike cold food, and it disagrees with others; but if you at least offer your guests a hot soup, it is then all right to have the rest of the meal cold.

Four of the following menus have been planned with the idea that you can have all the preparation finished in advance. But since the main dishes in the last one should be cooked and served at an exact moment, that menu should be saved until a day when you have some help in the kitchen.

Clam or Oyster Chowder with Oyster Crackers
Fruit Salad and Cottage Cheese
Melba Toast
Chocolate Mousse
Coffee

Curried Chicken with Rice Ring
Mixed Green Salad
Baking Powder Biscuits
Jello Made with Fresh Fruit
Coffee

Little Neck Clams, or Oysters
Cold Sliced Roast Beef, Horse-radish Sauce
Potatoes au Gratin
Watercress and Tomato Salad
Fresh Strawberries and Sour Cream
Coffee

For that very hot day:

Cold Salmon with Green Mayonnaise Sauce
Sliced Cucumber and Tomato
Protein and White Toast
Lemon Chiffon Pie
Coffee

Fresh Fruit Cup
Filet of Sole Amandine
Spinach Salad with Chopped, Hard-boiled Egg, Tart Dressing
Buttered Rolls
Orange Chiffon Cake
Coffee

BEVERAGES

Iced tea and iced coffee are delicious with luncheon, especially in the summer. It is nice to give your guests a choice by passing a tray with a pitcher of each or by having both available close to the buffet table. A bowl of fruit punch may take the place of iced tea or coffee and appears cool and refreshing if it is prepared with floating slices of orange and lemon and is surrounded by glasses or cups adorned with fresh sprigs of mint.

In the winter, many hostesses like to have hot coffee or tea in a convenient spot where the guests may help themselves.

A light wine may be served, although it is not necessary, especially if you have offered cocktails.

A pitcher of iced water, from which the guests may help themselves, should always be in evidence, or glasses of water should already be on the table if the luncheon is not buffet.

LATER IN THE AFTERNOON

On a hot summer day when people have been playing cards for an hour or more, a tray should be brought in with a large pitcher of iced water and perhaps another pitcher of iced tea and put down on a convenient table. The one thing that hostesses tend to forget is that five people out of six long for a cold drink in the afternoon more than anything else. Occasionally sandwiches and cookies are brought in as well as the iced tea, but these are not necessary when bridge follows a luncheon. If you invite people to come at two and play for the afternoon, light refreshments should be served between half past four and five o'clock.

31

Informal dances

Dances that are less sumptuous and less formal than balls may be given for any number of reasons, from the very specific—perhaps to celebrate a graduation—to the very general—your friends like to dance and no other excuse is necessary. Whatever the occasion and the degree of informality, certain points should be kept in mind if your dance is to be a success.

EVENING DANCES

If the dance is for adults, the invitations are usually written on an informal. They may be written in the same way for a dance for young people. But unless the dance is quite a formal affair, invitations are more often sent out on commercial party invitations, which have attractive drawings on the outside and spaces for writing time, address, and type of party on the inside. Remember to include at the bottom a hint about clothes. Parties, even dances, can be so informal that clothing may be anything from suits for the boys and "party" dresses for the girls to Bermuda shorts for both. An R.S.V.P. with a telephone number beside it is the surest way of having some idea of how many will be at the party. The invitation, too, may be by telephone. *For additional details, see Chapter Fifty-three.*

DECORATING THE ROOMS

When the dance is held in your own home rather than a public room of any sort, the most important thing is a large enough clear space and a floor properly prepared for dancing. If possible, all the furniture should be removed from the room, but if not, take out whatever you can and move the rest close to the wall. The rugs must be rolled and put away and the floor freshly waxed.

Decorations are not too important. A few flowers placed where they are not in the way—on a mantle, for instance—are sufficient. If the party is held during a holiday season, appropriate decorations such as Christmas ornaments or valentines on the walls add a festive note.

OUTDOOR DANCES

If you are fortunate enough to have a smooth terrace, a stone patio, perhaps beside a swimming pool, or even a built-in dance floor in the lawn, an outdoor dance on a summer evening is one of the most romantic and gay ways of entertaining. There should be tables and chairs available for those who are not dancing. The bar, if you are serving liquor, and the refreshments should be nearby.

Plenty of light is important. There must be light for members of the orchestra to see their music, and the bar should be well lit for the benefit of the bartender and waiters. Your guests may be delighted to dance in the moonlight, but when they are ready to sit down, uneven ground or steps may be a hazard if not well lighted. The most satisfactory lighting, because it is diffused and has a romantic effect, is achieved by placing floodlights in the trees—pointed up to reflect off the branches.

THE IMPORTANCE OF GOOD MUSIC

Probably the most important thing in assuring the success of any dance is good music. Therefore, although you may save as much as you can on decorations and refreshments, spend as much as your pocketbook can afford on the music. If it is within your means, hire the best orchestra you can obtain, even though you may only be able to afford three pieces. Rhythm, gaiety, and a knowledge of the taste of the age group at the party are the essential qualities that the orchestra must have. If the guests are people in their fifties, they probably will not want to dance the latest teen-age fad. By the same token, teen-agers would think a party a miserable failure if the orchestra played nothing but foxtrots and waltzes.

If you simply cannot hire an orchestra and are planning to use a phonograph, choose records that were specifically intended for dancing and ones that will appeal to your guests. If you borrow records from your friends—and many people do in such a situation—be sure the owner's name is clearly printed on the label in indelible ink or put on with marking tape.

DANCE MANNERS

Good manners at a dance are the same for young and old alike. Whatever the local customs about cutting in, double cutting (that is, switching partners on the dance floor), and so on, a man must dance with his hostess, and he must dance the first and last dances with the lady he brought to the party, whether it be his wife or a date. The exception is the dinner dance, when he dances first with the ladies seated beside him.

At a dance where the guests are married couples, there may be few or no extra men, and the only time to change partners may be during the intermission or when the music starts again. At this type of party there are almost always tables to which the couples return between dances. The men are expected to ask the women next to them, their wives, and their hostess to dance. If the hostess is at another table, a man should not ask her to dance until he is sure that all the women at his table have partners or at least that there is a group remaining at the table so that no one woman is left alone.

When the dance is over, every guest must, of course, find his host and hostess, thank them, and say "good night."

SATURDAY NIGHT AT THE COUNTRY CLUB

In many communities the Saturday night dance at the local country club has largely replaced small informal private dances. Usually a group of friends will attend a country club dance together after a cocktail party or similar gathering such as the one described in Chapter Twenty-seven. On arriving at the club you ask to be shown to the table that your hostess at the earlier party has already reserved. It is likely that you will arrive before her since she cannot leave her home before all her guests have departed. If she has not arranged to have place cards on the table, you should leave seats free at each end or at opposite sides for her and her husband.

Generally, in deciding where to sit, many husbands and wives split up, since much of the fun of a dance is to enjoy the company of different people.

As soon as possible a man should dance with the women seated on either side of him. If his wife is one of these two, and the woman on his other side has already been asked to dance, he then asks his wife for the first dance. After dancing with the women on either side of him, he should try to dance with as many of the other women at the table as possible, being certain not to forget either his hostess at the cocktail party or his wife! When she gets up to dance a woman leaves her bag, if it is a small one, on the table, or a larger bag on her chair.

When you make up a group to go to this type of party, try to choose couples who like to dance. It is inexcusably rude for the men to go off to the bar or otherwise ignore the women at the table. From time to time a man may of course cut in on a woman he knows who is sitting at another table, but after that particular dance is over he should escort her back to her own table and then rejoin his original group.

At a late party you do not have to stay until the music stops, although do not leave so early that your departure will be construed as breaking up the party. Since people do not always want to leave at the same time, it is far safer to take your own car to the club than to share a ride with another couple. Even though sharing a ride may seem practical and friendly before the dance begins, it can be very disconcerting to have to stay on at a party just because your earlier companions have decided to make a night of it.

32

Picnics

From early spring until late autumn the very proposal "Let's give a party" is almost certain to suggest a picnic to those who enjoy them. In its essential outline, going on a picnic means packing a cooler and baskets with things to eat and drink, and then walking or sailing, bicycling, or driving to some pleasant outdoor spot to eat this lunch or supper.

Although picnics can be utterly delightful when well managed, they can be perfectly awful when bungled! Therefore here are a few general directions for the benefit of those who want to have a successful picnic.

WHAT KIND OF PICNIC?

DUTCH TREAT OR HOST'S TREAT?

There are several ways of organizing a picnic.

The first is to give the picnic yourself, inviting the guests by telephone. If they accept, tell them the hour, where to meet, and possibly ask them to bring a blanket or back rest if the party is large and you do not have enough for everyone.

Or you may call and say, "Mike and I are trying to get a group together for a picnic Saturday night. We'll bring the steaks, and we're asking each couple to contribute one dish. Would you rather bring dessert or salad?" Others might be asked to bring the condiments, chowder, corn, or the drinks.

Lastly, a group of friends may simply arrange to picnic together, each family bringing their own food and cooking it over a community fire. It is fun to see what the others have prepared, and often there is considerable trading and sharing. "I'll trade you a chicken leg for a lobster claw," or "Do try some of this special steak sauce that Susie taught me to make." This sort of picnic is especially good if children are included, as each mother knows best what her young ones will eat most happily.

TAIL-GATE PICNICS

Tail-gate picnics have come into being with the universal popularity of the station wagon. They are particularly suitable on two occasions. First, if you are making a long trip and do not wish to take too lengthy a break for lunch, you may pull over to the side of the road (preferably in a "rest area" if you are on a big highway, because of the receptacles provided for garbage, etc.), let down the tail-gate, spread out your picnic on it, and eat, in no time at all.

The other occasion that has gained tremendous popularity is the lunch before a college football or baseball game. Call your classmate who lives in another town—"How about meeting us at the Number Two parking lot at the stadium, before the State versus Hometown game in October? We'll bring the food and you bring the drinks, and we'll have a reunion!" Having arranged the meeting place specifically, you load your whole family into the station wagon and enjoy the game after a sumptuous meal cooked on your folding grill and a chance to catch up on all the news of old friends. In fact, many of those friends may turn up in the same parking lot.

The tail-gate takes the place of a folding table, and the only other pieces of necessary equipment are the grill and a piece of oilcloth or plastic to lay on the tail-gate, which is likely to be dusty or sandy.

CLAMBAKES

The preparations for a clambake are quite specialized; but if you know how a seaweed oven is made (practically, as well as theoretically), and you have a loyal friend who is willing to help, nothing is more in keeping with a holiday at the seaside. To be successful, however, you or someone on your beach must have experience in preparing and timing the baking of corn on the cob and potatoes and the clams and lobsters. Before you think of a clambake make sure there is enough seaweed on your beach as well as rocks to line your pit—and I repeat, do not attempt one at all if you are not an expert, or if you are not willing to devote the entire day to the preparation. The fire must be lit in the morning and constantly tended from then on, or your pit will not be hot enough to cook the "bake."

YOU'RE THE HOSTESS

If you wish to entertain friends by taking them on a picnic, your first task is to consider your guest list very carefully. Nothing is so dampening to the enjoyment of a picnic as the presence of one or more faultfinders who never lift a finger but sit and complain of the heat, of the wind, of a possible shower, of the discomfort of sitting on the ground, or of their personal sufferings caused by mosquitoes or flies. On the other hand, if you select your company from friends who really enjoy picnics (and you are wise to stick to those), not only will they make everyone forget blowing sand and inquisitive ants or hungry mosquitoes, but most likely they will work like beavers.

Knowing that you have a congenial group and considering the ages and preferences of your guests—whether adults and children or just adults—you now decide whether you are going to provide an already-prepared outdoor lunch or supper, meaning that you will take only things that are ready to serve—sandwiches, or cold chicken and salad, and a thermos of liquids, for example—or whether you are going to build a fire and cook.

Next you must choose the location. If you live near the mountains, you may decide to climb or drive to a site that has a beautiful view, but if there are children in the party, be sure there is a field nearby for games or races or a stream in which they may swim. It should be scarcely necessary to remind you to select a site that you know something about—because you or your friends have picnicked there before. Be sure that the ground is not swampy, that it is not more mosquito- or ant-infested than anywhere else, and that it is not covered with poison ivy.

If you choose a beach, remember to make some preparation to shield both your guests and the food they are to eat from blowing sand. For this nothing is better than some five-foot garden stakes and a few yards of burlap with a wide hem at each end through which stakes are inserted. Thrust the stakes into the sand to form a windbreak. If you are going to be on the beach all day, an umbrella is a must for those who are not well tanned or accustomed to the sun.

If you are giving a large picnic and including a number of people who are not necessarily picnic addicts, it is important to select a site that is easy to get to or away from. You may have a jeep or "beach buggy" that allows you to reach a remote part of the beach with no effort at all, but if not, don't expect your average guest to tramp through miles of soft sand, carrying blankets, beach towels, and back rests.

Having made up your mind as to what to eat and where to cook it, you should plan as carefully as you would if you were inviting people to dine with you at home. You wouldn't ask guests to lunch at your house at one o'clock and then not serve until three; nor would you give them fish or chicken, raw on one side and charred to a cinder on the other. There is no more reason to do this at an outdoor meal than at an indoor one.

HOT OR COLD?

The very simplest type of picnic is a "continental" picnic, straight from the farmers of Europe. It consists of a loaf of bread, a piece of cheese, and a bottle of wine. If the cheese and wine are good and the bread fresh, this menu has all the advantages of being delicious and nourishing, requiring no preparation, and costing next to nothing. However, in spite of the ease of getting together and carrying the ingredients of a "continental" picnic, most Americans prefer to expand the menu in varying degrees. Using the three items above as a base, you may add whatever you wish—fruit for dessert, little tomatoes as a vegetable, tins of sardines or meats, and so on.

If there are children included at the picnic, sandwiches are the most popular food of all. Peanut butter and jelly seem to outstrip any other variety in popularity contests among the very young. Adults and children alike enjoy meat sandwiches, well-seasoned and with a little butter or mayonnaise to moisten the bread. Don't, however, make the mistake of using too much mayonnaise or too many tomatoes and other "runny" ingredients, as the sandwiches will turn to mush on the way to the picnic grounds. Don't attempt to take bread and fillings separately and let people make their own. The messiest picnic imaginable is one at which knives and plates and bread and butter and a half-dozen jars of jams and meat pastes are all spread around and flavored with sand or ants.

It is wise to offer a choice of two or three kinds of sandwiches, and by all means label each variety, especially if they are wrapped in foil. Wrapping and unwrapping and pulling apart to view the insides can make a hash of the most beautifully prepared sandwich.

To accompany the sandwich menu, offer a selection of potato chips, pickles, tomatoes, carrot and celery sticks, or jars of potato or macaroni salad. Cake or cookies or any other dessert that may be eaten with the fingers (seedless grapes are among the most popular with all ages) make a perfect ending. Thermos jugs of milk or soft drinks for the children, and beer, iced tea, or coffee for the adults complete the meal.

Cold menus may be much more elaborate than sandwiches. In fact, if you have the necessary equipment, you may have an entire buffet spread on a folding table. But most people prefer a simpler picnic, and the main requirement is that the food be the best of its kind. Cold fried chicken, or cold boiled lobster, accompanied by coleslaw or lettuce brought in a damp cloth and mixed with dressing when the group is ready to eat, bread and butter, and fresh fruit for dessert make a meal that is truly "fit for a king."

When the nights are cool, or simply because you prefer it, you may wish to serve a hot dish on your picnic. Again you have a choice to make. Do you wish to bring a main dish already made in an insulated container, or do you wish to build a fire and heat your meal at the picnic site? Stews complete with potatoes and other vegetables, creamed chicken with noodles, roast-beef hash made with potatoes, or filling chowders are all excellent choices. All keep indefinitely in big thermos jugs or any other well-insulated container.

Many men enjoy cooking meat over an open fire, and they generally have more assistance and suggestions than they need from their male guests. If the host—or the hostess—likes to do it, there is nothing more delicious than meat or fish cooked over coals. Steak, lamb chops, chicken, swordfish, or lobster are all superb when done in this fashion, and hot dogs and hamburgers change from an uninspired meal to a delectable treat. Whole potatoes or corn, wrapped in foil and roasted in the coals, and a mixed green salad make the best accompaniments, along with as many condiments such as mustard or ketchup as you can fit into your baskets. Cold sliced watermelon, or perhaps fresh strawberries, already sugared, might finish the meal.

Your plates for a "hot" picnic must be more substantial than uncoated paper. Plastic ones are really the most satisfactory, even though they must be taken home to be washed. Plastic bowls or cups for chowder are far more leak-proof and easier to hold than paper cups. As long as you are bringing the utensils for this type of meal, there is no reason not to accompany your main dish with a salad already mixed in a big bowl and breads kept warm by several layers of foil wrapping.

Good strong coffee in a thermos and plenty of beer and soft drinks kept cold in a tub of ice should be on hand for the singing around a roaring fire that should be a part of every evening picnic.

EQUIPMENT

Several items of equipment available at hardware stores, chain stores, or specialty shops are a delight to any picnic enthusiast. Styrofoam containers, which will keep food either hot or cold and weigh almost nothing, are a must. Another excellent item is an insulated wide-mouthed jug or thermos to carry anything from cold vichysoisse to hot lamb stew.

Portable grills with folding legs are a great help if you are planning to cook, although on the beach you may simply scoop a hole in the sand, put in the charcoal, and lay a grill from your oven across it, resting it on sturdy boards pressed into the sand on either side of the hole.

Charcoal briquettes in a cardboard container save the trouble of taking newspaper or lighting fluid, and they are easier to carry than a large bag of charcoal. All one has to do is to touch a match to the cardboard and the fire is started. And one warning—don't try to cook until the flame has died down and the coals have turned white, with a faint red glow here and there.

A two-sided grill, hinged on one end and with a long handle, is wonderful for holding and turning hamburgers, hot dogs, and steaks. It eliminates the danger of the hot dogs rolling between the rungs of a larger grill into the fire, or the hamburgers sticking and crumbling when they are turned.

A pair of long tongs is useful for arranging coals and for moving anything that is hot. They are ideal for turning corn or potatoes as they cook in the coals, and better for turning a steak than a fork, which pierces the meat and allows the juices to escape.

There are many other items that add greatly to the ease of preparing a picnic, and each picnic fan must decide which please him most. In general, choose those articles that are the most compact and lightweight and those that serve several purposes—without being limited either to a sandwich-and-cold-drink picnic or to a cooking picnic, but useful for transporting or preparing either.

A CHECK LIST

Like the perfect traveler, the perfect picnic manager has reduced the process to an exact science. She knows very well that the one thing to do is to take the fewest things possible and to consider the utility of those few.

Fitted hampers, tents and umbrellas, folding chairs and tables are all very well in a shop—and all right if you have a trailer or a station wagon for hauling them. But the usual flaw in picnics is that there are too many things to carry and look after and too much to clean and pack up and take home again.

Therefore, people who organize picnics frequently should make up a list of all items that may be needed and check it each time before leaving. All the equipment may not be necessary for every picnic, but a list will prevent the salt or the bottle opener from being omitted!

LEAVING THE PICNIC SITE

No matter where your picnic has taken place, be sure not only to tidy up before you leave so that no trace will be left, but to be careful, while you are eating and opening papers, not to throw them carelessly aside where they will blow out onto the road. Many of our highways have pleasant wayside parks for picnickers, equipped with rustic tables, safe drinking water, and incinerators. On the property of a private owner, the least payment you can make is to be sure that you do nothing that might despoil any of his property.

Most important of all, *never* leave a fire without being absolutely certain that it is out. In the woods, water may be poured on the logs until there is no sign of steam, or if you have a shovel or other means of lifting them, the embers may be carried to a nearby pond or stream and thrown in. On the beach the fire may also be put out with water. *Never* cover the coals with sand, as they will retain the heat for hours, and someone walking by with bare feet, unable to see the remains of the fire, may step on the hot sand and receive a terrible burn.

33

Barbecues

A barbecue is essentially a cooking picnic in your own yard, but because of the proximity to your house, your menu and equipment may be more elaborate than that for a meal transported in your car.

ARRANGING YOUR DINING AREA

If you have a built-in grill in your yard or patio, you are fortunate indeed, but it is not at all necessary. A portable grill, either one on wheels or the folding variety, serves just as well. There should be a table, or tables, near the fire to hold the food and the plates, cooking utensils, and any other necessary equipment. There must be seating facilities for every guest. If your garden has a wall or if the patio has steps leading to it, these may be used as seats, but it is thoughtful to provide cushions to cover hard stone or cement. If you do not have enough small chairs that can easily be carried to the yard, it is possible to rent them very inexpensively from a caterer.

SETTING THE BARBECUE TABLE

In setting the table for a barbecue, you may give your flair for color and decoration a free rein. Checked or striped tablecloths, ones with splashy designs of fruits or flowers, or those with bright red lobsters or colorful chefs' hats are eye-catching and set the tone for a gay party. They may be of cotton or linen if you wish, but plastic ones that can be wiped clean are more practical. Paper napkins in every imaginable color and design are available, but if your cloth is patterned, a solid colored napkin is best.

Disposable plates and cups of paper or plastic, which lighten the hostess's duties, can also be bought in many colors and varieties. Be sure, however, that they are of a sturdy material—plastic or plastic-coated paper rather than the somewhat flimsy cardboard-paper type. If you are serving a hot drink, paper cups must have handles or your guests will have difficulty holding them; and the package should be labeled "for hot drinks," or they will leak. Styrofoam cups or glasses are ideal in that they do not conduct the heat, and at the same time keep the liquid hot.

Hostesses who do not like to use disposable plates have many alternatives. Hard plastic sets of "china" come in lovely patterns and, although unbreakable, feel much like real china. Drink containers, too, come in many break-proof materials that are ideal for use outdoors, where uneven ground or stone patios add to the ordinary number of broken glasses.

Flame-proof pots and pans in gaily colored enamelware or ironware are very useful to the barbecue cook. What a joy to be able to cook or heat a casserole over your fire and serve it in the same handsome container! This enamelware also can be purchased for individual servings—little casseroles with covers, perfect for hot chowder, stew, meat pies, etc.

Types of centerpieces and decorations are unlimited, but you will receive more compliments if they are appropriate to the meal or the season. For example, Chinese lanterns strung above the table and a centerpiece of gay paper parasols might accompany a Chinese dinner. Or a fishnet tablecloth with colorful felt cutouts of fish is decorative on the table set for a lobster dinner. Half a watermelon, filled with fresh melon balls and other fruits and decorated with sprigs of mint, makes a cool and appealing centerpiece for a hot summer evening. And fresh flowers arranged in a container that fits the barbecue theme are always attractive —yellow daisies, for instance, arranged in a copper kettle.

THE HOST AS COOK

At most barbecues the host is the cook, but this is not a hard and fast rule. If he dislikes cooking and the hostess wants to entertain their friends in this way, there is no reason why she should not act as chef—and she is almost sure to be deluged with suggestions and assistance from her male guests. But the party will run more smoothly if she is relieved of the duties at the grill and is free to bring the other dishes from the kitchen, to help the guests serve themselves, and to see that everyone is having a good time.

MENU SUGGESTIONS

Rather than discuss menu possibilities generally, I am going to give you some sample menus, all of which may be enlarged upon or changed to fit the taste of the guests and the hosts. These suggestions are intended as a guide, to show the infinite variety that may be presented at this type of party; they are not in any way meant to be a complete list. In each case, the main dish—meat, fish, or fowl—is prepared on the grill. Unless specified, the others are prepared in advance and kept on the stove indoors or brought out to sit on a corner of the grill where the temperature must be neither too hot nor too cold.

The following meal is the least expensive, but always popular—especially with young people:

Hamburgers and/or Hot Dogs
Buttered Rolls
Casserole of Baked Beans
Potato Chips
Celery and Carrot Sticks
Watermelon Slices

This exotic menu calls for more preparation beforehand (pieces of meat or shrimp, mushrooms, tomatoes, onions, and bacon are marinated and threaded alternately on long skewers, ready to be laid on the grill):

Beef, Lamb, or Shrimp "Kabobs"
Rice
Watercress and Tomato Salad
Hot Rolls
Chocolate Eclairs

Especially good for the seashore are:

Grilled Swordfish
Casserole of Scalloped Potatoes
Spinach Salad
Croissants
Fresh Fruit Compote and Cookies or Cake

Spare ribs are messy to eat, but delicious. Be sure that your guests are informally dressed for this one:

Spare Ribs with Barbecue Sauce
Baked Potatoes
Coleslaw
Hard Rolls
Apple pie with Vanilla Ice Cream

This is the classic barbecue menu:

Sirloin Steak
Potato Chips
French Fried Onions
Mixed Green Salad
French or Garlic Bread
Assorted Pastries

Beer, any soft drink, and pitchers of milk all go well with the informality of a barbecue. In hot weather iced tea and iced coffee are delicious. Pots of coffee should be kept hot on the grill for serving either during or after the meal.

Cocktails may be served, but since the food is hearty elaborate hors d'oeuvres are not necessary. A few dishes of nuts or potato chips scattered about are sufficient.

A side table loaded with a variety of condiments is a nice idea. As each guest fills his plate (the host usually cuts and serves the meat), he passes by this table and helps himself to ketchup, mustard, relish, sauce, or whatever may be offered.

SOME GENERAL HINTS

Remember to have plenty of light; it is very difficult for the chef to tell whether the meat is done if he cannot see it. Floodlights directed up into the trees give a beautiful effect. Gay and colorful Japanese lanterns can be purchased strung on electric wires like Christmas-tree bulbs. Candles give a soft light, but must be placed in hurricane lamps to protect them from the breeze. Some candles contain an insect repellent—an excellent idea for a summer night.

Entertainment after the meal depends on your facilities and the preferences of your guests. A lunchtime barbecue may be followed by a swim if you have a pool or are near the beach. If not, you may want to organize a game of softball or badminton. Many adults enjoy a game of catch or touch football on a brisk day. When there are children present, suitable games and races are almost a necessity to keep them out of the chef's way.

In the evening you may dance to records if the patio or terrace has a suitable surface. Or, if you have a stone fireplace, build up the fire to a blaze so that the guests may gather round to sing or chat. If you notice your guests shivering or putting on sweaters or coats, you must be prepared to move the party into the house—one of the advantages of having a barbecue in your own yard—otherwise your guests will soon start to leave.

34

Other informal gatherings

There are many varieties of informal entertainment which have special descriptive names or specific purposes but which do not otherwise differ much from the informal gatherings discussed in earlier chapters. A housewarming, for example, may be a cocktail buffet with tours of the new house added, or a surprise party might be an informal dance given in someone else's house. Therefore, it may often be practical for a hostess to combine the suggestions made here with those from another appropriate chapter.

HOURS FOR PARTY-GIVING

The hour chosen for a meal, party, game, or visit should comply with local custom. To invite friends to dine two hours later than their regular meal hour is not likely to impress them with what may be intended as a fashionable innovation. People dine in London at nine and in Spain or Mexico at ten or even later, but this is no reason for upsetting the digestions of those who prefer to dine at seven. If weddings in the evening are customary in your neighborhood, then have your wedding in the evening too. If, on the other hand, a nine o'clock dinner hour and a noon wedding are customary, at nine you dine and at noon you marry.

If neighbors pay visits in the evening—or if morning is the hour preferred—you take your protesting husband with you in the evening—or go by yourself in the morning—no matter how inconvenient either hour may be to you.

The same is true of a dessert-bridge party or the meeting of your sewing circle. If you cannot manage to have the group at the time decreed by custom, find another way to entertain your friends that can be conveniently fitted into your schedule and theirs.

HOUSEWARMINGS

When you have put a great deal of time and effort into making a lovely home, you are naturally as eager to show it off as your friends are to see it. The nicest way to do so is to call your friends and ask them to a housewarming. Or you may invite them informally whenever you want. Invitations on informals are quite suitable, too. Because the object of the party is to show your guests the house, it is far better to have two or three small parties at which you will only have to make the tour a few times. If you have too many people at once, you may spend the entire time leading groups from one room to another.

A housewarming is generally a cocktail party or a cocktail buffet. It may be as simple or as elaborate as you wish, but it is fun to keep the style of your house in mind when you plan your decorations. For instance, if it is an Early American type, a brown tablecloth set with copper or pewter may be more appealing than lace with crystal or silver. *For additional suggestions, see Chapter Twenty-eight, "Cocktail Parties."*

The guest generally takes a small gift to a housewarming. It need not be expensive, but it is more thoughtful to find something that will be of permanent use rather than flowers, which will only last a short time, or paper napkins, which would soon be used up. An ash tray, a few pretty dish towels or place mats, a cigarette box, a brush for the fireplace are a few possibilities.

OPEN HOUSE

An open house is literally what the name implies. The door is open to all those invited at any time between the hours stated on the invitation. Today most open houses are held to celebrate a holiday—New Year's Day, perhaps, or Christmas Eve. They also may take the place of a housewarming.

In very small communities an announcement of the open house may be put in the local paper, and anyone and everyone who reads it is expected to attend if he wishes. When invitations are issued in church or club announcements, the host is saved from having to invite the entire membership individually. Personal invitations are generally sent out on informals or commercial cards bought for the occasion.

Because an answer is never expected, refreshments are simple and of a sort that may be expanded or not set out all at once. Dips, bowls of nuts, and a punch—rather than individual drinks—are good choices. People drop in to greet their hosts, and friends wish each other a "Happy New Year" or "Good luck to you in your new home." They generally stay no more than a half-hour to an hour.

If the open house is to celebrate a holiday, the decorations are generally appropriate to the season. At Christmas time, the tree would be trimmed, and whatever other decorations you might wish to use would be arranged as beautifully as possible. For a Fourth of July party, red, white, and blue streamers, balloons, or bouquets might add a note of gaiety. But if the open house is not held to celebrate any particular holiday, no decorations are necessary other than some vases of pretty flowers or greens.

The food and beverages may be arranged on the dining-room table if you have enough plates of cookies or sandwiches so that it will not look bare. If your refreshments are restricted to one or two plates of food and a punch bowl, they may be set out on any conveniently placed table in the hall or living room, or on a side table in the dining room. You may wish to surround a bowl of eggnog with holly twigs or a fruit punch with flowers, but otherwise, only the attractive arrangement of glasses, little napkins (cloth or paper), and food is necessary to assure the charm of your refreshment table.

BRUNCHES

Brunch—a combination of breakfast and lunch that relies heavily on breakfast for its menus but that is held closer to the usual hour for lunch—is a pleasant sort of informal, even casual, entertaining. It is not unusual to find brunches being given on the day after a large party, especially if there are many out-of-town guests who have come for the "big" occasion. However, no such excuse is necessary if you find the late morning hours convenient for you and your friends.

In any event informality is the rule. In the country, slacks or simple dresses may be worn by the women, or if the host is having the party beside his swimming pool, people may come in shorts and bring their bathing suits. In the city, any daytime dress or a suit is correct for a woman, and a man usually wears a sports jacket rather than a business suit.

Invitations may be telephoned ahead of time, but this kind of gathering is so casual that the host may simply say to his friends as they are leaving someone else's party, "Would you come over around 11:30 tomorrow for a late breakfast?" or "Would you all come for a late breakfast after church tomorrow?"

Sometimes a Bloody Mary or a mixture of chilled consommé and vodka is served, but tomato juice or consommé must also be offered without the liquor for friends who prefer it that way.

The food is arranged on a buffet table less elaborately set than for lunch or dinner, but attractively and conveniently laid out. Breakfast and lunch dishes are combined. For example, a platter of scrambled eggs surrounded with bacon or little sausages may be accompanied by hot rolls, toast, sautéed potatoes, and broiled tomatoes. Or platters of waffles can be covered with maple syrup by some or with creamed chicken by guests who prefer a heartier meal. Pitchers of fruit juice and pots of coffee should be on a table beside the buffet.

CARD PARTIES

ON PLANNING YOUR TABLES

In giving a card party, whether of two tables or of ten, the first thing to do is to plan the tables carefully. Divide the people who accept into groups of four, and try to seat at each table only those who like to play together. The tables may all be different—one with good players, another with beginners, one where the stakes are high, another where they play for nothing—but you must do your best to put those who play approximately the same kind of game at the same table. In addition to playing, it is important to remember temperament. Don't put people who take their game seriously (and "play for blood") with others who unceasingly chatter and keep asking, "What's trump?" Don't put someone who plays rapidly at a table with dawdlers who take forever to decide which card they'll play—and who even then take half as long again to lay the card face up on the table!

There are hostesses who apparently seat players by drawing names out of a hat without the slightest regard for the good players and the bad players or for what stakes they like to play. These hostesses will put two men who are the best players in town at a table with one woman who thinks of nothing but the next bright remark she can make, and a second woman who is beautiful to look at but who knows no more than a child of eight about bidding. A man will be delighted to find a pretty woman next to him at the dinner table, but at the card table he hopes for an expert partner. If she is pretty or charming, or both, so much the better, but these attributes are secondary. The real point is that one poor player spoils the whole evening—or afternoon—for the three who play well.

However, when a group of friends play together regularly, and they have approximately the same degree of skill, they may prefer to draw for partners and tables in order to have the opportunity of playing with different combinations of people.

And now your preparations: It seems scarcely necessary to say that the packs of cards on each table must be fresh and that the pencils laid beside the score pads must be sharp. On each table you leave a slip of paper on which you have written the names of the four players who are to play there, or you may simply tell each guest at which table he is to play. At parties where bridge is simply a diversion and is not taken too seriously, or when a group plays together frequently and they are all of the same caliber, the table grouping may also be arranged by lot. At each table the players cut for their seats and partners. It is important to see that each table is comfortably lighted. Poorly placed light that is reflected from the shiny surface of the cards is just as bad as darkness that makes red cards indistinguishable from black ones. If you have any doubt about the light, sit in each place, hold cards in your hands, lay a few on the table, and see for yourself.

REFRESHMENTS

The kind of refreshments you offer your card-playing guests depends, of course, on the time of day. While small sandwiches and tiny cakes, accompanied by tea or coffee, might be suitable when served at four o'clock to a group of women, they would hardly please the men at an evening gathering. Then a selection of cold meats and cheeses and a variety of breads for do-it-yourself sandwiches, served with coffee and beer, would be more appropriate. In either case, however, the food may be attractively arranged on the dining-room table, and, having served themselves, the guests may be asked either to return to the cleared card tables or to take their plates to the comfortable chairs in the living room.

A note of warning: If you have invited avid card players, you will be well advised not to interrupt their game to serve some lavish concoction of whipped cream, cake, frosting, and cherries, no matter how elegant you think it looks. Men in particular will be most unlikely to accept your next invitation if they feel that in your home card playing is secondary to such culinary productions. Give another kind of party if you wish to show off your prowess in the kitchen!

PRIZES

If it is customary in your community to play for prizes, then you must select a first prize for the highest score to be made by a woman and a first prize for the highest score to be made by a man. At a party to which no men are invited, a second prize is usually given. In any case, all prizes should be attractively wrapped before being presented. Those who receive the prizes must, of course, open the packages at once and show some evidence of appreciation when thanking the hostess. Needless to say, a well-behaved person does not show disappointment upon receiving a prize that happens not to please him or her, nor does he "forget" to take it home.

DESSERT CARD PARTY

A dessert card party is a happy compromise for the hostess who may feel that she cannot provide a full luncheon for her guests, yet wishes to do more than simply invite them to play cards. When there are four present, or even eight if her dining-room table is large enough to seat them, dessert may be served in the following way: The dining table is set for the dessert course only. Individual place mats are set with a china dessert plate, a lunch napkin on the plate, a fork at the left and a spoon at the right, and a glass of water. The table should, furthermore, be set with a coffee tray in front of the hostess; while her friends are having their dessert she pours the coffee, and it is handed around the table. After coffee they begin playing on tables already set up in the living room.

If there are more than eight, the dining table may be set as a buffet, using a tablecloth or place mats or round lace doilies (paper ones will do if you have no lace mats) under the stack of plates and the dishes on which the dessert is served.

The guests serve themselves and take their plates to the living room to eat. Unless the hostess asks them to, they do not sit at the card tables, which have already been set up and readied for bridge. They help themselves to coffee, and if they wish to start playing immediately, they may take their cups with them to the bridge tables.

STAG DINNERS

A man's dinner is sometimes called a stag or bachelor dinner and, as its name implies, is a dinner given by a man for men only. It usually celebrates some special event or person. It may be a welcome or farewell, or the bridegroom's last party with his good friends before his wedding. Occasionally a man may have a quantity of game that he has shot, or fish that he has caught, and want to share it with his friends.

Nearly always a man's dinner is given at the host's club or in a private room in a hotel or restaurant. But if he chooses to give a stag dinner in his own house, his wife (or mother or sister) should *not* appear. For his wife to come downstairs and receive the guests with him is most definitely out of place. No matter how much you may want to say "How do you do" to your husband's or son's friends—*don't.*

Therefore, if a man does decide he would like to entertain his friends at home, he must discuss his plans and the menu with his wife, who will then prepare it ahead of time and unobtrusively set out the dishes on a buffet table at the time agreed upon with her husband. After the men have eaten, she may remove the plates and clean up if they have gone to a living room or library separated from the dining room, but if they are still close by, she would do better to leave the cleaning up until the next day. If there are servants in the house, they may prepare and serve the meal as at any dinner party.

THE SURPRISE PARTY

Years ago, in the days of many servants, surprise parties were often arranged in the home of the guests of honor—with the cooperation of the cook, waitress, or whoever would be involved. The couple were spirited away on some pretext, and when they returned, the house was ready and the guests were hidden inside waiting to shout "Surprise!" as they entered.

Today, very few servantless couples would welcome a group when they have had no warning to prepare their home for a party. An exception might be made when a husband wishes to give his wife a surprise birthday party, or she wishes to surprise him with a party in honor of a special occasion—a promotion, for example. Then, with the help of friends, the one planning the party can arrange it in his own house.

Otherwise, surprise parties take place at a friend's house or possibly in a club. The couple to be honored is invited for a "quiet" dinner or evening by another couple, and when they arrive their entire circle of friends is there waiting to surprise them.

Such parties always consist of a group of intimate friends and usually take place on John's or Mary's birthday or their anniversary, particularly an earlier one.

Some caution should be exercised in arranging surprise parties, and thought given to whether the people honored would really enjoy the occasion. For example, a word of warning is necessary for persons who might be inclined to surprise their friends with a party for their golden wedding anniversary. If the bride and groom are young for their ages, it is possible that they would like this type of party. But if they were not married in their earliest youth, the excitement of too great a surprise might very well have the opposite of happy results.

SINGING, READING, OR DISCUSSION GROUPS

When neighborhood groups include both men and women, they usually meet in the evening at a time agreed upon as convenient for everyone. Therefore, the hostess has little to say about the hour. But a group of women interested, for example, in reading French together, may find that an afternoon or even a morning meeting is the only solution to the problem of family schedules. The convenience of the members carries more weight in such circumstances than any prescribed hour, and even neighborhood custom should not discourage a group from picking their own time or changing it by mutual consent.

Refreshments are usually served after the activity of the meeting, and of course the kind depends on the hour, the preferences of the group, and the inclination of the hostess-of-the-day. Coffee and sandwiches, Welsh rarebit and beer, cider and doughnuts would all be appropriate after an evening gathering. Earlier in the day, coffee and rolls or tea and cookies might very well be adequate.

Otherwise, there are no rules for such groups—except to be firm with those who can't keep in tune or with the gossipers who wander from the topic under discussion.

SEWING GROUPS

The hostess at whose house a sewing group meets should have a supply of different-sized thimbles, extra needles, and several pairs of scissors and spools of thread. What is sewed depends upon the purpose of the group, which may be to make garments for a nursery, hospital, or other organization. It may have no object other than to meet socially, in which case the members sew for themselves—doing needlepoint, darning socks, even knitting. Sometimes a sewing circle is also a lunch club that meets weekly or fortnightly at the houses of the various members. They sew from eleven until about one and then have a sit-down or buffet luncheon. More often coffee and light refreshments, such as coffee cake, cookies, or doughnuts, are served approximately halfway through a session that may run from ten to twelve or from two to half past four.

35

Showers

Showers are friendly gatherings held in honor of a bride-to-be, a new clergyman, or an expectant mother—in fact, they can celebrate almost anything you wish. So, too, the setting for a shower can be almost anything—a luncheon, a dinner, an afternoon tea, an evening party, or even a morning coffee. The only distinguishing characteristic of the shower is the giving of presents to the guest of honor.

Bridal showers are never given by members of the bride's immediate family, because a gift is obligatory. Whether a wedding present is sent in addition to a shower gift depends upon the custom of one's own community and on whether the wedding is to be restricted to family members. Generally people who are invited to a wedding reception send a wedding gift in addition to a shower present. It is perfectly permissible to give a shower for someone who is being married for the second time, whether she be widow or divorcée. But the hostess, as she plans her party, would do well to keep in mind the elaborateness of the wedding plans and make hers accordingly. In other words, the bride-to-be who for one reason or another is having a very quiet, simple wedding might easily be embarrassed by an extremely elaborate shower, however kindly her friend's intention.

THE INVITATIONS

Invitations to showers are often telephoned: "I'm having a kitchen shower for Betsy Jones on Tuesday at three o'clock." They may be written on a visiting card—"Housewarming shower for Dr. Smythe" or "Stork shower for Helen"—with the day and the hour. Or one of the shower cards found at stationers' shops is just as appropriate. Make certain, however, that it is perfectly clear to the guests exactly what kind of shower it is to be, including all details you have that may be helpful. For example, if you know that Betsy Jones's kitchen is to have red trim, do let the guests know, too, so that they can choose appropriately colored items. For a lingerie shower, it is essential to mention the bride's size.

THE HOUR

A shower for a bride may be given at any hour of the day or evening. Evening is chosen when the shower presents take the place of wedding presents, and when men as well as women are invited.

The shower for a clergyman is usually given in the early evening. Before the arrival of a baby, a stork shower is always given in the afternoon and only close girl friends of the mother-to-be are invited. When the baby is five or six weeks old, a stork shower may be held at the mother's house. Sometimes given as a surprise party, this is one occasion when it would be excusable for someone to give the new mother a hint at least half an hour in advance so that both she and the baby will be found ready for company. Also, the guests usually bring refreshments with them as at all typical surprise parties, including one for an unmarried clergyman.

GRANDMOTHER SHOWERS

When a women's club or social organization learns that one of their members is about to become a grandmother, the others may wish to give her a "grandmother shower." It is usually held during or at the end of their regular meeting or get-together, with some special refreshments served and a few extra minutes devoted to the opening of the gifts. However, it may be given in the usual way—by a close friend or group of friends of the grandmother-to-be as an afternoon tea or a morning coffee.

The main distinction between a grandmother shower and any other is that the gifts are not for the use of the recipient. Often they are gifts for the baby or the new mother which are given through the grandmother. They may also be articles to be used by the grandmother when she is caring for the new baby—diaper pins, a bathinette, a teething ring, bibs, etc.

Whatever the arrangements, the grandmother shower is a delightful way to honor a friend, and to make the prospective grandmother feel an important part of the coming event.

THE GIFTS

Many times the type of shower being given allows wide leeway in the choice of presents. At a stork shower they may include anything for a new baby. A kitchen shower, which is often given for a new clergyman, includes everything eatable. Showers for a bride are sometimes specified as linen showers, kitchen showers, lingerie showers, or general showers, for which a guest may bring anything at all that seems appropriate.

At a "round-the-clock" shower, each guest is given an hour of the day on her invitation and brings a present appropriate for the hour. For example, at a bridal shower, if her hour is ten in the morning she might take a dustpan and brush, or if it is six in the evening she might take a set of four or six cocktail glasses.

Although sometimes the shower presents are given in place of wedding gifts, more generally they are an extra expression of generosity and of much less importance than the wedding gifts. Sometimes they are the donation of the bride's bridge club or a small group of her most intimate friends who have been busy hemming or embroidering a set of table linens or kitchen towels, each piece of which is signed by the sewer. Such gifts have a charm and personal sentiment that the bride is certain to appreciate.

PRESENTING THE GIFTS

When everyone—or almost everyone—expected has arrived, Mary opens the packages one by one and thanks each giver. "Thank you, Susie—these towels will be just perfect with my wallpaper!" The cards of donors should be enclosed, because otherwise each giver must say more or less self-consciously as her present is unwrapped, "That's from me."

After that, if the party is at teatime, the guests are offered tea or coffee, sandwiches and cakes. If it is in the evening, coffee or punch and sandwiches are suitable, as are cider and doughnuts, or liqueurs or highballs, especially if men are included.

Although wedding presents are sent from the shop where they are bought, gifts for a shower are brought by hand and given personally—although sometimes the packages are taken at the door by the hostess and put unopened with the others on a table in another room.

In some localities all the presents are sent to the hostess several days beforehand. She leaves the packages as they are, but puts each in a uniform outer gift wrapping so that the whole stack of packages will be alike. For this purpose the wrapping-paper assortments to be found at all stationery counters are perfect. When all are wrapped, the presents are piled on a table in another room or behind a screen, or perhaps in the living room.

36

House parties and overnight guests

Although the day of the great house staffed by a horde of servants is almost gone, there is no reason why the simple house with a relaxed hostess and enthusiastic guests cannot be the setting for a house party that is just as much a success as the elaborate affair of other years.

The size of the house party in the houses of today is limited mainly by the number of available beds. Furthermore, for a hostess who has no help, it is certainly easier to cook, serve, and keep the house in order with two guests than it is with eight, a fact she should remember even after she has counted the beds.

THE INVITATIONS

Invitations are generally telephoned, but if your guests live in another town, they may be written on your notepaper.

June 15

Dear Ellie,

John and I are hoping that you and Bob and the children can spend the weekend of the fourth with us in Edgartown. If Bob could leave the office a little early on Friday the 2nd, there is a 4:00 P.M.

ferry that would get you here in time for dinner, and there are ferries leaving the island at 5:00 and at 8:00 on Sunday. The fishing should be great, and our children are counting on Sally and Jimmy for the annual picnic. Please come—we have wanted to show you our island for so long.

Much love,
Ann

With the rising popularity of winter sports, more and more people are acquiring lodges in the mountains, and ski weekends are becoming almost an institution in all sections of the country where there are nearby slopes.

January 4

Dear Joan,

The forecast is for snow and more snow, and Dick and I are hoping that you and Bill will spend the weekend after next skiing with us at Stowe. Come as early as you can on Friday the eighth, and stay until Sunday night so as not to miss a minute of it. The Hortons are coming, too, so maybe you could drive up together. To find us, you turn off Route 7 on Skyline Drive, exactly three-tenths of a mile beyond the traffic light in Hampton, and we are the second house on the right.

No formal clothes, only your ski outfits, and slacks or a skirt for the evening. Plenty of woolies and flannels—it's cold!

We're counting on you, so do say "yes."

Love to you both,
Barbara

In your letter or on the telephone, be sure to give the details of transportation, or the route if your guests are coming by car. If they will be arriving by public transportation, you must tell them to let you know at what hour they will arrive so that you can meet them at the station or airport.

To make it easier for a woman to know what to bring, it is wise to indicate what the main activities will be. "We're planning a deep-sea fishing expedition on Saturday," "The Joneses have asked us to a beach picnic on Sunday," or "There is to be a dance at the club on Saturday."

ROOM FOR YOUR GUESTS

TEMPORARY ARRANGEMENTS

Most families today do not have a room in their house that is intended solely for the use of guests. When they wish to have friends spend a night or a weekend (or more), the children are moved around to vacate a room; or the library or den, which is furnished with convertible sofas, is put in readiness. The toys are hidden from sight, the clothes are removed from the closet, sufficient drawer space is cleared so that the guest may unpack his suitcase, and the room is made sparkling clean. If he is to share a bath with other members of the household, his towels should be hung on a rack in his bedroom, so that children do not inadvertently use them. Although it may seem that not much more can be done to make a guest room out of one that is used every day, many of the suggestions made in the following section describing the permanent guest room can be adapted—to the comfort and convenience of your visitors.

THE GUEST ROOM

It is by no means idle talk to suggest that every hostess try her guest room by spending at least one night in it herself. If she doesn't do this, she should at least check the facilities thoroughly. She should go into the guest bathroom and check the drains to see that there is no stoppage and make sure that the toilet flushes properly. If a man is to utilize the bathroom, she should see that there is a receptacle for used razor blades and that there is a well-lighted mirror in which he can look to shave. Even though it may be adequate for powdering her nose, it would be safer to ask her husband to bathe and shave in the guest bathroom and then listen to what he says about it.

There must, of course, be plenty of bath towels, face towels, a washcloth, a bath mat, and fresh cakes of soap for the bathtub and on the washstand.

It is not expected, but it is a nice touch to place eau de cologne, bath salts or bath oil, mouthwash, bath powder, hand and sunburn lotion in decorated bottles on the washstand shelf or in the medicine chest. But to cover the dressing table in the bedroom with an array of these articles is more of a nuisance than a comfort. A good clothes brush and a pincushion with both straight and safety pins are always a welcome sight, and a new toothbrush in the bathroom has saved many a guest a trip to the local drugstore.

Good beds are most important. The mattresses should be firm—many people develop serious backaches from sleeping on a sagging bed. The most desirable arrangement is to have twin beds placed together, possibly with a single headboard. This satisfies both the couple who cannot sleep in the same bed and the couple who are used to a double bed. It also serves perfectly well for two girls (or two boys). If there is space, the beds may be pushed apart and a table put between them if the girls are not intimate friends.

It is nice but not necessary to provide two pillows for each guest, one medium hard and one soft, so that he may have a choice. Two pillows are also a comfort to those who like to read in bed. There must always be plenty of covers, of course, and in the winter there should be a quilt laid across the foot of the bed, unless you have electric blankets.

There must, of course, be a light at the head of each bed. Not just a decorative glowworm effect, but a 75- or 100-watt bulb with an adjustable shade that provides really good reading light. Moreover, if there are twin beds, each light should be so shaded from the other that the occupant of one can read while the other sleeps. A reliable clock, preferably with an alarm, is essential. And in case the visitor has not brought his own reading material, there should be books—chosen more to divert then to strain the reader's attention. The sort of selection appropriate for a guest room might include one or two nonfiction books of the moment, a light novel or a mystery novel, a book of short stories, and a few of the latest magazines. It is very important that this selection be revised from time to time. Otherwise the guest room can become a wastebasket for outdated magazines or a catchall for books selected because of a momentary timeliness.

There should be cigarettes, matches, and ash trays on the tables, and a wastebasket beside the bureau. In hot weather every guest room should have an electric fan if the house does not have some type of air-conditioning; and in August, even though there are screens, a fly swatter is a good idea.

The hostess should put on her makeup at the dressing table to learn whether the light is good both at night and in the daytime.

Facial tissues in pretty containers should be placed on the dressing table or beside the beds, and in the bathroom.

If there is a desk in the room, one must be sure that the ink is not a dried-up patch of black dust, that the pens are in working order, and that the writing paper matches the envelopes. The blotter should be fresh, and the calendar up to date. A thoughtful hostess puts a few stamps in the desk drawer.

The closets should contain wooden clothes hangers with bars for trousers, or plastic ones for dresses. Thin wire hangers from the cleaner's crease the shoulders of dresses and the knees of pants.

The paper lining in the bureau drawers must be fresh, and everything stored in them by members of the family must be removed to make space for the belongings of the guests.

People who like strong perfumes often mistakenly think they are giving pleasure in filling all the bureau drawers with heavily scented pads. Instead of feeling pleasure, some people are made almost sick by them, but a very lightly scented sachet is delightful. Everyone—except a hay-fever sufferer—loves flowers, and vases of them dress up rooms as nothing else can. Even a shabby little room embellished with a few wild flowers or a potted plant becomes inviting.

A shortcoming in many houses is the lack of a newspaper. The thoughtful hostess who has a servant and has a morning paper sent up with her guest's breakfast tray deserves a halo. When the visitor breakfasts in the dining room, it takes no effort to see that one is placed near his place at the breakfast table.

Guest rooms should have dark shades for those who like to sleep late.

If you have no thermos jugs to be placed by the guest-room beds, be sure that there are glasses in the bathroom, or suggest that your guest take a glass of iced water with him when says good night.

THE HOUSE WITH SERVANTS

When houseguests arrive at a house staffed by a number of servants, the personal maid of the hostess (if she has one—otherwise, the housemaid) unpacks the luggage, lays toilet articles on the dressing table and in the bathroom, puts folded things in the drawers, and hangs dresses in the closet. If, as she unpacks, the maid sees that something of importance has been forgotten, she tells the hostess; or, if she is a longtime employee and knows where to find a substitute for the missing article, she supplies it without asking. She also sees that the clothes are pressed if necessary.

In a house with a large staff, breakfast trays for the ladies are usually carried to the bedroom floor by the butler and are handed to the lady's maid or to the housemaid, who takes the tray into the room. In simpler households they are carried up by the waitress.

Trays for men visitors are less common, but when ordered they are carried up and into the room by the butler or, if there are no menservants, by the waitress.

Unless breakfast is at a set time and everyone comes down promptly, the advantage of having one's guests breakfast upstairs is that no delayed breakfast prevents the dining room's being put in order or the lunch table set. Trays, on the other hand, can stand all morning in the pantry and interfere much less with the dining-room work. Many hostesses therefore much prefer guests to have trays.

A breakfast set always has a coffeepot or teapot, a cream pitcher and sugar bowl, a cup and saucer, two plates, one bowl, an egg cup, and a cover. Hot cereal is usually put in the bowl, toast in a napkin on a plate, and eggs and bacon on a plate with a cover. Glasses for fruit juice and iced water complete the tray.

When a guest rings for breakfast, the maid goes into the room and pulls up the shades. In cold weather she closes the windows and turns on the heat. If the guest wishes a morning bath, she goes into the bathroom, spreads a bath mat on the floor and a big towel over a chair, and draws the bath. If the hostess has not asked her guests the night before, the maid asks what they would like for breakfast at this time.

Anyone breakfasting in the dining room is expected to dress before going down to the table. On some rare and informal occasions, the hostess may suggest the night before that dressing gowns are in order, but this is not usually the case in a household with servants.

TIPS

In the United States, when you dine in a friend's house, you do not tip anyone—ever. But when you go to stay overnight or longer as a houseguest, you are expected to give a gratuity.

For an average servant in an average house, two dollars is about right for a weekend. Mrs. Lavender, staying with the Littlehouses and causing very little extra work, might quite acceptably give no more than five dollars for a week. Intimate friends in a house with two or three servants tip perhaps only a dollar or two apiece, but no one is forgotten. In a very big house, this is never done; you tip only those who have served you. The least a bachelor can offer any of the menservants is two dollars and the most is usually five.

You give the maid her tip when she has finished packing your bag. You give the butler his or the waitress hers in the front hall.

In a small house, if the waitress is not in the hall you go to the pantry or kitchen and put the money into her hand. If you are a fre-

quent visitor and know her name, you say, "Good-bye, Anna, and thank you." If the cook is there you say the same thing to her. If not, you may, after giving Anna her own tip, hand her a second sum of money, saying, "Please give this to the cook for me." If Anna has pressed your dress, let us say, or sewed something that had ripped or done any other special service, you give her a dollar or two extra; and when you say good-bye, you add "Thank you" for whatever the service was.

This whole system is generally embarrassing to the visitor, the host, and frequently to the servant also. A far better method is for the employer to offer his servant, or staff of servants, a bonus when he entertains overnight guests. Houseguests should be informed of the arrangement at some time during their visit so that they will not leave money for the chambermaid in their room, or approach the other help with a tip. This should be clearly understood when the servants are hired, and they should be asked to refuse tips, should any visitors attempt to give them a "little gift" regardless of the host's request that they do not do so. This would insure a happier household in every way—the servants would look forward to visitors, knowing that it would definitely mean extra money, and guests would be relieved of the questions of "How much?" and "How do I leave it?" at the end of their stay.

MEALS IN THE HOUSEHOLD WITHOUT SERVANTS

If you are one of those who has servants, meals for your guests present few, if any, problems. Prepare the menus, discuss them with your cook, and think no more about them until you sit down at the table.

When you must entertain without help, the more planning and preparation that can be done ahead, the more effortless and pleasant the result. House parties do not generally last for more than two days and nights—at most three. With the help of a freezer, or even the freezing compartment of your refrigerator, your meals can be largely prepared in advance. A casserole kept warm in the oven can be ready at whatever hour your guests arrive, early or late. A steak cooked on the beach in summer or over the coals of the fireplace in winter, served with potato chips and salad, takes little effort. And you may wish to treat your guests to a dinner in a local restaurant that specializes in foods native to the region. At most summer resorts, yacht clubs or night clubs provide dinner and dancing on Saturday night.

For lunches, you may prepare the ingredients for a chef's salad, lobster rolls, chowder, and sandwiches in advance, ready to be mixed or spread at the last moment.

The one meal that the hostess cannot organize in advance is breakfast. Because one of the joys of a weekend away from home is being able to sleep as late as one wants, do not awaken the guests unless there is an activity planned in which they truly wish to participate.

The hostess should get up at an early enough hour to precede all her guests to the kitchen. She makes coffee, prepares fruit or juice, and cooks sausage or bacon enough for everyone. This can be kept warm on a hot plate or in a very low oven. She may then put butter, eggs, and frying pan—or pancake batter and griddle—by the stove, bread by the toaster, and an assortment of cereals and milk and cream on the table, which she sets with places for everyone. She may wait for her guests, or she may eat her own breakfast and be ready to help the latecomers as they arrive. If some of the group want to make an early start, to the beach or to ski, for instance, plans should be made the day before. The host and hostess may accompany the ones who are leaving, as long as everything is left in readiness for those who wish to sleep or relax and arrangements have been made for their joining the group later on if they wish.

This very friendly custom is gaining popularity everywhere when two or three couples go to visit good friends: they may offer to bring a roast or a casserole to provide one evening's meal. There is no reason why the hostess should not accept such an offer. On this type of intimate party, all guests feel more comfortable if they can contribute, and it certainly adds to the pleasure of the hostess.

THE PERFECT HOSTESS

The abilities of a perfect hostess are called upon long before the actual start of the house party. They begin with choosing guests who have the same interests and who will enjoy each other's company. There is little pleasure in having one couple who enjoys staying up all night to play bridge, while the others wish to go to bed early in order to be up at sunrise to go on a fishing expedition.

Arrangements for whatever activities you know your visitors will enjoy must be made ahead of time. If they like tennis, be sure that you sign up or reserve a court at a convenient hour, or if you are certain that they would love to go to the dance at your club, don't forget to make a reservation for a table or you may be disappointed when you arrive at the door. Don't try to fill every minute with strenuous projects, however. It is probable that your guests would like some time to relax and visit with you and the other guests, and they may very well have some suggestions of their own about a special landmark they would like to see, or a shopping trip to stores carrying merchandise made in the area.

A perfect hostess in a household with servants gives the impression that she has nothing whatever to do with household arrangements, which apparently run themselves. In a servantless household, she has the cleaning, marketing, and as much cooking as possible done in advance, so that an absolute minimum of her time is spent on these chores while her guests are with her.

Certain rules are easy to observe once they are brought to attention. A host or hostess should never speak of annoyance of any kind—no matter what happens. Unless actually unable to stand up, they should not mention their physical ills any more than mental ones.

If anything goes wrong with the household, the host and hostess must work a miracle and keep it from their guests. If, for instance, the stove breaks down, then a picnic must be held as though a picnic had been planned from the beginning. Should a guest be taken ill, the hostess must assure him that he is not giving the slightest trouble; at the same time, nothing that can be done for his comfort must be overlooked.

And above all, she must not be "overanxious." The overanxious hostess is one who fusses and plans continually, who thinks the guests are not having a good time unless they are being rushed—tourist fashion

—from one engagement to another every moment of their stay. She is always asking what you would like to do next. If you say you are quite content as you are, she nevertheless continues to shower suggestions that leave no time for peace and quiet.

DO'S AND DON'T'S FOR HOUSEGUESTS

Having accepted an invitation, guests may shorten their visit, but they must not stay beyond the time they were asked for unless very especially urged to do so. Even then they would be much wiser to go early and be missed rather than to run the risk of overstaying their welcome.

The laws governing the behavior of the ideal guest are by no means easy to follow. Whether it is easy or not, you as a guest must conform to the habits of the family with whom you are staying. You take your meals at their hour, you eat what is put before you, and you get up and go out and come in and go to bed according to the schedule arranged by your hostess. And no matter how much the hours or the food or the arrangements may upset you, you must appear blissfully content. When the visit is over you need never enter that house again, but while you are there you must at least act as if you are enjoying yourself.

If you know anyone who is always in demand, not only for dinners, but for cruises on yachts and weekend visits, you may be very sure of one thing—that person is either unselfish or else an extremely good actor, and very often both.

You must always be ready for anything—or nothing. If a plan is made to picnic, you like picnics above everything and prove that liking by enthusiastically making the sandwiches or the salad dressing or whatever you think you do best. If, on the other hand, no one seems to want to do anything, the perfect guest always has a book to be absorbed in, or a piece of sewing or knitting, or else beyond everything would love to sit in an easy chair and do nothing.

If you want to be an ideal guest, give your attention to these four details when you have accepted an invitation: selection of clothes to be taken, selection of luggage to put them in, selection of gifts, and development of the ideal guest's state of mind.

It is not only courteous but almost obligatory to take your hostess a gift—or, if she has children, to take presents to them. The conventional list of flowers, fruit, candy, or a book is acceptable, but be sure you know of a book she wants, or that she eats candy, or that she has no flowers in her garden or fruit on her trees. Some people prefer to send a present after their visit, having made note of something that their hostess would find useful or that would go perfectly in one of the rooms. As to the children, if they are young, a collection of small amusing articles from the ten-cent store often gives them more pleasure than a single more valuable present.

Your next concern when going on a visit is to condense your luggage in both quantity and size. If you are going in your own car, this is not so important; but if you are being taken in someone else's car or going by train to a place where there are no porters to carry heavy bags, excess luggage can be a near tragedy.

It is sometimes difficult to go for a weekend without a good deal of equipment. An athletic man who is likely to ride and play golf and tennis might easily be taken for a traveler about to make a six-month safari. Besides the necessary sports clothes, a dinner coat (if your host says it is necessary to bring one), one or two sports jackets, slacks, shirts, shoes, ties, etc. must all be included in the luggage.

If you are going where you are to swim or ride or take part in other sports, be sure you take your own bathing suit, riding habit, tennis racket, or golf clubs. Your hostess will want to have her things available for her own use, and you will avoid having to use borrowed clothes or equipment that may not fit or may be totally unlike that to which you are accustomed.

It too often follows that the borrower is likewise an abuser of the lender's property. The guest no one invites a second time is the one who dog-ears books, who burns cigarette trenches on table edges, who uses towels for cleaning shoes, who stands wet glasses on polished wood, who tracks into the house in muddy shoes and then puts them up on the sofa or bed, and who leaves his room looking as though it had been visited by a cyclone. Nor are men the only offenders. Women have been known to commit every one of these offenses and more besides. Think of what they can do to fine linen with their lipstick! Or to a dressing-table surface with nail polish!

Besides these actually destructive shortcomings, there are those guests whose lack of consideration is scarcely less annoying. They may be late for every meal, or they help themselves to a car and go off and fail to come back for meals on time. Then there are those who write no letters afterward, nor even take the trouble to go up and speak to a former hostess when they see her again. This abuse of hospitality is, of course, more often met with by hostesses of large estates whose frequent weekend parties include mere acquaintances. The hostess of a little house seldom has anyone staying with her except a really intimate friend.

Aside from the more or less general rule of behavior, there are a few more specific rules that are worthy of mention.

A guest in someone's home should never suggest taking his hosts to a meal in a restaurant. While you are their guest, you eat the food they provide. If, however, your host suggests dining at a restaurant, you might well say, "That sounds wonderful, and we would love to be *your* hosts for dinner—you are giving us such a wonderful time!" Otherwise, you show your gratitude by inviting them to a restaurant sometime when they are in town or by sending a suitable present.

If you have friends in the neighborhood and they invite you and your hosts over for a swim or to play tennis, you should never accept the invitation and then relay it to your hostess. It is better to leave the "door ajar" and make a noncommital reply such as, "May I call you back? —I'm not sure about Joan's plans."

If you are not needed to make up a foursome at bridge and you are tired and want to go to bed before your hosts and the other guests do, it is perfectly all right to say to your hostess that you've had a "rugged" week at the office and would like to say good night.

When you are visiting a house run with one maid or none, it is inconsiderate to make your visit a burden through the extra picking up that your careless disorder would entail. Even should you be staying in a house where there are many servants, remember that each has a share of work to do. If the housemaid offers to press a dress that has become mussed in packing, accept her offer and later give her a gratuity—but you should not ask this service unless the pressing is really necessary.

If the hostess does her own housework, you must make your bed, pick up your room, and offer to help in clearing the table and cleaning up in the kitchen.

When you are visiting in a large household, don't use the staff as your own servants; and unless you have been told to ring for breakfast, do not do so. If your hostess forgets to tell you the breakfast arrangements, ask about them before you go to bed.

One of the most trying things to people of set habits is an unusual breakfast hour. When you are one who wakes with the dawn and the household you are visiting has the custom of sleeping on a Sunday morning, the long wait for your coffee can truly upset your whole day. On the other hand, to be aroused at seven on the only day when you do not have to hurry to your office in order to yawn through an early breakfast and then sit around and kill time with the Sunday paper is just as trying. The farsighted guest with the early habit can in a measure prevent discomfort. He can carry his own little electric water-heating outfit and a package of instant coffee or tea, sugar, powdered milk or cream, and a few crackers. He can then start his day all by himself in the barnyard hours without disturbing anyone. Or, in an informal household, he may slip quietly into the kitchen and make himself a cup of coffee and a piece of toast to sustain him until the others are ready for a full breakfast. Few people care enough to fuss, but if they do, these suggestions for a visitor with incurably early waking hours can make a great difference to his enjoyment of the entire day.

Perhaps the entire guest situation may be expressed in one sentence.

If you are an inflexible person, very set in your ways, don't visit! At least don't visit without carefully looking the situation over from every angle to be sure that the habits of the house you are going to are in accord with your own. If you have confidence in your adaptability, go and enjoy yourself!

THE OVERNIGHT GUEST IN A CITY APARTMENT

Today an increasing number of people live in apartments, where a guest room is a rarity. Sometimes a couch in the living room can be converted into a comfortable bed at night for an overnight guest, or if a child is away at camp or boarding school, his room may be available. No matter how hospitable your host or hostess may be, a guest should remember that an extra person in small quarters is inevitably something of an imposition—no matter how charming the guest may be. Household regulations should be meticulously observed, and the visitor should stay no longer than necessary. He should take up as little room with his possessions as possible and keep his belongings neat. Above all, he should be prepared to fit in with the household schedule and not inconvenience his host or hostess.

Part SEVEN

SPECIAL OCCASIONS

37

The new baby

The first announcement of the birth of a baby is usually made to the nearest and dearest friends and relatives as soon as the proud father or delighted grandparents can get to the telephone. Some time before the blessed event actually takes place, or immediately thereafter, the parents may visit a stationer's and select an announcement card to be sent to their own friends and those of the grandparents who are close to the family. After the birth and as soon as the name is determined, the father notifies the stationer, and in a few days the cards are ready.

One of the nicest types of birth announcement consists simply of a very small card with the baby's name and birth date on it, tied with a white or pastel ribbon to the upper margin of the "Mr. and Mrs." card of the parents.

A large variety of commercially designed announcement cards with space for the baby's name, date of birth, and parents' names to be written in by hand are also available, and as they are much less expensive they are very popular. Some are in the best of taste, but those which include such data as the baby's weight and length and foolish phrasing or coy designs are better left on the rack. Good taste says that the simplest card is the best, *always!*

Robert Meadows, Jr.

July tenth

Mr. and Mrs. Robert Meadows

47 Pace Place

The arrival of a birth announcement does not mean that the recipient need send a gift. Parents sometimes hesitate to send cards for fear that that will be the reaction, but there is no such obligation, and there is no nicer way to let friends know about the happy event.

It is thoughtful, however, for those who receive announcements to send a note of congratulation to the new parents.

ANNOUNCEMENT OF ADOPTION

It is a nice gesture to send a card announcing this happy event to your friends and relatives. A card such as this will also bring reassuring comfort to the child later on, should he or she ever doubt his place in the hearts of the family who chose him.

Mr. and Mrs. Nuhome
have the happiness to announce
the adoption of
Mary
aged thirteen months

Or, if announcements are sent during the legal proceedings, the wording may be changed:

Mr. and Mrs. Nuhome
have the happiness to announce
the arrival
and prospective adoption of
Mary
aged thirteen months

NEWSPAPER ANNOUNCEMENT OF BIRTH

In the week following the birth, the father may send a release to the local newspapers announcing the event: "Mr. and Mrs. Robert Meadows of 202 Park Avenue, New York City, announce the birth of a son, Robert, Jr. on July 10, 1968, at Doctors' Hospital. They have one daughter, Jane, 4. Mrs. Meadows is the former Miss Mary Gilding." Or "A daughter, Mary Jane, was born to Mr. and Mrs. John Phillips of 19 Maple Avenue, Hillsdale, on February 9 at St. Joseph's Hospital. Mrs. Phillips is the former Miss Mary Star of New Haven, Connecticut." The same announcement may be sent to the editor of the church newsletter or bulletin.

CHOOSING A NAME

Parents should be careful to avoid giving the baby a name that will be a handicap because it is too long or difficult to pronounce clearly or forms an unpleasant combination with the last name. Simple or biblical names will go well with most family names. It is nice for a name to have some significance, perhaps because of its original meaning or because it is traditionally carried by some member of the family. A child may also be named for a highly respected national figure or a beloved friend.

Many Christian first sons are given the same name as their fathers; when a child is named for a parent he may be given a middle name different from that of the parent, and in adult life he may decide to be known as "R. William Meadows" instead of "Robert Meadows, Jr." The name of a Roman Catholic baby, by canon law, must include the name of a saint. Although he may be called by any diminutive, his baptismal certificate must record the saint's name as the baby's first or middle one. Most Jewish babies are traditionally named for a deceased relative, and thus the name of a loved one is perpetuated.

PRESENTS FOR BABY AND MOTHER

Anyone who wishes to send a gift to the baby may do so. It may either be addressed to the parents at home or brought with you if you visit the hospital. It is thoughtful to bring something for the new mother, too—cologne (if she uses it), a book, or perhaps a plant or flower arrangement.

CHRISTENINGS AND OTHER RELIGIOUS CEREMONIES

TIME OF CHRISTENING

At one time it was required that a baby in the Roman or High Episcopal church be baptized on the first, or possibly the second, Sunday after its birth. In the Catholic church, the baptism still takes place when the baby is very young—usually not over a month old—and always in the church or baptistry. In Latin countries, babies are often baptized in the hospital, within a day or two of their birth. In Protestant churches, the average age for christening is from two to six months, although in some denominations or under special conditions, children may not be christened until they are several years old. In all churches the mother should be present if she is able.

THE GODPARENTS

If your faith requires godparents, they should be asked and their consent obtained before the day of the christening is set. They may be asked to serve when the baby's arrival is announced to them, and in some cases they are asked even before the birth. In Protestant practice, there are usually two godfathers and one godmother for a boy, two godmothers and one godfather for a girl. A Catholic baby has one godparent of each sex, who must be Catholics, too. (Catholics are not allowed to serve as godparents for children of other faiths.)

It is perfectly correct to send a note if the godparent lives at a distance, or he may be asked by telegraph: "It's a boy. Will you be godfather?" But in any case do not write anything so formal as "My husband and I sincerely hope that you will consent to be our son's godmother." It would be the height of presumption to ask anyone so slightly known as this wording implies to fill so intimate a position.

If a godparent is unable to be present, a proxy acts for him or her at the ceremony, the consent of the real godparent having first been given. It is considerate for the real godparent to send a note to the clergyman authorizing the proxy.

One must never ask any but a most intimate friend to be a godmother or godfather, for it is a responsibility not to be undertaken lightly and also one difficult to refuse. Godparents are usually chosen from among friends rather than relatives, because one advantage of godparents is that they add to the child's stock of relatives. Should the youngster be left alone in the world, its godparents become its protectors. But when a child is born with plenty of relatives who can be called upon for assistance, godparents are sometimes chosen from among them.

The obligation of being a godparent is essentially a spiritual one; therefore, the godparent should be of the same faith as the parents. The godparent is supposed to see that the child is given religious training and is confirmed at the proper time. Beyond these obligations, he is expected to take a special interest in the child, much as a very near relative would do.

At the christening, he gives the baby as nice a present as he can afford. The typical gift is a silver mug or porringer, inscribed: "Robert Meadows, Jr./December 5, 1968/From his godfather/John Strong." Other typical presents are a silver fork and spoon, a silver comb and brush set, a government bond, or a trust fund to which the donor may add each year until the child is grown.

CHRISTENING INVITATIONS

Usually, christening invitations are given over the telephone or in a personal note.

> *Dear Jane,*
>
> *We are having Karen christened on Sunday at 3:00 in Christ Church. Would you and Bob come to the ceremony at the church, and join us afterward at our house?*
>
> *Love,*
> *Sally*

Or a message may be written on the "Mr. and Mrs." card of the parents, or on an informal, saying simply: "Karen's christening, St. Mary's Church, Jan. 10, 3 o'clock. Reception at our house afterward." All invitations to a christening should be very friendly and informal.

THE CHILD'S CLOTHES

The baby's christening dress is often one that was worn by the baby's mother, father, or even one of its grand- or great-grandparents. Everything the baby wears on this occasion should be white, although this is merely a custom and not a church requirement. The traditional christening dress is long, made of sheer, soft material with lace and hand embroidery trim, and worn with delicate, long petticoats. It is not necessary to go to the expense of buying a traditional christening dress if there is no family heirloom; any long, or even short, plain white dress will do. However, some very pretty christening dresses are available in the new miracle fabrics, which are quite inexpensive.

In Protestant churches, when the children are older, little girls wear white dresses, even though they may be well past the baby stage. Little boys, however, do not have to wear white suits. An Eton jacket, dark blue with matching shorts, is appropriate for very little ones, and older boys may wear a dark blue or dark gray suit.

WHAT THE GUESTS WEAR

The guests at a christening wear what they would wear to church. The mother wears a light-colored dress; she should not wear black on this occasion, and she should wear a hat or a veil. If she is not sure of the custom of the church, every woman should wear a hat—it is *never* incorrect.

THE CHURCH CEREMONY

The clergyman, of course, is consulted about the place and hour for the christening before the guests are invited. The ceremony may take place at the close of the regular Sunday service, the guests remaining after the rest of the congregation leaves. Roman Catholic parishes generally schedule baptisms for a specified time on Sunday afternoons, and the parents make an appointment at the rectory in advance. If a large number of guests are invited to attend a Protestant christening, it is best to choose a weekday and an hour when the church is not being otherwise used. Guests seat themselves in the pews nearest the front.

As soon as the clergyman appears, the baby's coat and cap are taken off and the godmother, holding the baby in her arms, stands directly in front of the clergyman. The other godparents stand beside her, and relatives and friends nearby.

The godmother holding the baby must be sure to pronounce his name distinctly; in fact, if the name is long or unusual it is wise to print it on a slip of paper and give it to the clergyman beforehand, because whatever name he pronounces is fixed for life. More than one baby has been given a name not intended for him. The godmother states the given name or names only, and not the surname.

In the Presbyterian church and others that do not require godparents, the father holds the baby and gives its name. There is no separate service—it is done during or immediately after the regular Sunday service.

As soon as the ceremony is over, the baby, the relatives, and the friends go to the house of the parents or grandparents, where a reception has been arranged.

Baptism is a sacrament of the church, for which no fee is ever required. A donation, however, is presented in an envelope to the clergyman after the ceremony, commensurate with the elaborateness of the christening.

A HOUSE CHRISTENING

If permitted by the church to which the baby's parents belong, the house christening is a most satisfactory ceremony—because a baby whose routine has not been upset by being taken to a strange place at an unusual hour is generally "good."

The arrangements for a house christening are quite simple, the only necessary decoration being the font. This is always a bowl—usually of silver—put on a small, high table.

Most people prefer to cover the table in a dark fabric such as old brocade or velvet—a white napkin suggests a restaurant rather than a ritual and is therefore an unfortunate choice. Flowers may be arranged around the bowl in a flat circle, the blossoms outside, the stems toward the center and covered by the base of the bowl.

At the hour set for the ceremony, the clergyman enters the room, the guests form an open aisle, and he takes his place at the font. The godmother, or the father if there are no godparents, carries the baby and follows the clergyman; the other participants walk behind, and they all stand near the font. At the proper moment, the clergyman takes the baby, baptizes it, and hands it back to the godmother or father, who holds it until the ceremony is over.

After performing the ceremony, the clergyman, if he wears vestments, goes to a room that has been set apart for him, changes into his street clothes, and then returns to the living room as one of the guests.

THE CHRISTENING PARTY

The only difference between an ordinary informal reception and a christening party is that the latter features christening cake and "caudle." The christening cake is generally a white "lady" cake elaborately iced. A real caudle is a hot eggnog, drunk out of little punch cups. But today champagne or punch is usually substituted for the caudle, and those who have an aversion to a punch are often offered a highball or a soft drink.

Guests eat the cake as a sign that they partake of the baby's hospitality and are therefore his friends, and they drink the punch to his health and prosperity. But by this time the young host or hostess is peacefully asleep in the nursery.

JEWISH CEREMONIES FOR THE NEWBORN

On the eighth day after birth, in the ceremony known as *brith milah,* a boy is initiated into the Jewish covenant between man and God. The circumcision is accompanied by a religious ceremony during which the boy is named. After the ceremony, which may take place in a special room in the hospital, there is a light collation. The guests drink to the baby's future and toast the parents, grandparents, and witnesses. Relatives and close friends are invited to the *brith* by telephone or informal note. They dress as they would for a service in a synagogue, and both men and women customarily wear hats.

Girls are named in the synagogue on the first Sabbath after birth, when the father is called up to the Torah. Sometimes the naming is postponed until the mother is able to be present. In some Reform congregations, boys are also named in the synagogue (in addition to being named at the *brith*) when both parents are present, and a special blessing is pronounced by the rabbi. The mother may be hostess at the reception following the service. Friends and relatives may be invited to attend the religious service during which the baby will be named.

The ceremony of redemption of the first-born, the *pidyon ha-ben,* which takes place only if the first-born is a boy, is performed when the baby is thirty-one days old. According to ancient custom described in the Bible, the first-born son was dedicated to the service of God. It became customary for a *cohen* (a descendant of the priestly tribe) to redeem the child from his obligation, entrusting him to the care of his father for upbringing in the Jewish faith. The *pidyon ha-ben*, consisting of a brief ceremony and a celebration, is held in the home. Informal notes of invitation are sent about ten days beforehand to close friends and relatives.

38

Confirmations and bar mitzvahs

CONFIRMATION

Catholic children are generally confirmed when they are eleven or twelve, Protestants a year or two older. However, if one was not confirmed as a child, it may be done at any age, and there is a special confirmation for those who change their faith.

The candidates for confirmation in all faiths undergo a period of instruction. Those who complete these lessons satisfactorily are confirmed by a bishop or other high church dignitary in the manner of a graduating class. The service, which in the Protestant church is held at a regular Sunday service, and which in the Catholic church is separate from the regular Mass, is attended by members of the families and close friends of the young people.

Some churches hold an informal reception after the ceremony, at which the parents and friends may have a chance to meet and chat with the visiting churchman who performed the confirmation.

Afterwards the family and a few friends may gather at the house for lunch, and those who wish to, give the newly confirmed youngster a gift. This is usually of a religious nature—a Bible with his name engraved on it, a prayer book, a gold cross, a medal or a charm of a religious nature are appropriate choices.

Catholic girls wear white dresses and sometimes a short veil. Some Protestant clergymen request that the girls wear white, but most simply ask that they wear simple, modest dresses in quiet colors. This is up to the discretion of the minister. In both Protestant and Catholic churches, the boys wear dark blue or dark gray suits.

Confirmation is a religious occasion rather than a social one. It is the moment when the young person himself confirms the vows that were made for him by his godparents at the time of his baptism. It is a thoughtful and serious event, and therefore is celebrated joyfully—but with restraint.

BAR MITZVAH

For a Jewish boy the ceremony which compares to the Christian confirmation is called Bar Mitzvah. In the Orthodox and Conservative branches, and in some Reform congregations, it takes place on the first Sabbath (Saturday) after the boy becomes thirteen. As in the Christian church, those candidates have undergone a period of religious instruction prior to the ceremony. Other Reform congregations have replaced the bar mitzvah with a "confirmation" service at which both boys and girls are confirmed, sometimes at an older age than the traditional thirteen. A Jewish boy's bar mitzvah or confirmation celebrates his acceptance as an adult member of his congregation.

Bar mitzvah differs from the Christian confirmation in that, in addition to being a deeply religious occasion, it is always celebrated socially as well. It is one of the most important events in the boy's life, and the family generally bends every effort to make it as wonderful an occasion as they can. The religious ceremony which takes place on Saturday morning may be followed immediately by a gathering in the social rooms of the synagogue. This is open to any member of the congregation who wishes to offer his congratulations.

The party—luncheon, dinner, or reception—which follows later in the day usually includes all the close friends of the parents as well as friends and classmates of the boy. Only those who receive invitations may attend.

Invitations may be formally engraved, they may be handwritten notes, or they may be telephoned. Often many more people are invited to the reception than can be accommodated at the religious ceremony, so the invitation must be quite explicit as to the hour, the place, and the occasion. They must, like other invitations, be acknowledged promptly, and in kind.

For the ceremony, guests wear the clothes that they ordinarily choose for a religious service. And if the party is a luncheon, they go directly to it without changing. If the celebration is later in the day, they change into clothes more appropriate for an evening party. If the affair is formal, this should be specified on the invitation. Otherwise the women wear cocktail or dinner dresses and the men wear dark suits.

Everyone invited to a bar mitzvah is expected to send, or take, a gift. Something of a permanent nature to serve as a reminder of the occasion is most appropriate, but gifts of money are also acceptable. A piece of jewelry, such as a tie clip or a set of studs for evening clothes, is typical, as well as a wallet, a leather desk set, a book on a favorite hobby —the list is limitless.

The boy must, of course, write thank-you letters promptly for each and every gift.

The reception itself is just like any other. Dinners and luncheons may be sit-down or buffet, and the party may be held at home or in a club, hotel, or restaurant. There may or may not be an orchestra, but if many young people are invited, they will enjoy dancing after the meal is over.

39

Graduation

INVITATIONS AND ANNOUNCEMENTS

Attendance at schools and colleges has grown so fast that the facilities of these institutions cannot always handle the crowds of parents and friends who would like to attend the festivities. Years ago graduates could invite their entire families, and often friends, too. Today almost every educational institution limits the number of visitors each student may invite—often to no more than four. The invitations are usually provided by the school, but if they are not, the parents or the graduate himself may write them, have them printed, or issue them by telephone. The graduate and his (or her) family must select the recipients very carefully so that there will be no hurt feelings. If, for instance, both sets of grandparents would like to be included, the ones who receive the invitations must be chosen with great tact. The choice might be made on the basis of which ones live closest, or are better able to travel. Whatever the reason, those not invited must be convinced that the choice is fair, and not guided by preference.

The restriction on the number of invitations allowed has led many people to send graduation announcements. This is all right as long as the list is restricted to very close family and friends who would otherwise be invited to the ceremonies. To go further afield may give the impression that one is boasting. Also, although it should not be so, those receiving announcements tend to feel that a present is expected, and this is an imposition.

Because the activities differ widely in each of our thousands of schools and colleges, no definite schedule for commencement week can be given. Graduation or commencement programs at the high school level are much the same as at the colleges, but on a modified scale. The senior class dance is more likely to be attended by the graduates and their dates only, with a few parents included as chaperones, although at some preparatory schools the graduates' families are invited, too. There may be a class play or a varsity game attended by parents and dates, or there may be nothing other than the graduation ceremony itself.

Although college and university "commencement week" festivities may start for the students a week or more in advance of the actual graduation day, the events to which families and friends are invited take place only on the last day or two before commencement. These events usually consist of any or all of the following: a senior class party—attended at some colleges only by the graduates and their dates, and at others by parents and brothers and sisters of the graduates as well; a senior class play—generally a comedy or review that sometimes involves the class history, and attended by everyone; fraternity parties, tea dances, or cocktail parties, to which the graduates' dates are invited; special events peculiar to a particular college, such as torchlight parades or barn dances. Finally, the baccalaureate service and the commencement exercises which are attended by every guest complete the festivities.

MAKING RESERVATIONS

It is essential in this day of large college classes for the families of the graduates to make reservations well in advance of graduation day. Because many hotels and inns have no rooms left to reserve by the time Christmas vacation arrives, it is well to think of this during the fall term, especially if the college is in a small town that does not have too many accommodations. Parents should find out how many guests each student may have and then consult with their son or daughter as to whom he or she wishes to invite. If the graduate has a fiancé or a serious boy or girl friend, the family makes a reservation for him, too.

REQUIREMENTS FOR THE SENIOR'S DATE

The senior's date, either boy or girl, and whether a fiancé or a very good friend, stays with the family of the student. He or she naturally attends all those events which are for graduates and dates only, but at parties or events to which all guests are invited, the dates goes with the parents and does not try to monopolize the attention of the graduate.

If a young man's family cannot attend the commencement or if he has no family, he or his date must try to find another graduate's family (preferably the parents of a close friend) willing to adopt her for the occasion. If this proves impossible, the young man may ask one of his favorite professors if it would be possible for her to stay in his house. In no circumstance should she stay alone in a motel or an inn.

CLOTHING

Clothing varies with the activities planned, of course, but it is much the same as for similar social events elsewhere. Guests are usually sent a program well in advance, either by their son or daughter or by the college, and can determine then what may be needed.

The senior dance is almost always formal, and if so, the date must bring an evening dress or a tuxedo. Girls generally wear shorts or simple cotton dresses for daytime sports events or picnics, and the boys wear shorts or slacks and sports shirts. Since June is graduation month and the weather is usually hot, the guests may be told to bring a bathing suit. Mothers and girl friends will look prettiest and be most comfortable in cool, short-sleeved dresses, in a print or a pastel color for the baccalaureate and commencement services. A grandmother may be happiest in a silk suit. Hats or veils are worn at a chapel service, but are not necessary if the commencement ceremony is held out-of-doors.

Men and boys wear lightweight suits of any conservative color for the formal services.

PRESENTS

Graduation presents are unlimited in variety, but the closer to the graduate the giver, the more elaborate the gift. Parents may give a fine watch, a set of evening jewelry, an automobile, or even a trip to Europe. If these gifts are beyond their means, anything that is lasting and of the best quality that they can afford is always appreciated. A nicely bound book on a favorite subject, for instance, or a set of cuff links or other simple jewelry can be a source of much pleasure.

A fiancé or a "steady" boy friend might choose a charm or a locket, and a girl friend might consider a handsome wallet or a gold or silver tie clip.

The gifts of other relatives and friends may depend on the future plans of the graduate. If he is taking a trip, a passport case or a suitcase would be a good choice. If he is about to be married, something for his home—a cigarette box with the college seal, perhaps, or a silver tray with the graduation date on it—would be appreciated.

THANK-YOU NOTES

A note of thanks, written by hand on notepaper, must go to everyone who has not been at the commencement to be thanked in person. This note need not be long, but it should express appreciation and be written as promptly as possible.

Dear Aunt Mary,

I can't thank you enough for the check you sent me, which will be such a help toward my summer in Europe. I'm looking forward to seeing you in the fall to tell you all about the trip.

With much love,
Jane

Or:

Dear Uncle Jim,

Thank you so much for the cuff links you sent me. How did you know they were the things I needed most of all? I was disappointed that you couldn't make the graduation, but I'll drive down to see you and thank you in person as soon as possible.

Thanks again,
Bill

40

Debuts

"Presenting a debutante to society" has a quaint flavor and today may seem to echo long-outdated social customs. Yet, when a young lady is eighteen—never before and rarely long after—her parents may want to present her to the adult world with a certain degree of formality. For this "coming-out," they have a choice of several forms.

The most elaborate, only possible for parents of considerable means, is a private ball. Less elaborate is a small dance that presents the debutante to her own and her parents' friends. Third is a tea dance. Fourth, and by far the most popular today, is the big dance given for, or by, a number of debutantes together. Sometimes it is given cooperatively by a group of parents who get together and share the expense of a single coming-out party for their daughters. In other cases, it may be given by an organization that invites a group of girls to participate. Many balls or cotillions of this kind are benefit affairs, handled by a committee of the sponsoring charity and thus serving a double purpose, since the parents of the girls invited to participate are expected to give a substantial donation to the charity involved. *The correct forms for the invitations and their answers to all these functions may be found in Chapters Fifty-two and Fifty-five.*

DEBUTANTE BALLS

THE RECEIVING LINE AT A PRIVATE DEBUT

The debutante's mother—or whoever is giving the ball and "presenting her"—stands nearest the entrance. The debutante stands next to her, and they are the only people who formally "receive." On entering, the guests approach the hostess, who introduces the debutante to those who do not know her. As the hostess shakes hands with each, she turns to the debutante and, repeating the name that has been announced to her, says, "My daughter" or "You remember Cynthia, don't you?" or merely "This is Cynthia."

Each arriving guest shakes hands with the debutante as well as with the hostess. If there is a queue of people coming at the same time, there is no need of saying anything beyond "How do you do?" and passing on as quickly as possible. If there are no others entering at the moment, each guest may make a few pleasant remarks.

At a ball, where the guests begin coming at eleven o'clock, the debutante receives until about twelve o'clock—or later if guests continue to arrive. Then she is free to join the dancing. She usually dances the first dance with her father and the next with the young man (or men) she has asked to be her escort for the evening.

SENDING FLOWERS AND GIFTS

It is customary in most cities to send a debutante flowers at her coming-out party. They may be bouquets or baskets or corsages, and they are sent by relatives, friends of the family, her father's business associates, as well as by the young men who are her escorts. These flowers are usually banked as a background for her when she stands to receive.

If she has only one escort, she wears the corsage he sends, but if she has two, she cannot very well wear both corsages. The best solution is to pin both—and any received from other guests—to a wide white velvet or satin ribbon which is then tied over her wrist. This is kept in place while she receives but must, of course, be removed when she starts to dance. At that time, to avoid favoring one escort, she might pin one corsage to her dress and the other to her evening bag.

Members of the family and close friends often wish to send gifts of a more permanent nature. Jewelry is the most appropriate choice—a pin, a charm, a necklace, or earrings are greatly appreciated by all young girls. The gift might also be an ornament for her room or an album or frame for her debutante pictures.

AT SUPPER

The debutante goes to supper with her escort. If she is very popular and does not wish to center her attention on one man, an easy way out is to ask a brother or other relative. She makes up her own table, which includes her most intimate friends. It is usually in the center of the dining room, is somewhat larger than the tables surrounding it, and has a card on it saying "Reserved."

DINNER DANCES

Since the times of the year when young people are free to give and attend parties are restricted to school vacations, there are often more girls who wish to come out at private parties than there are evenings available. In many communities, two girls whose guest lists overlap agree that one will be presented at a dinner dance and the other at a late dance on the same evening. This is a very convenient arrangement for both families. The parents who go to the expense of serving the dinner know that they need to provide drinks and refreshments for only a limited time after dinner. The other family only need to worry about a light supper served around one o'clock, and the champagne, punch, or whatever they choose to serve for the rest of the night.

The two debutantes attend each other's party, and the one giving the second party leaves, with her escorts, shortly after dinner to help her mother with last-minute arrangements. The dinner dance is usually held at seven-thirty or eight o'clock, and the debutante and her hostess receive until dinner is served at eight-thirty or nine. The late dance begins at approximately eleven.

SMALLER DANCES

The afternoon tea dance to introduce a debutante is described in Chapter Thirty-two, and the small evening debut party needs little comment, because its pattern is precisely the same as that of any dance. As at every coming-out party, the debutante and her mother or hostess stand in line and receive the guests as they arrive.

ASSEMBLIES, COTILLIONS, AND COMMUNITY DEBUTS

To come out as a member of a group and thus eliminate the expense and rigors of a private ball is becoming more and more common. If she wishes, a girl's mother may give a small debut party or tea at home and still accept an invitation for her daughter to participate in one of the assemblies or cotillions.

Customs vary widely in different areas, and because debutante balls are generally planned by knowledgeable people, it is safe to assume that whatever local practices have become traditional and are accepted by the participants are, in that city or town, quite correct.

The debutantes are expected to send in the names of their escorts as soon as they have accepted, and the committee then sends the young men formal invitations. The girls are expected to pay for their escorts'

tickets if the ball is charity-sponsored. At most multiple debuts, the committee does not invite guests, but each debutante's family is allowed a certain number of invitations, and they are responsible for paying for those they invite. Some committees, however, do invite extra boys—and girls—at their discretion.

There may be entertainment in the form of a dance performed by the debutantes and their fathers or escorts, or nothing more than the formal presentation, by their fathers, of the girls to the committee members who are acting as hostesses. There may or may not be professional entertainment—a singer or dancer, perhaps.

The party may be a dinner dance, but it is more likely to be a late party. When a ball is private, friends frequently give dinner parties preceding it; and when it is run by a committee, the members often have dinners for the debutantes and their escorts. This may also be done by the families of the girls themselves.

Whatever the local traditions, these "mass debuts" are a great success. By sharing the costs, many families can afford far more elaborate decorations, prettier dresses, and better music than they could otherwise hope to obtain. The debutantes, if they are at all shy, are spared the nightmare of being alone in the spotlight. And any mishaps that may occur seem smaller when the responsibility is divided, whereas sharing a success with friends makes it doubly sweet.

THE FATHER'S PART

The role of the father at a private debut is simply that of the good host at any party. He does not stand in the receiving line, but he stays nearby, greets friends and acquaintances, and sees that everything is running smoothly. He dances the first dance with his daughter, and then he dances with his wife, with the grandmothers if they are present and wish to dance, and then with the other guests, young and old alike.

At many cotillions and community debuts, the fathers participate in a parade and a simple cotillion dance with their daughters. They cross the ballroom, one couple at a time, and each father presents his debutante daughter to the hostess or to the committee giving the dance. Although today the young men guests may wear tuxedos to debut parties, the escorts of the debutantes who are coming out and their fathers must wear white tie and tails.

THE DEBUTANTE'S DRESS

At a ball, the debutante wears the very prettiest evening dress she can buy. Traditionally it is white, and suggests something light, airy, gay, and, above all, young. For the girl who prefers to wear colors, a very, very pale pastel is most suitable. But the dress may not be scarlet or a bright blue, and on no account black, no matter how sophisticated or chic the debutante thinks she would look in it. At a multiple debut, the girls wear the same color, almost invariably white, but they choose their own style. The mothers of the debutantes wear evening dresses in any color except black.

At an afternoon tea the debutante wears a cocktail dress. Her mother wears an afternoon dress, not an evening one. Both mother and daughter wear gloves, and neither wears a hat.

SOME HINTS FOR THE "BELLE OF THE BALL"

Let us suppose that you are a young girl on the evening of your coming-out ball! Of course you are excited! But don't let your excitement overwhelm your sense of courtesy.

It takes very little effort to listen to a name that is said to you, to look at the one to whom the name belongs, to put our your hand willingly and not as though you were bored, and with a smile say, "How do you do, Mrs. Holmes?" It takes no longer to be cordial and attentive than to be flustered and rude, yet the impression made in a few seconds of time may easily gain or lose a friend. When no other guests are entering, you can chatter to your own friends as much as you like; but as you turn to greet a new arrival you must show nothing but pleasure in giving her or him your attention.

As friends who have sent you flowers approach, thank them; later you must also write an additional note of thanks to older people. To your relatives or your own intimate friends, your oral thanks, if appreciatively made, are sufficient.

41

Anniversary parties

Anniversary parties may be given in honor of any anniversary, but first, fifth, tenth, twenty-fifth, and fiftieth are those most generally celebrated. The parties given for the first three are usually informal, not distinguishable from any other reception except that there would be toasts to the bride and groom, and close friends would bring gifts. The twenty-fifth and fiftieth anniversaries, however, are given much more importance, and certain customs—almost rituals—are followed. Therefore this chapter will deal principally with the latter two.

When it is convenient, the party should be given on the actual date of the anniversary. But should the couple prefer to have it on a Saturday night, for example, it is perfectly all right to move it forward or back a few days. If one member of the couple is ill or absent at the time, an anniversary may be celebrated several weeks after the true date. When the illness or the absence is prolonged, it is preferable to celebrate the anniversary which falls on the following year. There is no rule which says one must recognize the twenty-fifth rather than the twenty-sixth.

WHO GIVES THE PARTY?

Early anniversary parties are always given by the couple themselves.

By the time they reach the twenty-fifth, they may well have grown children who wish to make the arrangements, but it is perfectly correct for them to do so themselves if the young people do not, or cannot. Fiftieth-anniversary celebrations are almost invariably planned by the family of the couple.

PLANNING THE PARTY

The party may be held in the home of the couple, in the home of the person planning the party, in a church parish house, or in a room of a hotel, restaurant, or club.

If the party is a dinner or a small reception, the guests are primarily family, members of the wedding party, and closest friends. If it is to be a large reception or an open house, the list may include business acquaintances, church and club members, and in very small communities—everyone in town.

INVITATIONS

The form of the invitations depends entirely on the degree of formality of the party. They may range from an informal telephone call to an engraved "third person" invitation. In between lie the most common forms—handwritten notes or the necessary information written on a visiting card or informal.

For the large open house the invitation may simply be an announcement in the local paper or the church or club bulletin. The dangers in this form of invitation are that more people than the host and hostess expect may appear, or that some who are really wanted may fail to read the announcement or hear of the party. If the only invitation is the announcement in the paper, anyone who reads it is expected to attend, but if any invitations are extended personally, only those who receive them may go.

The following are some sample invitations.

When the couple are giving the party themselves:

1943–1968
Mr. and Mrs. Harvey Langdon
request the pleasure of your company
at a reception
in honor of
their silver wedding anniversary
on Saturday, the eighth of December
at eight o'clock
Barrymore Country Club

R.s.v.p.
12 Corning Road

On an informal or visiting card (name engraved):

1943–1968
Mr. and Mrs. Harvey Langdon
March 1 at 6 P.M.
12 Corning Road

R.s.v.p.

When the children of the couple give the party:

Dear Anne (or Mrs. Franklin),

Will you and Joe (or Mr. Franklin) join us for dinner on Saturday, May 4, at 7:00 P.M. to help us celebrate Mom and Dad's twenty-fifth anniversary? Hoping to see you then,

Helen and Bill
(or Helen & Bill Porter)

Or, if they prepare an engraved card:

In honor of the
fiftieth wedding anniversary of
Mr. and Mrs. Harvey Langdon

Mr. and Mrs. William Porter
(or "their sons and daughters")
request the pleasure of your company
on Tuesday, the fourth of July
at seven-thirty o'clock
10 Glenwood Road

R.s.v.p.

The newspaper or church bulletin announcement reads:

Open House
to celebrate the fiftieth anniversary
of Mr. & Mrs. Harvey Langdon. Sunday,
March 4, 4 to 6 P.M., 12 Osborn Road

REFRESHMENTS

The refreshments depend on the type of party being given. If it is a meal—a luncheon or a dinner—the hostess simply chooses whatever menu she thinks will please the couple and the guests most. Since the later anniversaries attempt to recreate the wedding day to some extent, the food might be the same as that served at the original wedding reception.

If the party is a cocktail party, hors d'oeuvres are served, but a wedding cake should be cut and passed with a round of champagne for toasting the couple before the guests leave.

At an afternoon reception or an open house, the menu varies according to the formality of the party and the pocketbook of the host and hostess. The refreshments may consist of sandwiches, snacks, and punch, or a complete buffet—cold ham, turkey, sliced fillet of beef, and chafing dishes filled with hot snacks or hors d'oeuvres. Whatever the other food, as close a replica of the couple's wedding cake as can be made is the main feature of the menu.

Drinks may range from tea and coffee at an afternoon reception to wine, champagne, or highballs at an evening affair. Soft drinks should always be available for those who prefer them. Punch is often served at open houses and other daytime parties, made either with or without liquor. When the family does not object to alcoholic beverages, a glass of champagne is the traditional drink for toasts—at any hour of the afternoon or evening. Otherwise, the toasts may be made with punch or whatever drinks are available. *For suggested anniversary toast, see Chapter Four, "Public Speaking."*

DECORATIONS

Decorations need not be elaborate, but the twenty-fifth anniversary party should feature white and silver ornaments and flowers, and the fiftieth, gold (or yellow) and white. Flowers make the loveliest decoration of all, and the bride should always be presented with a corsage.

WITH OR WITHOUT MUSIC

There need not be any entertainment, but a strolling accordian player adds a touch of romance, and he can be asked to play the couple's favorite tunes, wedding music, etc. If the host and hostess wish to hire an orchestra or provide records, dancing will be all the entertainment necessary.

THE RECEIVING LINE

One of the distinguishing features of an anniversary party is the receiving line. Except for a somewhat elderly couple celebrating their fiftieth, the couple and any members of their bridal party stand near the door, just as they did at their wedding reception. Their children may join them in the line, and if the party is given by another member of the family, that person always heads the line as hostess.

Older couples who tire easily, or who may not be well, may be seated in a central spot—in front of a fireplace, for example. The guests, after greeting the hostess near the door, move on to find the honored pair and offer their congratulations.

GIFTS

Gifts are almost always taken to the couple celebrating an early anniversary because they are always in need of household articles of every sort. But when a couple has been married twenty-five years or more, they frequently have all the material things they can use. If they wish, it is perfectly correct to say "No gifts, please" on the invitations, but there are other alternatives.

It is *never* in good taste for a hostess to request a gift of money either for herself or for the person for whom she is giving the party. But if she knows of something the couple longs for, she may enclose a note with the invitations explaining that the couple being honored wants terribly to go on a cruise, and if the guests would like to help make it possible, would they, instead of bringing a gift, send a small check to the "Anywhere Travel Agency." The hostess would then make up a packet of folders, tickets, boat plans, and a card signed by all the guests, to be presented at the party. In this way, neither she nor the couple would know the exact amounts contributed, and the mercenary aspect would be missing—replaced by the joy of knowing that the gifts would be truly appreciated.

Another wonderful solution to the gift problem is a card enclosed with the invitation, reading "In place of gifts, please, if you wish, send a contribution to Mother and Dad's favorite charity—the 'XYZ Research Foundation.' " The check may be sent with a note saying, "Please accept this contribution in honor of the fiftieth anniversary of Mr. and Mrs. John Doe."

When gifts are given they need not necessarily be of the traditional material allotted to each anniversary. But many people feel that it is more meaningful if they are, and the list has been modified to include modern materials in some cases. When an article of the original material cannot be purchased, something similar but not identical may be chosen—for example, a stainless steel or pewter platter instead of a silver one would be acceptable on a twenty-fifth anniversary. For all anniversaries a lovely flower arrangement or a plant which can be set out in the couple's garden is always appropriate.

Here are the traditional anniversary gifts:

1. Paper or plastics
2. Calico or cotton
3. Leather or simulated leather
4. Silk
5. Wood
6. Iron
7. Copper or wool
8. Electric appliances
9. Pottery
10. Tin or aluminum
11. Steel
12. Linen
13. Lace
14. Ivory
15. Crystal
20. China

25. Silver
30. Pearls
35. Coral and jade
40. Ruby
45. Sapphire
50. Gold
60. Diamond

THE MAIN TABLE

The table should be as much like the bridal table at the couple's wedding reception as possible. The bride and groom sit together at the center of a long table, or at the head of a round one. The bridesmaids and ushers, if any are present, are seated next to them; their husbands or wives are also included at the table. Other places are filled by close relatives. If none of the bridal party is present, the couple's children are seated with them, the oldest son on the bride's right and the oldest daughter on the groom's left. Their husbands and wives, their older children, and brothers and sisters of the couple are arranged in whatever way they will enjoy most.

When the party is given by a married son or daughter of the anniversary couple, the host and hostess sit at either end of the table. But the couple sit together at the center rather than the bride sitting on the host's right and the groom on the hostess's right like ordinary guests of honor.

The table is decorated with white flowers or, for a fiftieth anniversary, gold or yellow flowers. If there is room the wedding cake may be in the center, but if it is large it is more convenient to place it on a side table.

PICTURES

Because the event is such a memorable one, all anniversary couples enjoy having candid pictures made of their party. They are generally taken by one of the guests, although a professional photographer may be hired. These pictures, put into an album, make an ideal present for the couple, either for the anniversary itself or for the next Christmas.

REAFFIRMATION OF MARRIAGE VOWS

Some couples like the idea of reaffirming their marriage vows on their twenty-fifth or fiftieth anniversaries. They may have—insofar as it is feasible—a complete reenactment of their original ceremony, or they may have a much simpler repetition of the vows. In either case, as many as possible of the wedding party gather for the service, and the reception follows.

42

Funerals

As a person reaches the age when he should make a will, he must also consider how and where he would like to be buried. These wishes may be put into his will; and while they are not irrevocable, the family will naturally give them every consideration. If he does not include them in his will, he should at some point discuss the question with those closest to him so they will be able to arrange for the type of burial that he would have chosen himself. He may also leave a note giving burial instructions with his personal papers.

If his parents have a plot in a cemetery, he should know whether there is space for him (and his wife, if she wishes) to be buried there, or he should think about purchasing a plot for himself and his own family. If he wishes to be cremated, the law requires that his nearest relatives give permission, and in many states the deceased must have expressed this desire in his will. Therefore, he should make his desires very clear to his wife (or husband, if we are speaking of a woman), his children, and his brothers or sisters.

Although few people like to think of death in personal terms, it is wise for the head of the family, at least, to have a space set aside in which he keeps a copy of his will and the name of the attorney who drew it up, a deed to a burial plot if he has one, a list of the location of safe deposit boxes, mortgages, bank accounts, etc., and any personal instructions he may wish to leave in case of his death. The other members of the family should know the location of these papers and something about their contents. The small amount of effort necessary to put such a sensible precaution into effect is nothing compared to the help it can be to a stunned and confused family at the time of death.

IMMEDIATE STEPS

At the time of actual death, when the bereaved stand baffled and alone, etiquette performs its most valuable service by smoothing the necessary personal contacts and making sure that the last rites shall be performed with beauty and gravity.

At this time it is of immeasurable help if a very good friend is willing to take charge of the funeral arrangements. The persons closest to the deceased may be in such an emotional state that it is impossible for them to make rational decisions, and they may rush, or be pushed, into situations that they later regret. If no such friend is at hand, then decisions must be made by a relative, possibly one who is not of the immediate family, a nephew or a cousin, perhaps. This lot often falls to a son of the deceased, however, and he must exercise strict self-control.

NOTIFYING FAMILY AND CLOSE FRIENDS

If members of the immediate family are not already present, the first act of someone at the bedside of the deceased is to notify them. At the same time one or two intimate friends whose capability and sympathy can be counted on should be called. If the deceased has suffered a long illness, and the family has become attached to the trained nurse, no one is better fitted to help those who now have a very real need. She, a friend, or a member of the family can look after many details.

Members of the family and very close friends should be called on the telephone. Close relatives, even though they live at some distance, should also be called, but if expense is a factor, friends and more distant relatives may be notified by telegram.

THE DEATH CERTIFICATE

The death certificate is filled out and signed by the physician in attendance at the time of death. If the death was sudden or caused by an accident, or if for any other reason there was no doctor in attendance, the county medical examiner or coroner must be called in to ascertain the cause of death and sign the certificate. This must be done immediately, because no other steps can be taken until the death certificate is properly signed.

NOTIFYING AN ATTORNEY

The next step is to notify an attorney, preferably the one who has drawn up the will of the deceased. If he, or someone in his firm, is unavailable, then any other attorney who is reputable—perhaps one who has been retained by another member of the family or one who is a personal friend—may be called.

THE FUNERAL DIRECTOR AND THE CLERGYMAN

The next most immediate matter is that of selecting a funeral home. If the family belongs to a church or synagogue, they may call the church office, which will give them all the information about the funeral directors in the area and probably recommend one who will suit their needs. The family doctor can also provide this information.

The funeral director will come to the house as soon as possible after he is called and remove the body to the funeral home. Whoever is in charge for the family discusses all the arrangements with him at that time, telling him how elaborate a funeral the relatives wish or can afford and how the details which the funeral director will enumerate are to be handled. If the service is to be held at the funeral home or in the home of the deceased, the day and hour may also be settled. If it is to be held in a church, the clergyman must be consulted immediately to fix the time. If the family is not affiliated with a church, the funeral director or a friend can recommend a clergyman of any faith the family chooses to perform the service.

NEWSPAPER NOTICES

Notices of the death should go to morning and evening papers in a large city, and to the local paper (daily or weekly) in towns or suburbs. They usually contain the date of death, names of immediate family, place and time of funeral, and, frequently, a request that a contribution be given to a charity instead of flowers sent to the deceased. When this is done, the sum is sent to the charity with a note saying, "This donation is sent in loving memory of Mrs. Roy Haskell, of 10 Park Place, Mount Vernon." The address of the sender should appear on the note. The charity sends a notice of the contribution to the family of the deceased, and an acknowledgment to the donor. The latter in no way takes the place of a thank-you note from the bereaved family—one of whom must write in person to express their appreciation. The notice may be telephoned to the paper by the person making the funeral arrangements, but often the funeral director handles it as part of his services.

CONSTANTINE—Mary Phillips, on March 19, 1964. Beloved wife of Henry S. Constantine, devoted mother of Henry S. Constantine, Jr. and Barbara Constantine Franklin, sister of Dorothy P. Hill. Reposing at the Frederick Carter Funeral Home, Farmingdale, Mass., Monday and Tuesday, 2:00 P.M.–9:00 P.M. Funeral Wednesday, 11:00 A.M., at Christ Church, Farmingdale. In lieu of flowers, please send donations to the New York Cancer Fund.

HASKELL—John Woods, suddenly, on February 12, 1964. Beloved brother of Robert C. Haskell, George F. Haskell, and Sally Haskell Simpson. Funeral service Friday, February 14 at 11:30 A.M. at the Riverside Funeral Home, 10 Lawton Street, Clinton, Mass.

Occasionally the notice reads "Funeral private" and neither time nor place is given. Very intimate friends are given this information, either by telephone or on the personal card of the relative or friend in charge: "Mr. Brown's funeral will be at Christ Church, Monday at eleven o'clock." Others are not expected to attend.

When the notice reads "Please omit flowers," this wish should be strictly followed.

If the person who has died was prominent in any way, it is probable that the newspapers have a file on him and, in the case of an older person, an obituary already written. The information that they have should be checked by someone who is acquainted with the facts so that no errors will be made in the published articles. The paid notice of death is inserted as with less well-known people, to announce the details of resting place, funeral, flowers, etc.

THE CLOTHING FOR BURIAL

The person who has been put in charge of arrangements, with the help of someone who may know of the deceased's special preferences or a favorite piece of suitable clothing, delivers the clothes to the funeral director. Members of some faiths, the Orthodox Jewish among them, still prefer to bury their dead in shrouds, but most religions have no restrictions on clothing for burial. Dresses should be in solid, subdued colors, of a style that might be worn to church. Young girls are usually buried in white and children in their Sunday school clothes. Men are also dressed as for church; generally the family chooses a dark suit. Wedding rings are usually left on, but other jewelry is removed.

EMBLEM OF MOURNING ON THE DOOR

To indicate that there has been a death in the house, the funeral director may hang streamers on the front door: white ones for a child, black and white for a young person, or black for an older person. Flowers are, of course, most beautiful and the choice of those who can afford them. Usually they are ordered by the family directly from their own florist, but quite possibly the funeral director orders them. White flowers are used for a young person, purple for someone who was older.

Any emblem is removed by a member of the funeral establishment before the family returns from the services.

THE PART OF CLOSE FRIENDS

Immediately on hearing of the death, the intimate friends of the deceased are expected to go to the house of mourning and ask whether they can be of service. There are countless ways in which they can be helpful, from assisting with such material needs of the family as food and child-care to sending telegrams and answering the door. When you hear of the death of a less intimate friend, you call at the home or funeral parlor according to the directions contained in the newspaper notice. At the house, if there is no register, you leave your card with "With Sympathy" written on it. At a funeral home you sign the register and offer the family your sympathy in person. Unless the deceased was a very distant acquaintance, or you expressed your sympathy in person, you must also write a letter to the family at once. Telephoning is not improper, but it may cause inconvenience by tying up the line, which is always needed at these times for notifying members of the family and making necessary arrangements.

HONORARY PALLBEARERS

The member of the family who is in charge will ask six or eight men who were close friends of the deceased to be the pallbearers. This may be done when they come to pay their respects, or by telephone or telegraph. When a man has been prominent in public life, there may be eight or ten of his political or business associates as well as six or eight lifelong friends. Members of the immediate family are never chosen, as their place is with the women of the family.

There are almost never any pallbearers at the funeral of a Christian woman, but in the Jewish faith, both men and women may have pallbearers.

One cannot refuse an invitation to be a pallbearer except because of illness or necessary absence from the city. The pallbearers meet in the vestibule of the church a few minutes before the time set for the service.

Honorary pallbearers serve only at church funerals. They do not carry the coffin. This service is performed by the assistants of the funeral director, who are expertly trained. The honorary pallbearers sit in the first pews on the left, and after the service leave the church two by two, walking immediately in front of the coffin.

USHERS

Ushers may be chosen in addition to, or in place of, pallbearers. Although funeral directors will supply men to perform the task, it is infinitely better to select men from the family (not immediate) or close friends, who will recognize those who come and seat them according to their closeness to the family, or according to their own wishes.

When there are no pallbearers, the ushers sit in the front pews on the left and march out ahead of the coffin as pallbearers would. If there are pallbearers, the ushers remain at the back of the church.

SENDING AND RECEIVING FLOWERS

If there is a notice in the papers requesting that no flowers be sent, you send none. Otherwise, they are addressed "To the funeral of (name of the deceased)," either at the funeral home or at the church. When you did not know the deceased, but only his close relatives, flowers may be sent to them at their home. Addressed to one of the family is an enclosed card, on which you write "With deepest sympathy," or, if appropriate, "With love and sympathy."

If you do not know where to send flowers at the time of the funeral, or if you hear of the death some time later, you may still send them to the family of the deceased at their home. In fact, these flowers, arriving after the confusion and misery of the first days, are often appreciated more than those which arrive promptly.

To avoid confusion, whoever is making the arrangements for the family should appoint one person to take charge of flowers, and he or she must carefully collect all the accompanying cards which are sent to the house or funeral parlor. This person writes a description of the flowers that came with the card on the outside of each envelope. Sometimes this is done by the florist and the cards are delivered to the bereaved family after the funeral. For example:

> Large spray Easter lilies tied with white ribbon
> Laurel weath with gardenias
> Long sheaf of white roses—broad silver ribbon

Without such notations, the family has no way of knowing anything about the flowers that people have sent. Moreover, these descriptions are invaluable when writing notes of thanks.

If some friends have sent potted plants or cut flowers to the house, their cards are also removed and noted for later acknowledgment.

If the family is Protestant, one or two women friends go to the church an hour before the time set for the service to help the florist or someone on the church staff arrange the flowers, which have been placed in the chancel. Their duty is only to see that those sent by relatives are given a prominent position. Moving about and arranging heavy wreaths and sprays is difficult for novices, and the florist is capable of doing a more effective job than amateurs.

The sexton or one of his assistants should collect the cards, noting the variety of flowers as just described, and give them to these friends, who will in turn deliver them to the one who is responsible for all the arrangements.

Friends of any faith may send a "spiritual bouquet" (a Mass said for the deceased) to a Catholic family. Any priest will make arrangements for the mass and accept the donation. A card is sent to the family, stating the time and place of the mass and the name of the donor.

CALLING AT THE FUNERAL HOME

More often than not the body of the deceased remains at the funeral home until the day of the funeral. In that case some members of the family receive close friends there, rather than at home. The hours when they will be there to accept expressions of sympathy should be included in the death notice in the newspaper. People who wish to pay their respects but who do not feel that they are close enough to intrude on the privacy of the bereaved may stop in at any time and sign the register provided by the funeral parlor. Their signatures should be formal, including their title—"Dr. and Mrs. Harvey Cross" or "Miss Deborah Page" and not "Bill and Joan Cross" or "Debbie Page"—in order to simplify the task of anyone helping the family to acknowledge these visits. A visitor who sees and personally extends his sympathy at the funeral home need not write a note of condolence, unless he wishes to write an absent member of the family. Those who merely sign the register should, in addition, write a note. The family need not thank each and every caller by letter, but if someone has made a special effort or if no one of the family was there to speak to him, they may wish to do so.

The visit to the funeral home need not last more than five or ten minutes. As soon as the visitor has expressed his sympathy to each member of the family, and spoken a moment or two with those he knows well, he may leave. If the casket is open, guests are expected to pass by and pay their respects to the deceased, but if this is too difficult or repugnant to someone, he need not do so.

WHO ATTENDS THE FUNERAL

All members of the family find out when the funeral is to take place and go to it without waiting to be notified. But if the notice read "Funeral private," a friend does not go unless he has received a message from the family that they wish him to come. If the hour and location of the service is printed in the paper, that is considered an invitation to attend. It is entirely up to you to decide whether you knew the deceased or his family well enough to wish to be at his funeral. But it is certainly heartless not to go to the public funeral of a person with whom you have been closely associated in business or some other interest, to whose house you have often been invited, or whose immediate family are your friends.

It is no longer considered necessary to wear black when you go to a friend's funeral unless you sit with the family or have been asked to be one of the honorary pallbearers. However, you should choose clothes that are dark and inconspicuous.

Enter the church as quietly as possible, and if there are no ushers to escort you to a pew, seat yourself where you think you belong. Only a very intimate friend should take a position far up on the center aisle. If you are merely an acquaintance, you sit toward the rear of the church.

FUNERAL SERVICES

AT THE CHURCH

Some people find the church funeral most trying because they must leave the seclusion of the house and be in the presence of a congregation. Others find the solemnity of a church service—with the added beauty of choir and organ—helpful.

As the time appointed for the funeral draws near, the congregation gradually fills the church. The first few pews on the right side of the center aisle are usually left empty for the family and those on the left for the pallbearers, but this may be reversed if the vestry or waiting rooms are on the left.

The trend today is to have the casket closed. Protestants may follow their own wishes. At a Catholic or Jewish service it is obligatory that the casket be closed.

At most funerals the processional is omitted. The coffin may have a floral piece or a blanket of flowers on it. In some churches it may be covered with a pall of needlework, or, for a member of the armed forces, it may be draped with the flag. The coffin is placed on a stand at the foot of the chancel a half-hour before the service. The family usually enter through the door nearest the front pews.

If the family wishes a processional, it forms in the vestibule. If there is to be a choral service, the minister and choir enter the church from the rear and precede the funeral cortege. Directly after the choir and clergy come the honorary pallbearers, two by two; then the coffin; and then the family—the chief mourner first, walking with whoever can offer the most comfort to him or her.

Usually each woman takes the arm of a man. But two women or two men may walk together, according to the division of the family. For example, if the deceased is one of four sons and there is no daughter, the mother and father walk together immediately after the body of their child, and they are followed by the two elder sons and then the younger, and then the nearest woman relative. Although the arrangement of the procession is fixed, it is important that the people in deepest grief should each be placed next to the one whose nearness may be of the most help to them. A younger child who is calm and soothing would be better next to his mother than an older one who is more nervous.

At the chancel, the choir takes its accustomed place, the clergyman stands at the foot of the chancel steps, the honorary pallbearers take their places in the front pews on the left, and the casket is set upon a stand previously placed there for the purpose. The actual bearers of the casket walk quietly to inconspicuous stations on the side aisles. The family and pallbearers occupy the front pews; the rest of the procession fills vacant places on either side. The service is read when everyone is seated. Upon its conclusion, the procession moves out in the same order as it came in, except that the choir remains in its place.

If the family wishes, one of the male relatives may stop at the back of the church to thank those who have attended the services. He needs to say nothing more than "Thank you," with perhaps a special word for close friends, but the gesture will certainly be warmly received.

Outside the church the casket is put into the hearse. The family enter automobiles waiting immediately behind, and the flowers are put into a covered vehicle (far preferable to an open car parading through the streets). They may be taken by a different route and placed beside the grave before the hearse and those attending the burial service arrive.

AT THE HOUSE

Many people prefer a house funeral. It is simpler and more private, and it obviates the necessity for those in sorrow to face people. The nearest relatives may stay apart in an adjoining room where they can hear the service yet remain in seclusion.

Years ago there seldom was music at house funerals, because at that time nothing could substitute for the deep, rich tones of the organ. Now, however, phonographic recordings of organ and choir music are excellent and readily available and may be used as a beautiful addition to a house funeral.

Arrangements are usually made to hold the service in the living room. The coffin is placed in front of the mantel, perhaps, or between two windows, but always at a distance from the door. It is usually set on stands brought by the funeral director, who also supplies enough folding chairs to fill the room without crowding.

At a house funeral the relatives either take their places near the casket or stay apart in seclusion. If the women of the family come into the living room, they wear hats, as they would in a church.

All other women keep their coats on. The men, if they are wearing overcoats, keep them on or carry them on their arms and hold their hats in their hands.

Only a very small group of relatives and intimate friends go to the cemetery from the house.

AT THE FUNERAL HOME OR CHAPEL

In recent years, the establishments of funeral directors have assumed a new prominence. There is always a chapel in the building, actually a small and often very beautiful nonsectarian church. There are also many retiring rooms and reception rooms where the families may remain undisturbed or receive the condolences of their friends.

Services are conducted in the chapel just as they would be in a church, although sometimes there is a private alcove to one side so that the family need not sit in the front pews.

THE BURIAL

If the burial is in the churchyard or within walking distance of the church, the congregation may follow the family to the graveside. Otherwise, those attending the funeral, wherever the services are held, do not go to the interment. The long line of vehicles that used to stand at the church, waiting to be filled with mere acquaintances, is proper only for a public personage.

CREMATION

Many people whose religions allow it prefer the idea of cremation to burial. The service is exactly the same as that preceding a burial. The family may or may not, as they wish, accompany the body to the crematorium. If they do, a very short service is held there also.

The ashes are later delivered to the family to be disposed of in any way that the deceased would wish (as long as it is not contrary to any law). Often, however, the urn is deposited in a building or section set aside in the cemetery or churchyard, and sometimes it is buried in the family plot.

A MEMORIAL SERVICE

In some circumstances—if, for instance, the deceased has died in a far country—a memorial service is held instead of a funeral.

Notice of this service is put into the obituary column of the paper, or, in a small town, relatives and friends may be given short lists of their own nearest neighbors whom they are asked to notify.

These services are very brief. In general outline: two verses of a hymn are sung, short prayers follow, and a very brief address is given about the work and personality of the one for whom the service is held. It is closed with a prayer and a verse or two of another hymn.

Usually, no flowers are sent except a few for the altar. On those occasions when flowers are sent, they are arranged as bouquets (not sheaves) so that they may be put into the wards of a hospital without having to be taken apart and rearranged.

Since this is more like a church service than a funeral, some of the men in the family may, before joining the women, escort guests to their seats as at a Sunday service.

AFTER THE FUNERAL

The old custom of having a roaring wake after the funeral service may have served to take the minds of the bereaved off their tragedy, but it did not do much to show either their sadness or their respect for the deceased. Today a quiet luncheon or reception at the home of one of the relatives has taken the place of a real wake. If it is held at the house of the immediate family, other relatives and close friends provide the food. Members of the family who may not have seen each other for some time have a chance to talk, and it provides a meeting place and a meal for those who came from out of town.

Because the mourners from out of town undoubtedly will be leaving shortly after the funeral, the will is often read right after the luncheon, or at least that same afternoon. If this is not possible for any reason, it should be done within the next day or two at the latest. It may be read either in the home of the deceased or, if more convenient, in the office of the lawyer in charge.

CHURCH FEES

No fee is ever asked by the clergyman, but the family are expected to make a contribution in appreciation of his services and they should do so. The fee may be anything from ten dollars for a very small funeral service to one hundred dollars for a very elaborate one.

A bill rendered by the church office includes all necessary charges for the church.

ACKNOWLEDGMENT OF SYMPATHY

When impersonal messages of condolence mount into the hundreds, as may be the case when a public figure or perhaps a prominent business executive or a member of his family dies, the sending of engraved or well-printed cards to strangers is proper:

The Governor and Mrs. State
wish gratefully to acknowledge
your kind expression of sympathy

The family of
Harrison L. Winthrop
wish to thank you for
your kind expression of sympathy

If such cards are used, a handwritten word or two and a signature *must* be added below the printed message when there is any personal acquaintance with the sender. In no circumstances should such cards be sent to those who have sent flowers or to intimate friends who have written personal letters.

Perhaps as the result of the use of cards in these rare but permissible cases, a most unfortunate custom has sprung up. The funeral director supplies printed cards, and the recipient merely signs his or her name to it. This is a poor return, indeed, for a beautiful spray of flowers or even a sincere and comforting note.

A personal message on a fold-over card is preferable to any printed card, and it takes but a moment to write "Thank you for your beautiful flowers" or "Thank you for all your kindness."

If the list is very long, or if the person who has received the flowers and messages is really unable to perform the task of writing, some member of the family or a near friend may write for her or him: "Mother asks me to thank you for your beautiful flowers and kind message of sympathy." No one expects more than a short message of acknowledgment, but that message should be *personal* and written by hand!

For suggestions on writing letters of condolence, see Chapter Nine, "Personal Letters."

MOURNING CLOTHES

During the past fifty years, no changes in etiquette have been so great as those in the conventions of mourning. Until then, the regulations about dress were definitely prescribed according to the precise degree of relationship of the mourner. One's real feelings, whether of grief or comparative indifference, had nothing to do with the outward manifestation one was expected to show as a sign of respect.

A greater and greater number of persons today do not believe in going into mourning at all. There may be a few who believe that great love should be expressed in rejoicing at the rebirth of a beloved spirit instead of selfishly mourning one's own earthly loss. It is certain, however, that the number who can actually attain this spirit are few indeed. Most of us merely do the best we can to keep occupied, to make the necessary adjustments, and to avoid casting the shadow of our own sadness on others. The sooner that we can overcome our grief and turn our thoughts to the future, the better. Because mourning is a continual reminder of the past, it can only delay the wearer's return to a normal life.

A WIDOW'S MOURNING

A widow of mature years may still, if she chooses (and in some Latin countries she does), wear mourning for life. On the other hand, deep mourning for a year is now considered extreme, and for even more than six months is very rare.

The young widow, if she wishes to wear mourning, should wear all-black for six months. Black clothes are never appropriate in the country, however; any sports clothes may be worn, provided they are of an inconspicuous nature.

A woman *never* remains in mourning for her first husband after she has decided that she can be consoled by a second. But, it would be inappropriate to welcome the attentions of a new suitor while still in mourning.

MOURNING FOR OTHERS

A mother who has lost a grown son or daughter may wear all-black for six months or a year, depending on her inclination.

A daughter or sister, if she wishes, wears mourning for one season. Counting by season is very practical because of the expense of buying extra clothes. When going into mourning in the spring or summer, for example, wear deep mourning until winter clothes are appropriate; then go back to regular clothes.

MOURNING FOR BUSINESS WOMEN

Since mourning is the outward evidence of a personal frame of mind that has no place in the impersonal world of business, mourning that attracts attention is as unsuitable in an office as a black uniform would be on a soldier.

If a woman arrives at her office a day or so after the death of a close relative in the clothes she ordinarily wears, no one looks askance.

MOURNING FOR MEN

It is entirely correct (but rather unusual nowadays) for a man to go into mourning for a few months by the simple expedient of putting a black band on his hat and on the left sleeve of his clothes. Also, he wears black shoes, gloves, socks, and ties, and white instead of colored shirts. In the country a young man continues to wear his ordinary sports clothes and shoes and sweaters—no matter how gay—and without any sleeve band.

The sleeve band is from three and a half to four and a half inches in width and is of dull cloth on overcoats or winter clothing and of serge on summer clothes.

But a sleeve band on business clothes is an implied bid for sympathy, which most men want to avoid. Therefore, they go to the office with no evidence of mourning other than a black tie and black socks, if anything at all.

THE BEHAVIOR OF THE FAMILY AFTER THE FUNERAL

As soon as possible after the funeral the life of the family should return to its normal routine. There are many things that must be attended to at once, and while these may seem like insurmountable chores to a grieving husband or wife, the necessity of having to perform them and, in so doing, to think of others rather than oneself is in reality a great help in returning to an active life.

Letters must be written to the clergyman, thanking him for his services and his help. The pallbearers must also be thanked, and there are always others who have performed some service for the family who will appreciate a note of thanks. The gifts of flowers must be acknowledged, and each letter of condolence answered. As stated above, when thousands of letters have been received, it is correct to use printed cards of acknowledgment, but in the ordinary family a handwritten note should be sent, be it only two lines long.

The return of the close relatives of the deceased to an active social life is up to the individual. If he or she is not wearing mourning, he may start, as soon as he feels up to it, to go to a friend's house, to a movie, play, sports event, classes, or meetings. He may wish to avoid large gatherings for a time, but little by little he increases the scope of his activities until his life has returned to normal. A man or woman may start to have dates when he or she feels like it, but for a few months these should be restricted to evenings at the home of a friend, a movie, or some other inconspicuous activity.

Those who are wearing mourning do not go to dances or other formal parties, nor do they take a leading part in purely social functions. However, anyone who is in public life or business or who has a professional career must, of course, continue to fulfill his duties. The fact that many women have gone into business or are following careers is another cause of the lightening of mourning and the shortening of its duration. In sum, each year the number increases of those who show the mourning in their hearts only by the quiet dignity of their lives.

CHILDREN

On no account should children be put into black at any time. They wear their best church clothes to a funeral, and afterward, whatever they ordinarily wear.

Many people are uncertain about whether children who have lost a parent should participate in their usual school activities and after-school entertainments. The answer is "yes." They should take part in sports and in school concerts or plays. However, older children may not wish to go to a purely social party within two or three weeks, or even longer, after the death of a parent. The normal routine of a small child should not be upset—more than ever he needs to romp and play.

MEMORIALS

Many bereaved families wish to make a material gesture to honor their dead. For the very wealthy this may take many forms, from the building of a monument to the donation of a piece of equipment to the hospital that cared for the deceased. This type of memorial does not need a great deal of discussion in this book, because its very nature requires that it be considered carefully, and because time will be required for extensive planning before it can be done. The advice of other people will be involved, and that will put an automatic restraint on those who might otherwise be overcome by their emotions.

Most of us, however, are not in a position to provide an enormously expensive memorial, and the gravestone we choose for our loved one is the only permanent memorial that will exist. Therefore, it, and the inscription on it, should be chosen with great care. The worst mistake one can make is to rush into ordering an ornate stone with sentimental carvings and a flowery inscription which may later seem in poor taste or objectionable. For example, one might wish in the emotion of the moment to write something about the deceased being "the only love" or "the greatest love" of the spouse. This could conceivably cause considerable anguish to a future husband or wife.

The wisest course is to choose as handsome a stone as one can afford and refrain from ordering terribly ornate decorations. Almost invariably, the simplest constructions—be they monuments, buildings, or any work of art—are those which endure and continue to please forever. The inscription, too, should be simple and sincere. "Beloved husband of" expresses true devotion without excluding other members of a present, or future, family. Titles are not used for either men or women. A typical and correct inscription would read:

1900–1968
Helen Jones Schaeffer
beloved wife of
John Simon Schaeffer

Whatever you choose, remember that you must consider the feelings of the living. While the donation of a memorial is, in part, a solace to the bereaved, it is something which will be seen and shared with others. Surely the one who has died would not want a memorial that could ever be anything but an honor to him and a pleasure to those he leaves behind.

PLANNING FOR THE GRAVE

In cemeteries where it is permitted, some people plant a veritable flower garden around a grave. Others prefer to have only grass and to bring fresh flowers or potted plants regularly as an evidence of their continuing love. This can become quite a chore, however, as the first grief diminishes, and the garden flowers need constant care or they become a straggling weed patch in short order. A very satisfactory solution is that of using evergreen shrubs and ground cover, which look beautiful all year round with little attention.

Part EIGHT

WEDDINGS

43

Engagements

Courtship is a time of excitement and fun, but as it progresses and as the young people find themselves more and more attracted to each other, it also becomes a time of serious consideration. At some point, the girl begins to think, "This is the man I want to marry—I wonder if he feels the same way about me?" And the man is asking himself similar questions. Their conversation becomes more personal and more serious, and they start to "sound each other out." Very often the man never actually says, "Will you marry me?" They agree to marry through a sort of understanding and acceptance of each other that has grown with their deepening acquaintance.

During this pre-engagement time it is very important that these young people do not avoid the company of others. While the evenings when they are alone are surely their favorite ones, it is essential for them to get to know each other's friends. A marriage in which either partner is incompatible with people who have always been part of the other's life has one strike against it to begin with. This is even more true of the couple's families. Each should be entertained in the home of the other so that they can see the surroundings and the family to which they will be expected to adjust. Although it may not be possible if either or both of the families live in another area, an overnight or weekend visit can be helpful in making the decision as to whether to propose and whether to accept if the proposal comes. The family who are to entertain the young people should be advised beforehand what the situation is by their son or daughter, in order to avoid embarrassing their guest.

Dear Mother,

May I bring Sally Foster up for the night next Saturday? We have been seeing a lot of each other, and I'm eager to have her see Waterbury, and to introduce her to you.

Love,
Jim

Or:

Dear Mom,

I've met a most attractive man, Jerry Boyd, from Syracuse, and I'm very eager for you to meet each other. So I wondered if it would be convenient for us to spend next weekend with you and Dad.

Please let me know as soon as you can.

Love to you both,
Sue

The parents receiving such a note or a telephone call are prepared to meet their possible son- or daugter-in-law, but should realize that unless they are told otherwise when the couple arrives, the engagement is still in the future.

THE FUTURE BRIDEGROOM AND HIS FIANCÉE'S FATHER

The first thing the couple does after the man proposes and the girl says "Yes" is to see her father or whoever is head of her family, and the prospective bridegroom asks for his consent. If her father refuses, the girl then is faced with the problem of changing her "Yes" to "No" or else marrying in opposition to her parents. An honest young woman who has made up her mind to marry in spite of her parents' disapproval tells them that her wedding will take place on such and such a day and refuses to give her word that she will not marry. It is the height of dishonor to give her word while intending to break it.

In most instances, however, when John goes to see Mary's father, the latter has a perfectly good idea of what the young man has come to say and has been planning how he will word his answer to his prospective son-in-law. The conversation is usually more of a discussion of the couple's plans and the boy's prospects than a request for permission to marry.

It may be that John's finances seem to the father not to be quite up to supporting his daughter, and he may decide to give her some sort of an allowance. He might advise them to wait until John is more established, or Mary might suggest that she work for a time to help out. In any case, if they come to a satisfactory conclusion, he makes no objection to an immediate announcement.

THE ENGAGEMENT RING

It is doubtful that the man who produced a ring from his pocket the instant that the woman said "Yes" ever existed outside romantic novels. In real life it is both correct and wise for *him* to consult *her* taste. The fiancé first goes alone to the jeweler, explains how much he can afford, and has a selection of rings set aside. He then brings his fiancée to the store and lets her choose the one she likes best.

She might choose a traditional diamond ring, or she might prefer a ring of more important size with her own birthstone. If there are family heirlooms to be chosen from, the man may show them to his fiancée and have her selection set to her taste.

Today many girls choose to use semiprecious stones, beside which a tiny diamond loses some of its appeal.

An aquamarine is first choice as a solitaire diamond's substitute. An amethyst, or topaz, or transparent tourmaline are all lovely as selections for an engagement ring. But if a birthstone seems more appropriate, these are the traditional choices:

JANUARY—*Garnet* (Its rather dark glow makes a pleasing engagement ring). The *zircon*, a white, crystal-clear stone, makes a very attractive ring and closely resembles a diamond, particularly when square cut and kept brilliantly clean. But because it does look like a diamond, there is chance that a bride might fear that people will feel she is trying to fool them into thinking it really is a diamond. There is also a beautiful steel-blue variety.

FEBRUARY—*Amethyst* (A big one with a square cut is effective).

MARCH—*Aquamarine* first, then *bloodstone* or *jasper*. A square-cut aquamarine is very popular and a really beautiful substitute for a diamond.

APRIL—*Diamond* (The stone of stones, but very expensive).

MAY—*Emerald* (Also very costly if perfect in color and without noticeable flaw).

JUNE—*Pearl* (Nothing more becoming to a young girl with lovely skin).

JULY—*Ruby* (Of very high value when of the desirable pigeon-blood color).

AUGUST—*Sardonyx, peridot* (a rare and beautiful stone), or *carnelian.*

SEPTEMBER—*Sapphire* (A favorite engagement ring of the past and always beautiful).

OCTOBER—*Opal* (The opal is believed to be the stone of good fortune for those born in October, but unlucky for those not born in this month).

NOVEMBER—*Topaz.*

DECEMBER—*Turquoise* or *lapis lazuli.*

The engagement ring is worn for the first time in public on the day of the announcement. But *an engagement ring is not essential to the validity of the betrothal.* Some people confuse the engagement ring with the wedding ring and believe the former is as indispensable as the latter. This is not the case. The wedding ring is a requirement of the marriage service. The engagement ring is simply evidence that he has proposed marriage and that she has said "Yes!"

Countless wives have never had an engagement ring at all. Others receive their rings long after marriage, when their husbands are able to buy the ring they have always wanted them to have. Some brides prefer to forego an engagement ring in order to put the money it would have cost toward furnishing their future homes.

A WIDOW'S OR DIVORCÉE'S ENGAGEMENT RING

When a widow or a divorcée becomes engaged to marry again, she stops wearing her engagement ring from her first marriage, whether or not she is given another. She may continue to wear her wedding ring, if she has children, until the day of her second marriage. She and her new fiancé must decide together what they wish to do with her old engagement ring. If she has a son, she may wish to keep it for him to use some day as an engagement ring for his future bride. Or the stones may be reset and used in another form of jewelry—by herself or her daughters.

IF SHE GIVES HIM AN ENGAGEMENT PRESENT

It is not obligatory or even customary for the girl to give the man an engagement present, but there is no impropriety in her doing so.

The more usual presents include such articles as a set of studs and a matching pair of cuff links, or a watch band or a key chain, or a cigarette lighter. Probably because the giving of an engagement ring is his particular province, she very rarely gives him a ring or, in fact, any present at all.

THE PARENTS BECOME ACQUAINTED

Years ago, one of the most unbreakable rules of etiquette was that the parents of the groom should call on those of the bride as soon as their son made the engagement known to them. But the custom of "calling on" anyone formally has long since passed—replaced by the informal meeting, usually arranged by telephone.

It is still the parents of the groom who should make the first move to become acquainted with the bride-to-be's family. If they live in the same town, the young man's mother calls the girl's mother and tells her how happy she and her husband are about the engagement. She suggests that they come over as soon as possible for coffee, cocktails, dinner, or whatever she chooses.

If they live in different cities, it is also up to the groom's parents to write—or call if they wish—first. A visit should be arranged between the families as soon as possible, and whichever one can travel most conveniently should make the trip.

If for any reason the man's family does not contact the parents of the girl, her father and mother should be very careful not to permit an oversight or lack of knowledge to develop into a situation that may cause great unhappiness. The important thing is that this time should be a happy one for the young couple and that both sets of parents should act with spontaneity and in a spirit of friendship.

The girl, too, must try to understand and accept the attitude of her future family (whatever it may be), and she must *not* stand inflexibly upon what she unwittingly considers to be her own family's rights. The objective that she should keep in mind is the happiness of the relationship between her future in-laws and herself.

ANNOUNCING THE ENGAGEMENT

PERSONAL ANNOUNCEMENT

Usually a few days—perhaps a week—before the formal announcement the girl and man each write to or call aunts, uncles, cousins, and their most intimate friends to tell them of their engagement. If the news is to be announced at a surprise party, they ask them not to tell anyone else. This is so that those closest to them will not read of it first in the newspapers. These relatives should telephone or write the bride as soon as they receive the news. She must, of course, answer the letters as soon as possible.

In case of a recent death in either immediate family, the engagement should be quietly announced by telling families and intimate friends. (The wedding announcement in the newspaper serves to inform other acquaintances.)

THE FORMAL ANNOUNCEMENT

The formal or public announcement is made by the parents of the bride-to-be. This is done either by notes or at the engagement party, and then publicly through the newspapers. Engraved announcements are not correct.

NEWSPAPER ANNOUNCEMENTS

The newspaper announcement of the engagement with all the pertinent information is sent by the bride's parents to the society editor of all the papers in which it is to be printed. You may include a picture if you wish. If you live in the suburbs of a large city or in a small town, a copy should be sent to the local paper (which may be a weekly). Others go to the paper of your choice in the nearby city and to the paper suggested by the bridegroom's family in their locality.

The announcement should be sent to the papers a week or more in advance of the date on which you wish it to appear, and that date should be clearly stated so that the announcement comes out simultaneously in all the papers. If the couple wish to keep their engagement a surprise until it is announced at an engagement party, the newspaper announcement should appear on the day following the party. Otherwise, it may be printed on whatever day the families choose, with the party held shortly afterwards. Many people think it important to have it appear in the Sunday paper, probably because more people read the society page on Sunday than they do on weekdays. But there is a far better chance of having all the information printed, and the photograph used, on a weekday, when the demand for space is not so pressing. If your local paper is a weekly, the date given the other papers should coincide with the day on which it is published.

The usual form is as follows:

> Mr. and Mrs. Herbert Coles Johnson of Lake Forest, Illinois, announce the engagement of their daughter, Miss Susan Bailey Johnson, to Dr. William Arthur Currier, son of Mr. and Mrs. Arthur Jamison Currier of Atlanta, Georgia. A June wedding is planned.
>
> Miss Johnson was graduated from Bentley Junior College. She made her debut in 1966 at the Mistletoe Ball in Chicago, and in May will complete her nurse's training at Atlanta General Hospital. Dr. Currier was graduated from the Hill School, Yale University, and the Yale Medical School. He completed his residency at the Atlanta General Hospital and is now in practice in that city.

In unusual situations, the information as to schools and employment remains the same although the identification of the bride and bridegroom and their parents may vary.

When one parent is deceased: The announcement is worded the same whether made by the mother or father of the bride.

> Mrs. Herbert Coles Johnson announces the engagement of her daughter, Miss Susan Bailey Johnson, to Dr. William Arthur Currier . . . etc. Miss Johnson is also the daughter of the late Herbert Coles Johnson. . . .

When the bride is an orphan: The engagement of an orphan is announced by the girl's nearest relative, a godparent, or a very dear friend. If she has no one close to her, she sends the announcement herself:

> The engagement of Miss Jessica Towne, daughter of the late Mr. and Mrs. Samuel Towne, is announced, to Mr. Richard Frost. . . .

This form may also be used if her parents live very far away or if she has, for some reason, separated herself completely from her family.

If the parents are divorced: The mother of the bride usually makes the announcement, but the name of the other parent should be included.

> Mrs. Jones Farnham announces the engagement of her daughter, Miss Cynthia Farnham. . . . Miss Farnham is also the daughter of Mr. Henry Farnham of Worcester, Mass. . . .

If the parent with whom the bride lives is remarried:

> Mr. and Mrs. Samuel Harvey announce the engagement of Mrs. (or Mr.) Harvey's daughter, Miss Jane Barber Cutler (Harvey) to. . . . Miss Cutler (Harvey) is also the daughter of Mr. David Soames Cutler (or Mrs. James Little) of Menlo Park, Calif.

If divorced parents are friendly: On occasion, divorced parents may remain good friends, and their daughter's time may be divided equally between them. If this is true, they may both wish to announce the engagement.

> Mr. Gordon Smythe of Philadelphia and Mrs. Howard Zabriskie of 12 East 72nd Street, New York City, announce the engagement of their daughter, Miss Carla Farr Smythe. . . .

If the bride is adopted: If the bride has been brought up since babyhood by her foster parents and uses their last name, there is no reason to mention the fact that she is adopted. If she joined the family later in life, however, and has retained her own name, it is proper to say:

> Mr. and Mrs. Warren La Tour announce the engagement of their adopted daughter, Miss Claudia Romney, daughter of the late Mr. and Mrs. Carlton Romney. . . .

Older women, widows, and divorcées: A woman of forty or more, even though her parents are living, generally does not announce her engagement in the newspaper, but instead calls or writes her relatives and friends shortly before the wedding. A widow or divorcée announces her second engagement in the same way.

Occasionally a situation arises in which the parents of the groom would like to announce the engagement. For instance, when a boy in the service becomes engaged to a girl from another country, her parents may not have the knowledge or means to put an announcement in the paper in his hometown. Rather than announce it in their own name, the groom's parents should word the notice:

> The engagement of Miss Gretchen Strauss, daughter of Mr. and Mrs. Heinrich Strauss of Frankfurt, Germany, is announced, to Lt. John Evans, son of Mr. and Mrs. Walter Evans of . . . etc.

THE ENGAGEMENT PARTY

Invitations to engagement parties are generally written on informals or commercial cards, and do not necessarily mention the reason for the party. They are ordinarily sent in the name of the bride's parents or of the relative or friend who is announcing the engagement. Occasionally the parents wish to include their daughter's name with theirs, and add "To meet Mr. Robert Watkins." Or they may prefer "In honor of Sally Jones and Robert Watkins," clearly indicating the nature of the occasion. The invitations also may be issued by telephone.

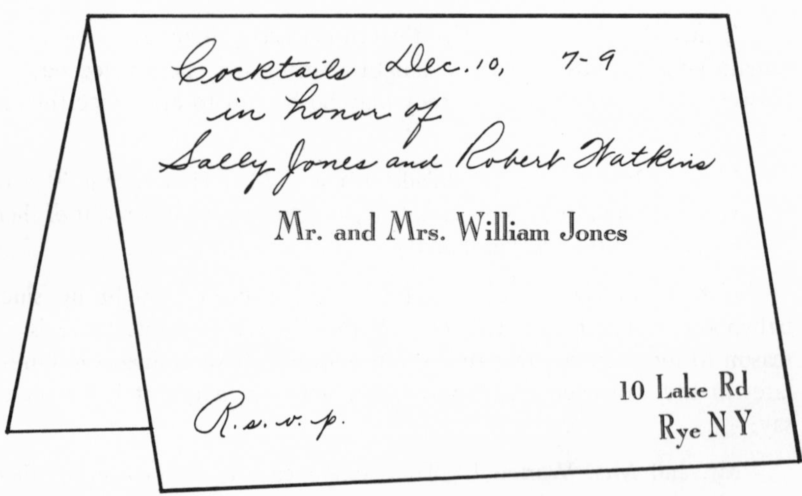

Cocktails Dec. 10, 7-9
in honor of
Sally Jones and Robert Watkins

Mr. and Mrs. William Jones

R.s.v.p.

10 Lake Rd
Rye N Y

Presents are rarely taken to an engagement party, even though it is not a surprise, because usually only intimate friends or relatives give gifts, and other guests might be embarrassed. Should some friends arrive with gifts, the bride should open them in private with only the donor present, rather than make a display of them in front of those who did not bring anything.

Cocktails
Dec. 10, 7-9
Mr. and Mrs. William Jones
Sally Jones
to meet Robert Watkins
10 Lake Rd.
R.s.v.p. Rye, N.Y.

The engagement party may be of any type that the bride and her mother prefer, but it is generally a cocktail party or a dinner. The guests are relatives, close friends of the bride and groom, and probably a few close friends of the parents. The news may be told by the girl herself, or by her mother as the guests arrive and find the fiancé standing with their hostess. There is no formal receiving line, but his presence beside the family, being introduced as the guests arrive, needs no further explanation. Perhaps, if the party is a dinner, the engagement is announced by the bride's father, who proposes a toast to the couple. Little announcing is necessary by the time dinner is served, however, when the young woman is wearing a shining ring on the fourth finger of her left hand.

To those who ask about using a novel way to announce an engagement, it can be said that there is really no logical objection to whatever may be pleasing to you. Whether you let a cat out of a bag with your names written on a ribbon around its neck, float balloons with your names printed on them, display a cake decorated with the couple's initials inside two hearts, or use place cards in the form of telegrams containing the announcement, there is not a rule in the world to hamper your own imagination.

THE TOAST

This is the conventional announcement made by the father of the bride at a dinner: After seeing that all glasses at the table are filled, the host rises, lifts his own glass, and says, "I propose we drink to the health of Mary and the young man she has decided to add permanently to our family, Tim Baldwin."

For other appropriate toasts, see Chapter Four, "Public Speaking."

Everyone except Mary and Jim rises and drinks a little of whatever the beverage may be. They congratulate the young couple, and Tim is called upon for a speech. He must stand and make at least a few remarks thanking the guests for their good wishes.

When the party is given on the afternoon or evening of the day of the newspaper announcement—or later—the engagement is never proclaimed to the guests as an assembled audience. The news is "out," and everyone is supposed to have heard it. Everybody congratulates the bridegroom and offers the bride-to-be wishes for her happiness.

BEHAVIOR OF THE ENGAGED COUPLE

There is said to be still preserved somewhere in Massachusetts a whispering reed, and through its long, hollow length lovers supposedly whispered messages of tenderness to each other while separated by a room's length and the inevitable chaperonage of the fiancée's entire family. At the opposite extreme is the engaged couple of today who persist in embarrassing everyone around them with constant displays of their emotion. It is not necessary to demonstrate one's feelings with caresses and kisses in public, but how attractive to indicate affection by frank approval of whatever the other may do or say and by a radiant look! That is love—as it should be!

NO OTHER SINGLE DATES

It is unnecessary to say that an engaged man shows no marked interest in other women. Often it so happens that engaged people are together very little because he is away at work, lives in another city, or for other reasons. Rather than sit home alone, he or she may, of course, go out with their friends, but they must avoid going out with any one man or woman alone.

CHAPERONING THE ENGAGED COUPLE

The question of a chaperon differs with locality. Southern girls used to be more carefully chaperoned than their northern sisters, and western girls have long been the most independent of all. But there are few places left today where an engaged pair may not spend as many hours alone together as they wish, so long as it is not overnight. In order to reach a destination where they will be chaperoned, they may travel overnight in a public conveyance, but their accommodations must not be adjoining and their behavior must preclude any possibility of criticism. They should never take an automobile trip that requires them to pass the night en route in a hotel or motel.

Unmarried friends are not suitable chaperons unless a large group is going on a weekend together, but a married couple, even though of the same age, is acceptable. Otherwise, for any overnight stay the engaged pair must be in the company of an older man, woman, or couple.

PRESENTS THAT MAY AND MAY NOT BE ACCEPTED BY THE BRIDE-TO-BE

The fiancée of a young man who is saving his pennies would be lacking in good taste as well as good sense if she were to encourage or allow him to send her many flowers or other charming but extravagant presents. On the other hand, if the bridegroom-elect has ample means, she may accept anything he chooses to select, *except* wearing apparel or anything that can be classified as maintenance.

They may, if they wish, open a joint bank account shortly before the wedding, in order to deposit the checks they receive as gifts. They may draw on this account to help in furnishing their future home.

It is perfectly proper for her to drive his car, and she may select furniture for their future home. But she should not live in the house or use its furniture until they are married. He may give her all the jewels he can afford; he may give her a fur neckpiece, but not a fur coat. The neckpiece is an ornament; the coat is wearing apparel.

If she cannot afford to buy a new dress, she may have to be married in the prettiest dress she already has, but her wedding dress and the clothes she wears away on her wedding day must not be supplied by the bridegroom or, in most circumstances, by his family. There are, of course, exceptions. If his mother has known the girl for years and loves her dearly, there is no reason why she should not give her everything she chooses. But a bride would be guilty of poor taste if she were lodged and clothed by any man, whether he is soon to be her husband or not.

THE LENGTH OF THE ENGAGEMENT

A long engagement is likely to be a strain on all involved. The ideal duration is from three to five months, which allows time for the wedding arrangements to be made and for the couple to come to know each other very well. If one or both are finishing school, they may want to be engaged during the last year so that they do not have to become involved in more social life than they wish. Or if a man is serving his military term and his fiancée wishes everyone to know that she will not be going out with other men, then it is right and proper to announce the engagement some time before the wedding. Nonetheless, it may be a somewhat trying period. The young people, trying to see as much of each other as possible and at the same time continue studying or working, are often exhausted. The bride has the added time-consuming responsibilities of planning the wedding, and her mother, who may be left to make the arrangements almost alone, is also in a difficult position. Therefore, unless there are good and sufficient reasons for a long engagement, a shorter one ensures that the bride, the bridegroom, and their families will arrive at the wedding in good health and a happy frame of mind.

THE BROKEN ENGAGEMENT

In the unfortunate event of a broken engagement, the ring and all other gifts of value must be returned to the former fiancé. Gifts received from relatives or friends should also be returned with a short note of explanation:

Dear Sue,

I am sorry to have to tell you that Jack and I have broken our engagement. Therefore I am returning the towels that you were so sweet to send to me.

Love,
Jane

A notice reading "The engagement of Miss Sara Black and Mr. John Doe has been broken by mutual consent" may be sent to the newspapers that announced the engagement.

If the man should die before the wedding, his fiancée may keep her engagement ring. If it happens to be an old family heirloom and she knows that his parents would like to have it remain in the family, she would be considerate to offer to return it. She may keep any gifts that were given her by friends.

BUYING THE WEDDING RING—OR RINGS

Shortly before the wedding, it is not only customary but important that the bride go with the groom when he buys the wedding ring. One reason is that since she may not intend to take it off—ever—she should be allowed to choose the style she prefers. No ring could be in better taste than the plain band of yellow or white gold or platinum. A diamond band, no matter how lovely, is more suitable as a guard than as a wedding ring, especially as any ring with stones must be taken off to be properly cleaned or to have a stone tightened or replaced.

If the bridegroom wishes to have a ring, the bride buys a plain gold band to match hers but a little wider—or it may be any type of ring he prefers and she is able to buy. Preferably a man's ring is worn on the fourth finger of his left hand, but the fourth or fifth finger of either hand is correct.

The wedding ring may be engraved with whatever sentiment the bridegroom chooses. On the broad rings of many years ago, it was not unusual to have a quotation of twenty-five letters or more, as well as initials. On the rings of today, however, only the initials and date are usually engraved.

The bridegroom's ring is marked similarly, or as the bride chooses.

ENGAGEMENT PRESENTS

It is not unusual for a bride-to-be to receive a few engagement presents sent either by her relatives, intimate friends, godparents, or by members of her fiancé's family as special messages of welcome to her. It is never necessary to give engagement as well as wedding presents. However, if one wishes to do so, the gifts are usually table linen, towels, bed linen such as a set of embroidered sheets, or possibly an inexpensive novelty gift—a "his and hers" cocktail shaker with two glasses, or an artificial flower arrangement. They are presents directed particularly toward the bride's pleasure, and if they are monogrammed, her married initials alone are used.

Shortly after the engagement is announced, it is wise for the bride to go to the local stores and indicate her preferences in colors and styles so the engagement presents will fit in with her choice of trousseau.

THE HOUSEHOLD TROUSSEAU

A trousseau, according to the derivation of the word, was the "little truss or bundle" that the bride carried with her to the house of her husband. Today, extravagant trousseaux are dwindling to items of actual requirement. Household linens enough to run an enormous house—and for a lifetime—are a thing of the past. Few modern linen closets would hold them. The well-appointed house of today's bride will be adequately equipped to start married life with the following items, although she may wish to add to them as her family and household expand:

BED LINEN (amounts are for *each* bed)

- 6 sheets (for master bed)
- 4 sheets (for guest bed)
- 4 pillow cases (for each single bed; 8 for double bed)
- 1 blanket cover (washable silk or drip-dry cotton)
- 2 quilted mattress pads
- 1 lightweight wool blanket for summer
- 1 electric blanket (dual control for double bed) or 2 heavyweight wool or wool-blend blankets
- 1 comforter for winter (preferably eiderdown)
- 1 bedspread

BATH LINEN (quantities are for each bathroom)

- 6 large bath towels
- 6 small towels to match
- 6 washcloths to match
- 6 hand towels for powder room
- 1 shower curtain
- 2 bath mats

KITCHEN

- 6 sturdy dish towels
- 4 dishcloths or 2 sponges

4 potholders

Hand towels and washcloths are needed for a maid who comes in by the day.

Remember that terry-cloth towels are very practical because they don't wrinkle. Linen towels rumple the moment they are used.

TABLE LINEN

1 damask tablecloth, white or pastel color, to fit your dining-room table.

12 dinner napkins to match

2 or 3 yard-and-a-half-square linen tablecloths for bridge tables; matching napkins optional

1 or 2 sets of linen place mats with matching napkins

12 linen or cotton napkins in a neutral color that will go with any odd place mats that you may be given

1 set (4 to 6) plastic mats with smooth, hard surface, or treated paper mats for everyday use

1 set (6 or 8) plastic, straw, or any attractive mats of a more elaborate design for use at informal parties

Optional, but very useful—large monogrammed paper napkins

Cocktail napkins, paper or cloth

A damask cloth is very useful for any buffet setting because, with a felt pad under it, every inch of space is available—which is not the case with the bare table spaces if mats are used. An embroidered linen cloth or one of lace is also practical with the addition of a heat-protecting mat under any exceptionally hot platter or dish.

Small place mats of linen with or without a runner to match are most practical. No matter how pretty your plastic mats may be, linen or lace ones always make your table a little dressier.

You should try your best to have cloth napkins to use with your tablecloths or linen mats. They need not be of the same fabric as long as they are appropriate. Paper napkins are so attractively made today that they can be used to solve the laundry problem very practically, but they *are* informal and should be used only with other casual table appointments.

If your dining room is very small, or if you have none at all, it may be practical to set three sturdy bridge tables with matching tablecloths and napkins. The color should, of course, go well with the colors in your room.

MARKING LINEN

Linen embroidered with a monogram or initials is very decorative. One initial with additional embellishment to give the appearance of a monogram is more effective than two initials—and usually the cost is less.

Towels are marked so that the monogram is centered when they are folded and hung on the rack.

The monogram should be in proportion to the size of the piece. If it is too small, it will look skimpy; if too large, it is overly conspicuous.

Years ago, when Muriel Barbara Jones married Henry Ross, not a piece of linen or silver in their house was marked otherwise than "MBJ." But because this proved a confusing and senseless custom, when initials are used it is now recognized as more practical to mark everything with the bride's future initials: "MJR" or simply "R."

Long tablecloths are marked on either side of center, midway between the table center and the edge. Small square tablecloths are marked at one corner midway between the table center and the point. Square monograms look well set in line with the table edge; irregular ones look best at a corner.

Very large damask napkins are marked in the center of one side, smaller ones in one corner—cross-cornered usually, but sometimes straight. To decide about the place for marking the napkins, fold the napkin exactly as it is to be folded for use and then make a light pencil outline in the center of the folded napkin.

Sheets are always marked with the base of the letters toward the hem—when on the bed, the monogram is right-side up and can be read by a person standing at the foot of the bed—and it is put at half the depth at which the sheet is turned back. Pillowcases are marked halfway between the edge of the case and the beginning of the pillow.

CHOOSING CHINA, GLASS, AND SILVER

Before her wedding invitations are sent out, every bride should go to the gift shops or department stores in her neighborhood, or anywhere that she knows her friends will be shopping, and select those patterns of glass, china, and other items that she would like to receive as wedding presents. All stores of this type are prepared to cooperate with the bride in keeping a record of her choice, and it is of an immeasurable help to those selecting gifts.

CHINA

Today stores are filled with such entrancing sets of pottery and china—thick, thin, plain, or decorated—that the problem is not to find sufficiently attractive table decorations but to choose one from among the many available. There is, however, one item of important advice. Keep in mind the subject of replacements. Any pattern not easily replaced means that breakage will leave you helplessly handicapped. It is always wise to ask if a pattern is in open stock. Remember, too, that soap-bubble-thin glass or glass that is very finely chased or cut naturally goes well with porcelains, whereas the heavier glassware is best suited to pottery.

Let us consider a few general principles that apply to a table set entirely with china. The one requirement is that the pieces be in harmony, meaning that they have some matching detail—such as a repeated note of color. In other words, dinner plates of one variety, bread-and-butter plates of another variety, a centerpiece of another, dishes for sweets of another would look like an odd-lot table unless the individual pieces were closely allied.

Whether you decide on decorated china or plain is your own choice. All white china of the same color and texture need not match in pattern or shape, but it would be unpleasing, for example, to use translucent milk glass with opaque white earthenware. The tastefulness of china in any other plain color necessarily depends upon the color of the cloth or table upon which it is to be set.

The following lists are what the bride should *basically* have to start out with. If her funds are limited and if she is not given enough dinner and dessert plates, for instance, to complete six or eight settings, she may add a piece or two as often as she can, completing one place setting at a time rather than buying two or three more dinner plates and still having an incomplete setting.

FOR EVERYDAY USE:

1 complete set of 4 or 6 place settings of inexpensive china, pottery, or unbreakable plastic ware—which now comes in most attractive patterns. This set should include:

- dinner plates
- dessert plates (may also be used for salad)
- cereal dishes (used also for soup, puddings, canned fruit, etc.)
- cups
- saucers
- cream pitcher and sugar bowl
- 2 platters
- 2 vegetable dishes

FOR ENTERTAINING:

The bride may choose between:

1. A complete service of fine matching china for 6 or 8 place settings. Each place setting should include:
   - soup cup (two-handled, for both clear and cream soups)
   - saucer
   - dinner plate
   - salad plate
   - butter plate
   - dessert plate

   Optional:
   - cups and saucers

cream soup plates
cream pitcher and sugar bowl
platters and vegetable dishes
demitasse cups
gravy boat
sauce bowls for hollandaise, mayonnaise, etc.

2. Odd sets of 6 or 8 dinner plates and dessert plates and additional items in any pattern she chooses.

If the bride prefers variety to a single set of china, she must choose her accompanying items carefully. Glass, silver, pewter, and the beautiful new easy-to-care-for stainless steel may be combined with any china to make a charming dinner table. To go with the odd dinner and dessert plates, the bride will need:

6 or 8 glass or silver butter plates
6 or 8 glass salad plates (the crescent-shaped ones are pretty and take up less space on the table)
12 cups and saucers in any pattern
6 or 8 demitasse cups and saucers in any pattern
2 platters and 3 vegetable dishes of silver or stainless steel
1 cream pitcher and sugar bowl—silver, glass, or stainless steel

Other essential items that may be of any material or style that the bride prefers are:

4 salts and peppers—silver, glass, stainless steel, wood, china, or a combination of silver and wood *or* salt and pepper dishes
1 salad bowl and servers—wood or glass
1 bread dish—silver or wicker
1 gravy or sauce boat—silver or china
3 condiment dishes—glass, china, or pottery
1 water pitcher—any material
8 or 12 fingerbowls—not essential, but nice for formal entertaining
silver tea service or china teapot
1 silver coffeepot, or a presentable coffee maker (stainless steel, glass, etc., whether an electric one or not) that may be brought from the kitchen for serving after-dinner coffee
8 deep dishes for serving ice cream with sauce or a "runny" dessert (glass dishes are best—they look very pretty on a plate with a colorful pattern showing through)
6 or 8 tiny dinner-table ash trays—china, glass, or silver
enamelware pots and casseroles, which come in innumerable sizes, shapes, and patterns—invaluable to a busy bride, as dishes may be cooked and served in the same utensil
1 electric warming tray—the most valuable thing in my kitchen!

4 trays—wood, tin, or plastic—necessary in this age of frequent meals out-of-doors or in front of the living-room fireplace

GLASSES

Glasses are so easily broken and good glass so expensive to replace that a bride who wishes to have a matching set for any length of time should have far more than she actually needs to start out with.

In order to save her good glass for entertaining, she should have for the everyday use of herself and her husband and for casual drop-in visitors:

8 "kitchen glasses" or tumblers
4 juice glasses
4 old-fashioned glasses
4 stem cocktail glasses (may also be used for wine)
4 iced-tea or highball glasses

Beyond this, she should have, depending on the amount and type of entertaining she intends to do:

goblets
wineglasses
liqueur glasses
sherbet glasses
8 highball glasses
8 stem cocktail glasses
8 old-fashioned glasses

Since the chances are that not all the guests at a party will request the same type of drink, this should be adequate for a party of twelve. Also, she may bring out her plainer cocktail and highball glasses if necessary.

SILVER

A large amount of silver is neither so desirable nor as fashionable as it used to be. In fact, many brides request that rather than silver they be given pewter or stainless steel, both of which require little care and are more durable. However, although the bride may ask for a set of stainless steel eating utensils for daily use, nothing can replace a set of beautiful sterling flat silver on the dinner-party table. There are innumerable patterns; the bride whose home is "traditional" may choose one of the older, more ornate patterns, and she who lives in a modern house or apartment will probably prefer a very plain design. Each has its advantages. The modern, undecorated piece is easier to clean, but it also shows wear and tear more quickly and is sometimes dulled by scratches.

Whichever the bride chooses, she should remember that it is probably the silver she will use all her life, and possibly her children after her. It is therefore safer to select a pattern that is neither too severely modern nor so ornate that it easily appears outdated.

As with china, it is wiser to complete one place setting at a time than to have twelve forks and no knives with which to cut the meat. If the bride is getting her china and silver a place setting at a time, she will simply start out with smaller parties. They will grow as her implements permit, and this is not necessarily a disadvantage. A girl who has had little practice in party-giving will do far better to start out with two or four guests and enlarge her group as her experience increases.

The necessary silver for one place setting is:

1 large fork
1 large knife
1 small fork
1 small knife
1 dessert spoon
1 teaspoon
1 butter knife

In addition—and these items need not be in the same pattern as the above list:

oyster forks
3 serving spoons (tablespoons in the chosen pattern may be used)
2 serving forks
12 after-dinner coffee spoons
2 gravy or sauce ladles
4 extra teaspoons (for sugar, condiments, etc.)

Optional—and often received as wedding presents:

salad or fish forks (broad tines)
sugar tongs
butter server
ornamented spoons for jellies or jams
cake knife
pie server

If the flat silver is monogrammed, either a single letter—the initial of the groom's last name—or a triangle of letters is used.

When Jane Ross marries Henry Cranmore, the silver may be engraved with the bride's married initials:

J R
 C

Or, with the last-name initial above and their two first-name initials below:

C
J H

Any initialing should be simple in style. Elongated Roman goes well on modern silver, and Old English is best on the more ornamented styles.

A wedding gift of silver may be marked if the giver is absolutely sure that it is something the bride truly wants and that no duplicate will arrive. However, generally it is safer to leave it unmarked so that it can be exchanged if desired.

44

Planning the wedding

A wedding, be it large and elaborate or small and simple, is an important occasion—beautiful, meaningful, and the bride's day of days. Also, it must be remembered that the groom's wishes should be consulted from first to last. There are so many details involved in even the simplest wedding that careful planning and preparation are necessary if everyone is to enjoy the day itself. For a large wedding, expert help should be arranged for well in advance. Without adequate preparation, father may be irritated, mother jittery, the bride in tears, and the bridegroom cross. This chapter and those that follow are dedicated to helping you avoid such needless unhappiness.

Let it be said at the outset that our discussion of wedding plans will be based on the most elaborate wedding possible. Very few will want or be able to have such an affair, but only by including every detail can we give the complete pattern. Then you can follow as many of these suggestions as you find pleasing and practical for you.

THE RESPONSIBILITIES, FINANCIAL AND OTHERWISE

The first fact to remember is that all the expenses of a wedding belong to the bride's parents. The cost of a wedding varies enormously.

A big, fashionable wedding can total several thousand dollars, whereas a lovely, simple one can be given for under five hundred dollars. A schedule of approximate costs follows, but remember that the prices listed will vary considerably depending on the area you live in, the type of music or food that you choose, and so on. Furthermore, you may substitute one expense for another. If you choose to borrow cars to transport the wedding party, for example, you may apply that expense toward more elaborate beverages or flowers.

TOTAL WEDDING BUDGET

	$500	$1,000	$2,000	$4,000
Type of Wedding	Informal or formal	Formal	Formal	Formal
Number of Attendants	1 or 2	2–4	4–6	6–8
Number at Reception	50	100	100–200	200–300
Place of Reception	Home or in church facilities	Home, club or restaurant	Club or hotel	Club or hotel
Type of Reception	Stand-up reception	Buffet at home or club, sit-down in restaurant	Buffet or sit-down	Buffet or sit-down depending on number
Refreshments	Sandwiches and snacks	Sandwiches and hors d'oeuvres	Sandwiches and hors d'oeuvres	Hot meal
ITEMS TO BUDGET:				
Wedding Clothes	$125	$200	$400	$ 680
Invitations, Announcements, etc.	25	40	80	200
Flowers, Attendants at Church and Reception	50	80	160	400
Music (Church and Reception)	35	40	160	400
Transportation for Bridal Party to Church and Reception	none	40	100	160
Photographs—Formal and Candids	50	100	200	240
Bridesmaids' Gifts	25	40	80	120
Reception (Food, Beverages, Wedding Cake, Catering Service)	185	430	760	1,600
Contingency Fund (Any additional expenses not planned in budget)	5	30	60	200

The inclusion of the chart above should not be taken to mean that a lovely wedding cannot be given for less than five hundred dollars. Actually, it is perfectly possible to have a beautiful and memorable wedding for two hundred and fifty dollars or even less. To illustrate I will describe a wedding and reception which I attended recently. The ceremony took place in the evening in a small chapel, decorated with two vases of white flowers. The couple received on the church steps, and then the wedding party (a maid of honor and best man) and the thirty-five guests went to the bride's home. Whiskey and soft drinks were offered, but no hors d'oeuvres. At eight-thirty a buffet dinner was served, consisting of shrimp newburg, sliced roast beef, salad, bread and rolls. There was a lovely wedding cake on display which later served as dessert. At the time the bride and groom cut the cake, one round of champagne was passed to drink a toast to their happiness.

The house was very simply decorated with vases of greens and white flowers from the family's garden.

The bride could not afford to buy the wedding dress she wanted, but she was fortunate to be able to borrow a lovely one. If this had not been possible she would have worn the prettiest dress she owned, as did her maid of honor.

The bride and groom issued the invitations by telephoning, eliminating that expense.

The total cost of this wedding was two hundred and sixty dollars. The expenses were as follows:

Food	
10 lbs. shrimp	$28.00
9 lbs. roast beef (eye round)	11.00
Cream	2.00
Salad	6.00
Rolls and bread	5.00
Miscellaneous	5.00
Wedding Cake	20.00
Beverages	
Whiskey, 6 bottles	36.00
Mixes, soft drinks	5.00
Champagne (domestic), 8 bottles	32.00
Catering help—cook and bartender	60.00
Flowers—church, table centerpiece, bride's and maid-of-honor's bouquets, corsages, and boutonnieres	50.00
Total	$260.00

Had the hostess been able to do the cooking herself, and had the host wished to serve the drinks, the cost of the help would have been eliminated. Other costs could have been lowered, too. A friend might have provided the wedding cake as a gift, and the champagne was not essential. The floral centerpiece could have been replaced by an ornament or less expensive paper flowers or figures. Corsages for the mothers of the couple were not necessary, although they were much appreciated. At the wedding described above, friends took pictures at the reception and gave them to the bride as wedding presents. Extra china, glasses, and silverware were lent by relatives and neighbors.

No element of a large and elaborate wedding was missing. The details were reduced only in amount or elegance. Even though this wedding was planned and given in less than ten days time, it will be remembered as a lovely occasion by everyone there. The bride will always know that she had as meaningful and beautiful a reception and ceremony as if she had planned and prepared three months in advance, and spent ten times the amount of money that she did.

DIVISION OF EXPENSES

THE BRIDE'S PARENTS PROVIDE:

The invitations to ceremony and reception, and the announcements. While true engraving is most beautiful and is required for a wedding of extreme formality, there are less expensive methods of simulating engraving that are very pleasing and entirely suitable.

The services of a professional secretary. She compiles a single guest list from the various ones provided her; addresses the envelopes, both inner and outer; encloses the proper number of cards; seals, stamps, and mails all the invitations or announcements. She may also handle such details as making arrangements with florists, orchestra, etc. This expense may be omitted if the work is done by members or friends of the family.

The service of a bridal consultant, if desired.

The trousseau of the bride, consisting not only of her clothing but of her household linen as well.

Floral decorations for church and reception, bouquets for the bride and bridesmaids, corsages for the bride's mother and grandmother, and a boutonniere for the father of the bride. In some American communities it is customary for the groom to provide the bouquet carried by the bride. In others it is the custom for the bride to send boutonnieres to the ushers and for the groom to order the bouquets of the bridesmaids. But in most areas the bride's as well as the bridesmaids' bouquets are looked upon as part of the decorative arrangements, all of which are provided by the bride's parents.

Choir, soloists, and organist at church, and the fee to the sexton. Some churches send a bill covering all these services; if not, they must be paid for separately.

Orchestra at reception. This may mean twenty pieces with two leader, or it may mean one violinist or a phonograph.

Automobiles for the bridal party from the house to the church and from there to the reception.

The refreshments, whether the most elaborate sit-down meal or the simplest afternoon tea.

The wedding cake and possibly boxes of cake (usually fruitcake) to be given to the guests.

Champagne and/or other beverages.

The bride's presents to her bridesmaids. They may be quite elaborate or carefully selected trinkets of negligible cost.

Hotel accommodations for bride's attendants if they cannot stay with relatives, friends, or neighbors.

A wedding present to the bride, often her flat silver or "good" china.

Photographs taken of the bride in her wedding dress and candid pictures taken the day of the wedding. If a bridesmaid or usher or guest wishes to have a wedding photograph, she or he may properly order and *pay for* a print from the photographer.

Awnings, tent for outdoor reception, and carpet for church aisle if desired.

The bride herself gives a wedding present or a wedding ring, or both, to the groom, if she wants to.

THE BRIDEGROOM'S EXPENSES:

The engagement ring—as handsome as he can afford.

A wedding present to the bride—jewelry if he is able, always something for her to keep forever.

His bachelor dinner—if he gives one.

The bride's bouquet, where local custom requires it, and in any case, a corsage for her to wear when they go away.

The marriage license.

A personal gift to his best man and to each of his ushers, and their hotel expenses unless they are invited to stay with neighbors or friends.

Even if the entire outfit is rented, he gives his best man and each usher his wedding tie, collar, and gloves.

He provides each of the above with a boutonniere, as well as his own and that of his father.

The wedding ring.

The clergyman's fee. Clergymen do not charge a regular fee, but a donation is expected, and it should be in accordance with the circumstances of the family and the elaborateness of the wedding. *See "Clergyman's Fee," Chapter Forty-seven.*

From the moment the bride and groom start off on their wedding trip, all the expenditure becomes his.

EXCEPTIONS

Whether a wedding is to be large or tiny, there is a tradition that the reception must be either at the house of the bride's parents or grandparents or other relatives or close friends, or else in rooms rented by her family. Etiquette has always decreed that the groom's family may give entertainments of whatever description they choose for the young couple after they have returned from the honeymoon, but the wedding and reception—however simple they may be—must be furnished by the bride's family.

There are circumstances, however, when it would be ridiculous not to break this rule. If, for instance, the bride were without family, or came from another country, she might perfectly well be married in a church or rectory and go to the house of the bridegroom's parents for the reception. After all, there are few rules that permit no exceptions under extenuating circumstances. But in the average case, to have the bridegroom's family hold the wedding would advertise the bride's family's inability to assume obligations which properly belong to them.

WHEN, WHERE, AND HOW BIG?

Before deciding the date of the wedding, the bride must find out definitely on which day her church or synagogue and the clergyman who is to perform the ceremony will be available. If it is to be a large wedding, she must also coordinate the time that the church is free with the time at which the caterer or hotel or club will be available.

Next she must decide on the time of day that will be best for the ceremony. Religion, climate, local custom, and transportation schedules may be important factors, as well as the bride and groom's own plans for their wedding trip. Also, due consideration should be given to the convenience of a majority of the relatives and friends who will want to come.

Having settled upon a day and hour, the bride next determines the number of guests who can be provided for, considering the type of reception intended, the size of the bride's house or club, and the amount that her family can afford to spend.

Remember, too, that if the reception comes at a customary meal hour, a substantial wedding breakfast is usually provided. In this case the number of guests invited to the reception may be restricted by the expense.

The number of guests invited to the ceremony need be limited only if the church or chapel is very small.

THE INVITATIONS

The bride-to-be and her mother go to the stationer's to decide on the invitations. Details such as size and texture of paper and style of engraving are considered. The order is given two months or more in advance for the estimated number of invitations or announcements. Once the plates are engraved, it is not difficult to increase the order if necessary. *For all details of the forms, see Chapters Forty-nine, Fifty, and Fifty-one.*

Invitations are sent out three weeks before a formal wedding and as little as two weeks or ten days before a small, informal wedding.

THE WEDDING LIST

Four lists are combined in sending out wedding invitations; the bride and the bridegroom each make one of their own friends, to which are added the list of the bride's family and the list of the groom's family.

The bride's mother consults with the groom or, if possible, with his mother, about how the list is to be divided between them. If the families are old friends and live in the same community, the invitations should be divided more or less equally between them. If it is decided that one hundred may be invited to the reception, this would suggest that some seventy names would probably be the same, and therefore each family would be able to add fifteen of their own to the seventy already on their shared list. But if they have never known each other well and their friends are unknown to each other, each list would have to be limited to fifty.

On the other hand, if the groom's people live in another place and not more than twenty will be able to come, the bride's mother will be able to invite as many people as will result in eighty acceptances. Both mothers may risk being a little overliberal because there are always a few who, having accepted, are then prevented for one reason or another from coming.

It is most important for future harmony that the family of the out-of-town groom estimate *realistically* the number of guests who will make the trip to the wedding. When the bride's mother tells them the total number that can be invited and how many acceptances she expects on her side, they should make every effort to stay within the total. It is up to the out-of-town family to respect the requests of the bride's family in this matter, as they may not be aware of the limitations of space or expense that are factors in the number of invitations to be sent.

Invitations to the reception should not be sent to distant acquaintances who could never be expected to attend, as they only appear to be invitations for a gift. These far-away friends should receive announcements or invitations to the church alone, neither of which carries any obligations.

The minister who performs the ceremony (and his wife) should be sent an invitation to the reception. If they are not acquainted with one family or the other, they may not wish to attend, but it would be discourteous not to include them on the list.

The bridal attendants and the groom's parents should receive invitations, simply because they generally enjoy them as mementos of the occasion. It is not necessary to send them to the attendants' families unless they are acquainted with the couple or their parents.

When a bride knows that one of her guests is engaged, she should, whether she knows the fiancé(e) or not, send him (or her) a separate invitation.

CHURCH INVITATIONS UNLIMITED

Invitations to a big church wedding may be sent to the entire list of personal acquaintances, and often to business associates of both families —no matter how large the combined number may be or whether they will attend or not. People in mourning are included, as well as those who live miles away, for the invitations to the ceremony only are messengers carrying the news of the marriage—with no attendant obligation.

At a typical wedding, friends are asked to the reception as well as to the church, and acquaintances to the church only. If the wedding is to be in the house or is otherwise small, so that only families and intimate friends are invited, announcements may be sent to all uninvited acquaintances. Little children who cannot be included at the reception because of limited space or cost are often thrilled by an invitation to the church ceremony.

LODGING FOR OUT-OF-TOWN GUESTS

If the groom lives far enough away from the bride so that his family and attendants cannot return home after pre-wedding parties and the wedding itself, the bride (or her mother) makes arrangements for their lodging. The groom's mother must, as soon as possible, tell the bride's family exactly how many of their relatives will definitely attend the wedding. Friends and neighbors of the bride, if they possibly can, offer accommodations for bridesmaids and ushers and occasionally (especially if they happen to be acquainted with them) for the immediate family of the groom. But aunts, uncles, cousins, and friends stay at nearby hotels, inns, or motels to avoid imposing on strangers in the usual servantless house of today. If the bride's family or some of their close friends are members of a club that has guest accommodations, it is an ideal solution for grandparents or older relatives, who can be provided with all services and meals when they are not attending wedding festivities.

Some weeks before the wedding, the bride's mother reserves the necessary number of rooms in the best hotels or motels nearby, or if there is a choice, she may send pamphlets or brochures (adding her own recommendation) to the groom's family. They select the one that appeals to them and make their own reservations or ask her to do so. In either case, unless the bride's family is very wealthy and that of the groom can barely pay for its transportation to the marriage, the cost of the accommodations is paid for by those using them.

CHOOSING THE ATTENDANTS

The bride's closest sister is always asked to be maid (or matron) of honor. If she has no sister of suitable age, she chooses a cousin or her most intimate friend.

In addition to a maid or matron of honor, a bride may have as many as eight or ten bridesmaids, flower girls, pages, and a ring bearer.

At the average wedding, however, there are from two to six bridesmaids. When a bride's best friends have married before her, the "maids" may be "matrons," but they are always called "bridesmaids" and not "bridesmatrons."

Although a bride need have no attendants, it is best that she have at least one. The picture of her father or the best man holding her bouquet and stooping to adjust her train would be difficult to witness with gravity.

As ushers and bridesmaids are chosen from the most intimate friends of the bride and groom, it is scarcely necessary to suggest how to word the asking. Usually they are told at the time the engagement is announced that they are invited to serve, or they are told whenever one happens to meet them. Those who live at a distance are invited by telephone, telegram, or letter. Only the most valid reasons could possibly excuse a man or woman so honored from accepting the invitation.

CHILDREN AS ATTENDANTS

Junior bridesmaids are young girls, usually between seven and twelve, who are too big to be flower girls and too young to be regular bridesmaids. They attend the rehearsal, of course, and usually the rehearsal dinner (for a little while, at least), but are not necessarily included in other festivities.

Flower girls used to scatter petals before the bride, but now they merely walk directly in front of her in the procession, often carrying old-fashioned baskets of flowers or bouquets. They are present at the rehearsal and at the reception, where they do not stand in line.

Junior ushers follow the older ushers in the procession and are dressed in the same clothes. They have no special duties.

A boy who is too big to be a ring bearer and too young to be a junior usher can be made responsible for running the ribbons along the ends of the pews. When there are two boys, one takes the right side of the aisle, the other one the left, and they stand beside the pews during the ceremony. *For information about the "ribbon" see "Reserved Pews," Chapter Forty-seven.*

If the bride would like to have her little brother or nephew be the *ring bearer,* he is dressed in white, carries the ring on a small, firm white cushion, and walks ahead of her. The ring is either lightly sewed to the cushion or fastened by having an ordinary pearl-headed flower pin thrust into the center of the cushion and the ring encircling this. The best man should be shown beforehand whether he is to pull or lift it off.

Train bearers, as the name implies, hold the bride's train. They, too, must be very little boys and dressed in white. Unless they have rehearsed their part thoroughly, the train trailing smoothly by itself is really safer than a train in the hands of small children whose behavior is apt to be uncertain, to say the least.

THE COST OF ATTENDING THE BRIDE

With the exception of the flowers they carry, which are presented by the bride, every article worn by the bridesmaids, flower girls, and pages is paid for by the wearers (or their parents).

It is unfortunate but true that an occasional young girl has to refuse the joy of being in the wedding party because a complete bridesmaid's outfit costs a sum that neither she nor her parents can provide. But it is seldom that the bride herself is in a position to pay for six or eight sets of dresses and accessories even if she wishes to make an exception to the rule. Therefore, unless her bridesmaids have unusually deep purses, the bride who has a conscience tries to choose clothes that will not be too expensive. Department stores as well as speciality shops offer enchanting ready-to-wear models that can be ordered in different colors or materials to fit almost any budget. Ideally, the bride should choose a model which will be useful to the bridesmaids after the wedding.

The other expenses are shared this way: All attendants of the bride and bridegroom pay for their own transportation from wherever they are to wherever the wedding is to take place. There, the girls are always guests of the bride and the men the guests of the bridegroom, whether the lodgings are in the houses of family friends or in motel or hotel rooms paid for by the bridal couple.

THE BEST MAN AND THE USHERS

No matter how small the wedding, the bridegroom always has a best man. It is not an unbreakable rule, but generally the closest brother of the groom is best man unless, of course, he is a great deal older or younger. When the groom has no brother, his next selection is his most intimate friend; or if deciding upon this is difficult, he perhaps chooses a cousin, or the brother of the bride. Frequently a son who is very devoted to his father will ask him to serve as best man.

The number of ushers is in proportion to the size of the church and the number of guests invited. At a house wedding, ushers are often merely honorary, and the groom may have many or none, as he chooses.

It is unheard of for a man to refuse the honor unless a bridegroom, for questionable reasons, asks someone who is not really a friend at all. Of course, the groom is careful not to ask someone who he knows will have problems of time and distance that will be difficult to overcome.

DUTIES OF THE BEST MAN

On the day of the wedding the busiest person is the best man. Quite literally, he finds himself thrust into a position that is a combination of secretary, valet, general manager of the entire wedding procedure, as well as the bridegroom's best friend. Naturally, his understanding and patience must be unfailing.

Bright and early in the morning (especially if it's to be a daytime wedding) he goes to the bridegroom's house. If the groom is calm and collected, so much the better. If he is overly nervous, the best man must calm him down as best he can.

BEST MAN AS BAGGAGE MASTER

The duties of the best man vary with the circumstances—the plans for the wedding and the honeymoon, the type of clothing the groom will be wearing, the amount of time he has free to place at the groom's disposal before the ceremony, and so on. The important thing is that he relieve the groom of as many details and as much responsibility as possible. Any or all of the following suggestions will smooth the groom's way and add to the couple's enjoyment of their wedding day. The best man should take care of as many of these situations as pertain to the particular wedding.

He may help the groom pack for his honeymoon, and see that in his nervousness he has not packed ski clothes for Bermuda or a tennis racquet for a winter vacation in Canada.

He sees that the clothes the groom will change into after the wedding are packed in a separate bag and taken to where the reception will be held.

He may deliver the luggage of both the newlyweds to the airport, dock, or station from which they will leave, seeing that it is properly checked. If he does this he must be sure to deliver the baggage claim checks to the groom!

If the couple are staying at a hotel or motel nearby, he may check their reservations and see that their accommodations are adequate. He may even register for them, delivering the key to the groom, so that they can go directly to their room.

If he is especially thoughtful, he may arrange to have flowers or a bottle of chilled champagne delivered just before their arrival.

When the couple are leaving the reception by car, the best man sees that the car is kept hidden until they are ready to go—to foil any practical jokes. He sees that their luggage is in the car, and he himself drives them to the hiding place or else arranges to have the car delivered at the moment of their departure.

BEST MAN AS VALET

His next duty is that of valet. He must see that the groom is dressed in plenty of time, and he must be prepared for any emergency: even to standing ready with a remedy should the groom cut himself shaving. He may need to find the cuff links or even to point out the "missing" clothes that he has laid out in full view. The marriage license must be safely stowed in the groom's wallet or pocket. He must also be sure to ask for the wedding ring and the clergyman's fee and put them in his own pocket.

When the couple leave to change out of their wedding clothes toward the end of the reception, he again becomes valet to the groom. He helps him dress, takes care of the discarded clothing, and finally sees that he has with him everything necessary for the wedding trip. Money or traveler's checks, car keys, baggage-check stubs, plane, train, or boat tickets, and (if the best man has registered in advance) hotel or motel keys are all too easy for the bridegroom to overlook in his excitement.

AT THE END OF THE CEREMONY

If the best man is not to walk out with the maid of honor, he leaves through a side door while the procession goes down the aisle. He quickly goes around to the front of the church to give the groom his hat and coat. The bridegroom or one of the bridal party helps the bride into her coat, which she left at the entrance to the church when she came in.

Sometimes the sexton takes charge of the groom's hat and coat and hands them to him at the church door as he goes out. But in either case the best man always hurries to see the bride and groom into their car, which has been standing at the entrance to the awning since she and her father alighted from it. If a chauffeur is not present to deliver the newlyweds to the reception, the best man generally performs this duty too.

The best man is responsible for giving the clergyman his fee on behalf of the groom. He may do it before the ceremony while they are waiting to enter the church, or if he is not driving the bride and groom to the reception, he may return to the vestry immediately after the recessional to deliver the envelope.

The amount may be from ten to twenty dollars for a very simple ceremony, fifty dollars for an average wedding with perhaps four attendants, one or two hundred (or more) for a very large wedding.

If the fee is given in the form of a check, it is made out to the minister himself rather than to the church.

If the father of the bride has reason to suspect that the circumstances of the groom or his family do not permit them to make a contribution commensurate with the elaborateness of the occasion, he may, if he wishes, make an additional contribution on his own later.

AT THE RECEPTION

After seeing that there is nothing he can do for the bridegroom while he is in the receiving line, the best man may mingle with the guests until the bridal party sit down at the bridal table. He sits on the bride's right, and it is his responsibility to make the first toast to the bride and groom. He is also the first man to dance with the bride after the groom, her father-in-law, and her father have had their turns.

When the couple is ready to leave, the best man escorts the groom's family to the dressing room for their farewells. He then leads the couple through the waiting guests to the door, and when they have pulled away in a shower of rose petals, he may at last breathe a sigh of relief and join the rest of the wedding party in a final celebration.

HEAD USHER

Unless there are special reasons to the contrary, the groom should choose the man who has had the most experience to be head usher. His first duty is to see that all the ushers arrive at the rehearsal on time. There he assigns, according to their height, the order in which the ushers are to walk in the processional and where each is to stand during the ceremony.

It is also the head usher's duty to see that the other ushers arrive at the church at the appointed hour and to decide which are assigned to the center and which to the side aisles. If the bridegroom has not already told them, he may suggest which of them will escort various members of the families to their seats. He himself accompanies the mother of the bride, unless one of her close relatives—a son or a nephew—is among the other ushers.

He also tells them which ladies of the family they are to escort to the back of the church after the recessional.

ANOTHER WORD ABOUT ATTENDANTS

RELATIVES OF THE BRIDE AND BRIDEGROOM AS ATTENDANTS

Unless attendants are limited to one or two, a brother of the bride, or if she has no brother, then her favorite cousin is usually asked by the groom to be an usher. The bride returns the compliment by asking the sister of the groom who is nearest her own age to be bridesmaid, or if he has no sister, she asks a cousin. If she is to have a number of bridesmaids and the groom has no sister, she may show her courtesy by asking the groom to name a close family friend. If the groom is choosing from six to ten ushers, he often includes one who is a special friend of the bride and asks him exactly as he asks the others.

When the homes of the bride and bridegroom are at such a great distance apart that none of the groom's immediate family can make the journey to the wedding, it is not unusual for him to choose (if he has no brother) his father or even stepfather as his best man. In such situations the ushers are chosen from among the friends of the bride.

MARRIED ATTENDANTS

It is entirely correct for a married man to act as usher, or for a married woman to be matron of honor or a bridesmaid. Neither the wife of the first nor the husband of the second need be asked to take part. The one not officiating is of course invited to the wedding and sits at the bridal table. It is unusual for a husband and wife to be attendants at the same wedding, but if they are both close friends of the bride and groom there is no rule against it.

PLANNING THE CHURCH SERVICE

Sometime before the day of the wedding, the bride and groom go together to visit the clergyman who will perform the ceremony. They discuss the service they would like to have, whether they wish the choir or a vocalist to sing, the selection of music (often consulting with the organist also), and any customs or rules peculiar to that church. In turn the clergyman may have, because of his experience with other marriages, suggestions as to decorations and other details. For example, if there are to be many elderly people in the audience or simply because it will be easier for the congregation to see the ceremony sitting down, the couple may ask the clergyman to announce that the guests may be seated, if he approves.

If the groom belongs to a different church, and if he or his family are close to the pastor there, the couple may discuss with the bride's clergyman the possibility of having the other assist at the ceremony. This is also frequently done when a member of either family is a clergyman.

If it is agreeable to the minister of the bride's church, the couple should visit both clergymen before the wedding takes place.

PLANNING THE "WEDDING BREAKFAST"

The "wedding breakfast" is a term applied to the meal served at the reception, whether it be morning, noon, or night. It may be an elaborate sit-down meal, it may be a buffet to which the guests help themselves, or it may simply be sandwiches and hors d'oeuvres passed on trays.

If the reception is held at a club or hotel, the staff will prepare the food and drinks. They may also provide some decorations, which are usually on hand for such occasions. The bride and her mother should discuss the menu and all other arrangements with the manager or person in charge of social activities as soon as the wedding date is set.

THE SIT-DOWN BREAKFAST

The sit-down breakfast is the most elaborate wedding reception possible. When not held at a club or hotel it is managed by a caterer, who brings to the home all the food, tables, chairs, napery, china, and glass as well as the necessary waiters. If there are servants in the house, they may assist or oversee or be detailed to other duties.

In the country a tent is erected on the lawn. Under the tent there is a platform surrounded by small tables, and at one end a large one is reserved for the bridal party. A second table is reserved for the immediate families of the bride and groom, the clergyman, and a few special friends.

Place cards at the bride's table and at the parents' table are usually of white bristol board embossed in silver to match the monograms on the wedding-cake boxes or the souvenir match boxes. Or plain white cards may have two small slits made in them through which the stems of small white flowers are inserted.

Place cards are not necessary on the small tables. All the guests, except the few placed at the two reserved tables, sit with whom they like. Sometimes they do so by prearrangement, but usually they sit where they happen to find friends—and room!

At very elaborate weddings small menu cards printed in silver may be put on all the tables. Sometimes these cards have the crest of the bride's father embossed at the top, but usually the initials of the surnames of the bride and bridegroom are stamped in silver to match the wedding-cake boxes.

There may be bouillon or vichyssoise, lobster Newburg or some other seafood. The main dish might be beef stroganoff with wild rice, sweetbreads and mushrooms, or creamed chicken.

Any variety of aspic or salad may be served.

Individual ices are accompanied by little cakes of assorted variety.

Lobster Newburg
Suprême of Chicken
Peas
Aspic of Foie Gras
Celery Salad
Ices
Coffee

At a wedding breakfast of this extreme elaborateness, the accepted beverage has always been champagne. For those who do not serve alcohol a punch of orange juice and ginger ale or white grape juice and ginger ale—with mint leaves, perhaps—can be satisfying substitutes.

THE STAND-UP BREAKFAST OR SUPPER

For the stand-up, or buffet, breakfast, a long table is set in the dining room of home or club. It is covered with a plain white damask cloth. The centerpiece is generally a bowl of white flowers. Piles of plates (preferably white, or white and gold), stacks of napkins, and rows of spoons and forks are symmetrically arranged on the table. This table should be situated so that the guests pass on directly to another table to help themselves to food, or if there is room, the plates of food may be arranged on the same table.

If there is a bridal table, it is set elsewhere. If not, the wedding cake is the feature of the buffet, placed at the center of the table with the centerpiece of white flowers behind it or two floral pieces flanking it. Cold dishes such as chicken or celery salad or ham mousse with chopped hearts of lettuce and hot dishes such as creamed crab meat, chicken à la king, or chicken croquettes are evenly spaced about the table. Whatever the choice is, there are two or three cold dishes and at least one hot dish. It is important to select food that can be easily eaten with a fork while the plate is held in the other hand. There should also be finger rolls and sandwiches, substantial yet small enough to eat easily.

There are dishes filled with fancy cakes or "petits fours" chosen for looks as much as taste. There may also be compotes of peppermints, caramels, and chocolates. Ice cream is the typical dessert, served with a slice of wedding cake.

After-dinner coffee is put on a side table, as is champagne or its substitute, punch. The cold beverages may also be passed on trays.

THE SIMPLEST RECEPTION REQUIREMENTS

A morning wedding followed by a high-noon breakfast would mean substantial food; and in the evening one rather expects an elaborate wedding—evening clothes, dinner, etc. An afternoon reception can, however, be very simple. All that is required is champagne or fruit punch, in order to drink the newlyweds' health, and the wedding cake. A slightly more elaborate reception would include either tea or coffee and thin sandwiches.

The table decorations and the wedding cake should of course be white. Although a number of small tables may be set up in the downstairs rooms of the house, the meal is usually set out on the dining table and the guests eat standing. The bridal table, if there is one at all, is necessarily placed in another room, or in summer, possibly, on the porch or in the garden. If the bride has only one attendant she chooses a few of her best friends to sit at her table.

In some areas there are two buffet tables, one called the bride's table and the other called the groom's table. The white wedding cake is served from the bride's table, and either chocolate cake or dark fruitcake from the groom's.

IF THERE IS TO BE NO RECEPTION

When the marriage takes place in a church and there is to be no reception afterward, the bride and the groom often follow the friendly and charming custom of receiving in the vestibule of the church with their parents and the bridal party. The guests stop for a moment and offer their good wishes as they leave the church.

THE WEDDING CAKE

Wedding cake is an essential of every wedding reception. Black fruitcake is traditional—but since it is very expensive, a white cake or a pound cake is the usual choice.

The wedding cake is almost always ordered from a caterer, who delivers it shortly before the hour of the reception. It is usually in several tiers, beautifully decorated with white icing, and topped by small figures of bride and groom, flowers made of frosting, or real flowers. It is large enough to serve the wedding party, the families, and often the close friends. If the reception is not too large, every guest may receive a piece.

THE GROOM'S CAKE

A nice custom that has become less prevalent because of the expense, but still seen at some weddings, is that of having a separate fruitcake called a "groom's cake" cut and put into individual white boxes tied with white satin ribbon and ornamented with the combined initials of the bride and groom. These boxes are stacked on a table close behind the front door, and each departing guest is expected to take one. When a member of a family has been prevented from coming unexpectedly, a second box may be taken home to him or her. Otherwise, it is very bad manners to take more than one's own box.

Although the cost of ordering such a cake may be prohibitive, the charm remains, and it might be an unusual and thoughtful wedding gift (after consulting with the bride) from a family friend who is skilled in the art of baking—or very rich. When made as a gift, the individual pieces of cake need not be put into expensive boxes, but may be wrapped in white paper and tied with white or silver ribbon, possibly with a little flower or greenery through the knot.

Another type of "groom's cake" is described above in "The Simplest Reception Requirements."

THE FLOWERS

When it is time to select the flowers, the bride and her mother consult their florist and ask him for an estimate for the decoration of the church and house and for the bridesmaids' bouquets. Whether they or the bridegroom order the bride's own bouquet depends upon the custom of the community, but in most places it is usual for the bride's parents to order her bouquet as well as the bridesmaids' when they order the flowers for the church and house.

The bridegroom sends the bride a corsage to wear when she leaves the reception with him. He always buys the boutonnieres for his ushers and himself—but not for the bride's father, who, unless he is a widower, receives his boutonniere from his own "bride," the bride's mother. In certain communities it is customary for him to send flowers for the mothers and grandmothers to wear at the wedding. When the bride's bouquet is the responsibility of the bridegroom, the corsage may be inserted in the center of the larger bouquet and removed when the bride dresses for going away or before she throws the bouquet to the bridesmaids.

At a very elaborate wedding the church is decorated with masses of flowers arranged as standards or sprays tied to the pew ends, as well as with the floral arrangements in the chancel. Later at the reception, not only is there floral background against which the bridal couple receives, but every room contains greens and flowers. The orchestra may be hidden behind philodendron or other greenery in the hall.

At a more typical wedding the floral arrangements are much simpler. The chancel of the church is decorated, but less lavishly—perhaps two bowls on the altar and a spray at the end of the choir stalls, or an arrangement on either side of the chancel steps. Sometimes there are flowers at the ends of the reserved pews or possibly only at the ends of the two pews that mark the beginning of the ribboned section.

There is very little floral decoration at the reception. There are usually flowers on the bridal table and the buffet table, but the decorations at all receptions in all seasons consist for the most part—and often wholly—of greens. It is in fact true that a profusion of flowers can detract from the dresses and bouquets of the bride and the bridesmaids.

Flowers for the church, incidentally, need not be white, but may blend with the color scheme of the bridesmaids' dresses and bouquets.

MAKING A BIG CHURCH SEEM SMALLER

If a small wedding is to be in a large church instead of a chapel and only a comparatively few pews are to be occupied, the effect of emptiness may be overcome entirely by making a hedge of branches or potted shrubbery behind the pews that form the boundary. Altar, chancel, and necessary pews should be lighted brilliantly and the pews behind the screen of greens left dark, thus making the church seem as small as need be.

An opening would be left in the aisle to admit the guests, but the bridal party would enter from the vestry or waiting room instead of going up the long aisle. Or at less expense, if there are choir stalls, they may be used as pews and the church so lighted as to include only the chancel. This arrangement gives to the smallest possible wedding all the solemn beauty of church surroundings, including the music of the organ.

OTHER DECORATIONS AND ACCESSORIES

Decorations and accessories, as well as flowers, must be ordered in advance. If a canopy is to be used at the church entrance, the sexton must know so that he can arrange for it to be put up the morning of the wedding day. A carpet is usually laid down the aisle of the church after the bride's mother is seated to protect the bride's train, and this must be ordered, either from the church or the florist. Tents or marquees are provided by the caterer for a home garden, or by a club where the reception is to be held. They must be put up a day or two in advance.

Many brides, especially when boxes of wedding cake are not to be distributed, provide mementos of the wedding in the form of white match boxes with the bride's and groom's names and the date printed on

them in silver. These are placed about in bowls as well as in or beside ash trays in sufficient quantities so that the guests feel free to take them home. Another attractive custom is that of having cocktail napkins imprinted with the couple's names. They are passed with sandwiches or hors d'oeuvres and also with glasses of cold drinks, which tend to drip on a warm day. These printed accessories should be ordered six weeks or two months ahead of the wedding date if the bride wishes to be sure of their delivery.

MUSIC FOR CHURCH AND RECEPTION

The choice of music to be played in the church and whether or not a choir or soloist sing are in the province of the choirmaster or the organist. At a majority of weddings, the march from Wagner's *Lohengrin* is chosen for the wedding procession and the recessional is Mendelssohn. However, members of some faiths, and individual clergymen or organists in others, feel that these pieces are frivolous and prefer that the young people choose more sacred music. If the bride and groom have their hearts set on music that is too worldly to be played in their church, they can, of course, have many of these selections played at the reception.

Sometimes a singer, or possibly an organist, who is a friend or member of the bride's or bridegroom's family is included in the musical arrangements. But it would be very discourteous to invite an outsider without consulting and receiving the consent of the church organist.

The size and formality of the wedding determine the type of music to be provided at the reception. If the reception is held in a large tent or ballroom, the bride's family usually hires a full orchestra, and the guests dance as well as watch the bride enjoy the most wonderful party of her life. For romantic effect, the orchestra leader generally features his string section rather than a large percussion or brass section. The bride and groom may give him a list of the pieces they would like to have played.

It is by no means necessary to go to this extent. For smaller, less formal weddings a trio or piano and violin, or even a phonograph, can easily provide music for a small dance floor—possibly one room of the house—cleared for the occasion.

If there is to be no dancing, a wandering violinist or accordionist, playing the music chosen by the couple, makes a happy background for toasts and conversation.

THE WEDDING PICTURES

THE FORMAL PHOTOGRAPH

At some time before the wedding, often at the final fitting of the bridal gown, the photographer takes the formal wedding pictures of the bride. If pictures are to be sent to the newspapers, they must be taken well in advance to allow time for choosing the ones to be used, the final printing, and mailing to the papers two to three weeks before the wedding day.

A small print of this formal picture in a silver frame, with or without date and the initials of the couple engraved on it, makes a charming present from bride to bridesmaid.

CANDID PHOTOGRAPHS

If the candid shots on the wedding day are to be taken by a professional, he must be engaged far ahead of time, especially if the wedding is to be in June. However, amateur photographers are often almost as well equipped and as skillful as the professional, and if you are fortunate enough to number one of these among your friends, he will surely be delighted to record the event. If he covers the entire day and uses quantities of film, the bride's family must certainly pay for the supplies and the printing, which, especially if color film is used, can be exorbitant. But if he uses a roll or two at the reception of his own volition and not at the specific request of the bride, this is not necessary, and often camera enthusiasts present these pictures as a wedding present to the bride.

A candid album may start with the bride's leaving the house before the wedding and continue through the day—her arrival at the church with her father (or whoever is giving her away), leaving the church after the ceremony, the bridal party and receiving line at the reception, shots of the bride dancing, the guests, the toasts, the cutting of the cake, throwing the bouquet, and finally, the departure of the happy pair on their honeymoon.

Pictures of the actual ceremony taken with flash bulbs are in poor taste because they detract from the solemnity of the service. One time exposure, if made with the clergyman's permission, would not be out of order. Once the service is over and the bridal procession is coming down the aisle, the camera may start to work, and pictures of the radiant bride and groom who suddenly realize that they are "Mr. and Mrs." are often among the best souvenirs of all.

Members of the bridal party who wish to have duplicates of the wedding pictures for their own scrapbooks may have them made at their own expense.

THE BRIDE'S TIMETABLE

In order to coordinate all the plans discussed in this chapter, the bride should have a definite schedule or timetable to follow. The list below is based on the time necessary to plan and prepare a large wedding. But even those of you who are getting married simply and on short notice will find one list helpful in organizing those procedures which will be a part of your wedding.

THREE MONTHS AHEAD OF THE WEDDING

1. *Decide what type of wedding you will have,* whether it will be formal, semiformal, or informal, and if it will be held at a church, club, hotel, or home. Be sure to consult your bridegroom and your family, whose expenses will be affected by the type of wedding you choose.

2. *Decide the hour of the ceremony and the type of reception to follow.* Remember, the degree of formality in your wedding ceremony should be matched in your reception.

3. *Decide the date of the wedding.* Find out when your clergyman is free to perform the ceremony, and when the church or chapel is available. Visit your clergyman with your fiancé to discuss personal matters as well as wedding details. At this time you should inquire about any restrictions as to the time of year, day of week, musical selections, floral decorations, or style of wedding clothes. You might also check with him on the rental fee for the church, organist's fee, whether the church chimes may be used, if a candlelight service is permissible, if the social hall is available that day for a reception, if arrangements for a policeman or parking attendant may be made through the church secretary.

Before confirming the church date, be sure that the club, caterer, or hotel selected for your reception can accommodate you and your party at the proper time.

4. *Decide how many guests and attendants you will have.* The bride should have at least one attendant—her maid or matron of honor. The groom always has a best man.

5. *Select your attendants.* The bride and groom usually ask their attendants to serve in their wedding at the time the engagement is announced or shortly thereafter.

6. *Compile your wedding lists for the church, reception, and announcements.* For a private ceremony, house wedding, or reception, where the guest list is limited, the bride's family may tell the groom's family how many guests they may invite.

While drawing up your invitation lists for the ceremony and reception, you may compile a special list of people to receive announcements only. Remember, guests at house weddings are always invited to the reception as well as the ceremony, although for church weddings the number of guests may vary for the ceremony and reception. Announcements are sent only to friends who are *not invited* to the wedding or reception.

7. *Order your wedding invitations and announcements,* and, if you wish, personal stationery for wedding-gift thank-you notes.

8. *Order your bridal gown, select gowns for the bridesmaids,* and urge the mothers to get together to choose their clothes.

9. *Set a date with your photographer for your bridal portrait* and/or candid pictures of your wedding.

10. *Begin to plan the decor of your new home or apartment,* and to shop for your household trousseau as well as your personal trousseau.

TWO MONTHS AHEAD OF THE WEDDING

1. Make your medical, dental, and beauty-shop appointments at appropriate times.
2. Select gifts for the groom and your bridesmaids.
3. Set the date for your bridesmaids' luncheon if one is planned.
4. Register your wedding gift preferences in your local stores.
5. Arrange for floral decorations for the church or ceremony, for the bride's and bridesmaids' bouquets, and for reception decorations after getting an estimate from your florist.
6. Arrange for your wedding music through your clergyman, sexton, or organist.
7. Make transportation arrangements for limousines or privately driven cars to take the wedding party and both sets of parents to the church. For a large church wedding, a policeman or parking attendant should be hired to help direct traffic and parking.

THE LAST MONTH BEFORE THE WEDDING

1. Mail invitations so that they are received at least three weeks before the wedding.
2. Record all wedding gifts and mail your thank-you notes as soon as each gift is received.
3. Make hotel reservations or housing arrangements for your attendants.
4. List what items you still need for your new household; make moving arrangements if necessary.
5. Prepare a list of things you will need for your honeymoon and begin to pack them in your luggage.
6. Set up your gift display shelves or table if you plan to display your wedding gifts.
7. Set aside everything you will use and wear on your wedding day and keep it together, in one place; check bridesmaids' apparel and accessories to be sure costumes are complete.
8. Make final arrangements with your caterer, florist, photographer, church secretary, or sexton on any last minute changes.
9. Send out wedding announcements and glossy prints of your picture to society editors.
10. Write out place cards for bride's table, if there is to be one.
11. Change your name on all important papers: driver's license, personal bank account, social security records, insurance policies, etc.

Relax and get ready to enjoy the most glorious wedding day ever!

WEDDING PRESENTS AND OTHER GIFTS

If the presents, which begin to arrive as soon as the invitations are out, are likely to be many, each one should be entered at once in a gift book or "bride's book." There are many kinds published for the purpose, but any book with ruled pages about eight to ten inches square will answer the purpose. The usual model spreads across the double page as follows:

PRESENT RECEIVED	ARTICLE	SENT BY	SENDER'S ADDRESS	WHERE BOUGHT	THANKS WRITTEN
May 20	Silver Dish	Mr. and Mrs. White	1 Park Place	Criterion's	May 20
May 21	12 Plates	Mr. and Mrs. Hardy	2 South Street	Crystal's	May 21

All gifts as they arrive should be numbered with a paste-on sticker, and the corresponding number should be listed in the gift book. Since there might be many silver dishes and also dozens of plates, this sticker provides the only means of identification.

THE BRIDE'S THANKS

In return for the joy of receiving the presents, there is a correspondence task that the bride may not evade. On a sheet of note paper—not a folded visiting card—and in her own handwriting, she must send a separate letter for each present she receives. If humanly possible, she writes each letter of thanks on the day the present arrives. If she does not, they may soon get ahead of her and the first weeks of her marriage are taken up with note-writing. A note of thanks is also sent to those who send congratulatory telegrams on the day of the wedding. *For the wording of the bride's notes, see Chapter Nine.*

It is not possible to overemphasize the inexcusable rudeness of the bride who sends a printed or even an engraved card of thanks for wedding presents. This is a flagrant affront to the traditions of common decency.

In unusual cases, such as the hurried marriage of a bridegroom who is unexpectedly being sent overseas, or the marriage of a person of such prominence that the gifts arrive in overwhelming numbers, a printed acknowledgment, *always* followed later by a note of thanks, is permissible. Even then it seems pretentious because it implies that so many presents were expected that special preparations were made in advance to take care of the avalanche.

There is no reason why a bride should not have every thank-you note written within two months. Even those who receive hundreds of presents can accomplish the chore by determining to write a set number —ten, for instance—each day. The donor who does not receive a note within two months is sure to think either that the gift was lost or that the bride is most unappreciative.

If circumstances demand it, however, the engraved note reads:

Miss Joanne Carter
(or Mrs. John Franklin,
if the notes are sent after the wedding)
gratefully acknowledges the receipt of
your wedding gift
and will write you a personal note at
the earliest possible date

WHEN THE PRESENTS ARE SHOWN

It is perfectly correct to show the presents at the wedding reception. The only reason for not showing them is lack of space. If there is an extra sitting room, such as a library, they are shown there. Otherwise a bedroom from which all the furniture has been removed is suitable. Tables covered with plain white damask tablecloths or sheets are placed around the sides of the room. They may be decorated with white ribbon or artificial flowers, and the sides may be draped with tulle net or pleated cheesecloth.

If the reception is not held at home, relatives and friends are often invited to the house shortly before the wedding day to see the display of presents.

ARRANGING THE PRESENTS

To do justice to the kindness of the people who have sent gifts, a bride should show her appreciation by placing each one in the position of greatest advantage. Naturally, all people's tastes are not equally pleasing to the taste of the bride—nor are all pocketbooks equally filled. Very valuable presents are better put in close contrast with others of like quality—or others entirely different in character. Colors should be carefully grouped. Two presents, both lovely in themselves, can completely destroy each other if the colors are allowed to clash.

Sometimes china is put on one table, silver on another, glass on another, but I think a more attractive arrangement can be made by combining textures and shapes. Pieces that "jar" when appearing together must be placed as far apart as possible and perhaps even moved to other surroundings. A badly designed piece of silverware should not be left among beautiful examples, but be put among china ornaments or other articles that do not reveal its lack of fineness by too direct comparison. To group duplicates is another unfortunate arrangement. Eight salad bowls or six sauce boats in a row might as well be labeled: "Look at this! What can she do with all of us?" They are sure to make the givers feel a little chagrined at least.

WHETHER CARDS ARE LEFT ON

There is no definite rule as to whether or not the cards that are sent with the gifts are removed. Some people prefer to leave them on, which certainly saves members of the family from repeating many times who sent this and who sent that, especially if the bride has received an unusual number of presents because her father is a well-known person. On the other hand, others feel that it is a private matter between the bride and the giver and do not wish the world to know how elaborate a gift they were able to send.

DISPLAYING CHECKS

Ordinarily it would be in very bad taste to display gifts of money. But because it would not be fair to a generous relative or intimate friend of the family to have it supposed that he or she sent no gift at all, it is quite proper to display checks with amounts concealed. This is done by laying them out on a flat surface one above the other so that the signatures alone are disclosed. The amount of the one at the top is covered with a strip of opaque paper and then a sheet of glass laid over them all.

EXCHANGING WEDDING PRESENTS

Some people think it discourteous if a bride changes the present chosen for her, but they are wrong. A bride may exchange all duplicate presents, and no friends should allow their feelings to be hurt unless they have chosen the present with a particular sentiment. She never changes the presents chosen for her by her own family or by the bridegroom's family unless especially told that she may do so. But to keep twenty saltcellars and six silver card trays when she has no pepper pots or coffee spoons would be putting sentiment above sense.

GIFTS FOR THE BRIDE'S ATTENDANTS

If the bridesmaids give a party for the bride shortly before the wedding or, if not, when they arrive to help the bride dress for the wedding, she gives each of them her present. The typical bridesmaid's present is a bracelet, a pair of earrings, a pin, or other jewelry, and according to the means of the bride, may have great value or scarcely any. The gift to her maid or matron of honor may match those given the bridesmaids or be quite different. If it is something that can be engraved, such as a small silver picture frame, the date and the initials of the bride and groom commemorate the occasion.

GIFTS FOR THE USHERS

The bridegroom's gifts to his ushers are usually put at their places at the bachelor dinner—if one is held. If not, they may be presented at the rehearsal dinner or just before leaving for the church. Cuff links are a popular gift. Silver or gold pencils, belt buckles, key rings, cigarette cases, billfolds, and other small and personal articles are suitable. The present to the best man is approximately the same as, or slightly handsomer than, the gifts to the ushers.

THE BRIDE AND GROOM EXCHANGE PRESENTS

He is a very exceptional and enviable groom who is financially able to take his fiancée to the jeweler and let her choose what she fancies. Customarily, and better, the bridegroom goes shopping alone and buys the handsomest ornament he can afford. Whether his gift is expensive or not, it must be something for her personal adornment.

The bride need not give a present to the groom, but she usually does if she can. Her favorite gift is something permanent and for his personal use—ranging from cuff links to a watch or ring.

RETURNING WEDDING GIFTS

When wedding plans are cancelled, gifts which have already been received must be returned. If it is an indefinite postponement but the couple intend to be married as soon as possible, the gifts are carefully put away until the time the ceremony takes place. If there is doubt as to whether it will take place at all, the bride after six weeks to two months must send back the gifts so that the donors may return them.

45

The clothes for the wedding party

Although the bride's gown is usually the center of attention at any wedding, the fact remains that all other members of the wedding party, as well as the parents of bride and groom, must appear in special and appropriate apparel. Nothing can be left to chance or a last-minute flurry, and as soon as the kind of wedding—formal or informal, morning, afternoon, or evening, large or small—has been determined, the bride must turn her attention to her own dress and the dresses of her attendants. The groom gives the necessary information about the arrangements to his best man, the ushers, and of course, his parents.

THE BRIDE'S COSTUME

In choosing her costume, the bride must consider several things. First, the degree of formality and the size of the wedding will affect the style of her gown. The probable temperature on the date chosen for the wedding will dictate the material. And she must also think of the setting and local custom. Will the reception be held indoors in a small house or will it be outdoors in a shady garden? Will the ceremony be held in a large cathedral, or a tiny chapel, or possibly in the living room of the bride's home? All these questions and many more must be answered before the bride can choose a dress that will be not only beautiful, but comfortable and appropriate.

THE DRESS

At her first wedding a bride suitably wears a dress of white and a bridal veil whether she is sixteen or forty! Beyond that age, she will probably feel more comfortable in a pretty cocktail dress in a pastel shade. Yards of billowing tulle would be too youthful for a bride of forty, just as a veil of yellowed lace might seem inappropriate for a bride of eighteen.

The traditional bridal material is satin for all seasons of the year. But few brides wish to wear such a warm material on a summer day. Therefore, although satin is the favorite choice for fall and winter, other materials have become more popular for the rest of the year.

Other suitable fabrics for autumn and midwinter weddings are faille, velvet, and moiré. In the spring, lace and taffeta are lovely, and in midsummer, chiffon, organdy, mousseline-de-soie, cottons, piqués, and linens. An infinite variety of synthetic materials has added to the bride's choice for every season.

A very young bride in a cloud of tulle is at her loveliest. Lace adds dignity and is most becoming to a mature bride. It is very important that a bride in her thirties or over choose both veil and dress in off-white, particularly if the dress is of satin. There is a very marked difference in the becomingness to the skin of an almost imperceptible accent of blue or pink or ivory.

The length of the train of the bride's dress depends somewhat upon the size of the church. In a large church the train can be very long; in a small chapel, short. A moderately short train extends one yard on the ground. The length of the train also depends to some extent on the height of the bride. The dress should be on the conservative side of fashion.

In the case of an informal marriage ceremony, such as a civil ceremony before a justice of the peace, or a second marriage when there is not to be a large celebration, the bride chooses the prettiest dress she has or can afford to buy, which will be appropriate to whatever the couple plan after the wedding ceremony. If a few friends are gathering to wish them happiness, she wears an afternoon or cocktail dress or suit. If they are leaving on a wedding trip directly following the ceremony, she may be married in the suit or traveling dress.

On rare occasions a wedding dress is borrowed rather than purchased. The wedding may take place on such short notice that the bride does not have time to find a dress which is becoming to her, or finances may prevent her from buying the one she wants. If she is fortunate enough to have a relative or close friend who offers to lend her her own wedding dress, there is no reason that she should not accept.

She must, of course, take extraordinary care with it and return it freshly cleaned and in perfect condition. The bride should also express her appreciation with the loveliest gift she can give.

THE BRIDE'S VEIL

The face veil is rather old-fashioned and is really appropriate only for a very young bride. Traditionally, she is a maiden too shy to face a congregation unveiled and reveals her face only when she is a married woman.

If she chooses to wear a veil over her face up the aisle and during the ceremony, it is always a short, separate piece about a yard square. Mounted by a milliner on a foundation, it need merely be put on the bride's head in front of her headdress. It is taken off by the maid of honor when she gives the bride's bouquet back to the bride at the conclusion of the ceremony, or if it will not destroy the headdress, it may simply be thrown back over the head.

SHOES AND GLOVES

The bride's slippers are of white satin or moiré. She should be sure that they are comfortable because she not only has to walk up the aisle in them, but she has to stand at the reception.

If she chooses to wear short, loose gloves, she merely pulls one glove off at the altar so that her ring can be put on. But if she wears elbow-length or longer gloves, the under-seam of the wedding finger of the glove is usually ripped open, and she only needs to pull the tip off to have the ring put on. If she prefers, she need wear no gloves at all.

JEWELRY SUITABLE FOR THE BRIDE

If the bridegroom has given the bride a piece of jewelry as a wedding gift, she always wears it, even though it may be composed of colored stones. Otherwise she wears colorless jewelry such as a pearl necklace or possibly a pin of pearls or diamonds.

MAKEUP

If the bride customarily wears makeup, naturally she will wear it for her wedding, but skillfully applied in moderation. Nothing could be more inappropriate than the bride and her attendants coming down the aisle of the church made up as though they were in a chorus line in a musical comedy.

THE BRIDEGROOM'S WEDDING CLOTHES

The bridegroom plans his outfit according to the degree of formality of the wedding, the season, and the *type* of dress the bride will wear. The ushers' suits are the same style as the groom's. The following are correct for every occasion:

1. FORMAL WEDDING, DAYTIME

Cutaway coat or, slightly less formal, black sack coat

Waistcoat, either to match or gray (or white or fawn in summer if the bridegroom prefers)

Gray-striped trousers or black with white pin stripes

Stiff white shirt for cutaway; soft white collarless shirt for sack coat

Wing or fold-down collar for cutaway; stiff fold-down collar for sack coat

Black-and-gray tie or gray or silver-gray ascot

Plain black kid shoes and black silk socks. Shoes should be freshly polished and have new soles and heels. Bridegrooms should blacken the soles of their shoes with waterproof shoe dye, so that when they kneel at the altar their shoes look dark and neat.

White boutonniere

White buckskin gloves preferred, but when gray is chosen, they should be as light as possible

Silk hat with cutaway; black homburg with sack coat. More often, no hats at all

2. INFORMAL WEDDING, DAYTIME (The bride wears a suit or daytime dress, or a very simple wedding gown with neither long veil nor train.)

Dark blue, black, or very dark gray suit

White shirt

Starched turn-down or soft fold collar

Four-in-hand tie in conservative stripe or dark solid color

Black socks and calfskin oxford shoes

White boutonniere

No gloves

Gray or black homburg or fedora

3. MOST FORMAL WEDDING, EVENING

Full dress (tail coat, stiffly starched white shirt, wing collar, white bow tie, white waistcoat)

White evening gloves

White boutonniere

Black fine kid or patent leather plain-front shoes or pumps

Black socks, silk or lisle

Silk hat, if worn at all

4. LESS FORMAL EVENING WEDDING (If the bride is in daytime dress, the groom wears outfit #2)

Dinner coat (tuxedo), black or midnight blue with matching trousers. In hot weather, a white dinner jacket is worn.

White shirt with piqué or pleated bosom, attached collar, or plain white soft shirt

Black waistcoat or cummerbund
Black silk bow tie
White boutonniere
No gloves
Black socks, silk or lisle
Black fine kid or patent leather, plain-front shoes or pumps
Black homburg or no hat

5. SUMMER DAYTIME WEDDING IN COUNTRY

Either dark blue or gray jacket with white flannel or linen trousers or white jacket with dark gray trousers
Plain white shirt
Dark four-in-hand tie, neat pattern
White buckskin shoes and white socks with white trousers, black shoes and socks with gray trousers
No hat
No gloves

6. INFORMAL DAYTIME WEDDING IN TORRID WEATHER

All-white Palm Beach or linen suit
Plain dark blue tie, four-in-hand
White socks
White buckskin shoes
White handkerchief

WHEN THE GROOM IS IN THE SERVICE

When our nation is not officially at war, military regulations ordinarily allow a member of the armed forces to choose whether or not he wears his uniform when he is off the base or off duty. Therefore, officers and enlisted men—with their fiancées' help—may decide if they wish to be married in uniform. A professional serviceman will undoubtedly choose to wear his uniform, and since his friends are probably regular service men too, they will also be dressed in uniform. A reserve officer or enlisted man has a more difficult decision. If his ushers are chosen from among his civilian friends, he must decide whether to give the wedding party a coordinated appearance by dressing in civilian clothes himself, or to ignore the look-alike question to show his pride in his service by wearing his uniform. Very often the wishes of his bride, who may feel very strongly one way or the other, will settle the problem for him.

Whatever the groom chooses to do, the ushers should be dressed alike. If some are civilians and some are servicemen, those in the service should be asked to conform to the civilians on that occasion, since it cannot be the other way around.

See Chapter Seventy-four for more information about the correct accessories for evening and daytime formal wear.

THE BRIDESMAIDS' COSTUMES

The costumes of the bridesmaids—slippers, stockings, dresses, bouquets, gloves, and hats—are selected by the bride. She may consult the bridesmaids if they live nearby, but she does not if they live at a distance, and in any case, the final choice is hers alone. Since long experience has proved that six girls almost certainly will have six different opinions, bridesmaids customarily wear and pay for what the bride chooses. That is the rule. They are always dressed exactly alike as to texture of materials and style, but sometimes their dresses differ in color. The two who follow the ushers might wear green, the next two chartreuse, the next two lemon yellow, and the maid of honor pale yellow. All carry the same kind of flowers. The dresses may be long or short, straight or full, light or dark, but the bride will do well to consider the coloring and build of her bridesmaids when making her choice.

Sometimes the bridesmaids wear the same color, but in graduated value. The first two would wear American Beauty rose, the next two a lighter tint, and the next two a still lighter color, while the maid of honor would be in palest flesh pink. Although a bride seldom cares to run the risk of having the white of her attendants detract from the effect of the single whiteness of her dress, a sash or other detail of color may solve the problem, and an almost all-white wedding can be entrancing, especially in a garden with a background of dense greens.

The material for the bridesmaids' dresses must complement the material of the dress of the bride. In other words, if the bride chooses austere satin, the bridesmaids should not be dressed in organdy or ruffled lace.

The dress of the maid or matron of honor, by the way, never precisely matches that of the bridesmaids. It is usually similar in style but different or reversed in color. For example, for an autumn wedding the bridesmaids might wear deep yellow and carry rust and orange chrysanthemums, and the maid of honor might wear rust and carry yellow chrysanthemums.

THE BRIDESMAIDS' FLOWERS

The bridesmaids almost always carry flowers—bouquets or falling sprays held in front of them, or sheaves which they hold on their outside arms. Those walking on the right side hold them on the right arm with the stems pointing downward to the left, and those on the left hold their flowers on the left arm with stems toward the right.

Although it gives an old-fashioned appearance, bridesmaids sometimes carry muffs in winter, or in summer, flower-filled baskets or hats made into baskets by tying their wide brims together with ribbons. Flowers matching those in the basket can be worn in the hair, in which case the bridesmaids need not wear either hats or hair ornaments.

Since nothing about a wedding should be artificial, fresh flowers only are used for the decorations and the bouquets. The only exception might be those worn as a wreath or hair ornament by bridesmaids and flower girls, and then only if they do not attempt to imitate the real flowers in the bouquets.

BRIDESMAID IN MOURNING

A bridesmaid who is in mourning may wear colors on this one day, as bridesmaids' dresses are looked upon as uniforms, not individual costumes.

CHILDREN ATTENDING THE BRIDE

Young girl attendants, aged from about seven to fourteen, who are too big to be flower girls and too young to be regular bridesmaids, are junior bridesmaids. The clothes of junior bridesmaids are modified copies of those worn by the bridesmaids.

Flower girls and pages may be dressed in quaint old-fashioned dresses and suits of white silk or satin of whatever period the bride fancies. Or perhaps they are dressed in ordinary white clothes, with wreaths and bouquets for the girls and white boutonnieres for the boys.

Ring bearers and train bearers are most often dressed in white suits, preferably with short pants.

At large weddings little girls sometimes wear picture bonnets. At simpler weddings they wear narrow wreaths on their heads. In this case, small artificial flowers are far better than real flowers, which are likely to be ragged as well as too heavy.

Tiny boys and girls wear slippers with a strap and white socks. If they are dressed in white, their slippers are white, but if they wear color, their slippers are colored, either to match their clothes or of black patent leather or a contrasting color—more often the latter.

Junior ushers may be dressed exactly like the other ushers. If not, they wear blue suits, as most suitable to their age group.

WHAT THE BEST MAN AND USHERS WEAR

At the formal daytime wedding, the best man wears precisely what the bridegroom wears. The groom and best man often wear ties that are different from those worn by the ushers and occasionally, if cutaways are being worn, white waistcoats. Otherwise the two principal men are dressed like the ushers.

To make sure that his ushers will be alike (in the event that the outfits are not being rented from one agency), a fastidious bridegroom sends each one instructions covering every detail of the equipment required. For example:

Please wear for the wedding:

- Black calfskin shoes
- Plain black socks
- Gray striped trousers—the darkest available
- Morning coat (cutaway) and single-breasted black waistcoat
- White dress shirt; cuffs to show three-quarters of an inch below coat sleeves
- Stand-up wing collar
- Tie and gloves are enclosed (Groom must find out size of gloves and size of collars, if bow ties have been selected)

When sending this list, the groom should include information as to when the usher should arrive in town, where he will be staying, what festivities are planned, etc.

Each usher's dress must be *almost* a counterpart of his fellows if the picture is to be perfect. Everyone knows what a ragged-edged appearance is produced by a company of recruits whose uniforms are from odd lots.

That one word "almost" is important: the clothes of the men of the bridal party—the bridegroom, the best man, and the ushers—need not and indeed should not match too precisely.

Their ties, boutonnieres, and gloves are exactly alike, of course, because they are gifts from the bridegroom and not bought individually. But otherwise, unless they have been rented in one group, there may be differences in stripes of trousers, shape of waistcoats, and slight but quite apparent differences in materials and measures of coats.

RENTING THE USHERS' CLOTHING

If the ushers are members of the diplomatic corps or in high government positions, they may very well own the cutaways or tail coats necessary for a formal wedding. Otherwise, since few young men possess such suits, the ushers' clothing is usually supplied by a rental agency.

Each may rent his own suit in accordance with the groom's instructions, or, for the sake of uniformity, the groom may prefer to rent them all from one agency in the area of the bride's home. In this case, he is responsible for obtaining the measurements of each out-of-town usher who cannot be measured by the store ahead of time, and he also arranges a time for a final fitting as soon as the ushers arrive, probably a day or two ahead of the wedding date.

One of the ushers who lives in the area is appointed to return the clothes on the first weekday after the wedding, or if they all must leave town immediately, a member of the bride's family should volunteer to take charge of this duty.

CLOTHES OF THE PARENTS

THE BRIDE'S MOTHER

At a wedding held at any hour between eight in the morning and six in the evening, the mother of the bride wears a daytime dress, light or bright in color but never solid black. The elaborateness of her dress varies according to the other wedding preparations. For example, at a formal wedding her dress follows an equally formal pattern—even, if she wishes, to a long skirt. She should always wear a hat and gloves, and she usually wears flowers, although these last are not necessary. Flowers or other hair ornaments or perhaps veiling or a lace mantilla would fill the requirements for head-covering in church if she prefers not to wear a hat.

In the evening, dinner dresses are in best taste. A low-cut dress is unsuitable in a church, but a fur piece or some other shoulder covering may be worn over it. As a rule, the mother of the bride leaves her wrap in the vestibule with those of the bridesmaids. If she knows that the church is likely to be cool and if she has an attractive fur piece, she carries or wears this. Otherwise, someone can put a light wrap in the pew for her just before she herself comes up the aisle. In other words, the bride's mother should not wear or carry anything that might spoil the effect of her dress.

THE BRIDE'S FATHER

There is no hard and fast rule governing the clothes of the bride's father. He may wear whatever is becoming to him, or he may wear whatever the bridegroom is going to wear. But since he will be escorting his daughter down the aisle behind the ushers, the party will have a more unified appearance if he elects to wear the same outfit as they do.

Ordinarily a young father wears a cutaway like that of the bridegroom and his ushers, and if they wear black sack coats he may very properly wear the same. But it would not be quite suitable for him to wear the less formal as well as more youthful sack coat when the younger men are wearing cutaways.

THE BRIDEGROOM'S MOTHER AND FATHER

Since the two mothers stand together to receive at the reception, the bridegroom's mother should if possible choose a dress similar in type to that chosen by the bride's mother. Obviously, one should not wear a tailored street dress if the other is wearing a long formal dress. It is up to the bridegroom's mother to get the necessary information by note or telephone call in order to plan her costume according to the style chosen by the bride's mother.

At a formal wedding, the bridegroom's father may wear the same type of clothes as those worn by the bride's father. He has, however, no official part in the ceremony and therefore may wear a dark suit if he is more comfortable in informal clothes.

Clothes worn by wedding guests are discussed in Chapter Forty-nine.

46

Events attending the wedding

THE PARTIES BEFORE THE WEDDING

THE BRIDESMAIDS' LUNCHEON

In many American communities the bridesmaids give the bride a farewell luncheon (or it may be a tea) in addition to the regular showers.

There is no special difference between a bridesmaids' luncheon and any other lunch party except that the table is more elaborately decorated, often in pink and white or the bride's chosen colors for the wedding. The bride may give her bridesmaids their presents at this time, and if they are giving her a single present from all of them, this would be the occasion for the presentation.

THE BACHELOR DINNER

Bachelor dinners are not held as often as they used to be, especially if the ushers are scattered far and wide or if they, as well as the groom, are working until the day before the wedding. If there is a dinner, it is generally held in the private dining room of a restaurant, or in a club.

Popularly supposed to be a frightful orgy, the bachelor dinner was in truth, more often than not, a sheep in wolf's clothing. As a matter of fact, the orgy was merely a gathering of young men—dedicated to the idea of getting the groom roaring drunk for the last time—whose idea of a smashing party was to make a tremendous noise, chiefly by singing at the top of their voices and breaking glasses. A boisterous picture, but scarcely a vicious one! Especially as a lot of the cheapest glassware was always there for the purpose.

The breaking habit originated with drinking the bride's health and breaking the stem of the wineglass so that it "might never serve a less honorable purpose." And this same time-honored custom is followed to this day. Toward the end of the dinner, the bridegroom rises and holding a filled champagne glass aloft says, "To the bride!" The men rise, drink the toast standing, and then break the delicate stem of the glass. The impulse to break more glass is natural and is seen at every county fair where enthusiasts delight in shooting or throwing balls at clay pipes and ducks and crockery.

Aside from toasting the bride and its glass-smashing result, the bridegroom's farewell dinner is exactly like any other stag dinner.

SHOWERS

For a full description of bridal showers, see Chapter Thirty-five.

PARTIES FOR OUT-OF-TOWN GUESTS

In order to take care of out-of-town family and guests who may arrive two or three days before the wedding, and also to relieve the bride's parents of extra meals and housework, friends of the family frequently give luncheons and dinners for the early arrivals as well as members of the wedding party who live nearby. These parties are likely to be much less formal than the actual wedding festivities and may be given at home, in a club, or in a restaurant. In warm weather they may be in the form of an outdoor barbecue or a swimming party; in the winter a sleigh ride or skating party could be organized for the young people, and a cozier fireside buffet for their elders. Whatever the party, the attendants, the families of the couple, their own close friends, and friends of their parents may be included.

LUNCHEON BEFORE THE WEDDING

A small luncheon for the bridal party may be held on the day of the wedding, again to relieve the bride's mother of extra responsibility. It is usually given by a relative or a friend of the bride's family and may be as simple or elaborate as the host and hostess wish. The bride and groom may not even attend. There is an old superstition that the bridegroom should not see his bride before the ceremony on the day of the wedding —but this is an outmoded idea, and they usually come for a short time, probably not together, but each with his own family.

THE REHEARSAL DINNER

A dinner is generally given the night before the wedding for the bridal party and the immediate families of the bride and groom. It may be followed by the rehearsal, but more often the rehearsal is in the late afternoon, followed at six or seven o'clock by the dinner.

It has now become an accepted custom all over the country, although it is not obligatory, that the parents of the groom give this party. This seems to be an extremely nice gesture—a slight repayment to the family of the bride for all the courtesies extended throughout the wedding activities to the family of the groom. If they come from another city, they may ask the mother of the bride to reserve a room in a club or restaurant for the dinner and consult with her on the number of her family who should be included so that they can make the reservations in advance. When they arrive for the wedding, they go at once to see the facilities and make the final arrangements. If the groom's family does not, or cannot, give the rehearsal dinner, it is arranged by some member of the bride's family or by a close friend.

INVITATIONS

Invitations are generally written on informals, or they may be simply a handwritten note. They may be telephoned, but since there are often out-of-town guests, the written invitation serves as a reminder of the time, address, etc.

Rehearsal dinner for
Pat and Bob

Mr. & Mrs. John Goodfellow

Friday, June 6th, 7:00 P.M.
Short Hills Country Club

RSVP
1700 Low Street
Short Hills

or

Dear Joan (or Mrs. Franklin),

John and I are giving a rehearsal dinner for Pat and Bob on Friday, June 6, at 7:00 P.M. It will be held at the Short Hills Country Club, and we hope you and Bill (Mr. Franklin) will be with us. We will look forward to hearing that you can come.

Affectionately (Sincerely),
Doris (Goodfellow)

1700 Low Street
Short Hills

THE GUESTS

All the members of the bridal party (with the exception of very young flower girls, pages, or ring bearers), the immediate families of the bride and groom, and out-of-town relatives who have arrived for the wedding are invited. If facilities and finances permit, a few very close friends are often included, especially those who come from a distance.

THE SEATING

A U-shaped table makes an ideal arrangement. The bride and groom sit at the base of the U with their attendants beside them. If there are many in the bridal party, some are seated opposite the bridal couple. The bridegroom's parents—or whoever are host and hostess—sit at either end of the U. The mother of the bride is seated on the right of the groom's father, and the bride's father sits on the groom's mother's right. Other members of the party are seated along the arms of the U in whatever way seems to make for the most congenial dinner partners. Grandparents are seated near the parents, and younger people may be grouped together.

DURING THE DINNER

The rehearsal dinner makes a perfect occasion for the presentation of the couple's gifts to the bridesmaids and ushers. In return, the attendants' gifts are often presented at the same time by the maid of honor and the best man, accompanied by a short speech or toast.

The host—generally the groom's father, makes the first toast, welcoming the guests and making some remarks about his happiness at the forthcoming marriage. This is followed by a return toast by the bride's father, and by numerous toasts proposed by the ushers and anyone else who wishes to get to his feet. *For suggestions on the content of these toasts, see Chapter Four.*

ENTERTAINMENT AND DECORATIONS

Music and dancing are not at all essential, and many rehearsal dinners offer no more than the meal and a pleasant gathering. Others are far more elaborate. A strolling violinist or accordionist may play romantic background music, or there may be a full orchestra and after-dinner dancing.

The bride and groom generally leave shortly after dinner to try to get a good night's sleep, but the guests may stay on to enjoy the festivities until the small hours if the host suggests it. Ushers and bridesmaids should remember that they have a responsibility to fulfill the next day, and refrain from either overindulging in champagne or staying so late that they look exhausted.

Decorations are simple. No matter how large the party may be, bowls of flowers—the number of arrangements depends on the size of the table—are all the adornment necessary.

THE REHEARSAL

The bride directs her wedding rehearsal with the help of her parents and her clergyman, but rarely takes part in it herself, as that is supposed to be bad luck. Someone else, anyone who happens to be present, is appointed to stand in for her. Some clergymen, however, feel that superstition has no part in religion and, unless she feels strongly, insist that the bride play her own part.

Most of us are familiar with the wedding service, and its form seems simple enough. But unless one gives strict attention to details, the ceremony can be rough and disjointed. It is not that awkwardness is a serious offense, but anything that destroys the smoothness of the general impression is disastrous to dignity, which is the qualification necessary above all in every ceremonial observance.

DRESS AND MANNER

People taking part in the rehearsal or attending as observers should remember that they are in a church and dress accordingly. The girls should wear simple dresses, never slacks or shorts, and the men should wear jackets and ties except in the heat of summer, when a neat sports shirt would be acceptable. A clergyman I know quite justifiably sent two bridesmaids home to change from shorts to skirts to preserve the dignity of his church and the ceremony.

In manner as well as dress, the bridal party should consider the importance of the occasion and attend the rehearsal seriously and with the desire to make the ceremony flawless. This means that they arrive on time, listen to instructions carefully, and avoid horseplay of any kind.

REHEARSING THE PROCESSION

A wedding rehearsal should proceed as follows:

First of all, since it is necessary to determine the exact speed at which the wedding march is to be played, the organist must always be present at the rehearsal. The ushers are asked to try it out. They line up at the door, walk forward two and two. The audience, consisting of the bride and members of the families, decides whether the pace looks well. It must not be fast enough to seem brisk, nor slow enough to be funereal.

Once the audience has decided upon the speed and the organist has noted the tempo, the entire procession, including the bridesmaids and the stand-in for the bride on her father's arm, goes out into the vestibule and makes its entry. Remember, the father is an important factor in the ceremony, and he must take part in the rehearsal. Each pair in the procession follows the two directly in front by four paces or beats of time. In the vestibule, everyone in the procession must pay attention to the feet directly in front; the pacemakers can follow the army sergeant's example and say very softly, "Left, left!" At the end the bride counts eight beats before she and the father put the left foot forward. The whole trick is starting; after that they just walk naturally to the beat of the music, keeping the distance between them and the preceding couple as nearly the same as possible.

REHEARSING THE MARRIAGE SERVICE

At the rehearsal the bride, if she does not take part, carefully watches how the substitute bride takes her left hand from the real father's arm, shifts her bouquet from her right hand to her left, and gives her right hand to the bridegroom. In the performance proper, the groom takes her right hand in his own right hand and draws it through his left arm, at the same time turning toward the chancel. If the service is undivided and all of it is to be at the altar, this is necessary, as the bride always goes up to the altar leaning on the arm of the groom. If, however, the marriage ceremony is to be read at the foot of the chancel, as is done at many weddings, he may merely take her hand in his left one and they stand as they are.

No words of the service are ever rehearsed, although all the places to be taken by the several participants in the marriage ceremony are rehearsed. The minister does explain the order of the service and the responses.

The substitute for the bride takes the bridegroom's left arm and goes slowly up the steps to the altar. The best man follows behind to the right of the groom, and the maid of honor, or first bridesmaid, leaves her companions and moves forward at the left of the bride. The bride, in pantomime, gives her bouquet to the maid of honor; the best man, in the same way, hands the ring to the groom. This is rehearsed merely to see that they are at a convenient distance for the services they are to perform.

Finally the bride must decide whether she wishes the bridal party to leave the church in the reverse of the order in which they entered, or whether the ushers and bridesmaids are to pair off and go out together. They practice taking their places to leave in the chosen order, but there is no further rehearsing because they walk out briskly at their natural pace. One admonition, however—the bride and groom should be reminded not to run from the church as if they were escaping from a penitentiary. One sees this often, and it not only destroys the dignity of the ceremony but deprives the guests of a good look at the radiant couple.

ENTERTAINING AFTER THE RECEPTION

In some areas it is an accepted practice that the bride's family invite out-of-town guests home for dinner or a late snack after the reception. But unless it is customary in your community, it is not necessary or expected. The bride's parents have had as much or more than they can do already, and are not expected to do further entertaining—unless they wish to.

Occasionally a few close friends are asked to dine with them, possibly because they have not had time to visit during the pre-wedding hours, or possibly because the bride's family simply does not yet wish to be alone to face the inevitable letdown of their daughter's departure.

47

The wedding day

THE HOUR APPROACHES

AT THE BRIDE'S HOME

Upstairs everyone is dressing. The father of the bride—one might think he were the bridegroom himself—is trying on his third shirt and desperately searching for his cuff links. The mother of the bride is hurriedly dressing so that she will be ready for any emergency, as well as to superintend the finishing touches to her daughter's dress and veil.

As the hour approaches everyone seems to be in the bride's room—her mother, her grandmother, three bridesmaids, four small children, and possibly a bridal consultant. Every little while someone brings a message or a package. Her father comes in and goes out at regular intervals from sheer nervousness. Those of the bridesmaids who have not dressed at the bride's house gradually appear and briefly distract the attention of the audience so that the bride has a moment to dress undisturbed. At last, even her veil is adjusted and everyone voices his approval: "How beautiful!" "Never saw anyone look so gorgeous."

Suddenly someone remembers:

Something old, something new,

Something borrowed, something blue,
And a lucky sixpence in your shoe.

"Let's see," says the bride. " 'Old,' I have old lace; 'new,' I have lots of new! But 'borrowed,' and 'blue'?" A chorus of voices: "Wear my ring," "Wear my pin," and someone's pin, which has a blue stone in it, is fastened under the trimming of her dress and serves both needs. Or a blue garter, purchased for the occasion but forgotten in the excitement, is presented by one of the bridesmaids. If the lucky sixpence—a dime in her shoe will do—is produced, she must at least pay in discomfort for her "luck."

PROCESSION TO THE CHURCH

Wherever they may dress, the bridesmaids always meet at the house of the bride, where they also receive their bouquets. When it is time to go to the church, several cars are waiting. The bride's mother drives away in the first, usually alone. She may, if she chooses, take her other children or one or two bridesmaids with her; but she must reserve room for her husband, who will return from church with her. The maid of honor, bridesmaids, and flower girls follow in as many cars as may be necessary.

Last of all comes the bride's car, which is often a rented limousine. She drives to the church accompanied only by her father. Her car stands in front of the church until she and her husband—in the place of her father—return from the ceremony and drive back to the breakfast or reception.

MEANWHILE, AT THE CHURCH

About an hour before the time for the ceremony, the ushers arrive at the church and the sexton turns his guardianship over to them. They leave their hats in the vestry or in the coat room. Their boutonnieres, sent by the groom, should be waiting in the vestibule unless the best man has distributed them beforehand. Each man puts one in his buttonhole and puts on his gloves.

Those of the ushers who are the most likely to recognize the various friends and members of each family should be detailed to the center aisle. A brother of the bride, for instance, would be chosen for this aisle because he should be best able to recognize and look out for the family's best friends. A second usher should be either a brother of the bridegroom or a near relative who is able to recognize the family and intimate friends of the groom.

RESERVED PEWS

The parents of the bride always sit in the first pew on the left, facing the chancel; the groom's parents in the first pew on the right. If the church has two aisles, her parents sit on the left of the right aisle, and his on the right of the left aisle.

A few pews on either side of the center aisle are reserved for the immediate families of the couple, and the people to sit there may have been given or sent pew cards (*see Chapter Forty-nine*) to show the ushers, who otherwise might not recognize them or know where to seat them. Sometimes pew cards are not sent, but the ushers are given a list of guests to be seated in the first few pews. These pews are called "in front of the ribbon." Formerly a ribbon was actually put across the aisle behind them and raised at one end by the usher to allow the guest to pass into the reserved section. Nowadays, however, these pews are generally designated by a bouquet or white bow on the end, and the aisle is not closed. Just before the procession starts, a ribbon is laid over the ends of the pews parallel to the aisle and ending at the last reserved pew. This task is assigned to two of the ushers, who are also responsible for removing it. Afterward the family is escorted out and leaves for the reception quickly, while the other guests must wait until the ribbon is removed.

A few pews may be taken from one family to give to the other when the one family is very small and the other large. Let us say the bride needs seven pews and the bridegroom three (as often occurs when he is from a distant part of the country and few of his family or friends can be present). Then the families may agree to instruct the ushers that behind the first three pews, those with pew cards may be seated evenly on both sides.

THE GUESTS ARRIVE AT THE CHURCH

It is the duty of the ushers to show all guests to their places. An usher offers his right arm to each lady as she arrives, whether he knows her personally or not. Only if the vestibule is very crowded and several ladies are together may he give his arm to the oldest and ask the others to follow. Customarily, he asks them to wait until he can come back or another usher is available.

The usher does not offer his arm to a man unless he is quite old and it is obvious that he needs assistance. If the older man is accompanied by a younger, the latter is asked to follow so that they can be seated together.

The ushers ask those guests whom they do not recognize, or who may be friends of both bride and groom, whether they wish to sit on the bride's side—the left—or on the groom's side—the right. If they fail to ask, the guest may offer the information: "I am a friend of Mary's—may I sit on her side?"

If the usher thinks a guest belongs in front of the ribbons though she fails to present her card, he always asks, "Have you a pew card?" If she has, he shows her to her place. If she has none, he asks which side she prefers and gives her the best seat vacant in the unreserved part of the church.

Ushers are not supposed to escort guests in total silence, even when they are strangers. A few casual remarks are made—in a low voice, but not whispered or solemn. The deportment of the ushers should be natural, but dignified and quiet, for they are in church. They must not trot up and down the aisles in a bustling manner; yet they must be fairly swift and efficient, as everyone must be seated as expeditiously as possible.

The guests without reserved cards should arrive early in order to find good places. Members of the families and the few guests who have places in front of the ribbon may come later.

SEATING DIVORCED PARENTS

THE BRIDE'S PARENTS DIVORCED BUT FRIENDLY

Because it is obviously happier for the children when friendliness rather than hatred exists between divorced parents, yesterday's ban against contact between them no longer exists. If a friendly relationship has been possible, not only Mary's parents but also both of her stepparents are present at the church and possibly at the house.

Her mother and stepfather sit in the front pew. If her mother has a "second" family, those stepbrothers or stepsisters are seated in the second pew. The bride's father (after giving her away in a Protestant ceremony) sits with her stepmother and their family in the next pew.

WHEN THEY ARE NOT FRIENDLY

In the entire subject of etiquette, there is perhaps no situation that brings such unhappiness as the wedding of a daughter whose parents are divorced and bitterly estranged. This is especially true for the bride who loves her father and all of his family quite as much as—sometimes even more than—her mother and her family. Yet according to convention, unless she has always lived with her father, the wedding must be given by her mother.

It is true that she drives with her father to the church, walks with him up the aisle, and has him share in the marriage ceremony. After giving his daughter away, he sits in the pew behind the immediate family of her mother. His second wife may sit with him if the bride wishes, or, if there is great bitterness involved, the stepmother does not attend at all. He does not have a chance to see his daughter after the ceremony, since he does not go to the reception given by his ex-wife and, quite possibly, her present husband.

It is also probable that no member of his family—neither the grandparents nor the aunts or uncles of his daughter—has so much as a glimpse of their granddaughter or their niece on her wedding day, since quite possibly they may not be invited even to the church.

THE WEDDING GIVEN BY THE BRIDE'S FATHER

When the wedding is given by the bride's father and stepmother while her own mother is also living, it is evidence that the daughter has made her home with her father instead of her mother.

The bride's own mother sits in the front pew with members of her family, but her second husband usually sits farther back. If the families are friendly, he may join his wife in the front pew. (She is not usually invited to the reception, although she may be if the bride requests it.) The father gives the bride away and then takes his place in the second pew with his present wife and their family.

SEATING DIVORCED PARENTS OF THE BRIDEGROOM

Even if they have remained on friendly terms, it would be in very bad taste to seat any divorced parents together. The groom's mother and whomever she would like to have with her should be given the first pew on the bridegroom's side of the church, and his father and others of his family are seated in the second pew. At a large reception their presence need not be conspicuous nor make anyone uncomfortable.

THE LAST FEW MINUTES

THE BRIDEGROOM WAITS

In a Christian ceremony, the bridegroom and his best man arrive at the church and enter the side door about fifteen minutes before the wedding hour. They sit in the vestry or in the clergyman's study until the sexton or an usher comes to say that the bride has arrived. They then wait for and follow the clergyman to their places.

At many Jewish weddings a reception is held in a room in the synagogue before the ceremony takes place.

THE LAST FIVE MINUTES

The groom's mother and father are waiting in the vestibule. As the bride's mother drives up, an usher hurries to tell the groom of her arrival, as the bride and her father will be close behind. Any brothers or sisters of the bride or groom who are not to take part in the wedding procession are now taken by ushers to their places in the front pews. The moment the entire wedding party is in the church, the doors between the vestibule and the church are closed. No one is seated after this except the parents of the young couple.

The groom's mother goes up the aisle on the arm of the head usher and takes her place in the first pew on the right; the groom's father follows alone and takes his place beside her. The same usher or a brother or cousin of the bride escorts the bride's mother to the first pew on the left. (When the bride has a stepfather—and especially when she is very close to him, even though he is not to give her away—the stepfather may follow her mother and the usher, in the same manner as the groom's father.)

If a carpet is to be laid, it is already arranged in folds so that two ushers may now pull it quickly down the aisle. At the last moment, the white ribbon is draped over the ends of the pews from the back of the church to the nearest reserved pew on each side of the center aisle. Having done this, the ushers return to the vestibule and take their places in the procession. The beginning of the wedding march should sound just as they return to the foot of the aisle.

To repeat: No person should be seated after the entrance of the mother of the bride. Nor must anyone be admitted to the side aisles while the mother of the bride is being ushered down the center one. Her entrance should not be detracted from by late arrivals scuttling into their seats behind her. Guests who arrive last must stand in the vestibule or—if there is one—go into the gallery.

THE BRIDE ARRIVES

At a perfectly planned wedding, the bride arrives exactly one minute after the hour in order to give the last arrival time to find a place. A maid or other volunteer is waiting in the vestibule to help the bride and bridesmaids off with their wraps and to help again after the ceremony. At simpler weddings the bridegroom, the maid of honor, or a bridesmaid helps the bride with her coat when they leave.

THE WEDDING CEREMONY

The sound of the music is the cue for the clergyman to enter the church, followed by the bridegroom and the best man.

ENTRANCE OF THE BRIDEGROOM

The groom stops at the foot of the chancel steps and takes his place at the right side of the aisle, as indicated in the diagram. His best man stands on his left, slightly behind him. The ushers and bridesmaids always pass in front of him and take their places as illustrated.

THE PROCESSION

At a Protestant wedding with choral service, the choir may enter in advance of the hour set for the ceremony and so take no part of the wedding procession. However, at a formal Catholic wedding and also at Protestant weddings, if the bride and groom wish it and the minister and organist agree, the choristers lead the wedding procession, singing as they go. The ushers immediately follow them.

The procession is arranged according to height, the two shortest ushers leading—unless others of nearly the same height are found to be more accurate pacemakers. Junior bridesmaids come next, if there are any. If not, the bridesmaids come directly after the ushers, two and two, also according to height, with the shortest in the lead. After the bridesmaids, the maid or matron of honor walks alone; flower girls follow, then the ring bearer, and last of all, the bride on the right arm of her father, with pages, if she has any, holding up her train. If there are both maid and matron of honor, the maid of honor immediately precedes the bride.

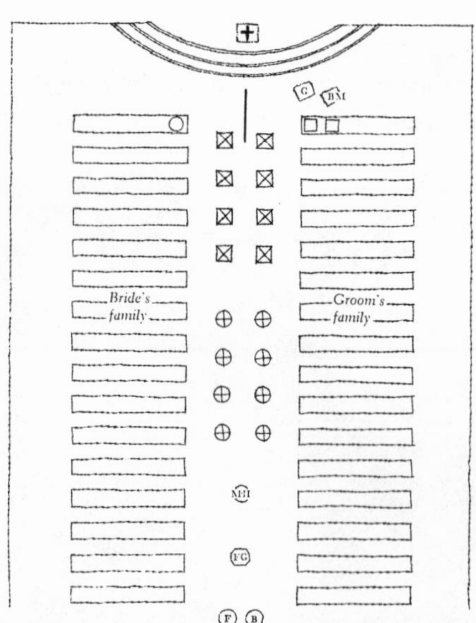

B, *bride;* F, *father;* FG, *flower girl;* MH, *maid of honor;* ⊕, *bridesmaid;* ⊠, *usher;* G, *groom;* BM, *best man;* ⊞, *clergyman*

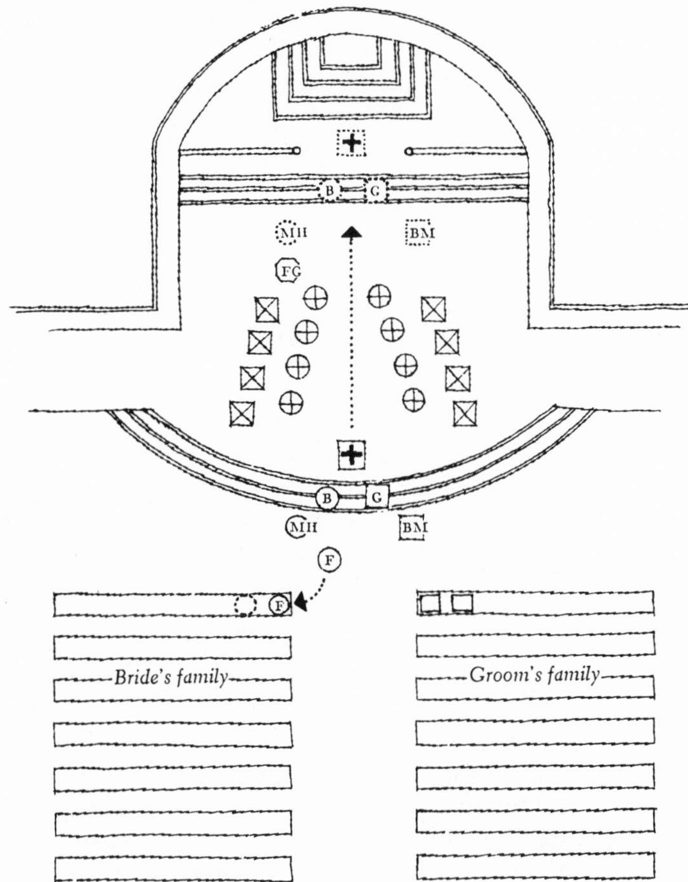

AT THE CHANCEL

At the foot of the chancel, the ushers divide. In a small church, the first two go up the chancel steps and stand at the top, one on the right, the other on the left. The second two go a step or two below the first. If there are more, they stand below. Chalk marks can be made on the chancel floor if necessary, which can be a great help to little children in remembering their positions.

In a big church the ushers go up farther, some of them lining the steps or all of them in front of the choir stalls with the line sloping outward so that the congregation may see them better. The bridesmaids also divide, half on either side, and stand in front of the ushers. The maid of honor's place is on the left at the foot of the steps, exactly opposite the best man. Flower girls are put above or below the bridesmaids, whichever makes the prettiest arrangement.

In a Roman Catholic ceremony, the father of the bride joins her mother as the groom joins the bride. He does not give his daughter away.

In a church with two main aisles, the guests are seated according to aisles and not according to the church as a whole. All the seats on the right aisle belong to the bride's family and guests. The left aisle belongs to the bridegroom.

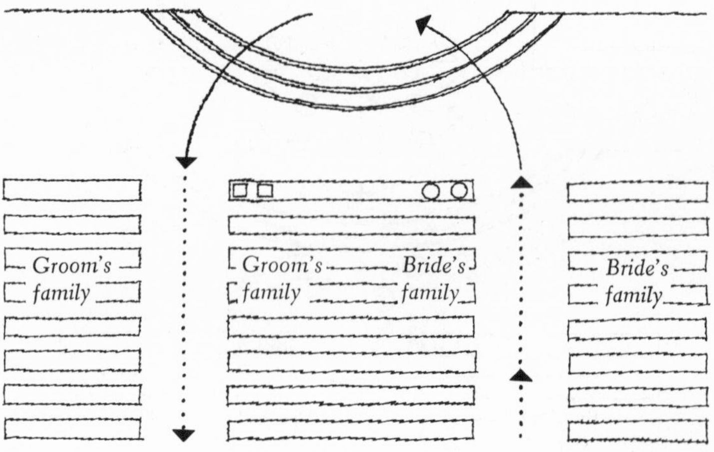

The bride's mother is seated in the front pew at the left (as always) of the bride's aisle—exactly as she would be in a center-aisle church. On the other side of the church the bridegroom's mother occupies the front pew on the right of the groom's aisle (also as always).

For the processional, the bride's (right) aisle is chosen because people naturally turn to the right rather than to the left. After the ceremony, the bride and groom come down the groom's (left) aisle. These directions make it quite clear why the aisles are necessarily chosen so as to place the immediate families in center pews. The left pew must be entered from the aisle at its right. If the bride's mother were to choose the left aisle, this would seat her in a side pew instead of a center one.

However, if the church is very large and the wedding small, the right aisle alone may be used. Then the bride's family sits on the left of this aisle and the groom's family on the right, while the marriage takes place at the head of this aisle.

THE SERVICE

As the bride approaches, the groom waits at the foot of the steps, unless he comes down the steps to meet her. If there are no steps, he waits at the head of the aisle. The bride relinquishes her father's arm, changes her bouquet from her right to her left arm, and gives her right hand to the groom. The groom, taking her right hand in his right hand, puts it through his left arm—just her fingertips should rest near the bend of his elbow—and turns to face the chancel as he does so. It does not matter whether she keeps his arm, or whether they stand hand in hand or merely side by side at the foot of the chancel in front of the clergyman.

In a Protestant ceremony, her father has remained where she left him, on her left and a step or two behind her. The clergyman stands a step or two above them and reads the betrothal. When he says, "Who giveth this woman to be married?" the father goes forward, still on her left, halfway between her and the clergyman but not in front of either. The bride turns slightly toward her father and gives him her right hand. The father puts her hand into the hand of the clergyman and says distinctly, "I do." In some parts of the country it is customary for the bride to give her father a brief kiss at this point to indicate her gratitude and affection. A recent innovation, which has caused many very favorable comments, is that of the bride's father replying, "Her mother and I do." He then takes his place next to his wife at the end of the first pew on the left. The clergyman, holding the bride's hand in his own right, takes the bridegroom's hand in his left and very deliberately places the bride's hand in the bridegroom's.

If it should happen that the bride has neither father nor any very near male relative or guardian, she may walk up the aisle alone. At the point in the ceremony where the clergyman asks, "Who giveth this woman to be married?" her mother stays where she is standing in her proper place at the end of the first pew on the left and bows her head very distinctly to indicate "I do." There is no rule against her going forward as the bride's father would have done, but this would be unusual.

The organist then plays softly while the clergyman slowly moves to the altar before which the marriage is performed. The bride and groom follow slowly, the fingers of her right hand on his left arm.

The maid or matron of honor moves out of line and follows until she stands behind the bride, slightly to her left. The best man takes the corresponding position behind the groom and to his right. At the termination of the anthem, the bride hands her bouquet to the maid of honor—or her prayer book to the clergyman. If the bride wishes her own prayer book to be used for her marriage, she carries it instead of a bouquet. And the bride and groom plight their troth.

When it is time for the ring, the best man produces it from his pocket, the minister blesses it, and the groom slips it on his bride's finger.

The wedding ring must not be put outside the engagement ring. On her wedding day a bride either leaves her engagement ring at home when she goes to church or wears it on her right hand. Afterward she wears it outside her wedding ring.

When it is to be a double-ring ceremony, the maid of honor hands the groom's ring to the bride at the moment that the best man gives her ring to the groom. The bride puts it on his finger immediately after she has received her ring from him. The ceremony then proceeds.

AFTER THE CEREMONY

At the conclusion of the ceremony, the minister congratulates the new couple. The organ begins the recessional. The bride takes her bouquet from her maid of honor, who then lifts the face veil, if one is worn. If they have decided to do so, the couple kiss. With her bouquet in her right hand, the bride puts her left hand through her husband's right arm, and they descend the steps.

The maid of honor hands her own bouquet to a second bridesmaid while she arranges and straightens the train and veil of the bride.

THE RECESSIONAL

The recessional is played, and the procession goes out in one of two ways. In reversed order the bride and groom go first—she on his right arm—then the maid or matron of honor, bridesmaids, and ushers, again all taking pains to fall into step with the leaders. In this form of recessional, the best man goes out through the vestry, picking up the groom's coat if he has one, and rejoins him at the front door.

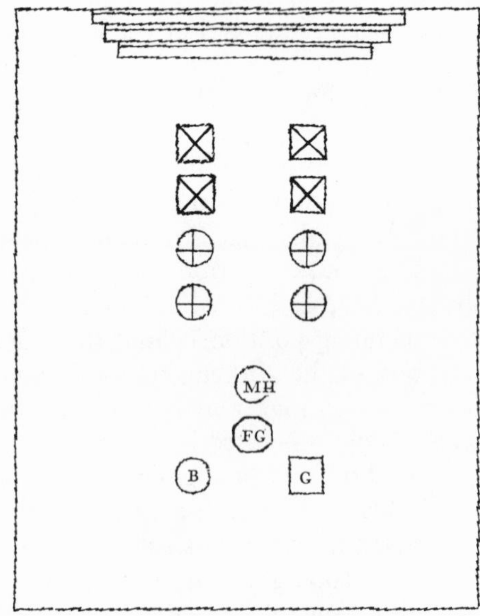

In the other form of recessional, the maid or matron of honor and the best man walk out together behind the bride and groom. Then the bridesmaids and ushers pair off and follow two by two. One of the ushers or the best man will have put the groom's coat in the vestibule before the ceremony so that he need not go back to the vestry or waiting room for it.

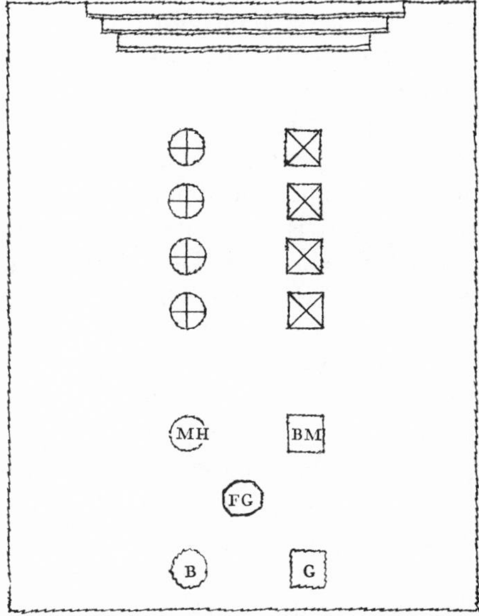

The automobiles are drawn up in the reverse order from that in which they arrived. The bride's car leaves first; next come those of the bridesmaids; next that of the bride's mother and father; next that of the groom's mother and father. The nearest members of both families follow, and finally all the other guests.

To return to the church for a moment: As soon as the recessional is over, the ushers hurry back and escort to the door all the ladies who were in the first pews, according to the order of precedence; the bride's mother first, then the groom's mother, then the other occupants of the first pew on either side, then the second and third pews, until all members of the immediate families have left the church. The husbands of these ladies follow immediately behind them, or walk with a young person who is not to be escorted out. At some weddings, only the two mothers of the couple are escorted by the ushers, and the husbands or escorts of the others walk out with them. Meanwhile it is a breach of etiquette for other guests to leave their places. As soon as the occupants of the first pews have left, the ribbons along the ends of the pews are removed by the two previously designated ushers, and all the other guests go out by themselves. The rest of the ushers are by that time hurrying to the bride's house to make themselves useful at the reception.

The best man goes back into the church, gives the fee to the clergyman (see page 357), collects his coat, and leaves for the reception.

ORTHODOX AND REFORM JEWISH WEDDINGS

The Orthodox wedding ceremony differs somewhat from the Reform Jewish ceremony. In the Orthodox ceremony, the bride is veiled and is escorted by her father and mother under a cloth canopy which used to be supported by four poles, carried by hand. Within recent years, the canopy, called "chupah," has been made stationary; that is, the posts rest upon a platform, and the bride's parents simply escort her up the aisle. Sometimes the canopy is of flowers instead of cloth—but the underlying idea is that there must be a covering over the heads of the couple to be married. The principals stand under the chupah before the Ark of the Covenant. The groom is escorted by his parents. Hats are worn by all men attending the ceremony.

The service is read in Hebrew. The groom places a ring upon the finger of the bride, repeating the following formula: "Thou art consecrated unto me with this ring, according to the law of Moses and Israel." The officiating rabbi than makes the benediction over the wine, giving the groom and bride the goblet, from which they drink. A document is read in Aramaic, giving in detail the pledge of fidelity and protection on the part of the groom toward the bride, and also indicating the bride's contribution to the new household. At the conclusion of the ceremony, a glass is broken, symbolizing the fact that one must never overlook, even at the height of happiness, the possibility of misfortune.

In the Reform service, English (or the native language) is used in addition to Hebrew, and the canopy may be dispensed with. If the young couple decide to include elements traditionally associated with the Christian wedding ceremony, they should consult with their rabbi about this beforehand. The groom is usually ushered in by his best man, and the bride is escorted on the arm of her father. The attendants function as in a Christian ceremony. The groom repeats either the Hebrew formula or its English equivalent. The bride and groom also drink wine out of the same cup, symbolizing the cup of joy. Usually the clergyman delivers a brief address on the significance of marriage.

ROMAN CATHOLIC WEDDINGS

The wedding of the Roman Catholic Church is customarily centered around the Nuptial Mass celebrated between eight in the morning and noon. Inasmuch as the Nuptial Mass follows the schedule of masses in most parishes, it is often necessary for the engaged couple to make arrangements at the rectory several months in advance. The banns, an announcement of intention to marry, are usually proclaimed from the pulpit three times or are published in the church calendar prior to the wedding. The couple should therefore complete church arrangements before making reception plans. It is also recommended, though not obligatory, that the Catholic members of the bridal party receive Holy Communion at the Nuptial Mass.

Whether the bride and groom and best man and maid of honor, or the whole bridal party are permitted within the altar rail is determined by individual church practice. Since the bride's father does not give her away, he steps into the front pew to join his wife after escorting her down the aisle. As some churches have strict rules about procedure, it is incumbent on the couple to ascertain the restrictions in advance and be guided by them.

Although afternoon weddings usually take place between four and five o'clock, they may be held any time from one to six. A Catholic wedding may take place any time during the year; but during the closed seasons of Lent and Advent, the Nuptial Blessing is not given, unless, under extraordinary circumstances, permission is granted by the bishop.

THE RECEPTION

On arriving at the house or club where the reception is to be held, the bridal party may pose for pictures before the other guests arrive. This finished, they form the receiving line, and the reception is under way.

THE RECEIVING LINE

The actual receiving line is made up of the mothers of the couple, the bride and groom, and the bride's attendants. The ushers and best man have no place in it.

The bride's mother greets the guests at the beginning of the line nearest the entrance to the room. Formerly she, with the bridegroom's mother and possibly his father, comprised a separate receiving line of three because they stood apart from the bridal party to greet the guests as they arrived. Today they stand next to the bridal couple so that they may introduce one or the other to older guests who may not have met them before. Possibly the bride's father joins the line, but more often the two fathers walk about together, leaving the two mothers to receive.

In any case, the bride's mother always stands nearest the door of entrance to the principal room. At an elaborate reception there may be an announcer, either the bride's family butler or one furnished by the caterer. He asks each guest his or her name and then repeats it aloud. The guests shake hands with the hostess and, making some polite remark about the "beautiful wedding" or "lovely bride," continue on to greet the bridal pair. If there is no one announcing, guests unknown to the hostess introduce themselves to her.

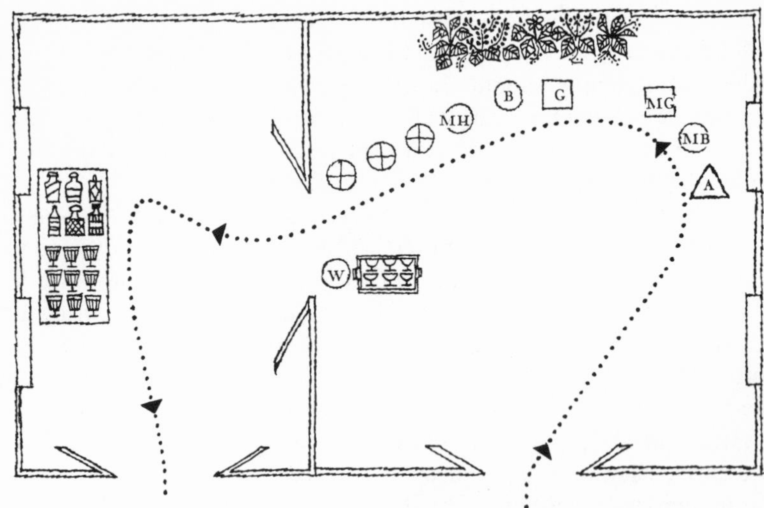

A, *announcer;* MB, *mother of bride;* MG, *mother of groom;* G, *groom;* B, *bride;* MH, *maid of honor;* W, *waiter*

The bride always stands on the bridegroom's right, the maid of honor next in line. The bridesmaids stand beyond the maid of honor, according to height. The direction of the queue depends upon the plan of the room. If, in the room shown in the diagram, the door to the dining room were at the right, the mothers would stand at the left and the queue would naturally swing away from that door and approach the line from the opposite direction, and guests would greet the bride first instead of the bridegroom.

Usually the bride and groom receive against the wall opposite the door of entrance; but this is not a fixed rule, and they choose whichever side of the room will make the most convenient background. This is usually decorated with leaves and flowers, but may equally well be the closed curtains of a window or a fireplace with flowers on the mantel.

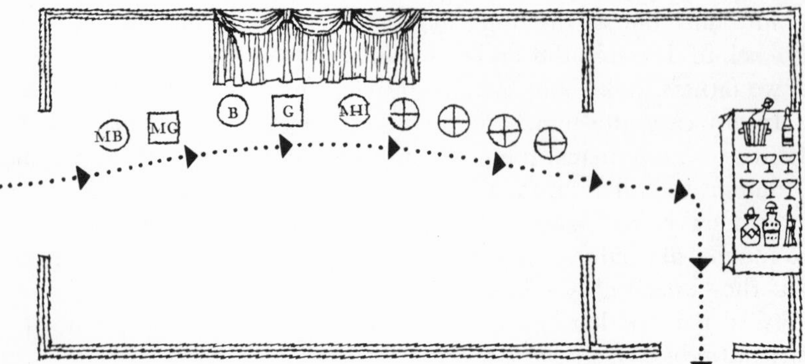

RECEIVING THEIR GUESTS

The bride always introduces her husband to relatives or friends, saying, "Aunt Kate, I want you to meet Jim," or "Mrs. Neighbor, this is Jim!" or, more formally, "Mrs. Faraway, I'd like you to meet *my* husband."

The bridegroom, on the approach of an old friend of his, says, "Mary, this is Cousin Carrie," or "Mrs. Denver, Mary," or "Hello, Steve. Mary, this is Steve Michigan." The young man says, "I'm glad to meet you, Mary." And she replies, "I'm glad to see you, Steve." When an older acquaintance comes through the line, the groom says, "Mary, I'd like you to meet Mr. Banker." She says "How do you do, Mr. Banker," and he replies "I'm so glad to meet you, Mrs. Newlywed."

The bride with a good memory thanks arriving guests for the gift sent her: "Thank you so much for the lovely candlesticks," or "The platter is just what we wanted." The person who is thanked says, "I am so glad you like it," or "I didn't have it marked so that in case you have a duplicate, you can change it." But these verbal thanks do not lessen her obligation to write a thank-you note. If she has received a large number of presents and if she doesn't trust her memory, she had better not run the risk of thanking Mr. and Mrs. Worthington for a glass ash tray when they sent a piece of sterling silver.

To all expressions of best wishes and congratulations, the bride and groom need only answer "Thank you."

It is wise to have the refreshments ready for guests as soon as they have passed down the receiving line—particularly if the reception is a large one. Some are sure to want to leave early or have other engagements.

THE BRIDE'S TABLE

Very frequently the bride and groom prefer not to have a bridal table but to mingle with the guests. When they do this, one of the regular tables should still be reserved for them so that they may sit down when they feel like it. When there is a bridal table, it may be at the side or end of a large room, or in a room apart decorated with white flowers. In front of the bride, the table's chief ornament is the wedding cake—always elaborately iced and often surmounted by little figures depicting the bride and groom, or by fresh white flowers.

When the queue of arriving guests has dwindled and melted away, the bride and groom go to their table or join their guests. Arm in arm they lead the way, followed by the ushers and bridesmaids.

The bride and groom always sit next to each other, she at his right, the maid or matron of honor at his left. The best man is at the right of the bride. Around the rest of the table are bridesmaids alternated with ushers. Sometimes one or two others—intimate friends who were not included in the wedding party and husbands or wives of the attendants —are asked to the table. When there are no bridesmaids, the table is always made up of such intimate friends. The bridal table is always served by waiters, even when the rest of the guests eat buffet style.

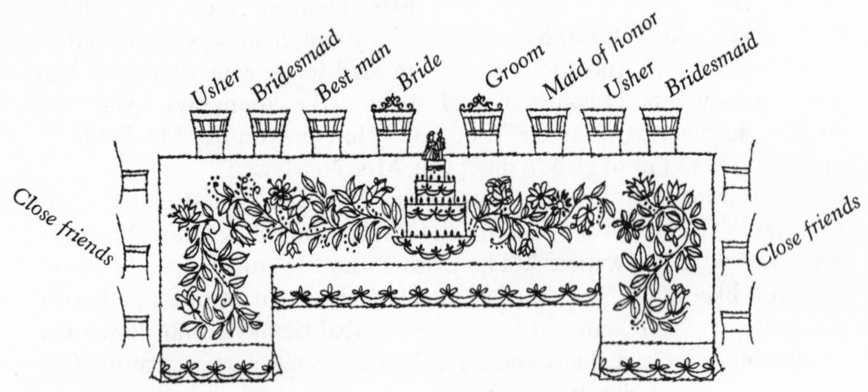

THE TABLE OF THE BRIDE'S PARENTS

The table of the bride's parents differs from other tables in nothing except its larger size and the place cards for those who have been invited to sit there. The groom's mother always sits on the right of the bride's father, and opposite them the groom's father is on the right of the mother of the bride. The other places at the table are occupied by grandparents, godparents, especially intimate friends of the bride's parents, or distinguished guests. The clergyman who has performed the ceremony is always included at this table and is placed at the left of the hostess. His wife, if present, sits at the bride's father's left.

When the wedding guests are to eat standing up, the only sit-down table is the one for the bridal party, and possibly one for elderly relatives of the bridal couple.

THE GRANDPARENTS

If possible, grandparents should be included at the parents' table. If space is limited, a separate table should be arranged for them and their close friends nearby. Although they have no official part in the wedding, they should at all times be treated as honored guests.

THE TOAST TO THE BRIDE AND GROOM

At a sit-down bridal table, champagne is poured as soon as the party is seated. The glass of the bride is filled first, then that of the bridegroom, and then on around the table, starting with the maid of honor

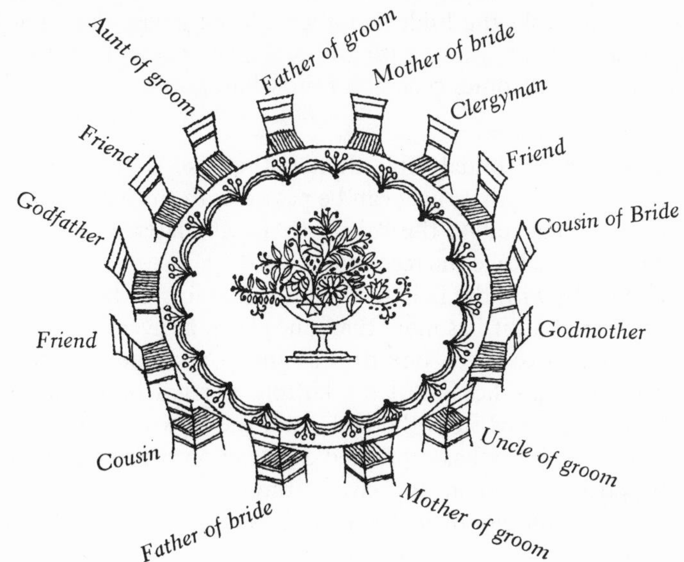

at the groom's left and ending with the best man seated at the right of the bride. Then someone—it is really the duty of the best man—proposes a toast to the bride and bridegroom. All (except the bride and groom) rise, raise their glasses, and drink the toast. Then the groom rises and replies with thanks from them both. Other toasts may be drunk should anyone care to propose them; for instance, the groom might wish to propose a toast to the bride's mother. At a large reception these are necessarily confined to individual groups, but at a small one, all the guests may join in drinking together to the couple's health and happiness. *For suggestions as to the wording of these toasts, see Chapter Four.*

DANCING AT THE RECEPTION

If a regular two- or three-course meal, or wedding breakfast, is to be served, the first course is passed shortly after the bridal party sits down. The dancing does not start until after dessert has been eaten and the cake cut. At a reception where no full meal is served, but sandwiches and snacks are passed or eaten from a buffet table, the bride and groom may start the dancing as soon as they have had a chance to rest a bit from standing in the receiving line.

All the guests watch and applaud while the bride and groom dance the first dance. Her father-in-law usually asks for the second dance and then her father. The bridegroom follows the same pattern and dances with his mother-in-law and with his mother.

After the bride and groom have danced alone for a few moments, the bride's father asks the groom's mother for the first dance, and the groom's father asks the bride's mother. As the groom dances with each bridesmaid and the ushers with the bride, the guests may start cutting in, and dancing becomes general for the whole group.

CUTTING THE CAKE

At a sit-down bridal table dinner, the cake is cut just before the dessert is served, so that slices can be passed with the ices or ice cream. If there is no bridal table, the cake may be cut later, often just shortly before the couple leave the reception.

The bride, with the help of the bridegroom, cuts the first slice from the bottom tier (if it has more than one) with a silver cake knife. Sometimes she cuts two slices, one for her groom and one for herself. After this, a waiter cuts slices until the bottom tier has been cut away. The cake then is removed from the table, and the tiers are separated and cut into slices. The baker has supported each tier on a heavy cardboard disk. When possible, the small top layer surmounted by figurines is set aside for the bride and groom to keep. At any rate, a large piece should be saved for them. The groom's cake (*described in Chapter Forty-four*) is put into individual boxes to be taken home by departing guests as a memento.

THE DIVORCED FATHER SHARES IN THE WEDDING

When the devoted but divorced father of the bride wishes to have a share in his daughter's wedding, there is a practical solution. The bride who, although she lives with her mother, is equally fond of her father and his family, knows very well that because bitterness exists between her parents, few if any of her nearest relatives on her father's side will be at the church. She also knows that her father will leave the church as promptly as possible and that neither he nor his immediate family, nor his special friends—many of them hers, too—will be at the reception given by her mother.

So at the same time that the wedding invitations are sent out by her mother, the following invitations to a small second gathering are sent out by her father:

Mr. John Pater
requests the pleasure of your company
at the wedding supper of his daughter
Mary
and her bridegroom
James Martin
Saturday, the tenth of April
at seven o'clock
4 Monroe Place

If he has remarried, the invitation may read:

Mr. and Mrs. John Pater
request the pleasure of your company
at the wedding supper of his daughter
etc.

One change in the mother's invitations is an earlier-than-usual hour for the reception. There is another deviation from the established wedding procedure: instead of leaving the reception at the bride's mother's in their traveling clothes, the bride and groom remain in their wedding clothes to drive to the home of her father.

After they greet his family and special friends, a buffet supper or a supper at small tables is served. At the end of this the bride and groom change into traveling clothes, which have been brought to her father's house earlier in the day, and depart under the customary shower of rose petals and confetti.

For the children, who care for both parents equally, a family divorce brings unavoidable unhappiness. To the bride whose love for her father and his family is quite as great as her love for her mother and her family, this plan can be a very important contribution to the thoughtful kindness that is always the test of perfect behavior!

THEY'RE OFF!

Sometimes the bride and groom continue dancing or chatting for so long that those who had intended to stay for the "going away" grow weary and leave—which is often exactly what the young couple wants! And unless they have to catch a train, they usually stay until the crowd thins before going to dress for their journey. At last the bride signals to her bridesmaids and leaves the room. They all gather at the foot of the stairs. About halfway to the upper landing as she goes up, she throws her bouquet, and they all try to catch it. The one who succeeds is supposed to be the next married. If the bride has no bridesmaids, she collects a group of other girls and throws her bouquet to them, and if there are no stairs, she throws the bouquet from whatever spot is most convenient.

Sometimes if a very close relative is too ill to attend the wedding, the bouquet is sent to her.

As soon as the bride has gone upstairs, followed by her mother, sisters, and bridesmaids, who stay with her while she changes into her traveling clothes, the groom goes to the room reserved for him and changes into the traveling clothes that the best man has already taken there for him. He waits upstairs until the bride appears in her going-away clothes. All the ushers shake hands with them both. His immediate family, as well as hers, has gradually collected. Any that are missing are sent for. The bride's mother gives her a last kiss. Her bridesmaids hurry downstairs to have plenty of paper rose petals ready and to tell everyone below as they descend, "Here they come!" A passage from the stairway and out the front door, all the way to their automobile, is left free between two rows of eager guests, their hands full of confetti and petals.

Down the stairs, out through the hall, into the car, slam the door, and they are off!

The wedding guests stand out on the street or lawn looking after them for as long as a vestige can be seen—and then gradually everyone disperses.

Many young couples spend a good deal of thought and planning on making their going away unusual and dramatic. Every sort of departure has been tried—on skis, in sleighs, on horseback or in horse-drawn carriage, and even in a helicopter! But the most memorable I have ever seen took place when the reception was held at a yacht club on a beautiful June evening. The bride and groom left on a handsome boat polished and shining, with all flags flying. They pulled away from the pier with horns of other boats tooting, and a carpet of rose petals floating on the water. It was truly an ending never to be forgotten by the bride and groom or by any who were there to see them go!

A THOUGHT FOR THE BRIDEGROOM'S PARENTS

At the end of the reception and as soon as she is in her traveling dress, a considerate bride will send a bridesmaid or someone out into the hall and ask her husband's parents to come and say good-bye to her.

It is very easy for a bride to forget this act of thoughtfulness and for a groom to overlook the fact that he should bid his parents good-bye before leaving the room where he dressed. Many a mother and father, seeing their son and new daughter rush past without even a glance, have returned home with a let-down feeling and an ache in their hearts. One might say, "How stupid of them! Why didn't they go upstairs?" But often the groom's parents are strangers; they may have met their new daughter only a few days or weeks before the wedding; and if by temperament they are shy or retiring, they hesitate to go upstairs in an unknown house until they have been invited to do so. So they wait, feeling sure that in good time they will be sent for. Meanwhile the bride forgets; and it does not occur to the groom that, unless he makes an effort while upstairs, there will be no opportunity in the dash down to the car to recognize his parents any more than anyone else.

THE NEWLY MARRIED COUPLE

A completely beautiful wedding is not merely a combination of wonderful flowers, beautiful clothes, smoothness of detail, and delicious food. These, no matter how pleasing, are external attributes. The spirit, the soul of it, must have something besides, and that something is seen in the behavior and in the expression of the bride and groom.

The most beautiful wedding in the world can be turned from sacrament to circus by the indecorous behavior of the groom and the flippancy of the bride. She must not reach up and wigwag signals while she is receiving, just as she must not wave to people as she goes up and then down the aisle, although she may relax and smile her joy on the way out of the church. She must not cling to her husband as though unable to stand, or lean against him or the wall or any person or thing. She must not swing her arms, she must not fidget, she must not shout; and she must not, while wearing her bridal veil, smoke a cigarette. No matter how young or natural and excited she may be, she must, during the ceremony and the short time that she stands beside her husband at the reception, act with dignity.

The happiness of both the bride and groom must dominate a perfect wedding. An unhappy-looking bride, an uncomfortable-looking groom, turns the greatest wedding splendor into sham—without love it is a sacrament profaned.

The radiance of a truly happy bride is so enhancing that even a plain girl is made beautiful. A happy bridegroom quite plainly may have the quality of radiance, but it is different—more directly glad. They both look as though there were sunlight behind their eyes, as though their mouths irresistibly turned to smiles in visible proof of perfect happiness that endears them to all beholders and gives beauty even to the simplest of weddings.

48

Weddings in special situations

The bride-to-be and her fiancé do not always choose to be married in church—for a number of perfectly acceptable reasons. These weddings require as much attention as any other, for they should be as perfect of their kind as the most elaborate church ceremonies. Then, too, there are variations on the usual form, as when two sisters wish to be married in a double wedding or when the bride has been married before.

THE HOUSE WEDDING

A house wedding involves somewhat less expenditure but a good deal more work for the bride's family than does the church wedding. It also has the disadvantage of limiting the number of guests. The ceremony is exactly the same as it is in a church, except that the procession advances from the stairs or hallway through an aisle of white satin ribbons to the improvised altar. Chairs for the immediate families may be placed within a marked-off enclosure, but if the room is small, space is merely kept free for them to stand in.

In the country a house wedding may be performed in the garden, with the wedding procession under the trees, and tables set out on the lawn. This can be a perfect plan for California or other rainless-season states, but often difficult to arrange along the Atlantic seaboard where the weather is all too likely to spoil everything.

When the couple's faith requires that they kneel during the wedding ceremony, a cushioned bench is provided for their use. It is placed directly in front of the space reserved for the clergyman and is often backed by an altar rail. The bench is usually six or eight inches high and between three and four feet long; at the back of it an upright board on either end supports a crosspiece of the altar rail. It can be made in the roughest fashion by any carpenter or amateur, as it is hidden under leaves and flowers or a drapery of some sort. Either end of the altar rail is usually decorated with a spray of white flowers.

At a house wedding, the bride's mother stands at the door of the room in which the ceremony is to be held and receives people as they arrive. But the bridegroom's mother takes her place near the altar with the rest of the immediate family. The ushers are purely ornamental, as no one is escorted to seats. The guests simply stand wherever they can find places behind the aisle ribbons. Just before the bride's entrance, her mother goes forward and stands in the front row on the left.

In a house, the procession usually starts from the top of the stairs. In an apartment, it starts in the hall or a room off the living room. The wedding march begins, and the ushers come in two and two, followed by the bridesmaids, exactly as in a church, the bride coming last on her father's arm. There are seldom many bridal attendants at a house wedding—two to four ushers, and one to four bridesmaids—unless the house is immense. The clergyman and the groom and best man have, if possible, reached the altar by another door. If the room has only one door, they go up the aisle a few moments before the bridal procession starts.

A HOUSE WEDDING WITH LEAST EXPENSE

At the simplest wedding possible, the clergyman enters, followed by the bridegroom; the bride then enters with her father, or alone; and the wedding service is read.

When there are no garden flowers to be had, a suitable background can be made by hanging a curtain of damask, velvet, or any other plain fabric across a flat wall space. Against this, the colorful clothes of the bride's attendants (if she has any) and her own white dress and veil are effective. For music, nothing could be more beautiful than the phonograph recordings of organ and choir made for just such weddings. The refreshments may consist of nothing but ginger ale or fruit juice, wedding cake, and a few varieties of sandwiches, placed on a small table covered with a tea cloth. But the spirit of the day remains, and the young couple should leave as joyously as if they had been wed in a cathedral.

THE DIFFERENCES

The chief difference between a church wedding and a house wedding is that the bride and groom do not take a single step together. The groom meets her at the point where the service is read. After the ceremony, there is no recessional. The clergyman withdraws, an usher removes the prayer bench, if there is one, and the bride and groom merely turn where they stand and receive the congratulations of their guests, unless the house is big enough so that they can receive in another room.

When there is no recessional and if bride and groom have decided in favor of the wedding kiss, it is always given before they turn to receive their guests. In any event, it is against all tradition for anyone to kiss the bride before her husband does.

AFTER THE CEREMONY

Usually, but not always, there is a bride's table, decorated exactly as described for a larger reception and placed perhaps in the dining room, but there is no special table for the bride's mother and her guests—or for anyone else.

The food would be the same as at a more elaborate reception, except that there would be only one hot dish and one salad. If green salad is served, there should be a hot dish of something like eggs or creamed shellfish. Or, if the hot dish is chicken croquettes or chicken à la king, there might be a salad of mixed vegetables. Bouillon and ice cream may be served.

SEATING AT A VERY SMALL WEDDING BREAKFAST

At the smallest wedding possible where only the immediate families and a few friends are present, they very often all sit together at one lunch or dinner table.

THE BRIDE'S DRESS

At a home wedding the bride has her choice of a formal wedding gown, long or short (without long train, however), or a daytime dress or suit worn with a hat. The other items of her costume correspond to those suitable for a similar church wedding.

The bridegroom and his attendants may wear sack coat and striped trousers if the bride chooses a formal wedding dress, but if she is dressed in an afternoon or cocktail dress, they would wear dark business suits. As in a church wedding, they would wear tuxedos for the more formal affair after six in the evening.

THE EVENING WEDDING

All through the South and generally throughout the West, many weddings are celebrated at eight or nine o'clock in the evening. There is a reason for the evening wedding in the South. The heat of the day has

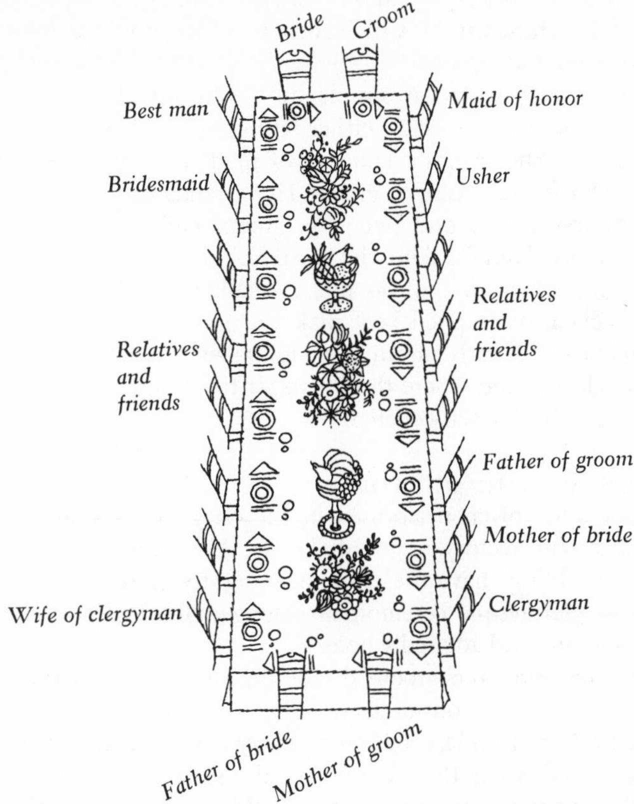

passed, and the coolness of the evening lends itself better to festivities and to dancing.

The details are precisely the same as those for the morning or afternoon. In large southern cities, the bride and bridesmaid may wear dresses that are perhaps more elaborate and more "evening" in type, and the bridegroom and ushers wear full evening clothes. Guests, both men and women, often dress as though going to a ball. For the church ceremony the women should wear light scarfs of some sort around their shoulders and over their hair, in compliance with the regulations forbidding the uncovering of women's heads and shoulders in places of worship.

At simpler ceremonies, especially in smaller communities, the guests wear exactly what they would wear to evening service in church—a good dress and hat for a woman and a dark daytime suit for a man.

THE EARLY MORNING WEDDING

Among Roman Catholics an eight o'clock morning wedding is not unusual, and its details may be precisely the same as for later hours. But for others, who are perhaps boarding an early morning train or ship and would like the informality to which such an hour lends itself, a wedding may be carried out as follows:

The bride may wear any simple dress. She might possibly wear a veil, but of tulle instead of lace, either falling to the hem of her dress or of finger length. She carries a bouquet of moderate size, unless she carries a prayer book, and wears no gloves. Her attendants wear the simplest sort of morning dresses and hats; the groom and his best man wear business suits or flannels. And the breakfast menu—really breakfast—might be fruit, coffee, and hot biscuits. A chafing dish of scrambled eggs, creamed chicken, or chipped beef makes a more substantial meal.

In fact, a small, early morning wedding—where everyone is dressed in morning clothes and where the breakfast truly suggests the first meal of the day—can be perfectly enchanting.

MARRIAGE AT THE RECTORY

Marriages are often performed in the clergyman's study or in another room at the rectory or parish house. Although the words "marriage" and "wedding" have the same meaning, the latter to most people connotes the picturesque ceremonial of long-established custom. "Marriage" is therefore used advisedly here.

When the bride and groom decide on a ceremony in the rectory, the clergyman must be consulted well ahead of time as to the date and hour. The bride and bridegroom go together and are met at the parsonage by the members of their families and any friends who have been invited. When all are assembled, the bridegroom tells the clergyman that they are ready. The clergyman takes his place. The bride and bridegroom stand before him, and the service is read. Afterward those present congratulate them, and that may be all. Or they may go to the house of the bride or of a witness or to a restaurant and have lunch, tea, or dinner together. At such a marriage, the bride rarely wears a white wedding dress and veil, but it is entirely proper for her to do so if she chooses—especially if there is to be a wedding dinner at someone's home afterward.

MARRIAGE BY A JUSTICE OF THE PEACE

The general procedure is exactly the same as that for a marriage at the rectory. However simple and informal the plans, there are always two guests, preferably relatives but often friends, who act as witnesses as well.

The traditional wedding dress and veil are not suitable in the circumstances, but the bride will certainly wish to wear the prettiest daytime dress or suit she has, or can afford to buy.

THE RUNAWAY MARRIAGE

To elope, according to the dictionary, is to run away from home with a lover, but to most of us an elopement means that a young couple has run off and been married without the consent of the girl's parents. I suspect, however, that many such marriages have had a quiet parental blessing; for some reason, financial or otherwise, the family felt that a big wedding would be impossible.

When the bride's parents have approved before the marriage or when they have decided after it to make the best of what has happened, they send out the announcements in their name. Should the parents be unalterably opposed, however, and wish the world to know that they are withholding their blessing, they do not send out the announcements. The newlyweds may, if they wish, send them out themselves. *See Chapter Fifty-one.*

If the bride's mother and father wish to give a belated reception after the marriage, it is generally an informal affair, attended by close friends and relatives. This is often done to introduce an out-of-town bridegroom. The invitations are telephoned or sent on informals. If written, they should include the bride's married name—"In honor of Mr. and Mrs. Harvey Kirk, Jr." or "In honor of Nancy and Bill." If the parents are truly enthusiastic about the marriage and wish to show it, they may give a much more formal reception, including a wedding cake, engraved invitations, etc.

THE DOUBLE WEDDING

At a double wedding, the two bridegrooms follow the clergyman and stand side by side, each with his best man behind him. The groom of the older sister stands nearer the aisle. The ushers—half friends of the first, and the others friends of the second bridegroom—go up the aisle together. Then come the bridesmaids of the older sister followed by her maid of honor, who walks alone. The older sister follows, holding her father's arm. Then come the bridesmaids of the younger sister, her maid of honor, and last, the younger bride on the arm of a brother, uncle, or nearest male relative.

The first couple ascend the chancel steps and take their place at the left side of the altar rail, leaving room at the right side for the younger bride and her bridegroom. The father stands just below his older daughter. The brother takes his place in the first pew.

The service is read to both couples, with the particular responses made twice. In a Protestant ceremony the father gives both brides away —first his older daughter and then his younger. Then he takes the place saved for him beside his wife in the first pew.

At the end of the ceremony the older sister and her husband turn and go down the aisle first. The younger couple follow. The bridesmaids of the older are followed by those of the younger, and the ushers follow last. Or bridesmaids and ushers pair off and go out together.

Each couple should have the same number of attendants. All of the ushers should be dressed alike. The bridesmaids' dresses, while not necessarily all the same, should harmonize.

"ATTENDING" EACH OTHER

It is not usual, but it is quite possible, for each bride at a double wedding to serve as maid of honor for her sister. Each in turn holds the other's bouquet during her sister's ceremony.

But the wise bridegroom, if he dispenses with a best man and uses the services of his brother groom, keeps his own bride's ring in his own waistcoat pocket.

SEATING THE PARENTS AT THE CHURCH

One difficulty of a double wedding is the seating of the parents of the two bridegrooms, who must either share the first pew or draw lots for the occupation of first or second. This question they must decide for themselves.

Occasionally the brides are cousins, in which case the front pew on the bride's side must be shared by both mothers, the older sitting in the aisle seat.

THE RECEPTION FOR A DOUBLE WEDDING

Since most double weddings involve two sisters, there is only one hostess—their mother. Therefore she, and her husband if he wishes, stand first in the receiving line. Next to her is the mother of the older sister's husband, and then the older sister and her groom. The younger sister's mother-in-law comes next, and then the younger couple. Both maids of honor follow them, but since there are so many in the line, the bridesmaids may be excused. The three mothers could stand togther at the head of the line, but if the two grooms' mothers stand next to their own children, they are in a better position to introduce their new daughters-in-law to their special friends.

At a sit-down wedding reception, the seating of the bridal parties depends on the numbers. If there are many attendants, it is best to have two tables, next to or facing each other, and arranged in the usual way. If, however, there are not too many in the parties, they may be seated at the same table. One couple would be placed at either end, or, if they prefer, opposite each other at the center of each long side. The bride always sits on the right of the groom. The maid of honor in either case would be on the groom's left and the best man on the bride's right. The other attendants would alternate—either on the same side of the table as their newlywed couple, or at the same end where their particular couple is seated.

In the rare case when the couples are serving as each other's honor attendants, they could sit together at the center of a long table, since there would be no need for spaces to be left on either side for the best man and maid of honor.

Each couple should have their own wedding cake. They cut the cakes one right after the other so that each may watch the other perform that ceremony.

All three sets of parents should be seated together at the same table. It is up to the brides' mother to discuss with her daughters' new mothers-in-law how many other relatives should be included with them.

In all other ways the reception is identical to that of a single wedding.

SECOND MARRIAGES

THE BRIDEGROOM'S SECOND MARRIAGE

The fact that a bridegroom has been married previously has no bearing on the wedding preparations made by his maiden bride. She may wear a white gown and veil, and the wedding and reception may be as elaborate as she chooses.

THE MARRIAGE OF A WIDOW

The marriage of a widow differs from that of a first-time bride in that she cannot wear a bridal veil, orange blossoms, or a myrtle wreath, which are emblems of virginity. Nor does she have bridesmaids, though she may have a maid or matron of honor.

If she has not done so long before, she should either remove her first wedding and engagement rings or else transfer them to the fourth finger of her right hand as soon as she becomes engaged. When her second engagement ring is given her, she of course puts aside the first. If her second marriage is to take place soon, she removes her wedding ring as well, unless she has children, in which case she may wish to wear it until the day of her second wedding. She may keep the engagement ring for her daughter by her first marriage, or eventually she may again wear it on her right hand. If the stone is valuable, she might have it reset into a clip or pin, either for herself or for her daughter. This, however, depends upon the feelings of her second husband. If she knows that he objects, her future happiness may quite possibly depend upon discarding it permanently.

Usually a widow writes personal notes of invitation to a quiet wedding, but this is no reason why she cannot have a lovely ceremony. Sometimes—especially if she is young and her family and the groom's are very large—it becomes necessary to send out engraved invitations. *For the correct form, see Chapter Forty-nine.*

Although she almost always chooses a dress and hat of color, she may wear white.

The most appropriate wedding for a widow is held in a small church or chapel or in her home, with a few flowers or some greens in the chancel or at the altar rail. There could be a few ushers or quite possibly only honorary ones, out of consideration for the bridegroom. There are no ribboned-off seats, as only very intimate friends are invited. Usually the bride wears an afternoon dress and hat or possibly a cocktail dress and tiny veil. There may be a fairly large reception afterward or the simplest gathering of friends. In any case, the breakfast, tea, or dinner is, if possible, at the bride's own house, and the bridal pair may stay where they are and have their guests take leave of them and then drive away afterward. They do not run off in a shower of confetti or rose petals as they would at a first marriage.

A DIVORCÉE REMARRIES

Whether or not a divorcée may be married in her church depends upon the circumstances of her divorce and the approval of her clergyman. Often the remarriage takes place in her own house, performed by either a clergyman or a justice of the peace. The ceremony is attended only by relatives and close friends. The reception may be larger than the wedding ceremony, but should still be relatively simple.

The bride may not wear a veil or orange blossoms, and she should not wear white. The dress should be a simple street-length gown worn with a hat, in any style she prefers.

Engraved invitations are not in good taste unless she is very young, her first marriage brief, and the guest list (because her bridegroom has not been married before) relatively long. Handwritten notes, a telephone invitation, or possibly messages on visiting cards are preferred. Her parents may send engraved announcements, or, in the case of a mature bride, she and her husband may send them themselves. *See Chapter Fifty-one.*

Children of divorced parents attend the marriage ceremony if they are reconciled to the situation and fond of their future stepparent. In any case, they may attend the reception if they wish.

MILITARY WEDDINGS

The only way in which a military wedding ceremony differs from a civilian one is the arch of swords through which the bride and groom pass at the end of the ceremony. This only occurs when the bridegroom is a commissioned officer. As soon as the service is over, the ushers line up on either side of the aisle at the foot of the chancel steps, and at the head usher's command, "Draw swords!" hold their swords up (blades up) in such a way as to form an arch. The couple pass through, and at the command, "Return swords!" the ushers return them to their sheaths. They then turn and escort the bridesmaids down the aisle.

If the weather is fine, the arch may be formed outside the entrance to the church. In this case, the ushers quickly leave by a side door and rush around to the front of the church to form the arch. The bridesmaids walk out two by two, unescorted, but stop short of the arch. Only the couple themselves pass through.

Should there be some civilian ushers in the party, they line up also and merely stand at attention while the arch is formed.

THE BLESSING OF A CIVIL MARRIAGE

When a couple has been married in a civil ceremony, and have had the approval of their church, they may later wish to have a religious ceremony held in a church or chapel to bless that marriage. There is such a service in the *Book of Common Worship*. It is similar to the marriage service, except that the minister says, "Do you *acknowledge* (rather than *take*) this woman . . . ," and makes other appropriate changes. No one, of course, gives the bride away, nor does the groom give the bride her ring again.

It is a lovely ceremony and most satisfactory for those who wanted but could not have a religious wedding originally.

The service is only attended by family and closest friends, and there are no attendants. It is, after all, a blessing rather than a celebration of the marriage. The bride wears a street dress, and the groom, a dark suit. She may carry a bouquet or wear a corsage. There may be music, and the altar is decorated with flowers.

If a reception follows the ceremony, it may be as simple or as elaborate as the couple wish. Presuming the blessing takes place shortly after the civil marriage, the reception may have all the trimmings of any other wedding reception.

49

The wedding guest

The mere fact of receiving a wedding announcement or even an engraved invitation to the church obligates you to much or to nothing, according to your own relationship to the bride or groom. In other words, an announcement informing you that a marriage has taken place between Mary Anthony and John Ballard may require no more attention than it takes to change the name of the bride in your address book. On the other hand, the wedding of a good friend or a relative necessarily entails certain responsibilities.

"THE HONOUR OF YOUR PRESENCE . . ."

As soon as you receive an invitation, whether to the ceremony, the reception, or both, and see that it includes R.S.V.P., you must reply at once. It is most inconsiderate as well as impolite not to do so. Remember that the family will have to make definite preparations for every guest who has not refused just as they have for those who do attend. Failure to reply causes extra trouble and expense.

As the wording suggests it is an "honour" to be invited to a wedding, and anyone so honored should have the common decency and good manners to sit down and write his answer in person. Therefore, although many people feel it is the only way of eliciting replies, I do not condone the sending of response cards with wedding invitations. If, however, you receive such a card, use it to answer the invitation, because the sender will be prepared to file and tabulate those cards rather than odd-sized letters. *For the correct form of acceptances and regrets, see Chapter Fifty-five.*

"AND FAMILY"

An invitation reading "and Family" includes each and every member of the family living under the same roof—and this means every child from walking and talking age (at about two) up to great-grandparents. Married daughters or sons who live in their own houses are not included because, if invited, they are sent separate invitations.

In general, however, guests should not take small children unless they themselves will look after them. Well-behaved chidren are very sweet at a wedding, but children out of hand can be most annoying to everyone and detract from the solemnity of the occasion.

No child may be taken unless he is specifically invited or the invitation does read "and Family." In some areas of the country this rule has been so ignored that brides have been at their wits' end to find a solution. It is scarcely in keeping with the atmosphere of a wedding to enclose a printed card saying in effect, "No Children." Therefore, the only remedy is by word of mouth. The bride may call those who are close to her, explain that she simply cannot include the children, and ask those friends to tactfully spread the word to others.

WHERE TO SEND PRESENTS AND RESPONSES

When the bride's address does not appear on the invitation, either under an R.S.V.P. or on the envelope flap, it may be very difficult to discover where presents are to be sent. If you have no way of getting her address, or her family's, the only solution is to send gifts and responses in care of the club, hotel, hall, or whatever is given as the site of the reception.

THE WEDDING PRESENT

Having sent your acceptance—or your regrets—you should next turn your thoughts to whether or not you will send a gift to the bride, for wedding presents should, if at all possible, arrive before the ceremony.

If you are not an intimate friend of the bride or groom or of their families and if you are not invited to the wedding reception, you need not send a present (unless, of course, you know that there is to be no reception). Of course, a gift always may be sent if you wish to, whether or not you receive any invitation at all. Obviously, the more personal the invitation the greater the obligation to send a gift. An invitation by written note definitely indicates that you are considered an especially close friend, and you will therefore certainly want to send a present. And you must always send a present to one who is marrying into your immediate family. It is considered obligatory to send a present when you are asked to a wedding reception, whether or not you attend.

PRESENTS FOR A SECOND MARRIAGE

Whether you are asked to the reception or not, there is no necessity for sending a present when both members of the couple have been married before. Often, however, special friends and perhaps close relatives send presents to someone being married for a second time. When one of the couple has never been married before, his or her friends will most probably wish to send gifts.

PRESENTS FOR ELOPERS

A person receiving an announcement of an elopement, either in the name of the parents or without their names, is no way obligated, nor even expected, to send a present. If, of course, out of love or affection for either the bride or the groom or their families, one wishes to give them something, it will be an especially appreciated gesture.

DELAYED PRESENTS

If, because of illness or absence, your present is not sent until after the wedding, a note should accompany it, giving the reason for the delay. Delayed presents are sent to Mr. and Mrs. Newlywed at their own new address. If you do not know their address, they may be sent in care of the bride's family.

WHEN YOU RECEIVE NO ACKNOWLEDGMENT FOR A GIFT

If, after several months, you have not received a thank-you note from the bride, you need not hesitate to write her and ask if your present ever arrived. You must word your letter carefully, not in any way implying that you are criticizing her for not writing, but making it clear that you only wish to know what happened so that you may send another gift if the first was lost in the mail. She, too, may have been wondering why a present from you had never arrived, and your letter will serve to clarify the situation for you both.

WHAT KIND OF GIFT

Typical wedding presents include almost anything ornamental or useful for the furnishing of a house or the setting of a dining-room table, from a piece of silver to a glass ash tray, a picture frame to a clock, a paper cutter to a lamp, a cigarette box to an occasional table or chair. Naturally, the less you know about the future living plans of the bride and groom, the more necessary it is to choose a gift that can be used by anyone living anywhere.

Many gifts are beautified by marking; a certain few require it. Objects of plain silver or untooled leather are enhanced by engraved or tooled initials. Linen, unless heavily embroidered or lace-inserted, may seem rather impersonal without an embroidered monogram or initials. However, unless you know for certain that your gift is something that the bride wants and that it will not be duplicated, it is safer to send presents unmarked.

The most important thing is that your gift be lovely and useful. To fulfill these two requirements it need not be expensive. No bride or groom would want you to spend more than you can afford. And one type of gift to avoid is the dust-catching and useless ornament.

PRESENTS FROM THE BRIDEGROOM'S FRIENDS

You seldom send a present to the bridegroom. Even if you are an old friend of his and have never met the bride, your present is sent to her—unless you send two presents, one in courtesy to her and one in affection to him. Rather often friends of the bridegroom do pick out things suitable for him, such as a decanter or a rather masculine-looking desk set, which are sent to her but are obviously intended for his use.

CHECK-GIVING

Near relatives may properly give their gifts in the form of money. Because checks given as wedding presents are often substantial and frequently intended for a definite purpose, they are not necessarily made out to the bride. Often they are drawn to the couple jointly; on occasion they are drawn to the bridegroom. The check to be cashed after the wedding is drawn to John and Mary Smith. Godparents also sometimes send checks so that the bride can choose her own gift—perhaps a coffee table or an occasional chair or whatever she wants. There is no formula as to the amount to be given—it depends on the donor's closeness to the bride or groom and what he can afford. *For display of checks with the other wedding presents, see Chapter Forty-three.*

Checks are generally sent to members of the Protestant or Catholic faiths before the wedding, as are other gifts. But in some faiths and ethnic groups, checks are presented to the couple as the guest passes through the receiving line. This is true at Jewish weddings, and in some Italian and Polish communities, among others. When it is customary it is quite correct.

CARDS WITH PRESENTS

If you have visiting cards one is practically always enclosed with a wedding present. Sometimes nothing is added, but usually you write "Best wishes" or "All best wishes for your happiness." If you have no visiting card at hand, write the same message on a blank card provided by the store, and sign it. If you are older than the bride you sign it "John and Mary Friendly"—friends of the same age simply write "John and Mary." If you use a visiting card and are a friend of the bride's parents or the groom's, you would write "With best wishes from" and place it so that "Mr. and Mrs. Your Name" engraved on your card forms the signature. Unless you are certain that the bride knows your address, be sure that it is included.

WHAT TO WEAR TO A WEDDING

The choice of clothes always depends upon the size and time of the wedding and the customary practices of the community. Wedding guests wear simpler clothes today than they used to.

At very large daytime weddings, correct clothes for men guests used to be gray striped trousers with a cutaway coat or the less formal black sack suit. Today this is unheard of except possibly at state weddings. Men wear nothing more formal than plain business suits, usually dark blue or dark gray. During hot weather, especially at simple seashore and country weddings, light suits or white or light gray flannel trousers with plain flannel coats are suitable. The sports coat is as out of place for a guest as it would be for a bridegroom!

In certain cities, especially in the South where formal evening weddings are customary, the tuxedo is often worn. In simpler communities, men wear plain navy-blue suits on all dress occasions in the evening as well as during the day.

As a general rule, at a formal evening wedding the women wear low-neck-and-no-sleeves evening dresses, with flowers or clips or hair ornaments or perhaps a lace scarf over their hair and shoulders in church. At a very simple wedding in the evening or during the day, they wear afternoon dresses, with small, becoming hats, a flower, or a hair ornament.

When not going to the reception, choose clothes that are habitually worn to church.

Children always wear their best party clothes.

Those in mourning should lighten it on this occasion by changing to lavender or white, or a subdued color. Or they may brighten their costumes by adding a touch of color in trim or accessory rather than casting a pall of gloom with unrelieved black.

AT THE CHURCH

On entering the church you go to the back of the center aisle and wait until one of the ushers comes up to you. If you are a member of either family or a very intimate friend of the bride or the groom, you tell him your name. If it is a wedding at which those to sit in the pews in front of the ribbons have been sent cards with a pew number, he will ask you for your card. At a wedding without pew cards he will ask your name and look on his "in front of the ribbons" list in order to seat you. If you say nothing to indicate that you should be seated in front, he will ask you whether you are a friend of the bride or of the groom, in order to seat you on her or his side of the aisle. In any case, a lady puts her hand on the inside of his proffered arm, and he escorts her to a seat. A gentleman alone walks beside the usher, or if he comes with a lady, he follows the usher and the lady unless there is room for the three of them to walk abreast.

AISLE SEAT NOT RELINQUISHED

If you have arrived early enough to be given an aisle seat, there is one rule of etiquette that is a seeming contradiction to politeness and therefore important to know: It is entirely proper for you to keep your aisle seat, no matter who or how many enter the pew later. Now and then an inconsiderate latecomer, seeing someone sitting on the aisle, unfairly demands, "Move up, please." Nine out of ten well-bred people do so instinctively and find themselves pushed along to the sixth seat in. To stand up where you are and to make room for the latecomers to pass you and take their places farther in is all that is required by etiquette, even though the one on the aisle be a young man and the newcomer an elderly woman. In other words, aisle seats at a wedding are held exactly as reserved seats are held in a theater.

GREETING OTHER GUESTS

At a wedding it is proper to smile and nod to people you know—even to talk briefly in a very low voice to a friend sitting next to you. But when you find yourself among strangers, you just sit quietly until the processional starts.

A STRANGER TO THE RITUAL

In most Protestant churches the congregation rises and stands throughout the service, although in some parts of our country it is the custom to remain seated. Whatever the sect, when you are in a church of a religion other than your own, observe those in front of you: stand if they stand, kneel if they kneel, and sit if they sit.

When the service is over and the recessional has passed by, those in the pews farther back must wait in their places until the immediate families in the front pews have left. If you wait until those around you start to leave, you will be sure of not making any mistake.

FROM CHURCH TO RECEPTION

When invited to the reception—if it is to follow the church ceremony—you are expected to go directly from the church to wherever the reception is to be held. But do give the bridal party a little while to arrange for wedding pictures and form the receiving line. No provision is ever made for taking any of the guests from the church to the house. You go in your own car, or you call a taxi, or if the distance is short, you walk.

AT THE RECEPTION

A woman arriving at the reception leaves her coat in the dressing room if she chooses to, but she does not take off her hat or gloves. Men always remove coats and hats. Then they go to the door of the room in which the reception is held. If there is an announcer, he asks each guest, "What name, please?" Guests give their names with title. If he says nothing, they say to him, "Miss Pauline Panic" or "Mrs. John Jones" or "Dr. Henry Roberts." He then repeats in a clear rather than loud voice, "Miss Pauline Panic," and she starts down the line.

The bride's mother will be standing closest to you. She offers you her hand, smiles, and if you are unknown to her, she says, "How do you do." If she knows you, she says whatever is suitable. In the first place, you also say, "How do you do"; in the second, you reply to what she says to you. If she says, "I am very glad to see you," you answer, "Thank you," or "It was very kind of you to invite me," and add something pleasant about the bride, the day, or the wedding in general. You shake hands with the groom's mother too, whether you are introduced to her or not. Even if you know both of the mothers very well, there is no time to say more than perhaps something such as "What a lovely day Mary and John have for the wedding!" or "How beautiful Mary looks!" There is, however, one real rule: Do not launch into a conversation about yourself, how you feel or look, what happened to you, or what you wore when you were married! Your subject should be confined to the young couple themselves, their wedding, their future.

Above all, be brief in order not to keep those behind waiting longer than necessary. If you have anything particular to tell them, you can return later when there is no longer a line. But even then, any long conversation is out of place.

You then move along with the queue of guests who are waiting to greet the bride and groom. You congratulate the groom, but you wish the bride happiness, because it is a breach of good manners to congratulate a bride on having secured a husband.

If you are in doubt about being known to either of them, you give your name, shake hands with the bride, and add, "I hope you'll be very happy!" Then you shake hands with the groom and say, "Congratulations, and all good wishes." If the bride does not introduce you because she is being greeted by someone following you, and the groom seems to be trying to remember your name, you tell him who you are. Otherwise, you don't.

In the excitement of the day the bride and groom may easily forget the names even of their best friends, and they are quite likely not to remember Aunt Mary, who last visited ten years ago. It is thoughtful for a guest to mention her name even though she thinks that the couple knows her. Never choose this moment to play "Guess who I am," as some unbelievably inconsiderate people do.

If you have been invited to bring a friend who is unknown to the bride and groom, you should introduce the friend to them both.

You greet any of the bridesmaids with whom you are acquainted. Otherwise you walk on—or smile perhaps if you happen to be looking directly at one of them who also looks at you. But there is no chance to stop and really talk to anyone unless you arrived early.

The bride's father sometimes stands beside his wife, but he usually circulates among his guests just as he would at a ball or any other party where he is host. Therefore, you speak to him either on your arrival or, as at other important occasions, whenever you encounter him acting as host.

Although the groom's father is a guest, it is certainly courteous—especially if he is a stranger—to introduce yourself and tell him how well you like his son or his new daughter-in-law or, best of all, both.

After greeting the bride and groom, you look around for friends of your own. If you see no one whom you know well enough to join, the best thing to do is to make your way slowly and nonchalantly to wherever refreshments are being served.

You take your time to look at the table and then either ask one of the waiters to serve you or help yourself to what you want. You can linger and nibble as long as you like or just sit down and watch people. And you may speak to anyone who is alone and looks willing to be spoken to.

A SIT-DOWN BREAKFAST

If you are a stranger at a sit-down breakfast, you cannot very well join a group of people whom you do not know. Therefore, it is best to sit down at an unoccupied table and let others join you. If you wait until every table has several people sitting at it, you have no alternative but to run the risk of making yourself an unwelcome intruder.

WHEN YOU MAY LEAVE THE RECEPTION

When you want to leave you just do so. It is not necessary or even polite to attract attention to your going if it means you will distract the hostess from her duties in the receiving line or from her other responsibilities. At a small, informal wedding, however, or if you are a close friend of the family, you should seek her out to bid her good-bye.

In the [illegible] and [illegible] they [illegible] not to remember [illegible] for [illegible] as [illegible]

[illegible] to the [illegible] both.

[illegible] you are acquainted. Otherwise [illegible] stop and [illegible] to [illegible] each.

The [illegible] where he [illegible] at other [illegible] occasions [illegible] tion.

Although the [illegible] you [illegible] you [illegible] himself and [illegible] you'll [illegible]

[illegible] your [illegible] best thing [illegible] everyone [illegible]

You [illegible] the [illegible] and [illegible] spoken.

[illegible]

[illegible] down [illegible] every [illegible] to the [illegible]

[illegible]

When [illegible] to [illegible] notice [illegible] to your [illegible] notices [illegible] friend of the family [illegible]

Part NINE

ON THE SUBJECT OF INVITATIONS

50

Invitations to weddings and receptions

The engraved forms of invitations and announcements that we use are almost as unchangeably fixed as are the letters of the alphabet. The third-person wording of an invitation and the replies of acceptance or regret have remained almost unchanged throughout countless years. It is true we no longer "present our compliments" and invite our neighbors to come in "for a dish of tea." On the other hand, third-person invitations to a formal wedding and reception are worded and engraved exactly as they have always been.

All formal invitations are recognized as such because they are worded in the third person, and their answers of acceptances or regrets are invariably written by hand in this same form. The words must be placed on specified lines and centered as evenly as possible. Names of hosts belong on the first line, the "request the pleasure of" on the second, the name of the guest on the third, and so on. Although this form of reply serves to baffle and dismay many people, actually, once learned, it is far simpler than any other. There is no reason to give excuses or regrets, and the only change in wording is the name of the person you are sending it to and the date.

Invitations to the largest and most elaborate of weddings consist of an invitation to the church ceremony, a card of admission or "pew card," and an invitation to the reception. But many variations are possible and perfectly correct, as we shall see.

When a guest is expected to attend the church service only, no invitation to the reception is enclosed.

If the wedding is to be in a very small church or chapel and the reception in a very big house or club, then many will receive invitations to the reception and few to the ceremony.

If it happens that not only the church but also the reception is limited to a small number who are sent handwritten invitations or are given oral invitations, then engraved announcements in place of invitations of any kind may be sent to the friends who could not be included, as well as to acquaintances.

The invitations to a large wedding are sent three weeks beforehand; those to a simpler wedding can be mailed as late as ten days before the wedding day.

See Chapters Fifty and Fifty-one for wedding announcements and reception invitations.

CORRECT STYLE

Correct invitations to any wedding, whatever its size, are engraved on the first page of a double sheet of heavy paper, ivory or white, either plain or with a raised margin called a plate-mark or panel. The invitation may be about five and a half inches wide by seven and three-eighths inches deep, or slightly smaller, and it is folded once for insertion into its envelope. Or it may be about four and three-eighths by five and three-fourths inches and go into the envelope without folding. The fashion varies from time to time, and other sizes may be used according to the current custom.

The engraving may be in whichever lettering style the bride prefers among the several offered her by the stationer.

Should the family of the bride's father have a coat of arms, this is one time when it is proper to have it (or just the crest) embossed without color at top center of the sheet. When the invitations are sent out by the bride's mother (or any woman alone), a coat of arms is not used. If the family has no coat of arms, the invitation bears no device of any kind. But if it does, plain script is the best taste for the engraving.

THE INNER ENVELOPE

Two envelopes are definitely associated with wedding invitations. The inner envelope has no mucilage on the flap and is addressed to Mr. and Mrs. Brown with neither first name nor address. Then it is put into an outer "mailing envelope," addressed side toward the flap. This envelope is then addressed by hand.

The names of children under thirteen are written on the inner envelope, "Joan, Robert, and Frederick," and inserted in an envelope addressed to "Miss and the Messrs. Greatlake" or "Miss Joan Greatlake" and below "Robert and Frederick Greatlake."

THE OUTER ENVELOPE

In all formal correspondence it is in bad taste to abbreviate the state name. Neither does one use initials for the first name—"Mr. and Mrs. Harold T. James" is correct rather than "Mr. and Mrs. H. T. James." When the middle name is known, that should be written out also.

When every member of a family under one roof is included in the invitation, the envelope may be addressed:

Mr. and Mrs. Joseph Truehart and Family

A daughter's name may be written below her parents'—"Miss Helen Truehart," or "The Misses Truehart." Boys over twelve or thirteen, however, are more correctly sent separate invitations.

INVITATIONS TO GUESTS UNKNOWN TO THE BRIDE OR GROOM

A girl may properly ask a bride if she may bring her fiancé to the wedding, if it will cause no inconvenience. If the bride has plenty of invitations, she should obtain the man's name and address and send him a separate one. If she has a limited number or cannot get his address, she may write his name below that of his fiancée on the inner envelope and enclose it in an outer envelope addressed to the girl only. This would also be done if the bride tells some of her friends to "bring an escort."

USHERS' AND BRIDESMAIDS' INVITATIONS

Although it may seem unnecessary, it is thoughtful to send invitations to members of the bridal party as mementos. These invitations are addressed exactly as they are to the other guests.

RETURN ADDRESSES

There are three excellent reasons for placing a return address on a wedding invitation, and, so far as I know, no very valid reason for omitting it. First, the Post Office Department requests that all first-class mail carry a return address. Second, it provides the wedding guest with a definite address to which to send a gift. Third, it also provides an address to which the guest may send a reply, especially when no R.S.V.P. is found on the invitation. Very often the only address in evidence is that of the church, or the club or hotel at which the reception is to be held.

The practice of stamping the address without ink on the back flap is somewhat helpful, but many people never notice it and discard the envelope before they think to look for the information there. Therefore, regardless of the many years in which it was considered in bad taste to put the return address on the envelope, I believe that it is time to change the rule, and I recommend that all stationers, at the request of their customers, put a legible return address on the back flap of the envelope (rather than in the front-upper-left corner, as on business envelopes).

FOLDING AND INSERTING

When preparing to send out the invitations, address all the envelopes first. An envelope-sized invitation is inserted in the inner envelope, folded edge down, with the engraved side toward the flap. An invitation designed to fit an envelope half its size will require a second fold, which should be made with the engraving inside. This is then inserted, folded edge down, into the envelope. With the unsealed flap of this filled inner envelope away from you, insert it in the mailing envelope. If the invitation is folded, all insertions (such as the reception card or pew card) are placed inside the second fold with the type facing the flap of the envelope. If the invitation is not folded a second time, the cards are inserted in front of it (nearest you), with the reception card next to the invitaion and any smaller cards in front of that.

Engravers generally use tissue sheets to protect the pages from the fresh ink. These tissues may be removed, but many stationers recommend that they be kept to prevent the ink from smearing.

WORDING OF INVITATIONS TO THE WEDDING

The wording of the wedding invitation varies as little as the conventions governing its size and mailing. For example, the invitation to the ceremony itself should always request "the honour"—spelled with a "u" —of your "presence" and never the "pleasure" of your "company." It is the invitation to the reception that requests the pleasure of your company. But it is perfectly proper for communicants of the Roman Catholic Church who so wish to use a form in which the phrase "at the marriage of" is replaced by "at the Marriage in Christ of"; and where appropriate there is added beneath the name of the bridegroom the lines "and your participation in the offering of the Nuptial Mass."

In the examples of correct wording, spacing, and styles of engraving that will be given, it is important to note the omission of punctuation, except after abbreviations and initials, and when phrases requiring separation by punctuation occur in the same line.

GENERAL FORMS

The following illustrations show proper forms for wedding invitations.

The wording of an invitation to a house wedding gives a house address in place of the name of a church, and R.S.V.P. is added at bottom left.

Mr. and Mrs. Charles Robert Oldname

request the honour of your presence

at the marriage of their daughter

Pauline Marie

to

Mr. John Frederick Hamilton

Saturday, the twenty-ninth of April

at four o'clock

Church of the Heavenly Rest

New York

Doctor and Mrs. John Huntington Smith

request the honour of

Miss Pauline Town's

presence at the marriage of their daughter

Mary Katherine

to

Mr. James Smartlington

Tuesday, the first of November

at twelve o'clock

St. John's Church

WEDDING AND RECEPTION INVITATION IN ONE

Occasionally, when every guest is invited to both ceremony and reception, the invitation to the reception or to the breakfast is included in the invitation to the ceremony.

Mrs. Alexander Oldname
requests the honour of your presence
at the marriage of her daughter
Barbara
to
Mr. James Town, junior
Tuesday, the twenty-first of October
at three o'clock
Church of the Resurrection
Ridgemont, New York
and afterwards at the reception
Bright Meadows

R.s.v.p.

WHEN THE BRIDE HAS A STEPFATHER

When the bride's own father is not living and she has a stepparent, or her mother has divorced and remarried, the invitations are worded:

Mr. and Mrs. John Huntington Smith
request the honour of your presence
at the marriage of her daughter
Mary Alice Towne
etc.

WHEN THE BRIDE'S MOTHER IS WIDOWED OR DIVORCED

If the bride's mother is giving the wedding alone:

Mrs. Bertram Jones
requests the honour of your presence
at the marriage of her daughter
Helen Jeffrey Jones
etc.

INVITATION TO A WEDDING IN THE HOUSE OF A FRIEND

Invitations are issued by the parents of the bride even though the wedding takes place at a house other than their own. The names of the parents at the head of the invitation means that *they* are giving the wedding (and probably assuming all expenses) but not in their own house.

Mr. and Mrs. Richard Littlehouse
request the honour of your presence
at the marriage of their daughter
Eleanor
to
Doctor Frederic Robinson
Saturday, the fifth of November
at four o'clock
at the residence of Mr. and Mrs. James Sterlington
Tuxedo Park, New York

R.s.v.p.

WHEN THE BRIDE'S PARENTS ARE DIVORCED

When the bride's parents are divorced, the wedding invitations are issued in the name of the parent who pays for and acts as host at the reception. In the event that relations are so friendly that they share the expenses and act as co-hosts, both names should appear on the invitation.

Mr. and Mrs. Henry Smith
(or Mrs. Jones Doe, if she has not remarried)
and
Mr. and Mrs. Robert Doe
(or Mr. Robert Doe)
request the honour of your presence
at the marriage of
Mary Doe
to
William Hughes, etc.

The bride's mother's name, whether she has remarried or not, appears first. If neither parent is remarried the wording would be:

Mrs. Jones Doe
and
Mr. Robert Doe
request the honour of your presence
at the marriage of their daughter
Mary
etc.

WHEN THE BRIDE IS AN ORPHAN

It is important to remember that ordinarily good taste does not permit "Miss" or "Mrs." as titles before the bride's name, but the cases that follow are exceptions.

If the bride has no relatives and the wedding is given by friends, the wording is:

Mr. and Mrs. John Neighbor
request the honour of your presence
at the marriage of
Miss Elizabeth Orphan
to
Mr. John Henry Bridegroom
etc.

If she has brothers, the oldest one customarily sends out her wedding invitations and announcements in his name. If another relative has taken the place of a parent, his or her name is used. When the bride is living with a married brother or sister, and that couple plans to give the wedding, the invitations go out in their name. The bride whose several sisters or brothers are younger than she may prefer to send her invitations in her own name. The following form is used:

The honour of your presence
is requested
at the marriage of
Miss Elizabeth Orphan
to
etc.

WHEN THE BRIDE IS A WIDOW OR DIVORCÉE

Invitations to the marriage of a young widow or divorcée are sent in the name of her parents exactly as were the invitations for her first wedding, except that her name, instead of being simply "Priscilla," is now written "Priscilla Banks Loring," thus:

Doctor and Mrs. Maynard Banks
request the honour of your presence
at the marriage of their daughter
Priscilla Banks Loring
to
etc.

A more mature woman, or one whose parents are dead, may send out her own invitations:

The honour of your presence
is requested
at the marriage of
Mrs. John Kerr Simons
to
etc.

This same woman would drop the "John" and use "Mrs. Kerr Simons" if she were a divorcée.

The fact that the groom has been divorced does not change the invitation to, or announcement of, his new bride's marriage.

WHEN THE BRIDE HAS A PROFESSIONAL NAME

If the bride has a career for which she uses a professional name, she probably has business friends whom she would like to invite but who might not recognize "Pauline Marie Oldname." The invitations may therefore have her professional name engraved in very small letters and in parentheses under her Christian name:

Pauline Marie
(Pat Bond)

to

Mr. John Frederick Hamilton

This is most practically done by having the name (Pat Bond) added to the plate after the order for regular invitations has been completed. As many invitations as are to go to her professional friends are then struck off with this addition.

WHEN PRINCIPALS ARE IN THE SERVICE

On the wedding invitations, the name of a bridegroom whose rank is below Lt. Commander in the Navy or Captain in the Army, is given this way:

John Strong
2nd Lieutenant, United States Army

or

Robert Todd
Ensign, United States Navy

The title of higher ranking officers precedes their name, and the service may or may not be included on the line below.

Colonel John Spring
United States Air Force

The name of a noncommissioned or an enlisted man in the armed forces is engraved "John Strong," and "Signal Corps, U.S.N.R.," or "Coast Artillery, U.S.A.," or whatever his particular designation is, in smaller type directly beneath the name on the wedding invitations. Or if the bride chooses to include "Private First Class, U.S.A.," or "Apprentice Seaman, U.S.N.R.," she may do so.

The name of the bride who is in the armed forces is engraved:

marriage of their daughter
Alice Mary
Lieutenant, Women's Army Corps

When the bride's father is in the armed forces and absent on duty, his name appears as follows:

Major (overseas) and Mrs. John Jones
request the honour of your presence, etc.

An officer in the Reserves does not use his title unless he is on active duty.

High-ranking regular officers continue to use their titles and include their service on the line below with "retired" following the service.

General George Harmon
United States Army, retired

THE DOUBLE-WEDDING INVITATION

Mr. and Mrs. Henry Smartlington
request the honour of your presence
at the marriage of their daughters
Marian Helen
to
Mr. Judson Jones
and
Amy Caroline
to
Mr. Herbert Scott Adams
Saturday, the tenth of November
at four o'clock
Trinity Church

The elder sister's name is given first.

It is unusual but not unheard of for two brides who have been life-long friends—or who are cousins, but with different names—to have a double wedding.

The wording of such invitations must necessarily include the surnames of both parents and brides:

Mr. and Mrs. Henry Smartlington
and
Mr. and Mrs. Arthur Lane
request the honour of your presence
at the marriage of their daughters
Marian Helen Smartlington
to
Mr. Judson Jones
and
Mary Alice Lane
to
Mr. John Gray
etc.

WHEN THE BRIDEGROOM'S FAMILY GIVES THE WEDDING

When the young bride comes as a stranger from abroad, or from any distance, without her family, it is entirely proper that the bridegroom's family give the wedding and send the invitations in their name. This is the only other case where the title "Miss" is used.

Mr. and Mrs. John Henry Pater
request the honour of your presence
at the marriage of
Miss Marie Mersailles
to
their son
John Henry Pater, junior
etc.

Announcements, but not invitations, may be sent from abroad by her own family.

INCLUDING THE BRIDEGROOM'S FAMILY IN THE INVITATION

On occasion the bridegroom's family, even though the bride's parents are alive and nearby, share in, or even pay for the major part of the reception, which is sometimes held in their home. When this occurs, it seems only fair that their names should be included on the invitation, since they are actually co-hosts. The wording would be:

Mr. and Mrs. Charles Goodman
and
Mr. and Mrs. George Gonzalez
request the pleasure of your company
at the wedding reception of
Julia Goodman
and
Roberto Gonzalez
etc.

A separate invitation to the wedding ceremony should be sent in the name of the bride's parents.

In some foreign countries it is customary for the groom's family to be included in the wedding invitation also, and the invitation is a double one—in the name of the bride's family on the left inside page and the groom's parents on the right. This form is sometimes followed by these nationalities here in the United States, and in many ways is a thoughtful and friendly custom.

Mr. and Mrs. Bruno Cairo
request the honour of your presence
at the marriage of their daughter
Julia
to
Mr. Francisco Conti
etc.

Mr. and Mrs. Roberto Conti
request the honour of your presence
at the marriage of their son
Francisco
to
Miss Julia Cairo
etc.

PERSONAL INVITATIONS

The most flattering wedding invitation possible is a note personally written by the bride. Even though she is sending engraved invitations to most of the guests, she may, as a special gesture of affection, send a few handwritten ones to those she cares most about.

Dear Aunt Jane,

Dick and I are to be married at Christ Church at noon on Thursday the tenth. We hope you and Uncle Dick will come to the church and afterward to the reception at the home of our friend, Mrs. Tilden, at Two South Beach Street.

With much love from us both,

Affectionately,
Helen

This type of note is also written when the wedding is to be very small, or when it is held on short notice. In these circumstances, telephone invitations are also perfectly correct.

WHEN THE BRIDEGROOM IS ABOUT TO RECEIVE A DEGREE

When the bridegroom is a medical student at the time the invitations are sent, but will be a graduate by the date of the wedding, his name should be written with his title—"Doctor John Jones." This would hold true for any man in a profession in which the title is ordinarily used.

WHEN WEDDING DATE IS CHANGED

It happens on occasion that the date of the wedding must be changed after the invitations have already been engraved. To order a new set of invitations would involve an enormous and unnecessary expense. Instead, the bride may enclose a small printed card saying, "The date of the wedding has been changed from . . . to. . . ." or, if the number of guests is small, she may write the same information on a small card by hand.

WHEN A WEDDING IS POSTPONED INDEFINITELY

When a wedding must be postponed indefinitely after the invitations have been mailed, it is necessary to send the news out as fast as possible. If it is possible to have cards printed in time, that is the best solution. If not, the bride and members of her family and bridal party who can help must send out handwritten notes at once. The wording, depending on the cause, would be:

Owing to the sudden death of
Mrs. Henry Miller
The marriage of her daughter
Sarah
to
Mr. Robert Sage
has been postponed

WORDING OF INVITATIONS TO THE RECEPTION

The correct form for the invitation to a wedding reception depends upon the combined plans for wedding and reception. That is, the invitation sent to guests who are also invited to the church differs from that used when the ceremony is private and invitations are sent out only for the reception.

INVITATIONS TO A RECEPTION FOLLOWING THE CEREMONY

The invitation to the breakfast or reception following the church ceremony is usually engraved on a card to match the paper and engraving of the church invitation. If the latter is folded for the envelope, then the card is a little smaller than half the full size of the invitation. If it is to go with the smaller invitation that does not fold, it may be from two and one-half to three inches high by three and one-half to four inches wide. The most commonly used form is this:

Reception

immediately following the ceremony

Essex County Country Club

West Orange

The favour of a reply is requested
Llewellyn Park, West Orange

Although the longer form below is perhaps better suited to the unfolded church invitation because of the larger size of the reception card, it is always perfectly correct.

Mr. and Mrs. John Huntington Smith
request the pleasure of

Miss Pauline Town's

company at the reception
following the ceremony
43 Park Avenue

R.s.v.p.

The forms R.s.v.p. and R.S.V.P. are both correct. In diplomatic circles the capital letters are the correct form.

INVITATION TO THE RECEPTION ONLY

When the ceremony is private and a big reception follows, the invitations to the ceremony are given orally, and general invitations to the reception sent out for a later hour. The size and style of these invitations are exactly the same as those to the wedding itself. The wording follows this form:

Mr. and Mrs. John Huntington Smith
request the pleasure of your company
at the wedding reception
of their daughter
Millicent Jane
and
Mr. Sidney Strothers
Tuesday, the first of November
at half after twelve o'clock
55 Clark Lane
Hillsdale

R.s.v.p.

A RECEPTION FOLLOWING A HOUSE WEDDING

When the reception follows a house wedding, it is not necessary to send any sort of separate invitation as it is assumed that those attending the wedding will stay on.

ENCLOSURES

CARDS FOR RESERVED PEWS

To the family and those intimate friends who are to be seated in specially designated pews, a card (approximately two by three inches) may be enclosed, with "Pew No. " engraved and the number filled in by hand. The style matches that of the invitation.

The more usual and less expensive custom is for the mother of the bride and the mother of the bridegroom each to write on her personal visiting card the number of the pew that each member of the family and each intimate friend is to occupy.

Pew No. 7

Mrs. John Huntington Smith

600 East Fifty-Seventh Street

A similar card for a reserved enclosure consisting of a certain number of front pews—although for no special pew—and inscribed "Within the ribbon" may be enclosed with the invitations. Or "Within the ribbon" may be written on a visiting card and included with the invitation.

Pew cards are often sent or given in person after acceptances have been received, when the families of the bride and groom know how many reserved seats will be needed.

ADMISSION CARDS

Except in the case of a wedding held in a cathedral or other church which attracts sightseers, admission cards are no longer used. If it is necessary, a card of approximately two by three inches is engraved in the same style as the invitations:

Please present this card

at

The Washington Cathedral

Saturday, the first of August

Only the holders of these cards will be admitted to the church at the time of the wedding.

AT HOME CARDS

If the bride and groom want their friends to know what their address is to be, an At Home card is included with the invitation. These cards have traditionally followed these forms:

At home

after the fifteenth of November

3842 Olympia Drive

Houston 19, Texas

Or:

Will be at home

after October sixteenth

1730 Taylor Street

Del Monte, California

The size of the cards is about four by two and three-fourths inches, slightly smaller than the reception card. *For At Home cards to accompany wedding announcements, see Chapter Fifty-one.*

Many people receiving these cards, however, put them away, intending to enter them in an address book or file. Later they come across the card, only to find they have entirely forgotten *who* would be at home at 1730 Taylor Street after October 16. Even though the couple are not married at the time the invitation is sent, in the interests of helpfulness and practicality, these cards should be engraved:

Mr. and Mrs. Howard
will be at home
etc.

INVITATIONS TO A BELATED WEDDING RECEPTION

A belated wedding reception is frequently held some time after the ceremony—perhaps after the honeymoon, or on occasion, even later when the couple returns after an extended absence. Although the party is held to celebrate the wedding, a true "wedding reception" immediately follows the ceremony, and the invitation for the belated reception omits the word "wedding."

These invitations may be formally engraved as follows:

Mr. and Mrs. Henry Peterson
request the pleasure of your company
at a reception
in honor of
Mr. and Mrs. Floyd Smith
on . . . .

If you prefer to send a less formal invitation, you may write the necessary information on an informal and at the top write "In honor of" the young couple.

Dinner for Nancy and Joe
Greenpoint Yacht Club
Horizon, New York

Mr. + Mrs. John Carr Doe
Friday, September 17th
7:00 P.M.

R.S.V.P.
6 Ridge Street

Formal

51

Wedding announcements

When the number of guests who can be accommodated at the marriage service or the reception is limited, announcements are sent to those friends of both families who would otherwise have been invited to be present. They require no gift or acknowledgment except what your own interest and impulse suggest. Announcements are never sent to anyone who has been invited to the wedding or the reception. And while they should always be sent as soon after the wedding as possible, there is no restriction on how long afterwards they may be sent. For instance, parents might wish to announce a daughter's secret marriage as much as six months or a year later.

CORRECT STYLE AND WORDING

The form of the wedding announcement resembles the form of the wedding invitation in almost everything except wording. The note paper, the styles of engraving, the use of a crest, the two envelopes, the manner of addressing the envelopes are all the same. *See Chapter Forty-nine.*

The standard wording is this:

Mr. and Mrs. John Fairplay
have the honour of
announcing the marriage of their daughter
Madeleine Anne
to
Mr. George Followes Highseas
Ensign United States Navy
Tuesday, the twenty-seventh of March
One thousand nine hundred and sixty-five
Washington, D. C.

Three forms of phrasing are equally correct: "have the honour to announce," or "have the honour of announcing," or merely the one word "announce." Although "Tuesday, April 24, 1965" is not incorrect, the use of "Tuesday, the twenty-fourth of April" on one line and "One thousand nine hundred sixty-five" on the next is most formal.

The variations in wording necessitated by special circumstances (when the bride has a stepfather, or professional name, etc.) correspond to the variations in wedding invitations (*see Chapter Forty-nine*) with these few exceptions:

Whenever possible, announcements go out in the name of the bride's nearest relatives, whether they have been present at the wedding or not. For example, invitations to a wedding given by the bridegroom's parents carry their names, whereas announcements of the same marriage carry the names of the bride's parents.

Announcements for a young widow's marriage are the same as for a first wedding:

Mr. and Mrs. Maynard Banks
announce the marriage of their daughter
Priscilla Banks Loring
etc.

The announcement of the marriage of a widow of maturer years reads differently:

Mrs. William Phillip Hoyt
and
Mr. Worthington Adams
announce their marriage
on Monday, the second of November
One thousand nine hundred and sixty-five
at Saratoga Springs
New York

The parents of a young divorcée may announce her second marriage in the same form as if she were a widow.

Mr. and Mrs. Harvey Strong
announce the marriage of their daughter
Mary Strong Brooks
etc.

Or a divorcée may, with her husband, announce her own marriage.

Mrs. Strong Brooks
and
Mr. Robert Hanson
announce their marriage
on Saturday, the tenth of May
etc.

The bride who is an orphan and the bridegroom may announce their own marriage this way:

Miss Elizabeth Orphan
and
Mr. John Henry Bridegroom
announce their marriage
etc.

When the bride comes from a foreign country, the bridegroom's parents may announce the marriage in the name of the bride's parents. If they do not wish to do this, the announcement may be worded exactly as that of the bride who is an orphan.

If the wedding was given by a relative or friend, the announcement may be made in this way:

Mr. and Mrs. John Neighbor
announce the marriage of
Miss Elizabeth Orphan
etc.

"AT HOME" NOTICE

When announcements are sent, the At Home notice may be engraved in the lower left-hand corner.

After the first of December
25 Elm Street, Greattown

Or cards in the same form as those used with wedding invitations may be enclosed (*see Chapter Fifty*).

Mr. and Mrs. John Newlywed
will be at home
after November twelfth
25 Elm Street
Greattown

52

Other formal invitations

All formal invitations at one time were engraved on white cards—either plain or plate-marked like those for wedding receptions—or written by hand on personal notepaper. There are now fine printing processes available which are equally acceptable.

Formal third-person invitations are sometimes written on paper headed by a very small monogram, but are never engraved on paper headed by an address. If the family has a coat of arms, it or the crest may be embossed without color on engraved invitations.

The size of the card of invitation varies with personal preference. The most graceful proportion is three units in height to four in width, or four high by three wide.

The lettering is a matter of personal choice, but the plainer the design the safer. Punctuation is used only when words requiring separation occur on the same line, and in certain abbreviations, such as R.S.V.P. The time should never be given as "nine-thirty" but as "half past nine o'clock" or, the more conservative form, "half after nine o'clock."

If the dance or dinner or other entertainment is to be given at one address and the hostess lives at another, both addresses are always given.

The replies are addressed to the person, or persons, from whom the invitation comes. The full first name, rather than initials, is used, and the name of the state is also written out in full. A return address should appear on the back flap of the envelope.

BALLS AND DANCES

TO A PRIVATE DANCE

The forms most often used are the following:

Mr. and Mrs. Harold Gilding

request the pleasure of

Miss Sally Waring's

company at a small dance

Monday, the first of January

at ten o'clock

400 Lake Shore Drive

R.s.v.p.

The expression "small dance" is sometimes used no matter what the size of the ball, but it is not necessary.

Mr. and Mrs. Sidney Oldname

request the pleasure of your company

at a dance

Monday evening, January the third

at ten o'clock

The Fitz-Cherry

Kindly send response to
Brookmeadows,
Long Island

Even when the ball is given for a debutante daughter, her name does not necessarily appear, and the forms just shown may be used.

Other proper invitations for debutante parties are these:

Mr. and Mrs. Davis Jefferson

At Home

Monday, the third of January

at ten o'clock

Town and Country Club

Kindly send reply to
Three Vernon Square

Dancing

THE INVITATION TO A PUBLIC BALL

The word "ball" is rarely used except in an invitation to a public one—or at least a semipublic one—such as may be given by a committee for a charity or by a club or association of some sort. For example:

The Entertainment Committee of the Greenwood Club
requests the pleasure of your company
at a Ball
to be held at the clubhouse
on the evening of Thursday, the seventh of November
at ten o'clock
for the benefit of
The Neighborhood Hospital
Tickets five dollars

INVITATIONS TO A DEBUTANTE ASSEMBLY

An invitation to present the debutante at an assembly reads:

The Committee of the Westchester Cotillion

invites

Mr. and Mrs. David S. Williams

to present

Miss Penelope Williams

at the Cotillion

on Friday, the ninth of September

at ten o'clock

Shenorock Shore Club

Rye, New York

An invitation to debutantes *not* being presented at the ball reads thus:

The Committee of the Mayfair Assembly

has the honor to extend to

Mrs. David S. Williams

an invitation for her daughter

Miss Penelope Williams

to attend

The Mayfair Assembly Dinner Dance

on

New Year's Eve

Saturday, December 31, 1964

Hotel Pierre Roof

nine o'clock

R.s.v.p.

An invitation to other guests invited to the ball:

The Governors of the Tuxedo Club
invite you to subscribe to
The Autumn Ball
to be held at
The Tuxedo Club
on Saturday, the twenty-second of October
Nineteen hundred and sixty-six
at eleven o'clock
Tuxedo Park, New York

R.s.v.p.

These invitations are accompanied by a card stating the amount of the subscription, where it should be sent, etc. Names of the debutantes being presented, the committee, and sometimes the patrons are printed inside the invitation.

INVITATION TO BE A PATRON

If the list of those invited to become patrons is very long, the correct wording is as follows:

The Committee of the Midwinter Ball
has the honour to invite
Mrs. James Beale
to be a Patron of the Ball
for the benefit of
The Children's Hospital
at the Hotel Grand
Friday evening, the thirtieth of October
at nine o'clock

Usually a card with return envelope is enclosed with the invitation for the convenience of the patron's answer.

INVITATIONS TO RECEPTIONS AND TEAS

Invitations to receptions and teas differ from invitations to balls in that the cards on which they are engraved are usually somewhat smaller. The words "At Home" with capital letters may be changed to "will be at home" with small letters or "at Home" with a small "a." The time is not set at a certain hour, but is limited to a definite period indicated by a beginning and a terminating hour. Also, except for very unusual occasions a man's name does not appear. If the tea is given for a debutante, her name is put under that of her mother, and sometimes under that of her sister or the bride of her brother.

When a reception is held in honor of someone, "In honor of Mr. and Mrs. Robert Fuller, Jr." may be written by hand at the top of the invitation. This is true whether the rest of the invitation is fully engraved, or is a fill-in "card of general invitation."

An invitation to a tea dance:

Mrs. Grantham Jones
Miss Muriel Jones
at Home
on Tuesday, the third of December
from four until seven o'clock
The Hilton Hotel
3751 Wildwood Boulevard *Dancing*

Or to a tea for a debutante:

Mrs. James Town
Mrs. James Town, Junior
Miss Pauline Town
will be at home
Tuesday, the eighth of December
from five until seven o'clock
850 Fifth Avenue

Because afternoon teas are supposedly given by women, Mr. Town's name is omitted from this invitation. Mr. Town shares his wife's responsibility if the party is given in the evening; and if he is present at an afternoon party, he naturally assumes the duties of host.

Probably Mr. Town's name would appear with that of his wife if he were an artist and the reception were given in his studio to view his pictures; or if a reception were given to meet a distinguished guest, such as a bishop or a governor. In this case "In honor of the Right Reverend William Ritual" or "To meet His Excellency the Governor of California" would be engraved at the top of the invitation.

Suitable wording for an evening reception:

To meet the Honorable George Stevens
Mr. and Mrs. James Town
at Home
Tuesday, the eighth of December
from nine until eleven o'clock

THE CARD OF GENERAL INVITATION

Invitations to important entertainments are nearly always specially engraved so that nothing is written except the name of the person invited. But the hostess who entertains frequently will find a card that is partially engraved with spaces left to be filled in by hand very helpful. These cards may serve for dinner, luncheon, dance, or whatever she may care to give.

Since cards of general invitation need not be specially ordered, they are also useful for people who do not wish to go to the expense of having the full form engraved.

Mr. and Mrs. Harold Foster Stevens

request the pleasure of

company at

on

at o'clock

Two Knob Hill

INVITATION BY MORE THAN ONE HOSTESS

There is no rule about the order in which the names of two or more hostesses should appear, but the one at whose house the party will be is usually placed first. Or if one is a great deal older, her name may head the list. The invitation should make very clear where the event is to take place and where the acceptances and regrets are to be sent. For example, if the luncheon is to be at Mrs. White's house, the correct form would be this:

Mrs. Walter David White
Mrs. Henry Edward Black
Mrs. Theodore Jamison Gray
request the pleasure of your company
at luncheon
Tuesday, the tenth of November
at half after one o'clock
123 Sutton Place

R.s.v.p.
Mrs. Walter David White

If, on the other hand, the luncheon is to be at a club or hotel, the form is this:

Mrs. Walter David White
Mrs. Henry Edward Black
Mrs. Theodore Jamison Gray
request the pleasure of your company
at luncheon
Tuesday, the tenth of November
at half after one o'clock
Hotel Carter

R.s.v.p.
Mrs. Walter David White
123 Sutton Place

INVITATION SENT BY AN ORGANIZATION

An example of this type of invitation:

The Alpha Chapter
of
Beta Chi Delta
requests the pleasure of your company
at a reception
on Monday, the twenty-third of February
at four o'clock
at the Beta Chi Delta House
2 Campus Row

INVITATION TO COMMENCEMENT

Each school, college, and university follows its own established customs for Commencement Week. *See Chapter Thirty-nine.*

Of the varying forms of invitation to commencement exercises sent, the following is the most usual:

The President and Faculty
of Hotchkiss College
request the pleasure of your company
at the Commencement Exercises
on Wednesday morning
the twentieth of June
at eleven o'clock
in the Sterling Gymnasium

HANDWRITTEN INVITATIONS

When the formal invitation to dinner or luncheon is written instead of engraved, plain white or cream notepaper or paper stamped with house address or personal device is used. The wording and spacing must follow the engraved models exactly. The invitation must be written by hand—it may not be typewritten.

Mr. and Mrs. John Kindhost
request the pleasure of
Mr. and Mrs. Robert Gilding Jr.'s
company at dinner
on Tuesday, the sixth of December,
at eight o'clock.

If the device stamped on the paper does not contain the address, it is important to write this below the hour. It is never proper for a telephone number to appear on a formal invitation. Note that "Jr." is used when appropriate.

An invitation should not be written like this:

Mr. & Mrs. J. Kindhost request
the pleasure of Mr. & Mrs. James
Town's company at dinner on Tuesday
etc

This incorrect example has three faults:

1. Invitations in the third person must follow the prescribed form, and this does not.

2. The "and" should be written out.

3. The full name "John" should be used instead of the initial "J."

53

Informal invitations

With the exception of invitations to house parties, those sent to out-of-town guests, and those requiring a certain amount of formality, the invitation by note is almost a thing of the past. On informal occasions, the attractively designed and decorated invitations sold for every sort of entertainment are widely used. Many of these are charming, and in the best of taste. The telephone is also a perfectly acceptable means of extending an informal invitation, and nothing needs to be said about the correct form beyond a reminder that you should be perfectly clear about dates and hour and leave your guests in no doubt about what is intended. If you feel that a written invitation is needed, you have a choice of several possibilities. However, as is true with more formal invitations, the informal one should not be typewritten unless the sender is truly unable to write by hand.

VISITING-CARD INVITATIONS

For an informal dance, a tea to meet a guest, or bridge, a lady may use her ordinary visiting card. (*See Chapter Fifty-six for their style and form.*) Because the Post Office will not accept very small envelopes, a practical size should be ordered for visiting cards or other small-sized cards. These larger envelopes, being thinner but of the color and texture of the cards, need not look unmatched.

The following examples are absolutely correct in every detail—including the abbreviations. They should be written, if possible, in black ink.

To meet
Miss Millicent Gordon

Mrs. John Kindhart

Tues. Jan. 7
Dancing at 9. o'ck.
1350 Madison Avenue

Wed. Jan. 8.
Bridge at 2. o'ck.

Mrs. John Kindhart

R. s. v. p. 1350 Madison Avenue

INFORMALS

The use of informals (small folding cards, described in Chapter Fifty-six) for invitations is correct and practical. If the card is engraved with your name, the invitation is written in this way:

Cocktail Buffet

Mr. and Mrs. Allen Burns

Sunday, June 9th
6:30 o'clock

10 Haverstraw Rd.

On informal invitations it is correct to put "regrets only" instead of R.S.V.P. if you prefer.

If the card is monogrammed or unmarked, the informal invitation must include your name, since the recipient may not know by whom it was sent. If the card is going to a close friend, the signature need only be the first name; but if there should be any question whether the receiver knows from which "Lucy" the invitation comes, it is safer to include the last name.

GBT

June 6

Dear Sally,
Could you and Jim join us for a barbecue dinner on Sat. June 12th?

Lucy Brooks

9 Holly St.

THE "SINGLE NOTE" CARD

A useful variation of the informal is an unfolded card, about four and a half by three and a half inches, with the address engraved in the upper right corner and the name slightly above the center, leaving room beneath for the message.

HANDWRITTEN NOTES AND ANSWERS

Informal invitations are those which are written in the second person. Although called informal because they have greater latitude than the utterly prescribed pattern of the third-person invitation and reply, they, too, follow a fairly definite formula. The colon is not used after the form of address in a social note. Use either no punctuation or a comma, as you prefer.

The informal dinner and luncheon invitation is not spaced according to set words on each line, but is just written in two paragraphs. From a younger to an older couple:

January 2

Dear Mrs. Steele

Will you and Mr. Steele have dinner with us on Thursday, the seventh of January, at eight o'clock?

Hoping so much to see you then, I am

Very sincerely,
Caroline Robinson Town

Or to a woman engaged to a man unknown to the writer of this invitation:

January 2

Dear Phyllis

Will you and your fiancé lunch with us this coming Saturday, at one o'clock?

Looking forward to meeting him,

Affectionately,
Caroline Town

Acceptance:

January 5

Dear Mrs. Town

We would be delighted to have dinner with you on Thursday the seventh at eight o'clock.

Thanking you for thinking of us,

Sincerely yours,
Phyllis Steele

Regret:

Dear Mrs. Town

We are so sorry that we cannot accept your kind invitation for Saturday because of another engagement.

With many thanks for thinking of us, and I will bring John over to meet you soon.

Sincerely,
Phyllis Steele

For invitations to a house party, see Chapter Thirty-seven; to an engagement party, see Chapter Forty-one.

REMINDER CARDS AND NOTES

When invitations have been telephoned, cards reminding guests of the occasion are very sensible. People who entertain a great deal have cards engraved with blank spaces to fill in with the word luncheon, dinners, playing bridge, or whatever.

Otherwise you write on your visiting card: "To remind you—Wednesday 10th, 7:30."

To expected houseguests, one perhaps writes a note.

Dear Helen

Just to remind you that we are expecting you and Dick on the sixth.

Love,
Muriel

A SINGLE PERSON'S INVITATIONS

The invitations of someone living alone are the same as those sent out by married couples.

In giving a party of any size, they may use their visiting cards or informals:

Saturday, April 7.
at 4. o'clk.

Mr. Anthony Dauber

To hear Tonini play.

Park Studio

54

Recalling and requesting invitations

If invitations have to be recalled because of illness or for some other reason, the following forms are correct. They are always printed instead of engraved—there being no time for engraving. In an emergency the message may be handwritten or given by telephone.

Owing to the sudden illness of their daughter
Mr. and Mrs. John Huntington Smith
are obliged to recall their invitations
for Tuesday, the tenth of June

When an engagement is broken after the wedding invitations have been issued:

Mr. and Mrs. Benjamin Nottingham
announce that the marriage of their daughter
Mary Katharine
to
Mr. Jerrold Atherton
will not take place

ASKING FOR AN INVITATION

One may never ask for an invitation for oneself anywhere! Nor ordinarily does one ask to bring a houseguest to a meal, unless one knows it is a buffet at which one or two unexpected persons could make no difference.

When regretting an invitation, it is quite all right to explain that you are expecting to have weekend guests. Ordinarily the hostess-to-be says, "I'm sorry!" But if it happens that she is having a big buffet lunch or a tea or cocktail party, she may say, "Do bring them. We would be delighted to have them!"

An invitation for any general entertainment may be asked for a stranger—especially for a houseguest—still more especially for a man.

Dear Mrs. Eminent,

My nephew, David Park, is staying with us. May he come to your dance on Friday?

Very sincerely yours,
Caroline Robinson Town

If the nephew had been a niece instead, Mrs. Town would have added, "If it will be inconvenient for you to include her, please do not hesitate to say so." This would give Mrs. Eminent a chance to answer, if necessary, that her list of men was rather short and that she would be glad to have Mary at the dance if Mrs. Town can find a man to escort her. Most probably Mrs. Town would call Mrs. Eminent on the telephone, which would enable them to discuss the problem, if there were one, and arrive at a solution at once.

A young girl may of course ask her hostess if she may bring a man to her dance; and in fact several men would almost certainly be welcomed!

55

Acceptances and regrets

The form of acceptance or regret depends upon the form of the invitation received, for the degree of formality or informality must be the same. On the telephone, of course, this presents no problems, but for the handwritten answer there are formulas that are invariably used. Once learned, the formal reply is the easiest to write, because no changes or embellishments are necessary other than in the names and the dates.

THE FORMAL ACCEPTANCE OR REGRET

Whether the invitation is to a dance, a dinner, or whatever, the answer is identical, with the exception of the pertinent word—that is, the following form may be used with the substitution of "a dance," etc. for "dinner."

Mr. and Mrs. Donald Lovejoy
accept with pleasure
the kind invitation of
Mr. and Mrs. William Jones Johnson, Jr.
for dinner
on Monday, the tenth of December
at eight o'clock

Also used but not quite so formal is this form:

Mr. and Mrs. Donald Lovejoy
accept with pleasure
Mr. and Mrs. Johnson's
kind invitation for dinner
on Monday, the tenth of December
at eight o'clock

Note that in the first form the full name, including "Jr." when appropriate, must be used, whereas in the second, "Mr. and Mrs. Johnson's" is sufficient.

The formulas for regret:

Mr. and Mrs. Timothy Kerry
regret that they are unable to accept
the kind invitation of
Mr. and Mrs. Harvey Brent Smith
for Monday, the tenth of December

Mr. Sidney Hartford
regrets that he is unable to accept
Mr. and Mrs. Worldly's
kind invitation for dinner
on Monday, the tenth of December

"Monday, December the tenth" is sometimes used, but the wording above is better.

In accepting an invitation, you must repeat the day and hour so that any mistake can be rectified. A guest is thus prevented from arriving on the wrong day or hour. But if you decline an invitation, it is not necessary to repeat the hour.

TO MORE THAN ONE HOSTESS

If the names of two or more hostesses appear on an invitation, the envelope is addressed to the one at whose house the party is to take place; or if it is to be at a club or hotel, to the name and address indicated below the R.S.V.P. (Without such indication, you must address it to all of them at the hotel or club.)

When you write your answer, you repeat the same order of names that appeared on the invitation, no matter how the envelope is to be addressed:

Mrs. Donald Lovejoy
accepts with pleasure
the kind invitation of
Mrs. White and

Mrs. Black and
Mrs. Grey
for Tuesday, the tenth of November
at half after one o'clock

TO A WEDDING

An invitation to the church only requires no answer whatever (except when the wedding is so small that the invitation is a personally written note). The answer to an invitation to the reception or breakfast is written on the first page of a sheet of full-sized letter paper or on fold-over notepaper; and although written by hand, the words must be spaced as though they were engraved.

Acceptance:

Mr. and Mrs. Robert Gilding, Jr.
accept with pleasure
Mr. and Mrs. Smith's
kind invitation for
Tuesday, the first of June

Regret:

Mr. and Mrs. Richard Brown
regret that they are unable to accept
Mr. and Mrs. Smith's
kind invitation for
Tuesday, the first of June

The alternative form is equally acceptable:

the kind invitation of
Mr. and Mrs. Roger James Smith
for Tuesday, the first of June

COMBINATION ACCEPTANCE AND REGRET

It is entirely proper for a wife or husband to take it for granted that either one alone will be welcome at a general wedding reception and to send an acceptance worded as follows:

Mrs. John Brown
accepts with pleasure
Mr. and Mrs. Smith's
kind invitation for
Saturday, the tenth of June
but regrets that
Mr. Brown

will be absent at that time
(*or*
"*will be unable to attend*")

If it were the wife who could not attend, the wording would merely transpose Mr. and Mrs.

FORMULAS FOR OTHER OCCASIONS

TO AN ORGANIZATION

Miss Mary Jones
accepts with pleasure
the kind invitation of
The Alpha Chapter
of
Beta Chi Delta
for Monday afternoon, February 23rd

TO A COMMITTEE

If the name of the committee or its organization is very long or complicated, you may write your reply in the following form:

Mr. and Mrs. Geoffrey Johnson
accept with pleasure
your kind invitation
for a Ball
on Saturday, the first of January

TO A MULTIPLE DEBUT

Doctor and Mrs. Ronald Graham
Miss Joan Graham
accept with pleasure
your kind invitation
for a dinner dance
Saturday, February tenth
at nine o'clock

INFORMAL REPLIES

When an invitation is sent on a visiting card or an informal, the reply may be telephoned or written briefly on your own card.

VISITING-CARD REPLIES

The reply is no more than this:

Accepts with pleasure!
Wednesday at 4.

Mrs. Robert Gilding, junior

14 Water Street

Sincere regrets
Wed. Jan. 8

Mr. and Mrs. Henry Osborn

INFORMALS

In replying on an informal, you use the same degree of formality as was used in the invitation.

EPL

June 4

Dear Sue

We'd love to come
to dinner on June
10th at 8:00.

Thanks so much
Betsy

Brook Street Holyoke Mass.

So sorry we can't
make it on the sixth.
We'll be at the Cape.

Gloria

If your informal is engraved as a visiting card, you may write:

Accept with pleasure
Sat. at 7:00

Mr. and Mrs. Carl Keeley

On a plain informal you might write:

Accept with pleasure

Saturday at 7:00

Fran and Carl Kelley

ANSWER CARDS

It is regrettable that it is necessary to write this section at all, but the custom of sending "answer cards" with invitations to debut parties and subscription dances is so widespread that it must be discussed.

This custom has risen out of sheer necessity. Years ago, even teenagers would not have thought of appearing at a party without having answered the invitation. Also years ago, when parties were given in houses with large staffs it was not as important to the hostess to know the exact number of guests she might expect. Both costs and service were more flexible than they are today, when parties are served and food prepared by catering services, who must know the exact quantity of food to be sent and waiters to be hired.

Therefore, while the lack of manners which makes the sending of these cards necessary is deplorable, we recognize the problem of the hostess who sends them. It must be admitted that it seems the only way to obtain the answers.

An answer card is usually small and engraved in the same style as the invitation with a box to check, indicating whether the invited guest will attend or not.

Mr. Allen Lordyce

☐ accepts

☐ regrets

Friday, January second
Columbus Country Club

Many invitations to private parties also include a self-addressed stamped envelope with the card. Subscription dance committees may send the envelope, but generally do not stamp it as they are more concerned with costs. Another arrangement is to enclose a self-addressed stamped postcard.

Etiquette has been made so simple for the receivers of these invitations that they can hardly fail to answer them. Having returned the card, they should not also send a formal reply, as the hostess or committee undoubtedly is keeping a filing box, and does not wish to receive the answers in a variety of shapes and sizes.

WHEN IT IS NECESSARY TO CHANGE YOUR ANSWER

DECLINING AFTER AN ACCEPTANCE

If for any reason you find you cannot attend a function which you have already accepted, it is essential that you let the hostess know immediately. If it is a seated dinner or a bridge party, it is obvious that it would be most inconsiderate not to do so at once, since she will want time to invite others in your place. Even at a large catered party it is important, because the hostess pays for the number of guests expected and not for how many actually arrive. In the case of an open house or a big cocktail party it is not so much a practical matter as one of common courtesy.

In most cases a telephone call is best, as it is quick and gives you a chance to explain your problem and express your regrets. If you prefer, however, and there is ample time, you may write a short note, giving the reason and your apologies.

ACCEPTING AFTER A REGRET

Sometimes a person refuses an invitation for perfectly legitimate reasons and then finds that circumstances change and he can attend after all. If the affair is a party involving a limited number, such as for bridge, a theater party, or a seated dinner, he must swallow his disappointment and hope to be asked again. The hostess will surely have filled his place, and it would only embarrass her if he asked to be "reinstated." However, if the party is a large reception, a cocktail buffet, a picnic, or any affair at which another guest or two would not cause any complications, he may call the hostess, explain his situation, and ask if he might change his regret to an acceptance.

Part TEN

CARDS AND CALLS

56

Visiting cards, business cards, and informals

Today, while one seldom leaves his card at the house of another, the "visiting card" or "calling card" is still the proper name for these small but useful objects. Business or professional cards differ somewhat in format, but should be considered in conjunction with their social counterparts. To these two long-familiar forms has been added a third—the informal. Although it cannot substitute for a business card or perform all the functions of a visiting card, it has in recent years earned a well-deserved place of its own.

VISITING CARDS

Cards used to be left in great quantities at the homes of acquaintances, but today the formal call is a thing of the past as is its attendant custom of leaving cards. Only in military and diplomatic circles is it still an accepted formality.

Not many years ago, the visiting card (in its matching envelope) was used for an invitation to informal parties of every description. Now it has been almost entirely replaced by an informal, a commercial invitation, or a telephone call. Messages of condolence or congratulation are sometimes written on visiting cards. But their most common use is as an enclosure when one sends a present. If you do not have your own visiting card with you, the small white card and envelope provided by many shops may be substituted.

SIZE AND ENGRAVING

Of necessity, the size of visiting cards varies according to length of the name, but a married woman's card is usually from three to three and one-half inches wide and from two and one-fourth to two and one-half inches high. (Very young girls customarily use a smaller card.) A man's card is narrower, from three to three and one-fourth inches long and from one and one-fourth to one and five-eighths inches high. The cards are made of white or cream-white glazed or unglazed bristol board of medium thickness, and they are not plate-marked.

The engraving much in use is shaded Roman, and script is always good form. Various other letterings brought out by engravers from time to time have a temporary vogue, but all overly large or ornate lettering should be avoided.

ADDRESSES

People who live in cities, especially if they have unlisted telephone numbers, sometimes have the address engraved in very small letters in the lower right corner. This is perfectly correct, but not often seen today.

ENVELOPES

When visiting cards were frequently mailed as invitations, it was necessary to order a supply of matching envelopes meeting postal regulations. Mailing envelopes are somewhat larger than the cards themselves, but color and quality of paper prevent any seeming mismatch and the larger size ensures their safe delivery. Today, because informals have largely replaced visiting cards for such uses, the special envelopes are not generally necessary.

CORRECT NAMES AND INITIALS

To be impeccably correct, one should not use initials on a visiting card. A gentleman's card should read "Mr. John Hunter Titherington Smith"; but because names are sometimes awkwardly long, he may have his cards engraved "Mr. John H. T. Smith" or "Mr. J. H. Titherington Smith," as suits his fancy. His wife's card must, of course, be the exact duplicate of his, and not read "Mrs. J. Hunter Smith" when his reads "Mr. John H. Smith." She uses "Jr." if he does, and drops it, if he does, when his father dies.

CARDS OF A MARRIED COUPLE

A married woman's card: As just stated, a married woman uses her husband's name in exactly the same form that he does, and her card is approximately three and one-fourth inches by two and one-fourth inches.

Mrs. John Foster Hughes

"Mr. and Mrs." cards: "Mr. and Mrs." cards are just as useful as individual cards. They are used for invitations, as enclosures with presents, or for any communication that comes from both husband and wife. They are approximately three and one-half inches by two and one-half inches.

Mr. and Mrs. John Foster Hughes

14 Willow Road

A married man's card: A man's card is engraved with his title, "Doctor" or "Mr.," even though he may have "junior" after his name.

"Mr." is *never* written "Mister," but "Doctor" rather than "Dr." is preferred. The size is three and one-fourth inches by one and one-half inches.

Mr. John Foster Hughes, Jr.

CARDS FOR OTHERS

A widow's name: A man gives his name to his wife for life—or until she herself through remarriage relinquishes it. A widow, therefore, should always continue to use her husband's Christian names. She is Mrs. John Foster Hughes—never Mrs. Sarah Hughes—if she cares at all about good taste.

If a widow's son has the name of his father, the widow may have "Sr." added to her name when her son marries. This use of Sr. is necessary if they live at the same address—or in a small village where no street numbers are used. If they live in different cities, both mother and daughter-in-law can be Mrs. John Foster Hughes.

If the widow lives in the same city but at a different address from her son and his wife, she can have her address engraved in small letters at the lower right-hand corner and so identify herself.

The use of "Jr." and "2nd" on cards: The fact that a man's name has "Jr." added at the end in no way takes the place of "Mr." His card should be engraved "Mr. John Foster Hughes, Jr." and his wife's "Mrs. John Foster Hughes, Jr." "Junior" may be engraved in full; when it is, it is not spelled with a capital *j*. John, second, or John, third, may have 2nd or 3rd after their names, but II or III in Roman numerals gives a very handsome appearance.

A divorcée's card: The proper name on a divorcée's card is her maiden name combined with her husband's surname. Miss Susan Coleman who is divorced from Franklin Butler becomes Mrs. Coleman Butler, and her cards should be engraved in this form. Because some surnames are overly long and awkward, there is a tendency for a woman to let herself become Mrs. Susan Butler, but this should not be condoned on anything as formal as a visiting card.

A professional woman's card: A woman who has earned a professional title uses her title or professional name in public, while in private life she uses the name of her husband. A spinster who is a practicing physician uses the title of Doctor socially as well as professionally. But if she is, for instance, a doctor of philosophy, a woman should not call herself "Doctor" except in a classroom or when she is introduced as a speaker.

The best solution for a woman who is a medical doctor is to have two cards—one for business purposes engraved "Helen Corbin, M.D." or "Doctor Helen Corbin," and one for social use engraved "Mrs. Richard Ford Corbin." On a "Mr. and Mrs." card, she would remain "Mrs.," not "Dr.," as it would be most awkward to have "Mr. and Dr. Richard Ford Corbin" on one card. If her husband is also a doctor, the card is engraved "Dr. and Mrs. Richard Ford Corbin."

A boy's card: A boy never puts "Mr." on his cards until he leaves school or becomes eighteen.

Cards of a young girl: A young girl's cards have "Miss" before her name after she is thirteen. She should use her real name, never a nickname: "Miss Sarah Smith," not "Miss Sally Smith."

Cards for children: It is not so "silly" as might be supposed that very little children should have visiting cards. Since it is through lifelong familiarity with good behavior that many fine manners are acquired, mothers often think it good experience for children—especially little girls—to have their own cards, even though they are used only to send with gifts. Children's cards are always smaller than regulation size, and the younger the child, the smaller the card. They may seem a bit extravagant, but as a present from a doting grandmother or aunt, they need not be.

Titles on cards: Doctors, clergymen, military officers on active duty, and holders of title-bestowing offices all have their cards engraved with their titles: "Doctor Henry Gordon" (an M.D.), "The Reverend William Goode," "Colonel Thomas Doyle," "Judge Horace Rush," "Senator James Widelands." But a person holding a high degree does not add its letters to his name, and his cards are not engraved "Professor." Double cards read "The Reverend and Mrs. Henry Gordon," "Judge and Mrs. Horace Rush," etc.

It is always best to engrave titles in full.

The correct card for a governor is:

The Governor of Nevada

on a card that is slightly larger or more nearly square than an ordinary man's card. Less correct, but not inadmissible, is his ordinary card with "Governor of Nevada" added in small letters under his name. Occasionally an overmodest incumbent objects to the correct form because he thinks it looks too self-important. But he must remember that the card is representative of the highest office of his state and not the card of a private citizen.

The card of mayor may read:

The Mayor of Chicago

or, if he prefers:

Mr. John Lake
Mayor of Chicago

A diplomat uses his title and "United States of America" rather than "America" or "American."

It is unnecessary to continue this list, as each official certainly knows his own name! But it may be as well to add that titles of courtesy have no place either in a signature or on a visiting card: the American title of courtesy, "The Honorable," unlike this title given to sons of British earls, viscounts, and barons, is never correct on a card.

The professional card of a doctor or surgeon is "James Smith, M.D." His social card is "Doctor James Smith."

THE P.P.C. CARD

The P.P.C. card is almost unheard of nowadays. But for those readers who might unexpectedly receive a card with those initials, I include this explanation. It is merely a visiting card, whether of a lady or a gentleman, on which the initials P.P.C. (*pour prendre congé*—to take leave) are written in ink in the lower left corner. This is usually sent by mail to acquaintances when one is leaving and means nothing except "I've gone away—good-bye." It is in no sense a message of thanks or farewell and no acknowledgment need be made.

MESSAGES WRITTEN ON CARDS

"With sympathy" or "With deepest sympathy" is written on your visiting card with flowers sent to a funeral. This same message is written on a card and left at the door of a house of mourning, if you do not know the family well enough to ask to be received.

Any message such as "With best wishes for your happiness" or "Congratulations" or "Happy birthday" may be written on cards accompanying gifts.

At the house of a lady whom you know well and whom you are sorry not to find at home, it is friendly to write "Sorry not to see you!" or "So sorry to miss you!"

INFORMALS

The small fold-over cards known as informals are convenient when you want, for example, to write a very brief note, but one that requires more space than is afforded by a visiting card.

Plain white informals of good quality are available at all stationers and are perfectly acceptable. If you wish, however, you may have them engraved. This should be done exactly as you would have your visiting cards engraved. Or you may simply have your monogram in the upper left corner.

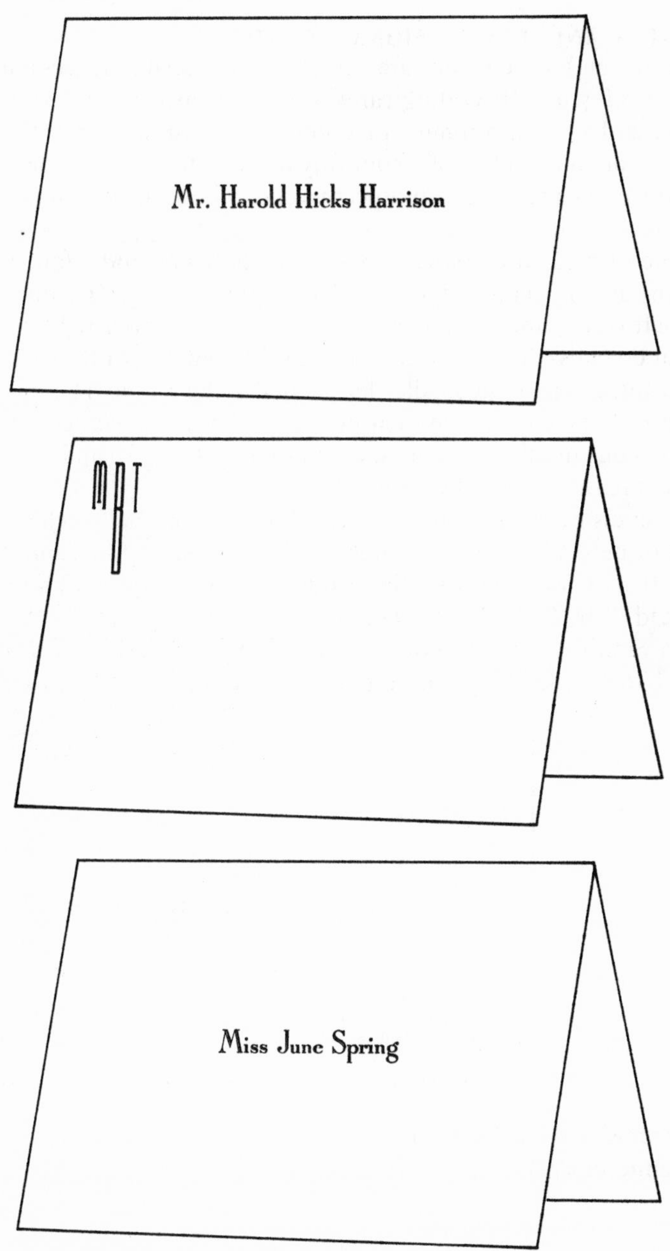

Because informals are usually somewhat larger than visiting cards, the envelopes present fewer problems when it comes to the size acceptable for mailing.

Informals are correct and practical for invitations (*see Chapter Fifty-three*), but they cannot be substituted for visiting cards when you make a formal call. They may be enclosed with a gift only if you wish to write a personal message on the inner page.

BUSINESS AND PROFESSIONAL CARDS

Although business cards are never used for social purposes and must not be confused with visiting cards, their principal use is very like the original and now uncommon function of the visiting card: When an employee or an executive of a company makes a business call on another company or on a client or a prospective client, he sends his card or leaves it as a record of his visit.

The card of an employee usually has the name and address of the company in the center of the card with the employee's name in the lower left corner and the telephone number in the lower right corner.

An executive has his or her name in the center with his or her position in the company in smaller letters under the name. The name and address of the company are then put in the lower left corner. Although the telephone number is sometimes omitted, it is helpful and convenient to have it in the lower right corner.

Business cards are approximately three and one-half inches by two inches in most cases. They do not require the use of full names to the extent that is usual with visiting cards. That is, a man's business card may read "Mr. John Smith" (whereas his social card reads "Mr. John Hunter Smith") if he is known simply as "John Smith" in his business life and, for example, signs his letters in that form.

HAROLD HICKS HARRISON

500 WALL STREET
NEW YORK, N. Y.

MARKET 6-7272

Professional cards may differ from business cards in that no company name appears.

57

Formal calls and informal visits

The custom of making formal calls is no longer a part of our lives. But there are circumstances in which even those most indifferent to social obligations must call and leave their cards: In Washington, members of diplomatic or military circles exchange calls. Members of the military or the diplomatic service arriving at a new post call on their superiors. Calls are exchanged between officers on military posts. Each of the services publishes its own books and pamphlets on military etiquette, which thoroughly cover the subject of these military calls.

In addition to official calls, there are certain visits that all of us must make, although few of them require that we leave cards.

VISITS THAT EVERYONE MUST PAY

A visit of condolence should be paid at once to a close friend when a death occurs in the immediate family, and in this case you ask if Mrs. Jackson feels like seeing you. Furthermore, the visitor asks if there is anything he or she can do. A lady does not call on a man, but writes him a note of sympathy.

When going to visit a friend who has been ill, whether or not you ask to see her depends upon how well you know her. In any case it is always proper as well as thoughtful to take a gift of a book or fruit or flowers, or if you know of something she particularly likes and that she is allowed to eat, a treat from your kitchen.

A visit of congratulation is often paid a new mother, and, of course, it is always very pleasing if you take a present to the baby.

HOW TO MAKE A FIRST VISIT

In large cities, neighbors seldom call on each other. But when strangers move into a neighborhood in a small town it is proper and friendly of the residents nearby to call on them. The newcomers should wait for the old residents to issue the first "formal" invitation, but if contact has been established casually through gardening activities, through children, in an apartment house, in the laundry, perhaps the new arrival could further the acquaintanceship by suggesting the other's child come over to play, by inviting the neighbor to join her for a soft drink, or by asking advice on stores, doctors, etc. These openings may well lead to an invitation to dine at the older resident's home, after which the newcomer may reciprocate with any form of entertainment.

Everyone invited to a wedding may go to see the bride on her return from the honeymoon. And when a man marries a girl from a distant place, courtesy demands that his friends and neighbors visit her as soon as she is at home.

WHAT TO DO

Before planning a visit to a stranger who has come to live in your neighborhood, telephone to be sure it's convenient. But if you are passing by and you find her planting flowers along her walk, you say, "Hello—I'm Nancy Jones. I live in the brick house across the street."

The new neighbor says, "How do you do. I'm very glad to see you," or "How nice of you to come to see me." She then invites you into her house or asks whether you think it would be cooler on the porch. In any case you sit and talk.

From ten to fifteen minutes is the time suggested for a first visit. This is not a strict rule, but it is well to keep within this time unless you have much to talk about, and unless your hostess says, "Oh, do stay a little longer," or "Let's have a glass of iced tea." Then you stay for a few minutes longer if you wish or reply, "I'm sorry! I'd love to, but I can't today. Do come and see me soon!" The new neighbor says, "I'd love to." You both say, "Good-bye," and that's all.

RETURNING A FIRST VISIT

People who are old friends pay no attention to how often or how seldom one goes to see the other, unless there is an illness, a death, or a birth in the family. Nor do they ever consider whose turn it is to invite whom. But first visits should be returned with considerable punctuality—especially after a *first* invitation to lunch or dine. The casual "first visit" described above allows the newcomer to "drop in" on her neighbor but not to issue a formal invitation to lunch or dinner.

If hospitality has been shown you by two or more hostesses together, you are indebted to both or all equally—if you know them equally. But if you know only one of the hostesses, it is not necessary that you return the hospitality of the other (or others) unless opportunity offers. In any event, when returning the hospitality of these several hostesses, it is never necessary that you invite them together.

CALLS OF CONDOLENCE

Calls of condolence should be made as soon as possible after hearing of the death of a friend or a member of a friend's family. If the friends are very close, you will probably be admitted to speak to them; and if you are, you should offer your services to help in any way that you can. If they do not need anything, you offer your sympathy and leave without delay. *For further detail see Chapter Forty-two, "Funerals."*

When you are not well acquainted with the family and do not wish to intrude on their privacy, you may leave your card with "With deepest sympathy" written across the top. Visits of condolence need not be returned.

SOME SPECIAL SITUATIONS

THE BUSY NEWCOMER

If a new neighbor, struggling to get her house in order, opens her door to an unexpected visitor, she may be faced with having to ask the visitor in to an embarrassing scene of confusion and mess or of requesting that she come back another time. Because this is so likely to happen when someone has just moved in, it is a good idea for the older resident to telephone first, introduce herself, and ask when it might be convenient to drop by.

IF THERE ARE SERVANTS

Years ago, in a household with servants, the door was opened by a maid—or butler—and if the hostess was at home, the guest was led into the living room. In a very formal household, the butler presented a tray for the card, read it himself, and, going to the living room, announced, "Mrs. Henry Stowe is here to see you." If the lady of the house was at home but upstairs, the visitor was asked to take a seat in the living room, and the servant took the card to the hostess.

Today, when a maid who knows you opens the door, she simply says, "Please come in; Mrs. Franklin is in the living room," and if you know the way you walk in by yourself. Or she may say "Mrs. Franklin is upstairs; I'll tell her you're here." If you are unfamiliar with the house, she should show you to the living room to wait while she takes the message. When the visitor is not known to the maid, she says, "May I tell Mrs. Franklin who is calling?" and the guest simply gives her name rather than presenting a card. When the visitor is ready to leave, the maid should stand with the front door open until the guest gets into her car, or if she is walking, until she has reached the sidewalk. It is bad manners ever to close the door in a visitor's face or while she is still going down the front steps.

"NOT AT HOME"—NO DISCOURTESY

Today, except in very special circumstances such as when a lady actually feels ill, she receives a visitor if she is home. Years ago, this was not always so. When a servant at a door said, "Mrs. Jones is not at home," this meant that the lady of the house was "not at home to visitors." While "not at home" was merely a phrase of politeness, for Mrs. Jones to have said "I am out" *after* a card had been brought to her was both an untruth and an inexcusable rudeness. Or to have had an inquiry answered, "I don't know, but I'll see," and then to have had the servant, after taking a card, come back with the message "Mrs. Jones is out" could not fail to make the visitor feel rebuffed. Once a card was admitted, the visitor had to be admitted also, no matter how inconvenient receiving her might be. Mrs. Jones might send a message that she was dressing but would be very glad to see her if she could wait ten minutes. The visitor could either wait or say she was pressed for time. But if she did not wait, then it was she who was rather discourteous.

CORRECT NUMBER OF CARDS TO LEAVE

The following information may seem outdated and unnecessary, but should you unexpectedly be faced with the occasion to make a formal call, it is wise to be familiar with the correct procedure.

When the visitor rings the doorbell and the message is "not at home," the butler or maid proffers the card tray on which the visitor lays a card of her own for each lady in the house and a card of her husband's for each lady and gentleman. In a less formal household the card tray is on a table in the hall, and the visitor finds it and deposits the cards there herself. The number of cards to leave is very simple. A woman leaves her own cards for ladies only, because she does not call on a gentleman. But her husband's card is left for every man as well as for every woman.

That is all there is to it. But three is the greatest number ever left of any one card. In calling on Mrs. Town, who has three grown daughters and her mother living in the house and a Mrs. Stranger staying with her, a card for each would mean a packet of six. Instead, the visitor should leave three—one for Mrs. Town, one for all the other ladies of the house (not one for each), and one for Mrs. Stranger.

CALLING WITHOUT A CARD

It is certainly not necessary to have a visiting card to pay a call. If the person on whom you are calling is home and greets you herself, she obviously knows that you have made the effort to see her. If no one is home, you may leave a note in her mailbox, "So sorry to have missed you, Sally." If she does not know you well, you sign it "Sally Brown."

When the door is opened by a maid who tells you that Mrs. Franklin is not home or cannot see you, you may ask for a pencil and paper and leave her a note or ask the maid to tell her that you have called.

INFORMAL VISITS

There is no need to discuss the casual visit between very close friends. There are no rules at all except those which might be set up between them. For instance, one might say, "Give me till ten o'clock to pull myself together before you come over." Or they might agree to take turns making sandwiches for lunch while the babies are napping. Whatever they may enjoy, it is a personal matter, and etiquette only requires that they are considerate to each other and offend no outsiders.

There are, however, many visits made between less intimate friends which are not at all in the category of a formal call. Friends making or receiving these informal visits should know and follow certain rules.

THE UNEXPECTED VISITOR

No one, with the exception of closest friends and immediate family, should ever be an "unexpected visitor." Formal calls are never "unexpected" because in the strata of society where they are made there are always servants to announce a visitor or say "Not at home." In military circles etc., since the hours for calls are strictly proscribed, the callers are always welcome. While occasionally an unannounced "drop-in" works out well, far more often it is most inconvenient to the one visited. She may have previous plans, her hair may be in curlers, her child may be sick, she may be in the middle of preparing dinner, or she may simply be resting or relaxing. The sight of an eager visitor at the door, neatly dressed and ready for an hour or two of conversation, is rarely an undiluted pleasure.

Therefore, do not make a visit without making your intentions known, and agree to a time convenient to both of you. It may be done by a telephone call, or, if you live some distance away, by a note. In the latter case, it should be written far enough in advance so that there is time for a reply. It should not say, "We are coming on Saturday etc." but rather, "If you and John are free Saturday, may we drop by . . . ?"

When you are the recipient of one of these unannounced visits, you have every right to carry on with any previous plans you might have. If Aunt Sally arrives unexpectedly from three hundred miles away, and you had been planning to go to a church supper, you might suggest that she go along with you. If, however, you were expected at the Howard's for bridge, you would simply ask her to make herself at home until your return. You should, if possible, find something in the refrigerator or the cupboard which would serve as a snack or light meal. But you need not make yourself late for your appointment by taking the time to prepare a full dinner, although you should get out the ingredients for her if she wishes to do so herself.

When the visitor is a friend or acquaintance from nearby, you merely say quite frankly, "I'm terribly sorry, but we were just leaving for dinner at the Hornsbys'. Could you come back another time?" And make the future date definite then and there. "Another time" left at that means little, but a firm invitation proves that you would really enjoy a visit at a more convenient moment. If your earlier plans were such that they could be carried out on another day, it would, of course, be more polite to postpone them and stay at home with your visitor.

If by chance you have just started your dinner when a caller drops in, you must try to make the meal stretch to include her. If she says, "Oh, no thank you—I've just eaten," you may pull up a chair for her and ask her forgiveness while you finish your meal No one who drops in unannounced can expect you to postpone your meal or let it get cold while you visit.

CHILDREN AND PETS

Unless they are specifically invited it is far better to leave children—and pets—home when you visit friends. This is not always practical, however, and couples with young children should think carefully about their visiting manners.

A smart housewife who knows that she will have young visitors from time to time—either children of friends, nieces, nephews, or grandchildren—makes preparations in advance.

She removes breakable articles and those which might be dangerous from low tables. She shuts the doors to rooms she wishes to make "off limits," and she sees that doors to cellar steps and low windows are tightly closed. Then, when safety precautions are taken care of, she checks her supply of recreational materials. A basket or sack of simple toys—coloring books, blocks, comic books, wind-up cars, and many others—goes a long way toward making the visit enjoyable for both mother and hostess. And, of course, this same clever lady has a supply of cookies and milk or soft drinks ready to fill in when the novelty of the toys wears off.

The mother herself can make her child a welcome guest in many ways. She should not take him visiting until he learns the meaning of "No." She also may bring a basket of his favorite toys to keep him occupied. And above all, she should set herself a time limit for her visit, knowing that no toddler has a very long span of concentration. Her call should end well before that limit is reached.

Pets, no matter how well behaved at home, should not be taken along on visits unless they are invited. Fido may be irresistible to you, but to your hostess who has new rugs or upholstery, or may be allergic to dog hairs, he may be anything but a welcome visitor.

VISITING THE SICK

"Making calls" brings to mind one subject that certainly is at one time or another in the thoughts of all of us. This is the occasional visit we must make to a hospital when members of our families or our close friends are ill. The same general rules apply to visiting a sick person at home, although if he is well on the way to recovery, they may be slightly relaxed.

The whole routine of a hospital is highly organized and kept in smooth running order by the doctors and nurses and staff. When visiting a friend in the hospital, we should try to make our presence there fit into an orderly pattern so that the hospital's staff can do its best for the patients. If we were hospital patients we would certainly appreciate the same consideration from visitors.

Far too often visitors are thoughtless and careless. One should think of the problems that a visitor makes under the busy, crowded hospital conditions of today. Courtesy to nurses and the other hospital personnel, quietness of manner and approach in the hospital buildings, avoidance of asking for special attention from busy people, these we can show—and above all we must not act in any way that will be tiring or harmful to the patient we are visiting. We must make our visits short and friendly, leaving our small gifts without fuss or any expectancy of more than a simple thank you for them. We must not engage the patient in long discussions, nor ask questions about his or her illness that properly are in the sphere of the doctor and the nurse. We must time our visits so that the patient becomes neither tired nor anxious and, of course, we must always follow the rules as they are given to us by the staff. A surgeon that I know claims that visitors kill more patients than do operations, certainly an overstatement, but one with more than a kernel of truth. Here a few do's and don'ts that may be helpful for visitor and patient.

Don't bring as your gift foods such as chocolates or cakes that the patient may not be permitted to have.

Whenever it is possible, bring your flowers with their own container and let them be of a size that can easily be handled. Hospitals are invariably short of containers, and it is an additional chore for the nurses to have to hunt for a suitable vase. Most florists realize this, and if you mention that your purchase is to go to a hospital, they will arrange the flowers in inexpensive (sometimes even disposable) containers at no additional charge.

Patients often prefer potted plants to cut flowers. They are easy to care for, last longer, and can be taken home by a member of the family if more space is needed for those which arrive at a later date. There they continue to give the patient many further moments of pleasure.

It should be clear that heavily scented flowers have no place in the sickroom.

Don't think that the hospital routine has been devised to bedevil you as a visitor or the patient himself. It is only a part of a long-range plan carefully worked out to serve everyone in the best way possible. Limited visiting hours, early meals, and rules governing smoking may seem unreasonable to you, but you must remember that they have not been made just for the benefit of your sister Susie, who may have nothing more than a broken finger, but rather for the sicker patients, who, without a carefully planned routine and the best possible conditions for rest and quiet, might not recover at all.

Don't talk about his illness in front of the patient. Ask for the necessary information quietly, from those who are competent to give it, out of the patient's hearing and sight. Also, remember that floor nurses are not allowed to answer certain questions. If one of them says to you, "You will have to ask Dr. Smith about that," you need not feel that she is hiding information from you or that she is being deliberately unfeeling; it is a hospital rule, and she has no choice.

Don't worry a patient about anything that you feel might upset or disturb him. The fact that Bobby is failing algebra, or the dog had a disastrous fight with the neighbor's cat, is not news calculated to improve the mental outlook of the patient. In any case, he or she can do nothing about your problems. The best thing you can do, if you wish his speedy return home, is to bring him cheerful, encouraging news that will make him want to get there quickly.

Remember that the average patient is not his normal self and the burden of good behavior is on your side, not his. He may show little enthusiasm for the things that usually interest him, or he may react overexcitedly to a minor incident. If he does either, simply tell yourself that this reaction is only temporary, and change the subject to a safer one. But it is up to you to lead the way.

Don't overstay your welcome. Visit briefly, cheerfully, and leave the patient rested and encouraged. Make up your mind before you arrive that you will stay no more than fifteen or twenty minutes, and stick to it, no matter how much your friend may beg you to stay. If other visitors arrive while you are there, leave sooner, so that they may have their share of the patient's time without overtiring him. Nothing is more exhausting to a person in bed than to have to try to follow a conversation among several people who may be seated on all sides of the room. If it is possible, when two or three people are present, stand or put your chairs on the same side of the bed.

If, possibly because of the shortage of nurses in many hospitals, the doctor or a member of the family asks you, as a close friend, to stay with the patient, do not let him feel that he must entertain you or even talk. Take a book along, attend to any simple things he may wish you to do, and settle yourself where he may know that you are there, but at the same time indicate that you are quite happy to have an hour or two in which to enjoy your book quietly.

SEMIPRIVATE ROOMS AND WARDS

The number of private rooms in every hospital has been greatly decreased, partly because of the shortage of nurses, partly because they are too costly for most people, and partly because there always seems to be a need for more hospital beds than exist. The vast majority of hospital patients today find themselves in semiprivate rooms or larger wards.

The rules governing visitors to these rooms must be stricter than those for visitors to patients in private rooms. Your friend may not object to cigarette smoke, but it may cause the man in the next bed to have a coughing attack which could be the worst thing for him. Therefore, if it is allowed at all, it is essential to ask the others nearby if it will bother them if you smoke. And please, cigarettes only! Cigar and pipe smoke can actually cause nausea in many people.

Voices must naturally be kept lower, not only for privacy's sake, but in order not to disturb the other sick people who may badly need their rest.

If you are going to the snack bar or restaurant to bring a dish of ice cream or a candy bar to your friend, it is only thoughtful to ask the other person in a semiprivate room if you can bring him anything at the same time. This would not be necessary in a larger ward, unless one of the patients actually requested you to do an errand for him.

If there is a television set in the room—and this rule applies between patients as well as visitor and patient—do not turn it on without asking the other's permission and consulting him as to his choice of program. Unless he shows real enthusiasm, keep the volume very low.

If another patient in a room wishes to rest, draw the curtains between the beds to give him as much privacy and quiet as possible. On the other hand, if he and your friend have become friendly, include him in the conversation, and your visit will be doubly appreciated.

TIPPING

The question of tipping the nurses may arise, but its answer is simple—don't. It is perfectly proper, however, to bring a box of candy or the like that can be shared by all the staff caring for the patient. The package should be left with the nurse on duty at the desk nearest his room, with a word or two to the effect that "this is for everyone who has been so nice."

Part ELEVEN

PROTOCOL IN OFFICIAL CIRCLES

58

Precedence and titles

Although most people who have been long in government service instinctively try to help the inexperienced, it is imperative that each new arrival in Washington—whether an official or a private citizen who expects to take part in the social life of the capitol—learn first of all the proper titles by which each diplomat, government official, and military officer is addressed and the order of his rank. When a man has been promoted to high position, the respect due his office should not be overlooked. And placing a foreign representative below his proper seat at a dinner table, showing less than proper concern for his rank, may actually endanger diplomatic feeling between nations.

Precedence is the bane of the Washington hostess. It is easy enough to know that a general outranks a lieutenant, a duke a count, or a member of the President's cabinet a state assemblyman. The difficulty begins in determining, for instance, whether a general of the army should rank the governor of a state, or whether a rear admiral, a major, or a justice of a state court should go in to dinner first, or where to seat the Archbishop of X and Duke of Y. If there is any doubt about which of two officials bears the higher rank, the hostess is safer to avoid inviting them to the same dinner party.

The hostess who plans to entertain several government officials, military officers, or foreign diplomats must try to arrange her seating without slighting any of her guests.

In an American house, the ranking foreigner should insofar as possible be given precedence.

In a foreign embassy in Washington, the ranking American is given precedence. The President of the United States takes precedence over the representative of the country that is receiving him. In the President's absence, the Vice-President, the Chief Justice, or the Secretary of State —whoever represents the United States—outranks all foreign ambassadors. In the diplomatic service, the highest ranking ambassador is the one who has been longest in residence in Washington—not longest in service of his country.

Wives of officials, whether their husbands are present or not, assume their husband's rank. Widows are merely given a courtesy position. Exceptions are wives and widows of former presidents, who do have a definite ranking in precedence.

Even though there is a guest of honor, men (or women) of higher rank are given the seats of honor on either side of the hostess (or host).

As the Protocol Staff of the Department of State has explained, "The White House and the Department of State prescribe the protocol to be used only for ceremonies of state. The protocol differs somewhat for each ceremony, and the rules used are not considered as binding at private functions. For this reason it is the policy of the White House not to make the rules public or to give out the order of precedence of Government officials." Therefore, the following list must be understood to be an unofficial order of rank among those in government service.

The President of the United States
The Vice-President of the United States
The Speaker of the House of Representatives
The Chief Justice of the United States
Former Presidents of the United States
The Secretary of State
Ambassadors of Foreign Powers
Widows of former Presidents of the United States
The Secretary General of the United Nations
United States Representative to the United Nations
Ministers of Foreign Powers (Chiefs of Diplomatic Missions)
Associate Justices of the Supreme Court of the United States and Retired Associate Justices
The Secretary of the Treasury
The Secretary of Defense

The Attorney General
The Postmaster General
The Secretary of the Interior
The Secretary of Agriculture
The Secretary of Commerce
The Secretary of Labor
The Secretary of Health, Education, and Welfare
The Secretary of Housing and Urban Development
The Secretary of Transportation
Senators
Governors of States
Acting Heads of Executive Departments (in the absence of the Cabinet member)
Former Vice-Presidents of the United States
Members of the House of Representatives
Under Secretaries of State
Administrator, Agency for International Development
Director, United States Arms Control and Disarmament Agency
Chargé d'Affaires of Foreign Powers
Secretaries of the Army, the Navy, and the Air Force (ranked according to date of appointment)
Director, Bureau of the Budget
Chairman, Council of Economic Advisers
Chairman, Board of Governors, Federal Reserve
Under Secretaries of the Executive Department and Deputy Secretaries
Chairman, Joint Chiefs of Staff
Chiefs of Staff of the Army, the Navy, and the Air Force (ranked according to date of appointment)
Commandant of the Marine Corps
Five-Star Generals of the Army and Fleet Admirals
The Secretary General, Organization of American States
Representatives to the Organization of American States
Director, Central Intelligence Agency
Administrator, General Services Administration
Director, United States Information Agency
Administrator, National Aeronautics and Space Administration
Chairman, The Atomic Energy Commission
Director, Defense Research and Engineering
Director, Office of Emergency Planning
Administrator, Federal Aviation Agency
Chairman, Civil Service Commission
Director, The Peace Corps
Special Assistants to the President

Deputy Under Secretaries of the Executive Departments
Assistant Secretaries of the Executive Departments
United States Chief of Protocol
Members of the Council of Economic Advisers
Active or Designate United States Ambassadors and Ministers (career rank, when in the United States)
Under Secretaries of the Army, the Navy, and the Air Force (ranked according to date of appointment)
Four-Star Generals and Admirals
Assistant Secretaries of the Army, the Navy, and the Air Force (ranked according to date of appointment)
Lieutenant Generals and Vice Admirals (Three-Star)
Ministers of Foreign Powers (serving in Embassies, not accredited)
Deputy Assistant Secretaries of the Executive Departments
Counselors of Embassies or Legations of Foreign Powers
* Major Generals and Rear Admirals (Two-Star)
Brigadier Generals (One-Star)
Assistant Chiefs of Protocol
The Secretary of the Senate

OFFICIAL TITLES

Just as there is a certain order of precedence within official circles, so there are forms of address that differ somewhat from those to which we are accustomed in unofficial life. For example, the following sentences indicate the way persons in the diplomatic world are introduced, announced, spoken of, and spoken to.

"Mr. Ambassador, may I present Mr. Worldly?" (Mr. Worldly finds out for himself, if he does not already know, *which* ambassador.)

But in the case of Mrs. Worldly the order is reversed.

"Mrs. Worldly, may I present the Speaker?"

"Mrs. Worldly, may I present Mr. Justice Lawson?"

"Mrs. Worldly, may I present the British Ambassador?" Or more formally: ". . . his Excellency the British Ambassador?"

A man of lesser rank is always introduced to one of greater.

Members of the Cabinet are usually "Mr. Secretary," but if several are present, one is designated "Mr. Secretary of State," the other "Mr. Secretary of Commerce." And you say, of course, "Mr. Chief Justice" or "Mr. Justice Lawson"—even after he has retired. You also say "General Pershing" and "Admiral Sim" and "Senator Lake," and not merely "General," "Admiral," or "Senator" without a surname.

* The rank of Rear Admiral is divided into two categories; the "upper half" and the "lower half." Those of the "upper half" are equivalent in rank to Two-Star, or Major Generals. Those of the "lower half" are equivalent to One-Star Brigadier Generals, and may even be, depending on date of rank, outranked by a Brigadier General.

The Chief Executive and the Vice-President are *always* spoken to without a surname:

"I appreciate the honor, Mr. President."

"Thank you, Mr. Vice-President."

If the conversation is prolonged, any official (including the President) may be spoken to as "Sir."

It is utterly improper to call a governor "Mr." no matter how informal and simple his own inclinations may be. And only those who know him well say "Governor" without adding his surname. In public he is "Governor Jones" or "the Governor."

Captains and commanders and those of higher rank are generally addressed by title and surname—"Captain Brown," "Commander Gray," "Colonel Steel"—but to call them by title alone is not objectionable, as it would be in the case of a governor.

Military and naval titles are used only by officers in active service or retired "regulars." It is not in good taste for reserve officers or those who held temporary commissions during the war to continue having their social cards engraved "Captain," "Major," or "Colonel." They do, of course, use the titles if they have, or resume, an active status in a Reserve unit or in the National Guard. Sometimes a man is affectionately called "Colonel" by his friends, but he should not have the title engraved on his visiting cards; neither should he use it as a part of his signature.

In contrast to the abbreviations of "Mr." and "Mrs.," which are *never* written in full, it is both correct and courteous to write out all military and naval titles—especially when addressing a social note. Impersonal communications may be sent to "2nd Lieut. John Smith," "Lieut. Johnson," or "Lt. Col. Graham," but other ranks are more properly written in full.

When introducing or addressing a letter to someone who has both a military and an inherited title, military rank is put first: "Colonel, Lord London."

TITLES ON PLACE CARDS

Place cards present another problem, for at official functions some carry only the title whereas others have title and surname. The following appear without names on all formal occasions:

The President
The Vice-President
The Archbishop of . . .
The Ambassador of . . .
The Minister of . . .
The Chief Justice
The Speaker

The Secretary of . . . *or* The Attorney General *or* The Postmaster General

So, too, at public dinners place cards are inscribed "His Excellency, the Archbishop of New York," "His Honor, the Mayor of Chicago," etc. "The Assistant Secretary of the Navy" is never used alone, however, because there is more than one assistant secretary in all executive departments. The same in true in the case of the following and similar titles:

Mr. Justice Fox
Senator Essex
Governor Lansing
Rev. Father Stole
Dr. Saintly

At a private dinner, when the title alone sounds overly stiff and formal, the hostess may modify the official form (except in the cases of the President and Vice-President) by adding the surname: "Ambassador Santorino," "Chief Justice Howard," "Secretary Knowles." For other notables, she uses the name by which she would address them in speaking: "Governor Street, will you sit here?" "Father Gaines, I'd like you to meet . . ." Everyone else appears as Mr., Mrs., or Miss. Remember that the object of a place card is twofold: to show the owner of the name (or title) where he is to sit and to give his neighbors at the table a clue about how to address him.

59

An invitation to the White House

An invitation to lunch or dine at the White House is a command and automatically cancels any other engagement that is not of the utmost importance. The reply must be written by hand. It must be mailed the day the invitation is received if it is not delivered by hand to the White House. There are very few acceptable excuses for refusing such an invitation, and the reason must be stated in the note of regret—unavoidable absence from Washington, the recent death of a close relative, or actual illness.

The correct forms for replies are:

Mr. and Mrs. Richard Worldly
have the honour to accept
the kind invitation of
The President and Mrs. Washington
for dinner on Thursday, the eighth of May
at eight o'clock

Mr. and Mrs. Robert Franklin
regret extremely
that owing to Mr. Franklin's illness
they will be unable to accept

the kind invitation of
The President and Mrs. Washington
for dinner on Friday, the first of May

The note to a disappointed hostess:

Mr. and Mrs. Richard Worldly
regret extremely
that an invitation to The White House
prevents their keeping
their previous engagement for
Tuesday, the first of December

INFORMAL INVITATIONS

Informal invitations to dinner or luncheon at the White House are now used more frequently than formerly. They may be sent by letters, telegrams, or telephone messages from the President's secretary or his wife's secretary. The replies should be sent in the same form to whoever issued the invitations. Acceptances (or regrets, when the reasons are valid) should be written on personal stationery, either engraved or plain.

A typical invitation might be worded something like this:

Dear Mrs. Heathcote,

Mrs. Harrison has asked me to invite you to have lunch with her at the White House on Thursday, the sixteenth of May. Luncheon will be at one o'clock.

Yours truly,
Eleanor Smithers
Secretary to Mrs. Harrison

The reply might read:

Dear Miss Smithers,

Will you please tell Mrs. Harrison that I shall be delighted to lunch with her at the White House on Thursday, the sixteenth of May. Thank you very much.

Sincerely,
Frances Heathcote

To the luncheon Mrs. Heathcote wears a dress that she might wear to any similar gathering, but in this instance she should wear hat and gloves as well.

DINNER AT THE WHITE HOUSE

An engraved invitation to the White House means black tie unless white tie is specified on the invitation. Women wear evening clothes, and if it is a white-tie dinner, they wear long gloves.

All the names of guests expected at the White House are posted with the guards at the gate. You announce your name and wait a few seconds until you are recognized.

After the guests arrive, the President and his wife enter and speak to each guest and shake hands. Guests, of course, remain standing.

At a formal dinner, the President goes into the dining room first with the highest ranking woman guest. His wife follows with the highest ranking man guest.

DETAILS OF WHITE HOUSE ETIQUETTE

Although customs vary somewhat during different administrations, the following details represent the conventional pattern from which each administration adapts its own procedure.

When you are invited to the White House, you must arrive several minutes, at least, before the hour specified. It is an unpardonable breach of etiquette not to be standing in the drawing room when the President makes his entry.

The President, followed by his wife, enters at the hour set and makes a tour of the room, shaking hands with each guest. When your turn comes, you bow. If he talks to you, you address him as "Mr. President." In a long conversation it is proper to vary "Mr. President" with "Sir" occasionally. You call the wife of the President "Mrs. Washington" and treat her as you would any formal hostess. You do not sit down as long as either the President or his wife remains standing. No guest, of course, ever leaves until after the President has withdrawn from the room, but they then bid each other good night and leave promptly.

Requests to see the President on a business matter should be made through one of the Presidential aides—the one closest to the subject you wish to discuss—or through your congressman. Your reason should be a valid one, you should be sure that no one else can solve your problem, and your letter should be stated in such a way that, if possible, the matter can be settled without a personal interview.

If you have a business appointment with the President, it is most important that you arrive a few minutes ahead of the appointed time. No doubt you will be told how much time you are allowed. Make your call brief and, if possible, take less time than that allotted.

If a buzzer should ring when you are in a corridor, an attendant will ask you to step behind a closed door. The buzzer means that the President or members of his family are leaving or entering. This precaution is for their safety and their privacy.

Don't smoke unless you are invited to.

Gentlemen always remove their hats as they reach the portico.

Do not take a present unless you have cleared it with an aide.

GIFTS TO THE PRESIDENT

Not only should you avoid taking a present to the President unless it has been cleared with an aide, but you should not *send* anything to the White House without receiving permission from his secretary or one of his aides. You may have had a successful hunting trip and wish to send the President a brace of pheasants. The gift must be cleared with the proper authority; otherwise he will never see or taste it.

60

The flag of the United States

There are certain rules and customs that all of us who love this symbol of the United States should know and always follow because it shows our true respect for our country.

It is proper to fly the flag every day in the year between sunrise and sunset, though customarily it is not flown in inclement weather unless there is a particular occasion that requires its display. It may also be displayed at night as part of a patriotic display.

On Memorial or Decoration Day, May 30, the flag is displayed at half-staff until noon and at full staff thereafter until sunset. Flag Day is June 14—the day when we especially celebrate this emblem. It is a widespread custom also for most of us to display the flag on other national holidays.

There are certain clear-cut situations in which the flag should never be used—for example, as decoration on a portion of a costume or athletic uniform, as embroidery on cushions, scarves, handkerchiefs, or applied to paper napkins or boxes. Of course, it should never be used as a covering for articles on a speaker's table, or so placed that objects may be put on or over it. When a statue or monument is unveiled, the flag should never be used as a covering for the object to be displayed. It is unlawful to use the flag in a registered trademark which comprises "the flag, coat of arms, or other insignia of the United States or any simulation thereof."

It goes without saying that the national emblem is never displayed in connection with advertising of any kind. When festoons, rosettes, or other draperies are desired, bunting of blue (uppermost), white, and red should be used, but never the flag itself.

DISPLAYING THE FLAG

When displayed over the middle of a street, the flag should be suspended vertically with the union (the blue field) to the north in an east-west street, or to the east in a north-south street.

When displayed with another flag from crossed staffs, the flag of the United States should be on the right (the flag's own right) and its staff should be in front of the staff of the other flag.

The flag should be raised briskly and lowered slowly and solemnly.

When flown at half-mast, the flag should be hoisted to the peak for a moment and then lowered to the half-mast position. And the flag should again be raised to the peak before being lowered for the day.

When flags of states or cities or pennants of societies are flown on the same halyard with the flag of the United States, the latter should always be at the peak. When flown from adjacent staffs, the national flag should be hoisted first and lowered last.

When the flag is suspended over a sidewalk from a rope extending from house to pole at the edge of the sidewalk, the flag should be hoisted union first.

When the flag is displayed from a staff projecting horizontally or at an angle from a window sill, balcony, or the front of a building, the union of the flag should go all the way to the peak of the staff (except when at half-mast).

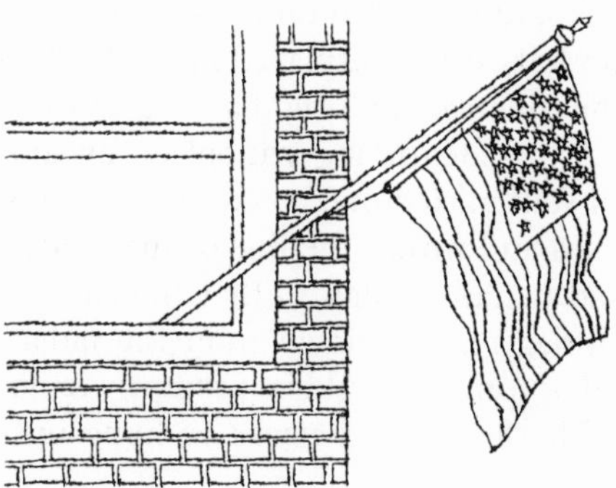

When used to cover a casket the flag should be placed so that the union is at the head and over the left shoulder. The flag should not be lowered into the grave or allowed to touch the ground.

When the flag is displayed in a manner other than flown from a staff, it should be flat, not tucked or draped, whether indoors or out. When displayed vertically against a wall, the union should be uppermost and to the observer's left. When displayed in a window it should be displayed in the same way, with the union to the left of the observer in the street.

When carried in a procession with another flag or flags, either the American flag should be on the marching right or, when there is a line of other flags, it may be in front of the center of that line.

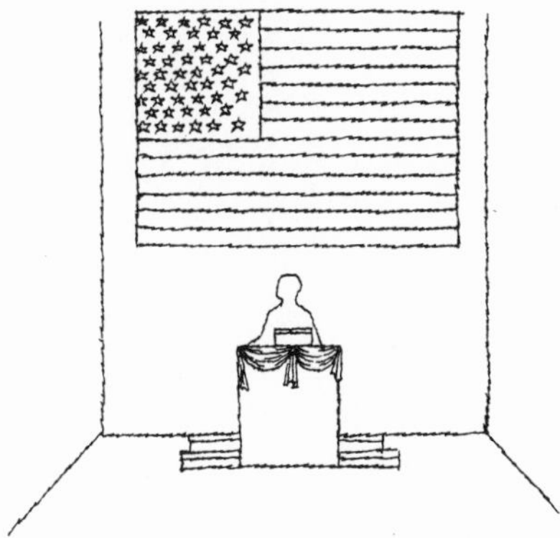

When a number of flags of states or cities are grouped and displayed from staffs, our national flag should be at the center or at the highest point of the group. If the flags of two or more nations are displayed, they should be flown from separate staffs of the same height, and the flags should be of approximately equal size. International usage forbids the display of the flag of one nation above that of another nation in time of peace.

When the flag is used in a church—on the chancel or on a platform —it should be placed on a staff on the clergyman's right; other flags are on his left. When displayed in the body of the church, the flag should be on the congregation's right as it faces the chancel.

As an identifying symbol on an automobile the flag is flown on a small staff affixed on the end of the front bumper, on the right looking forward and within the line of the fender. When used this way, the staff should be tall enough so that the flag clears the car hood. Alternately, a small flag may be flown from the radiator cap. If the flag has become soiled or torn, it should be promptly removed and replaced.

The flag should *never* be hung upside down except as a signal of distress.

CARE OF THE FLAG

The flag of our country should be carefully protected in storage and in use so that it will not be damaged. Every precaution should be taken to prevent it from becoming soiled or torn. It should not be permitted to touch the ground, or water, or a floor. In handling the flag do not let it brush against other objects.

If it should get wet it should be hung smoothly until dry—never rolled or folded while still damp.

Flags should be dry-cleaned, not washed.

61

The United Nations

Because of the diversified membership of the United Nations, precedence and protocol have always evidenced a kind of fluidity quite in keeping with its multinational character. Therefore, when entertaining guests of almost equal rank, the host and hostess may consult the Chief of Protocol (Protocol and Liaison, United Nations, New York).

It is quite understandable that members of an organization comprised of persons from countries of widely varied systems of diplomatic protocol and social custom will largely follow the customs of their home countries in such matters. On the other hand, since the United Nations Headquarters is located within the United States, very often—but by no means always—the American custom is followed.

In general there are three broad principles: First, the order of diplomatic precedence—prime minister or chief of state, cabinet minister, ambassador extraordinary and plenipotentiary, envoy extraordinary and minister plenipotentiary, counselor of embassy, and attaché—is observed. Second, no seniority in length of membership is recognized; the various member countries are listed alphabetically as they are spelled in the English language. Third, the administrative branch of the United Nations—

the Secretariat—is international in character, and the rank of its members is derived from the positions they hold in that branch and not from their national diplomatic status.

As there is a system of rotation employed in many of the component organizations of the United Nations, the determination of precedence is often qualified by a date—as in the Security Council, where the presidency is rotated monthly. Thus an individual who normally has the rank of Ambassador of his nation to the United Nations is raised in precedence temporarily while serving as President of the Security Council. He, of course, returns to his rank as Ambassador when his term as President expires.

Remembering that those serving at the United Nations are in a sense the guests of our country (and some are very distinguished guests indeed), the thoughtful host or hostess will get from the Chief of Protocol the necessary information about his or her guest-to-be.

Part TWELVE

GOOD MANNERS FOR EVERY DAY

62

On the telephone

When you talk on the telephone, whether in your home or in an office, the quality of your voice and your ability to express yourself clearly and concisely are of utmost importance. The person at the other end of the line cannot, after all, see your facial expressions or gestures, and the impression he receives must depend entirely on what he hears.

The telephone is designed to carry your voice at its natural volume and pitch. It is not necessary to shout. In fact, raising your voice, especially during a long-distance call, will only distort it. The telephone transmitter should be held about one inch from your lips and the earpiece close to your ear. Speak clearly and distinctly, with the same inflections that you would use in a face-to-face conversation. If you must put the telephone down during the conversation, do it gently, and when you hang up, do not slam the receiver down. The person at the other end may still have the phone close to his ear, and the sudden sharp bang can be quite deafening.

THE BUSINESS TELEPHONE

ANSWERING THE OFFICE PHONE

When telephone calls go through a switchboard, the operator often answers the ring by giving the name of the company. Some firms, however, feel that a more friendly impression is made on the caller by the greeting "ABC Company, good morning," or "Good afternoon, ABC Company."

When the call goes directly through to an office or has been transferred by the switchboard operator, it should be answered promptly. The person answering should identify himself and his department: "Mr. Hugo, accounting department." If answering for someone else, as a secretary does, she should give her employer's name as well as her own: "Mr. Carlson's office, Miss Norton speaking." If her employer is not in, or if she wishes to protect him from unnecessary calls, she should then offer to help the caller if she can, or if not, take a message: "He's not available at the moment. May I take a message?" or "He's out of the office just now. May I have him call you?" or "He's attending a meeting this morning. Could I help you?" If he is in his office, she asks, "May I tell him who is calling?" Any of these phrases should elicit the necessary information without the abruptness of "Who's calling?" But if the caller is evasive, you may have to ask for his name more directly. "Who is calling, please?" is sometimes necessary.

A pad and pencil must be kept next to the phone to avoid the irritating "Just a minute. I have to find a pencil" when you are asked to take a message.

PLACING A BUSINESS CALL

When placing a call, be sure that you have the correct number. Next to all business phones there should be a list of the numbers frequently called.

As soon as your call is answered, you must identify yourself; and unless the person you are calling knows you well, you must also name your organization. "This is Mr. Kramer of the Hobbs Company. May I speak to Mr. Hughes?"

It is not in good taste for a salesman to announce himself as Sam Sales to the operator or secretary who answers. Correctly he says, "This is Mr. Sales of the Blank Company." But when he reaches the man he is calling, he omits the "Mr." and uses "Sam."

A young woman in business says, "This is Miss Caesar of the Wheel Tyre Company."

All names must be given as briefly but as explicitly and as clearly as is humanly possible.

The most discourteous telephone habit is that of the businessman who tells his secretary to call Mr. Jones and then is not waiting to take the call. For example, the secretary dials the number; a voice announces, "A. B. Jones Company"; the secretary says, "Mr. Frank Brown is calling Mr. Jones." Promptly Mr. Jones says, "Hello, Frank," but instead of hearing Frank's voice, he hears a secretary explain, "Mr. Brown is busy on another wire. He'll be with you in a moment." Mr. Jones listens good-temperedly a few seconds—and less patiently for more seconds. Mr. Brown is evidently unaware that seconds seem minutes to a busy person listening to a dead receiver.

Initiating a call on a second line after putting in a call on the first shows nothing but rudeness to someone who, having been called to the telephone, is then asked to wait!

The correct form for a wife calling her husband at his office is, "This is Mrs. Jones; is Mr. Jones in?"

THE TELEPHONE IN THE HOME

"HELLO" CORRECT AT HOME

The correct way to answer a house telephone is still "Hello." "Yes" is abrupt and a bit rude, but "This is Mrs. Jones's house" leaves the door standing open wide, and "Mrs. Jones speaking" leaves her without chance of retreat.

This is not nonsense. It is a really important aspect of modern telephone etiquette. In all big cities telephones are rung so persistently by every type of stranger who wants to sell something to Mrs. Householder, to ask a favor of Mrs. Prominent, or to get in touch with Mr. Official (having failed to reach him at his office) that many prominent people are obliged to keep their personal telephone numbers unlisted. The last thing that they want to do, therefore, is to announce, "Miss Star speaking." It is far more practical to say "Hello" and let the one calling ask, "Is Miss Star there? Mr. Director would like to speak to her." If she herself answers, she must, of course, simply say, "Yes, this is Miss Star speaking."

WHO IS CALLING, PLEASE?

When the telephone in the home is answered by someone other than the head of the household, the response to "May I speak to Mrs. Brown, please?" is usually "Just a moment, please." However, if Mrs. Brown has told the maid, or a child, that she is very busy and cannot take any calls, the one who answers is correct in saying, "Mrs. Brown can't come to the phone just now; may I have your name, and she will call you as soon as she can."

If the caller should say, "I want to speak to Mrs. Brown personally," whoever has answered replies, "I'm sorry, but I can't interrupt Mrs. Brown. May I give her a message?" If he then refuses to leave a message or give his name, he can hardly expect Mrs. Brown to speak to him, nor is there any reason why she should.

Some women instruct their maids or their children to ask, "Who is calling, please?" so that they are prepared when they reach the telephone. However, others who feel that this gives an impression of prying may prefer that the one who answers say no more than "Just a moment, please."

When a woman is alone in the house, she definitely *should* ask "Who is calling?" before giving out any information as to her husband's whereabouts or return. This is not only correct—it's a necessary safety precaution.

GIVING ONE'S NAME

Whether to give one's name with or without title is a question often raised. When talking with strangers, titles are always used, but in other situations usage may vary.

The following rules hold good: An older person announcing herself or himself to someone much younger says, "This is Mrs. Elder" or "Miss Spinster" or "Mr. Elder."

A younger lady, whether married or single, says, "This is Marie Manners." To an older woman whom she knows socially she says, "Hello, Mrs. Knox? This is Mary Bailey." Mrs. Knox answers, "Good morning, Mrs. Bailey!" (Or "Mary," if she knows her well.)

A gentleman calling a lady never, under any circumstances, announces himself to her as "Mr. Smart." Instead, if the call is social, he says, "This is George Smart."

If you are a young man calling a friend and the answering voice is that of a friend or a member of the friend's family, you say, "This is Jim Brown," or probably "This is Jim." If the voice is that of a maid or a butler, you say, "This is Mr. James Brown. May I speak to Mr. Allen Gray?" or if the friend is the only man in the house, "to Mr. Gray."

INVITATIONS BY TELEPHONE

When Mrs. Jones issues an invitation by telephone, there is no long conversation, but merely:

Mrs. Jones: "Is that you Sally? This is Helen Jones." (*If she is much older* than Sally, she would say "This is Mrs. Jones.") "Could you and your husband (or John) dine with us next Tuesday?"

Sally: "I'm sorry we can't. We are going to the theater Tuesday night," or "We'd love to." And probably she repeats "Next Tuesday at eight" to be sure there is no misunderstanding of date or time. Before hanging up, she would add, "Thanks so much," or "We'll look forward to seeing you."

It is not correct to preface an invitation with, "Hello, John. What are you doing Saturday night?" or, "Are you going to be busy Monday afternoon?" This maneuver puts John in the embarrassing position of saying "Nothing" and then wanting to refuse after being told that he is expected to dine with the Borings or to play bridge with the Revokes. On the other hand, if he answers, "I have an engagement" and is then told that he would have been invited to something he likes very much, it is disappointing not to be able to go—without seeming rude to the person he has at first refused. A young woman who says she has an engagement and is then told, "Too bad you can't come, because John Brilliant was looking forward to meeting you," cannot change her mind and say, "Oh, then I'll get out of my dinner somehow and come." To do so would be the height of rudeness to all concerned.

In responding to a telephone invitation, it is very rude to say, "I'll let you know," unless it is immediately followed by an explanation such as "I'll have to ask John if he has made any commitments for that weekend," or "We have tickets for the high school play for that night, but perhaps I can exchange them for two on Friday." Without this sort of definite reason, "I'll let you know" sounds as if you were waiting for a better invitation to come along before saying "Yes."

THREE IMPORTANT DON'TS

When you get a wrong number, don't ask, "What number is this?" Ask instead, "Is this Main 2-3456?" so that you can look it up again or dial more carefully the next time.

Don't answer and then say, "Wait a minute" and keep the caller waiting while you vanish on an errand of your own. If the doorbell is ringing and you can't listen at that moment, say "I'll call you back in a few minutes!" And do so.

Don't let too young a child answer the telephone. A lot of the caller's time is wasted trying to make the child understand a message and relay it to the right person. If there is a long silence, there is no way of knowing whether the child is hunting for Mother or playing with his dog, quite forgetful of the caller and the telephone.

TERMINATING TELEPHONE CALLS

Under ordinary circumstances, the one who originates the call is the one who terminates it. This is not a matter of great importance, but it is helpful to know if a call seems to be dragging on and getting nowhere. The caller simply says, "I'm so glad I reached you—we'll be looking forward to seeing you on the seventh. Good-bye," or any appropriate remark.

We have all been trapped on the telephone by a long-winded caller —a determined salesman, perhaps, or a loquacious friend. When you have made several tentative efforts to end the conversation, which have been completely ignored, you may take more aggressive measures. At the first pause, or even interrupting if necessary, you may say, "I'm terribly sorry, but I simply must hang up—the baby's crying," or "My bath is running over," or even, "I'm late for an appointment now."

Another occasion on which a call should be terminated quickly is when the one who receives it has a visitor—either in a business office or at home. It is very inconsiderate to carry on a long chat while your visitor tries to occupy the time and avoid listening to your conversation. When you answer the phone and find it is not a call which can be terminated in a moment or two, you should postpone it for a more convenient time. At home you might say, "Joan just dropped in for a visit, so may I call you back in a little while?" The businessman could say, "I have a customer with me at the moment. If you will give me your number, I'll call you back when I am free."

In either case, be sure that you do return the call as soon as you can.

LONG-DISTANCE CALLS

When making a long-distance call, remember not to shout—amplifiers on the circuits will step up your voice all the way. On some overseas calls, it is also important to wait for the other person to finish speaking before you start. It can be a one-way-at-a-time circuit, and if both speak at once, both are shut off until one or the other stops talking.

Keep on the tip of your tongue what you have to say, and say it promptly. If you have several things to say, write them down and read them off.

If you call long distance often, a telephone timer is a must. It is a small second-counting gadget that rings a bell before each three minutes. If you are making a personal call and the person on the other end of the line likes to talk on and on, when you put in your call you may ask the operator to interrupt when the three minutes are up. But in these days of direct dialing, you will do well to have a timer at hand, for you may never have a chance to speak to the operator.

INFORMATION, PLEASE

It is quite true that the telephone operator who answers when we dial Information is prepared to answer our questions, but it is not at all true that she can be expected to overcome our lazy carelessness.

Strangely enough, it is not our oldest generation who find it difficult to read the small print in the telephone book (a small magnifying glass near the telephone will help the farsighted). On the contrary, investigation by the telephone company has found that the numerous unnecessary calls made to Information which at times literally cripple service—especially in our greatest cities—are made by the young. If for some reason you have to ask for a number, and it is one you think you will call again, write it down.

ON A PARTY LINE

The usual number of families sharing a party line is four and the maximum ten. When you realize that as long as one person is talking no outside call can reach any other person on that line, it is obvious that each one must show consideration for the others.

Ordinarily, when you find the line in use, you hang up for three minutes before signaling again. In an emergency, it is permissible to break in on a conversation and call out clearly "*Emergency!*" and then "Our barn is on fire," or "Johnny's had an accident," or whatever it is. But unless everyone on the line hangs up, your telephone is cut off.

Callers on a party line should limit their calls to five minutes—ten at the very most.

A personal memory: During the last war, a soldier tried to say a few last words to his wife before sailing. For fifty minutes the long-distance operator repeatedly received a "busy wire" signal. He left without a word to her. What he could have done (and we can all do) is remember that while the operator is not permitted to cut in on a busy wire, her supervisor can. In this case, the husband could have asked for the supervisor of the station and briefly explained the situation to her. At her discretion, she could then have cut in, announced a long-distance call for Mrs. Soldier, and asked those talking to hang up, please, so that she could receive it.

PAYING FOR YOUR CALLS

ON A NEIGHBOR'S TELEPHONE

Today almost everyone has his own telephone, but sometimes, especially in resort areas, there are those who become embarrassing and expensive nuisances by using a neighbor's telephone over and over again, not only for local calls, but for long-distance ones, too.

Those who live in a town where local calls are not charged for individually or who seldom use their allotted number of calls may find frequent use of their telephone annoying, but not an added expense, unless long-distance calls are made. In a city where even a local call is charged for, it should be just as correct to present an itemized bill for the charges on your telephone bill as it would be to present a bill for eggs or chickens, a thing you would never hesitate to do.

For an occasional local call, you might let it go; but for telephone users who make many long-distance calls, it is simplest as well as most accurate to show them the toll list so that each can check his calls and pay his total. Local calls that are charged individually will also be listed on the bill, and should be shown to the person who made them.

Try to avoid making calls from a busy doctor's office; but if you must do so, pay the nurse for the call.

BY VISITORS AND HOUSEGUESTS

Many visitors forget to offer to pay for their calls. The definite rule is this: Should a houseguest be obliged to make a local call or two, he would not ordinarily offer payment for it, but it is absolutely required that he pay for every long-distance call. Moreover, this is the only way in which a houseguest can feel free to telephone as often as he or she may want to. The guest can call the operator as soon as he has finished speaking and ask for "the toll charge on 212 468 9121." The necessary amount should be left with a slip, giving date and number called. Or if a visitor has used the telephone a great deal during a long stay, the complete list of calls or telegrams with the amounts of each and their total should be handed to the hostess and paid for when he leaves. This is not humiliating, and no matter how rich the host may be, it is the correct way to pay this debt.

An even more satisfactory way is to charge the call to your own home number. This may be done even though you do not have a Telephone Company credit card. The operator calls your home and asks whoever is there if he will accept the charge. You must, of course, warn those at home, in advance, to do so. This system saves you the annoyance of finding correct change or cash to pay your hostess, and saves her the inconvenience of a larger bill. If you have a credit card, by all means use that.

THE TELEPHONE COURTESY TEST

If it interests you to know how good your telephone manners may be, the number of times you can answer "Yes" to the following questions will give you your rating. If every one is "Yes," you deserve not merely a crown, but a halo!

1. Do you make sure of the correct number so as not to risk disturbing strangers by "calling from memory?"

2. Do you make sure that your conversations with busy people are as brief as possible?

3. When calling intimate friends who do not recognize your voice, do you resist playing a game of "guess who?" and announce yourself promptly?

4. Do you try to time your calls so as not to interfere with the occupations of those you call most often?

5. Do you make business calls well before the close of office hours, especially if calling a person you know is a commuter?

6. In a business office, do you explain to personal friends inclined to talk at length that you will call them after hours?

7. Do you treat wrong-number calls as a mutual inconvenience and answer, "Sorry, wrong number," in a tone of polite sympathy instead of showing ill-tempered annoyance?

8. On a dial telephone, do you always wait for the dial tone?

9. When the number you are calling is not answered quickly, do you wait long enough for someone to lay aside what he or she may be doing and to reach the telephone? It is very annoying to have been disturbed just to pick up the telephone and find the caller has hung up.

10. When making a number of calls on a party line, do you space them so that others on the line may have a chance to use their telephones?

63

The courteous driver

If every driver would follow the rule "Do unto others as you would have others do unto you," there would be very few accidents on our highways. No one who has a license to drive can fail to appreciate the good manners of the driver who signals his turns, makes his stops smoothly, and gradually pulls into the proper lane well before making a turn. This type of consideration not only shows "good manners," but may actually save the lives of others—as well as his own.

Really fine drivers do exist, and very good ones are not uncommon. This chapter is certainly not for either of these groups, but for the tens of thousands who swarm out on the highways to have their lives saved time and again (though they don't know it) by the experts—or by Lady Luck. If we think seriously of the power in all these machines running freely over our streets and roads and realize that no examination in driving courtesy is required of one applying for a license, the wonder is not that there are accidents, but that there are not more.

Courtesy is essential to safe driving. The courteous driver constantly considers how his actions will affect those behind, in front of, and beside him, and is alert to what other cars are doing as well. Because of this attitude, he is invariably a safe driver. Many men and women whose behavior in all other circumstances is beyond reproach become transformed into bad-mannered autocrats behind the wheel of a car. Even calm and considerate drivers become jittery when exposed to repeated experiences with rude motorists. These otherwise safe and well-mannered people, when impatient and irritated, often become "accidents going somewhere to happen."

A polite driver no more cheats at a red light or stop sign than he would cheat in a game of cards. Often the man who tries to force his way ahead of others in a line of cars would not think of trying to force himself ahead of others in a box-office line—if he accidentally did such a thing he would probably be mortified by his own rudeness. However, let him get behind the wheel of a car, and his courteous instincts may fly right out the window.

"DO UNTO OTHERS . . ."

Every driver has innumerable chances to observe the golden rule each time he steps into his car. How do *you* feel when there is not one polite driver in the solid line of traffic into which you must turn from a side street? Are you that polite one who will pause to let a car in, or do you stay glued to the bumper of the car ahead. Are *you* the driver who swears at the heavy pedestrian traffic slowing your turn in the city, or are *you* the one who waits patiently until there is a break in the flow, remembering that you may have to cross a street yourself when you leave the car?

Put yourself in the other person's place when he causes you to wait or startles you in some way. Ask yourself if there isn't a good reason for his action. You will find, if you are honest, that many times his sudden swerve was to avoid a child or an animal, or his seemingly long wait was to let an older person cross the street safely. Don't just give lip service to the golden rule; act on it, and you will not only become a better driver, but a more relaxed and therefore a safer driver.

AT TRAFFIC LIGHTS

The courteous driver stops for a red light in a position that does not block the crosswalk. In heavy traffic he doesn't enter an intersection unless he is sure he can complete the crossing before the light changes.

It is both illegal and impolite to start up with a rush when the light turns orange in the other direction. But it is equally discourteous to linger lazily after the light has changed since the drivers behind you will be caught by the next red light.

If you know that there is a right- or left-turn arrow at an intersection, stay out of those lanes when you intend to go straight through so that you do not prevent others from turning with the arrow.

CASPAR MILQUETOAST

Traffic police are well equipped to deal with those who exceed the speed limit. On many highways there is a minimum limit as well as a maximum, but where there is not, the offender against courtesy is not always just the fast driver, but also the slow! The snail who pokes along thirty miles an hour slower than the other cars is a menace to everyone. He is frequently ill-mannered enough to drive in the left or center lane, causing overtaking cars to change lanes—often too suddenly. If you wish to drive slowly, please stay off the super highways entirely, or if you must use them, have the courtesy to keep to the right where the slower traffic belongs.

OTHER OFFENDERS

Another discourteous menace is the "weaver." He scoots back and forth from lane to lane, cutting drivers off, causing them to jam on their brakes or swerve into the lane beside them. He rarely looks beside or behind him, and shows complete lack of consideration for the other motorists on the highway.

The well-mannered traveler on a highway always signals well in advance before he switches lanes or makes a turn. He keeps an eye on his mirror to be sure that drivers behind him have noticed his signals before he makes his move.

A thoughtful motorist always gets into the proper lane well before he reaches his turn or exit. There are few people more dangerous on the road than the man who suddenly realizes that he has reached his turnoff or that he needs gas at the service station, and who disregards the cars in the lanes behind him as he cuts through, in front of, or into them in order to reach his destination.

PASSING POINTERS

One of the worst offenders on the road is the driver who pulls out of a solid line of cars to steal his way forward. Finding himself in sudden danger of a head-on collision, he makes a frantic effort to push his way back into the line—possibly forcing someone off the road or at the very least crumpling fenders.

Of course, the one who causes him to take his rash action is also to blame. He is the same Caspar Milquetoast who drives well below the speed limit, this time on a narrow twisting road through hilly country with a long line of impatient drivers behind him. In their exasperation these drivers take desperate chances, passing too close to a curve or the top of a hill, and the net result is that Caspar is more likely to be involved in a serious crash than if he were to drive a little faster.

A final word about good passing habits: When you have reached that safe stretch of road with adequate visibility, make your move smoothly, quickly, and without changing your mind. And when you are the driver being passed, slow down a little to allow the other car plenty of space to pull back into line ahead of you.

NIGHT DRIVING

There are two very important rules of safety and courtesy to be followed when driving at night. First, the careful driver lowers his speed in the darkness because he simply cannot see as far ahead in the dark no matter how excellent his headlights. Second, whether his state laws require it or not, he dims his lights when meeting other cars at night. Blinding another driver by a blaze of light is not only rude but dangerous. When drivers courteously dim their lights first, they automatically invite others to do the same. If you are driving with lights on low beam, it is reasonable to turn them high momentarily to remind an approaching driver to turn his down, but keeping on your high-beam lights to "get even" with someone who has not dimmed his is both impolite and stupid. After all, you can be the victim of the driver you "blind."

USING THE HORN

If more people realized that the horn, as the voice of the car, is in reality the voice of the driver, there would be less thoughtlessness in its use. If it is necessary to prevent an accident, use your horn, of course, but no polite driver ever blows his horn at an individual, a crowd of persons on foot, or other automobiles as if to blast them out of the way. In other words, a courteous driver sounds his horn as a warning only in emergencies. Otherwise he beeps it gently as a polite signal.

No well-mannered young man would announce his arrival at his date's home by standing at the curb and yelling for her. Yet this is just the impression given by the man who arrives by car, sits at the wheel, and blasts away at the horn.

I have the greatest sympathy for the man in the following story. His car had stalled in heavy traffic, and although he was obviously trying to remedy the trouble, the driver behind was impatiently honking and swearing at the embarrassed victim. After standing the noise and rudeness for as long as he could, our driver politely walked back to the other's car, and said, "Sir, if you would be kind enough to start my car for *me*, I would be delighted to stay here and blow your horn for *you!*"

PARKING

The two most important parking rules, the observance of which separates the thoughtful driver from the inconsiderate one are: first, never take up more space than necessary, and second, never park so close to the car behind or in front of you that he will be unable to pull out.

In addition to those two rules, it should be pointed out that it is considerate to park as close to the curb as possible to leave more room for passing cars. And most important, when the car in front of you obviously wishes to back into a parking space, stop in time to give him room to do it without rushing him by creeping forward, or worse, blowing your horn! It is, of course, the most glaring breach of good manners to sneak into an empty space when another car is about to back in.

Courteous drivers stay within the lines for parking spaces, they take care not to block driveways, and they park off the pavement on rural roads or when forced to pull off a highway. They don't monopolize unmetered parking spaces in busy shopping areas for long periods, and they don't pull out without carefully looking in all directions. They also always look behind them before backing up to make sure there are no pedestrians about to step off the curb.

ENTERING A CAR

The custom of a man opening the door and assisting a woman into a car is still correct—in fact many women feel slighted if the gesture is not made. However, when the car is parked on a busy street, no considerate woman would expect her escort to help her in and then walk into the stream of cars to get in on the other side. In this case the man excuses himself for preceding her, and slides in from her side. Safety for everyone concerned is far more important than unthinking obedience to an old established rule of etiquette. On a wide or lightly traveled street a gentleman naturally enters the car on his own side after first assisting any ladies into the car on the curb side. Obviously passengers in the back seats should also enter from the side nearest the curb whenever possible.

DRINKING AND DRIVING

It should be unnecessary to emphasize the menace of the drunken driver; certainly there is nothing to be said in his defense, nor could anyone want him to escape the full penalty of the law. But not half enough blame is laid on the exhilarated driver who has had one or two cocktails and cannot be called drunk by any standard. With joyful recklessness he takes chances that he would not think of taking when he has had nothing to drink. Alcohol and gasoline do not mix. If you have had a drink or two and realize that your senses are not as sharp as they should be, DO have the intelligence to refuse to take the wheel. It could be nothing but a display of the finest type of courtesy to ask, when the stakes are so high, that some other man or woman do the driving. Furthermore, any host, seeing that one of his guests is showing the signs of his liquor, should do his best to persuade him to stay away from the wheel.

IN AN EMERGENCY

If in spite of all precautions you have an emergency such as a flat tire or broken fan belt, it is not only essential to your safety, but is also courteous to the other motorists to pull well off to the side of the road. Raise the hood, and tie a white handkerchief or cloth to your door handle, as this is the universal signal of distress. Any policeman, and often a kindhearted passerby, will stop to offer assistance. On a super highway, stay in your car until help arrives. Walking for help on such a road is dangerous both for yourself and to the cars who swerve to avoid you.

DRIVERS WE LIKE—AND DISLIKE

The perfect driver is one with whom you never find yourself driving the car. If you are constantly tensing your muscles and pressing your feet on imaginary controls, this is an indication that you are with a poor driver. Rapid accelerations and sudden stops can only mean that the person driving has not been planning ahead and concentrating on his responsibility. The last two characteristics are always evident in the driving of the well-mannered motorist.

AS FOR THE MANNERS OF PEDESTRIANS . . .

When anyone is run over by an automobile, the driver's guilt is *invariably* taken for granted. Often the blame belongs to him, but often it does not. In other words, motor manners are every bit as important to people who want to escape being injured as to people who want to avoid injuring them. First rules for pedestrians include:

Don't cross before the light turns green or the signal reads "Walk." Don't cross streets in the middle of a block. Don't dart forward after hiding behind a parked car and imagine that an oncoming driver, whom you yourself could not see, could know by means of clairvoyance that you were there! Don't, when the lights change while you are in the middle of the street, turn and run back to the side you started from. If you keep on going exactly as you were, drivers will automatically wait and give you time to pass in front of their cars. But those you have already passed cannot possibly be prepared to have you about-face and suddenly dash back again in front of the wheels.

One of the serious causes of pedestrian accidents is the practically universal (and a very natural) habit of walking on the right side of a road that has no sidewalk. A pedestrian on the right side cannot see a car overtaking him. If another car is coming from the other direction, the pedestrian cannot even hear the car coming from behind him. Pedestrians should walk on the left-hand side of the road—always.

SOME TIPS FOR MOTOR TRIPS

YOUR CAR AND EQUIPMENT

When starting out on an automobile trip that will take you away from your normal garage or repair shop, make certain that your equipment is in the best possible condition. Tires are the most important item—never start on a trip on which you will undoubtedly be driving at higher speeds than you normally would with worn tires, or if you are likely to find winter driving conditions, without snow tires or chains. Your fuel, oil, brakes, and automatic transmission fluid should be checked before starting, as well as frequently during the trip. In strange territory you have no way of knowing when you will find the next gas station. Windshield-wiper blades should be replaced if rough or worn, and headlights, turn indicators, and brake lights checked. And of course, your car registration must be in order and easily available, as well as your driver's license.

AVOID FATIGUE

On long trips it is essential to make frequent stops to stretch your legs, take some refreshment, and allow your engine and tires to cool off. If you are accompanied by a licensed and capable driver, you should, of course, take turns at the wheel. A good rule is to stop and change drivers every hundred miles or every two hours, whichever comes first.

If you are stopping at motels along the way, it is wise to make a reservation for the following evening before you set off in the morning. The many chains of excellent motels all over the United States are delighted to help you estimate the distance you will cover and call ahead, free of charge, to one of their member motels to reserve a room for that night. You will find yourself much less tired if you plan to arrive at your destination by four in the afternoon to allow time for a rest, a little sightseeing if there are attractions in the neighborhood, and a leisurely dinner.

TRAVELING WITH CHILDREN

Traveling with children who are old enough to read, write, or play games need not be a problem. By taking along a supply of papers, crayons, or one of the excellent game books that are sold just for the purpose, the time can be made to fly. Verbal games, too, such as "Twenty Questions," help to pass the hours. You may find that frequent stops are necessary—young stomachs seem to demand a steady flow of nibbles when motoring—but the stops will help to avoid restless wriggling while in the car.

For little children, a mattress laid in the back of the station wagon, or a little playpen with a well-padded mat on the back seat is a boon to the parents. The baby is free to move about safely, rather than endure the restraint of a car seat or his mother's lap. Even the older child will enjoy the luxury of being able to stretch out on such a mattress if you can afford to use the space in this way. Usually children will sleep away many hours if they can lie down comfortably.

FOR COMFORT AND SAFETY

It is required by law that all new cars be equipped with safety belts, but there is no law which says you must use them. However, you are very foolish if you don't. Figures on accident deaths prove that while they do not prevent accidents, fatalities are far less frequent among drivers and passengers wearing properly installed belts or shoulder harnesses. They should be snugly fastened, so that you are not thrown hard *against* the belt by a sudden stop. Not only should the driver use his own belt, but he is correct in asking his passengers to do the same.

It is an excellent idea to keep a pair of sunglasses in the glove compartment of your car, since many people find that prolonged glare can cause severe headaches. If the glasses are always there, you will never be caught unprepared by an unexpected change in the weather.

Your clothing should be loose and comfortable. A girl who is comfortable in slacks or shorts will find that they are excellent for traveling. They allow maximum mobility, and now that there are so many motels available, a woman need not be seen in public until after she has had a chance to wash and change. A man, even though he may be dressed in a business suit, will probably be more comfortable if he removes his tie and replaces his jacket with a loose sweater or, if it is warm, drives in his shirt with the collar loosened.

CAR POOLS

Many thousands of Americans go to work in a "car pool." As a practical and economical arrangement it allows the other members of their families to have the car except on those days when it is their turn to provide the transportation.

For people who are about to join a car pool there are several basic rules of courtesy to be observed.

1. Be on time! If you keep the others waiting you may cause them to be penalized for late arrival at work.

2. Don't carry quantities of articles. If you must take a package or two, don't pile them where they will obstruct the driver's view, either directly or in the rear-view mirror.

3. Don't open or close windows without asking the permission of the other passengers.

4. Don't bring an extra passenger without asking the driver if there is room. For example, some drivers do not object to three in the front seat, but others might find this a considerable annoyance.

5. Ask the permission of the other riders before smoking. When you do smoke, make sure that a window is opened, if only a little, to allow the smoke to escape.

6. If you are a woman, don't use the rear-view mirror to fix your makeup. Carry a compact with a mirror or a small mirror in your purse.

7. If you must carry an umbrella when it rains, shake it well (and your raincoat, too) before getting in the car so that you won't soak your neighbor.

8. If you are not planning to use the car pool, let the driver know in advance so that he does not go out of his way to pick you up or wait for you unnecessarily before continuing his trip.

64

For those who smoke

The universal custom of smoking in nearly all places at nearly all hours and by all sorts of people makes it seem advisable to gather in this special chapter rules that will permit the enjoyment of smoking by those who smoke with the least unhappiness to those who don't.

TIMES WHEN NO ONE MAY SMOKE

One may not smoke in a church, or during any religious service or ceremonial proceedings.

One may not smoke in a sickroom unless the patient himself is smoking or unless he specifically says that his visitor is welcome to smoke. Even though ash trays are in evidence in a doctor's waiting room, it is thoughtful to ask if others waiting object to smoking.

Good taste still forbids smoking by a woman on a city street. It should be unnecessary to say that no one should think of smoking or carrying a lighted cigarette when dancing.

Smoking is forbidden on local buses and on some coaches on the railroad. These cars are clearly marked "No Smoking."

Smoking is permitted in the mezzanine or loge seats in some movie houses, but never in the main orchestra. Whether it is allowed at all depends on local or state ordinances.

Smoking is forbidden in most museums, although some have designated areas where it is allowed.

Legitimate theaters do not allow smoking in the theater proper. It is usually allowed in the outer lobby, and those who wish to smoke during the intermission go there to do so. It is perfectly correct for a man who wishes to smoke to leave a lady who doesn't, but he should hurry back, and not leave her too frequently.

To these restrictions should be added those in business (regulated by the rules of each firm) and those of consideration for the customs of the community which you may be visiting or for the prejudices of the people with whom you personally come in contact.

Most important of all, and so frequently disobeyed, is the rule never to light a cigarette, pipe, or cigar when a "No Smoking" sign is displayed.

In private situations when there may be some objection, before lighting your cigarette, always ask "Do you mind if I smoke?" If there is any hesitation in the reply, do your best to refrain from smoking until you leave.

WHEN GUESTS SMOKE

The answer to the hostesses who ask how they can protect their possessions from careless guests is that hospitality need never be helpless. It is true that after a guest has burned a hole in the upholstery or a groove on a table edge, nothing can be done about it, although the guest should insist on paying for whatever repairs are necessary. But when a hostess sees a smoker pick up an ornament of value to use in place of an ash tray, she can certainly take it away and put an ash tray in its place. Perhaps she says nothing or perhaps she smiles and says, "Let me give you this," as though she were thinking of the smoker's convenience.

The sensible solution for the wise hostess is to see to it that there is an ash tray within easy reach of every seat that may be occupied by a smoking guest. A thoughtful hostess, even one who does not smoke herself, will see that there are cigarette boxes with fresh cigarettes in them and a lighter that is filled and that works—or plenty of match boxes—for the comfort of her smoking guests. Ash trays should be reasonably large and have a wide lip or groove to hold a cigarette.

Cigars need be passed only after dinner and when the ladies have left the dining room.

SMOKING DON'TS

First of all, it is unforgivable to lay a cigarette (or cigar) on the edge of a table or other piece of furniture—ever! Forgetting it and letting it burn a charred groove on a table edge or a brown scar on a marble mantel is the inevitable result of putting it down on the wrong place to begin with. Find an ash tray to lay it on—or ask for one.

Striking a match directly toward someone is dangerous—the head may fly off and cause a painful burn.

Never press a cigarette out without being sure that the object pressed on is intended for that purpose. Cigarettes put out against lamp bases, ornaments, and the like may mar or destroy objects of value. And potted plants do not thrive on ashes or unburned tobacco!

Lighted cigarettes should not be thrown into fireplaces. If the fire is laid, a roaring blaze started on a hot July day may be the reward of such carelessness, and if it is not, remains of cigarettes or unburned filter tips look dreadfully messy in a freshly swept fireplace. Never toss a cigarette out the window—it may land on an awning or the top of someone's new convertible parked outside.

Other don'ts include such untidiness as spilling ashes on the floor or upholstery, or throwing filter-tipped cigarettes on a lawn or terrace where the fireproof, rainproof tip will remain until someone rakes or sweeps it away. And worst of all is the smoker who leaves his lighted cigarette in the ash tray to burn itself out, making even the other smokers present ill from the smell.

CIGARETTES AT THE TABLE

Whether it is proper to smoke at table depends upon the setting of the places. If each place is set with cigarettes, a lighter, and an ash tray, naturally people may smoke as soon as they choose. However, in the houses where cigarettes are not on the table or where they are passed only after dessert, it is still bad manners to light one's own cigarette and smoke throughout the meal.

It is also extremely bad manners and thoughtless to pay no attention to whether smoke from the cigarette you are holding is blowing into the face of someone who may not be smoking.

A FEW HINTS ON SMOKING MANNERS

Smokers should carry their own cigarettes. Even though a hostess has filled her cigarette boxes (to put filter tips in some boxes and "regulars" in others is thoughtful), she will appreciate the guest who does not depend entirely on her supply.

When a man is about to smoke, it is polite to offer a cigarette to people next to him or in his immediate group, but he need not pass them farther afield. And a warning to the ladies: the feminine cigarette "sponge" is no more popular than the masculine.

A man should light a woman's cigarette if he is close to her, but not if he is on the other side of a table or if it would be awkward in any way.

A woman smoker should carry her own matches or lighter and *use* them. She only looks ridiculous sitting with a dangling cigarette, waiting for a group of men to break up their conversation in order to provide her with a light.

Pipe smokers must exert extra caution when emptying a pipe, since it sometimes takes a sharp rap to loosen the burned tobacco in the bowl. They should select a sturdy ash tray, for they may shatter a delicate glass or fine china receptacle or, if it is too small, find their ashes spraying all over the table top.

And two final words to the cigar smoker. First, don't leave cigar butts in ash trays. They *do* smell, and they *are* unattractive in appearance. Unless you see that someone is prepared to remove the ash tray when you have finished smoking, try to find another means of disposing of the cigar butt—into a lighted fire, down the toilet, anywhere, as long as it is out of sight.

Second, you *must* ask permission to smoke a cigar in mixed company. Naturally, when cigars are passed to the men after dinner or offered (traditionally) in an office to celebrate the birth of a baby, or at any male gathering, you are expected to smoke them. However, since many women find cigar smoke unpleasant if not actually nauseating, your popularity with the opposite sex will quickly wane if you do not check with your companion before lighting a cigar.

65

In clubs

A society is an organization composed of persons who band together for a common purpose and who are not infrequently obligated to one another by bonds of brotherhood. A club is an organization composed of persons who have joined it for their individual convenience or pleasure. Its membership, whether composed of men or women or both, may be limited to a dozen or may include several thousands, and the procedure of joining may be easy or difficult, according to the type of club and the standing of the would-be member.

Membership in many athletic associations may be had by walking in and paying dues, and many country golf clubs are as free to the public as country inns. But joining an exclusive club is a very different matter. To be eligible for membership in such a club, a man must have among the members friends who like him enough to be willing to propose him and second him and write letters for him; furthermore he must be disliked by no one—at least not so much that a member might raise a serious objection to his company.

There are two ways of joining a club: by invitation and by having application made for you. To join by invitation means that you are invited when the club is started to be one of the founders or charter members; or if you are a distinguished citizen, you may at the invitation of the governors become an honorary member; or in a small or informal club you may become an ordinary member by invitation or at the suggestion of the governors that you would be welcome. A charter member pays dues, but not always an initiation fee. An honorary member pays neither dues nor initiation fee; he is really a permanent guest of the club, or a temporary one—as in the case of a mayor, for example, who may be an honorary member just for the duration of his term in office. A life member is one who after paying his dues for twenty years or so in a lump sum is thereafter exempted from dues even though the annual dues should be greatly increased in later years or he should live to be a hundred.

Different clubs offer different types of membership. At a country club you might be a "golfing member," using only the golfing facilities, or a "house member," using only the restaurant and facilities of the clubhouse. Or it may depend on where you live—the ordinary members of a club might be resident, meaning that they live or have their office within fifty miles of the club, or nonresident, living beyond that distance and paying smaller dues but having the same privileges.

BECOMING A MEMBER

"PUTTING UP" A NAME

Since no sensible man is likely to want to join a club in which the members are not his friends, he says to a member of his family or an intimate friend, "Do you mind putting me up for the Nearby Club? I think that Dick would second me." The friend answers, "Delighted to do it!" and Dick says the same.

More likely the suggestion to join comes from a member, who remarks one day, "Why don't you join the Nearby Club? It would be very convenient for you." The other replies, "I'd like to," and the friend says, "Let me put you up, and I'll ask Dick to second you." And he arranges with Dick to do so.

It must be remembered that a man has no right to ask anyone who is not really one of his best friends to propose or second him. It is an awkward thing to refuse in the first place; in the second, recommending someone involves considerable effort and on occasion a great deal of annoyance, to say nothing of responsibility.

For example, let us suppose that Jim Struthers asks Donald Cameron to propose him and Henry Bancroft to second him. Donald informs the club secretary, and at the proper time Jim's name is posted—meaning that it appears among a list of nominees put up on the bulletin board in the clubhouse. In many clubs, a list of proposed names is also sent to each member. It is then the duty of Donald and Henry each to write a letter of endorsement to the governors of the club, to be read by that body when they hold the meeting at which Struthers' name comes up for election.

Board of Governors
The Nearby Club
Dear Sirs:

I am delighted to propose Mr. James Struthers for membership in The Nearby Club. I have known Mr. Struthers for many years and consider him qualified in every way for membership.

He is a graduate of Northsouthern University, class of 1951, and is a member of the Center Club. He is now with the firm of Jones, Fairbanks, & Co.

Yours very truly,
Donald Cameron

In most clubs, the number of members is limited by the bylaws. Therefore, there may be a waiting list, necessitating a considerable delay before Jim's name comes up for consideration. Before making a decision as to which clubs you wish to join, find out about the length of waiting time, and discuss the possibilities with your sponsor.

MEETING THE GOVERNORS

Cameron must also select with Struthers the required number of friends who are members of the club (but not governors) and ask them to write letters endorsing him. Furthermore, the candidate cannot come up for election unless he knows several of the governors personally so that they can vouch for him at the meeting. Donald and Henry must therefore take Jim to several governors and personally present him.

At many clubs the governors set aside an hour on several weekend afternoons before elections for meeting candidates in the visitors' rooms at the clubhouse. Or a large reception may be held, attended by the governors, the candidates, and their sponsors.

IMPORTANCE OF GOOD LETTERS OF ENDORSEMENT

Jim Struthers, having popular and well-known sponsors and also being very well liked himself, is elected with no difficulty.

But take the case of young Breezy. He was put up by two not very well-known members who wrote half-hearted endorsements themselves and did nothing about getting letters from others. They scarcely knew any of the governors, and trusted in the fact that two members who knew Breezy slightly would do. As he had no friends strong enough to stand up for him, he was turned down. A man is rarely blackballed, as such an action could injure him in the eyes of the community. (The expression "blackball" comes from the custom of voting for a member by putting a white ball in a ballot box, or against him by putting in a black one.) If a candidate is likely to receive a blackball the governors do not vote on him at all, but inform the proposer that the name of his candidate had better be withdrawn, which is almost invariably done. Later on, if the objection to him is disproved or overcome, his name may again be put up.

QUALIFICATIONS FOR ELECTION

The more popular the candidate, the less work for his proposer and seconder. A stranger, if he is not a member of a comparable club in his own city, would need strong friends to elect him to an exclusive club in another community. An unpopular man should never be proposed.

However, in all but very rare instances events run smoothly; the candidate is voted on at a meeting of the board of governors and is elected. A notice is mailed to him next morning, telling him that he has been elected and that his initiation fee and his dues make a total of so much. The candidate at once draws his check for the amount and mails it. As soon as the club secretary has had ample time to receive the check, the new member is free to use the club as much or as little as he likes.

THE NEW MEMBER

The new member usually, though not necessarily, goes to a club for the first time with his proposer or his seconder, or at least with an old member, who briefs him on unwritten information: "That chair in the window is where old Snodgrass always sits. Don't sit in it when you see him coming in or he'll be disagreeable to everybody for a week." Or "They always play double stakes at this table, so don't sit at it unless you mean to." Or "There's an unwritten rule that we never walk on the grass in the circle." "The roasts are always good, and that waiter is the best in the room." And so on.

A new member is given or should ask for a copy of the Club Book, which contains, besides the list of the members, the constitution and the bylaws or "house rules," which he must study carefully and be sure to obey.

COUNTRY CLUBS

Country clubs vary greatly in both characteristics and expense. It is quite as difficult to be elected to some of them as to any of the exclusive clubs in the cities—more so, if anything—inasmuch as they are open to the family and friends of every member. Whereas in a man's city club his membership gives the privilege of the club to no one but himself personally, in a country club his family and possible guests must be as agreeable to the governors as he is.

Nearly all country clubs have, however, one open door unknown to city clubs. People taking houses in the neighborhood or vacation visitors in a resort are often granted "season privileges"; that is, on being proposed by a member and upon paying a season's subscription, new householders are accepted as transient guests. In some clubs this membership may be indefinitely renewed; in others a man must come up for regular election at the end of three or six months' or a year's time.

Apart from the few that may be called very exclusive country clubs, there are hundreds—more likely thousands—that have very simple requirements for membership. Merely having one or two members vouch for a candidate's integrity and good behavior is sufficient.

In almost all country clubs the atmosphere is less formal than in a city club. Members speak to each other without introductions, form tennis games and golf foursomes with comparative strangers, and otherwise behave in a more casual and informal manner.

WOMEN'S CLUBS

In every state of the Union, there are women's clubs of every kind and grade: social, political, sports, professional. Some are housed in enormous and elegant buildings designed especially for them; others are in only a room or two, usually in a hotel. Most women's clubs work for, or support, various charities, but some merely provide lodging facilities or a place for the members to meet socially.

IN THE CITY CLUB

Good manners in clubs are the same as good manners elsewhere—only a little more so. A club is for the pleasure and convenience of many people; it is never intended as a stage setting for a star or clown or monologist. There is hardly any place where a person has greater need of restraint and consideration for others than in a club. In every well-appointed one there is a reading room or library where conversation is discouraged. There are books and easy chairs and good light for reading by day and night, and one important unspoken rule is not to speak to anybody who is reading or writing.

It is courteous of a governor or long-time member, on noticing a new member or a visitor—especially one who seems to be rather at a loss—to go up and speak to him. In the dining rooms of many clubs, there is a large table, sometimes known as the social table, where members who are lunching alone may sit and where the conversation is general. All are expected to talk whether they are friends or total strangers.

VISITORS IN A CLUB

When a men's club moves into new quarters, it is quite usual for the members to give an opening reception to which ladies are invited to see the house. After this, in some clubs, women are barred, except perhaps for one day a year on which they are invited to a cocktail party or dinner.

Today, most men's clubs have a dining room to which ladies as well as gentlemen who are not members are admitted. When a woman gives a lunch or any party in a club, either a women's club, or in the "open" dining room of a men's club, she waits for her guests in the lobby, entrance hall, or, if there is one, the reception room. As her guests arrive, they join her and stand or sit near her.

All men's clubs have private dining rooms where members can give dinners that include nonmembers, either men who are local residents but who do not belong to the club or men who are merely visiting the city.

In almost every club in the United States a member is allowed to extend club privileges to a stranger—one who lives beyond a specified distance—for a varying length of time determined by the bylaws of the club. In some clubs, guests may be put up for a day only; in others, the privilege extends for two weeks or more. Many clubs allow each member a certain number of visitors a year; in others, visitors are unlimited. In many city clubs the same guest cannot be introduced twice within the year. In country clubs members usually may have an unlimited number of visitors. When these are golf or tennis players, the host is responsible for greens fees or court charges.

As a rule, when a member introduces a stranger, he takes him to the club personally, writes his name in the visitors' book, and introduces him to those who may be present at the time. If for some reason it is not possible for the host to take his guest to the club, he writes to the secretary for a card of introduction.

Secretary
The Town Club
Dear Sir (or *Dear Mr. Jones*):
Kindly send Mr. A. M. Stanton, of Wilkes Barre, Pa., a card extending the privileges of the Club for one week.
Mr. Stanton is staying at the Carlton House.

Yours very truly,
Henry Bancroft

Note the degree of formality. One does not write "Dear Jim," because this is not a personal letter, but a formal request to be put on file.

The secretary then sends a card to Mr. Stanton:

The Town Club
Extends its privileges to
Mr. Stanton
from Jan. 7 to Jan. 14
Through the courtesy of
Mr. Henry Bancroft

Mr. Stanton goes to the club by himself. A visitor who has been given a card to a club has, during the time of his visit, all the privileges of a member except that he is not allowed to introduce others to the club and he cannot give a dinner in a private dining room. The guest must arrange at the club's office to have his charges rendered to himself. He must be scrupulous about asking for his bill upon leaving and pay it immediately and without question. Otherwise his bill must be paid by the member who issued the invitation—a poor reward for the latter's kindness.

The visitor's status throughout his stay is founded on the courtesy of the member who introduced him, and he should try to show an equal courtesy to everyone about him. He should remember not to intrude on the privacy of the members he does not know. He has no right to criticize the management, the rules, or the organization of the club. In short, he behaves exactly as a guest would behave in a private home.

UNBREAKABLE RULES

Failure to pay one's debts or behavior unbefitting a gentleman is cause for expulsion from every club.

If a man cannot afford to belong to a club, he must resign while he is still in good standing. If later on he is able to rejoin, his name is put at the head of the waiting list; if he was considered a desirable member, he is re-elected at the next meeting of the governors. But a man who has been expelled—unless he can show that his expulsion was unjust—can never again belong to that club. In fact, it would probably be difficult for him to be elected to any other club since his expulsion from one will almost certainly come to the attention of another considering him for membership.

RESIGNING FROM A CLUB

When one wishes to resign from a club, it is necessary to write a letter of resignation to the secretary well before the date on which the next yearly dues will be due. The letter would read something like this:

Mrs. James Town
Secretary, Colonial Club, New York
My dear Mrs. Town,

It is with great regret that I find it necessary to resign from the club and to ask you therefore to present my resignation at the next meeting of the governors.

Very sincerely,
Mary Smarlington

66

At the table

All the rules of table manners have been made for a very few basic reasons, and keeping them in mind can solve many problems automatically. There are, in addition, a number of trifling decrees of etiquette, some of them unreasonable and silly, others merely finicky. No one will disapprove if you follow the latter quietly and without ostentation, but before you concern yourself with them, you should be sure that you have thoroughly mastered the basic ones.

THE "WHYS" OF GOOD TABLE MANNERS

Most rules for the table were made to avoid ugliness. To let anyone see what you have in your mouth is offensive. To make a noise is repulsive. To make a mess is disgusting. But if you consider the impression your behavior will make on the others at the table, few problems will arise that cannot be solved by common sense alone.

The second "why"—and it should not even need mention—involves the comfort of the eater and those around him. To saw away at one's meat with elbows high is to risk hitting one's neighbor. To wave one's arms about is to endanger one's own back or his neighbor's if just then a waitress is about to serve a plate of scalding soup.

The third is the general principle that we have met before: Do not attract attention to yourself in public. Chairs scraped on the floor, knives and forks rattled against the plate, and other unnecessary noises can only cause disapproval among those nearby.

A certain easy gentleness will prevent many an unfortunate experience at table. It will do much to keep accidents from happening, and it will be noticed, if at all, with pleasure and appreciation.

ARRIVING AT THE TABLE

At informal social gatherings a man holds the chair for the woman on his right. However, at family meals if the men or boys do not arrive simultaneously with the women, as may happen when Mother calls "Dinner's ready" to her homeworking children, the women (and girls) seat themselves without delay.

GRACE BEFORE MEALS

The custom of giving a family blessing or thanks before meals is a very gracious one, though it is not observed as widely as it used to be. Some families are seated with bowed heads and touch nothing until the grace has been said; others remain standing. Both forms are correct.

Usually the mother or the father offers the prayer, but it is nice to allow the younger members of the family to take turns in asking grace. There are a number of shorter and longer variations, but the following three are typical examples.

> *Bless us, O Lord, and these Thy gifts, which we are about to receive from Thy bounty. Through Christ our Lord. Amen.*

> *Lift up your hands toward the Sanctuary and bless the Lord. Blessed art Thou, O Lord our God, King of the universe, who bringest forth bread from the earth. Amen.*

> *Bless, O Lord, this food to our use, and us to Thy service, and make us ever mindful of the needs of others, in Jesus' Name. Amen.*

POSTURE AT THE TABLE

The distance from the table at which it is best to sit is a matter of personal comfort. One should not sit so close that his elbows are bent like a cricket's, nor so far back that food is likely to be dropped in transit from plate to mouth.

Elbows are *never* put on the table while one is actually eating. To sit with the left elbow propped on the table while eating with the right hand or to prop the right one on the table while lifting fork or glass to the mouth must be avoided.

There are some situations when elbows are not only permitted on the table but are actually necessary. This is true in restaurants where people are lunching or dining at a small table and, to make oneself heard above music or conversation without being overheard at other tables nearby, one must lean far forward. A woman is far more graceful leaning forward supported by her elbows rather than doubled forward over her hands in her lap as though she were in pain! *At home,* when there is no reason for leaning across the table, there is no reason for elbows. At a formal dinner, elbows are rarely if ever seen on the table except perhaps at the ends of the table, where again one has to lean forward in order to talk to a companion at a distance across the table corner. And even in these special situations, elbows are *never* on the table when one is eating.

Slouching or slumping at the table is most unattractive, too. Tipping one's chair—a most unfortunate habit among young people (and, occasionally, grown men)—is unforgivable. It not only looks dreadfully sloppy, but it is fatal to the back legs of the chair.

Ideal posture at the table is to sit straight, but not stiffly, leaning slightly against the back of the chair. Your hands, when you are not actually eating, are best off in your lap; this position will automatically prevent you from fussing with implements, playing with breadcrumbs, drawing on the tablecloth, and so forth. Hands should also be kept away from the face, from nervous scratching, and from twisting or touching the hair.

It is correct to reach for anything on the table that does not necessitate stretching across your neighbor or leaning far across the table yourself. When something is out of reach, simply ask the person nearest to it, "Would you please pass the jelly, Mrs. Betts?"

THE NAPKIN

As soon as you are seated, you put your napkin on your lap. It does not matter how you do it, so long as you do not give it a violent shake to open it up. You take it from the table, place it on your lap (if it is large enough, you may tuck a corner under you to keep it from sliding off, or if it is not, you arrange it as safely as you can), and unfold it as much as necessary with both hands.

A man should never tuck his napkin into his collar, his belt, or between the buttons of his shirt.

When using the napkin, avoid wiping your mouth as if with a washcloth. Blotting or patting the lips is much more delicate.

When the meal is finished, or if you leave the table during the meal, put the napkin on the right side of your place, or if the plates have been removed, in the center. It should not be refolded, nor should it be crumpled up; rather it is laid on the table in loose folds so that it does not spread itself out. At a dinner party, the hostess lays her napkin on the table as a signal that the meal is over, and the guests then lay their napkins on the table—not before.

SERVING ONESELF AND BEING SERVED

When helping yourself, the first rule is to pay attention to what you are doing and not handle a serving fork or spoon in such a way as to spill food over either the floor, the table, your neighbor, or yourself.

Anything served on a piece of toast should be lifted from the platter on the toast. Squab or quail might be lifted, leaving the toast on the plate, but foods such as mushrooms, sweetbreads, or asparagus must remain on the toast. It is not only difficult to serve them otherwise, but it would leave a soggy, unattractive piece of toast on the platter. The toast with its topping is lifted on the spoon and held in place with the fork. If there is only a serving spoon and no fork in the dish, you must balance the food with great care.

When helping yourself, you say nothing; but when declining a dish offered by a waiter, you say, "No, thank you." Your voice is barely audible, and in fact a negative shake of the head and "No thanks" more nearly describe the usual refusal.

Gravy should be put *on* the meat, potatoes, or rice, and the condiment, pickles, and jelly *at the side* of whatever they accompany. Olives, radishes, or celery are put on the bread-and-butter plate if there is one, otherwise on the edge of the plate from which one is eating. Salted nuts are put on the tablecloth or place mat.

When passing your plate to the head of the table for a second helping, always leave knife and fork on the plate and be sure the handles are far enough on not to topple off.

It is good manners to take at least a little of every dish that is offered to you, but if it is a food you especially dislike and if you are among friends, you may refuse with a polite "No, thank you." In fact, because it is definitely impolite not to finish the food on your plate, it is better to refuse it; that which remains on the platter can be used again, while that which remains on your plate must be thrown away. You need not give your reason for refusing a dish, but if it is because of an allergy, diet, or other physical cause, you may avoid hurting your hostess's feelings if you quietly tell her your problem, always without drawing the attention of the entire table.

WHEN TO START EATING

At a small table of two, four, or even six people, when the delay will not be sufficient to cause the food to become cold or the soufflé to fall, it is certainly polite to wait to start eating until all have been served. In this case, the hostess should pick up her implement first, and the others follow suit.

If the group is larger, however, it is *not* necessary to wait until all have been served. The hostess, if she is at all aware of her guest's comfort, will say, as soon as the first two or three guests have their food, "Please start

—your dinner will only get cold if you wait," and the guests take her at her word and start immediately. If the hostess says nothing and you realize that her attention has been devoted to serving or supervising, or that she has simply forgotten to say anything, it is not incorrect to pick up your spoon or fork after five or six people have been served, and the others will soon follow your lead. At family meals, as Mother or Father fills and passes the plates, the children should say, "May I please begin?" if they are not old enough to be expected to wait.

THE SILVER

There should never be any question of which silver to use: *You always start with the implement farthest from the plate.* This question arises again and again, and the answer is always the same, with one exception. If the table is incorrectly set, possibly by a maid who is not experienced, and the error is such that you cannot use the implement for the course that its position indicates, you must, of course, choose the next one that is appropriate. For example, if the small shellfish fork has been put next to the plate, you would not use the dinner fork for the shrimp cocktail and leave the little fork for the main course, even though they were placed in that order. Otherwise, you assume that the table is correctly set, and starting at the outside, you work your way with each course toward the center.

When you have finished the main course, the knife and fork are placed beside each other on the dinner plate diagonally from upper left to lower right. The handles extend slightly over the edge of the plate. The dessert spoon or fork is placed in the same way. If a dessert such as cut-up fruit or custard is served in a bowl or cup with a plate under it, the spoon is laid on the plate to the right of the bowl, again diagonally.

USING THE KNIFE AND FORK

The proper way to use the knife and fork can best be explained by the accompanying illustrations. Study them carefully and you will see that they depict easy and graceful ways of cutting food and bringing it to your mouth.

The American custom of "zigzag" eating (changing the fork from left to right hand after cutting meat) is not incorrect, but it is unnecessarily complicated. Therefore, it does not have as pleasing an appearance as the simpler method of leaving the fork in your left hand after you have cut your meat. You eat the meat from your fork while it is still in the left hand, rather than turning the fork over and switching it to your right hand.

Dessert may be eaten with spoon or fork or both. Stewed fruit is held in place with the fork and cut and eaten with the spoon. Peaches or other very juicy fruits are peeled and then eaten with knife and fork, but dry fruits, such as apples, may be cut and then eaten with the fingers.

FINGERS OR FORKS

All juicy or soft fruit and all cakes are best eaten with a fork; in most cases it is a matter of dexterity rather than rule. If you are able to eat a peach or ripe pear in your fingers and not smear your face or make a sucking noise, you are the one in a thousand who *may*, and with utmost propriety, continue the feat. If you can eat a Napoleon or a cream puff and not let the cream ooze out on the far side, you need not use a fork. But if you cannot eat something—no matter what it is—without getting it all over your fingers, you must use a fork, and when necessary, a spoon or a knife also.

PUSHERS

There is no better pusher than a piece of dry crust. Lacking this, the knife is also correct—if properly used. Held in the left hand in the same position as it is when held in the right hand, with the tip of the blade helping to guide and hold each mouthful for the fork to lift, it is a natural motion in no way incorrect.

OTHER THAN THE MAIN COURSE

SOUPS

Either clear soup or thick soup may be served in a cup with one handle or with handles on both sides. After taking a spoonful or two you may pick up the cup, if the soup is cool enough. Use both hands if the cup has two handles, or continue to use your spoon.

Clear soups are sometimes served in a soup plate rather than in a cup. When the level of the soup is so low that you must tip the plate to avoid scraping the bottom noisily, lift the near edge in your left hand and tip the plate away from you. Then the soup may be spooned away from you or toward you, whichever is less awkward.

Both soup cups and soup plates should be served with a saucer or plate beneath them. The spoon, when not in use or when the soup is finished, is laid on the saucer when a soup cup is used, but it is left in the soup plate rather than on the dish under it.

BREAD AND BUTTER

Bread should always be broken into moderate-sized pieces—but not necessarily single-mouthful bits—with the fingers before being eaten. To butter it hold a piece on the edge of the bread-and-butter plate, or the place plate, and with a butter knife spread enough butter on it for a mouthful or two at a time. If there is no butter knife use any other knife you find available.

This buttering of bread is not an important rule. There are always common-sense exceptions. For instance, hot biscuits can of course be buttered immediately, since they are most delicious when the butter is quickly and thoroughly melted. Bread must never, however, be held flat on the palm and buttered with the hand held in the air. If a table knife is used, care must be taken not to smear food particles from the knife onto the butter. Jellies and jams as well as butter are spread on bread with a knife, never with a fork, though you do put butter on vegetables and jelly on meat with a fork.

BREAD AND GRAVY

You may sop bread into gravy, but it must be done properly—by putting a small piece down on the gravy and then eating it with knife and fork as though it were any other helping on your plate. A good sauce may also be finished in this way—in fact, to do so is a compliment to the cook.

SALAD

Why one should not cut one's salad in small pieces—if one wants to—makes little sense unless, that is, one cuts up a whole plateful and makes the plate messy. Until stainless steel was invented, a steel knife blade was not usable for salad or fruit since the metal turned black; but silver-bladed knives have always been used for salads as well as for fruits, and today stainless steel has joined its older brother silver.

Anything more difficult than managing leafy salad with a fork alone —especially the fresh, crisp, springing variety—is difficult to imagine. At all events, beware of rolling the fork and wrapping springy leaves around the tines in a spiral. Remember what a spring that lets go can do! At present, and happily ever since stainless steel was introduced, there has been no possible reason why anyone should be denied the efficiency of a salad knife.

BEVERAGES

Many people today are using mugs instead of cups and saucers for coffee, tea, or hot chocolate. Since saucers are not used with mugs, the problem arises of what to do with the spoon—which should never be left in the mug. Mugs are not proper on a formal table and are rarely seen on any table covered with a cloth, so the solution depends somewhat on the place mats. If the mats are informal, of paper or plastic, perhaps, the spoon may be wiped clean with the lips, and laid on the mat or on the table beside the mug. If the mats are of fine quality it would be thoughtless to risk staining them. The bowl of the spoon, face down, should be rested on the edge of the butter plate or dinner plate, with the spoon handle on the table.

Iced tea or iced coffee presents the same problem, although a smart hostess serves a coaster or saucer under the glass. Iced tea spoons may be left in the glass and held against the rim with the forefinger when drinking. However, this is awkward, and the procedure just mentioned for removing the spoon is generally more practical.

When dining informally one may use a teaspoon to put a small piece of ice from the water glass into a steaming beverage to cool it slightly. This may only be done, however, with a clean, unused spoon.

Tea bags are naturally placed on the edge of the saucer, but they should be pressed gently against the side of the cup with the spoon to remove excess liquid. Should the tea be served in a glass or china mug without a saucer, you may ask for a dish on which to place the bag. Otherwise you must put it on the edge of the butter or dinner plate, where it inevitably leaks drops of tea into the food on the plate.

In spite of an outdated idea to the contrary, tea which is too hot to drink from the cup may be sipped from the spoon, as may coffee or any other hot beverage.

When coffee is spilled into the saucer, the best course is to replace the saucer with a clean one. This is always true at home, where one may get the replacement oneself, or when dining at a friend's house or in a fine restaurant where one may request the exchange. It is sometimes impossible, however, in some restaurants or in a cafeteria. Rather than drip coffee each time you lift the cup to your mouth, it is permissible to pour the liquid back into the cup and use a paper napkin (if one is available) to dry the bottom of the cup.

SALT IN A SALTCELLAR

If there is no spoon in the saltcellar, use the tip of a clean knife. If the saltcellar is for you alone, use the top of your knife to sprinkle the salt on your food or take a pinch with your fingers. Salt that is to be dipped into should be put on the bread-and-butter plate or on the rim of whatever plate is before you.

FRUIT AT TABLE

The equipment for eating fruit at table consists of a sharp-bladed fruit knife and fork, and a finger bowl. In a restaurant, when no knife is given you, it is proper to ask for one.

Raw apples and *pears* are quartered, usually with a knife. The core is then cut away from each quarter, and the fruit is eaten in the fingers. Those who do not like the skin pare each quarter separately.

Bananas may be peeled halfway down and eaten bite by bite at table, but it is better to peel the skin all the way off, lay the fruit on your plate, cut it in slices, and eat it with a fork.

Berries are usually hulled or stemmed ahead of time, served with cream and sugar, and eaten with a spoon. When especially fine or so freshly picked that they are still warm from the sun, strawberries and other berries are often served with their hulls on and sugar placed at one side of each person's plate. The hull of each berry is held in the fingers, and the fruit is dipped in the sugar and then eaten.

Cantaloupes and *muskmelons* are served in halves, or sometimes quarters, and eaten with a spoon.

Honeydew, Persian, and *Casaba* melons are cut into new-moon-shaped quarters or eighths, depending on size, and eaten with either spoon or knife and fork—whichever you prefer.

Watermelon is cut into large-sized pieces or slices and usually eaten in the fingers. If using a fork, remove seeds with tines and then cut pieces with side of fork.

Raw cherries and *plums* are eaten in the fingers, of course. The pit of the cherry should be made as clean as possible in your mouth and dropped into your almost-closed cupped hand and thence to your plate. The plum is held in your fingers and eaten as close to the pit as possible. On occasion when you do remove a pit in your fingers, you should do it with your thumb underneath and your first two fingers across your mouth, and not with your fingertips pointing into your mouth.

Hothouse grapes are eaten in two ways: One, lay a grape on its side, hold it with fingers of left hand, cut into center with point of knife, and remove the seeds. Two, put a whole grape in your mouth, chew it, swallow the pulp and juice, and drop the bare seeds into your almost-closed fist.

With *garden* or *Concord grapes,* you press the stem end of a grape between your lips and against your almost-closed teeth so that the juice and pulp will be drawn into your mouth and the skin left to be discarded.

Little *seedless grapes* are no problem since they are eaten whole.

Oranges often served at the table are the rather rough-skinned, firm variety, usually seedless. An enjoyable way to eat them is to slice the two ends of the rind off first, and cut the peel off in vertical strips with the knife. You then cut the peeled orange in half at its equator. After this, each half is easily cut and eaten mouthful by mouthful with knife and fork together. Oranges can also be halved, the sections loosened with a curved grapefruit knife, and then eaten with an orange spoon or teaspoon.

A thin-skinned orange, filled with seeds, is extremely difficult to eat. About the only way is to cut it into eighths, take out the seeds from the center with the tip of the knife, and eat the new-moon-shaped pieces as daintily as you can in the fingers.

Tangerines seemingly present no problem because the skin is removed easily and the segments separate readily. But the pulp, seeds, and fibers must be taken neatly from between the lips with the thumb and first two fingers (fingers above and thumb underneath).

A *freestone peach* or a *nectarine* is cut into the pit, then broken in half and eaten. A *clingstone* you can't break apart; therefore if you don't mind the fuzz, as most of us do, you eat it whole. If you do this you take very small bites to prevent the juice from running down your wrist. It is better to peel the peach whole and then eat it with knife and fork.

THE FOODS THAT ARE SOMETIMES DIFFICULT

ARTICHOKES

Artichokes are always eaten with the fingers; a leaf at a time is pulled off, and the edible portion dipped in the sauce and then bitten off. When the center is reached, the thistlelike part is scraped away with a knife, and the heart eaten with a knife and fork.

ASPARAGUS

By reputation this is a finger food, but the ungraceful appearance of a bent stalk of asparagus falling limply into someone's mouth and the fact that moisture is also likely to drip from the end cause most fastidious people to eat it—at least in part—with the fork. That is, cut the stalks with the fork to where they become harder, and then pick up the ends in the fingers if you choose. But don't squeeze the stalks or let juice run down your fingers.

Asparagus that has no hard end is eaten entirely with a fork. All hard ends should be cut off asparagus before serving it at a dinner party, since picking up stalks in the fingers is scarcely compatible with formal table manners.

BAKED POTATO

Baked potato, whether white or sweet and not otherwise prepared before serving, is usually eaten by breaking it in half with the fingers (cutting a slit with a knife first if necessary), scooping all the inside of the potato onto the plate with a fork, and then mixing butter, salt, and pepper in it with a fork.

Another way to eat baked potato is to break it in half with the fingers and lay both halves, skin down, on the plate. Mix a little butter in a small part of one half with a fork and eat that. Then mix a little more, and so on, eating it out of the skin without turning it out onto the plate.

A third way—for those who like to eat the skin as well as the inside —is to cut the baked potato into two halves with the knife and fork. Then cut them again into pieces, a few at a time, of eatable size. Butter the pieces with the fork alone and eat, of course, with the fork held in right hand, tines up. If you wish to eat the skins separately they may be placed on the side of the plate, or on the butter plate, and eaten a small piece at a time, exactly as you would bread and butter.

BACON

Breakfast bacon should, when possible, be eaten with a fork. But when it is so very dry and crisp that it scatters into fragments when broken by the fork, fingers are permitted.

BUTTER

Every sort of bread, biscuit, toast, and also hot griddle cakes and corn on the cob are buttered with a knife. But corn that has been cut off the cob, or rice, or potato—or anything else on your plate—has seasoning or butter mixed in it with a fork.

CHEESE

Cheese is one food that may be spread with either a knife or a fork. If eaten with a salad with which one is using no knife, a piece of cheese may be broken off and put on lettuce or a cracker with one's fork. Runny or soft cheeses, such as Brie, Camembert, or Liederkranz, should always be spread with a salad knife or butter knife if there is one.

CONDIMENTS

The thought of smearing condiments with a knife on food already impaled on a fork is quite unpleasant if more than a small amount is taken. The proper way to manage a quantity of cranberry sauce, dressing, jelly, pickle, etc. is to lift it onto the fork and either eat it as a separate mouthful or take some of it with a small piece of meat on the tips of the tines.

CORN ON THE COB

To attack corn on the cob with as little ferocity as possible is perhaps the only direction to be given, and the only maxim to bear in mind when eating this pleasant-to-taste but not-very-easy-to-manage vegetable is to eat it as neatly as possible. It doesn't matter whether you break the ear in half, or whether you hold it by its own ends or by special little handles. The real thing to avoid is too much buttering all at once and too greedy eating. If you like much butter, then spread it across only half the length about two rows at a time. If you take a moderate amount of butter, you can spread it across the whole length of two rows, add salt and pepper, hold the ends in both hands, and eat those two rows. Repeat the buttering and eating until all is finished.

Cutting corn off the cob easily is chiefly a question of the sharpness of the knife. Considerate housekeepers should supply small sharp vegetable knives (steak knives would do nicely) to guests who like to cut the corn off. Corn served at a dinner party should be cut off the cobs in the kitchen and creamed or buttered.

CHICKEN (ROAST OR BROILED), SQUAB, GAME HEN, AND OTHER SMALL BIRDS

At a formal dinner, no part of a bird is picked up in the fingers. Among family and friends, however, it is permissible to eat as follows:

The main body of the bird is not eaten with the fingers. You cut off as much meat as you can and leave the rest on your plate. If you know how to manage very small bones, such as joint or wing, or the second joint of a squab, you put the piece of bone with meat on it in your mouth, eat it clean, and remove the bare bones between forefinger and thumb. Larger joints, such as the drumstick of a roast chicken, may be picked up after the first few easily cut-off pieces have been eaten.

CRACKERS OR CROUSTADES WITH SOUP

Croustades, which are very small forcemeat pastries, are scattered on soup after it has been ladled into the plate to be served. Croutons (tiny French-fried cubes of bread) are either floated on the soup or else passed separately in a dish with a small serving spoon so that each person may put a spoonful in his soup. Oyster crackers, as well as any others, are put on the bread-and-butter plate—or on the tablecloth—and dropped two or three pieces at a time into the soup.

FRENCH-FRIED POTATOES

When French-fried potatoes accompany a hamburger, hot dog, or other sandwich, they may be eaten in the fingers. At other times they should be cut into reasonable lengths and eaten with a fork.

LAMB CHOPS

At a dinner party or in a formal restaurant, lamb chops must be eaten with knife and fork. At the family table or among an informal group of friends, the center may be cut out and eaten with the fork, and the bone picked up and eaten clean with the teeth. This is permissible, too, with veal or pork chops, but only if they are broiled or otherwise cooked without gravy or sauce.

LOBSTER, BROILED

This is called a finger food because unless the claws have been broken in two their meat cannot be eaten at all. You must therefore pick up the claw in its shell to pry out the meat with a lobster fork, but you put the meat (and that from the main body) on your plate, cut it with a knife, and eat it with the fork.

Properly, a big paper napkin (or bib) is used. Finger bowls with hot water and lemon slices should be put at the side of each place as soon as people are finished eating. These are carried away after the dinner plates have been removed.

OLIVES

Eat them with your fingers. Bite off the meat, but don't nibble too avidly around the stone. Bite a large stuffed one in half. Put only a very small stuffed olive in your mouth whole.

OLIVES, ONIONS, AND CHERRIES IN COCKTAILS

When the glass is drained, it is easy enough to tip the glass and drop the cherry, onion, or small olive into your mouth. Since a large olive is too much of a mouthful, lift it out with the fingers and eat it in two or three bites.

SANDWICHES

All ordinary sandwiches, not only at picnics but everywhere, are eaten from the fingers. Club sandwiches and other inch-thick and whole-meal sandwiches are best cut in smaller portions before being picked up and held tightly in the fingers of both hands, or if literally dripping with mayonnaise they should be served on a plate with a knife and fork. If you are not sitting at table and you have no knife, you bite into an over-large and hugely thick piece as nicely as you can or, following previous advice on eating corn on the cob, attack it with as little ferocity as possible.

SHRIMP

Shrimp as a first course present one of the most difficult problems encountered by the diner. If not too impossibly large, each shrimp should be eaten in one bite. But when they are of jumbo size, the diner has no alternative but to grasp the cup firmly with his left hand and cut the shrimp as neatly as possible with the edge of his fork. It is impractical to use a knife because the stemmed shrimp cup will tip over unless held with one hand. At home the problem can be avoided by arranging the shrimp attractively on a small plate—where they can be cut easily with knife or fork—and I can see no reason why restaurants should not do the same.

SPAGHETTI

The method of eating spaghetti by winding it on a fork held against a spoon is correct neither here nor in Italy. A few pieces are held against the plate with the end of the fork, which is then twisted to wrap the spaghetti around the tines and conveyed to the mouth. If necessary this can be done against the curve of the plate, which will substitute for the spoon in keeping the slippery pieces on the fork while they are being wound. An extra amount of grated Parmesan cheese will help a novice because it makes the strands less slippery.

EMBARRASSING DIFFICULTIES

If food is too hot, quickly take a swallow of water. Never, NEVER spit it out! It is offensive to take anything out of your mouth that has been put in it, except dry fish bones and equally dry fruit pits or seeds. If you choke on a fish bone, cover your mouth with your napkin and leave the table quickly. To spit anything whatever into the corner of your napkin is not permissible. It is unpleasant to see anyone spit wet skins or pits on a fork or onto the plate, and it is excusable only if you get a bad clam or something similar into your mouth. Even then the best—because it is the least noticeable—method is to take it from your mouth in your fingers: thumb underneath and four other fingers forming a screen over whatever it is from lips to plate. And then wipe off on your napkin any moisture still on your fingertips.

THE TECHNIQUE FOR BONES, PITS, AND SEEDS

Fish bones or other incidental bones are taken between finger and thumb and removed between compressed lips. Pits and seeds must be eaten quite bare and clean in the mouth and dropped into the cupped fist and then into the plate. The pits of stewed prunes or cherries that are eaten with a spoon are made as clean and dry as possible in the mouth with the tongue and teeth, dropped into the spoon with which you are eating, and then conveyed to the edge of the plate.

SPILLS

If you should spill jelly or a bit of vegetable or other solid food on the table, pick up as much as you can neatly with a clean spoon or the blade of your knife. If it has caused a stain, apologize to your hostess, who, in turn, should not add to your embarrassment by calling attention to the accident but quietly assure you that "No harm was done—the cloth will be washed tomorrow in any case."

If you spill wine or water at a formal dinner or in a restaurant, try quietly to attract the attention of the butler or waiter, who will bring a cloth to cover the spot. At the family table or informal dinner without servants, offer to get a cloth or sponge to mop up the liquid, and help the hostess clean up in any way you can.

SOME TABLE DON'TS

Don't encircle a plate with the left arm while eating with the right hand.

Don't push back your plate when finished. It remains exactly where it is until the person serving you removes it. If you wait on yourself, get up and carry it to the kitchen.

Don't lean back and announce, "I'm through," or "I'm stuffed." The fact that you have put your fork or spoon down shows that you have finished.

Don't *ever* put liquid into your mouth if it is already filled with food—this really means filled. You might have a little bread in your mouth when you drink your coffee, if it be so little as to be undetectable to others. But a good habit is *never.*

Don't dunk, although according to the movies it is an approved practice in lunch wagons. If you must soften your doughnut or slice of toast, at least break it in half and dip an end, or cut the toast into one-inch strips and dip them lightly. Better, break a small piece at a time into your coffee, milk, or soup, and eat it with a spoon.

Don't apologize and thus call unnecessary attention to anything so unpleasant as having to blow your nose at the table. The only thing to do is to end it as quickly as possible.

Don't wait until all the plates are served; after a few guests have been served it is perfectly all right to start eating.

Don't wipe off the tableware in a restaurant. If you do happen to find a dirty piece of silver at your place, call a waiter or waitress, show him the soiled article, and ask for a clean one.

Don't, if you are a woman, wear an excessive amount of lipstick to the table, out of consideration for your hostess's napkin, and also because it is very unattractive on the rim of a glass or on the silver.

Don't spread jelly or jam directly onto a piece of bread from the dish in which it is served. Put a small portion on your butter plate, or the rim of your dinner plate if there is no butter plate, using the spoon provided to serve the condiment. If there is no spoon with the jelly, you may use a clean knife to put a little on your plate.

Don't crook your finger when picking up your cup. It's an affected mannerism.

Don't—ever—leave your spoon in your cup. Not only does it look unattractive; it is almost certain to result in an accident.

Don't leave half the food on your spoon or fork to be waved about during conversation. One often sees this done with ice cream, but the coldness is no excuse. One should put less on the spoon and eat it in one bite.

Don't cut up your entire meal before you start to eat; it only makes a mess on your plate.

Don't bend your head so low over the plate that you seem to be bobbing up and down for each bite like a robin for a worm. Of course, you must lean forward slightly to avoid carrying the food too far and risking a spill on your lap, but there is a happy medium.

WHEN CHILDREN COME TO THE TABLE

No child under five can be expected to use a napkin instead of a bib, although, if he wishes, he may be given a napkin in addition to the bib to become accustomed to using it to wipe his mouth. No matter how nicely behaved he may be, there is always the present danger of his spilling something, sometime. Soft-boiled egg is hideously difficult to eat without ever getting a drop of it down the front, and it is much easier to supply him wth a clean bib for the next meal than to change his clothes for the next moment. By experimenting with the individual child you can easily ascertain just when he is ready for the next step in the training program. But until he is ready to accept the new way do not force the issue unduly.

Very little children usually have warming plates—made as a double plate with hot-water space in between—on which the food is cut up and the vegetables "fixed" in the kitchen. It is brought to them before other people at the table are served, not only because it is hard for them to wait when their attention is too easily attracted by food not for them, but because they naturally eat slowly and deliberately. As soon as they are old enough to eat everything on the table, they are served, not last, but in the regular rotation in which they come at table.

When children are learning to help themselves, they must especially try to handle the serving spoon evenly and to guard against "flinging" it quickly and so spattering the table. In fact, this principal cause for a spotted tablecloth is something to which even grown people should pay attention.

THE LEFT-HANDED CHILD

To the many who ask whether it is best to set the place at table in reverse of usual order for a left-handed child who has to "cross over" for every implement, the answer is definitely "No!"

Nothing could turn out to be a greater handicap than letting him become accustomed to a reversed place setting. It is only by being obliged to make this maneuver at every meal at home that he becomes adept at it. If his place is set especially for him at home, he will be conspicuously awkward at every meal he ever eats away from home where his place will not be so set.

TABLE TRICKS THAT MUST BE CORRECTED

To pile mashed potato and other vegetables on top of meat on the convex side of the fork for two inches or more of its length is an ungainly habit dear to the hearts of schoolboys and sometimes of their fathers—a habit that is more easily prevented in the beginning than corrected later. In fact, taking a big mouthful (next to smearing the face and chewing with mouth open) is perhaps the worst offense at the table.

To sit up straight and keep their hands in their laps when not occupied with eating is very hard indeed for children, but it should be insisted upon in order to forestall a careless habit that all too readily degenerates into flopping this way and that and fingering whatever is in reach. The child must not be allowed to warm his hands on his plate, or drum on the table, or screw his napkin into a rope, or make marks on the tablecloth. If he shows talent as an artist, give him pencils or modeling wax in his playroom; do not let him bite his slice of bread into the silhouette of an animal or model figures in butter at the table. And do not allow him to construct a tent out of two forks, or tie the corners of his napkin into bunny-rabbit ears. Food and table implements are not playthings, nor is the dining-room table a playground.

Children should be taught from the time they are little not to talk at table about what foods they like and don't like. A child who is not allowed to say anything but "No, thank you" when offered something he doesn't want at home will not mortify his mother in public by screaming, "I *hate* spinach. I *won't* eat potato. I want ice cream and cookies!"

Older children should not be allowed to jerk out their chairs, to flop down sideways, to flick their napkins by one corner, to reach out for something, or to begin by eating candy, fruit, or other table decorations. A child as well as a grown person should sit down in the center of his chair and draw it up to the table (if there is no one to push it in for him) by holding the seat in either hand while momentarily lifting himself on his feet. It makes no difference whether he approaches the chair from the left or the right. The only rule is for him to take his place quietly, and not to jump or rock his chair into place at the table. In getting up from the table, again he must push his chair back quietly, using his hands on either side of the chair seat. He should *not* hold onto the table edge and give himself, chair and all, a sudden shove!

SPECIAL RESTAURANT PROBLEMS

Many accompaniments to meals in restaurants are served with paper wrappers or in cardboard containers. The question of what to do with, for instance, paper sugar packets, comes up frequently. They should be crumpled up tightly and either tucked under the rim of your plate or placed on the edge of the saucer or butter plate. This is preferable to putting them in the ash tray where a lighted cigarette may easily set them on fire.

When jelly or marmalade is served in a paper container, it should be taken out with the butter knife (or dinner knife if there is no butter knife) and put on the butter plate. The top is put back in the empty container, which is left on the table beside the butter plate.

Vegetables which are brought to the table in small individual dishes may be left in the dishes if the dinner plate is crowded with portions of meat or fish. It is equally correct to spoon the vegetables onto the plate and ask that the dishes be removed, leaving a less cluttered table. If no serving spoon is provided, the small dish may be tilted over the dinner plate, and the vegetables pushed carefully out with the dinner fork.

Meat pies or stews should be removed with a serving spoon from the dish in which they are presented, taking as much as you think you will want. Ask the waiter for a spoon if one is not served with the pie container. If only one fork (or knife) is provided, and it is used for the first course, it may be placed on the butter plate when the used plate is removed, and used again for the main course. It should never be wiped clean and replaced on the table.

If toothpicks are on the table or counter, help yourself, but leave the table before using them. Go to the rest room, or someplace where you will not be observed, because nothing is more disgusting to other diners than the sight of someone digging at the food stuck in his teeth!

67

In business

Every successful executive knows how important etiquette is, both in managing his office and in dealing with other businessmen. No man can ever tell when a knowledge of it may be to his advantage, or when the lack of it may suddenly turn the scale against him. The man who remains "planted" in his chair when a lady speaks to him, who receives customers in his shirtsleeves, who does not take off his hat when talking with a lady or take his cigar out of his mouth when addressing her, impresses others, not only by his lack of good manners, but by the business incompetence that his attitude suggests.

THE WELL-MANNERED BUSINESSMAN

The more important the executive, the greater courtesy he shows to those with whom he has an appointment. A president of a large industry chooses his assistants partly because of their tact and good manners. If a man who has no appointment asks to see Mr. Prominent, one of these aides finds out what the visitor's business is and attends to it himself if possible. If it seems important that the visitor see the president, the aide arranges for an appointment as soon as possible.

The president has a courteous manner that makes every visitor feel there is nothing in the day's work half so important as what he, the client, has come to see him about. Nor is this manner insincere, for he has made a practice of giving anyone he talks with his undivided attention. Should his time be short and the moment approach when he is due at another appointment, his secretary comes in a few minutes before the hour and reminds him, "I'm sorry, Mr. Prominent, but your appointment with the traffic committee is due." Mr. Prominent uses up most of these few minutes in an unhurried close of the previous conversation so that the visitor has the impression that the subject he introduced is the president's main interest.

This is neither sincerity nor insincerity, but merely bringing social knowledge into business dealing. To make a pleasant and friendly impression is not only good manners, but equally good business. That this is understood by modern businessmen is shown by the importance they give to public relations. The less experienced man might show his eagerness to be rid of his visitor, offending the latter's pride by the discourtesy of inattention. Mr. Prominent not only gained the good will of his visitor, but had plenty of time for his own appointment.

When visiting another firm, executives and salesmen alike show the same courtesy they would in a social situation. They give their names clearly to the receptionist, and present a card to be shown to her employer. They wait patiently if they cannot be seen at once, and they do not bother the employees with conversation in order to pass the time more quickly. Once admitted they present their business as concisely and clearly as possible, to save valuable time for both themselves and the man they are seeing.

WOMEN IN BUSINESS

Women have come to stay in not only every branch of business but every profession as well. Women are the successful heads of their own offices, and very few are the businesses that do not have women secretaries, bookkeepers, receptionists, switchboard operators, clerks, and typists.

The ideal business woman is accurate, orderly, quick, and impersonal, whether she is a typist or the top executive of a great concern. Here the word "impersonal" means exactly that! Her point of view must be focused on the work in hand, not on her own reactions to it or on anyone's reactions to her. If she is an executive, she avoids being dictatorial and still maintains her dignity.

At the very top of the list of women's business shortcomings is the inability of many of them to achieve this impersonality. Mood, temper, jealousy, especially when induced by a "crush on" her employer or a fellow worker—these are the chief flaws of the woman in business and a constant source of annoyance in every office where she works. The greatest handicap to woman's advancement in business is her inability to leave her personal feelings and affairs at home.

An anonymous expert on business gave as the recipe for success: "The ability to work efficiently and pleasantly with other people." The recipe is pefect—there is nothing to add except to acknowledge that it takes no small amount of will and self-control to get on with any constant companion under the daily friction of an enforced relationship that is unrelieved day after day, week after week. It is wonderful that human nature stands the strain as well as it does, especially in situations where one's own work is dependent upon the cooperation of others for its complete efficiency.

Women who work must learn not to waste their employers' time. And employers should know that the effect on morale of a ten-minute makeup repair or coffee break more than makes up in increased efficiency for the actual loss in time. No employer, however, will stand for a coffee-break atmosphere throughout the working day. During working hours women should avoid wasting time in idle conversation, which only interrupts the office routine and is a very unbusinesslike habit.

SEX IN A BUSINESS OFFICE

A woman who goes into an office because she hopes to meet romance in the form of her employer, or at least to rise quickly because of her physical charm, has clerkship and show business mixed up. Sex is one thing that has no place in business. Much as a man may admire a pretty or magnetic or amusing woman in his leisure hours, in his hours of work he wants someone to help him with that work. The more help she can give him, the more he values her and the more salary he is willing to pay.

Naturally he prefers someone who is attractive, but business personality and leisure personality are two different things. They are sometimes combined in one person, and sometimes romance is an outcome of business, but that is the exception that proves the rule. And every time the prospect of romance intrudes into a business situation, think not just twice but a dozen times before allowing an office relationship to become a personal one. The woman who happens to work in an office with her husband should remember to be as impersonal and efficient during working hours as any other woman would be.

Every businessman likes a woman who is neat, impersonal, and efficient, just as he likes an automobile that is ready to go any distance without any danger of breaking down. A successful business personality has as its first attribute *efficiency*, not sex appeal.

THE PERFECT SECRETARY

The function of the perfect secretary is to complement her employer's endeavor and not make any intrusions which would be more likely to impede than help.

Needless to say, a secretary must not betray the secrets of her employer. His business dealings must be regarded as professional secrets. No matter how inconsequential they may seem to her it would be dishonorable for her to divulge them.

She makes his appointments, sees that he is reminded of them, protects him from unwanted calls and visitors, handles small details without bothering him, and in general, attempts to relieve him of all time-consuming chores. He is thus free to concentrate on his more important business.

THE CORRESPONDENCE OF HER EMPLOYER

Business training teaches every secretary to know everything she can that will be of service to her employer, but to know as little as possible about the things that are not her concern. When sorting his mail, she leaves unopened the obviously private letters—envelopes written by hand on stationery not suggestive of business—and having opened his other letters and arranged them in whatever order he prefers, she should then clip a sheet of blank paper on the top of each pile, or put the mail in a manila folder, so that visitors or others who have access to his office will not have the contents of letters displayed before them.

TAKING DICTATION

When a secretary enters a man's office in response to his summons or because it is the hour set for her appearance, she should take a chair and place it near enough to hear him easily. Where she sits depends very much on the office—where the light comes from and where she can best hear his voice. It is not expected that he get up and offer her a chair or show her the sort of personal attention that a man in social life shows to a woman.

IN UNCONVENTIONAL SITUATIONS

The young woman who is a confidential secretary to an executive may very well on occasion be required to stay late into the evening working with him alone; or if the nature of his business or profession requires that he take long trips to distant cities, she may accompany him on these purely business trips. Theoretically nothing could be more improper than a young woman—an attractive and personable one, no doubt—traveling about the country with a man alone. But practically, and according to the exigencies of the modern business world, it is necessary that every professional or business woman shall write her own code of propriety. She must! In the case of Miss Secretary, no one in the world can advise her as well as she can advise herself. She knows exactly how necessary she is or is not to the work her employer must do; she knows his attitude toward her, and certainly she knows her own attitude toward him. Therefore, she knows beyond the shadow of a doubt whether she must or whether she need not go with him.

It is true the business woman is free from criticism—unless she herself gives cause for it. It isn't the bald fact of taking planes and staying in hotels and being off in a distant state alone with Mr. Employer that will hurt Miss Secretary's good name. Nothing will hurt her good name except her own or Mr. Employer's unprofessional and therefore improper attitude of mind. And now having said that Miss Secretary may defy convention, I must add a fairly formidable array of qualifying rules that the critical world expects her to follow.

In preparation for the journey the secretary orders whatever accommodations the employer always expects. In hotels she engages a suite for him, and a room and bath on another floor for herself. To put herself in another hotel would be a mistake, because she will make her employer conscious of the fact that she is conscious of him, to say nothing of the inconvenience should he need her services unexpectedly.

If she should by chance find herself shown into a room adjoining that of her employer, the question of what to do depends somewhat upon the type of man he is. She may accept the situation, or if she has reason to suspect he might take advantage of it, she goes down to the desk and tells the clerk that her room is not the one that was ordered and tries to get another.

HER BEHAVIOR OUTSIDE BUSINESS HOURS

Today the private secretary traveling with her employer will frequently—especially if clients or associates are with them—lunch with him or have dinner with him in hotel dining rooms or restaurants. When there is no time to spare she may have to eat in his rooms where they are working. In other words, she takes eating alone or eating with him as incidental to convenience. However, the better part of discretion is that they dine in a public eating place rather than in his hotel room.

WHEN SHOULD A SECRETARY RISE?

A question often raised is whether a secretary should rise when visitors enter the office. Many a young woman thinks it very rude not to meet the friendliness of such persons as she would do were she at home.

The answer to this is that unless the visitors are persons of importance to her employer—so important that the time she takes from her work is spent in her employer's interest—it would not be expected of her, or even proper, to greet them in such a way as to encourage their talking to her at length. On the other hand, if she is the private secretary of an executive and part of her job is to make a pleasant impression, she would naturally leave her desk to greet a stranger or an important customer. However, if she is otherwise busy she does not rise to greet someone who comes into the office constantly. A secretary's duties do not include helping a visitor off and on with his coat, unless he actually needs help. The same approach to these problems applies to all similar office personnel.

A secretary does not rise when a member of the company who is in a superior position approaches her desk on a business matter. If, however, an employee stops by to inquire after her family, offer congratulations, or hold some similar social conversation, a younger girl would rise to say "Thank you" and to chat for a moment or two.

THE RECEPTIONIST

A tactful person at the reception desk in an office is of great importance. Neither a condescending nor a gushing attitude is suitable—anywhere! A pleasant, quiet, but cordial attitude can do much to further the good will of the firm for which you work.

When a recumbent, gum-chewing office boy flings at you from behind a locked gate "Who d'ja wanna see?" and then shuffles off and returns with "Mr. Brown's busy. Can't see ya t'day! Try t'morrer if ya like," the customer will *not*, unless he really must see Mr. Brown and cannot take his business to anyone else. Many offices—especially those which have many personal contacts—are putting middle-aged women at the reception desk because it has been found that people do not resent being refused admittance by a tactful older person as they resent being barred by someone who is young and callous.

THE WELL-RUN OFFICE

OFFICE DISCIPLINE

An employee should take as much pride in helping to keep up the tone of the office he works in as he takes in his own efficiency. A company in which everyone contributes to a spirit of enthusiasm and participation is a happier place for both employer and employee.

Possessing tact and knowing how to please people and make them pleased in turn with your firm can be one of the surest ways of getting an increase of salary. Putting on airs and thinking yourself too good for your job is pretty close to asking for a job not half so good as the one you hold.

Do not bring your personal problems to the office. You may rest assured that no one is interested. Leave them at home or, if you must, discuss them with a friend during lunch.

In the office of a large company the executives should call their employees "Miss [or Mrs.] Jones" rather than "Mary." The employees, in turn, always call the executives "Mr. Smith." There are, however, varying degrees of formality in business organizations. Offices today tend to be more casual than formerly. Many employers feel that in a more relaxed atmosphere employees will be more efficient, more reliable, and more loyal. These employers try to hire personnel who will be congenial and who will work well together to the benefit of the company. The employer or ranking executive determines the degree of formality in his office. He may, for instance, prefer to be on a first-name basis with his staff, and the informality does not itself imply a too-familiar relationship. This is invariably true in the office of a small company, where the total staff may not exceed ten or twelve people.

A wise young woman in a subordinate position does not go out to lunch with her superior or employer. There is always the danger that it would lead to a more personal relationship which would make it most difficult for two people to work together at maximum efficiency. But a woman in a commensurate position, especially if she has matters of business to discuss, may on occasion lunch with a man in her firm. It would, however, be courting criticism should their going out together become a habit.

A man does not rise when a woman employee comes into his office. But he must stand to receive a woman visitor and remain standing until she is seated. He stands again when she prepares to leave and usually goes with her to the door, opens it for her, and "bows her out."

Personal messages over the telephone are at times unavoidable, but long, chatty conversations are not only out of place but wasteful of time that does not belong to the employee. Social "chatter" annoys other people in the office who can't help overhearing your discussion of the movie you saw last night. Personal calls that interfere with the routine of office procedure, either incoming or outgoing, are inexcusable except in genuine emergencies.

Discourage visits from your family and friends at the office. Your baby brother may be a most enchanting child, but his place is not in the office where you work.

Don't be a borrower. Constant requests for a cigarette, a dime for a candy bar, the use of a comb, etc. will make you thoroughly unpopular. If it is absolutely necessary on occasion, make sure that you repay the lender promptly or return the borrowed article in perfect shape.

BUSINESS GIFTS

Gifts from a firm to its employees are usually in the form of a bonus or a proportion of one's salary. It is not necessary to write a note of thanks for such a bonus, because it is not in the nature of a personal gift. At Christmas a man may give his personal secretary a present. Candy is conventional, although when she has been with him for some time, he might choose something he thinks she would rather have. It is hardly necessary to add that wearing apparel is NOT suitable. A private secretary known well to a man's wife is sometimes, but not usually, remembered by the wife at Christmas. Occasionally employees give presents to their employers, but it is not common. If one of the members of the office staff gets married, or if a baby is born, then the other employees may all contribute and send a gift. They also as a group may send flowers to a funeral. A committee usually collects contributions and makes an appropriate selection. No one should feel obligated to contribute more than he can afford, or anything at all if he does not wish to do so. People who do participate should all sign the card which accompanies the gift.

Giving gifts to one's fellow workers who are also personal friends should always be arranged for out of office hours.

SOCIAL AMENITIES

A man who is new in a company or who has been transferred to another branch does not entertain his employer until he has first been entertained. Shortly afterwards, it is fitting that the newcomer and his wife return the compliment in some way. It need not be "in kind." If the employer takes a young executive and his wife to an expensive restaurant for dinner, the young couple are not expected to entertain him in the same way. They may invite an older couple to a simple buffet supper, including another couple or two if they wish.

There are exceptions. If the employee has known his superior for some time he might invite him over as he would any friend. Also, if he should be giving a large party—an open house or housewarming, perhaps—including all the other members of the office, it would be nothing short of insulting to leave his employer out.

The most important thing for a young wife to remember in entertaining her husband's boss is that she recognize that he knows her situation and her means, and she need not "put on the dog." She, and her husband, should do their best to relax and act naturally, and to make the evening as pleasant as possible for their guests. The hosts' aim is to have their guests go home thinking, "What a charming friendly couple—we're lucky to have them with our company!"

STORE ETIQUETTE

The technical aspects of salesmanship are much too specialized to be discussed by anyone who has not learned the subject at first hand and practiced it with success—success, moreover, that is measured by tangible proof of satisfactory sales slips, and best of all, an increasing number of customers who ask for Mrs. Keen or Miss Personable when they come again to buy. A saleswoman can be very helpful, but she can also be a nuisance.

The aspects of salesmanship that depend for their success upon tactful and pleasing manners belong very decidedly in a book such as this. Also very decidedly belong good manners that are to be expected of all customers who make any pretense of being well-bred.

First let us consider the point of view of a customer, since this is something that we all know from personal experience. We surely do not all agree as to the type of saleswoman we like or dislike. A clever saleswoman must have different methods with different customers. After all, if customers were identical, perfect salesmanship would not be the difficult accomplishment it is. It is quite possible for methods that are unendurable to some of us to be acceptable to others.

THE SUCCESSFUL SALESWOMAN

Really great saleswomen have cultivated not only an expert knowledge of the commodities they sell, but an equally expert ability to appraise each of the customers to whom they sell. It is essential to know, therefore, whether a customer likes to be "dearied" or "madamed" or chatted to about every topic under the sun, whether she is one who likes to have her mind made up for her, or whether she is one who, knowing exactly want she wants, prefers to have her own questions answered intelligently without any unasked-for advice.

The saleswoman whom an intelligent customer is certain to like best—and return to—is one who listens to what the prospective buyer says and tries to give her what she wants, instead of trying to sell her what the store seems eager to be rid of.

For example, if you asked for something the store couldn't supply, the ideal saleswoman would listen attentively to what you say and answer, "I am very sorry, but we have nothing at all like that in the color you want; I could give you something in a small pattern of yellow," and then with certain eagerness she would ask, "Have you time to let me show it to you?"

You are pleased, because the saleswoman showed eagerness to help you find what you want, and you as a customer would be very lacking in courtesy not at least to let her show you what she so much hopes may please you. When she brings the article you are inclined to like it because, though you know it is not just what you want, you are sure it is not going to be thrust upon you. And the possibilities are that if you can make it do, you will take it. And even if you do not, you will certainly come back to that saleswoman another time when you are looking for something else.

Of all the varieties of poor saleswomen the worst is she who simply brushes aside what you say you want and blandly spreads before you something that is exactly what you have explained to her you do NOT want. At the same time she tries to force you to like it be extolling its beauties or its bargain values, and caps the climax by telling you that Mrs. Uppity thinks this is exquisite! That kind of saleswoman would have difficulty in selling a steak to a starving man.

I do not think that any person likes high-pressure salesmanship or that it ever pays in the long run. One wonders how many customers who have been high-pressured into buying what they did not really want or into spending more than they could afford have thereafter avoided not only that particular salesperson, but that particular store as well.

THE INCONSIDERATE CUSTOMER

The behavior of the customer is as important as that of the saleswoman. Indeed, a saleswoman is, so to speak, at the mercy of any customer who is ill-bred or unreasonable for as long as that customer chooses to keep her in attendance. Moreover, an unjustifiably irate customer can cause by her complaints a mark against a saleswoman, and whether deserved or not, many such marks may mean loss of a job.

As a guess, one might say that an inconsiderate customer can be at her worst and cause the greatest strain upon a saleswoman's sportsmanship and good temper in a ready-to-wear clothing department. And what a careless customer often does to the merchandise is scarcely believable. Perhaps she smears the dresses with lipstick as she pulls them on or off; perhaps she tears them in her haste or sheer carelessness; perhaps she scorches one with her cigarette, although smoking is not permitted in stores. Rarely does she think *she* did the damage. And in the end she orders none, or perhaps she buys several and then returns everything looking still more shopworn the next day.

It is true that we all at some time buy something which for one reason or another we are obliged to send back. But neither this practice nor that of being inconsiderate of salespeople or careless with the merchandise belonging to the store is typical of any thoughtful person.

Another lack of consideration is shown by people who go shopping ten minutes before closing time. The salespeople have had a long day and have routine chores to do before they can leave.

Another fault—but probably only belonging to housewives who have had no business experience—is to think it fair or honest to expect favors from their friends who are no longer women of leisure and who are not in a position to give below-cost prices or to put all other customers aside and spend their time in gossiping with a friend. Finally, it is hard to believe but there are women who, with no thought of buying anything, will go into a dress department solely to pass an hour or so before a lunch date, and waste the time of a saleswoman who is paid at least in part by commissions on the dresses she sells—and not on the ones she shows.

Is the customer always right? It would not seem likely. Unfailing patience and good temper are qualities expected of every saleswoman, whereas there is nothing to restrain the ill humor or unreasonableness of a customer—except her own good manners.

68

In games and sports

The basic requisite for good manners at any game table or sports area is that age-old quality *sportsmanship*. The training schools for sportsmanship are three: first, easiest, and best, the nursery; second, school and college; third, the adult school of competitive tournaments.

The quality that perhaps more than any other distinguishes true sportsmanship is absence of any show of temper, not temper brought along and held in check, but temper securely locked and left at home. After all, if you can't take sports with grace and good temper, don't go in for them. Cursing your faults or your luck, excusing, complaining, and protesting against unfairness won't get you anywhere—except in trouble. You win or you lose; that is all there is to it! Never to display ill-humor is the first rule of sportsmanship. This does not mean that never by expression or gesture may you show either satisfaction or chagrin. Stoicism is often a means, not an end. The imperfect sportsman, whether he has traits of character that he cannot otherwise control, or whether he is a child or novice at the sport and still uncertain of his own reactions, learns that stoicism is the rule of safety.

The perfect sportsman meets every situation with easy grace. He shows chagrin, he shows elation, but only for the briefest moment and never without a smile. He is a favorite with onlookers because he is "human." Every now and then his expression lights with a distinctly happy grin, or it creases into a grimace at a bit of bad luck or a bungled play. There is no reason whatever why a player may not on occasion smile, unless the smile broadens into triumphant affront or verges on the smugness of conceit. When he wins, he takes his satisfaction lightly, or perhaps the better word is transiently. If he loses, he takes it good-naturedly —and still more transiently. Furthermore, when the game is over, the subject is finished. Why he won or lost or how he felt or played is not to be talked about.

It is entirely proper, even advisable, for the tournament player to win popularity if he can. One often notices that a player does almost better than he knows how to when the public is cheering him—no champagne is equal to it. On the other hand, silence for himself and cheering for his adversary are quite as real a handicap as extra pounds strapped on his back—a weight that every player must at least sometimes steel himself to bear.

The second rule is always to give your opponent the benefit of the doubt. Nothing is more important to your standing as a sportsman, though the loss of the particular point in question may seem very important at that moment. Never argue with the umpire. If he rules a line ball on the tennis court is out, it is out. You do not turn toward the spectators with an expression that says, "See how unfairly I am being treated!"

Among the lesser shortcomings of an unsportsmanlike player is his practice of understating his ability before a match. It is not necessary to point out the lack of fair play in this procedure before the handicaps are given out, but it is a commonplace occurrence to hear from a man who is perfectly satisfied with his skill, "I am not much of a player," or "I know I'll make a poor showing; I've got a 'bad' arm!" The motive is not necessarily dishonest—though on many occasions it is difficult to see it as anything else—but is often a show-off impulse to create admiring surprise should he play brilliantly on the one hand and on the other to save face should his game be off. The only time a player may declare himself unskilled is when he really is, and would otherwise be a source of annoyance in a game beyond his class.

One last and earnestly urged "don't" is the loser's practice of complaining of illness after having lost a match. "I had such a pain in my side [or knee, or back] that I don't know how I ever got through the match!" is heard so frequently that one consciously resists the temptation to taunt the loser, "I'm *sure*, poor dear, you were in such pain you could not see the ball!"

For the benefit of those who seem to believe that a man is rated a good sport because he spends money freely, it should be stated clearly that they have confused the term "sportsman"—one who competes fairly in any contest—with "sporting man," a man of far from admirable habits. A player's reputation as a good sportsman is the one thing that money *cannot* buy. Neither by giving away boxes of tennis and golf balls, nor by offering colossal silver cups, nor even by a million-dollar endowment, can the richest man ever increase by the thickness of a leaf of beaten gold his rating in sportsmanship.

Sportsmanship can be very well acquired by following a few simple rules. Keep your mind on the game, but not on your feelings. If you win, don't at once begin to fancy yourself a star. A gloating winner is detested even more than a bad loser. But when you lose, don't sulk, or protest, or long-windedly explain. If you are hurt, whether in mind or body, don't nurse your bruises. Get up and lightheartedly, courageously, good-temperedly get ready for the next encounter. This is playing the game—and the only successful way to take life.

CARD PLAYERS, PLEASANT AND UNPLEASANT

Bridge is probably the most popular "mixed-company" card game, but the same rules of etiquette apply to players of gin rummy, hearts, poker—mixed or stag—and any other game.

That no one likes a poor partner—or even a poor opponent—goes without saying. In a "team" game the ideal partner is one who never criticizes or who never even seems to be aware of your mistakes, even though you trump his ace unnecessarily; on the contrary, he recognizes a good maneuver on your part, is pleased over a clever play, and gives you credit for it whether you win the hand or lose. The inferior sportsman is likely to judge you merely by what you win and blame you if you lose, though your play may have been exceptionally good and the loss occasioned by a wrong move on his part. To be continually found at fault makes you play your worst, whereas appreciation of your good judgment acts as a tonic, and you seem to play better than you know how to.

Nothing more quickly reveals the man whose gentlemanly appearance is only a veneer than the card table, for that veneer melts quickly with success or failure. Carried away by the game, he forgets to keep on his company polish. If he wins, he becomes an insufferable gloater; if he loses, he complains constantly about the cards he has been holding and sneers at the luck of others.

ANNOYING MANNERISMS

Mannerisms must always be avoided like the plague. If there is one thing worse than the horrible postmortem, it is the incessant repetition of some jarring habit by one particular player. A common offense is that of snapping down a card as played, or picking it up and trotting it up and down on the table.

Other pet offenses are drumming on the table with one's fingers, making various clicking, whistling, or humming sounds, massaging one's face, scratching one's chin with the cards, or holding the card one is going to play aloft in the air in smart aleck fashion as though shouting, "I know what you are going to play! And my card is ready!" All mannerisms that attract attention are unpleasant—and in the long run even unendurable—to one's companions.

Many people whose game is otherwise admirable are rarely asked to play because they have some such silly and annoying habit. Don't hold a postmortem on anybody's delinquencies, unless you are actually teaching.

THE GOOD LOSER

The good loser makes it an invariable rule never to play for stakes that it will be inconvenient to lose. The neglect of this rule has been responsible for more bad losers than any other reason, and needless to say a bad loser is about as welcome at a game table as rain at a championship tennis match. Of course, they *are* people who can take losses beyond their means with perfect cheerfulness and composure. Some few are so imbued with the gambler's instinct that a heavy turn of luck, in either direction, is the salt of life. But the average person is equally embarrassed in winning or losing a stake that matters, and the only answer is always to play only for what one can easily afford.

THE THOUGHTFUL HOSTESS

There is one point of consideration which every hostess owes her guests: protection from being forced into playing for stakes which can embarrass them. Giving a guest a chance to decline her invitation beforehand is really much more important for a man than for a woman. A woman usually feels free to say, "I'm sorry, but I never play for more than so much." But a man sometimes feels that his refusal is an embarrassing confession of financial failure—a position into which no good hostess would ever put him. If people coming to her house, for instance, are known to play together, nothing need be said; but if strangers are invited to play with others who play for certain stakes, the hostess should say when she invites them, "The Smiths and Browns and Robinsons are coming. They all play for a cent. Is that all right?" The one invited can either say, "I'm sorry. I don't play for money," or "My limit is a tenth of a cent," or "They must be way out of my class! Do ask me again when you are having people who play for less."

CONTRACT BRIDGE

A trick that is annoying to moderately skilled players is to have an overconfident opponent (who usually is a better player than they are) throw down his hand, saying, "The rest of the tricks are mine!" Often it is quite possible that they might not have been his if the hand had been played out. Knowing themselves to be poorer players, the others are not likely to challenge the move, even though they feel that their rights have been taken away.

A rather trying partner is the nervous player who has no confidence in his own judgment and will invariably pass a good hand in favor of his partner's bid. If, for instance, he has six perfectly good diamonds, he doesn't mention them because, his partner having declared a heart, he thinks to himself, "Her hearts must be better than my diamonds, and if I have to play the hand, I'll probably butcher it."

An equally serious failing—and one that is far more common—is the habit of overbidding. In poker you play alone and can therefore play as carefully or as recklessly as you please; but in contract bridge your partner has to suffer with you, and you therefore are in honor bound to play a sound game—the best you know how—and the best you know how will surely keep you from overbidding more than very occasionally indeed.

If luck is against you, it will avail you nothing to sulk or complain about the awful cards you have been holding. Your partner is suffering just as much in finding you a "poison vine" as you are in being one—and you can scarcely expect your opponents to be sympathetic. You must learn to look perfectly tranquil and cheerful even though you hold nothing but poor cards for days on end, and you must on no account try to defend your own bad play. When you have made a play of poor judgment, the best thing you can say is, "I'm very sorry, partner," and let it go at that.

Always pay close attention to the game. When you are dummy, you have certain duties to your partner, so do not wander around the room or look into your opponents' hands. If you don't know what your duties are, read the rules until you know them by heart and then—read them all over again! It is impossible to play any game without a thorough knowledge of the rules that govern it.

Don't be offended if your partner takes you out of a bid, and don't take him out for the glory of playing the hand. He is quite as anxious to win the rubber as you are. It is unbelievable how many people really seem to regard their partners as third opponents.

VARIOUS SPORTS

There are fixed rules for playing every game—and for proper conduct in every sport. The details of these rules must be studied in the books of the game, learned from instructors, or acquired by experience. A small boy perhaps learns to fish by himself, but he is probably taught by his father how to hunt with a gun or ride a horse. But apart from the technique of each sport, or the rules of each game, the basic principles of good sportsmanship are always the same. In no sport or game can any evasion of rules be allowed. Sport is based upon an impersonal and indiscriminating enforcement of all rules on everyone alike.

It would be impossible to discuss good manners in every game played by sports-loving Americans. Nor is it necessary, as most are governed by a combination of adherence to the rules of the game and common courtesy.

I have chosen four sports, however, in which good manners beyond the rule book are most important. They are boating, tennis, golf, and skiing. The latter two I will dwell on at some length for three reasons. First, because of the enormous number of people who enjoy them. Second, because their popularity has increased so tremendously in very recent years that there are more people who do not know the rules—in fact, the rules are still being formed. And third, in both cases, adherence to the rules of etiquette is essential to the safety of the sport.

BOATING

If you are the proud owner of a new boat, be it sail or power, and especially if it is your first venture in ownership, you must learn thoroughly and completely the rules of safety on the water. These rules and regulations can easily be obtained from the United States Coast Guard. After complying with the rules affecting other boats, the captain may establish the routine for his own boat in as rigid or as relaxed a way as he wishes. But since there are certain procedures that have come to be regarded as most correct and most practical, every guest should be acquainted with these conventions before accepting an invitation to go cruising.

On all but the most elaborate yachts or houseboats, space is very limited. Therefore, one takes as few clothes as possible. If you are going on an extended cruise, you must find out where and in what circumstances you will be going ashore. You may attend receptions, cocktail parties, or dances in five different ports; but remember that because the people ashore will not have seen you in the other ports, and the people on other boats understand the space problem, the same dress or two will serve for several trips to shore. Most captains keep foul-weather gear on their boats, but before you sail be sure that he has sufficient, and if not, bring your own.

Some cruises, for example the New York Yacht Club cruise, do not allow laundry to be hung on deck. All participants should find out the regulations and plan their wardrobes to last the number of days between ports where a laundromat can be found.

Although many boat owners do not object to hard shoes on board, it is only polite to find out how your captain feels. If he does object, carry your party shoes in your hand until you reach shore, where you may change into them. Remember that regular rubber soles are slippery. If you are to be on board a boat that will be "heeling" (tipping with the wind) or one small enough so that it will pitch about in a rough sea, you should have grooved, nonskid sneakers especially made for sailors.

All clothing must be packed in canvas bags or duffel bags, never in a hard suitcase. The latter is impossible to stow away, whereas the canvas ones can be squashed into a minimum of space.

If cruising on a luxurious yacht, you treat the crew exactly as you would the servants in a house on land. They should be regarded with friendliness and respect, and if a steward has taken care of you and your clothing, you may leave him a tip, just as you would a chambermaid, before going ashore.

There are no other rules that are not simply those of good manners anywhere. Remember that, even more than a host on shore, the skipper is boss, and, as much for safety as for politeness, his word is law. He, after all, is the one who knows the limits of his boat and also the capabilities of his guests or crew, and he has planned for the greatest enjoyment (and in racing, the greatest chance of success) that he possibly can.

Because of the close community living on board a boat, consideration for the other people with you is of utmost importance. Before you make any move, ask yourself if you will disturb one of the others, and try to be constantly aware of the special habits and likes and dislikes of your fellow cruisers.

TENNIS

Good manners on the tennis court are generally the rule, but one does see enough violations of etiquette to make them worth mentioning. More often than not tennis is a partnership game, and one cannot, as he can in golf or skiing, play alone. Therefore, the most important rules of etiquette are those which deal with considerate manners between players.

First of all, never question the ruling of the linesmen or referee. You may think your ball landed "in" by a foot, but he is in a better place to see each line, and his decision must be final.

If your ball bounces out of your court and into the occupied court next to you, wait until those players have finished the point. Don't call "Ball please" or dash over to retrieve it while their ball is still in play.

Change sides on every odd game if the sun or wind give an advantage to one court. This is a requirement in tournament play, and even in a friendly game the offer should be made.

Children and beginners should not sign up for courts (at many clubs they are not allowed to) on weekends or other days that are the only ones on which the businessmen can play. If those happen to be the only times available to the novice as well, he should arrange to play very early in the morning or late in the afternoon.

When you arrive at the hour for which you have signed up and find the players on the court are playing what are probably the last points, wait patiently without pacing, bouncing balls, or glaring at them. In fact, it is polite to say, "Go ahead and finish. We don't mind waiting a few minutes." At the same time, when you are the one on the court, don't try to finish if you are not near the end of a set. Never finish out more than the game you are playing, and if that does not end the set, leave the court anyway.

At the end of a match it is not necessary to hop over the net as the players do in the movies, but do go up to the net and, shaking hands with your opponents, congratulate them for the good game if they won, or thank them for the excellent match if they lost.

Clothing for the tennis court is fully described in Chapter Seventy-five. Suffice it to say here that white is the tennis color, if it is not actually required, as it often is, and that clean, neat, modest shorts or dresses are correct on every court in every locality.

GOLF

Golf was originally considered (and with reason) a rich man's game. Today, however, with the appearance of the thousands of public courses that eliminate the necessity of joining an expensive club, millions of people are enjoying the game. For those who have recently started to play, there are—above and beyond learning to hit the ball correctly—some important rules of etiquette to be learned.

Golf places a particularly severe strain upon the amiability of the average person, and in no other game, except possibly bridge, is serenity of disposition so essential. No one who is easily ruffled can keep a clear eye on the ball, and exasperation at lost balls seemingly bewitches successive ones into disappearing like puffs of smoke. In a race or other test of endurance a flare of anger might even help, but in golf it is safe to say that he who loses his temper is almost certain to muff his shot and lose the match.

Golf players, of course, know the rules and observe them; but it quite often happens that idlers, having nothing better to do, walk out over a course and watch the players. If they know the players well, that is one thing, but they have no right to follow strangers. A diffident player is easily put off his game, especially if those watching him are so ill-bred as to make audible remarks. Those playing matches of course expect an audience, and erratic and nervous players ought not to enter tournaments—and certainly not into two-ball foursomes where they will handicap a partner.

Let us first consider those rules which help to eliminate the danger on a crowded golf course.

Never, in any circumstances, hit your shot until the group ahead of you is out of range. On weekends, there is generally a starter on the first tee who will tell you when to drive, but if not, you *must* wait until those who teed off before you have hit their second shots. And this rule is followed on every one of the eighteen holes. The only exception occurs when the group ahead feels that they are holding you up and signals to you to "go through." In this case, at least wait until they have moved to the edge of the fairway, and also be sure that they are all watching your ball in case it should go astray.

If you hit a wild shot that heads toward a player on another fairway, or if someone appears unexpectedly from behind a bush where he was searching for a ball, shout "Fore!" at the top of your lungs. Although he will not have time to locate your ball in flight and dodge, your shout will generally cause him to throw his arms over his head and possibly avoid serious injury.

On a blind hole (a hole where the green is not visible from where you are hitting), send a caddy or another player to the point at which he can see the area where your ball may be expected to land. If there are still other golfers in range, he holds up his hand to signal you to wait and then, when it is safe for you to hit, waves and steps to the edge of the fairway.

While waiting on a tee for your turn to drive, look around before taking a practice swing. Not only may you hit someone with your club, but if you are swinging toward them you may blast them painfully with bits of stone or turf from the ground. This is true while playing other shots as well—your caddy or companions may be closer behind you than you think—and it is always safer to look before you swing.

In addition to these rules affecting safety on the golf course, there are many that add to the pleasure of the player and the orderly progression of the game.

Never speak, rattle your clubs, or move when another player is making his shot. This is especially true on the green, where intense concentration is required, but it can be disturbing on any part of the course. Even though you may think you are far enough away from the player whose turn it is to hit, the wind may carry a sound right to him, or he may catch your movement from the corner of his eye in the middle of his backswing.

It is a matter of convention rather than etiquette, but should be mentioned because it is important to the smooth functioning of the twosome or foursome, that the person whose ball is farthest from the pin, or hole, plays first. Around the putting green there are certain set golf rules that apply to special situations, but in an informal match the ball farthest from the hole is played, even though it is not on the green, or putting surface. Usually, however, it is agreed that if a player's ball stops close to the hole, he will "putt out," or tap it in, to save the time involved in marking the spot, moving his ball, waiting for the others to play, replacing the ball, and then sinking the putt.

A foursome is obligated to allow a twosome to "go through," or pass them, if there is an empty hole ahead of them. This "if" is important, because when there are players directly in front, the twosome will be prevented from moving on, there will be a pile-up of six or more players on the same hole, and those behind will have an even more lengthy wait. In the case of a foursome following a foursome, or a twosome following a twosome, the first one obviously holding up the second, it is very rude of the slower one not to allow the others to go through.

It is customary for the player who has had the lowest score on the previous hole to "tee off," or drive, first on the next hole. If two or more are tied for the "honor," as this privilege is called, the one who had the lowest score on the last hole on which there was a difference plays first. In the case of teams, all members of the team that won the last hole go first and usually keep the same order no matter which one of them had the low score.

The final three rules relate to the proper care of the course. It should hardly be necessary to say that divots (pieces of turf dug up by the club head) should be replaced, but if one walks over a course after a busy weekend, it becomes apparent that golfers' education has been sadly neglected in this area. Equally important is the need for repairing the little pits made in the green by a high approach shot.

After playing a shot out of a trap (or bunker), the player must see that his caddy rakes the sand to eliminate his footprints and the hole made by his club. If he has no caddy, he must do it himself. In the event that there is no rake by the trap, he may do his best to smooth the sand with the head of his club.

In addition to these rules, all golfers will continue to enjoy the sport more and more if tempers are restrained and everyday rules of courtesy are observed.

SKIING

The number of people who have recently become enthusiastic about skiing in winter makes this sport comparable to golf in the summer, and as in golf, many of the rules of etiquette for skiers have developed from a need for safety regulations. In fact, on the ski slopes, except for the ordinary rules of good behavior and consideration for others, almost all the etiquette is derived from an effort to eliminate dangerous situations.

Never ski alone. Even the most expert skier in the world can have an accident—in fact the best skiers may have the most serious falls, as a result of their speed—and cold and emptiness are no respectors of skill if one falls on a lonely trail when no one knows his whereabouts.

Never ski on a closed trail. The commonest reason for blocking it off is that it is considered too dangerous for skiing at the time. Some daredevils, thinking that nothing is too difficult for them, are occasionally tempted to ski a trail that has been marked "Closed." First and foremost, this is foolish, as the ski patrols have no obligation to patrol that slope and in case of accident the skiers are far from help. Second, the trail may be closed in order to keep the snow in condition for a time later in the season or for a special competition. In the latter case, using it is thoughtless to the management of the area as well as to the skiers who are to use it when it opens.

Never ski on a trail or slope that is too difficult for you. All ski areas mark their trails "Novice," "Intermediate," or "Expert," or possibly a combination of two—"Novice-Intermediate." If you have only been skiing a few times, don't assume that because in other sports you are as good as your friend Sally, who has been on the slopes since she was three, you are capable of accompanying her to the top of the mountain to try the new "expert" trail. Not only are you likely to break a leg, but you will infuriate the true experts who are entitled to use the trail and who will hardly appreciate rounding a curve at high speed only to find a novice "snow-plowing" down the middle of the trail in front of them.

The other side of the coin must be cited, too. If you are an expert, high-speed-loving skier, stay off the novice and intermediate slopes as much as possible. There is no need to make them more crowded than they ordinarily are, and nothing is more terrifying to a beginner than a hurtling skier rushing past him or even, as I have seen so often, running over the tips of his skis or actually knocking him down.

Skiers cannot be put on little tracks labeled *10 mph, 20 mph, 40 mph,* and so forth, however, and there are certain to be occasions when a faster skier must pass a slower skier on a narrow trail. In order to warn him (or her) that he is about to pass, he calls "Track, right" or "Track, left," indicating that he will pass on that side, thereby warning the slower skier to pull to the other side—or at least not to make a sudden turn toward him as he passes.

If, because of a miscalculation, or for any reason whatever, you do knock another skier down, STOP! Apologize, and make absolutely sure that he is not injured before you continue on down the hill.

If he appears to be having difficulty in regaining his feet, it is only common courtesy to go back and assist him. If he is unable to move or get up or is in pain, do not fly off hysterically looking for help, but stay with him, doing whatever you can, such as undoing his harnesses, to make him more comfortable, until another skier approaches. Then, and only then, having asked the new arrival to stay with the injured person, you may go as fast as you possibly can to the nearest ski patrol. Never try to move the fallen skier. If he is suffering from a broken bone you may cause a much more serious injury if you move him incorrectly. The ski patrol are trained to do this and will have the proper equipment with them when they arrive.

Remember that the mountain may be very large, and it is very difficult to find another person at any given time. When you are a member of a group, family or friends, it is wise to set a specific place and time at which to meet for meals, to go home, or just to "check in."

Otherwise, good manners for skiers are simply a matter of employing consideration for others at all times. Don't ridicule the novice even jokingly, and don't boast of your own skill. When the line waiting for the lift is long, don't shove ahead of those already waiting, but take your place patiently and cheerfully. If you are with a group, don't hold the better skiers up by insisting that they wait for you, and if you are one of the more expert, don't insist that the beginners accompany you where they are not capable of staying in control.

Skiing is a wonderful sport, both for physical thrills and for the social life that is a part of it. But more than in almost any other sport, consideration of others and good manners are essential to the enjoyment and safety of everyone.

69

For the newcomer

Becoming settled in a new community presents problems to all but those who are thoroughly accustomed to moving. Mrs. Engineer, whose husband stays in one spot only long enough to complete a bridge and then transports his family to another river halfway across the continent, may after a few years develop her own packing and moving system to a high degree of perfection and find it not too difficult to adjust to a new neighborhood. But Mrs. Youngbride, leaving her hometown for the first time, can find the change very difficult, and it is primarily, but not solely, to her that these remarks are directed.

THE NEW BRIDE

The young bride who is a stranger, but whose husband and his family are well known in the community, has no problem other than to make herself liked in her new surroundings. The best way to do this is to be ready to like others, to be interested in what interests them, and to try to adapt herself to their points of view. This does not mean that she is to be double-faced, but merely that she is not to ride roughshod over their pet prejudices before she has even discovered what they are. The bride, for example, who comes from Chicago or San Francisco and goes to

Bright Meadows and then rudely criticizes the smaller town's ways, who insists on comparing Bright Meadows' new six-story office building with fifty-story skyscrapers, is being not merely discourteous but stupid.

The best ingredients for likableness are an unaffected manner, a sympathetic attitude, and a cheerful disposition. A young woman with an affected pose and bad or conceited manners will never make friends anywhere. The best rule to follow, as always is: Be your own natural self.

The newcomer, whether a new bride or not, should avoid forcing herself on her neighbors. It is fatal to push or be presumptuous. A smile, the friendlier the better, is never out of place. Enthusiasm should, of course, be shown to friends, in contrast to the more impersonal courtesy displayed to strangers.

WHEN BOTH ARE STRANGERS

Let us say the young Lakes from Chicago are about to move to Strangetown, where John Lake will be employed in the new branch office his firm has just opened. Business is the usual reason for moving to a new community. John will, of course, meet a few people through business, but they will not necessarily be congenial socially.

If the town is small and friendly, Mary will probably get to know her neighbors without too much difficulty. By becoming members of the church and by participating in a variety of community activities the Lakes will gradually enlarge their acquaintance.

BREAKING THE ICE

The old rule that the new neighbor must sit and wait—perhaps forever—for an old resident to make a move is one that I would like to change. In this day of informality I can see nothing contrary to the basic rules of etiquette in asking a neighbor you meet on the street to come in for a cup of coffee, or to bring her child over to play with your toddler. No one in his right mind would consider this "pushy." Asking for advice —where to find the best butcher, or who may be the best pediatrician— is always a fine opener.

The new neighbor should not, however, be the first to extend an invitation to a meal, at least until an informal preliminary meeting has been achieved. Once an older resident has made the first move, the newcomer is free to ask her to any function she wishes, although she might do well to get to know the wife a little better before the husbands are brought together. This could avoid establishing a relationship too quickly, which might later be difficult to break off if it were not satisfactory.

A LETTER OF INTRODUCTION

Before the Lakes left Chicago, they told Mrs. Oldname about

John's new location, and Mrs. Oldname offered to send a letter introducing the young couple to a friend of hers in Strangetown.

A letter of introduction is better sent than taken in person by the newcomers. If the Lakes themselves were to take a letter to Mrs. Welcome, this lady would be obligated, whether she felt like it or not, to show them immediate and particular hospitality, or risk affronting both the newcomers and the writer of the letter. A letter of introduction sent by Mrs. Oldname telling her friends about Mary and John Lake gives Mrs. Welcome time to consider when and how best she may introduce the young couple to other and congenial young people. It does not force the Lakes upon the intimate hospitality of Mrs. Welcome as a letter taken by them to her would do.

NEWCOMERS TO A BIG CITY

Many young people have the notion that life in a big city is glamorous, and those who come from a small, neighborly community into a huge metropolis are likely to be greatly disappointed and unhappy. The young bride will find herself without a position such as she had at home and would have had in almost any other small community. This is not because the great city refuses to accept her; it simply doesn't know of her existence. In a small town she would not remain unrecognized for long. After she had walked down Main Street a dozen times, dozens of people would know her, by sight, at least.

If you plan to move to one of our large cities, try not to go into a neighborhood where you will know no one at all. If you have any friends or relatives in the city, try to find an apartment within easy traveling distance of them. Or perhaps a man's business associates in a new city can recommend a neighborhood with which they are familiar. If you know no one in the city, you may be more at home in a suburb where the casual informality will provide new friends more easily.

But even if you do take an apartment in, let's say, the heart of New York, you will, in time, find a circle of friends. Even in an enormous city, people can be friendly. Just give a few of them a chance to get to know you. You'll meet your next-door neighbors in the laundry room or the elevator, or in the park a block away. If you, as well as your husband, have a career, you will meet people of similar interests through business. Become an *active* member of the nearest church of your denomination; perhaps it has a young couples' club, a Bible study class, or some other activities you both can participate in. The YMCA and similar organizations sponsor a variety of clubs and classes. And every large city has several universities offering evening extension courses. Study French literature or interior decorating and make friends with the others taking the same courses. Above all, be sure to keep busy; never stay at home moping about the town you came from. The bigger the city you move to, the more there is for you to do and discover in it.

YOUR FIRST VISITORS

Very possibly some of your new neighbors will come to call before your home is ready to receive visitors. If they find you at the top of a stepladder or in a paint-spattered smock, you are really in luck. If you think about it, you will realize that this is a far more friendly setting than a formal hostess-visitor scene could be. Before you know it, you will be showing your neighbors what you have painted and the curtain material you are going to sew; and before they know it, they are giving you their best advice, which perhaps you take or perhaps you don't. By the time they go they seem like friends, and probably they soon become just that. *For the more formal first call, see Chapter Fifty-seven.*

BEWARE OF IMMEDIATE INTIMACY

Beware of rushing into intimacy with every welcoming but not necessarily congenial neighbor. You will only appear to be a snob if you later break with your earlier acquaintances when you meet people you really like. After you have been in your new home for a while, you will come to know people whose interests are the same as your own. You can avoid suddenly having to neglect those with whom you were too intimate at first if you are selective and somewhat reserved from the beginning. If you *are* a snob, and transfer yourself from the Nextdoor circle to the Highhills, who are richer or more important, you will deserve the opinion that others will most certainly have of you.

Between being a snob and being selective is the entire distance between being contemptible and admirable—between worst and best.

70

With regard to artists, entertainers, and other celebrities

When we meet a performing artist or a distinguished lecturer or a celebrity of any kind, ordinary good manners and common courtesy SHOULD cover almost every situation, but only too often problems arise. Indeed, the forms of impoliteness may cover a very wide range—from the debutante's mother who shows no consideration for the musicians hired to play for the tea dance to the lion-hunting hostess who invites a celebrity to dinner not because of any genuine feeling of friendship for him, but merely because of a misguided wish to impress her other guests, which she certainly will not do in any desirable way.

THE ARTIST IS EMPLOYED

Apart from the courtesies that every hostess instinctively shows to friends, acquaintances, or strangers when they are admitted to her house, there are rules that apply particularly to professional artists who are hired to entertain.

Unless their presence is to be a surprise, all entertainers should be admitted at the front door, of course.

Musicians who play at a dance or at a wedding reception necessarily arrive before the guests, and they are shown to a room where they may wash up or change, and then to the place where they are to play. They should be greeted briefly by whoever is in charge of arrangements. Refreshments should be taken to them at the times that fit in best with their program.

Soloists or actors who are to make their entrance on a stage should be shown to the dressing rooms and then to a lounge or other convenient spot to await the hour of their performance. They should be greeted as soon after their arrival as possible by the host or hostess or master of ceremonies, who asks whether there is anything that would add to their comfort. Whether they meet the guests after their performance or not depends upon their personality and their wishes. When musicians or actresses or actors are especially charming or talented, or both, guests will almost surely ask to meet them, and the true professional is always delighted to comply.

COURTESY TO A CELEBRITY IN ONE'S HOME

A real celebrity, whether a star in the entertainment world or a notable person who is to lecture, is usually the guest of honor and treated as such in every particular. Since the hostess may be busy with other guests, the host is delegated to greet the celebrity upon his arrival and to conduct him to wherever he is to wait until it is time for his entrance. The host (or delegate-host) remains with the artist or speaker until the hostess herself appears. She greets the celebrity and conducts him to the room where he is to perform and introduces him to the audience. At the end of the program, the hostess stands beside him and introduces those of her guests who wish to meet him.

No matter in which category an artist belongs, there is a certain purely business matter-of-factness to the situation of a professional fulfilling an engagement. He goes prepared to do to the best of his ability what he has agreed to do, and at the close of his performance he receives the sum that has been agreed upon. Whether in addition to this he has a delightful evening or a trying one is, as far as his business contract goes, beside the point.

THE ARTIST IS A FRIEND

For obvious reasons, the hostess who considers that professional friends' talents are assets to which she has proprietary rights is intolerable. Do you know Mrs. Hi Wayman, who invites Mr. Barrytone Tops or Mr. Hitshow to dine on Sunday evening? After dinner she coyly announces that she just knows that Mr. Tops will be delighted to sing, or that Mr. Hitshow will *of course* do that delicious scene that is the only reason why the theater is packed to bursting every night in the week!

It is often true that at a party of considerable size an entertainer can, or possibly must, decline on the plea that contracts prohibit his performance. But at an informal dinner at which one or two others of lesser talent may have contributed their part, it can be embarrassing to refuse because it seems ungenerous to those who eagerly looked forward to it. But actually it is distinctly unfair to expect someone to return the courtesy of a little food and a place at dinner between pleasant companions with an entertainment commercially valued at possibly surpassing four figures! And even if he is not at or near the top of his profession, remember that your guest is not a trained poodle to be put through a bag of tricks for the entertainment of your other guests.

FAVORS TOO MUCH TAKEN FOR GRANTED

Much can be said about the unthinking casualness with which people do ask favors of their professional friends. Put bluntly, one would not go to a butcher and ask to be given a steak, nor to the shop of a milliner and ask to be given a hat, and yet the friends of a professional artist will think nothing of asking for a sketch or a recital. And the work of every professional is his livelihood. If he gives to one person, how can he refuse to give to another—and who will want to buy what is given so freely?

Of much less importance, but merely illustrating the point: The barest acquaintances of an author think nothing of asking him for his books. Apparently most people imagine that books grow like daisies in the field and that an author need merely pick them at random. Doctors and lawyers are constantly asked for professional advice by people they meet casually in the houses of their friends. In nearly all cases they are delighted to give generously to someone they care for or to a cause in which they are interested; but when they are asked to give, a conventional "I'm so sorry" should be respected without forcing them into a position that seems to make them appear ungracious.

If musicians are amateurs, however, their friends can perfectly well ask them to play at a party. But they should not be asked to provide a background accompaniment to chatter. No one with any sensibility would invite artists to play or sing and then make no effort to preserve a courteous silence during their performance. On the other hand, professional dance orchestras and other party musicians who play at dances and at weddings do not expect, or even want, to face a room full of completely silent people.

AUTOGRAPHS

The number of people who recognize the celebrity on the street and the number who wait outside the stage door to get his autograph are among the principal measures of his success. If he is rude or impatient with these fans, it can only have an adverse affect on his popularity, and therefore most entertainers or professionals whose success depends on their public image are willing to be watched, followed, and hounded for their signatures. The greater the degree of friendliness and tact with which they submit to these annoyances, the greater their success with the public.

By respecting the fact that their idol cannot defend himself against invasions of his privacy without alienating people, his fans should confine their efforts to the times when he expects to sign their books and otherwise fulfill his obligations as a public figure. When a prominent person is in his home or dining out, even though he may be in a public restaurant, shopping, seeking relaxation in a sport or a hobby, or otherwise attempting to lead a normal life, he should be allowed his privacy.

71

With the handicapped

It is probably true that a majority of the people in the world have little contact with the unfortunate ones who are handicapped or disabled. If we have a cripple of any sort in our homes, or in the home of a relative or friend, we quickly become accustomed to the situation and learn how to act so as to be of the most help to him and to those around him. Should the disabled one be a member of our own family, we make every effort to learn all that we can about his problem, to seek professional advice, and to make his life, as well as our own, as normal as possible. This chapter, therefore, is devoted to people who meet the handicapped only from time to time and who, in making an effort to be helpful, may go about it, through lack of knowledge, in the wrong way. Their intentions may be the very best, but an act of kindness, tendered in the wrong way, may be a cause of much embarrassment and even actual harm to the very person they are trying to help.

There are certain rules that apply to your behavior in regard to all handicapped people, and the most important by far is this: NEVER stare, or indicate that you are conscious that the person is different from others in any way. People who are getting themselves about in wheelchairs, who have mastered the use of crutch or brace, or who can manipulate a mechanical hand dexterously take great pride in their independence and approach to normalcy. The last thing they wish is to be reminded by curious or overly solicitous persons that they have not achieved their goal. An offer of help to a man in a wheelchair who must navigate a steep curb in order to cross the street or an arm proffered to a lady with a cane and a leg brace who is trying to get down a rail-less set of steps is, of course, in order. But before grabbing the wheelchair or seizing an arm, ask politely if, and in what way, you can be of assistance.

Another important rule is never to make personal remarks, or ask personal questions of one with an obvious disability. If he wishes to talk about the accident that caused it or discuss his condition, let him introduce the subject, but never, never pry into his feelings or his clinical symptoms—subjects that he may be doing his best to forget.

Of all forms of disabilities, deafness and blindness are the two with which the greatest number of people come into frequent contact. Therefore, I am making some suggestions, not only for those meeting deaf or blind people, but for those so handicapped themselves.

DEAFNESS

There are, of course, all degrees of deafness, from partial loss of hearing in one ear to the more unusual extreme of complete deafness, which cannot be helped even by a hearing aid. It may only be necessary to speak a little more distinctly to one who is partially deaf or to repeat a remark that he may have missed. If you know that the hearing loss is in one ear, it is considerate to sit on the side of his good ear in movies, restaurants, or any place where you may not face him. In the case of total hearing loss, the only means of contact is visual—through lip reading—so the rules are quite different from those applying to someone with partial hearing.

You must speak distinctly and reasonably slowly.

Don't use exaggerated mouth movements. Distorted lip motions may confuse him, as he has been taught to read normal lip movement.

To attract his attention, it is useless to shout. If he is not facing you, tap him gently on the arm or shoulder.

Be patient in talking to him and willing to repeat or make your statement in words that are easier for him to understand.

Encourage him to participate in family and social activities. Persons with severe handicaps tend to withdraw into themselves, but it is not to their own good, and it only upsets their family and friends. A little extra urging and enthusiasm over their presence can make the handicapped feel much more like leading a normal life. On the other hand, try to be sensitive to their reactions, because too much pressure can have the opposite from the desired effect.

Between the slightly deaf and the totally deaf fall the many thousands with intermediate degrees of the disability. The first thing to be recommended for them is that they wear a hearing aid. There is no more stigma or embarrassment in this than in wearing glasses, and the family and friends of the hard of hearing who are reluctant should do their best to encourage them to overcome their hesitation. Once persuaded, they will find that their life will attain a normalness they had never thought possible. Here are some rules that should be observed for conversation with the partially deaf:

Don't raise your voice or shout—his hearing aid is probably adjusted for a normal voice.

Call him by name to attract his attention.

As with the more severely handicapped, be patient—willing to repeat if necessary. And if you must repeat, don't shout or appear annoyed. This will only embarrass him and make it harder for him to understand.

Don't exclude him from conversation, but try to place him so that he may see you or the group. Even normal people read lips unconsciously, and it is a great help to one handicapped by partial deafness.

If you are one of those handicapped by deafness yourself, a few of the following suggestions may add to your comfort and that of your friends.

DO wear a hearing aid—they are now made in such a way as to be almost invisible, and even if they weren't, loss of hearing is no more "shameful" than loss of sight, and few people refuse to wear glasses.

Having gotten a hearing aid, wear it! A strained expression of concentration, a constant, "What did you say?" and answers that make no sense make you appear inattentive, or stupid, when there is no need to. Keep your aid turned on, and gain the admiration of your friends for so capably overcoming your handicap.

With or without your aid, do listen attentively and concentrate on what people are saying. Even people with normal hearing miss many remarks through inattention.

Look at the people talking to you—their expression and their lips will help you to "hear" them.

Don't take advantage of your impairment by trying to arouse sympathy. There is no justifiable reason for sympathy—a deaf person can, with a little extra effort, lead a perfectly normal life.

BLINDNESS

The most important thing to remember when coming in contact with someone handicapped by blindness is that in every other respect he is exactly like you. His other facilities are in no way impaired; his interests and his way of life may be much the same as yours. He certainly has a problem to overcome that a sighted person does not face, but it is a problem with which one can learn to live, and most blind people have done so with considerable success.

Therefore the cardinal rule is this: Treat the blind man as you would any other person. Talk to him, in a normal voice, about the same subjects that would interest your other friends, including blindness, if it should come up. Don't avoid the use of the word "see." Blind people use it as much as anyone else. There is no reason to show surprise that he can dial telephone numbers, light a cigarette, dress himself, or perform any of the daily chores that we all do. He has simply made a little more effort to learn to do them by touch or sound.

Aside from your attitude, there are several specific suggestions that will make your contacts with a blind person more pleasurable to you both.

When you are with, or pass by, a blind person on a street corner, you are perfectly correct in asking if you can help him to cross; but never grasp his arm or try to give assistance without first asking whether he wishes it or not. If he does, let *him* take *your* arm, which will give him far more confidence than being propelled forward by you. If he should ask you for directions, be sure to use left and right from his viewpoint—the direction he is facing.

If you go to a restaurant with a blind person, do not hesitate to read him the menu, including the prices if the occasion demands. You certainly may tell him quietly where the salt and pepper are and help him to the sugar and cream if he wishes. You may tell him how the items on his plate are arranged and help him cut his meat if necessary. But much of this he will prefer to do himself if you simply locate the food for him.

When he visits your home lead him to a chair and then just place his hand on the arm or back. If he is staying with you for any length of time, remember to tell him where the furniture is, inform him if anything is rearranged, and keep doors open or closed—never halfway.

When taking him to a strange place, tell him quietly where the furniture is located and who is present. And before you leave him alone, be sure that he has someone to talk to—one thing he cannot do (unless he is among good friends whose voices he recognizes) is single out a person who would, from his appearance, be congenial.

When there is a blind person in a room you have just entered, make your presence known, and tell him, if he does not recognize your voice, who you are. Tell him also when you leave, so that he will not be left talking—to himself.

Last of all, if the blind person has a Seeing Eye dog, do not attempt to play with or distract the dog in any way. His attention must remain fully on his master, whose safety and well being may depend entirely on his strict adherence to his training.

72

For pets and people

A dog may be man's best friend and a cat by the hearth a very cozy sight, but all who own pets are responsible for seeing that they behave in such a way as to make them the real friends of everyone with whom they come in contact. Pets other than dogs and cats may be fewer in number, but their good manners are just as important. And, if your children's rabbit cannot be trained not to make a nuisance of himself, *your* good manners take over and you must insist that he be kept in his pen when visitors are in the house.

DOGS

For years people have complained to me about the unnecessary problems created by neighbor's pets. Is there anything that the Joneses can do to protect themselves from the ill-mannered dogs of neighbors or visitors or even houseguests? I could quote instances by the dozen of pleasant neighborhood friendships that have become strained and even broken by the Smith dog that barks all night, or the Pope dog that runs through flower beds and possibly rolls or digs in them. Then there are other dogs brought by their owners into friends' houses and allowed to jump up on the furniture, in spite of muddy paws or sharp claws that dig into the sofa cushions. We have all known owners who complacently believe that their pet is perfectly trained to stay exactly where ordered. It never occurs to them, engrossed in conversation, to notice that less than a minute after being told to stay there, their pet has quietly slipped away on an exploring expedition. If he is a dog of mature intelligence, he may, it is quite true, make an entirely impersonal and dignified survey of the premises. But if he is young and eager to test the taste, texture, and toughness of every new thing he sees, his investigation may all too well become a foray of destruction. *For suggestions about the note of apology to be written after such an unfortunate episode, see Chapter Nine.*

The behavior of a dog—like that of the rest of us—is seldom better in company than it is at home. If Kiltie (bright little Scottie though he is) is allowed to run around the dinner table and beg, he will do the same in every other house. Moreover, he is naturally more restless where new surroundings tantalize his curiosity than he is at home where everything is familiar and where he can be allowed the freedom of the house.

On the subject of that seemingly unaccountable lapse from trustworthy behavior that *can* overtake a dog who is allowed to wander at liberty in a strange house—particularly a new house—owners sometimes fail to realize that it is the thoroughly impregnated scent of "human habitation" that tells him he is indoors. To his sense of smell, new upholstery or a newly laid carpet, which has had almost no human handling, is easily mistaken for outdoors. He can't tell the difference between indoor decoration and outdoor view just by sight! It is always safest in a strange house to keep him on a short leash unless his obedience to command is so complete that wherever he may be, he pays attention to nothing but his position at his master's side. On the street, he does not even glance in the direction of another dog unless his master releases him by saying in a changed tone, "Go run," and he is free to go where he pleases. At the command "Heel!" he takes his place at his master's side with the precision of a soldier obeying the command of his sergeant. In fact, you might test your own dog's training by noticing when you take him out whether he is welcomed by your neighbors', "Hello, Topsie," "Good morning, Blackie!" or by a frown that clearly says, "Oh dear, there's that dreadful dog again!"

It is true, some people do not like dogs at all. Plainly then, if you are invited to stay with friends who do not welcome four-footed visitors, this is one of the occasions when ownership of a dog exacts its payment, and you must stay home unless you have someone with whom you can leave him or a good kennel at which you can board him. On the other hand, no absolutely obedient dog has ever—so far as I know personally—been objected to by anyone, even as a houseguest. But the dog who is told "Come here" only to have him run in the other direction, the puppy who nips people on the ankle, the one who chews on everything in sight, the big, loose-lipped dog who on hot days drools like a teething baby over the suits and dresses of visitors—are not social assets even in the opinion of dog-lovers.

To train a dog to such a degree that he obeys on the second every word spoken, or every wordless gesture made to him, requires consistent as well as persistent patience directed by practical common sense. That perfect training is entirely possible has been proved not only by the miracle dogs that are Seeing Eyes for the blind and by the dogs trained as assistants to the police, but by all other breeds of dogs that perform in the theater, by those which herd sheep, and by those which work flawlessly in the hunting field. Surely then, it is not too much to ask that adequate education be given to the four-footed members of the family. One thing is certainly true: the rewards of beautiful manners are very great. Not only does the behavior of a canine gentleman (or lady) quite actually enhance the social prestige of his master, but the dog himself acquires stature as a companion, a guardian, and a friend—in short, a recognized personality.

CATS

In some ways cats present different problems, for they are taken visiting far less often. When your cat has the run of the neighborhood, however, you may have to take steps to see that he does not become an inadvertent but regular visitor to the house of someone who once innocently set out a saucer of milk in the kitchen, only to find the cat perched between the Dresden figurines on the mantel. It is perfectly proper, before the accident has a chance to occur, to ask your neighbors not to feed your pet, as the habit is hard to break and can easily become a neighborhood problem.

In your own house you may be quite accustomed to having your cat jump into your lap without warning, but remember that your guest probably isn't. Not only will there be a suit or dress covered with hairs and possibly snagged; there may be a broken teacup or a burned carpet as a result of the natural and involuntary start of surprise. Until you know your visitor well, it is far safer to put Fluffy securely in another room. This is in no way unkind to your pet, for very likely you are saving him from the discipline his overenthusiasm might cause.

Some people, of course, have real aversions to all cats, even the best behaved, and you should no more force Fluffy's presence on them than you would force crabmeat on a guest who is allergic to it.

OTHER PEOPLE

If you are one of those who have an allergy or an aversion to dogs, cats, hamsters, white mice, or any of the other pets you are likely to encounter, it is only polite of you to tell your host or hostess quietly and unobtrusively, just as you would mention a food allergy to avoid embarrassment at the dinner table. No one will wish you to suffer while a guest in his house, and a few words can usually prevent much discomfort and possibly an unpleasant misunderstanding.

On the other hand, if you are fond of household animals, you should take every care to respect their training and encourage their good habits. Don't, for example, thump the sofa beside you and invite Kiltie to jump up until you have asked whether he is allowed to sit on the furniture. Don't feed an animal without his owner's permission, any more than you give a child candy without asking his mother first. If you wish your pet-owning friends and neighbors to respect your rights, do remember that your thoughtless actions may undo months of careful training.

73

Gifts and giving

A gift, above all, is an expression of affection. It need not be large or expensive, but it should show thoughtful consideration of the interests of the person to whom it is given.

MONEY AS A WEDDING PRESENT

The custom of giving money as a wedding present is a long established tradition in Jewish communities and among various other groups. Even in those weddings where most guests give presents, close relatives and intimate friends of the bride's or groom's parents sometimes prefer to give money. To set maximums or minimums on a sum given as a gift is against every principle of etiquette. The amount you spend should depend on your affection for the receiver and the closeness of the tie between you. In some groups it is accepted that one gives five or ten or twenty dollars as a gift. If this is the custom in your area, you must go along with it or risk criticism. Otherwise, for anyone to say "You must give thus-and-so" is entirely wrong.

A check given before the wedding is made out in the bride's maiden name, or if the couple have opened a joint account, it may be written to both the bride and groom. A check to be presented at the reception may be made out to the bride's married name or to the couple jointly.

Checks may be displayed along with other presents but should be arranged so the amounts are hidden. When money is given at a reception, the cash or a check is placed in an envelope with the couple's first names written on the outside and handed to them as the guests go down the receiving line. The bride and groom both thank the donors, and the envelopes are put into a receptacle to be opened later. In addition to her verbal thanks, the bride must write a thank-you note as soon as possible.

OTHER GIFTS OF MONEY

Although giving money is often a lazy way of avoiding the trouble of choosing a gift, there are occasions when a check is the most welcome present of all. There are many elderly couples with a limited income who love the opportunity of shopping for some long-desired object, and there are few teen-agers who don't relish the idea of a little extra cash.

For people who dislike the idea of giving cash or a check a gift certificate is a good compromise. One couple I know took the trouble to buy such a certificate in the leading department store of the town to which their neighbors were moving, and presented it at their going-away party. Somehow the thoughtfulness of this gesture made the gift seem far warmer and more personal than a check.

It is never correct to include a request for money on the invitation to any private party such as an anniversary or open house. If, however, the people giving the party have planned a special group present such as tickets for a vacation trip, a new television set, or a fine painting, it would be proper to enclose a short note with the invitation explaining what has been planned, and asking the guests if they would like to make a contribution in place of bringing an individual gift. Each guest who contributes should sign the card accompanying the gift.

THANK-YOU LETTERS

All thank-you letters should be written as soon as possible. A bride should try to write her thanks the day wedding gifts arrive. When a quantity of gifts arrives at the last minute, letters may be postponed until after the honeymoon, but three months should be the outside limit for acknowledging every one. Thank-you letters are not necessary for presents that have been given in person on a birthday, at a house party, a shower, or other similar occasions. Although it is in no way wrong to write a note, sincere verbal thanks at the time you receive the gift are sufficient. Nor do thank-you or "bread-and-butter" letters themselves require any reply: that would be inviting a never-ending exchange of correspondence. A thank-you gift sent with, or in place of, a bread-and-butter letter should, however, be acknowledged. Sending printed cards of thanks is inexcusable, unless a personal note is added. In cases where a delay in sending handwritten notes is unavoidable, a printed card acknowledging receipt of the gift and stating that a letter will follow is the best way of keeping people from wondering what happened to their present. But the handwritten note must follow as soon as physically possible.

When a gift is received from a married couple, the thank-you note is generally written to Mrs. Doe, but some reference to her husband should be made in the text of the note: "I want you and Mr. Doe to know how much we like the . . ." It is not incorrect, however, to address these notes to both man and wife: "Dear Mr. and Mrs. Doe." The same procedure is followed when a wife writes a thank-you letter for a gift given to both her husband and herself. She generally writes and signs the note, but refers to her husband in the text.

RETURNING AND EXCHANGING GIFTS

If an engagement is broken, the woman must return to her former fiancé the ring and all other gifts of value that he gave her. Gifts received from relatives or friends should also be returned with a short note of explanation. Once the wedding has taken place, however, gifts are not returned, no matter how short the marriage. Strictly speaking, the presents belong to the wife, but the usual procedure is for the husband to keep those items that came from his own family and friends, and those particularly meaningful or useful to him, while the wife keeps the others.

If a gift arrives broken, take it, with its wrappings, to the shop where it was purchased. If it comes from another city, return it by mail, accompanied by a letter explaining how it arrived. Any good store owner will replace the merchandise on reasonable evidence that it was received in damaged condition. Do not involve the donor in this transaction, nor even let her know what happened if you can possibly avoid doing so.

Although a bride should not change presents chosen for her by her own or her bridegroom's family—unless especially told she may do so—other duplicate wedding gifts may be exchanged. In fact many people refrain from marking or initialing the present they send in order to make such an exchange possible. Just as a bride never mentions the fact that she is exchanging a present when writing her thank-you letter, a donor doesn't ask on a subsequent visit, "Where is that lovely bowl we gave you?" The time-honored custom permitting the exchange of duplicate wedding presents is so practical and sensible that no one should be offended by it.

Exchanging gifts received on other occasions, however, may require a little more tact. A present should not be exchanged just because it doesn't happen to be exactly what you want. If it is a duplicate, it would be thoughtful to call the giver and say, "Mary, I happen to have two bottle warmers already. Would you mind terribly if . . . ?" Then in your thank-you note tell Mary how much you are enjoying what you got as a replacement. An exchange to correct the size of a present of clothing need not be mentioned.

OPENING PARTY PRESENTS

Half the fun of giving and receiving presents at any party is to see and enjoy what everyone else brought. The nicest way to do this is to collect all the presents in one place until after everyone has arrived, at which time the guest of honor opens them. Whether a gift is a fifty-cent "joke" present or a more expensive article is not important. The recipient reads the cards enclosed, particularly if they are funny ones, and shows enthusiasm for each gift. It is important to include a card with a gift you are planning to deliver personally because many people like to collect and save the cards they receive at these times as mementos of the occasion. If anybody has given money instead of a present, the amount should not be mentioned but the recipient may well say something like, "This is a really welcome contribution toward the china we are saving for," or whatever else may be appropriate.

On occasions when gifts are not necessarily expected, but two or three people bring them regardless, they are opened in the donor's presence but without drawing the attention of other guests. This might happen, for instance, when a couple brings a gift to a dinner hostess. She must show her appreciation, but making a display of the present could embarrass guests who did not bring one.

FLOWERS AS PRESENTS

Flowers may be sent by almost everyone to almost anyone. There are certain times when sending them—if you can possibly afford it—is obligatory. They may be used in place of, or in addition to, the gifts suggested for many occasions mentioned here.

Some thoughtful people are constantly sending flowers; others seldom do. The majority of us send them much less often than we might because we think those we can afford to buy are not good enough. This reminds me of our daughter who, as a teen-ager, received at times corsages and gifts of flowers. I can truthfully say the one she treasured most was a single red rose from a boy whose knowledge of how to please a girl was well in advance of his years.

SUGGESTED GIFTS FOR DIFFERENT OCCASIONS

R—Gift required
O—Gift is optional
R & O—Gift may or may not be required depending on relationship and circumstances

O *Engagements*

Presents are expected only from close relatives and intimate friends and are almost always intended especially for the bride.

Towels for bathroom
Luggage for honeymoon
Blanket cover
Jewelry
Lingerie (negligee, slips)
Plastic mat set
Bar or kitchen towels
Table linen

R *Showers*

Gifts should be chosen to meet the specifications (including color and size) given in the invitation

Literally, any useful or decorative article appropriate to the particular occasion is acceptable, but it should not be elaborate, and should not be intended to take the place of a wedding present. Something made personally by the donor is traditional, and often, no matter how simple, is the most appreciated gift of all.

R & O *Weddings*

Anything to furnish a house or apartment including:
Set of folding tables on rack
Mirror for an entry or hall
Leather box containing decks of cards
Crystal or china vase
Planter
Electric hot tray
Carving set
Large pepper grinder
Painting or prints
Glasses or china
Lamps
Hors d'oeuvre tray
Salad bowl
Items of china or silver pattern selected by bride

R *Wedding-party attendants to bride or groom, or both*

Silver after-dinner coffee spoons, each engraved with

name of one attendant
Silver tray, pitcher, or cigarette box engraved with attendants' names

R *From bride to her bridesmaids*

Small silver picture frame with bride's picture
Bracelet with disc engraved with wedding date
Gold charm for bracelet

R *From bridegroom to his ushers*

Monogrammed key case or ring
Initialed silver belt buckle
Monogrammed stud box

R *Anniversary parties*

Picture album (to be filled later if possible with pictures taken at party)
Picture frame with family portrait
Bottle of wine or champagne
Plant—one which may be planted outside if couple has yard

It is not necessary to limit gifts to the traditional materials for each anniversary, but for those who wish to, the following list may be useful:

* 1 year—Paper or plastic
2 years—Calico or cotton
3 years—Leather or simulated leather
4 years—Silk
* 5 years—Wood
6 years—Iron
7 years—Copper or woolen
8 years—Electric appliances
9 years—Pottery
*10 years—Tin (aluminum now included)
11 years—Steel
12 years—Linen
13 years—Lace
14 years—Ivory
*15 years—Crystal (includes glass)
*20 years—China
*25 years—Silver (the best-known anniversary)
30 years—Pearls
35 years—Coral and Jade
40 years—Ruby
45 years—Sapphire
*50 years—Gold
*60 years—Diamond

* The eight anniversaries which are traditionally celebrated.

O *Farewell parties*

I *For those permanently leaving a neighborhood:*

- Scrapbook with mementos of years spent together (if you have the imagination and inclination)
- Gift certificate from department store in future hometown

II *Bon voyage parties*

- Books
- Small game
- Trip diary
- Guidebook
- Champagne or wine (especially if you arrange with the wine steward to have it served as a surprise during the voyage)
- Passport folder
- Money exchange guide
- Playing cards in case
- Small leather picture frame and family picture
- Travel kit of cleaning and laundry products
- Camera film

R *Housewarmings*

- Cigarette box
- Wastebasket
- Bookends
- Magazine rack
- Leather or silver stamp holder (especially nice when filled with postage stamps)
- Potted plant
- Seeds or bulbs for garden
- Address book including names, addresses, and phone numbers of recommended local services and stores

O *New babies*

- Sweater, other clothing
- Blanket or comforter
- Crib toys
- Baby food
- Bath articles
- Furnishing for room (picture, little chair)
- Spoon and fork
- Bibs

R *Christenings*

- Silver porringer
- Hair brush and comb
- Savings bond
- For a girl—one pearl or charm—to be added to later
- Baby's memory book or album

R & O *Birthdays*

I *For teen-agers*

- Clothing
- Sports equipment
- Records
- Books
- Money (perhaps one dollar for each year of age)

II *For a wife or husband*

Any little present you know he or she wants but has avoided buying because *you* think it foolish or extravagant

III *For an older couple*

- Travel tickets for a special vacation
- Gift certificate
- Plant

IV *For friends*

Any foolish "gag" present. Unless very close friend, to avoid embarrassment, don't give expensive gifts.

R *First Communion*

- Bible
- Prayerbook
- Jewelry
- Fine book

R *Bar Mitzvah* A gift of money is most generally given. The amount depends on the closeness of the donor to the youngster.

R & O *Graduation*

- Money, gift certificate, savings bond, or stock
- Initial deposit in a new savings account
- Watch or bedside clock or clock-radio
- Desk pen and pencil set or desk lamp
- Books (especially those useful for chosen career or standard reference works)
- Camera
- Sports equipment
- Stereo or hi-fi equipment
- Jewelry

R *For weekend visit*

- Gourmet hors d'oeuvres
- Cocktail or highball glasses
- A set of good scissors
- Toys for young children
- Liquor or wine

Steak or casserole dish ready for heating (check with hostess in advance)
Record album
Flowers or plant
A new game or jigsaw puzzle (especially good if hostess has children)
Cookies, a cake, or candy

R & O *Christmas* I *Girl to a boyfriend*
Key case
Wallet
Imprinted stationery
Picture frame with her picture
Something she has knitted or personalized herself, such as a sweater, mittens, or golf club covers

II *Boy to a girlfriend*
A pair of tickets to a hit show
Costume jewelry
Inexpensive charm
Clothing accessories (gloves, scarf, belt, etc., but not "personal" clothing)
Books
Records
Stuffed toy animal

O *To nurses, doctors, and professional people in appreciation of special care*

I *For hospital nurses*
Cookies, candy, or fruit sent to nurses' desk on patient's floor

II *For doctors*
Desk set
Food specialty (homemade fruitcake)
Liquor or wine
Golf balls
Carving set
Contribution to his favorite charity

O *For sick people or hospital patients*
Light reading matter
Homemade soup
Cookies or other specialty (clear all food gifts with doctor first)

Flower arrangements or potted plants (not loose cut flowers)
Autobridge game
Crossword puzzle book
Bed jacket or dressing gown
Pillow-type backrest

R & O *For a debutante*

Flowers or corsage
Simple real jewelry
Pretty ornament for her room
White leather picture frame for debut picture
Perfume
Good stationery
Gift certificate at local beauty shop

O *For a teacher* Give a combined class present in place of individual gifts. This might be an atlas or leather-bound dictionary or any other professional book, or something more personal, such as a sweater, or ornamental, such as a desk clock or a picture for the wall.

R & O *For a nun*

Check or cash
White linen handkerchiefs
Religious picture or statue
Book (including light novels)
Small luxury items (lotion, powder, bath accessory)
Black gloves
Black stockings
Magazine subscription
Cookies and candy
Warm blanket or shawl

R & O *For a newly ordained priest or minister*

Magazine subscription
Leather diary
Pen and pencil set
Gift certificate at local department store
Pipe and/or pipe rack
Leather address book
Wristwatch
Briefcase or wallet

GIFTS TO AVOID

Many people are far more sensitive than their friends suspect. For this reason it is important never to choose a gift that might be construed as criticism. A present of a cookbook can be most welcome providing your friend knows that you have enjoyed her cooking and—even more important—knows that you know she likes to cook. This same cookbook given to someone whose abilities lie outside the kitchen and at whose home the food is at best mediocre might easily be resented.

Presents requiring constant care when given to people who are not interested or able to give that care can be a real disaster. Foremost among these are live birds or fish or animals. The cruelty involved in unsolicited gifts of baby ducklings and rabbits at Easter should be obvious, and the well-meaning family friend who gives a young child a puppy or kitten without first clearing the matter with his parents will not long remain a family friend.

Finally, there are the white elephants that seem to grow in every gift shop. Before buying any present in this category think to yourself, "What would she do with it?" and if you can't find an answer to that, then don't buy it.

GIFT WRAPPINGS

Just as a picture needs a frame so does a gift need a pretty wrapping as well as a card to go with it. Most department and gift stores now provide special gift wrapping free, or at a slight extra charge. For those who have neither the time nor inclination to wrap their own presents this is a great boon. On the other hand, devising a clever or entertaining way to present a gift can add to the fun of giving it. In many cases an unusual or attractive package adds greatly to the present itself. Wine bottles packaged in picnic baskets or golf balls sold in cigarette boxes are examples of this. The original packaging you do yourself, however, can be even more entertaining or useful. A friend of mine camouflaged his Christmas present of ski poles for his teen-age daughter as a poinsettia plant. The handles of the poles were stuck into a pot filled with sand, and red and green construction paper was used to make the petals and leaves to complete the illusion.

MARKING GIFTS

Discussion of a gift's appearance leads to the question of whether to personalize or monogram it. The obvious drawback is that once an article has been initialed, it can never be returned. Before you have anything of value marked, therefore, be sure it is something you know is wanted and also that it is the right size, color, and style. If you *are* sure of this, then initials are a handsome addition to many gifts. Muriel Barbara

Jones uses the initials "MBJ" before she plans to be married, but when she marries Henry Ross, her initials become "MJR." (Wedding presents are usually marked with her married initials or, on her flat silver, it may be just "R," the first letter of her new last name). A man uses all three of his initials and should include "Jr." after them when applicable.

QUESTIONS

The queries below have been selected from those I am most frequently asked by my readers.

Q. Does an invitation to a wedding ceremony require that the receiver send a gift?

A. An invitation to a wedding ceremony carries no obligation. Neither does a wedding announcement. People receiving invitations to a reception, however, are expected to send gifts, of course, whether they attend or not. It is perfectly correct for the recipients of a church invitation or an announcement to send a present if they feel so inclined.

Q. Do engaged couples send joint or separate wedding presents?

A. It depends a little on their relationship to the bridal couple. If each of them knows one member of the couple well, they may wish to send separate gifts. If one is closer to the couple than the other, or if one does not know the bride or groom at all but is included on the guest list, they may send a joint present.

Q. What do you do when your neighbor arrives Christmas Eve with an unexpected Christmas present?

A. It's a wise idea to have a supply of small gifts on hand for just such an emergency. When you see something you really like, and it's not too expensive, buy half a dozen instead of one, and put the others away —later on you'll thank your lucky star for your foresight.

Q. Are the cards that accompany wedding presents displayed with the gifts?

A. There is no firm rule. Some brides feel that it is complimentary to display them, and also that it relieves the family of explaining, "This came from Aunt Millie," "That is the Gardners' present," etc. Others feel that displaying the cards invites comparisons—"I see Mrs. Brown didn't give as many glasses as Mrs. Green"—or that some donors who could not afford to give as much as they would like dislike having the fact advertised. It is entirely up to the bride. It is correct to display cards —it is equally correct to leave them off.

Q. How can you let guests know that you do not wish gifts brought to a birthday or anniversary party?

A. You may write "No gifts, please" on any invitation. If the invitations are issued by telephone, you must tell the guests that you do not expect, or want, a gift. When this is indicated, the guests should respect the wish, and not say, "Oh, I'll just take some little thing."

Q. What should you say when someone asks you what you want as a present?

A. Try to help them out, although they may have shown ill-judgment by putting you in an embarrassing position. Rather than saying, "I don't know," or "I'd rather you chose something yourself," attempt to make a suggestion or two. If you can't, tell them you'll let them know, and then remember to do it.

Part THIRTEEN

ON HOW TO DRESS

74

Women's clothes and fashions

Clothes do more than add to our appearance; in a sense, they are our appearance. The first impression that we make upon others depends almost entirely upon what we wear and how we wear it. Manners and speech are noticed next, and character last of all.

Character is, of course, the true essential; but for the transient impression that we make everywhere in public, two superficial attributes are indispensable—good manners and a pleasing appearance. And such an appearance is impossible without an average degree of smartness.

THE CLOTHES THAT SUIT

The woman who knows how to wear clothes is like a stage director who skillfully presents—herself. This skill in presentation is something for which it is difficult to give directions, because it is a talent rather than a formula. Naturally, someone who is young, whose skin is clear, and whose figure is size ten or twelve can wear almost any dress she fancies and it will be becoming. And yet a woman who lacks the knack of choosing what is suitable will find buying a becoming hat such a trial that she finally buys, not one she likes, but the one she dislikes least.

The sense of what is becoming and the knack of wearing clothes well are the two greatest assets of smartness, but neither is attainable by anyone unwilling to look at herself as she really is.

SHORT WOMEN

There are certain basic principles that all women should consider when they are buying their clothes. Very short women should choose clothes with long vertical lines rather than those broken at the waist by a belt or band of contrasting color. High heels add height, but it is better to wear a moderate heel than a "spike" if one is unable to walk gracefully on the latter. Hairdos that are high on top of the head and tall hats add inches to the short woman.

TALL WOMEN

Tall girls should feature outfits with a break in the middle—a wide belt, a suit with a fitted jacket, or contrasting colors in skirt and blouse. Pretty shoes are sold for the tall girl, with slim graceful heels of low or moderate height. When a hat is worn, it should not add inches to the head, nor should the hairdo.

FAT WOMEN

The plump woman must avoid large prints, wide plaids, and bulky materials. Black and navy blue are the most slimming colors, but any solid color or small print also looks well if it is becoming to her complexion. Clothes should not be tight enough to reveal a bulge, but neither should they be "baggy" or gathered at the waist. A flared skirt (called the A-line) is much more flattering than either a "dirndl" or a straight style. Upswept hairdos, if becoming to the face, and long earrings help to lengthen a short neck. Evening dresses should be as simple as possible, and, if practical, a style that covers the upper arm (having a matching stole, for example) is desirable. Bathing suits with a skirt of a reasonable length help to hide chubby thighs, and please, no "stretch" suits "to hold in the tummy!" Bikinis and two-piece suits may be charming on a slender figure, but if you have even a suggestion of a "roll," you MUST stick to the one-piece suit. The fat girl, alas, must give up wearing shorts and slacks in public.

THIN WOMEN

The thin girl has relatively few problems, as most clothes look well on a slim figure. If the neck bones are prominent, however, a low neckline should be avoided, and because a long neck often goes with a thin figure, turtle neck blouses, high collars, and scarves are usually most becoming. The interesting "nubbly" materials, which so many women cannot wear, look nice on the thin girl, as do more extreme styles, such as short, straight skirts. This type is also fortunate in being able to wear shorts or slacks with style.

THE AVERAGE FIGURE

If you have a more or less average figure, choose clothes in the colors and styles that exaggerate your good points. Minimize your poorer features, heavy hips, perhaps, or a thick waist, by choosing clothes that disguise those faults. And consider your age. The older woman may feel she is still a "sport," but she might better carry on her athletics in a smartly tailored skirt than brief shorts. Nor does graying hair look well in a long, loose hairdo; the shorter, fuller, or upswept styles are more becoming to a mature face.

FAD FOLLOWERS

Fashion has the power to make any style seem acceptable, even though it has few elements of flattery or beauty. If you doubt it, look at old fashion plates. Even a woman with excellent taste succumbs occasionally to the epidemics of fashion, but she is more immune than most. All women who have any clothes sense whatever know more or less the types of things that are their style—unless they have such a temporary attack of "fashionitis" that they are completely irresponsible.

There is one unchanging principle which must be followed by everyone who would be well dressed—*suitability*. A great number of women do dress with this in mind, but there are many others who, like sheep, follow every turn of style, without the slightest sense of whether it is a good one or absurd, or even if it is in the least becoming to them. As each new season's fashion is defined, they all run and dress themselves one in a replica of the other; their own types and personalities have nothing to do with the case. Fashion says, "Wear your skirts six inches above the knee," and daughter, mother, and grandmother wear the same length. Utility, becomingness, suitability, and beauty are of no importance. Fashion is followed to the letter—therefore they fancy, poor sheep, that they are the last word in smartness.

VULGAR CLOTHES

To define differences between clothes that are smart and clothes that are merely conspicuous is to define something very elusive. Vulgar clothes are those which are too elaborate for the occasion, are immodest, are too exaggerated in style, or have accessories out of harmony with the dress and the wearer.

Beau Brummell's remark that when someone attracted too much notice he could be sure of being not well dressed but overdressed has for years been the comfort of the dowdy. It is, of course, very often true, but not invariably so. A person may be stared at for any one of many reasons. A woman may be stared at because she is ill-behaved, because she looks like a freak of the circus, or because she is simply "lovely to look at."

THE WOMAN WHO IS CHIC

The woman who is chic is always a little different. Not different in being precisely in fashion, but always slightly apart from it. Chic (pronounced *sheek*) is a borrowed adjective, but unfortunately no word in our language expresses its meaning. Its nearest description today is the combination of sophistication and fastidious taste. By way of comment, the word chi-chi (pronounced *she-she*) is not a synonym for chic, but a flashy imitation of it.

The woman who is chic adapts fashion to her own personality. This is in contrast to the woman who will merely buy the latest hat or dress and adapt herself to it, whether the fashion suits her or not. When it conspicuously does *not*, it is likely to be chi-chi.

ACCESSORIES

Accessories are as important to the budget-conscious woman as the basic dress. They provide the accents that can vary the costume, giving it versatility as well as adding to its beauty. In planning your wardrobe, it is well to stick to a narrow range of colors so that the same accessories may be used with a number of outfits. That is not to say, however, that accessories should limit your wardrobe; instead they should broaden it. A simple black dress may be perfect for lunch at a restaurant or an afternoon shopping when it is worn with a gold circle pin, single-pearl earrings, and a daytime watch or wide gold bracelet and accompanied by black kid pumps and a plain leather pocketbook. But change these accessories to a diamond or zircon clip (or add a single or double strand of pearls), diamond (or pearl drop) earrings, a bracelet, perhaps, or a ring of glittering stones, suede pumps, and a small suede purse, and you may appear at any but the most formal party that night.

JEWELRY

The wearing of too much jewelry is, at most times, considered ostentatious and in poor taste. However, with the improvement in quality and the consequent rise in popularity of costume jewelry, smart women all over have increased the amount of jewelry they wear in public as well as at home. Certain gems, such as sapphires, can actually be manufactured now, and others are beautifully imitated. Cultured pearls rival "real" pearls in beauty, and such semiprecious stones as zircons, garnets, or jade come in an infinite variety of colors. With the lower cost of these substitutes for expensive gems many more women than ever before are able to wear beautiful jewelry.

Jewelry, like clothing, should be chosen and worn with an eye to suitability rather than to fad. A woman with stubby, unattractive hands, for example, should not draw attention to them with a large, flashing ring, no matter how fine a gem it may contain. Furthermore, the type of jewelry worn changes with the time of day and the activity. When engaging in an active sport, jewelry of any kind is out of place. In the daytime, gold and silver, pearls, and enamels, wood, and semiprecious stones are more suitable than the brilliant gems that go well with evening clothes. In the afternoon, a gold link necklace, a pendant, or a string of pearls is ideal. Bracelets, earrings, and a pretty pin or clip to set off a dress or suit are lovely at any hour. In short, the choice of jewelry is limited only by the good taste and the budget of the wearer. When she has occasion to wear a formal evening gown, a lady may bring out her most brilliant precious stones—as long as she does not overload her wrists and fingers.

GLOVES

Gloves are worn on city streets, to luncheons, dinner parties, and other social gatherings, to churches, restaurants, theaters, and all other public places of entertainment. At a restaurant, theater, or the like, they may be removed on arrival, but they are generally left on in church except during communion or when it is very warm.

A lady never takes off her gloves to shake hands, no matter when or where, and *never* apologizes for not doing so. But she *always* removes them for dining. On formal occasions the hostess should wear gloves to shake hands with her guests—and keep them on until food is served. Gloves are *always* worn when standing in a receiving line. When long gloves are an intrinsic part of your costume at a ball, they may be left on for dancing—otherwise they are taken off. A bracelet may be worn outside a long glove, but never a ring. Gloves which come above the elbow are worn only with sleeveless or strapless evening dresses. Wrist-length or three-quarter length gloves are correct with less formal gowns. At informal dances it is not necessary to wear gloves at all if you prefer not to do so.

HATS

If you look well in hats, wear them! A well-chosen hat may add dash and distinction to your outfit that a bare head can't possibly achieve. If you are one of the many women who feel that there is no hat in the world becoming to you, settle for a little veil or a band or bow on those occasions when it is necessary to cover your head. You *must* wear a hat to all Roman Catholic church ceremonies, and it is always correct at churches of every faith. At official luncheons and receptions they are almost a requirement, and beyond that, hats may be, and are, worn at any time and on any occasion that you wish to during the day. A small hat or veil is appropriate, but not necessary, with a cocktail dress. Except for the necessary head covering at an evening wedding, a hat, even the smallest veil, is never worn with an evening dress. The only exception, and it is not truly an exception, is the practical one of wearing a plastic or net scarf tied over your new hairdo to protect it from wind and rain on the way to a formal party.

FUR CAPES AND STOLES

For many years ladies adhered to an arbitrary and, to me, inexplicable rule that fur capes, stoles, and jackets should not be worn before five o'clock in the evening. I have always enjoyed the story of the Midwestern lady who went to spend a weekend at a fashionable Eastern resort. She appeared at a luncheon at the exclusive club with her beautiful mink stole over her shoulders. One of the dowagers, looking down her nose at the visitor, said, "My dear Mrs. Newcomer, don't you know you can't wear a fur before five?" Mrs. Newcomer smiled politely and replied, "That's what I thought, too, Mrs. Goldbrick, until I had one."

Actually, there is no reason for a fur stole's not being worn to any "dressy" affair from noon on if the costume the fur is worn over is of a comparable degree of elegance. Morning wear is invariably less formal, and therefore a short fur of any sort would not be in keeping. But for luncheons, receptions, weddings, etc. held at or after noon, it would seem most ridiculous to leave a lovely fur hanging in the closet. Women who have a choice might prefer to wear a cloth coat in the daytime and save their fur for evening, but those who can only have one "dress" coat, and prefer a fur to all others, may feel free to wear it at almost any hour.

Mink and other luxurious and expensive furs should never be worn with sports clothes such as wool suits or slacks.

SHOES

The first consideration in buying shoes—and this cannot be stressed too strongly—is the importance of comfort. The most beautiful pair of shoes in the world will destroy the appearance of the wearer if the height of the heel causes her to teeter or hobble, if the tightness of the toes causes her to stand painfully—first on one foot and then the other—or worse yet, if she has to sink thankfully onto the nearest chair, saying, "My feet are killing me—do you mind?" and kick off the offenders! When you find a last (the form on which the shoe is made) that really fits your foot, you will do well to continue to choose shoes produced by the maker of that last.

When picking out shoes, try to find colors and styles that will go with more than one dress. Red, for instance, is an excellent choice for spring and summer, as it goes well with black, navy, white, and many of the light summer shades.

If you are more comfortable in "flats" or low heels, stick to them for daytime wear—there are attractive styles available even for city wearing.

Dressier shoes are now made with low, medium, or high heels to fit every requirement. Loafers, sneakers, sandals, and gaily colored flat-soled shoes in every conceivable material and to fit any budget are cool and comfortable in summer. Patent leather, which until recently only appeared in black and was traditionally worn only in the summer, now comes in every conceivable color and is accepted the year round.

In winter a pair of handsome wool-lined boots is invaluable for daytime use in the country, and city dwellers have found them a wonderful replacement for galoshes or rubber boots, which must go on and off a dozen times a day.

The working girl who is on her feet much of the day should sacrifice some smartness for comfort and choose a shoe that has a thick, soft sole and gives her foot some support. A good suggestion, if feasible, is to keep an extra pair of shoes at your place of business, as a change in the middle of the day is very restful to the feet.

Shoes to be worn with more formal clothes should match or blend with the costume in color and be appropriate in material and style. You wouldn't, for example, wear alligator pumps with a satin dress, even though they might both be brown. Generally speaking, leather shoes such as alligator or kid, in dark colors, are correct for daytime in the winter. Black shoes go well with almost every winter costume. Suede or satin shoes in black or a color matching your dress are worn for more formal occasions or in the evening. Pumps in gold, silver, or a color matching your dress, or gold or silver sandals, are worn with a formal evening dress. During the summer months shoes of any color of the rainbow are attractive as long as they complement the rest of the outfit. But if you do not wish to buy a variety of colors, a pair of "spectators" (white pumps trimmed with black, brown, or navy) or straw pumps for daytime occasions, and white linen or patent leather pumps for after dark will go happily with almost any summer ensemble.

HANDBAGS

Styles in handbags have changed as much as those of any accessory or clothing. The result is that over the years the best features of many types have been retained, and bags can now be found in a literally unlimited variety of colors, styles, and materials. There is little to be said about color—you simply decide on one that will go with a special outfit or will blend with all of your costumes, depending on your need. Your own taste will be your guide in selecting your purse, but there are a few suggestions that may be helpful. A good quality black leather bag, large enough to contain all the items you may need for a whole day, will last for years and pay for itself many times over in usefulness, durability, and beauty. A straw handbag for daytime use in the summer will go with all cottons and sport clothes, and on some the decorations may be changed to match a special costume. Small linen fold-over bags are so inexpensive that two or three in different colors will not strain your budget.

The bag with changeable covers is one of the more practical innovations. These are not inexpensive, but the cost is more than made up for by the versatility, and one bag may make up your entire pocketbook wardrobe. For a winter bag of this type, the basic purse might be black leather, and the covers (which are cleverly designed to snap on so that the result appears to be an ordinary purse) might be of brown kid, black lizard, or possibly, for dressier occasions, suede. The summer bags are less expensive, as the covers may be of cotton or linen, and they have the added advantage of being washable!

Evening bags, which come in many materials and colors, can add greatly to your costume. Gold metallic bags, sometimes adorned with artificial (or very occasionally, real) jewels, are popular; and for older people, embroidered black velvet, silk, or satin is a good choice. For cocktail time, small suede or satin bags come in a variety of pretty colors and shapes. They should be small and easy to carry, since one is apt to remain standing and a large bag is heavy and difficult to manage. Also, a small bag is less in the way if kept on a table.

CORSAGES

There is no rule in existence about how a woman wears a corsage. She pins it wherever and however she thinks most becoming to her dress, to herself, and to the flowers themselves. In short, she stands in front of her mirror, holds the flowers against her dress in different places until she finds where they are most pleasing, and that is where she places them. If the dress is so designed that a corsage does not go well on it, or if the wearer is afraid of crushing the flowers while dancing, she may also pin them on a cloth evening bag.

A WORD ABOUT SLACKS

Slacks as sports wear have been accepted for a number of years. They are certainly the most practical dress for an active woman engaged in sailing, hunting, heavy housework, gardening, or many other activities. However, a woman who has a weight problem or who is particularly heavy through the hips should avoid wearing slacks on all other occasions. They may be comfortable, but unless the wearer is reasonably slim they are anything but flattering.

The same is true of evening slacks and the popular "pants suits." They cannot be surpassed for comfort, and for smartness when worn by the right woman, but on anyone else a long "at home" skirt, or a cocktail or dinner dress is far more appealing.

MAKEUP AND HAIR STYLES

To the present generation, it must seem fantastic that not so very long ago all makeup was considered wicked. Today the only restraint in the use of every item in the cosmetic catalog lies in the answer to the question: Are you sure you are not exchanging a face for a mask?

Except for special occasions a little powder to dull the shine on your nose, a touch of rouge if you are pale, lipstick of a color becoming to your complexion, a little eye makeup if you live in the city, and a neatly combed hairdo are sufficient to make every woman appear well groomed. A good powder base which contains a lubricant for the skin is an excellent idea for older women. The powder should be applied lightly and evenly over the base, and when properly done, the two together will cover the natural blemishes and wrinkles that come inevitably with the years. This, however, is not necessary for a young girl whose skin is fresh and lovely.

Eye makeup, if used, should also be applied with discretion. A heavy outline intended to enlarge the eye can, if badly applied, destroy the natural line and appear nothing short of grotesque.

Lipstick should follow the line of the lips. An attempt to enlarge or change the shape of the mouth by running the lipstick over the natural outline of the lips generally gives the appearance that your hand has slipped.

Hairdos should be chosen to flatter your face. Of course, if you are young and pretty, many styles will be becoming, and it is great fun to attempt different effects and to experiment with current fashions. It is not worth doing, however, if the latest thing could be harmful to the hair—such as spraying with excessively drying lacquers. The well-groomed woman finds a style that is pleasing to her and not difficult to maintain, and while she may vary her coiffure on special occasions, she returns to the simple, becoming style for ordinary dress.

Finally, always remember that a mask can never take the place of a face. The face of a clown is grotesque, for it is meant to be. If cosmetics are to add to beauty, they must be the allies, not the enemies, of nature.

BUDGET BUYING

The woman of means has little problem in buying clothes, for she may have an outfit for every occasion and a set of accessories for each outfit. But the vast majority of us must plan our wardrobes carefully and take advantage of all the available means of stretching our pennies.

To begin with, sales can be of great help to the budget-conscious woman, but only if taken advantage of with thought and planning. End-of-season sales are generally limited to leftover odd sizes and the less attractive styles, but if you happen to fit those sizes or wear a rather unusual color well, you can sometimes find a wonderful bargain for the following year. Beware, however, of buying anything "high style" at these sales—the dress will probably be "out-of-style" in a year's time.

In buying at one of the "cut-rate" stores, you may also find fabulous bargains, but again, take care! These stores get their merchandise from the stocks of more expensive houses for several reasons. The clothes may be defective in workmanship, faulty in cut, or out of style. Or (and you are in luck if you happen to go in on the day this shipment arrives) they may be bargains simply because too many of one design were ordered. If you are knowledgeable about clothes and able to recognize good design and workmanship, as a penny-wise shopper you will do well to frequent these stores.

Wherever you decide to do your shopping, you must plan your needs in advance. If you wish to be able to use the same accessories with all your clothes, your color scheme must be in harmony. For example, for fall wear, you might choose dresses and suits in olive greens, golds, browns, and beige. With all these colors, you may use the same pair of brown alligator or kid pumps, brown or dull green leather "flats," a brown purse, and a brown or beige coat. A camel's hair polo coat would be a good choice in the country, but you would probably want something a little dressier in the city.

Outfits that can be changed to fit different occasions are helpful. Skirts are most versatile—with a sweater they are practical for everyday use, but if not too "tweedy" they can be dressed up by a silk blouse or a decorated sweater for informal evenings with friends or at home. A short-sleeved or sleeveless wool or silk dress with a jacket is a good choice. Without the jacket, it may be worn for a dinner party or an evening of theater and night clubs. By putting on the jacket, you are ready for a luncheon, movie, or informal cocktail party.

To make your budget wardrobe truly adequate, you should try to choose two or three basic dresses—one for afternoon and two for evening—of good quality. The higher cost of these will be amply repaid in durability and excellent fit. They should not be conspicuous in color or style, but rather, becoming to you, so that you can wear them time and time again without feeling that your friends are saying, "There comes Janey in her polka-dot dress again!"

Coats are a problem to the budget-minded. Not only are they the most costly item to buy, but no one coat can cover all your needs. A polo coat or a lined gabardine is most practical for country wear, and both go well with all daytime clothes from slacks to afternoon dresses. But for winter evenings it is essential to have a second coat—a well-cut black wool will fit any occasion—but best of all, if your budget allows, or if you have a generous husband or parents, a fur coat. A full-length fur coat, cut in a simple style, will last for years, and of all coats it provides the greatest warmth and beauty. In choosing a fur coat you will do well to follow the recommendations of a reputable furrier.

Some imitation furs are so beautifully made that they are an acceptable substitute. They must be of good quality however, or they will seem exactly what they are—a cheap copy of the real thing.

Spring and summer coats are less expensive and more versatile. A lightweight wool in white, beige, or red (strangely enough red goes well with most summer colors) can serve for daytime or evening, although a small fur cape or stole, if one can afford it, is a comfort on a cool summer night. Raincoats come in such attractive fabrics now that they can also serve as summer coats even when the sun is shining.

DAYTIME CLOTHES

There are so many wonderful synthetic fabrics on the market today that it would be impossible to list them by name each time that a specific fabric is mentioned. The drip-dry materials or blends are in many ways preferable to plain cotton, as they need little or no ironing. There are various forms of synthetic linen, silk, and cotton which do not wrinkle, making them ideal for traveling. Therefore, each time that a material is specifically mentioned here, the reader must assume that any of the newer (and often improved) fabrics having the same visual effect are in equally good taste, as well as very often even more attractive and practical.

By the same token, since it is impossible to list the best clothing material for each climate in all parts of the United States or for traveling all over the world, we have chosen to speak in terms of the four seasons as represented in a temperate climate. The reader who lives the year round in southern Florida or in the desert of the Southwest will realize that even in the so-called "winter" months she may never need the basic wool dress or suit, nor will she often wear very dark colors, even in the city, because they simply are not appropriate in very hot weather. One must use one's own judgment and consider her own circumstances, but the material and colors mentioned in connection with a certain season are the most comfortable and in the best taste over the largest area of the country.

MORNING

The housewife busily doing her chores in her house or apartment should certainly wear whatever clothes are, for her, most comfortable. In the country this often means shorts or slacks for all morning activities, and in the city these are certainly proper in her own apartment, or if she is hurrying out for a moment to a shop in her block or to walk the dog to the corner. No matter how informal the outfit, if it is neat and clean (of course, you may have dirt from the garden on your hands or smudges from cleaning the oven on your face, but if your chores for the day have been of this sort, do them first and wash and change before going on to something of a less demanding nature), you need make no apology when a salesman comes to the door or your friendly neighbor drops in.

Two cardinal rules must be mentioned: *Never* go shopping or to any public place with your hair in curlers, unless they are so skillfully concealed with a scarf or hat as to be completely invisible. *Never* wear short shorts or a bathing suit on the street. Because in many communities it is actually illegal to appear dressed in this way, if you don't wish to change into other clothes to do your errands, you must cover your *lack* of clothing with a skirt, a beach coat, or a shift.

AFTERNOON

Dresses for luncheons, card parties, and the like vary so widely in different sections of the country that it would be impossible to recommend any one type. One must generalize and say that during the cool months women wear wool dresses or suits (not "tweedy" checks or stripes) to luncheons. Hats are usually worn, although they are not essential. Cottons are the most popular choice in the summer, with darker colors being chosen for the city. Clothing for other afternoon parties, perhaps for bridge, is the same, but at a formal tea one would choose a somewhat more elaborate wool or a silk in a solid color or print.

CLOTHES FOR THE EVENING

For evenings at home—either with your family or good friends—nothing is more comfortable than a smartly tailored pair of evening slacks, velvet or satin in the winter, cotton or silk in the summer. Equaling these in popularity are the "hostess skirts" that come in enchanting colors and fabrics and are often matched by gay blouses.

But for evenings away from home you must have a separate wardrobe. For cocktail and dinner parties the winter wool (not too tailored) or the gay summer cotton is the most common costume. For more formal parties a silk or satin cocktail dress or suit is almost a necessity, and the dress, worn without a jacket, serves as a dinner dress. A true dinner dress is long (unless current fashion dictates that all dinner and evening dresses are short), but is not made of as dressy a material or cut as low as an evening gown. It may be of wool or velvet in winter, or cotton or silk for summer. The dinner dress is always worn at formal dinners and may be worn to informal dinners and dances, the opera or theater, and to any party that is "black tie." An evening dress is worn only at dances, to the opera, opening nights at the theater, and on a few other very special occasions. It is sleeveless, sometimes strapless, cut low in back and usually in front, and made of the most elegant materials—satins, brocades—

and with endless variations in decoration and embroidery. As already stated, hats and veils are never worn with dinner or evening dresses.

In deciding what to wear to any function when the invitation has not made it clear, you may follow one rule that is fairly safe. If you have no way of finding out what the correct attire is, wear the plainer dress. If you must decide between a ball dress and a dinner dress, wear the dinner dress, or between velvet and wool, choose the wool.

IN A RESTAURANT

Afternoon dresses or suits are worn to restaurants for both lunch and dinner. If you are going to a dinner party given at a restaurant, you would wear the somewhat more elaborate cocktail dress or, if formal, a dinner dress. Hats are optional with the daytime dress, but are rarely worn with the cocktail dress and never with the dinner dress.

CLOTHES FOR THE BUSINESS WOMAN

The first requirement is neatness. The unfailing directions for clothes worn in an office are that they be tailored, smart, in good taste, but in no way conspicuous. Above all, avoid wearing clothes that need constant arranging. If you have to keep fussing at your belt or your neckline or your wrists, if anything dangling drips into things or catches on knobs or typewriter keys, discard the distracting detail quickly. It is not necessary to sacrifice prettiness to exaggerated sleekness, but do avoid everything that interferes or catches or keeps getting out of place.

Also wear clothes that properly cover you. Scant attire may be very alluring in a musical revue, but men do not look for, or want to find, that allure in their offices. In hot weather sleeveless dresses are permissible.

YOUR TRAVELING WARDROBE

When you plan a wardrobe for a trip, whether it be by airplane, car, train, or boat, there are two considerations—space and weight. Air travel is not the only means of transportation where weight is a factor. Have you ever tried to carry your own fifty-pound suitcase through the train station when no porter can be found, as is now so often the case? Or have you seen your host take your bag from your car trunk and stagger gasping up his steps because the days of the butler and houseman have passed?

Even more consideration should be given your travel wardrobe than your regular outfits, because of the need for traveling with as few accessories as possible. Nothing takes up more space or weighs more than handbags and shoes. If you can plan your costumes so that one pair of the most comfortable, sturdy shoes available for sightseeing can be exchanged in the evening for a pump of the same color, your packing and overweight problems will be almost solved. The handbags with changeable covers mentioned earlier in this chapter are ideal for traveling. You may carry the bag itself onto the boat or plane and pack only the lightweight covers. For evening, a small flat silk or satin bag will look well with any costume and add little to the weight of your suitcase.

Dresses of wrinkleproof material are a "must," and they can now be found in all styles and weights for summer or winter travel. Take along a cleaning fluid or powders put up specially for travelers—a spot on a dress that forms an important part of your clothing scheme can be a disaster.

Think again of the versatility of your clothes. Sweaters should be chosen because they go well with *all* your skirts, shorts, and dresses. A skirt with a matching coat makes a stunning costume for cruise or country wear and is better than dress and coat, because with a change of blouses the skirt can give the appearance of several outfits. One rarely needs an evening dress when traveling, but a sleeveless cocktail dress with a jacket may be worn in any restaurant or theater or at any party to which you are invited.

Shorts and slacks, incidentally, are rarely worn by foreign women except at such resorts as the Riviera, and therefore American women should "in Rome, do as the Romans," or they will appear conspicuous and typically "tourist." If you are traveling on the Continent rather than on a cruise ship (where the same clothes are appropriate as those worn in any resort at home), save space by not taking more shorts than you will need for the day or two you plan to spend in Cannes. But don't forget a bathing suit—even a wayside stream can provide a refreshing relief from the heat of southern France, Italy, or Spain in summer, and swimming pools and lakes are found near resort hotels all over the world.

For clothes appropriate to special occasions, please consult the Index.

75

Men's clothes

Although the clothes a man wears are certain to reveal his background, fashion is not as important or as changeable as is the case with a woman's clothes. Recently, however, radical departures from the conservative clothes considered essential for many years have occurred, and men are at last permitted a wider choice of colors and styles than has been true for many years.

Fashions in business suits have not changed drastically. A well-made suit bought ten years ago should still be perfectly wearable today, although its age would be noticeable in some details. Lapels have become narrower, trouser legs slimmer, and neckties, too, are much narrower than they used to be. A particular style may come and go, and the well-dressed businessman may choose to follow these styles if they are not overly flamboyant and if they are becoming to him. Certain colors have a temporary vogue—in shirts, for instance. One year yellow shirts may appear with gray or brown suits; the next year they will be replaced by blue. Bow ties are popular in some years; in others one sees only the four-in-hands.

Whatever the fashion of the moment, if a man's suit fits him well, is appropriate to whatever he may be doing, and is not overly conspicuous in style or color, he may rest assured that he will be labeled "well-dressed" in any community.

Outside of the business office a man may now choose from an infinite variety of "new looks." Most of the fads are temporary, but they have had the happy effect of releasing the male population from the rigidity and stuffiness which characterized men's wear for so long. Since there are few rules governing fads other than those of decency and cleanliness, this chapter is devoted mainly to appropriate clothing for the business and social worlds.

THE IMPORTANCE OF FIT AND GOOD CARE

Whether you buy your clothes at a men's store or a department store or have them made by a tailor, the most important consideration is excellent fit. Although you may be on a strict budget and are buying your clothing as inexpensively as possible, be sure to spend the extra time and money required to have any necessary alterations made. Any suit appears more costly than it is if it hangs well and does not sag or stretch.

Another means of adding years to the life of your clothes and adding immeasurably to their appearance is the care that you give them. Suits and sports jackets should be pressed, brushed, and spot-cleaned after two or three wearings. But if it is important to you to lengthen the life of your clothes, they should only be sent for general cleaning when they are soiled all over, or have a stain which cannot be removed at home. Trousers should be pressed each time they are worn if the crease is gone or if they are very wrinkled at the seat or knee. But if you invest in a good "silent valet" (a stand over which you hang the trousers, which are then pressed by another hinged board that is clamped tight against the hanging legs) a suit, because the jacket does not show signs of use to the extent that the trousers do, may be worn many more times before either a pressing or a trip to the cleaner's is necessary.

The immediate replacement of a missing button is a "must." Not only does it ruin the appearance of the clothing, but it can actually cause the material of the suit or jacket to lose shape if it is left unrepaired for a long period of time.

Another worthwhile investment is a pair of shoe trees for each pair of shoes. Nothing increases the life of the shoes so much as being properly stretched on trees each time they are removed, and nothing improves the appearance or preserves the leather so much as proper shining.

THE MAN ON A BUDGET

The man on a budget is more fortunate than the woman in the same situation. A man does not need so many complete changes of outfit as a woman, because the same suit with different shirts, ties, and socks may be used for almost every day and for any occasion. But the budget-minded man must consider the same things as his female counterpart. If a limited supply of ties, shirts, socks, and shoes must go with all his suits and jackets, then he must restrict himself to one or two colors. A gray suit for business, a dark blue suit for evening, and a sports jacket in a gray-blue tweed could be worn, for example, with blue and red neckties, white, blue, or yellow shirts, and blue, maroon, or black socks. Since a white shirt is more formal than a colored one, it is always correct with the blue suit in the evening as well as at any other time. Dark brown shoes could be worn with all three, although most well-dressed men prefer black with a blue suit. A good solution for a two-pair wardrobe would be a black pair to wear with the two suits, and a pair of brown loafers or other casual shoes to wear with the sports jacket.

Because of its versatility, a dark gray flannel suit is an invaluable asset to the man on a limited clothes budget. It may appear anywhere in the daytime and yet go to the theater, a restaurant, or any informal gathering in the evening. In addition, the trousers may be worn separately with a sports shirt or jacket.

INFORMAL DAYTIME WEAR

Rules for daytime clothes are less rigid than they used to be, but the man who works in an office in the city must dress according to a set pattern if he wishes to impress his clients and his employers or superiors favorably. Sports jackets, open-necked shirts, and loud plaids are worn in the city only on weekends (for a picnic in the park, for instance) or in your own home. For weekday wear during office hours, a suit is the proper attire.

THE BUSINESS SUIT

The business suit is supposed to be an inconspicuous garment and should be. Today's suit usually consists of trousers and a single-breasted coat. Some men do wear double-breasted suits—they go in and out of style. Vests, like double breasted suits, come and go. A few rules to follow:

Don't choose striking patterns or materials, although a quiet plaid or muted stripe or herringbone pattern can be very handsome. Suitable woolens come in endless variety, and any that look inconspicuous at a short distance are safe.

Dark gray (charcoal), dark blue, and brown are first color choices, although olive greens and lighter grays are also correct. But don't get too light a blue, too bright a green, or anything suggesting a horse blanket. If you must be eccentric, save your efforts for the next fancy-dress party, but at business clothing should be reasonable.

It is better taste not to wear silk socks in winter, except in the evening, but lisle or cotton are correct for those who are not comfortable in wool. Above all, don't wear white socks with a suit. Don't cover yourself with chains, fobs, lodge emblems, etc., and don't wear plaid shirts and neckties. If a salesman offers you anything that has "never been seen before," the safest rule is to shun it unless your judgment is very experienced.

White shirts are always correct with a business suit, but solid-color and pin- or narrow-striped materials are also acceptable.

Summer suits are lighter in color as well as weight, and their accessories can be much less conservative. Socks are entirely proper not only in browns and grays, but in other colors as well. Ties of printed silk or any of the new synthetic fabrics can be gaily colored, but patterns should be small, and stripes should not be too wild.

A tan, gray, blue, or olive green suit in the new lightweight, crease-resistant summer fabrics has the advantage of being correct for the city and not looking out of place in the country.

Some of the new materials are so cool and light that the wearer is comfortable in even the hottest weather, and the necessity of removing the coat has been almost eliminated.

THE COUNTRY OFFICE

Many men who work in offices in the country prefer to wear a sports jacket rather than a suit. Some companies require their employees, even in small towns, to wear suits, however, because they feel it is more dignified and makes a better impression on clients or customers. Unless the company specifies the color, suits worn in the suburbs or country may be lighter in color or a little gayer in pattern than those worn in the city. While a suit is always correct for business wear, if your work is such that you do not have to meet outsiders—as does, for instance, a salesman—it is certainly not incorrect to wear a comfortable sports jacket in your office.

WHEN NOT AT WORK

It would not be possible to go into all the types of clothing that may be worn out of working hours. But there are certain general observations that may be made.

Clothing should be appropriate to the occasion. If you have been asked to spend a weekend at a fishing camp, you would be foolish to take light-colored, easily spotted linen slacks rather than dungarees or khakis. Nor would you be wise to appear at an exclusive beach club in clothing appropriate for a weekend on a farm. Don't wear loafers on board a boat. Not only might you slip and fall overboard, but most owners will shudder at the marks that the hard soles may make on their polished decks. In other words, choose your vacationtime clothes with an eye toward what your activities will be, and if you don't know, ask! No one has ever been criticized for wanting to have the appropriate clothes, but many a friendship has been dampened by the need to outfit or loan clothing to someone who didn't take the trouble to find out what might be needed.

See also Chapters Thirty-seven, Sixty-eight, and Seventy-five.

In general, men in the city wear the same clothes in their own homes as do their brothers in the country. But when they appear in public, they should put on jacket and tie, and for most social activities, suits are usually worn.

The country dweller need not be so formal. Open-necked polo shirts and slacks are standard attire in any warm climate, and in the cooler months, flannel shirts and sweaters are seen all over the country. But even the suburbanite or farmer puts on his sports jacket and tie when going to any sort of social gathering, from a friendly brunch to a morning meeting of the "Little League" fathers. Men attending weddings, cocktail parties, luncheons, or any other daytime function, unless it is specified as "formal," wear the same dark suit, white shirt, and conservative tie and socks that they would wear to informal evening affairs.

FORMAL DAYTIME WEAR

When it is necessary to dress more formally, the cutaway or a black sack coat and striped trousers are worn at any affair that takes place before six o'clock in the evening.

THE CUTAWAY

The cutaway is the most formal afternoon attire, and it is rarely seen except at large afternoon weddings, on pallbearers at a large funeral, or at official teas or receptions. For this reason, few men not in the diplomatic corps or in high government positions have cutaways, but they can always rent them.

When renting *any* formal attire, make your arrangements well ahead of the date on which it is to be worn if you possibly can, so that it may be perfectly fitted to you. This is particularly true of cutaways and tailcoats.

The cutaway (sometimes called morning) coat—Black or oxford gray worsted or cheviot, with peaked lapels. Edges may be bound, but generally plain ones are preferred. Buttons are bone or self-covered.

Waistcoat—Double-breasted. In winter, black wool to match the coat or pearl-gray fine wool (doeskin). In summer, white or fawn linen or white piqué.

Trousers—Black and gray striped worsted or cheviot. Cuffless.

Shirt—White, with starched bosom and starched cuffs.

Collar—Detachable wing or starched fold collar.

Tie—For weddings, ascot, in gray or silver-gray silk, plain, figured, or striped. Worn with wing collar. For funerals, black four-in-hand, worn with fold collar. Other occasions, a bow tie with a wing collar, or a four-in-hand with either wing or fold collar. Tie may be gray, black, or silver-gray, with traditional patterns.

Socks—Black or dark gray. Any material except very heavy wool.

Shoes—Black calf oxfords.

Hat—Black silk hat. Less appropriate, a black homburg.

Topcoat—Black, dark gray, or dark blue.

Gloves—Gray, any material of good quality.

Accessories—Jewelry: pearl pin with ascot, gold cuff links. With stiff shirt with bow tie, single stud should be gold. Boutonniere, white or red carnation. Boutonnieres are not worn at funerals. At a wedding, the bridegroom may wear a small sprig from his bride's bouquet. Handkerchief: white or gray silk scarf, white linen handkerchief. Handkerchief should be initialed in white, with all initials, or that of last name only. It is folded square and shows no more than one-half inch to one inch above pocket.

THE SACK COAT

The sack coat is a less formal version of the cutaway. It is worn by the participants in morning weddings, afternoon weddings, large funerals, and on any daytime occasion when the formality of the cutaway is not essential.

Sack Coat—Black or oxford gray worsted, single-breasted.

Waistcoat—Double-breasted. Black or oxford gray, same as the sack coat, or pearl-gray fine wool.

Trousers—Same as for cutaway.

Shirt—White, soft bosom, starched French cuffs. Starched fold collar.

Tie—Black or gray-and-black pattern, silk. Four-in-hand style.

Hat—Black homburg or soft black felt.

All other clothing and accessories are the same as for a cutaway.

EVENING CLOTHES

For all informal evening wear, the dark—navy or charcoal gray—suit, with white shirt, dark tie, and dark socks, is the accepted outfit. For formal evenings, either full evening dress, called "white tie" or "tails" (sometimes "white tie and tails"), or a dinner jacket, called "black tie" or "tuxedo," is worn.

If ever in doubt about what to wear, the best rule is to err on the side of informality. If you are not sure whether to put on your full dress suit or your tuxedo, wear the latter.

On the other hand, when an occasion is important and a man wants to make sure that his clothes will be correct, it is entirely proper for him to call his host or his hostess on the telephone and ask, "Do I wear a black tie tonight, or a white one?" or the question may be: "Day clothes or tuxedos?"

Variations of the above attire come into vogue from time to time, but few have had more than a brief span of popularity. Typical are the string ties popular recently, and currently, turtlenecks worn instead of conventional shirts. Those who want to show their up-to-dateness are quick to adopt these fashions, but they are just as quick to drop them when they lose favor. This they invariably do because a majority of men find the traditional costume either most comfortable or most handsome.

BLACK TIE

To go out for the evening dressed in "black tie" means that you are wearing a dinner jacket or tuxedo. The term "tuxedo" appeared in the early nineties when the dinner jacket was introduced in the Tuxedo Club to provide something less formal to wear than the "swallowtail" or full evening dress. Today black tie is accepted as correct on almost every formal occasion, and few men have any need to dress often in a more formal manner. Therefore, while it is more practical for most men to rent a "set of tails" when the occasion demands, it is advisable for those who can to invest in a good quality, well-fitted tuxedo, which will last for many years. It consists of:

Jacket—In winter or summer, black or midnight blue is always correct, and the material is usually tropical worsted or, if it is not shiny, one of the new blended materials. The lapels are faced with satin. In hot weather, white linen is worn for formal affairs, but for less formal parties, plaid (madras) or a solid-color cotton, dacron, or other blend is appropriate, attractive, and gay. On all jackets the lapels may be rolled or peaked and of whatever width current fashion demands. Dinner jackets are usually single-breasted, but a few men still prefer the double-breasted form, which requires neither waistcoat nor cummerbund.

Trousers—When a dark jacket (black or midnight blue) is worn, the trousers are always of the same material. If a colored jacket is worn, the trousers are of a good quality black material, usually the same pair worn with a black jacket. In either case, they do not have cuffs and do have a single stripe of black braid or satin.

Waistcoat or cummerbund—The waistcoat is of white piqué or plain or patterned black silk. Today, instead of a waistcoat, a cummerbund is usually worn. The most formal are of black or maroon silk, but it may also be plaid or figured, especially in the summertime.

Shirt—A daytime white shirt with fold collar may be worn, but for a formal occasion, a piqué or pleated bosom makes a better appearance.

Tie—Black silk bow with waistcoat or black cummerbund. If cummerbund other than black is worn, the tie should be of matching color and material.

Socks—Black silk or lisle.

Shoes—Black patent leather.

Hat—A black homburg or black or gray soft-brimmed fedora in the winter, gray fedora in the spring or fall, and a Panama in the summer. However, if the weather does not necessitate the wearing of a hat, many men prefer not to do so.

Gloves—Gray chamois or buck.

Topcoat—Black, dark gray, or navy coat, with or without velvet collar.

Accessories—Jewelry: pearl or mother-of-pearl or black onyx studs. Cuff links may be gold or mother-of-pearl to match the studs. Handkerchief: white linen, with or without initials. White silk scarf. Boutonniere: white or red carnation.

WHITE TIE

Full evening dress is required only occasionally for some men, and never for most. Therefore, relatively few men own their "tails," and the great majority rent them for those special occasions. This is perfectly correct, as long as they are rented from a reputable establishment that has excellent tailors to do alterations, because there is no outfit whose appearance is so ruined by poor fitting as the tailcoat.

A tailcoat *must* be worn by the fathers and escorts of debutantes at their coming-out parties. It *must* be worn to any affair when the invitation reads "white tie." Otherwise, it *may* be worn to formal dinners or balls, or to official or diplomatic parties, or when sitting in a box at the opera. It is often worn by the principals involved in an opening night at the theater, or by those in charge of benefits or charity affairs.

Tailcoat—Black worsted or tropical worsted. Lapels are peaked and faced in grosgrain or satin. The tails should hang to the break at the back of the knees.

Waistcoat—White pique. Usually single-breasted, but may be double-breasted.

Trousers—Match the coat. Single stripe of satin or braid; no cuffs.

Shirt—White, made to wear with detachable wing collar. Piqué or plain linen bosom, stiffly starched. Cuffs are single, starched. Shirt may have either one or two buttonholes for studs.

Tie—White piqué bow. Current fashion favors straight ends rather than "butterfly" shape.

Socks—Black silk or nylon.

Shoes—Black patent leather pumps or oxfords.

Hat—High silk or opera hat is most formal, but a black homburg is more frequently worn. Many men prefer not to wear a hat with tails.

Topcoat—Black, dark gray, or dark blue.

Gloves—White chamois or doeskin.

Accessories—Jewelry: pearl or mother-of-pearl studs for shirt, mother-of-pearl for the waistcoat and cuff links, or of platinum or white gold. White linen handkerchief and white silk scarf. Boutonniere: white carnation or small white gardenia.

COATS AND HATS

Men's topcoats come in an infinite variety of colors and materials. For the man who lives a very active social life and frequently wears evening clothes, a solid black, navy, or dark gray coat is a necessity. For daytime wear, he must also have a less formal coat in the color that goes best with his suits.

The dress coat may or may not be double-breasted—the daytime sports coat, never.

For the average man, and especially the young man who is starting his wardrobe, a coat that will look well in any circumstance is preferable to the very dressy or very sporty one. For the city dweller, a dark gray herringbone tweed is most practical. Brown tweed is handsome, but should not be worn with formal evening dress. For either city or country wear, a polo coat for the cold months and a straight gabardine (or one of the newer waterproof materials) to double as a topcoat in the summer are ideal solutions.

Some men, in both city and country, prefer not to wear hats unless it is absolutely necessary. For these men, or for anyone whose wardrobe is limited, a gray felt fedora is the best choice. It can be worn with any color, and in any circumstance except with full evening dress. Men who wear white tie frequently should certainly have a black homburg or silk hat to go with it. Derbies, which used to be worn with business suits, and the high silk hat have almost disappeared.

Men who live in the country may choose a fedora in a rougher material than the regular felt. They may have special bands of braid or cloth other than black silk, and occasionally they have a feather or other ornament tucked into the band at the side. This type of hat should not be worn with a tuxedo, however.

In the summertime coconut straw hats (fedora-shaped) are handsome and cool. The bands may be of any solid color, or figured or plaid. These are accepted for all daytime wear, even in the city, but with evening clothes the conservative Panama hat is correct.

LIFTING OR TIPPING THE HAT

Lifting or tipping the hat is a conventional gesture of politeness shown to strangers or mere acquaintances only. In lifting his hat, a gentleman merely lifts it slightly off his forehead—by the brim of a stiff hat or by the crown of a soft one—and replaces it. Hats are generally tipped whenever a man says "Excuse me," "Thank you," "Allow me . . . ," or when he greets, or is greeted by, a lady in passing.

WHEN TO REMOVE A HAT AND GLOVES

A gentleman takes off his hat and holds it in his hand when a lady enters the elevator in an apartment house or hotel—any building which can be classified as a dwelling. He puts it on again in the corridor. A public corridor is like the street, but an elevator in a hotel or apartment house has the character of a room in a house and there a man does not keep his hat on in the presence of women.

However, in public buildings, such as offices or stores, the elevator is considered as public a place as a bus or train. What is more, the elevators in such business structures are usually so crowded that the only room for a man's hat is on his head!

A man who stops on a city street to speak to a woman must show considerable dexterity in taking his hat and right glove off, and (should he be smoking) in getting his cigarette out of the way. He must hold the cigarette (or pipe) and hat in his left hand while removing the right glove and offering his hand to the lady. If they walk on together he puts his hat on, but while he is standing in the street talking to her he should remain hatless unless, of course, she thoughtfully says, "Please put your hat on—you'll catch pneumonia in this freezing wind." In the country he may very well be bareheaded and also be smoking, but in a city street it would be in very poor taste for a man to stand talking to a lady with his hat on and a cigar, pipe, or cigarette in his mouth.

I hope that it is not necessary to add that, out of doors, every American citizen stands with his hat off at the passing of the flag, and both indoors (in a public place) and outdoors when the national anthem is played. Also, every man should take his hat off in the presence of a funeral and in all Christian churches.

A gentleman wearing *outdoor* gloves never shakes hands with a lady without first removing his right-hand glove. But at a formal ball, or when he is usher at a wedding, he does *not* remove his glove, which is intended to be worn indoors. When outside, if for some reason he cannot get his right glove off, he may say, "Excuse my glove," but he does not ask that an indoor glove be excused.

SHOES AND SOCKS

Shoes, like all men's clothing, should be conservative in style and color. Dark brown, cordovan, and black are the best choices and go well with all business or sports clothes. If you have evening clothes you must have black patent leather shoes to go with them.

The better quality shoes you buy, the more wear they will give you.

Good leather, properly cared for with wax polish, will last for many years. Good shoes are well worth resoling, and you should have it done before they become too worn. Since the more expensive shoes will also fit your foot better, the added cost is quite justified, especially if your work requires many hours of standing.

As to style, plain leather (like "cordovan"), perforated insteps and toes, or "capped" toes are chosen according to your taste. It is well to avoid pointed toes and higher-than-average heels. Loafers are fine for country wear, but tend to look too casual during business hours in the city. Open-work, suede, and novelty leathers may ruin an otherwise well-chosen outfit.

Socks are selected according to the color of your suit. Black, navy, and maroon are best with blue suits; black, gray, green, or maroon with gray; and brown or green with brown. They may be solid color, ribbed or plain knit, with or without clock, and they may have a small stripe or a tiny pattern.

When you are selecting socks, remember that there is nothing attractive about an expanse of bare masculine leg below the trouser cuff. Unless you sit primly with both feet on the floor at all times—as is not likely—you will do well to avoid anklets, especially with a business suit; and you should invest in a good pair of garters unless you prefer a style of sock that has built-in support.

NECKTIES

Neckties should, of course, go well with the color of your suit, and often they match the socks as well, but ties that match shirts—white on white, for example—are not in good taste. Solid colors, muted paisleys, narrow stripes, or small patterns go well with business suits. They may be of foulard (silk), knit, or smooth wool in winter, or cotton or silk in summer.

Choosing a tie to go with a sports jacket can be difficult. With a loud plaid, you must avoid stripes or a bold pattern. A solid-color knit or wool is the safest choice with a wool jacket, and the color should match one of the tones in the plaid. A tie with a very sparse pattern—perhaps two or three flying birds, or a single emblem of some sort—can also be worn with a sports jacket. Cotton or silk ties are worn with madras or patterned lightweight jackets.

The four-in-hand is by far the most popular style, but the bow tie is very becoming to some men and provides a good way of giving your outfits a little variety. When choosing a bow tie, try several lengths and shapes, as certain styles are definitely better suited to one shape of face than others. And practice tying the bow until you are truly adept—if you can't avoid a flying end or a sagging loop, stick to the four-in-hand!

An ascot in gray or silver-gray silk is worn by the bridegroom at a formal wedding—with a cutaway.

A less formal type of ascot is one made of patterned silk in any color. It is worn, tucked inside an open-necked shirt, at sports events in the country and sometimes at informal gatherings such as barbecues or brunches.

VESTS OR WAISTCOATS

The vest, or waistcoat (those worn with evening clothes are always called "waistcoats"), rises and falls in popularity. Many men, however, wear them for added warmth and extra pockets, as well as for the appearance.

When worn with a business suit, the vest is of the same material as the suit. With a sports jacket, it may be of gaily colored flannel, a check or plaid wool (often called "tattersal"), or other pattern. Many wives enjoy embroidering vests with the emblems of their husbands' schools or with designs derived from a favorite sport or hobby. Vests such as these make wonderful "conversation pieces" and add a distinctive note to a man's sports clothes.

One warning, however: if you are wearing a vest, remember to remove it if you take off your jacket for any reason. Vests were never meant to be seen uncovered from the rear.

JEWELRY

The two most important requisites for men's jewelry are first, that it be of good quality, and second, that it be inconspicuous.

Naturally everyone cannot go out and buy solid gold or platinum tie clips or cuff links. So until you can buy expensive jewelry, exercise great care in choosing what you can afford. The best rule is to select the simplest design that can be found—it invariably gives the appearance of being more costly than does ornate or gaudy jewelry. There is a great deal of imitation jewelry available that is handsomely designed and well made. The problem is to choose something that not only looks very smart, but will not tarnish, lose its finish, or otherwise fall apart.

Cuff links for wear with a business suit should be made of solid metal—usually gold or silver—and should be of moderate size. They may be initialed, have a personal or other crest, or a raised or etched design. Flashing stones in the daytime are not in good taste.

For evening wear, mother-of-pearl cuff links are usually accompanied by matching studs. They may or may not have a circle of tiny diamonds around the edge. Darker pearl and black onyx are handsome with a tuxedo, and white gold or platinum may be worn. But other colored stones are to be avoided, as they do look conspicuous.

Collar pins are made of gold, and tie clips may be of almost any metal or combination of metals. The width of the clip depends on the taste of the wearer, and its length, on the width of the tie. Tie pins to hold ascots or scarves in place may be set with a pearl, diamond, or other stones.

The most attractive man's ring, in my opinion, is one of gold, with initials or crest, worn on the little finger. Rings may also be set with a single stone. Onyx, opals, moonstones, star sapphires, or rough-cut stones are more masculine than other gems. Seal rings from school, college, or military service are popular and handsome. These are often worn on the fourth finger of either hand rather than the little finger. Wedding rings are almost always of plain gold, although occasionally they have a pattern or design. They are usually chosen to match the ring of the bride.

Other than the articles mentioned above, accessories for men are of a practical rather than an ornamental nature. Money clips, cigarette lighters, and watches are all utilitarian, but although they may not, in the strictest sense of the word, be *jewelry*, they may be *jewelled*. A cigarette case or lighter used in the evening may bear a design or initials done in precious stones, and a watch may be so beautiful and have such a fine gold band that it is as decorative as jewelry. But all these things and the many more, like key chains or gold pencils, that have not been discussed, must be carefully chosen to suit the taste of the wearer and the purse of the buyer.

For clothes appropriate to special occasions, please consult the Index.

76

Clothing for various sports

Although there are no "do's and don't's" at all about the proper dress for certain sports, others require considerable knowledge of the right clothing if you do not wish to appear a rank amateur. To people about to go on a trout fishing trip, it is hardly necessary to say that they need waterproof waders or hip boots, or to hunters that they wear red hats or shirts in order not to be shot by other hunters. Except for this sort of essential clothing, there are no rules as to what one wears—it is simply a matter of most practical and most comfortable.

And this actually is the basis for the choice of clothing that, over a period of time, has come to be considered correct for a number of other sports. Some of these rules for dress have become so much a part of the game that one is required to dress in a prescribed style in order to be allowed to participate.

TENNIS

For some years tennis players have recognized that in the heat of the summer, white clothes were the coolest (white actually does not absorb heat as do darker colors) and the freshest looking on the court. Today many clubs and organizations will not allow players to play in colored clothes at any time, and almost all others require white on week-ends or for tournaments.

MEN'S CLOTHES

Shorts and polo shirts are standard attire for the men. The flannel "Bermuda" short is the smartest for spring and fall, but too hot for the summer months or in a Southern climate. Shirts may be open collared or round neck, and they may have a narrow band of color at the neck or a shield on the pocket, often the colors of the club, school, or team that the player represents. Plain white socks and sneakers and a visor or cap complete the outfit. For after the game, a heavy ribbed or cabled v-neck sweater with or without a stripe of color at the neck will mark you as a well-dressed tennis player.

WOMEN'S CLOTHES

Women play in either shorts or short skirts, depending on their age and figure. The short (above the knee) tennis dress with full or pleated skirt and matching "short shorts" underneath is so becoming that even very young girls are wearing it instead of shorts. There is no rule as to style or material—round neck, shirtwaist, or any other design that is comfortable and attractive—but, unless the wearer has lovely slim legs, it must not be too short. If shorts are worn, they should be of medium or "Bermuda" length—not as brief as a bathing suit.

Women, unless their hair is worn very short or smoothly knotted or pinned, should wear a cap, net, or band. It is untidy and distracting to any player to have hair flying wildly over the face in the middle of a fast rally. In any case, it is safer for older women to wear a hat when playing in the hot sun.

GOLF

SHORTS AND SLACKS

There are few golf clubs left that do not allow members of both sexes to play in shorts and permit women to wear slacks in cool weather. Most clubs specify, however, that they be long shorts or "Bermudas." As long as this rule is followed, and if you have reasonably presentable legs and at least a "medium" figure, shorts are acceptable. Many women prefer very short skirts. They are more becoming to most, and in very hot weather, cooler. There is no limit to color combinations for both men and women. Solid-color shorts or skirts with blending, printed shirts or blouses are a popular style, but the scheme may be reversed. Also, the same color may be used for the whole outfit. Plaid or madras shorts are favored by many men.

The male golfer may prefer slacks to shorts and has his choice of linen, cotton, or any other lightweight material. In cool weather, flannel is the most popular choice, and although gray or brown are the most prevalent colors, gray-blue, green, and many other shades are often seen. Slacks should be cut reasonably full for ease in bending and walking, and shirts should be generously cut to allow free movement of the arms. In chilly weather the men may prefer a flannel or wool shirt so that they need not wear a sweater or jacket.

SKIRTS AND DRESSES

Women who feel that their figures are not suited to shorts—or whose clubs do not allow them—should choose dresses or skirts of a comfortable, simple design. Any color is acceptable, and dresses are sometimes sold with a matching sweater. Skirts should be flared—not pleated or gathered, as these kinds will blow in the wind and may distract the most avid golfer just as she is about to sink a putt. Short skirts, ending above the knee, are popular with many women. In cool weather, slacks, if becoming, are the warmest and most comfortable clothing, but if they do not look well, or are not allowed, flannel or wool skirts and knee-length socks or wool stockings will ward off the chill.

JACKETS

Golf jackets for both men and women come in all colors and styles. They may be open-down or pullover, long or short, but they must be windproof, waterproof, lightweight, and loose fitting.

SHOES

Shoes should be chosen for comfort, waterproofing, and durability, and therefore they must be of good quality. Men's shoes should be brown, black, or a combination of either of these with white. They should not be yellow or any other light color. They may have a flap over the laces or not, as the wearer chooses.

Women's shoes are much the same as men's, with the addition of navy blue to the list of colors.

HATS

The poor frustrated male who must restrict himself to conservative business clothes may indulge himself and go "all out" in his choice of a golf hat. Be it straw, felt, or cloth, he may pick any style or color that will keep the sun out of his eyes and the rain from his head. He may decorate it with golf insignia, feathers, colored bands, or anything else he likes, and as long as it stays on when it should and suits him well, the wilder it is the more admiration it will arouse in his foursome.

SKIING

The newest sport to reach the zenith of popularity is skiing, and styles in ski clothes have changed, and are changing, so fast that is hard to keep up with them. But in spite of this, certain types of clothing have proved to be most practical as well as attractive to look at, and the best features of these have been retained, although such details as color, belts, and hats may vary from year to year.

The main differences between men's and women's ski outfits are the colors, the use of fur or fancy trimming, and hat styles.

TROUSERS AND SHIRTS

"Stretch" pants have proved to be most flattering to almost every sort of figure, as well as most practical, because they do not buckle, flap, or sag out of shape. While they must fit snugly, without fullness or wrinkles, there must also be enough "give" so that the seams do not split with the first fall. They come in every color of the rainbow, but the best men skiers stick to the more masculine colors—browns, olives, dark blues, blacks, and the like.

Any type of shirt that is comfortable and goes well with your outfit is perfectly correct—cotton, flannel, turtleneck, man-tailored, whatever becomes you best.

PARKAS

Parkas come in an infinite variety of colors and should be chosen to match or blend with the pants. Girls—especially those who are seen around the base lodge more than on the slopes—usually choose wildly printed, fur-trimmed, or solid fur (I have even seen mink on occasion!) parkas. The more serious lady skiers tend to choose more conservative patterns or solid colors in the same style as those worn by the men.

The lightweight quilted parka is standard for both men and women—it is waterproof, windproof, and warm. Many are reversible, a good idea for those who ski frequently and cannot afford more than one outfit. The tendency now is toward longer parkas, a fine idea as they protect the upper legs and seat from bitter winds (especially while you stand in the ever-present line for the lifts) and from the wet or freezing seat of the chair lift. The parka may be belted or not, according to your own taste, but it should have a hood, which usually rolls up under the collar when not in use.

SKI BOOTS

The heavy ski boot, with inner and outer laces or adjustable clips for ease in doing up the outside boot, is the most important item of your ski clothing. Before buying your boots, wear them for several hours with the socks you plan to use when skiing. Many, many pairs of boots have been bought without taking this precaution, only to be exchanged after the first ski trip because blisters have appeared on the skier's heel, ankle, or toe after the first hour's skiing. Boots should be bought from a reputable ski shop, and it is wise to seek the advice of a knowledgeable salesman who can tell you which is the best boot for the price you can pay. As this will be your most expensive clothing investment, choose carefully, remembering that the better quality boot, though more costly, will give you many more years of wear.

Ski boots must be well cared for to keep the leather pliant and waterproof. They must be put on racks made for the purpose immediately upon removal, and from time to time they should be treated with a leather conditioner and waterproofer. These supplies are sold at all ski shops.

UNDERWEAR

Ski underwear is especially designed to give the greatest warmth possible. It is usually double-layered wool or a wool and synthetic or cotton blend. Long pants and long-sleeved round-necked or turtleneck shirts are standard equipment.

SOCKS

Two pairs of socks are recommended—one lightweight pair of silk, nylon, or thin wool, and a heavy wool pair of "duotherm" socks, which are double-layered.

GLOVES

Gloves may be self-lined or worn with a thin nylon, cotton, or silk liner underneath. Mittens are warmer than gloves and are preferred by the average skier. They also may be self-lined, but an outer "shell" with a wool mitten inside is more practical because the inner one can be changed for a dry one when soaked by melting snow.

HATS

No particular style of hat is correct or incorrect for the skier. Whatever the style, it should be chosen for warmth, comfort, a fit that will not let it fly off, and, especially for the girls, appearance. Fur and make-believe-fur hats are very popular with the ladies and are attractive as well as warm. Wool hats in all colors, knits, and shapes can be found to match any parka, and the men are often seen in caps with flaps that come down to cover the ears.

SNOW BUNNIES

As I have said all through this chapter on sports clothing, the most important thing of all is appropriateness. And one of the least appropriate sights I know is a "snow bunny"—a girl dressed in lavender stretch pants so tight that they appear to have been painted on, a pink and purple fur-trimmed parka, an enormous white fur hat, and a face made up for a night club act—struggling miserably down the beginner's slope on Skiball Mountain. Or worse yet, sitting at the bar in the lodge attempting to look as if she had just come in from the expert trail! These women are not there to ski, and their outfits announce the fact by their very conspicuousness. The true enthusiast, be he an earnest novice or an ardent expert, dresses in a well-matched, good-looking outfit, chosen as much for comfort and wear as appearance. He—or she—makes no attempt to catch the eye of all the members of the opposite sex on the slope.

BOWLING

A full skirt or slacks, worn with a loosely cut cotton or cotton knit blouse, is the standard outfit for women who bowl. If you are blessed with a figure that looks well in slacks, they are the most practical choice, as they combine complete freedom of movement with modesty. A skirt must be flared to allow for a full stride, and long enough not to ride up too high in the back when you bend over. A box-pleat skirt is ideal, as it hangs smoothly and yet allows freedom of movement. The short-sleeved blouses may be of any style most comfortable and becoming to the wearer, with either slacks or a skirt.

A man wears slacks and any open-necked sports shirt or whatever shirt is worn by his team or club.

Most bowlers have their own shoes, but if you don't, you must rent them. Almost all alleys have shoes available, because they require them for the protection of their alleys. If there is no such regulation, sneakers will do, but never hard-soled shoes.

Except by young children, shorts are not worn at the bowling alley.

RIDING

A riding habit, no matter what the fashion happens to be, is the counterpart of an officer's uniform; it must be beautifully fitted, smart, and utterly conventional. Don't wear loud plaids, pockets, or eccentric cuffs or lapels. The best choice for the coat is a plain dark color, but small checks, herringbone tweed, or muted plaids can be handsome, too. A medium-weight closely woven material holds its shape better than a light loose weave. The trousers are solid color, usually fawn or gray.

There are two accepted types of riding habits for women—the jodhpur and the high boot—but men are more correctly dressed in the high boot.

Jodhpurs are breeches that widen slightly in the lower leg so that they fit *over* a low boot rather than inside a high one. For both men and women the rest of the outfit is the same as that worn with high boots.

The boots should be low heeled and have a straight line from heel to top of back. The tops should be no wider than absolutely necessary to get the boots on and off, and they should not be curved or fancy in shape. Be sure that there is no elbow sticking out like a horse's hock at the back.

Low boots for wear with jodhpurs should be of plain leather. The ornamental Western boots that are available in some sections of the country are suitable only with Western riding pants or blue jeans.

Hats must fit the head well, and the shape must be conventional. The peaked velvet cap is most often worn, but derbies are correct, especially for show riding. Hats are worn straight—never on the back of the head or tipped over the nose.

Gloves should be leather.

Neckties or stocks should be tied so as to make them as flat and neat as possible and anchored so securely that nothing can possibly come loose.

If you are asked to ride with a hunt, your wear your most formal riding clothes, with collarless shirt and stock, and a derby if you have one.

Members of a hunt, on special occasions, wear the red (but called pink) coats peculiar to the sport, white or fawn breeches, high black boots, and a black derby. The style is rigidly prescribed, although some details may be varied to identify a particular hunt.

The riding habit is proper for riding in city parks or in horse shows. Riding clothes for the country are completely casual, and shirts, sweaters, or jackets may be chosen according to the weather. Open-necked cotton or flannel shirts, turtleneck or polo shirts are all comfortable and attractive, and sweaters may be worn instead of jackets. Jodhpur boots are easier to care for than the highly polished boots, and therefore jodhpurs are often worn in the country by those who ride a great deal.

IN GENERAL

There are many other sports that we could discuss in this chapter, but most of them either need no particular costume or require clothing so prescribed that those taking part know what they are to wear without having to read a book. The figure skater, for instance, knows without being told that she wears a short flared skirt and tights to keep her legs warm.

If you are taking up a new sport, make a point of observing those who are old hands—they will know what is correct. Then you can choose the features that will be most becoming to you and most suited to your degree of skill. The rank beginner need not choose the very expensive equipment that the expert requires, but remember, as in choosing all clothes, quality, simplicity, and appropriateness are the most important requisites of dressing well.

Part FOURTEEN

THE WELL-APPOINTED HOUSE

77

The personality of the house

Every house has an exterior to be made as presentable as possible, and an interior which must be continually set in order and cleaned. There are meals to be prepared and served, clothes to be laundered and mended, and perhaps children to be cared for. The devices or appliances essential to these needs must be provided to the best of the ability of the head of the household.

Beyond these fundamental necessities, luxuries can be added indefinitely. A little house cannot be a splendid mansion, nor should it attempt to be. But the little house, beautifully furnished and perfectly kept, can display the taste and discrimination of the family which lives there, whereas the large house in bad taste and improperly run only reveals the ignorance of its owner.

A gem of a house may be tiny, but its lines must be good and its painting and furnishing in good taste. As for its upkeep, its path or sidewalk is neat, the steps clean, the brasses polished, and the bell is answered promptly—all these things contribute unmistakably to the impression of quality.

However, the mansion of bastard architecture and ornate detail, with its brass unrecognizable, the steps covered with leaves and mud, and the bell answered by a sloppy and disinterested maid, clearly advertises that the wealth of the owner has not succeeded in giving him a knowledge of charm and good taste. As a matter of fact, the knowledge of how to make a house distinguished both in appearance and in service is harder to learn than how to present such an appearance oneself and to acquire presentable manners.

The personality of a house is indefinable, but there never lived an attractive woman whose home, whether a mansion or a tiny apartment, did not reflect the charm of its owner. Houses without personality are a series of walled enclosures with furniture standing about in them. Sometimes their lack of appeal is baffling; every article is correct and perhaps even beautiful, but one has the feeling that the decorator made chalk marks indicating the exact spot on which each piece of furniture is to stand. Other houses are filled with things of little intrinsic value, even with much that is shabby, and yet they have that inviting atmosphere, that air of unmistakable rightness, which is an unfailing indication of people of excellent taste.

"BECOMING" FURNITURE

Suitability is a test of good taste always—the dress to the occasion, the article to the place, the furniture to the background. To combine many periods in one and commit no anachronism—to put something French, something Spanish, something Italian, and something English into an American house and have the result the epitome of American taste is a feat that has been accomplished time and again—by those who know how!

An intelligent woman follows fashion in house furnishing in general principles only, just as she follows fashion in dress. She wears what is becoming to her own type and personality, and she puts into her house only articles that are becoming to it.

That a quaint old-fashioned house should be filled with antique or old-fashioned pieces of furniture, in size proportioned to the size of the rooms, and that rush-bottomed chairs and rag rugs have no place in a marble hall, should be obvious. But to an amazing number of persons, proportion seems to mean nothing at all. They will put a huge piece of furniture in a tiny room so that the effect is one of painful indigestion, or they will spoil a really good room by the addition of senseless and inappropriately cluttering objects in the belief that because they are valuable they must be beautiful, regardless of suitability.

Sometimes a room is marred by "treasures" clung to for reasons of sentiment. If you happen to collect old glass, keep it in one room, easily accessible in order to show it to other people who are interested, but not scattered over table tops everywhere so that your house has the appearance of a museum or antique shop.

THE BLINDNESS OF SENTIMENT

It is almost impossible for any of us to judge accurately things we have been accustomed to throughout a lifetime. A chair that was Grandmother's, a painting Father bought, the silver that has always been on the dining-room table—all are so much a part of ourselves that we are sentiment-blind to their defects and incongruity in new surroundings.

For instance, the portrait of a Colonial officer, among others, had always hung in Mrs. Oldname's dining room. One day an art critic whose knowledge was better than his manners blurted out, "Will you please tell me why you have that dreadful thing in this otherwise perfect room?" Mrs. Oldname, somewhat taken aback, answered rather wonderingly, "Is it dreadful? Really? I am so fond of him and his dog!"

The critic was merciless. "If you call a cotton-flannel effigy a dog! And as for the figure, it's equally false and lifeless! It is amazing how anyone with your taste can bear looking at it!" In spite of his rudeness, Mrs. Oldname saw then that what he said was quite true—when the fact was pointed out to her. Gradually she grew to dislike the poor officer so much that he was finally relegated to the attic. In the same way, most of us have possessions that have "always been there," or perhaps "treasures" that we love for some association rather than for their appearance. Habit has blinded us, though we would recognize their hideousness if we saw them in the house of another. Or perhaps they are not bad in themselves. Perhaps they are quite beautiful, but unsuitable in the place in which they are and to the objects surrounding them.

Of course, most people cannot afford to throw away every esthetically unpleasing possession, but those whose pocketbook and sentiment permit would add greatly to the beauty of their houses by throwing out the bad. Far better to have stoneware plates that are good in design than ugly but costly porcelain. Expensiveness, in other words, is never a criterion of taste.

The only way to determine what is good and what is horrible is to study and try to understand the principles underlying what is good—from books, in museums, in art classes at the universities, and in the magazines devoted to the decorative arts.

Be very careful, though. Do not mistake fads for "art." There are, quite literally, frightful things in vogue at times—flamboyant and discordant colors, grotesque deformities, designs that cannot possibly be other than bad. In fact, aside from striking novelty there is nothing good about them.

78

Household help—old and new

When I was planning this present edition of *Etiquette,* I had thought of leaving out of it entirely the sections about the duties of the butler, the footman, the housekeeper, and so on. I thought so few of these people remained that the information would be superfluous. And then I heard this story. A young bride was given a copy of *Etiquette* by her aunt. She raved so much about it, saying she could not run her house without it, that her aunt asked what she meant. "Why," she said, "I carefully read the chapter about the work done by the cook, the chambermaid, and the butler, and I did it."

This seemed such a sensible approach that instead of omitting the chapter, I decided merely to change the emphasis. Also, since it is true that a modern housewife's chores are much the same as those performed by yesterday's staff, it is still interesting to read about how they were carried out in the days of enormous households. When you read the following description on the "great house" of years ago, it is hard to believe that most of today's housewives take care of all of the duties described there by themselves—with only the aid of a few appliances or, possibly, part-time help. But they do, and a well-run, beautifully kept home is something in which a woman should take great pride.

THE STAFF OF A LARGE ESTABLISHMENT—FIFTY YEARS AGO

The management of a house of great size was usually divided into several distinct departments, each under its separate head. The housekeeper, if there was one—otherwise the lady of the house—was in charge of the appearance of the house and of its contents, the manners and appearance of the maids as well as their work; taking care of linen was also her responsibility.

The butler took charge of the pantry and dining room. He engaged the footmen, apportioned their work, and was responsible for their appearance, manners, and efficiency. He was also responsible for silver and wines.

The cook was in charge of the kitchen and the kitchen maids, if any.

The nurse, the personal maid, and the cook were under the direction of the lady of the house. The butler and the valet as well as the chauffeur and gardener were usually engaged by the gentleman of the house. When garage or garden required more than one person, the head chauffeur usually engaged his own assistant, and the head gardener always did so.

THE BUTLER

The butler was not only the most important servant in every big establishment, but it was by no means unheard of for him to be both steward and housekeeper. However, although he perhaps supervised the cook's orders or even went to market, the cook was not otherwise under his supervision, and neither, of course, was the children's nurse or the lady's maid.

Where there was no housekeeper the butler engaged not only the menservants but the housemaids, parlor maids, and even on occasion the cook. In the smaller house the butler had charge of the dining room and pantry or possibly the whole ground floor. In all smaller establishments, and in many great ones, he was valet to his employer. In a small house the butler worked a great deal with his hands and not so much with his head. In a large establishment the butler worked very much with his head and with his hands very little.

At Golden Hall, when guests used to come in dozens at a time, his stewardship was not a job that a man of small ability could fill. He had perhaps twenty men under him at big dinners, ten who belonged under him in the house always; he had the keys to the wine cellar and the combination of the silver safe. He also chose the china and glass and linen as well as the silver to be used each day, and he oversaw the setting of the table and the serving of food.

At all meals he stood behind the chair of the lady of the house so that at the slightest turn of her head he need only take a step to be within reach of her voice. The husband, by the way, is "head of the house," but the wife is "head of his table."

In a smaller house where the butler worked alone, he did all the work—naturally. When he had a parlor maid or waitress, he cleaned the silver and answered the front door and telephone and passed the main courses at the table. The assistant passed the secondary dishes and also washed dishes and cleaned the dining room and pantry. Every other afternoon they took turns in answering the door and serving tea. The butler was also valet not only for the gentleman of the house but for any gentlemen guests as well.

FOOTMEN

Even in 1922, when the first edition of *Etiquette* was published, the position of "live-in" footman was almost nonexistent, and when the butler needed extra help for a special occasion, the footmen were hired from a caterer or an agency. They were provided by the agency with regulation "liveries" consisting of trousers and tailcoat to match, buttons of either brass or silver, stiff-starched collar and shirt, white lawn tie, striped waistcoat, and white cotton gloves. Usually there were three buttons on each side of the front of the coat in addition to two linked together on each side of the front edge to hold the coat nearly closed over the waistcoat. There were also twelve buttons on the tails of the coat.

In the rare establishment large enough to require a permanent assistant to the butler, his duties were the following: cleaning the dining room, pantry, lower hall, entrance vestibule and sidewalk, attending to the furnace, carrying wood to any open fireplaces in the house, cleaning the windows, cleaning brasses, cleaning all shoes and boots, carrying everything that was too heavy for the maids or moving furniture so that they could clean behind it, valeting all gentlemen who were guests in the house, assisting the butler in setting and waiting on table, attending the front door, answering the telephone and writing down messages, and cleaning and polishing silver.

The butler himself usually answered the telephone; if not, it was answered by the footman. The footman was deputy butler and took his place whenever the butler was off duty.

THE CHAUFFEUR

The position of chauffeur differed from that of other domestic employees in two respects. The first was that he usually had no regular days off. Second, he usually found and paid for his own board and lodging.

Sometimes a single man might eat with the servants in the kitchen, but this was not common. Sometimes, too, there was a room over the garage —or a whole apartment—for him and his family.

His duties were irregular, sometimes extremely so. In a large family, particularly where there were half-grown sons or daughters, a chauffeur's life could be inhumanly strenuous. He was, for example, expected to take the younger children to school, come back and take the lady shopping, go back to school for the children, drive various members of the family during the afternoon, come back and take his employers out to dinner, go back later to fetch them, and perhaps take a debutante daughter to a night club or ball. Or, if his employers were entertaining that evening, he might perhaps have had to stand on the sidewalk to open the car doors of the arriving guests, and then do so again when they departed.

On the other hand, there were places in which the chauffeur was almost a man of leisure; his employer was an old lady, perhaps, who went to church on Sunday morning from eleven to half-past twelve, who liked to drive from three to five every afternoon, and who went out to dinner or to a concert or to the theater not oftener than once a week. The typical schedule was midway between the two. As far in advance as he could every considerate employer would tell his chauffeur when he was not going to want the car, because only in these circumstances could the chauffeur make any personal engagements.

A chauffeur never carried a robe on his arm when waiting at the car door for his employer. Properly, the lap robe was laid in deep full-length folds on the far side of the seat. As soon as the occupants had taken their places, the chauffeur reached across and, holding the edge of the fold, drew it toward him across their laps. Upon arriving at a destination, if a doorman or a chauffeur was stationed on the sidewalk, he remained seated; otherwise he left his seat and held open the door for the occupants to alight.

THE COOK AND KITCHEN MAID

The cook was always in charge in the kitchen. In a small house or in an apartment she did all the cooking and all the cleaning of the kitchen and pantry, answered the back door bell, set the servants' table, and washed their dishes as well as her kitchen utensils.

In a larger house the kitchen maid prepared vegetables, did all cleaning of the kitchen and pots and pans, answered the bell, set the servants' table, and washed the servants' table dishes. She also carried the housekeeper's meals to her.

In most houses the cook did all the marketing, usually by telephone. She saw the lady of the house every morning and submitted the day's menus for her to approve or change. The butler always went into the kitchen shortly after the cook had had the menus checked and copied the day's menus on a pad of his own. From this he knew what table utensils would be needed.

The cook always wore a white dress and usually a high apron with pockets, stockings (often white), and white shoes. She was expected to furnish her clothes herself, but her aprons and uniforms (and her hair coverings if she wore them) were laundered for her. A few fastidious cooks wore small white kerchief-shaped caps or hair nets when they were preparing food.

THE PARLOR MAID-WAITRESS AND CHAMBERMAID

The parlor maid or waitress kept the drawing room and library in order and laid the fire. In some houses she took up the breakfast trays; in others the butler did this himself and handed them to the lady's maid or the chambermaid to be taken into the bedrooms. She cleaned the windows and the brasses if there was no utility man.

The parlor maid-waitress assisted the butler in waiting table and washing dishes and took turns with him in answering the door and the telephone.

The chambermaid did all the bedrooms, cleaned all silver on dressing tables, polished fixtures in the bathroom—in other words took care of the bedroom floors. She also took care of the rooms of the other servants.

In a larger house the head housemaid had charge of the linen and did the bedrooms of the lady and gentleman of the house and a few of the guest rooms. The second housemaid did the children's rooms, extra guest rooms, and the servants' floors. The larger the establishment, the more housemaids, and the more the work was divided.

The waitress or parlor maid and the housemaid were dressed alike. Their work dresses were of plain cotton in whatever color the lady of the house preferred, and had just-above-elbow sleeves edged with a turn-back attached white cuff. The dresses were finished at the neck with a matching turned-down collar. Large white aprons with high bibs were worn with them.

In a formal house at mealtime, the waitress changed to a long-sleeved dress of taffeta or silk, in black or a dark color, with embroidered white collars, cuffs, and a matching white apron.

A maid's hair had to be smooth and neat. Anything suggesting a faddist hair style or curls flying long and loose was in almost as bad taste as a butler's wearing a mustache!

THE LADY'S MAID

A first-class lady's maid, often called a "personal maid," was required to be a hairdresser, a good packer, and an expert needlewoman.

Her duty was to keep her employer's clothes in perfect order and to help her dress and undress. She drew the bath, laid out underclothes, dressed the lady's hair, and got out the dress to be worn, as well as the stockings, shoes, hat, gloves, handbag, or whatever accessories went with the dress selected.

As soon as her lady was dressed for the day, everything that had been worn was gone over carefully. Everything mussed was pressed, everything suspected of not being immaculate was washed or cleaned, and, when in perfect order, was placed where it belonged. Stockings were looked over for threatening runs or holes and mended if possible. Fine stockings and fragile underwear, as well as washable gloves, were always washed by the maid. In many cases the meticulous maid refused to let anyone but herself launder items of special fineness. This was more reasonable than it perhaps appeared since mending these fragile items was her very special task.

Most ladies' maids were never asked to wait up for their employer beyond a reasonably early hour. Those who sat up late were permitted to sleep comparatively late in the morning.

On duty, a lady's maid wore a dark skirt, a white blouse, and either a small white apron, the band of which buttoned in the back, or else a small, round-cornered, black taffeta apron with a narrow self-ruffle. This neither tied nor buttoned at the back. Her aprons were supplied by her employer; otherwise she always wore her own clothes. These, however, were very quiet in color and of shirtwaist plainness. She never wore a cap.

THE VALET AND HOUSEMAN

The valet (pronounced VAL-et, not valLAY) was what Beau Brummell called a gentleman's gentleman. He kept his employer's clothes in perfect order, brushed, cleaned, and pressed everything as soon as it had been worn, laid out the clothes to be put on, and put away everything that was a personal belonging. Some gentlemen, particularly those who were very old, liked their valets to help them dress, run the bath, shave them, and hold each article in readiness as it was to be put on. But most merely required that their clothes be laid out for them in good order.

The valet also unpacked the bags of any gentlemen guests when they arrived, valeted them while there, and packed again when they left. He always packed for his own gentleman, bought tickets, looked after the luggage, and made himself generally useful as a personal attendant, whether at home or when traveling.

THE CHILDREN'S NURSE

Everybody knew fifty years ago that the children's nurse was either the comfort or the torment of the house. Many an excellent cook left an otherwise satisfactory job because the nurse was upsetting the kitchen routine. Not only was it important to have a sweet-tempered, competent, and clean person. Her character was of utmost concern, for she was the constant and inseparable companion of children whose whole lives were influenced by her example, especially if busy parents could give only a small portion of time to their children.

When the mother of the children cared very much about appearances, their nurse was always dressed in white in the house. On the street she might have worn a simple suit or dress and hat. To dress any nurse in the cloak and cap of the English nurse was suitable only if she actually was British.

OTHER HOUSEHOLD ASSISTANTS

In addition to those regularly employed on the staff of any large establishment there were others whose assistance was required from time to time or on special occasions—the tutor, the registered nurse, and so forth. The companion was sometimes a permanent member of any staff, or she could be employed on a temporary basis in a home with no staff at all. In the same way, one household might have required the services of a social secretary at all times, whereas another family employed her for only a few months, to handle the details of their daughter's elaborate wedding, for example.

THEN—AND NOW

And so, back to the present day.

Gone are the footmen, and most of the butlers and chambermaids, but the chores they performed remain, and must be taken care of by the help which is available today. Thanks to the conveniences and appliances found in modern homes, the work that used to be done by many can now be done by one or two. This is not to say that there are no homes with a large staff. There are some, and the duties of those staffs are divided in much the same way as they were in the "great house" of yesterday. Their work, of course, is considerably lighter—thanks to modern appliances—than that described above.

But the vast majority of home owners who have live-in servants have no more than one or two, and it is to these people that the rest of this chapter is devoted.

COUPLES

A satisfactory solution to the problem of household help for many families who have large houses but cannot or do not wish to employ many servants is the married couple who are hired together. The work is divided according to the abilities of the man and wife, but the most usual arrangement is for the woman to do the cooking and to clean the bedroom floors, while the man waits on table, cleans the living rooms, dining room, halls, etc., and also does some driving and takes care of the cars. They share the work of cleaning up after meals, and he may also help with their preparation, especially if the employer is entertaining.

The couple must have an apartment of at least two rooms, preferably with a private entrance, perhaps over a garage. Some employers do not object if a child lives with the parents, but it must be understood in advance that he or she will not be disturbing in any way and will not be allowed the run of the house except when playing with the children of the employer.

THE BABY-SITTER

With smaller family houses and small-apartment living, the shortage of a "live-in" staff has, especially for young people, created a special demand—and baby-sitters have achieved both amateur and professional standing. Age of sitters may range from the early teens, if he or she is a responsible youngster and fond of children, up to elderly ladies. In the intermediate group, many high school and college boys and girls and young business women are glad to supplement their allowances or salaries by baby-sitting a few times a week.

In many large cities, girls who live in residential clubs post their names to indicate their availability for baby-sitting, and mothers in the neighborhood may avail themselves of this service. In some communities there are agencies that provide approved sitters at standard rates.

As the rate of payment varies in different localities, no set schedule can be fixed. But the customary rate of the community should be observed, and the sitter should be paid at the end of the evening. The sitter should be told that after the children are asleep she (or he) may use the television set or play the radio, read, or do homework. In some households a sitter is permitted to ask a girlfriend to keep her company, but she may never entertain a boy when "sitting." In other words, it should be clearly understood what she is expected to do and what she may not do. It is thoughtful to leave a snack in the refrigerator—the hours can become long and tiresome. Be specific about where you are going—leave address and telephone number, as well as the name, address, and telephone number of the children's doctor. Always tell the sitter when you expect to be back—and try to be on time.

Adequate transportation must be provided for the sitter's safe return home, and this applies for sitters of any age.

PART-TIME HELP

The maid, or "cleaning woman" who comes by the hour or day should be treated with the same courtesy that is expected by the permanent servant. She should be paid promptly, daily, weekly, or in any other way agreed upon.

If the house is far from public transportation, the employer must see that she is transported to bus or train or, if she is not, that her pay is augmented to cover taxi fare.

If the lady of the house wishes her to wear uniforms, she naturally provides them for her. The part-time cleaning woman often prefers to wear her own clothes covered by a large apron, but if she wishes to wear a uniform in order to save her clothes, she may ask her employer to buy one or two.

The maid's duties should be carefully outlined in advance. Will there be cooking to do? Are washing and ironing expected, and what about heavy cleaning like waxing floors and washing windows? All these points should be clearly understood on both sides, and if she is asked to do any unusual work or stay on late, to help with a dinner party, for example, her hourly rate for this extra service should be agreed upon beforehand.

THE REGISTERED NURSE

The social position of a registered hospital nurse is, of course, that of a deputy physician and, if on a long case, the closest of the family's friends. She always eats her meals with the family or has them served to her on a tray in a sitting room. She never eats in the kitchen unless that is where the family also eats.

When on duty in her patient's room or anywhere in a private house, she wears her uniform. But when going into the street, going downstairs in a hotel, or traveling with her patient, she dresses as does any other lady.

THE MOTHER'S HELPER

Many young couples with young children need an all-around helper more than they need a specialist such as a cook or a nurse.

The duties of a "mother's helper" are generally related to the care of the children—their meals, their rooms, and their clothes. If there are only one or two children, her chores may also include some light housework, some laundry, some cooking, and some washing up. It is essential, because of the loosely defined nature of the job, that the areas and amount of work to be done are discussed and settled upon before the position is accepted. Too often a woman is hired to "take care of the children" and, because no guidelines were laid down in the beginning, eventually finds herself taking care of the whole house as well.

The relationship of a "mother's helper" and her family is usually quite different from that of other servants and employers. She often, over a period of time, becomes almost a member of the family. In some cases she may eat her meals with them, but this can become somewhat of a strain, because every couple is entitled to its privacy and the privilege of being alone. When there are young children in the family, the ideal solution is for her to eat dinner with them at an earlier hour, except, perhaps, on Sundays and special occasions. Some perceptive "mother's helpers," in order to avoid imposing, simply say that they prefer to eat earlier, or to watch television at that hour, or make some other excuse. But she, with the children, may join the family for a while before dinner if she wishes, and once the children are in bed, her time should be her own.

A great many young girls come from abroad to fill this position, and they have their special problems. They generally contract to come for a ridiculously low salary, for a period of one year. But the housewife who does not realize that the wage, even though agreed upon, is often completely inadequate in our economy, will find herself with a very unhappy employee. She will also find, if she does not voluntarily offer to pay a reasonable amount, that her mother's helper may suddenly be wooed away by an offer of higher wages from one of the neighbors. These girls are often highly educated, and take the job as a means of getting to the United States. Their background is frequently the same or better than that of the people they are working for. When this is so, it is even more necessary, if the year is to be a success, and possibly to extend to more years, that her employers make every effort to make their "helper" feel at home. Although she need not be included when they are entertaining or when they are alone as a family, she should be a welcome member of the group.

79

The employer-servant relationship

In these days of "do-it-yourself" housekeeping, a large household staff is rare indeed. A moderate number of households have one maid living in, but the most that a great majority of the women of today expect is to have help with the housecleaning chores once or twice a week. Beyond that, they may hire a combination cook-waitress to assist on a special occasion.

Everyone who ever employs a servant is at some point faced with the problem of doing so for the first time. Even the young woman who has grown up in a household with a large staff is confronted by a new situation when she begins to look for her own maid for her own home. Too many people give too little thought to what is involved in the employer-servant relationship, not only when they interview applicants, but throughout the months and years that follow.

If you have never kept house before and do not know what a maid should be able to do, you can go to a reliable employment office where the personnel will tell you about hours and wages and an average working plan. On the other hand, if you advertise in the paper, then you could perhaps ask a friend whose household is similar to your own to give you advice on making a fair and practical schedule.

INTERVIEWING AN APPLICANT

If the applicant has a written reference from her last employer, read it carefully but do not put too much stock in it. Most housewives hesitate to write down derogatory comments and then give them to their ex-employees. A written reference is worthwhile only if it gives the name and telephone number of the writer. Before hiring anyone, the housewife should take advantage of that information because she will get a far more complete and honest appraisal over the phone than the note of reference can possibly give.

Let us say that the references of an applicant are good and that the wages you can pay meet her expectations. Let us say, too, that you find her personality pleasing. (Perhaps this feeling is not always reliable, but it is an important point to consider.)

The next move is to give her briefly but accurately the schedule of both working and time-off hours. Accuracy is emphasized because careless misrepresentation of facts or intentions is unfair. It is unfair, for example, to assure the maid that she is to have no care of the baby and then gradually ask that she do just about everything that would be expected of a nurse—as well as her other work.

Another important point is to try to visualize what you offer her as well as what you expect of her. Don't say that you are always prompt when you are not; don't say that your meals will be very simple and then expect her to be an expert chef. Don't say that you don't entertain much, when you regularly give Saturday night dinner parties. Don't say that her work will take a certain number of hours a day without having the vaguest notion of how much work can be reasonably expected in this length of time. At the other extreme, it isn't necessary to exaggerate whatever inconveniences there may perhaps be, particularly when there will be much compensating pleasantness that could make her quite happy with you.

HOW MUCH WORK?

The details of just how much, and just what, one maid should do constitute a subject that is almost impossible to treat in a general statement, because her work must be adjusted not only to the needs of the particular family by whom she is employed, but also to her own capability.

Out of every twenty-four hours, every normal human being should have at least nine hours for sleeping, dressing, and undressing, in addition to plenty of time for eating three meals. During the rest of the day, she must find the time for rest and recreation as well as for work. It is impossible to establish a fixed schedule for working hours and time off, because these are in many cases subject to personal requirements and agreements. But her days off should be clearly stated and respected. If it is absolutely necessary to change a day off, she must be given ample warning so that she may change her own plans.

MAY SERVANTS ENTERTAIN FRIENDS?

Of course they may! Domestic help often enjoy entertaining friends just as their employers do, and whenever their duties are finished, and it does not interfere with plans of the people they work for, they should be allowed this privilege.

In a house where no sitting room for a maid is possible, one end of the kitchen can sometimes be attractively fixed up for her leisure hours. Or the maid's room, especially one on the ground floor, may be furnished as a sitting room.

In homes with one servant, the relationship is sometimes on such a friendly basis that the use of the living room is offered the maid when the family is not at home. Naturally, she and her friends should not abuse this privilege by helping themselves to cigarettes or liquor. If he wishes, the man of the house may suggest that her caller will find a beer or soft drink in the refrigerator. The maid, of course, makes the room immaculate when her friends leave.

UNIFORMS

All maids' uniforms as well as aprons and collars and cuffs are furnished by the employer, with the exception, possibly, of those worn by a cook, for whom the employer furnishes only the aprons.

AN ATTRACTIVE ROOM

Now let us go to the day of your new maid's arrival. Try to imagine yourself in her place and take pains to make her room as attractive as possible. Surely nothing could be more discouraging to any normal young woman—or to an older one, for that matter—than to arrive in a strange place, which is to be her "home," and be taken to a drab and comfortless room, all too plainly furnished with the family discards.

After all, a comfortable bed, attractively painted furniture, and a little becoming chintz are not very difficult to supply, especially in this day of spray paints which can be put on by the merest amateur. In other words, dingy brown and "landlord cream" are inexcusable. The same attention to attractiveness and convenience should be evident in the kitchen—where most maids work and take their meals, and where they may also spend much of their leisure time.

COURTESY ON BOTH SIDES

Years ago the Worldlys' butler was called Hastings, not John. The housekeeper was Mrs. Jones, and the nurse was called by her name or a nickname such as "Nanny." In the less formal household of today, the maid may be called by her nickname, or if she is an older woman, she may be called Mrs. Helper.

Every courteous person says "please" in asking that something be brought to her or him. "Would you turn on the lights, please," or "Some bread, please." One can, of course, put a smile into one's tone and say, "A little more bread!" But usually one who is well mannered instinctively adds "please." No lady or gentleman barks, "Turn on the lights!" or "Give me the bread!" In refusing a dish at the table one says, "No, thank you," or "No, thanks." Children must be taught these courtesies at the earliest possible age.

ON THE OTHER SIDE

The satisfactory maid is neat in appearance, quiet in manner, and speaks in a low voice.

She answers her employer, "Yes, Mrs. Grant" or "Mr. Grant." Possibly she may say, "Yes, Sir," but never "Yes," "No," "O.K.," or "Sure."

The nurse, and all other maids, call the young children by their first names or nicknames.

SUCCESS IN HOUSEHOLD MANAGEMENT

Those who have servant trouble might do well to remember a basic rule that is often overlooked: Justice must be the foundation upon which every tranquil household is constructed. Work must be as evenly divided as possible; one servant should not be allowed liberties not accorded to all.

This, perhaps, explains why some people are always having a trouble—finding servants difficult to get and more difficult to keep. It is a question whether the servant problem is not more often an employer problem. I'm sure it is! Because, if you notice, families who have woes and complaints invariably have them continually, just as others never have any trouble at all. It does not depend on the size of the house; the Lovejoys never have any trouble, and yet their one maid-of-all-work has a far-from-easy job.

It is not fair to be too lenient, any more than it is just to be unreasonably demanding. To allow impertinence or sloppy work is a mistake, but it is also inexcusable to show causeless irritability or to be overbearing or rude. And there is no greater example of injustice than to reprimand people about you because you happen to be in a bad humor, and at another time to overlook offenses that are greater because you are in an amiable mood. There is also no excuse ever for correcting an employee in front of anyone else.

In analyzing the spirit pervading happy houses, I think it will be found to consist of the understanding and fairness that are shown by both sides. Proper pride on the part of an employee demands that he or she give fair value for wages received. On the other side, the obligation of the lady of the house and the other members of the family is to show understanding and fairness in what they require. If their point of view is just, and if they themselves are kind and trustworthy, then they naturally believe that people serving them have the same traits, and they are very unlikely ever to have any housekeeping difficulties.

80

Setting the table for family meals

In the average home the lady of the house (or possibly one maid) prepares, serves, and cleans up after the meals, and as a result, the number of courses, dishes, and implements is kept to a minimum. But simplification should not mean sloppiness, and the following suggestions are important in the most informal of households.

THE TABLE

In many of today's houses and apartments, the pressures of space and expense have caused the formal dining room to disappear. The dining table appears in any one of a number of other places—in an ell or an alcove off the living room, in the end of the living room nearest the kitchen, sometimes in a wide hall, or in the kitchen. The location of the table does not affect its use, however, and even though it may not have the formal surroundings that it did in Grandmother's day, it should be thought of as a pleasant center of family gatherings.

The table itself should be large enough to accommodate the entire family comfortably. A pretty cloth or attractive place mats (in any material that is easily wiped clean or laundered) should always be used, not only to protect the table top, but also to lend an air of graciousness to even the simplest meal. Although not necessary, a centerpiece is pleasing. With a little help, children can arrange a few flowers or make a simple table decoration for some particular holiday or special occasion. Such contributions add to the family's enjoyment of mealtime and help the children recognize the importance of household appointments as well.

Seating arrangements at table depend entirely on the convenience of the family. Most often, when there is no maid, the mother sits nearest the kitchen door with the youngest children who may still need help from time to time next to her. The place opposite hers is the father's. Some families make a tradition of seating a birthday child as the guest of honor would be seated at a formal dinner, a custom that is flattering to the child and at the same time provides practice in the behavior that will be expected of him when he is older.

KITCHEN DINING

Some families, even though they have a formal dining room, prefer the coziness and convenience of the kitchen when dining alone. Many others, as mentioned above, have no dining rooms. In either case, if space permits, it is most desirable to have an end or corner of the kitchen set apart, furnished or decorated in such a way that children growing up in the home feel the importance of good manners at any table, no matter where it may be. When there is no such space, the ordinary kitchen table must do, but an extra effort should be made to make the room attractive and to make sure that the table is uncluttered and clean.

Even a kitchen table should be nicely set for dinner, with place mats (even though they may be paper doilies), spotless utensils (although they may be stainless steel), and pretty plates and glasses, attractive in color and pattern (no matter if they were bought at the local "five and ten").

THE PLACE SETTINGS

The main difference in setting a table for guests and setting a table for the family is that for family a minimum number of utensils is put at each place—only those absolutely necessary for each course. Very often there may be no more than two or three pieces of silver: a fork, a knife, and a spoon or fork for dessert. At a family dinner it is certainly not necessary to have a separate fork for salad, but a salad plate is another matter. Who could wish to have the gravy and salad dressing run together into an unsavory soup, or the salad wilt on a heated plate?

Butter plates and knives are often omitted, and the bread and butter are placed on the edge of the dinner plate, but with the convenience of an electric dishwasher, it is far nicer to have a separate plate. This is especially true if the dinner plates are, as they should be, heated, because butter put on them melts at once. Or you may place the butter on the side of the salad plate to reduce the number of dishes.

The table settings described in the following sections indicate the correct positions of whatever articles might be used. No china or silver that will not actually be used needs to be put on the table—no dessert spoon if you are not serving dessert, no bread and butter plate if you have no bread.

BREAKFAST

More often than at other meals, there is a wide difference in the tastes of breakfast-eaters. Some people, teen-age girls especially, prefer to eat no breakfast at all—or perhaps a piece of toast and a glass of milk. Many women take only a cup of coffee and a glass of juice, while others eat a hearty morning meal and watch their calories at lunch time. Men and boys generally like a more substantial meal, sometimes two or three courses, including fruit, cereal, and eggs. Unlike other meals, breakfast may, and should, be prepared "to order." That is, if daughter Susie truly dislikes eggs, she may be given a dish of cold cereal, but Father should not therefore be deprived of his scrambled eggs and bacon.

In setting the breakfast table, Mother puts out just those utensils which will be needed by each person.

A variety of cold cereals, milk, cream, sugar, salt and pepper, and jams or jellies may be placed in the center of the table or on a convenient side table, but whoever is doing the cooking serves the hot food directly onto the plates and places them in front of those sitting at the table. If your table is large enough, a "lazy susan" or turntable is most convenient and makes each item easily accessible to everyone.

If breakfast is served by a maid in the dining room, the setting is as follows:

Fork at left of plate.

Knife at right of plate.

Spoon for cereal at right of knife.

Teaspoon for fruit (but not for coffee) at right of cereal spoon.

Butter knife across bread-and-butter plate, which is to the left and above fork.

Napkins at left of plates if fruit or fruit juice is at places; otherwise, napkins at the center of each place.

Coffee cups with spoons lying at right of saucers, at the right of each plate if coffee is served from the kitchen. If it is served by the lady of the house at the table, cups and saucers and tea- or coffeepot are beside her place.

Glass for milk or water, to the right and above spoons.

LUNCH

For the busy woman of today, lunch usually consists of a sandwich, a bowl of soup, or a salad. It may be served at the dining-room table if there is a maid, or it may be brought to the living room or patio on a tray. When children are home for lunch, it can be served either at the dining table or in the kitchen, according to the preference of the family. If the man of the house has lunch at home, he will probably want a more substantial meal, and the table is set in accordance with the food to be served. In the simple household—unless the main meal is eaten at midday, in which case the table is set as for dinner—no more than three courses are ever served for lunch, and even that number is most unusual. The setting is as follows:

Salad fork at left, next to plate, if salad is to be served after meat.

Meat fork at left of salad fork.

On the right, a meat knife; and at the right of this knife, a bouillon or fruit spoon, if necessary.

Butter plate and knife above forks at left.

Because dessert, if served, is brought in after the main course, the dessert fork or spoon may be brought in with the dessert plate.

DINNER

If the food is to be passed, the dinner plates are at each place on the table when the family sits down or they are stacked in front of the head of the household if he is to serve. However, many women prefer to serve the plates directly from the stove in order to avoid the use of extra platters and serving dishes. The table setting for dinner is similar to that for lunch:

At left of plate, salad fork (if necessary), then dinner fork.

At right, the dinner knife next to plate, then the soup spoon or the oyster fork or fruit spoon on the outside (if necessary).

Glass or goblet for beverage at right above knife.

Butter plate to left and above fork, with butter knife laid on it diagonally from upper left to lower right.

In every case, the implements necessary for each course are arranged in order of their use. The one to be used first goes on the outside; that to be used last is put nearest the plate. Dessert spoon and fork may be brought in on the dessert plate after the table is cleared; otherwise the fork goes next to the plate on the left, and the spoon immediately to the right of the knife.

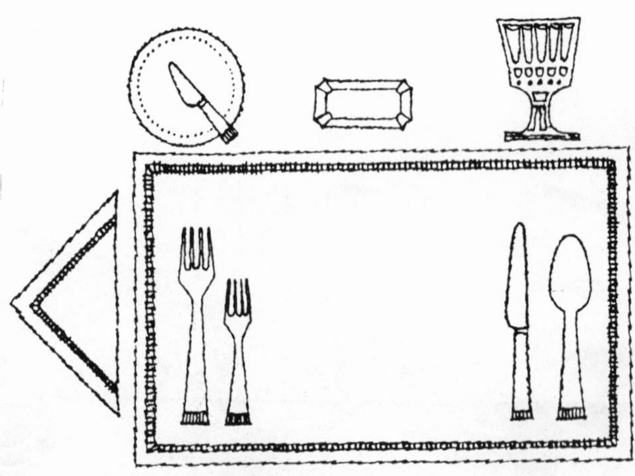

THE MEALTIME TRAY

Although few women in a simple household are served breakfast on a tray, there are many occasions when a member of the family is ill and must remain in bed for his meals. An attractive tray with a flower in a little vase or a gay napkin and tray cloth can do much to aid a lagging appetite and a sagging spirit.

For all meals, the tray is covered with a tray cloth or, if you do not have special tray linen, a doily of any sort. The setting is the same as the individual place setting at the table insofar as space permits. The dessert plate and the coffee cup and saucer are usually brought when the main meal is finished because of lack of room. The dinner plate should be heated and covered if the meal is hot. If you do not have a regular domed plate cover, a piece of foil laid over the food will keep it warm while the tray is carried to its destination.

Individual breakfast sets for trays are available and often given as wedding presents. They generally include an egg cup, a cereal bowl, two or three plates and a cover, coffee cup and saucer, sugar bowl, cream pitcher, and a small coffeepot. They come in gay patterns or lovely solid colors and by the very charm of their appearance make the morning more cheerful.

Part FIFTEEN

FAMILY LIFE

81

The young child

I have often been asked how best to teach rules of etiquette to young people, and whether there are special rules which they should be taught. The most important thing to realize is that etiquette applies to everyone, old or young, and that the best way to teach etiquette to children is the best way to teach anything—by instruction, consistency, firmness, and example. Indeed, children are people—and parents and teachers will do well to remember it.

Children who are spoken to in baby talk and treated as if they were adorable idiots are inclined to act like babies or idiots. But children who are treated as interesting individuals with minds of their own will react by trying to prove that they *are* intelligent and that they *are* individuals.

Children can scarcely be too young to be taught the rudiments of etiquette, nor can the teaching be too patiently or too conscientiously carried out. Any child can be taught to be well behaved with no effort greater than patience and perseverance, whereas to break bad habits once they are acquired is a herculean task.

FAIR PLAY

Quite young children are able to understand the principles of justice, and they should be taught, even before they go to school, to "play fair," to respect each other's property and rights, to give credit to others, and not to take too much credit to themselves. They must be taught to share playthings and to take good care of their own toys as well as those that belong to other children. A bright, observing child should never be encouraged to brag about his own achievements or to tell his or her mother how inferior other children are. If he wins a medal at school or is praised, the family naturally rejoice, and it is proper that they should; but a wise mother teaches her child that selfishness and conceit will get him nowhere.

"BECAUSE EVERYONE ELSE DOES"

All young people feel a need to conform to the activities of others of their age. This they express in their speech, their play, their choice of clothing, and their relationships to each other. This conformity is quite normal and is to be respected as part of the development of individual personality as well as of social responsibility. Adults, after all, conform to their world too. Young people in time learn that through conformity with most of the social customs of the adult world they will be able to take their place in that world.

Children should be permitted to follow the customs of their community, so as not to differ too radically from the other children in the neighborhood. However, there are necessary and obvious qualifications to this advice. It is possible for children to be well brought up even though the community where the family lives may seem to have accepted lower standards of behavior than the family's own. The phrase one hears so often from children—"Everyone else does thus-and-so"—is not sufficient excuse for lowering standards. Surely, to take an extreme example, no one could condone cheating at games or on examinations just "because everyone else does."

Of course, parents sometimes must make a decision at the risk of having their children a little different in some particular from their friends. There are times when children should be required to set an example, rather than following others. There is a certain element of risk involved in this position, but there is also an element of discipline that is far more important.

Parents and teachers must never underestimate the problems that a child has in adapting himself to a world full of contradiction that can only be explained by experience.

EATING HABITS

The first requirement in table manners is neatness. When children are a year and a half to two years old, they will begin to learn to feed themselves, and while they are too little to be taught the refinements of truly good manners, it is not too soon to start them in the right direction. From the very first, they can be encouraged to keep the food on the plate, taught how to hold a cup so that it will not spill, and shown the use of a bib or napkin. These skills do not come naturally, but with patient repetition and gentle insistence they can be acquired.

As soon as the child has learned to eat well enough so that his presence at the table is not offensive, he should be allowed to eat with adults, occasionally at first, and more often as his manners improve. When he becomes a member of the family group at meals, there are more advanced lessons to be learned.

He must be clean and neat when he comes to the table.

He must chew quietly, with his mouth closed.

He must not overload his spoon or fork.

He must not interrupt the adults, but at the same time, he should be included in the conversation. If it is beyond his understanding, his mother or father should from time to time introduce a subject that is within his range of interests.

He must not fidget or play with his food or the implements at his place.

He must use his fork and spoon properly and never leave the spoon in his cup or bowl.

If he finishes before the others, he must ask, "May I please be excused?" and wait for permission before leaving the table. Very young children should be given this privilege, because if they are forced to remain at the table when their food is gone, they are sure to resort to wriggling, fiddling, and noise-making to pass the time.

If he refuses to be good, the best course is to say nothing but lead him as quietly as possible from the table. The child will learn much more quickly to be well behaved if he understands that good behavior is the price of admission to grown-up society.

There are many ways in which the child's mother can help to pave the way for him. His plate should be brought to the table ready for him to eat. The portions should be of small or moderate size—never a heaping plateful. Meat should be cut in small bite-size pieces, as should vegetables such as asparagus and string beans. To avoid accidents, his glass or cup should have a broad base and be of plastic or pottery. If he is very small, his fork and spoon should be of appropriate size. He should wear a bib large enough so that an accidental spill will not ruin his clothes. And he should either sit in his high chair or have cushions on a regular chair that will raise him to the proper height. If you think this is unimportant, try sometime to eat neatly while kneeling at a table that comes approximately to the level of your chin.

All these small aids put together help to make the child look forward to his meal with pleasure, rather than as a time of strain. Mealtime should, above all, be pleasant. The child who sees his family enjoying their food and enjoying each other's company cannot help but follow their example. Constant nagging and correction are as detrimental as a total lack of instruction. If older children are allowed to complain about the food, if Father refuses to eat anything but steak and potatoes, and if there are continuous arguments at the table, the young child will come to dread the dinner hour, and the unhappy associations will result in antagonism to food and to good manners in eating.

MONEY MATTERS

From the time a child is old enough to buy a candy bar or an ice cream cone for himself, he should be given a small, regular allowance. In return, he should be expected to perform certain chores, such as helping with the dishes or keeping his room neat. But extra duties—washing the dog or running an errand—deserve special consideration and are paid for separately if the parents feel that they merit a reward. Only by having money of their own can children begin to appreciate its value, and they should be permitted to use an allowance as they wish. The amount must be decided upon by considering what uses the money will be put to and the approximate amount small friends are given. It is as bad for a child to have twice as much as the neighborhood children (even though his parents can well afford it) as it is to have him always saying, "I can't go to the movies with you—I don't have enough money." Some parents give the child more allowance but insist that a part be set aside for the weekly church contribution or that a certain sum be put in a piggy bank or otherwise saved for birthday presents or a special hobby or treat. This seems to me to be a wise system, as the child acquires a sense of the value of money that he cannot have if the parents simply put his quarter in the plate each Sunday or pay for the birthday presents as the dates arrive.

As the child grows, so must his allowance, and so must the expenses he is expected to pay for himself. If he is working toward something worthwhile that he really cares about, his parents will be wise to encourage him by giving him extra chores which they may pay for at an hourly rate and by adding to his fund with a small check for Christmas or birthday.

A CHILD'S APPEARANCE

Speaking of children who wish to buy a bit of extra clothing with their allowance brings up the subject of clothes. As soon as a child shows any interest in what he is wearing, he should be allowed a voice in choosing his clothes. Naturally, his mother must make the final decision, as a little child will not consider cost, practicality, or suitability, but within the limits of these requirements, the child can be given a choice of garments. He will thus absorb some principles of dressing well, and he will also be happy to wear the clothes that are bought for him.

There are several offenses committed by doting mothers that should be avoided.

Don't overdress your child. If he or she is invited to a party, ask the mother of the host or hostess what type of clothing will be appropriate. Nothing could make a little girl more miserable than to wear a frilly organdy dress to a party that turns out to be an outdoor barbecue. Even school clothes should conform to those of the other children. If wearing ties is not required of the small boys, let your son go in a sports shirt, and if the girls all wear brown loafers, don't insist on patent-leather slippers.

Never dress your child in clothes that are too old for him. Your three-year-old dressed in long gray flannels and a sports jacket may look, to you, too "cute" for words, but it is as inappropriate as his father going to business in shorts and an Eton jacket.

Little girls should never wear high heels, even moderately high, before they reach their teens.

Don't let little girls wear makeup or dress their hair elaborately. Of course they want to imitate Mommy, but let them play at being grown up in the privacy of their rooms or at a costume party, but never in public. This is not to say that their hair should not be arranged in an attractive, simple style and neatly combed. They have many years ahead when they will need makeup to enhance their looks, but until then, the natural fresh glow of youth is the most attractive sight in the world.

CHILDREN'S PARTIES

A child's party that has been well planned can be a joy to everyone. Parties for very young children, under six, let us say, should be quite short, preferably not more than two hours long. The span of attention of tiny children is very limited, and they also tire quickly, which leads to crankiness and naughtiness. Refreshments should be simple to allow the mother and her assistants more time for supervision and less time in the kitchen. Also, a large amount of rich food can upset little stomachs that are already in a turmoil with excitement. Finally, to avoid confusion and permit better organization, the guest list should be short. Five or six guests would be ample for a second birthday party, and ten or twelve should be the limit for a six- to eight-year-old. The formula for a successful party for the very young is as follows:

Guests arrive at four. One half-hour is allowed for opening presents and letting off steam. One hour of organized games or entertainment follows. A magician is always popular, and comedy movies, if you have a projector or can borrow one, are invariably a great success. Treasure hunts, "pin-the-tail-on-the-donkey," musical chairs for tiny children, and guessing games, a "three-legged" race, or other contests for older ones, all help to make the hour fly. At five-thirty refreshments are served. A sandwich (peanut butter and jelly cannot be surpassed for popularity), ice cream, and the birthday cake are all that are necessary. If the weather is warm, a fruit punch, soda, or ice-cold milk may be served, and in the winter hot chocolate is always welcome.

Parties for older children can be extended to two and a half or three hours if enough entertainment is planned. Games can be more complicated, thus taking more time, and a short feature movie could be shown rather than "shorts." A scavenger hunt is always popular outside the city, or if you have the use of a swimming pool, that may be all that is necessary to have a successful summer party. As children reach the age of ten or eleven or even older, hay rides, sleigh rides, trips to baseball or football games, or circuses or rodeos become more fun than the "game party" at home. When a group is taken to this sort of entertainment, the invitation should make it clear whether or not lunch or supper will be provided and whether the guests should take money of their own for snacks or souvenirs. Remember, when planning a trip to the ball park or anywhere, a small group will be easier to chaperon, it will be less expensive, and your child will enjoy it every bit as much as a large rambunctious crowd.

If the birthday child is old enough, he may help in deciding on the guest list, sending out invitations, and setting the table. A girl may even help prepare the refreshments—mixing the cake batter or making sandwiches.

Whether they are three or ten, the essential manners for party guests are identical. They must say "Hello" to their host and the host's mother when they arrive, and they must shake hands and say, "Good-bye, and thank you for a wonderful time" when they leave. The young host or hostess must, in turn, greet them when they come and, in answer to their farewell, say, "Good-bye, and thanks again for the present," or "Good-bye. Thank you for coming."

PARENTS AND CHILDREN

First and foremost, every parent must realize that each child is an individual and, as such, must be treated with respect. There are thousands of books and articles in print on the subject of bringing up children, and many of them offer valuable advice, but their suggestions must be tempered to suit the personality and the specific problems of your child.

THE PARENT'S ATTITUDE

The first outward sign of respect you can show your toddler is not to talk *down* to him. Of course you must use simple words and sentences or he will not understand you at all, but "baby talk" is an insult to the intelligence of a normal child and does nothing to encourage him to increase his vocabulary or to speak as fluently as possible.

This same attitude of treating a child as an individual carries through to your judgment of what he can or cannot do. I have found that most children are far more capable than their elders can believe. If you expect good behavior or assume that your child will react to a situation in a reasonable way, you will generally find that he will live up to your expectations. If, however, you start out by saying to Johnny, "I'll cut your meat for you, dear—you're too little," he will certainly not be encouraged to make the effort to learn to do it himself. One word of warning, however: This can be overdone, and nothing will frustrate Johnny more than being required to do things that he simply is not capable of handling. To scold him for not being able to do up his snaps or buttons will quickly cause him to rebel against all attempts to teach him to dress himself.

Study your child as an interesting person, increase his responsibilities as he seems able to cope with them, reprove him when he falls short, and praise him when he takes a step forward. Include him in your conversation, correcting his mistakes and teaching him new words, and share as many family activities with him as you can. Don't laugh at his mistakes or ridicule him, but at the same time, try to appreciate his developing sense of humor, and laugh *with* him. Encouragement, appreciation, and lots of love are the most essential elements in a baby's happy environment.

OBEYING THE RULES

Little children must be taught from their earliest years that there are certain rules that have to be obeyed. You may be one of the many parents who believe in self-regulating schedules for small children (I happen to believe that a certain amount of regulation is better for both children and their parents), but this does not mean that they cannot be taught the rules that govern the relationship between themselves and other people. I firmly believe that too much permissiveness can contribute to delinquency. Young people, no matter what they may say aloud, want and need direction and correction, and the more honest ones will even admit it. I have actually heard a young girl say, "I wish my mother would say 'No'—then I woudn't have to make up my mind."

PUNISHMENT

The single most important thing about disciplining a child is to make your point and stick to it. If you say "No" to an extra half-hour at bedtime, and then say "Yes" when Susie says, "But Mommy, this is my favorite TV program," how will Susie ever know whether you mean what you say or not? Nor will she have much respect for your decisions.

The severity of the punishment should be directly related to the seriousness of the misdeed. If it is a minor infraction, it should not result in a major penalty, or you will have nowhere to go when a more serious misdeed is committed, and the child will have no way of differentiating between an important and an unimportant offense. If possible, the punishment should be related to the error. If Judy, who loves cherries, insists on throwing her cherry pits on the floor, she might be deprived of her favorite fruit for several meals. Or if Johnny refuses to remove his muddy rubbers time after time, he might be forbidden to go out and play in the mud puddles the next time his best friend calls him.

Unless you know that you will be able to hold to them, don't make threats. When you have broken a threat once, your child will pay little attention when you make another. A simple one such as "Bobby, if you don't stop throwing the wrappers on the floor, I will have to take away the rest of your chewing gum" is all right, because it is simple and easily carried out, but to say, "Karen, if you don't go to bed at once, I won't let you go to kindergarten for a week," when you know perfectly well (and so does Karen) that she will be there the next morning, carries no weight at all and only makes you appear ridiculous in her eyes.

When a child has committed a serious misdeed, especially if he has repeated it after being corrected, take the time and trouble to explain the reason for the rule. The most obvious example of this, and unfortunately one of the commonest, is lighting matches and setting fires. I am not of the school that believes you should burn the child to prove your point, but for an offense as dangerous as this, punishment should be quick and severe. First show him, with paper or kerosene or however you can make it the most impressive, how quickly a fire can spread and explain the consequences from his point of view—his favorite toy would be burned up, his dog might be killed, etc. And then decide on the punishment that you think will make the deepest impression. It might be deprivation of certain privileges like watching television, or the cancellation of a longed-for treat, or something equally important. In extreme cases, where repeated admonitions and punishments have not brought any results, I believe there is no substitute for a good hard—not brutal—spanking, with the palm of Daddy's hand!

RESPECT

In the relation between children and their parents today, the quality that is most lacking is respect. In a large part, this is the result of the atmosphere that modern psychologists advocated when they went overboard in recommending that parents be "pals" with their children rather than continuing the normal relationship that has existed for centuries. If children are taught that their parents should have no authority over them and are simply their equals, regardless of age, education, and experience, how will respect arise? This trend, which fortunately has been somewhat modified and even reversed, showed itself in families whose children called their parents by their first names, where they were never required to rise when older people entered the room, nor adhere to any other special conventions. This resulted in a directionless youth, and rather than being mature, independent people, these children grew up as lazy, confused individuals, lacking respect not only for their parents, but for all society. If you as parents lead your youngsters to believe that your experience, your education, and your attitudes are worth emulating, respect will follow of its own accord. This, in turn, will be expanded, as your children grow up, to include relatives, friends, and, finally, more mature people of every sort.

82

The teen-ager

Boys and girls who have reached their teens have a whole new set of problems to face. This is the time when they really begin to emerge from the constant supervision of their parents and to develop independence and a social life of their own choosing. Because they are well on their way to becoming adults, they are expected to act in an adult manner, and they must make the adjustment from childhood, with its complete dependence on parental care, to adulthood, which brings not only the joys of independence but the trials as well.

Parents of teen-agers must try to recognize this transition. The wise mother and father will, from the very early teen years when the child is still "in between" and under a good deal of supervision, encourage him to make his own decisions, and offer him guidance and help rather than dictate to him.

THE EARLY TEENS

If parents have had a loving, intelligent relationship with their sons and daughters during childhood, with confidence and respect growing on both sides, the problems will be greatly modified. Even though the emotional makeup of a teen-ager is vastly more complicated and often more high-strung than that of younger children, the same characteristics of patience, give-and-take, and restraint will tide the family over what can be difficult years.

However, this is not a book designed to discuss the psychological aspects of the young, but rather to discuss their manners and what they should or should not do. Just remember, when making a rule or saying "No" to a teen-ager, to consider the importance of the decision to him (Does it really *matter* if Bob stays out a half-hour longer?), the customs of his friends and classmates, and whether it will actually help him, either from his own point of view or in the eyes of others. The last reason in the world for making a regulation is "Well, I always had to wash the dishes when I was your age!"

A family is a unit, but it is made up of individuals. Each of these individuals has his own likes and dislikes, his own talents, his own personality, which may clash violently with the characteristics of other members of his family. Parents must recognize these differences—there may even be actual antipathy between certain of their children—and in order to make the home a livable place, must work out a mode of conduct.

Every member of the family has a right to his own separate life and his privacy. Don't insist on involving yourself in every problem. For instance, if you see Sally and Anne having a serious discussion, don't ask, "What are you two talking about?" Leave them alone—if either one wants to tell you about it, or ask for advice, that is her choice, not yours.

It is most important that your teen-agers share, willingly, in the chores. It is up to you as parents to decide in what areas you need their assistance, and together you should settle on a reasonable schedule. In the interest of fairness, chores should be rotated, so that the monotony of doing the same old thing day after day will be avoided.

Enthusiasm for family projects is important, and up to a certain point you should insist that your youngsters participate. However, we all have moods and times when we just don't feel like taking part in a group activity. When this happens to one of your children, respect his feelings and don't force him. On the other hand, don't let him be a "wet blanket." Suggest that he go to his room and read, play records, or snooze until the mood passes.

In every way the parents must set the example. If they don't act in a reasonable and considerate way, their children certainly won't. There's nothing wrong in admitting a mistake, so when you are at fault, say so. If an apology is in order, make it. This will not lower your image in your children's eyes—it will only heighten their respect for your honesty and "human-ness."

If your children practice their manners with the family and your guests, they'll never have any problems in other homes, or among strangers. Of course you are going to relax some of the formalities at home, and life wouldn't be much fun if you didn't, but you must insist on unselfishness and consideration, the basic principles of etiquette.

One informality that should not be allowed is that of letting the youngsters call their parents by their first names, or cute nicknames. This is happening more and more today, and it is indicative of, and contributes to, the lack of respect many teen-agers feel for their elders. Parents are older and presumably wiser—if only because they have learned by more experience. They are entitled to respect from younger people, and the effort to put children and parents on an equal footing by such means as this first-name habit is unnatural and wrong.

When adult guests come to your home, your children have a wonderful chance to practice their manners. Teach them that a prompt, firm handshake is the proper response to an introduction. Urge them to come in and chat with your guests for a few minutes so that they will learn to be at ease with adults and to talk with them without self-consciousness. When they bring a stranger of their own age to the house, insist that they introduce him to you in the proper way, and by your own example, show them how much an enthusiastic and proper response to an introduction means.

Mealtime provides another opportunity for teaching good manners. Because it may well be the only hour of the day when your family is together, you should try to make it as pleasant as possible. Don't use that time to scold Jimmy for the mess in his room, or Sue for borrowing your sweater without asking. Try to keep the conversation on subjects of interest to everyone. A good, honest difference of opinion can be stimulating and educational for the youngsters. Let them hear your side, and pay them the courtesy of listening to theirs.

It is important for their own sakes—for the good impression they will make on others—as well as for the enjoyment of people who eat with them, that young people learn good table manners. Slouching, tipping the chair back, and fiddling all seem to be within the special province of the teen-ager, but not even the gangliest sixteen-year-old should be incapable of sitting still and upright in his chair. It is up to the parents to instill in him the importance of good posture. Since teen-agers' appetites are generally tremendous, they must be constantly reminded not to bolt their food, and to wait for the others at the table. Their faults are more likely to be errors committed than good habits omitted, and because they can hardly be sent to eat in another room like a child, their mothers and fathers must improve their manners with firm, patient, repeated corrections. In many cases, it is not willful disregard of directions

—they simply do not absorb them. Their minds are on a thousand other more interesting matters—girls, boys, parties, school, sports, ad infinitum—and the only hope of penetrating the screen is repetition, in the hope that eventually your words will "sink in." By the tone of your voice and the way you say it, repeated correction can avoid the undesirable effect of "nagging."

APPEARANCE

Most teen-agers from thirteen to nineteen have one trait in common. They apparently *like* to be sloppy. This applies not only to themselves but to their rooms and possessions. It doesn't seem to do much good to remind them that they will be more popular with the opposite sex if they have their hair combed and their clothes clean, nor are they interested in keeping warm in cold weather if no one else is wearing a coat. Shoes seem to be a forgotten item of clothing in the summer everywhere except in the largest cities. My feeling about this general attitude is that they be allowed to dress as casually as they please during vacations, in their own homes, on the beach, or at picnics. But at school (fortunately most schools set certain standards which the pupils must adhere to), at meals, on any excursion with adults, on all public conveyances, and at all social functions, they must be properly and neatly dressed. This does not mean that they should not go to an informal gathering without a tie and jacket. Of course they may wear a sports shirt, shorts, and sweater, or whatever the favorite local costume is, but the sweater and shirt should be clean, the hair combed, and shoes ON.

Young boys must be constantly reminded to wash and to shave. Nothing looks dirtier or messier than a stubble of whiskers on a young face, but many boys who are not accustomed to regular shaving habits simply do not realize that their beards are becoming heavier each year. The only way to achieve this is to keep after them day in and day out until it becomes a habit.

Teen-age girls need less urging to fix their hair—in fact most of them spend interminable hours under a hair dryer. What they do need is guidance as to style, length, becomingness, and good hygiene. Extreme styles should be avoided in the younger teen years—the simplest hairdo currently popular is generally the most becoming. As they get older, they will want to experiment with more complicated arrangements, and the only restriction should be that they refrain from becoming too extreme, for such styles invariably make a young girl look "cheap."

The same suggestions apply to makeup. A thirteen or fourteen year old may wear lipstick to a party, but it should be light in color and application. As she gets older, she may use a more vivid shade, and by the time she is sixteen or seventeen, she may choose any shade that goes well with her complexion as well as powder, a *very light* rouge if she is pale, and inconspicuous eye makeup. Heavily made-up eyes belong only on the stage or in the chorus line.

CLOTHING

Styles in clothing change so much that it is impossible to make hard and fast rules, but there are certain ones that are, and always have been, important. Again, avoid extremes. As always, those people, young or old, who have the most delightful manners and the greatest charm are those who do not go out of their way to attract attention.

ALLOWANCES

As children advance into their teens, allowances may become a question of what the parents can afford and how much responsibility the youngster himself wants to assume. Teen-age boys have more expenses than girls of the same age, and therefore their allowances may be raised sooner. They have to pay for their dates, they are likely to have the use of a car at a younger age than girls, and they generally wish to attain economic independence much sooner than their female counterparts.

The question of a "clothes allowance" usually arises in the middle teens. Some youngsters can't wait to be given enough money to dress themselves and pay all their own expenses, while others cling to the security of letting their parents pay for their clothes and receiving a small weekly or monthly "daily expenses" allowance. As a general rule, the year a boy or girl enters college, or reaches college age, is the time to give him or her financial independence.

But there is no set rule—the time might come a year or two earlier for a boy who is responsible and understands the value of money and the danger of wasting it, while the girl who has had little experience in shopping or managing a checking account should perhaps wait longer.

A system that seems to me to be excellent is practiced by one of my neighbors. Her daughter of fourteen, a sensible, intelligent girl, was most anxious to be given a clothes allowance. Rather than telling her that she was just too young or putting her on a large allowance all at once, the parents started her out with a monthly sum that was to cover school clothes—blouses, skirts, shoes, socks, underwear, etc.—but no expensive ones such as party dresses or overcoats. In this way she is learning to shop carefully and to understand the handling of money, but she does not have a large sum at her disposal, which might prove to be a temptation to spend irresponsibly. They plan to increase the sum and the variety of clothing she is expected to buy each year so that by the time she finishes high school, she will be completely responsible for her clothes and incidental expenses.

Most parents pay as much of their children's tuition at school and college as they can, but if it is too severe a strain on the family budget, teen-agers should certainly help as much as possible by applying for scholarships, working part-time at one of the jobs (in the cafeteria, dormitories, or library) that most college provide, or taking an evening job, preferably one like baby-sitting that will allow the student to study during those hours. Parents should never be ashamed to discuss the need for financial assistance of this sort with their children. Young men and women, if they really care about a good education, are more than willing to do what they can to attain it. If they have been brought up with love and respect for their families, they will never criticize parents who may not have amassed great wealth, but rather will take pride in what has been achieved.

As to the actual amounts for suitable allowances, it is impossible to say, because the requirements vary so in different areas. A city child needs more—every time he takes a bus or subway it costs him something, while his country cousin can ride the same distance on a bicycle. Prices are higher, too, in the city. Movies, food, and entertainment are much bigger budget items than the equivalent items in the country. The country boy might take his date to a square dance at the local grange for fifty cents or so, while the city boy, if he wishes to dance, must go to a night club or dance hall where the admission or cover charge may be as high as several dollars.

A possible scale for a weekly allowance, necessarily subject to change to fit the circumstances, might run something like this:

13–14 years	$1.00–2.00
15–17 years	4.00–5.00

When the teen-ager is older and it seems advisable to add a clothing allowance to his pocket money, he might receive a monthly amount something like this:

16–18 years	$25.00–35.00
18 and over	75.00–100.00

Naturally, a boy or girl receiving as much as one hundred dollars a month would be expected to pay all expenses such as school books, cleaning bills, etc.—everything, in other words, except tuition and doctors' bills.

LEARNING TO ENTERTAIN

Youngsters who learn how to entertain their friends nicely during their adolescence will have a good background for more formal and ambitious entertaining later on. Parents who encourage a child to invite his or her friends in reasonably often and who help him to plan and prepare parties will be more than rewarded by the young person's gratitude and enthusiasm. Because girls are more inclined to give parties than boys—just as it is the wife who plans a couple's social activities—my suggestions may be of special interest to young girls and their mothers. However, a boy who is planning a party may profit from them, too.

Although the following subjects should be discussed and decided on by mother and daughter (or son) together, the word "hostess" will refer to the daughter, since the party will, of course, be hers.

The most attractive written invitations for young people are the colorful cards available at all stationery stores. Your daughter may pick any one which is appropriate, and fill in the blanks with the necessary information. She may add R.S.V.P. with your telephone number below it, or she may, if she wishes, put "regrets only" with the number.

If she prefers to issue her invitations by telephone in order to get definite answers immediately, she may do so, but she runs the risk of her guests forgetting the date, the hour, or the location of the party.

THE GUEST LIST

Like adults, young people must choose congenial guests who will enjoy each other's company. A group of friends who all know each other well is easy and fun, but not particularly interesting or stimulating. On the other hand, a group of strangers who have little in common, or don't know that they do, can be a nightmare for the young hostess trying to get the party off the ground. A combination of a few friends and two or three "outsiders" works best, as long as the hostess sees that the strangers are included in conversation and activities.

The number of guests invited depends on, first, the size of your home, and second, the amount you can afford to spend. Discuss these questions frankly with your daughter. Overcrowded rooms and lack of space can ruin an otherwise good party, and grandiose ideas on your child's part, forgetting the family exchequer, must be restrained before she goes too far.

If it is to be a "singles" party, with invitations issued to both boys and girls, the hostess must see that there are even numbers, or extra boys. If only boys or only girls are sent invitations with "bring a date" written on them, those receiving them should let the hostess know whether they are successful in finding a date, and if so, who he or she is.

When a boy or girl is going steady, or has a previous date for the night of a "singles" party, it is perfectly proper to call and ask if the date may be included. At the same time, if it makes too many people, or upsets the boy-girl ratio, the hostess has every right to refuse—politely, and with an explanation, of course.

Since teen-agers like to get dressed up once in a while, don't be afraid to suggest a "jacket and tie" or "dress" party. Then dress up the party to suit the outfit—fancier food, prettier decorations, and perhaps, live music. The whole affair will take on a glamor that a less formal party never has.

There are a few things that you should insist on, no matter how informal the party. Guests should wear shoes and socks. At VERY informal parties, they may sometimes kick them off later, but at a dance girls should not be allowed on the floor without shoes. It lowers the tone of the party, and the tone is what makes a more or less formal party rather special. The same is true of jackets and ties—at a formal party they should be kept on.

When an invitation says "black tie" or "formal," a boy should not try to go unless he is wearing a tuxedo, or, in some communities, a dark suit. The hostess has set the tone of the party, and he should respect her wishes.

MAKING A PARTY "GO"

There is no question about it—young people love to dance, so be sure that your youngster has good records available and cleared floor space. The most popular parties are those which combine the opportunity to dance with the chance to sit around and talk and eat. Boys especially, but most girls too, like to take time out between dances to relax and enjoy a little conversation.

A piano is a tremendous asset if one of the group can play, and so is a guest with a guitar. Active games such as ping-pong, pool, carpet bowls or Twister are not to be scorned. If one or two people start playing, the rest of the group is often quick to join.

FOOD AND DRINK

The most important consideration in thinking about food and drink is quantity. It doesn't matter too much *what* you serve, and your daughter will know the preferences of her guests. But it is a calamity to run short before the end of the evening. For an after-dinner party, count on the guests drinking two soft drinks apiece, and add half again as many for emergencies.

Food is generally very simple. It may be that snacks such as pretzels, popcorn, corn chips, etc., are all that are necessary. If your daughter likes to bake, or if you have a special cake or cookie recipe, those foods will disappear as fast as you serve them. You and your husband might offer to help cook up a batch of hot dogs and hamburgers around midnight, and if you help serve, it gives you an excellent opportunity to check on how things are going without seeming to "chaperon." Other popular late-evening foods are pancakes, pizzas, or cheese fondue. If you serve a fondue, be sure to cover the table with a plastic cloth, for it is almost impossible to eat without dripping.

As long as there are teen-age parties, there will be boys who try to smuggle in liquor. You and your daughter must decide in advance how you will cope with this if it occurs. Your daughter, because she will be there all the time, must keep her eyes open for signs of hidden flasks or bottles. If she does not have the self-assurance to handle the situation by asking the offenders to stop drinking, to remove the liquor, or to leave, she should come to you. Ask the boy or boys to hand their liquor over to you for the duration of the party, and when it is over, if they are of legal age to drink, return it to them before they go home. If they are not of legal age, notify their parents. As for allowing your own teen-agers to serve liquor in states where it is permissible, my advice is—don't do it. If you do, be sure that there are plenty of soft drinks available for those who want them.

ENDING THE PARTY

When your daughter sends out, or issues, her invitations, she should give an "until" time as well as an "at" time. She should state "eight to twelve" or whatever the hours may be. In that way, parents of nondrivers will know what time to come for their youngsters, and that will automatically start a break-up of the party.

It is also a good idea to cut off the supply of food and drink a half-hour or so before the party should end. Tell your daughter that if all else fails, and nobody seems to have the slightest intention of leaving, she may ask you to put in an appearance, and that will be a sufficient hint!

83

College years

Young men and girls during their four years in college not only receive an academic education, but also take part in the social life of their school. Etiquette on the campus must cover some rather specialized situations, but there is one simple truth: Whatever constitutes proper and decent behavior for young men and girls anywhere is correct in any college situation.

PERSONAL POPULARITY

Your decision to attend college is a very serious one, of course, and should be made chiefly because of your wish to further your general education or to study for a particular career. As is true of everything, you may expect to gain from your studies in proportion to the time and interest you devote to them. But surely you do not want or expect your years in college to be a "grind," devoted solely to academic work. To be able to make people like you, to get on easily with those who are thrown into close and continued contact with you, and to make friends is of vital importance to you now, as it will be all the rest of your life.

The best way to make yourself liked and to make friends is to like people enough to become interested in what interests them and to be outgoing and friendly. Most of us go through life mentally wrapped in the cotton wool of our own affairs. We go about thinking of what we are going to do, what we hope or fear is going to happen to us, instead of thinking or caring about what happens to those about us.

Sensitive awareness of the reactions of other people is a priceless gift. There are far too many of us who never note the effect that our thoughtlessness is having upon the feelings of others.

Good looks are an asset, certainly, but a bright, responsive personality is far more attractive than great beauty—even for a girl. Men will find that the possession of a pleasant personality will be of more value than a movie-star appearance. Good grooming, however, is the one aspect of good looks that always counts. Campus clothing may be casual and comfortable, suited to the informal activities of the college day, but it should always be clean and neat.

THE FRESHMAN ARRIVES AT COLLEGE

Your first days in college will be harried and hurried, but they'll also be a lot of fun. You'll be learning new things, meeting new people, and adapting to a whole new life. Orientation or Welcome Week is included in the first-of-the-semester activities at many colleges. It is a time devoted exclusively to the freshman, for in this week there are group meetings to explain such matters as study programs, registration routine, the faculty-advisor system, and other facts of campus life. Faculty members are available for the new students to meet and talk with. There are also meetings devoted to a presentation of extracurricular activities, with representatives from each student group describing its program and membership qualifications.

Orientation Week is a busy procession of events, all devoted to helping the new student feel at home in his new environment. If you approach the Welcoming Committee with interest and cordiality, you will receive the full benefits from this special time—in addition to acquiring many first-of-the-year friends that will be yours for four years and possibly for life.

DORMITORY LIFE

Consideration is the key to successful dormitory living, whether it be for a roommate, your hall mates, the dormitory personnel, or the maintenance staff. The facilities of the dormitory are yours, but they're also your roommate's. This means sharing the mirror, the shower, the desk, the lounge; it means preserving the life of all dormitory property; it means keeping "your side" in order. It also means being considerate of your roommate's sleeping and studying habits and observing the quiet hours that the dormitory imposes.

Obeying the regulations that every dormitory must enforce will not make you a "goody-goody." It is merely showing thoughtfulness to people among whom you must live, for dormitory rules are designed to make the lives of many strangers living together run more smoothly.

A custom much to be deplored, but not likely to disappear, is that of borrowing among dormitory mates. Avoid borrowing if you can, but you must of course respond graciously when asked to lend an article of yours, whether you accept or refuse the request. If you must borrow, never do so without asking permission, and always take better care of borrowed property than of your own. Whether you borrow a book or a sweater, its prompt return to the owner as soon as you have finished with it is essential.

The housemother is there to guide you, not to guard you. Treat her with the respect you would show any older person, but also with friendliness. Dropping into her apartment now and then with a few friends for a chat before dinner is a gesture that takes little time, but will be appreciated for its thoughtfulness. Never, of course, allow yourself to impose on her time or otherwise become a nuisance.

Christmas gifts to the housemother and tips to the staff are certainly in order. The manner of presentation depends on campus custom. Usually a box is passed, with a sum being collected for those on the household staff, and a gift from all presented to the housemother; otherwise, a small remembrance can be given individually.

IN CLASS AND AFTER

The professor or lecturer in a college classroom may be more remote than was the teacher in your high-school classroom, but you nevertheless owe him quiet, attention, and your fully alert mental powers.

In college, the responsibility for handing in assignments on time is yours, and you will not be pressured or reminded to do so.

When you recite in class, speak so that you can be heard by the professor as well as your fellow students. But talk only if you have something to contribute, or if you really don't understand a point. Killing time in the classroom is a trick of many pseudo scholars, but such vocal antics fool no one but the student himself!

The student encounters faculty members not only in the classroom, but also at joint student-faculty committee meetings, departmental teas, extracurricular activities, and on the campus. A professor should never be addressed as "Doc" or "Prof." If a graduate assistant himself requests it, it is all right to call him by his first name, but in general faculty members should be treated with the respect due to their position and age.

With a host of extracurricular activities confronting him, the student must selectively determine which ones interest him the most. He may choose among those that supplement academic interests, such as a history, education, or foreign-affairs club that offers opportunities to speak the language of his major, or among those that provide a contrast to them, such as religious organizations, student government, and any kind of athletic club.

You will miss a lot if you don't join in any of these activities during your years in college. On the other hand, if you're inclined to be an "organization man," remember that moderation is always the wisest course. Consider Joe College, for example: he is an officer of the Men's Athletic Association, a member of the Dramatic Club, the basketball team, and a fraternity, and he writes for the humor magazine. Always busy, Joe has no time for his studies. Even worse, he has made too many acquaintances and too few friends.

Participating in extracurricular activities is an excellent way to make new friends. You will encounter fellow students whose leisure interests are similar to your own, but whom you might not meet during your regular academic hours.

Fraternities and sororities are an integral feature of most campuses throughout the country, but it would be a mistake to believe they are essential to a collegiate social life. Whatever the fraternity picture on your campus may be, follow your own individual tastes and needs in deciding whether to affiliate with one or remain an independent.

You should remember that the homecoming or reunion weekend is in honor of the alumni. Members of the class of '27, having their reunion, may seem pretty far removed from your college situation. They may even be "old fogies"! But they are loyal alumni, giving financial and moral support to your school, and they should be given respect and consideration. A little out-goingness from your group can do much to make these returning alumni enjoy their visit to your campus.

THE BIG COLLEGE WEEKEND

To the students at a college, one of the most important events of the year is their special annual weekend. It may take place in the fall or in the spring, and—at a men's college—it brings an influx of girls to the campus. There may be a Friday-night informal party at the fraternity houses; on Saturday, a picnic or a game to watch, or perhaps a ski excursion in mid-winter. Saturday night is a more formal dance, often preceded by a sit-down dinner. Sunday, students and their dates may go to church together and organize an excursion or informal party. After Sunday dinner, the weekend closes.

Though the girl pays for her own transportation to and from the campus, the man should, as soon as she has accepted his written invitation, inform her of the train or bus schedules. If it is impossible for him to meet her, he should arrange for a friend to be there or see that a taxi will be available.

The girl may stay in the college's chapter house of her sorority, in a dormitory made ready for the visitors, or at a local hotel, where she may share a room with another "import." The man should make all the arrangements, and do it far enough in advance to enable his date to have the most comfortable and convenient accommodations available. He, of course, assumes the financial obligations. He must tell his girl exactly what her accommodations will be, and if he does not, she should be sure to ask.

He also pays for all her meals and for all transportation after she arrives at the local railroad depot. He would be well advised to inspect his wardrobe more than one week in advance of the weekend and make sure the clothes he intends to wear are clean and ready for use.

Whether the man's date is from his campus or from out of town, he owes her all the courtesies due a guest. He shouldn't leave her alone while he hobnobs with his pals and fraternity brothers. Though he is in his element, she may not be in hers, and his thoughtful attentiveness to her will enhance the enjoyment of the weekend for all.

DON'TS FOR ALL HOUSE PARTY VISITORS

To begin with packing: DON'T put off looking at your bag until the last moment, unless it is new or you know it is in perfect condition. Don't arrive with a shabby, down-at-heel suitcase with handle half off or lock broken, or packed with straps carelessly hanging out. Neat, compact, good-looking luggage will please a man much more than you might suspect.

DON'T forget to dress mentally as you pack. Stockings? Now, shoes? Slip? Dress? What goes with it? Belt, clips or other accessories, bag, etc. No one is less likely to be pleasing than the girl who begins to borrow from the other girls or sends a boy on repeated trips to the drugstore for the comb or toothpaste or whatever else she forgot. And yet: DON'T make your luggage one inch bigger or one ounce heavier than necessary, unless you are driving your own car! Any girl who brings more than one moderate-sized bag will not add to her popularity either with the others who are going in the same car or with her host who meets her at the station and perhaps has to carry this extra weight up a steep hill to the house where she is to stay. Don't forget that on holiday occasions in small college towns there may not be taxis or cars for more than about one out of ten. Therefore DON'T count on being that one.

Upon your arrival at the house, DON'T greet the housemother and other chaperons as though they were inanimate objects upon whom you need waste no attention. DON'T show an alive and interested manner toward the boys and total indifference toward the girls. When you are shown to the room which you are to share with another girl, DON'T claim the bed you like best by throwing your bag on it. At least make the gesture of asking the other girl if she cares which she takes.

DON'T take up more than exactly your share of the closet space and drawer space. If you have brought too many things for the space that is yours, you must leave some of them packed in your bag and leave the bag neatly closed.

DON'T monopolize the bathroom; remember that others are waiting. If you have a bathroom to yourself at home, all the more reason for remembering this. DON'T leave your personal belongings around on all the bedroom furniture. DON'T leave powder scattered over everything. Later, when you pack to leave, DON'T leave powder or smears of lipstick or bobby pins in the bureau drawer. Also, open dresser drawers wide to be sure you have not left panties or other personal items behind. DON'T leave rubbish behind you, either. Remember that the regular occupant of the room may have to move back in before there is time to have the rooms cleaned. DON'T forget, throughout your stay, to respect the wishes of the housemother and other chaperons. Be sure to say good-bye to her and to the others, and to thank them for their kindness.

But now, to turn back to the evening of your arrival—at the time, let us say, when you all congregate before dinner and introductions are made. In a fraternity house with no outsiders except each brother's best girl, the introductions would very likely be not only by first names but by nicknames: "Sally, this is Slim," or Babs, and so on.

DON'T, however, wait for introductions under the house roof. Friendliness should be your natural inclination. It would be too bad to be thought a snob when you are really only shy. If you are afraid you won't make friends, don't forget that nearly every other girl is feeling exactly the same!

If you don't know anything about the boy seated beside you at dinner, ask your own date, who should be seated at your left, about him first so as to know what to talk to him about. It is cynical advice, but it is as true today as it was in the day of Cleopatra that a man is rarely bored if you talk—but with some intelligence—about him. DON'T, however, get his abilities confused with those of someone else, and DON'T in any case lay flattery on with a trowel!

At the dances, greet the chaperons as though you liked them. The moment of enthusiastic attention that courtesy demands is one of the easiest and most rewarding social investments you can make.

DON'T refuse to dance with anyone who cuts in, unless he is drunk or objectionable.

Throughout the days of your visit, DON'T think only of what you like to do; that is, DON'T insist on playing ping-pong if your host would like you to make a fourth at bridge—unless your ping-pong is expert and your bridge is very bad indeed. In this case tell him you would be delighted to play, only you know how sorry everyone else will be if you do. But in general, to do whatever the majority suggest is no more than what is expected of you everywhere—unless what is suggested is something you think is wrong. For instance, there is no obligation to drink anywhere at any time—unless you choose to.

DON'T be jealous of every attention your best boy friend pays to another girl. The more you show your dislike for this interest, the more jealous he is likely to try to make you. DON'T show that you hate to be teased, or you'll be a target for even those who never thought of teasing until you showed how badly you take it.

DON'T show chagrin or disappointment. The fundamental secret of the popular houseguest is to show delight in everything pleasing, and to be blind, deaf, and insensible to annoyance or disappointment. Above all, DON'T do anything that can seem unappreciative of the efforts made for your pleasure by the man who is your host. It is not playing the part of a fascinating woman of the world to try to impress him with your powers by attracting one of his classmates; on the contrary, it is the maneuver of an extremely stupid as well as vain young woman, whose lack of loyalty to a friend is resented by every member of his crowd.

Above all, DON'T forget that the friendship of other girls is the crown of your own success. Popularity with girls may not make you popular with men, but earning their dislike by treating them with contempt and by trying to take their boy friends will end in ostracism of yourself. The really popular girl is popular with girls as well as boys.

In short, DON'T try to be the house-party coquette in an attempt to see how many of the men you can add to your chain of admirers! It is natural that every man wants the girl he asks to this big social event to be liked by all his friends. But you must not confuse the friendliness shown you in these circumstances with that which might otherwise be given to you for yourself alone.

84

Chaperons and dates

It is hard for the present generation to understand the position of the chaperon of another day. We are likely to think of a chaperon as having been a kind of policewoman employed to look after the morals, as well as the manners, of a young girl. Although the chaperon has largely become a lost convention, there are still a few situations in which she is required. Today, however, parental training has largely taken the place of the chaperon's protection.

MODERN CHAPERONAGE

From an ethical standpoint, the only chaperon worth having in the present day is a young girl's own efficiency in chaperoning herself. The girl who has been taught to appraise every person and situation she meets needs no one to sit beside her and tell her what to do. She must be able to handle any situation herself, because the modern girl is on her own. She must be able to gauge the reactions of various types of persons, particularly men, in varying circumstances. She must learn to judge which man has the instincts of a gentleman and which is likely, if given the opportunity, to exhibit quite different traits. The girl who, in addition to trained judgment, has the right attributes of proper pride and character needs no chaperon—ever. But if she lacks these qualities, not even Argus could watch over her!

Apart, however, from the consideration of ethics, which is concerned with what the girl herself thinks or feels or the motives behind what she says or does, there still remain the appearances to be considered. Many young people today are inclined to ignore them, to feel that they can act independently of public opinion.

It is necessary to act properly for the same reason that one does not make a scene in the street: if you want to keep your affairs private and your reputation intact, you should never let yourself become a subject for public discussion. There are too many people like Mrs. Grundy even in this modern day, whose gossip still influences a world that seldom takes the trouble to sift appearance from fact.

Many parents, unfortunately, become overprotective of their teen-aged children, and restrict their activities and friendships unreasonably. Perhaps they are afraid that more lenient guidance would give the impression that they are indifferent to their daughter's well-being. They should realize that overzealous guarding will hamper their child's development of responsibility and judgment and that unnecessary restriction may separate her from her friends. It is admittedly difficult to achieve the middle road of reasonable supervision, but it is important to the child's social development to receive freedom as well as guidance during these years of adolescence.

THE NECESSARY PROPRIETIES

If a young girl's family is not at home, she should not, on returning from a party, invite or allow her date to "come in for a while." If he persists, she should tell him firmly, "Sorry, another time," and bid him "good night." However, if her parents are home and have been notified, it is perfectly all right to invite him in for a snack. He should not stay overly long, and if he shows no inclination to leave, the girl should tell him that her parents have set a definite "curfew" hour.

Some families insist on a practice that is quite sensible—merely that their daughter telephone home just before leaving a dance if she plans to go on to someone's house or bring friends to her own. This is not unreasonable from the daughter's point of view. If she has poise and loyalty and is sure of herself, she can make her practice of telephoning an evidence of respect for her mother, and there will be no more question about her going to the telephone than about going to get her coat!

An unmarried girl should not go alone on overnight trips with any young man, even with her fiancé. However, a girl of eighteen or older may perfectly well go on a weekend trip with several couples to a ski resort or a beach resort. In this case, the presence of a few other girls in the party is sufficient protection from idle and malicious gossip.

It is perfectly proper, not only for a college girl but also for her teen-aged sister, to invite friends to a party without the necessity of chaperonage other than that of her parents' presence in some part of the house. They should, however, arrange to put in an appearance at some time during the party. They could say "Hello" when their daughter's guests arrive and then leave the young people alone, returning to serve the refreshments or, at the younger girl's party, to bid the guests good-bye.

A girl of sixteen or more can invite a small group to her home on an evening when her parents are dining out, as long as they are returning shortly after dinner. She must be responsible for seeing that the kitchen is left clean so that her mother does not return to a stack of dirty dishes in the sink. After all parties are over, the teen-aged host or hostess should empty ash trays, dispose of empty bottles, wash glasses, dispose of paper plates or other trash, and generally "pick up." If this is faithfully done, parents will rarely object to another party in their home.

THE HOUSEMOTHER AS RESIDENT CHAPERON

The housemother, as her title implies, is a substitute mother for the girls or young women in her charge. She is to be found in preparatory boarding schools, college dormitories, or metropolitan women's residence hotels.

The housemother should be neither inquisitive nor interfering, except for seriously considered, valid reasons, since she serves as an advisor to the young girls. Charm is a necessary quality, because she will be meeting and greeting the parents, girl friends, and beaux of her charges. She'll also be asked to serve at teas, be at the head of reception lines, and preside at luncheons, dinners, and other social occasions.

Genuine friendliness and kindness are at least as important as being charmingly gracious when a visiting V.I.P. is on hand. A housemother must offer friendship to all the girls under her wing, and not show favoritism to the few to whom she may feel partial.

THE CHAPERONS AT A DANCE

Chaperons for a dance may be recruited from among the faculty, the parents of the students, or other townspeople; they may be single persons or married couples. Chaperons are the ringside participants at the dance, responsible for the general discipline and order of those dancing. A school dance should be fun, and the chaperons should never put a damper on it, but instead should enhance the party by their own enjoyment of it. While a chaperon is not expected to serve as a "bouncer," he or she should be prepared to put down the firm foot of authority if a young person gets too boisterous.

A committee may be in charge of securing the chaperons for the gala evening. The committee should select two or three chaperons who will enjoy the party and who will be congenial to one another. It is thoughtful to invite chaperons at least two weeks in advance so that they can obtain baby-sitters or make any other necessary arrangements. If you are asking single persons, they should be told they may bring escorts. The same committee is responsible for writing thank-you notes to each chaperon after the dance.

And, of course, everyone must bid the chaperons good night and thank them for having come to the dance.

DATES

The age at which a girl may go out alone with a boy in the evening and how late she may stay out will vary according to the responsibility of the girl herself and the custom of the community. Only a parent can make the exact decision. A girl of thirteen or fourteen might go out with a boy as part of a group of four or more to an early movie, dinner, sports event, or some other special occasion. Most of her dates will, however, be those at the homes of friends or dances organized by her school. Her parents should at all times know where and with whom she is and at what time she will be home. As she grows in age and experience, her dates will naturally include many more activities, she will go out more frequently alone with a boy, and her hours will be later.

HOMECOMING HOURS

The hour at which a teen-ager must be home is one of the most difficult problems to be settled between children and their parents. The customs of the community, the hours kept by friends, the amount of sleep the individual child needs, and the confidence of the parents in a girl's escort, all are important factors. During the early teen years, when children do not have the wisdom to recognize their own needs, the parents must set time limits on dates and see that they are kept, even though it may mean waiting up to greet the returning son or daughter. This is a simple matter of good health, as well as setting a high standard of behavior. It is wise to discuss homecoming hours with other parents and try to arrive at an hour to which everyone, including the children, agrees. If this is impossible, try to choose a time you think sensible—not the earliest, for this will only cause resentment and disobedience, or the latest, which may cause criticism, as well as be detrimental to the child's health.

Dates should be absolutely restricted to weekends and vacations. Even high-school students who are "going steady" should not be permitted to date during the week, even to study together. The only exceptions might be very special occasions, such as if a boy were given theater tickets to an excellent and difficult-to-see show, or to a championship game or some other extraordinary event. In these cases, the young people should study especially hard in advance to be sure that their work is ready for the next day and get extra sleep the nights before and after the date.

As a general rule, ten-thirty or eleven is a reasonable time for a thirteen- or fourteen-year-old to be home. On occasion, he or she may attend a school or club dance or other special party until twelve. The hours should be made a little later each year, so that sixteen- or seventeen-year-olds might stay at parties until twelve-thirty or one. For an ordinary movie date, this age group should still return by eleven or thereabouts. If they plan to go to a friend's house or a snack bar afterward, their parents should know in advance or be called on the telephone so that they may know the whereabouts of the child and readjust the hour when he must be home. When a youngster reaches his late teens, his hours should be regulated only by his or her own need for sleep or the rules of his school or university. Parents of a child living at home should realize that were he away at college, he would be making his own rules as to hours, and allow him the same privilege. They may, of course, point out that he is not getting enough sleep, or suggest that he needs a "health night," as my teen-agers call an early-to-bed evening. But many eighteen-year-olds live away from home—they work, they are in the armed forces, and they are even married—so it seems a little ridiculous for parents, simply because they are fortunate enough to have their youngster at home, to attempt to treat him as a child rather than an intelligent, if young, adult.

MAKING CONTACT

When a boy (or man) sees someone he thinks he would like to know, it is fairly simple for him to make contact. All he has to do is find someone who knows the girl and will introduce them. Then he can chat with her for a bit, and if she is as attractive as she appeared from a distance, he may ask her for a date.

If a girl wishes to avoid giving the impression that she is chasing a boy, she must be more devious. Boys are flattered, of course, when a girl obviously wants to meet them, but they are often scared by an overzealous attack, and she will do well to be subtle. Without seeming too eager, she may:

Give a friendly smile and an enthusiastic "Hello" whenever they meet.

Persuade a mutual friend to invite them both to a small party.

Go to all school events in which he takes part.

Join school, church, or community organizations to which he belongs.

Get a girl who knows him to arrange a blind (double) date.

After the contact is made, and it's clear that they would like to get to know each other, the boy may ask for a date by telephone, or simply when they meet. He should remember to mention the following details:

What time he will call for the girl.

Their means of transportation.

What kind of date it will be—movies, a party at a friend's, a picnic, etc.

If he forgets to offer any of this information, the girl may, and should, ask for it.

Unless a boy and girl are going steady, he should ask for a date:

Two to four days ahead for an ordinary date.

At least two weeks ahead for a formal dance.

A month or more ahead for a big college weekend.

There are exceptions, such as when a party is planned on the spur of the moment, but these are good general rules.

ACCEPTING OR REFUSING A DATE

Ordinarily accepting a date presents no problem. If she wants to go, the girl need only say, "I'd love to!" promptly and enthusiastically. The worst mistake she can make is to be evasive. If she promised to baby-sit and doesn't know if she can get a substitute, or if she is not sure if the family is going to the country for the weekend, she must say so. But it must be true, and she must be sincere, or he will surely know it. No one should ever say, "Can I let you know tomorrow?" without saying why.

Once a girl has accepted, she must keep the date unless a real emergency arises. One can *never* break one date to accept another.

To refuse a date politely, a girl only need say, "I'm so sorry, but I already have a date for Saturday night." If she is no more specific, she is free to accept someone else who calls. If, however, she would really like the man to ask her again, she should give him a more detailed excuse which sounds, and is, true.

OTHER DATING DATA

A girl should introduce a new friend to her parents on her first date with him. She should brief her parents a little before he arrives so that they can carry on the conversation easily. Five or ten minutes is enough for the visit, and it is up to the young lady to suggest that they had better be on their way.

Men—and boys—must call for their dates at their homes. Only if he knows her well and has a good reason (such as an early dinner reservation at a restaurant) might he meet her at a convenient spot.

Unless a couple have been going steady and have agreed to share at times, the man pays all expenses on a date. The girl may help considerably by suggesting inexpensive entertainment—a movie instead of the theater, for example—or choosing the lower priced items on a menu.

It is the man's responsibility to make all the plans for the evening. Provided the activity he suggests is not one of which she does not approve, the girl should participate with enthusiasm. At the end of the evening, it is she who decides that it is time to go home.

The man should arrive for the date on time, and the woman should be ready. There is no truth in the old idea that she makes herself more desirable by keeping him waiting.

The girl should be dressed suitably, assuming the man has told her what they are going to do. If he has been vague, a simple rather than a "dressy" costume is a safer choice. Should she discover that her date is dressed for bowling when she thought they were going to a cocktail party, she should excuse herself for ten minutes—no more—while she hastily changes into something more casual.

THE BLIND DATE

The "blind date" is a peculiarly American variation of the formal introduction, which in this case is made indirectly and for the express purpose of arranging a date. It is sometimes arranged by a third person such as Mrs. Towne, who thinks that Gloria Gorgeous and Harry Handsome would enjoy each other's company. She first makes sure that Harry would be interested in calling Gloria; then she asks Gloria if she would like to meet an attractive man. Only after both parties have indicated that they are willing to be so introduced should Mrs. Towne give Gloria's telephone number to Harry.

The date may also be arranged by a girl who is asked for a date by a boy she does not know well or does not wish to go out with alone. She might say, "Jane Harvey is spending the night with me, so I would love to go out with you if you have a friend who would like to take her out, and we'll make it a foursome."

The most frequent type of blind date, however, occurs when a host or hostess arranges a date for his or her overnight guest. A girl may call a good friend and say, "Tom, Sally, my roommate at college, is spending the weekend with me, and I think you'd like her, so how about taking her to a movie with Jim and me on Saturday night?"

Dates arranged in any of these ways should not be expected to result in anything more than a pleasant evening. Even close friends do not always agree on whom they like or dislike, and while Cindy may think Charley is divine, her friend Jane may well be bored to death in his company. So make the best of a blind date, and no matter what you may think to yourself, act as if you were enjoying every minute. After all, it is probably better than sitting at home by yourself, and whether he or she is enchanting or not, you may meet more attractive people through your new acquaintance.

"GOING STEADY" AND "PINNING"

The dating habits of young people today include some customs that were unknown a short generation ago. To the chagrin of many parents and teachers, "going steady" has become a fact of American teen-age life. Gone is the traditional stag line at the high-school dance; today a girl usually dances only with her escort. When a boy and girl date each other consistently, they are considered by their contemporaries to be "going steady." Usually they have an agreement that neither is to date anyone else, and this may even be formalized by an exchange of friendship rings or identification bracelets.

For several reasons, this is an unfortunate practice, and it is the wise young person who widens rather than narrows his circle of friends. Many girls fear not having a date for Saturday night, and some boys are afraid to be told "no" when they call a girl for a date. But these young people are putting limits on the development of their own social personalities when they limit their dating friendships. Only by meeting many other young people of varied backgrounds and interests can a boy or girl broaden his or her own experience and gain enough insight to be capable of making a good choice of a marriage partner when the time comes.

The presentation of a fraternity badge by a college man to his girl, known as "pinning," may be merely another type of "going steady," or it may mean that the couple are "engaged to be engaged," depending on the customs of that particular college. Generally the couple intends marriage but in the somewhat distant future, and this relationship allows them to examine their compatibility without committing themselves formally to an engagement. It is not right for a girl to collect fraternity pins as trophies of her dates. If the "pinned" couple "breaks up," the girl is expected to return the pin to the young man. In many cases, "pinning" does lead to a formal engagement and then to marriage.

After leaving college, of course, unmarried young men and women do not follow these customs, which seem to have significance only in the high school or college community. Although a couple in their twenties or thirties may be dating each other exclusively, there will usually be no formalizing of their relationship until they decide to become engaged.

DON'T NEGLECT YOUR GIRL FRIENDS!

Many girls make the mistake of boasting of boredom when compelled to be with girls alone, as though this boredom were an asset. The girl who tells other girls that she understands men—implying that the others, poor things, are less perceptive—is not instilling feelings of envy and admiration in the hearts of her hearers, but feelings of resentment against her conceit, and contempt for her stupidity.

The mistake, of course, is in boasting, and not in her preference for the companionship of men. Most popular girls recognize the necessity of having friendships with girls as well as men. The girl who really has a capacity for friendship with men rarely boasts of it.

85

A happy marriage

There are no two people in the world, no matter how much in love they are when they get married, who do not have to make adjustments to each other. There is simply no way of getting to know each other completely when still living apart, and the first months, and even years, of married life are an exciting, stimulating time of discovery and deepening affection. If, that is, each partner is willing to make concessions to the habits of his mate that annoy him and to look for and enjoy the traits that please. The wife who starts nagging soon after marriage because her husband does not hang up his suit every night or the husband who can't stand her stockings drying in the bathroom will have a difficult period of adjustment. Of course, he should try to improve his bachelor habits in order to make his wife's housecleaning easier, and she should do her wash early enough so that her stockings can be put away before he gets home, but this type of irritation should never be allowed to become so important that the happy times are forgotten in a constant stream of recriminations.

HINTS FOR THE NEWLYWEDS

I don't know why people should feel that because they have married, they may give up all pretense of good manners and treat their partner as an "old shoe." During courtship, both men and women put their best foot forward, and rather than being a trap to catch their mate, this should set the pattern for their marriage. But it does not always work that way, and many a marriage has failed because one or both of the partners allowed their attitude toward the other to become careless, ill-mannered, or just plain bored. It takes effort to keep a good marriage going, and the close proximity of home life makes the constant presence of good manners more important than in any relationship with those outside the family.

THE WIFE'S PART

How many times does a woman say, "No one is coming in. That old dress will do." Old clothes! Sloppy manners! And what is the result? One more wife wonders why her husband neglects her! Curious how the habit of careless manners and the habit of old clothes go together. And how many women commit esthetic suicide by letting themselves slide down to where they feel natural in an old housecoat, not only physically but mentally.

She who changes her dress and fixes her hair for her husband's homecoming is sure to greet him with greater charm than she who thinks whatever she happens to have on is good enough. The very fact of *looking* more attractive makes one feel less tired and therefore more charming and better company.

So many women save up all their troubles to pour on the one they most love, the idea being, I suppose, that no reserves are necessary between lovers. Nor need there be, really. But why, when the roses burst into bloom this morning, does she never show them to him instead of insisting that he look at the hole dug in his garden by the neighbor's dog?

She who complains incessantly that this is wrong or that this hurts or that some other thing worries or vexes her, so that his inevitable answer to her greeting is "I'm so sorry, dear," or "That's too bad," is getting very decidedly into an old housecoat! If something is seriously wrong, if she is really ill, that is different. But beware of the petty things that are only told in order to gain sympathy. There is a big deposit of sympathy in the bank of love, but don't draw out little sums every hour or two. By and by, when perhaps you need it badly, it is all drawn out, and you yourself don't know how or on what it was spent.

Not many husbands can endure the wife who smears her face with cream and rolls her hair in curlers before going to bed. With a handy portable drier, there is no reason that hair cannot be dried while doing chores, feeding the baby, paying the bills, or performing any other household duties during the day. And the wife who prepares and sees her husband off to work in a dirty bathrobe, with hair uncombed and face unwashed, sends him off with a thoroughly unflattering picture of her in his mind. No wonder many a man has found his neat, efficient, pretty secretary more appealing than his unkempt, uncaring wife!

The intelligent woman will listen and care about her husband's problems at the office. Many wives complain after being married for some years that their husbands never talk to them when they come home. This may be because at the beginning of their married life, John eagerly started out, "Guess what, darling, I have an appointment with the President of the Fix Corporation, and he may give me their account . . ." but Joan, not fully understanding the importance of the meeting to him, interrupted, "Oh really? But you must come and see Junior's new tooth, and then please repair the stopper in the sink, and . . ." John soon gave up trying to discuss his business with Joan, and a rift was started that was never quite healed with talk of babies, household repairs, etc.

Even though a girl may loathe cooking, she should make an effort to cater to her husband's likes and dislikes and to make meals appetizing and interesting. If he hates liver, she should not serve it once a week because "it's good for the blood." If she is on a diet, she must not feed her husband a dinner of one lamb chop and a small green salad. And no matter how noble he may be about claiming he likes it, she never feeds him frozen dinners except in emergencies. A little surprise now and then —something he especially likes, such as a homemade apple pie or a special cut of steak ordinarily beyond her budget—will do wonders toward making her seem a marvelous cook and clever wife.

A considerate wife doesn't make plans without consulting her husband, unless she knows the event is something he will enjoy. If he is working very hard, it is terribly thoughtless of her to plan a dinner party for Friday, to accept an invitation for a dance on Saturday, and to organize an all-day picnic with the children on Sunday. Of course, a girl who has been tied down to babies and household chores all week looks forward to a little gaiety on the weekend, but here again there must be compromise and she must remember that her husband, while he also enjoys a little diversion, may need some extra rest.

If her husband is the type who enjoys an evening of poker with his friends, the smart wife will cheer him on his way and even offer to provide refreshments for his gang at home when it is his turn to invite them there. She leaves everything in readiness and disappears—completely! But if he is bringing a business acquaintance home, she must be a gracious hostess until after dinner, when she excuses herself, washes up quietly, and goes to her room to leave them to their business discussion.

THE HUSBAND'S PART

For some reason, it seems that the bride generally has to make more effort to achieve a successful marriage than the bridegroom, but it is certainly a two-sided partnership, and she cannot do it alone. The man who rushed to open the car door or light her cigarette when they were engaged is still the same man, but he will soon fall far short of her expectations if he drops these little politenesses as soon as they are married.

It is just as true that a husband must show some interest in his wife's daily activities as that she should listen to his business news. The worst of evenings begins when the husband—whose wife has had no one but the baby to talk to all day long—grunts and buries his nose in the newspaper when she tries to carry on a conversation.

He may have been accustomed to living alone or in a bachelor apartment where no one cared, or at home where his mother picked up for him, but the new husband must learn that trousers dropped in the middle of the floor, a sink spattered with shaving soap, and soggy towels on the bathroom rug can be an unpleasant shock to his bride.

Many men do not care too much for babies until they are old enough to respond or even to show interest in things about which Daddy cares. But this can be a very sore point with a young mother who firmly believes that every move her baby makes is without equal, and her husband's lack of interest seems callous and cruel. If Daddy will take the time to really observe and play with, as well as discipline, his children when he comes home, it will not only please his wife, but he will find himself more interested in the babies than he thought possible.

The husband who will keep his wife company in the kitchen while she is finishing the dinner preparations, rather than retire to the television set or his newspaper, will find himself more than repaid by her appreciation. A girl who has been alone all day doing household chores is desperately anxious to have someone to talk to, and a comfortable chair where her husband may sit and chat with her is well worth the expense. A helping hand with the dishes after dinner is never amiss, although many men, and some wives too, feel that this is the woman's department.

A considerate husband never brings home unexpected guests without giving his wife some warning. He and the guests can hardly wish to walk in on her in her negligee and with her hair in curlers, any more than she could welcome their arrival. And he certainly cannot expect, without advance notice, that she produce a succulent meal for four when she has chopped meat for two hamburgers.

It has been said many times before, but it is still true, that it is important to women that their husbands remember special occasions. If the budget is limited, the remembrance need only be a card for Mother's

Day, a single rose for an anniversary, or a simple little gift for a birthday. It is the thought that counts, and women, generally more sentimental than men, attach tremendous importance to these little gestures.

Unless a man has come to an agreement with his wife, it is very selfish for him to spend all his free time pursuing a sport or hobby that does not interest her. Of course, he should follow his interest within reason, but the husband who spends all weekend on the golf course, making his wife into a "golf widow," may find that she will look for interests other than his, which may include a man who has tastes more similar to hers. A Saturday golf game with his friends, and a Sunday picnic with his family, plus, perhaps, an hour's workout at the driving range one evening or two during the week can be a happy solution for the whole family.

One of the most important things a man can do to please his wife is to plan occasional entertainments that will appeal to her—especially a dinner at a restaurant if he can afford it. He may surprise her, or they may plan it together, but a trip to the theater, an overnight jaunt to some favorite spot, or even an evening at the movies can be a wonderful treat to a girl who spends much of her time at home. If a man's budget simply cannot stretch this far, he can still make his wife very happy by offering to plan and cook the dinner occasionally, or by taking her on a picnic at a beach or lake, or to a free concert or museum or lecture, depending on her interests. In any case, she will appreciate the effort he has made to plan something for her, and it will give her something to look forward to and, afterward, a happy memory to share.

AIRING THE PROBLEMS

There are endless other suggestions that might well be considered by the newlyweds. Although the problems just named seem to be the principal bones of contention in many marriages, there are lesser ones—interrupting each other, making fun of idiosyncracies, not laughing at his or her jokes, never being on time, the wife's using the husband's razor, and a thousand others that can build up a huge wall of resentment. And there are greater ones—basic differences of opinion on bringing up children, on spending vacations, on watching television in the bedroom, and so on—that can undermine an otherwise sound marriage. But great or small, the only way to handle these problems is by bringing them into the open and keeping the lines of communication free between husband and wife. The moment that one or the other feels he cannot discuss a problem and it is left to fester and grow inside is the moment the marriage begins to dissolve. The couple who agrees not only to listen to each other's problems, but to make an effort to see the other side and to DO something to correct the situation is certain to stay out of the divorce courts.

IN-LAW SITUATIONS

One is likely to overlook the fact that when John Jones marries Mary Smith, a number of Smiths and Joneses are suddenly forced into the closeness of family relationships. Even when a bride or bridegroom has no family, he or she becomes son or daughter, sister or brother to those who may have hitherto been total strangers.

The two most difficult situations to meet happily and successfully are those between the husband and his father-in-law and between the wife and her mother-in-law. The other positions are easy and there is little reason for failure. In any case, the very first rule that every father-in-law—and especially every mother-in-law—must learn is DON'T INTERFERE. Never mind what small blunders your daughter or daughter-in-law or your son or son-in-law may make; remember that it is their right to live and do and think as they please. If you are asked what you think, answer truthfully, of course; but don't, upon being given one opening, cram in every item of good advice that you've been storing up for just this chance—or you will risk never being asked again.

LIVING WITH RELATIVES

When a young wife, for any one of many reasons, goes to live with her husband's family, she must in this difficult situation adapt herself not only to their mode of living but also to the dispositions of the various members of the family. In this way alone can she herself be happy. On the other hand, it is essential that the mother-in-law encourage the younger woman's efforts to become adjusted to completely new surroundings instead of showing irritation over the shortcomings, of which she will certainly have at least a few.

When a mother or father must live with a married child, the situation demands the wisdom of a Solomon, the tact of a Recamier, and the self-control of a stoic. Moreover, she or he must conscientiously practice the art of "invisibility" at frequent and lengthy intervals. This does not mean that the mother, for example, must scuttle out of sight like a frightened mouse, but that she should have or make occupations of her own that keep her from being idly, plaintively, or forcefully present—particularly when special friends of her daughter-in-law or even old friends of her son are present. Perhaps she can find some friends and pay bridge or canasta one or two evenings every week. Her room should be equipped with radio and television so that she can always be free to enjoy her own favorite programs. She should assist with household chores or caring for the children as much as she easily can, but she should not be imposed upon or made to feel like a built-in baby-sitter.

On the other hand there is no excuse for the ruthless unkindness that certain wives show when they are obliged to have a parent-in-law live in their house. This attitude not only is distressing to the helpless victim of their cruelty, but is certainly resented by all who see it.

IN-LAW RELATIONSHIP AT ITS BEST

An in-law relationship should be unhampering, uninterfering, uncriticizing.

Whether we are a mother or father, a bride or a groom, the safe rule for our own happiness is to take things as we find them, take pleasure in the assets, not to search for flaws, and never to permit ourselves the weakness of feeling sorry for ourselves. Nothing is harder to build than this impersonality of mind, and the first step is to keep our thoughts and feelings focused not upon ourselves, but on someone or something else.

If it is physically possible, it is far better for parents to live apart from their married children. The young people should, if necessary, help to support the older ones, especially a widow, but the parents should be allowed to feel that they are handling their own affairs and managing their own lives until they are no longer capable or do not wish to do so. Love and affection will flourish in an atmosphere of independence, supplemented by close family ties. But people of different generations living together are bound to find some friction even though they may feel great affection for each other.

SEPARATION AND DIVORCE

Unfortunately, there has been an epidemic of divorce raging in this country for the past fifty years. There are cases, of course, where divorce is the best—sometimes the only—solution for everyone concerned. If two persons are truly mismated, they certainly, and perhaps their children too, are better off if they part. The only consideration of vital importance is that they shall not part because of a love-for-another attack that might prove to be transient.

Sometimes a period of separation can solve the problem of too-hasty divorce, for separation and divorce are different not only in terms of the law, but to some extent in terms of the behavior expected of the people involved.

A separation may be legal or it may simply be arranged by unwritten consent of both parties. It may be a "trial" separation, or it may be viewed from the beginning as permanent. This is often true if the faith of the couple forbids divorce, as does Catholicism.

A trial separation is exactly what it sounds like. Two people have found it increasingly difficult to live together and wish to find out if they can readjust, and be happier, living alone. But for one reason or another, because of children, finances, or any number of other situations, they want time to consider before taking the final steps toward divorce. If they find they are better off apart, and if they are not interested in remarriage or are forbidden by their church to remarry, they may make the separation legal, and papers making property settlements, arrangements for children, financial support, and so on, will be drawn up by their lawyers.

When a couple separates, it is never publicly announced, although the news generally spreads quickly. Because they are still legally married, the woman continues to use her husband's name and wears her wedding ring. He quietly moves out of their home, or she may take her children for a visit to her family. They refuse invitations that come to "Mr. and Mrs.," although if they accidentally meet, they should act as friendly and normal as possible. Friends, of course, should respect the situation and never invite them both to the same party without their knowledge and consent.

If they decide that life together was better than life apart, they simply move back together and make as little of the separation as they can. For this reason, it is wise for the wife, or husband, whichever has remained there, to keep the home and other property intact, rather than selling or renting in a moment of bitterness.

When a divorce is finally and irrevocably decided upon, both parties must accept the fact that their marriage no longer exists. The husband who insists on "dropping in" to see the children or the wife who keeps calling his office to ask his advice on this or that is only prolonging the agony and achieving nothing but more unhappiness. People who have made the decision to part should have done so with enough serious thought so that once accomplished, all ties are severed, and they can start to make new lives for themselves and leave their ex-partners to do the same.

A divorce is almost always a tragic experience for at least one of the couple. Therefore, it should not be announced publicly and certainly never, even in private, treated as a matter for celebration. The fact that a woman discards her wedding ring and substitutes her maiden name for her husband's first name (Mrs. McCallum Ford) is sufficient announcement in itself. In the happy event that the couple resolve their difficulties after the divorce is final, they should remarry quietly, with only their families or closest friends as witnesses. The divorced couple's friends should extend their sympathetic friendship—never criticism or censure—but at the same time respect their privacy, and avoid prying or questioning the reasons for or the mechanics of the divorce.

There is no longer any stigma attached to divorce in this country, but neither should anyone approach it lightly.

In the thousands of cases where children are involved, it is far, far better that the divorced parents make every effort to remain on friendly terms. Nothing in all the world is so devastating in its destruction of character and of soul as living in an atmosphere infused with hatred. Anything is better for children than that!

At present the breaking up of homes is so widespread it may be that young people who grow up never having known the completeness of home will find it unessential. Or will it be the other way around? Perhaps the children of today's divided houses will be twice as earnest in their efforts to provide their own children with the priceless security of a father and mother together in one place called HOME!

INDEX